North Atlantic Seafood

Alan Davidson, who counts himself a Scotsman, was born in 1924. He won a scholarship from Leeds Grammar School to the Queen's College, Oxford, and took a double first there in Classical Greats. His studies sandwiched several years' wartime service in the RNVR, including a spell in the Mediterranean.

He joined the Diplomatic Service in 1948 and served in Washington, The Hague, Cairo, Tunis and Brussels as well as in the Foreign Office. He was appointed British Ambassador in Vientiane, Laos in 1973. At the end of 1975 he left diplomacy in order to write full time.

His other publications include *Fish and Fish Dishes of Laos*, *Seafood of South-East Asia*, *Mediterranean Seafood*, which won the Glenfiddich gold medal for 1972, and – with his American wife Jane – *Dumas on Food*.

His main current task is writing the *Oxford Companion to Food*, a completely new work of very wide scope. He is co-founder, with Dr Theodore Zeldin, of the Oxford Symposia on Food History.

Alan and Jane Davidson, who have three daughters, live in Chelsea. They are the active Directors of Prospect Books, a small publishing house which specializes in serious works on food, cookery and cookery books; including an eccentric journal, *PPC*, which comes out thrice yearly and covers the same field.

In 1979 Alan Davidson was awarded a Glenfiddich gold medal for *North Atlantic Seafood*.

A View of a Stage & also of ye manner of Fishing for, Curing & Drying Cod at NEW FOUND LAND.
A. The Habit of ye Fishermen. B. The Line. C. The manner of Fishing. D. The Dressers of ye Fish. E. The Trough into which they throw ye Cod when Dressed. F. Salt Boxes. G. The manner of Carrying ye Cod. H. The Cleansing ye Cod. I. A Press to extract ye Oyl from ye Cods Livers. K. Casks to receive ye Water & Blood that comes from ye Livers. L. Another Cask to receive the Oyl. M. The manner of Drying ye Cod.

NORTH ATLANTIC SEAFOOD

Alan Davidson

Penguin Books

PENGUIN BOOKS

Published by the Penguin Group
Penguin Books Ltd, 27 Wrights Lane, London W8 5TZ, England
Penguin Books USA Inc., 375 Hudson Street, New York, New York 10014, USA
Penguin Books Australia Ltd, Ringwood, Victoria, Australia
Penguin Books Canada Ltd, 10 Alcorn Avenue, Toronto, Ontario, Canada M4V 3B2
Penguin Books (NZ) Ltd, 182–190 Wairau Road, Auckland 10, New Zealand

Penguin Books Ltd, Registered Offices: Harmondsworth, Middlesex, England

First published in Macmillan 1979
Published in Penguin Books 1980
5 7 9 10 8 6 4

Printed in England by Clays Ltd, St Ives plc
Filmset in Monophoto Times

This book is dedicated to Elizabeth David, with much gratitude for her kind help and encouragement to myself; and in homage to the literary and gastronomic menu, displayed below, which she has provided for us all over the last quarter of a century.

1950	A Book of Mediterranean Food
1951	French Country Cooking
1954	Italian Food
1955	Summer Cooking
1960	French Provincial Cooking
1970	Spices, Salt and Aromatics
	in the English Kitchen
1977	English Bread and Yeast Cookery

The commendable practice of selling fish alive used to exist in many countries and still does so to some extent in Russia, as Pamela Davidson explains on page 338. This picture, which comes from a battered fragment of a nineteenth-century publication called *The Pictorial Museum of Animated Nature*, is introduced therein as follows.

'[This figure] represents one of the Fish-barks of St Petersburg, floating fishmongers' shops, in which are bought and sold all the fish consumed in that capital during the summer. This ark is surrounded by numerous floating cisterns and boats, either pierced with small holes to admit the clear waters of the Neva, or filled with salt water for the natives of the sea. In these are kept various kinds of fish alive, while the bark is the fishmonger's residence, which communicates with the quay by means of a railed plank. On the application of a customer for a fish, the person is conducted down a sloping plank to the reservoirs, and makes choice of the fish, which are secured by means of a small landing-net; those which are not approved being returned to the proper vessels. In winter this mode cannot be practised, for the water is ice . . .'

Contents

RECIPES

Acknowledgements

The extent of the travel and visits involved in preparing this book makes it impossible to name here everyone who helped me. I must have recourse to an omnibus expression of gratitude to all those experts, librarians, authors, professional and non-professional cooks, interpreters and former colleagues in the Diplomatic Service who have helped me with information, bibliographical clues, introductions, hospitality and the elucidation of a host of particular problems and questions to do with both marine biology and seafood cookery.

This said, I should like to express special thanks as follows. In BRITAIN, to Geoffrey Burgess, Director of the Torry Research Station at Aberdeen, for many acts of help, including a critical reading of the whole draft of the catalogues; Alwyne Wheeler of the British Museum (Natural History), who kindly read the catalogue of fish in draft; Anthony Fincham, Ray Ingle, Peter Whitehead, Solene Whybrow and many others in the same institution; Melvile Clarke at the Marine Laboratory, Plymouth; Gerald Watkins of the Worshipful Company of Fishmongers in London; Jack Shiells and others at Billingsgate Market; Fred Smith at Grimsby; Nora McMillan; Ian and Kath Smith in Orkney; Jimmy Fraser and the County Librarian in Lerwick, Shetland; June Chatfield at the National Museum of Wales and Minwel Tibbott of the Welsh Folk Museum at St Fagans. In IRELAND to Arthur Went, and also Colm Duggan and Paul Hillis of the Department of Fisheries; the Folklore Commission of University College, Dublin; the Irish Countrywomen's Association; the National Museum and the National Library; Eileen Kieran of the Fish Cookery Advisory Service of the Irish Sea Fisheries Board; and Joan Crichton.

In PORTUGAL, to Fernando Lima and Judite Jesus de Cabo. In SPAIN, to José Castillo and Diego Bustamante. In FRANCE, to the Laboratory at Boulogne of the Institut des Pêches Maritimes; and to Mireille Mathieu (for help unwittingly given, which I hope some day to explain to her). In BELGIUM, to the Rijksstation voor Seevisserij at Ostend; the Fischermuseum at Oostduinkerke; and Roland Desnerck. In the NETHERLANDS, to the Rijksinstituut voor Visserij Onderzoek in The Hague; Dolf Boddeke of the Fisheries Laboratory at IJmuiden; Ka. Taal of the Herring Control Service at Scheveningen; and Françoise Berserik. In GERMANY, to the various institutions in Hamburg of the Bundesforschungsanstalt für Fischerei; the Bundesverband der Deutschen Fischindustrie; Peter Frisch; Eberhard Putter; Heinrich Katz of Bremerhaven; and Edith Harrington. In POLAND, to the Sea Fisheries Institute at Gdynia; Jan Jokiel; and Anna Lubinska. In the SOVIET UNION, to the scores of people who helped my daughter Pamela compile her collection of recipes there. In FINLAND, to Gösta Bergman of the Fisheries Division of the Ministry of Agriculture and Forestry; Guy-Stephan Catani; Annuka Harma; Henrik and Inger Antell; and Lylli Lauka. In SWEDEN, to Harald Alander; the Natural History Museum at Göteborg; Bo Essvik; Inga Dixon; and Ray Bradfield. In NORWAY, to Knut and Nancy Fægri for most extensive and generous assistance; the Biological Station at Espegrend of the University of Bergen; the Fisheries Directorate and the Institute of Marine Research at Bergen; Hroar Dege; and Elizabeth Bogstad. In DENMARK, to Vagn and Lise Hansen for both master-minding and largely contributing to my Danish researches; Dyrnesli Nielsen; Alice Bruun; and Margaret Moody. In ICELAND, to Alda Möller of the Iceland Fisheries Laboratories in Reykjavik; Maria Petursdóttir; Finnbogi Gudmundsson. Director of the National Library; the National Museum; Hilmar Jónsson; and Margret Bjornsdóttir. In CANADA, to W. B. Scott, Director of the Huntsman Marine Laboratory at St Andrew's, N.B.; Michael Dadswell and John Caddy of the Marine Biological Station at the same place; Graham Bligh, Director of the Halifax Laboratory, and Cathy Sinnott; Derek Davis and Niels Jannasch of the Nova Scotia Museum; and the Library of Canada House in London. In the UNITED STATES, to Warren F. Rathjen of the New England Fisheries Development Program at Gloucester, Mass.; Robert Livingstone, Jr, of the Northeast Utilisation Research Center, also at Gloucester; Robert Livingstone, Jr, of the Northeast Fisheries Center at Wood's Hole, Mass.; Daniel and Anne Cohen at the Smithsonian Institution for innumerable acts of kind help; Ray Manning and Isa Farfante of the same institution; R. Tucker Abbott; the National Marine Fisheries Service in Washington, D.C.; William P. Davis and Alston C. Badger of the Bear's Bluff Field Station, S.C.; Gene R. Huntsman of the Beaufort Laboratory, N.C.; Frederick H. Berry of the Miami Laboratory; George and Priscilla Macmillan; and May Louise Zumwalt.

To my own family, four bouquets with my love. My wife Jane accompanied and helped me on many of my research journeys and acted unfailingly as the 'Voice of the Practical Cook' whenever this was necessary, as it often was. My three daughters all made notable contributions. Caroline undertook a large share of the testing of recipes and criticized the whole recipe section in draft. Pamela provided the most interesting of the recipe chapters, that on the Soviet Union. Jennifer composed the indexes with care and enthusiasm.

The testing of recipes was by no means confined to our own kitchen. My warm thanks to Judith Baum and Jenny Kenrick for doing much of this; and to Audrey Ellison and the Flour Advisory Council in London for technical advice on certain recipes involving pastry.

I have been triply blessed in working not only with my commissioning editor, Jillian Norman, but also with two co-editors in other publishing houses, Caroline Hobhouse and Barbara Burn. My affectionate thanks go to them all; and likewise, for the third time in three years, to Janet Lovelock for preparing a typescript impeccably tailored to match the printed page.

Finally, I wish to thank the André L. Simon Foundation for generously offering to provide a substantial grant towards my travel expenses. The Foundation thus made it possible for me to pay my particularly fruitful visits to Norway and Iceland, for which I am most grateful.

ILLUSTRATIONS

These come from a variety of sources, partly from necessity, but partly also by choice; since it seemed to me that it would add to the interest of the book to present the work of different artists in it, while preserving a certain harmony of style.

I thank William Scott in Canada, Lipke B. Holthuis in the Netherlands and Bent Muus in Copenhagen for helping me to obtain some of these in the best possible form, in some instances in the original; and the Smithsonian Institution in Washington, D.C., for providing me with reproductions, barely distinguishable from the originals, of many of the famous drawings of fish by H. L. Todd and kindred material. I am likewise grateful to Cressida Pemberton-Pigott for photographing many of the drawings.

Wendy Jones did the following drawings expressly for this book: those on pages 24, 195,

200, 207, 213, 222, 225, 227, 244, 251, 261, 262, 274, 276, 305, 343, 347, 348, 356, 365, 410, 411, 451, 454, 460 and 462.

The dedication page was designed by Marco Valdivia.

The maps on pages 15 to 18 were prepared by Illustra Design.

The sources of the other illustrations, except for those given in the text, are as follows:

From Rondelet, *Libri de Piscibus Marinis*, 1588; that on page 165.

From Bonaparte, the volume on fish in his *Iconografia della Fauna italica*, 1832: those on pages 110 (lower) and 158.

From Parnell, *Fishes of the Firth of Forth*, 1838: those on pages 30, 140, 141 (upper and centre) and 152 (upper).

From De Kay's *Zoology of New York*, Vol. 5, 1843; that on page 226 (lower left).

From Forbes and Hanley, *A History of British Mollusca*, 1849–53; those on pages 210, 214, 215, 216 (right), 218, 219, 220, 226 (upper), 228 (upper), 229, 230, 231 (lower), 234, 235, 237, 238, 239 and 240 (upper).

From Chenu, the volume on crustaceans and molluscs in his *Encyclopédie d'Histoire naturelle*, 1858: those on pages 193 and 242.

From Yarrell, *A History of British Fishes*, 3rd ed., 1859: those on pages 42 (lower), 47 (lower) and 122 (lower).

From Blanchard, *Les poissons des eaux douces de la France*, 1866: that on page 47 (upper) and the subsidiary drawing on page 176.

From Day, *The Fishes of Great Britain and Ireland*, 1880–84: those on pages 31, 32, 33, 38, 48 (upper), 56, 58, 60, 64, 69 (upper), 71 (upper), 79 (lower), 80, 89 (lower), 99, 100 (lower), 104, 113 (upper), 116, 117, 124, 134, 144, 145, 156, 157, 172, 173 and 176 (main drawing).

From the *Smithsonian Institution Collection* (of drawings done in the late nineteenth century and mostly published for the first time in the two works cited under Goode in the Bibliography, although some first appeared in the work of Jordan and Evermann): those on pages 25, 26, 34, 35, 52, 55, 63, 70, 71 (lower), 72, 79 (upper), 87, 89 (upper), 90, 91, 92, 95, 96, 97, 98, 100 (upper), 101, 102, 103, 105, 107, 108, 109, 110 (upper), 111, 112, 113 (lower), 115, 119, 120, 121, 128, 129, 137, 139, 141 (lower), 150, 151 (lower), 153, 154, 155 (upper), 161, 163, 166, 187, 188 (lower right), 192, 196, 197, 198, 203 (upper), 228 (lower), 233 (upper), 236, 247 (upper) and 426. The drawings of fish were mostly done by H. L. Todd; those of crustaceans by Richard Rathbun.

From an advertisement in *Mrs A. B. Marshall's Cookery Book*, c. 1890: that on page 336.

From Smitt, *A History of Scandinavian Fishes*, 1893–5, those on pages 82, 146 and 155 (lower).

From Stuxberg's *Sveriges och Norges Fisker*, 1895: those on page 175.

From Augusta Foote Arnold's *The Sea-Beach at Ebb-Tide*, 1901: those on pages 231 (upper), 232 and 240 (lower).

From Joubin and Le Danois, *Catalogue illustré des animaux marins comestibles . . .* (of France). 1925: that on page 233 (lower).

From Lily Newton's *A Handbook of the British Seaweeds*, 1931: those on pages 251 (upper), 252 and 253.

From Poll, *Poissons marins (de Belgique)*, 1947: those on pages 40 (upper), 57, 62, 66, 68, 88, 118, 147 (lower) (all after Smitt); those on pages 60, 148, 149, and 151 (upper) (all after Day); those on pages 74, 76, 94 and 123 (all after drawings in the collection listed under Conseil Permanent International pour l'Exploration de la Mer in the Bibliography); those on pages 77, 78, 84, 168 (upper), 169, 170, 171 and 180 (all after Bonaparte); those on page 142 (after J. Travis Jenkins); and those on pages 147 (upper) and 162 (original drawings by Henri Dupond, who also did the drawings adapted from other sources).

From *Fishes of the Western North Atlantic*, published by the Sears Foundation from 1948 onwards: those on pages 81 and 179.

From the volumes by Holthuis in *Fauna van Nederland*, 1950: those on pages 186, 188 (upper left) and 190; and from an unpublished volume in the same series that on page 194.

From the volume edited by Ushakov on *Invertebrates of the Far-Eastern Seas of the U.S.S.R.*, 1955: those on pages 204 (lower), 224 (lower) and 250.

From the volume by Muus on cephalopods in *Danmarks Fauna*, 1959: those on pages 245, 246, 247 (except the uppermost one) and 248.

From Oskarsson's work on Icelandic bivalves, *Samlokur i Sjó*, 1964: those on pages 216 (left) and 226 (lower right).

From Austin B. Williams's *Marine Decapod Crustaceans of the Carolinas*, 1965: those on page 182 (lower) and 206.

From Leim and Scott, *Fishes of the Atlantic Coast of Canada*, 1966: those on pages 36, 37, 40 (lower), 42 (upper), 45, 46, 48 (lower), 49, 65, 67, 85, 86, 126, 130, 131, 132, 135, 138 (upper), 152 (lower), 167 (adapted) and 174. These drawings were all the work of D. R. Harriott, except for the upper drawing on page 174, which was done by the firm Todd and Stackhouse.

From Isabel Pérez Farfante's *Western Atlantic Shrimps of the genus Penaeus*, 1969: those on pages 184 and 185 (the work of the artist María M. Diéguez).

From Wheeler's *The Fishes of the British Isles and North-West Europe*, 1969: those on pages 50, 69 (lower), 114 and 122 (the work of Valerie du Heaume).

From Marit Christiansen's *Decapoda Brachyura* (of Scandinavia), 1969: those on pages 202, 203 (centre) and 205.

From Graham's *British Prosobranch and other Operculate Gastropod Molluscs*, 1971: those on pages 211 and 212.

From my own *Mediterranean Seafood*, 1972: those on pages 138 (lower), 209 and 224 (upper) (the work of Peter Stebbing).

From the F.A.O. *Species Identification Sheets for the Mediterranean and the Black Sea*, 1973: those on pages 183 and 191.

From the U.S. *Marine Fisheries Review* of August 1975: that on page 204 (upper).

From *Oceanus*, summer number of 1976: that on page 254 (artist Ihsan Al-Shehbaz, illustrating an article by Richard A. Fralick and John H. Ryther on Uses and Cultivation of Seaweed).

The drawing of *Crangon crangon* on page 182 is by Dolf Boddeke.

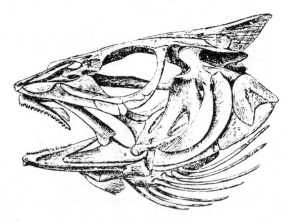

The bones of a cod's head – see page 395

Introduction

Having lived on both sides of the North Atlantic, I have been struck by a small paradox. Traffic between the two sides is intense. The relationship between the cuisines of Europe and those of North America is obvious and interesting. The fauna, marine or other, on the two sides are often identical and almost always closely related. Yet books are usually about one side or the other, not both.

I have written this book with various purposes in mind, one of which has been to illuminate some of these relationships for travellers and for cooks. In writing the book, I have visited or revisited almost all the countries of the region. These travels have fortified my belief that transatlantic links in this field, as well as the relationships to be seen within Europe and within North America, deserve to be chronicled; but they have also made me realize how much more could be done than I have managed to do. Suggestions and corrections from readers will be very welcome.

Since the scope of the book is unusual, I ought to say what I mean by the North Atlantic. The definition which its inhabitants, the fish, tacitly furnish by their distribution and movements would approximate to 'the waters north of a curving line drawn from Cape Hatteras in the west to the northern part of the Bay of Biscay in the east'. Species from further south are found above this line, and species from the north below it; but it does indicate in a general way the division between marine fauna of the colder northern waters and those of the warmer, sub-tropical waters to the south.

However, this would not quite fit my purpose. I wish to take account of the distribution and migrations of human beings as well as of fish; and of the flow of culinary influences as well as that of ocean currents. I have therefore defined the North Atlantic area in a manner which covers the whole seaboard of western Europe, including the Baltic, and virtually the whole of the eastern seaboard of Canada and the United States. I omit only the State of Florida, since in the present context it patently belongs to a different region, that of the West Indies and the Gulf of Mexico.

Vientiane and London 1973–8

The North Atlantic

The Atlantic Ocean is vast. It stretches from the Arctic to the Antarctic. At its point of greatest width it is 5000 miles wide. It is a single ocean. However, these few remarks and the accompanying maps are intended to illuminate only the northern part, its adjacent seas and its fisheries.

Fish, crustaceans and molluscs have distributions, ranges or habitats which are determined by several criteria. One is the temperature of the water, another its salinity. A third, which is not of direct concern to pelagic fish, i.e. those which swim at the surface, is the depth of the water. A fourth is the availability of the foods on which the various species nourish themselves. A fifth, which applies to demersal fish, i.e. those which live on the sea bottom, is the nature of the bottom and its suitability to various needs, such as the requirement of many flatfish for sandy bottoms in which they can half bury themselves and that of lobsters for rocky crevices in which they can lurk. Finally, many species make migratory movements which may be determined by yet another factor, namely the need to find suitable places in which to spawn.

The movements of fishermen and fishing fleets depend, obviously, on the whereabouts of their prey. Although some fishing techniques, such as bottom-trawling, bring in varied catches, most fishing operations are directed at a particular species. They must take place where that species is present in numbers which make the fishing worth while economically, and where the fish are accessible to whatever catching gear is available. But there are other considerations. One is the legal one, namely the fishing limits, either exclusive or controlled by a quota system, which the various maritime countries set in the waters contiguous to their coasts. These limits have been changing to such an extent and so fast in recent years that I have not attempted to show them on the map. A further consideration is that there are various international institutions and agreements which are concerned to prevent over-exploitation of stocks by setting limits to the quantities which may be caught in a given year. These limits also change, in the light of continuous research into the size of the stocks and the habits of the species.

The main map, on pages 16 and 17, gives a conspectus of the whole

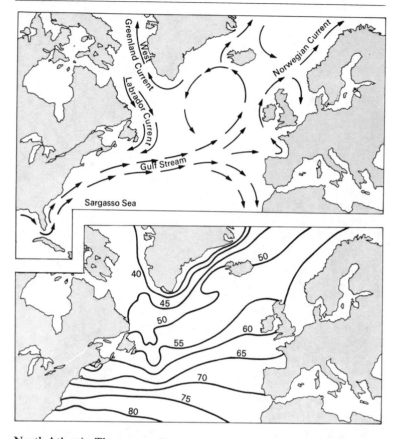

North Atlantic. The two smaller maps above illustrate in a simple manner the flow of certain important currents in the North Atlantic, and the general pattern of the variations in temperature which these currents and other factors bring about. The most important current is the Gulf Stream. Warm water pouring westwards into the Gulf of Mexico, as a result of the prevailing winds, finds its exit between Florida and Cuba and is propelled towards the north-east with such force that its effects are felt as far away as the north of Norway.

Thus the lines representing different water temperatures do not run more or less straight across in an east/west axis, but are considerably convoluted; and this fact of course affects the distribution of species. But the temperatures vary with the seasons. Certain fish will swim as far north as, say, Cape Cod or the south coast of England in the summer, although they would never be found there in the winter.

The large map above has been kept as simple as possible. Its most important purpose is to indicate the varying extent of the continental shelf, i.e. the shallow waters (down to 200 metres or so) adjacent to land; and thus to illustrate the importance for fishermen of such famous fishing areas as the waters around Iceland and off Newfoundland. Progress in technology makes it possible to fish in waters deeper than these. But the continental shelf still provides and will continue to provide the richest fishing grounds, since it is there that the principal edible species congregate in the largest numbers. There are fish in the very deep waters known as the 'abyss'; but abyssal species are on the whole not worth catching.

THE NORTH ATLANTIC

Continental shelf
(waters down to a depth of 200 metres.)

1000 kms
1000 mls

The continental shelf is only one feature of the submarine geography. There are also 'trenches' of particularly deep water, and lofty submarine ridges. The most important of these, the mid Atlantic ridge, extends from Iceland down to Tristan da Cunha in the South Atlantic. Iceland itself and the Azores represent peaks in this submerged mountain chain. Another ridge runs from Iceland to the Faroes, Shetland and north Scotland. Most of it lies below the surface, and it does not significantly affect surface temperatures; but there is a marked difference in temperature between the deeper waters on either side of this sill, and a corresponding difference between the fauna of the two sides.

Salinity levels in the Baltic Sea.

The salinity level in the North Sea is about 35%. This map shows how sharply and progressively the figure decreases in the Baltic Sea.

The North Atlantic Ocean has many important seas which can be regarded as part of it or as adjacent to it. Among these are the Irish or Celtic Sea, the Norwegian Sea and the North Sea, with its famed and heavily exploited fishing grounds (including the renowned Silver Pit, discovered in 1837 to be a rich source of fine soles). The sea which I have chosen to illustrate separately, above, is, however, the Baltic Sea. It is more clearly separated from its parent ocean and has unusual characteristics, of which the most important is that, as the map shows, the level of salinity in it decreases remarkably from its mouth to its inner extremities. The result of this is that it contains a relatively limited range of marine species, since few such species can tolerate very low salinity; but that by way of compensation a number of species which are normally regarded as freshwater fish are taken in such areas as the Gulfs of Bothnia and of Finland. The fisheries in the Baltic are, naturally, controlled by the littoral states; and the cooperation between them in sharing out their resources of seafood, which can be defined with more accuracy in this separate and special body of water than in most parts of the North Atlantic region, is close.

Catalogues

The lobster, the crab, and the crayfish are borne in heraldry. The lobster, as an enemy to serpents, was sometimes used as an emblem of temperance, and two lobsters fighting as an emblem of sedition.

Argent, a lobster gules, is the armorial ensign of the family of Von Melem of Frankfort; the crest, two wings argent, each charged with a lobster.

The suits of armour, on the principle of the lobster's shell, consisting of laminæ, being made with overlapping plates, which enabled the steel to give way to every motion of the body, were called *Ecrevisses*, from their resemblance to the lobster, by the French knights of the reign of Henry IV. when these suits were much used. (Moule, *The Heraldry of Fish*)

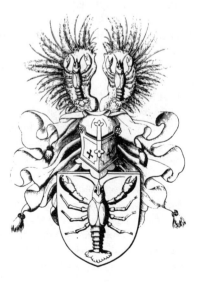

INTRODUCING SOME NINETEENTH-CENTURY AUTHORS

I quote frequently from these authors and would like to introduce them to my readers in advance, and to acknowledge a special debt to them.

FRANCIS DAY (1829–89) was not a natural historian by training. He went out to India as an army surgeon, but made ichthyology his hobby and eventually his new profession. He was appointed Inspector-General of Fisheries in India in 1871, and became the author of two of the greatest books on fish in the English language: *Fishes of India* (1875–80) and *Fishes of Great Britain* (1880–84). He displayed in his work that prodigious application which many Victorians possessed, but spiced his writings agreeably with scholarly anecdotes. The picture shows him in his forties.

FRANK BUCKLAND (1826–80) began a career as a surgeon, like Day, and also developed into an Inspector of Fisheries, in Britain. Unlike Day, he was one of the great Victorian eccentrics; yet combined his amusing eccentricities with much serious work. He is best remembered now for his books, such as the *Logbook of a Fisherman and Zoologist*. To gain a full impression of his manifold activities and exuberant character, read *The Curious World of Frank Buckland* by Geoffrey Burgess.

GEORGE BROWN GOODE (1851–96) was one of the greatest American ichthyologists. He was also a talented museum administrator and became Secretary of the Smithsonian Institution, in charge of the national collections, in 1887. This was also the year in which his great work on the natural history of the fishes of the U.S.A. was completed. This work, gracefully and often wittily written, formed part of the monumental report, in seven volumes, on *The Fisheries and Fishery Industries of the United States*, which he edited with a team of associates.

Finally, I mention the anonymous PISCATOR, whose book *Fish: how to choose and how to dress* was first published in London in 1843. His real name was William Hughes, and he was a barrister. His work was, I believe, the first cookery book devoted entirely to fish to be published in Britain.

1. Explanation of the Catalogues

The catalogues which follow include almost all the species of sea fish, crustaceans, molluscs and miscellaneous seafoods which are both indigenous to the North Atlantic region, as I have defined it on page 13, and likely to be found in fish markets or restaurants. I say 'almost' because I have left out all marine mammals, for reasons explained on page 249.

I have listed some species which are rarely or never marketed, but which readers may catch or gather for themselves. With an eye to the future, I have also included some species which are not marketed at present, but may be before long. The blue whiting and the grenadier are examples.

Some species really belong to the warmer waters of the Central Atlantic, but make excursions to the north, usually in the summer. Depending on their importance and the scale of their presence in northern waters, I have listed, mentioned or ignored them.

The sequence in which the species are catalogued conforms in a general way with current scientific practice. In particular, I have taken the useful list published by the American Fisheries Society (see Bibliography) as a guide in ordering the fishes; but I have made a few adjustments. Thus the non-bony fish (sharks, rays, etc.) do not appear in their usual position at the beginning, where they would provide an uninspiring start for those interested in cookery, but have been moved to the end.

There are, of course, many more North Atlantic species than I have listed. Some are inedible or not worth eating. Some are rare or inaccessible. Readers who would like to consult comprehensive works will find these in the Bibliography, e.g. Wheeler's *The Fishes of the British Isles and North West Europe* and Leim and Scott's *Fishes of the Atlantic Coast of Canada*. (Very few scientific books treat the North Atlantic as a whole.)

SCIENTIFIC NAMES

In the catalogues the name of each species is given in a Latinized form. This is the scientific name. It usually consists of two words, the first indicating the genus and the second the species within the genus. Some species are shown with more than one scientific name. The explanation is that different naturalists have given them different names and that more than one have recently been or still are in common use.

The first scientific name is the preferred name and is followed by the name of the naturalist * who bestowed it on the species in question. Sometimes the name of the naturalist appears in brackets, sometimes not. The brackets are used to show that the specific name bestowed by the naturalist has been retained, but that the generic name has been changed, since the species is now assigned to a different genus. If the name of the naturalist is not in brackets, this means that the whole of the name which he bestowed is still accepted. There are now relatively few instances of this, since the pace of change in taxonomy has quickened during the last few decades to a full gallop. Changes which bring greater clarity and precision must be welcomed, but it sometimes seems a pity that names which have stood for centuries, which may even have been given by the great Linnaeus himself, must be replaced by new and unfamiliar ones.

So much for species and genus. The catalogue entries also show to what family each species belongs. The family is the next step up in the sequence: species, genus, family, order, class, sub-phylum, phylum . . . But I need go no further. Even at the fifth level, there are only two classes of fish, those with a bony skeleton and those with cartilaginous 'bones'. There are, however, quite a lot of Orders. (This word, and Class, are often thus capitalized, as if to emphasize what a Belgian house-agent would call their 'haut standing'.) The reader who would like to know to what Order a species belongs will find the information in the introductory passages which preface each group of catalogue entries.

COMMON NAMES

Common or vernacular names are those which people normally use in their own languages. These can be confusing in various ways. It is not always easy to tell whether they are general names or specific ones. They may have only local validity. They can have different meanings in different parts of a country, or in different countries (for example, hake in Britain and the United States). They may be ambiguous (for example, monkfish in Britain). They may be misleading (for example, Dover sole, if it makes people think that there is a distinct species inhabiting the waters near Dover). And it is often difficult to know which of two or three widely used names is the best (for example, sea trout or salmon trout?).

In short, common names present an unruly tangle of imprecision and ambiguity, quite apart from the additional confusion produced by the use

---

* Occasionally abbreviated. Thus C. and V. for Cuvier and Valenciennes; and B. and S. for Bloch and Schneider.

of euphemistic names, such as rock salmon. It is not surprising that various international and national authorities seek to tidy up the mess by publishing lists of 'approved' names. I wish them well, but am glad that they will not achieve success overnight. The existing common names are, to put it mildly, the ones which are most useful to most people.

Common names are given in the catalogues, with certain subtractions and additions, in English (including American and Canadian English where these differ from English English), Portuguese, Spanish, French (including French Canadian where appropriate), Dutch, German, Polish, Russian, Finnish, Swedish, Norwegian, Danish and Icelandic.

The subtractions are of names which exist but are hardly ever used. The Finnish language has names for almost every species in this book, but only a few of these species are marketed in Finland, and even fewer are found in Finnish waters. The irrelevant names have been left out. I have likewise omitted names from the other Nordic countries for species which do not range north of the English Channel; and Spanish and Portuguese names for species which are confined to northern waters.

The additions are various. I have included Basque, Breton, Welsh, Irish, Scots Gaelic, Faroese, Greenlandic, Estonian, Latvian and Lithuanian names for at least some of the species which are important to those who speak these tongues. I have also put in some local names and some obsolete ones, where these have taken my fancy.

The transliteration of Russian names is a problem to which several solutions are available, but none which commands universal support. I have followed the (revised) system of the British Standards Institute, which has also been used by my daughter Pamela in her 'Recipes from the Soviet Union' (page 338). I take this opportunity to praise the dictionary of Russian fish names, cited under Ricker in the Bibliography.

The Icelandic language has two letters which require explanation. þ (capital Þ) is pronounced like 'th' in thing; and ð (capital Ð) like 'th' in them. The second of these letters also occurs in Faroese.

THE DRAWINGS

These come, necessarily, from a variety of sources; but the variety is partly intentional, since it seemed to me that to use the work of a number of different artists and draftsmen or draftswomen, presented in a harmonious fashion, would add to the interest of the book. The sources of the drawings reproduced in the catalogue are given in the Acknowledgements. Here I need only ask the reader to keep in mind that the drawings are not to a uniform scale; and that a fish out of water will not, of course, have its fins erect as shown in the drawings.

REMARKS

Under this heading I give various pieces of information, including almost always maximum length and colour.

It is usual to measure the length of a fish from its snout to the base of its tail fin, as shown in the diagrammatic drawing below. This is the method which I have tried to follow in giving maximum and normal lengths. But some writers in the past have included projections such as the tail fin at the rear and the sword of the swordfish at the front. Some measurements of this kind may have crept into my text.

However, what I would particularly ask readers to remember is that the maximum length is that of an unusually large adult; and that very many fish are caught before they even attain normal adult length.

Information about colour may also be useful in identifying fish. But many species can modify their own colours to match their habitat; and colours often change when fish are taken out of the water and die. Surer clues to identification are provided by such features as the shape of the fish, the number and position of the various fins and the course of the lateral line along the fish's side. The diagram below explains the technical terms used in the catalogues with regard to such features.

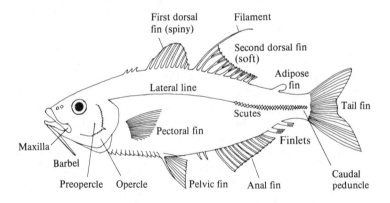

USING THE CATALOGUES

In each catalogue entry the reader will find under the heading 'Cuisine' a summary indication of how the fish or other sea creature can best be cooked or otherwise prepared for eating; and sometimes the outline of a recipe which could not be included in the recipe section. In many catalogue entries a further heading 'Recipes' covers signposts to full recipes which are specifically suitable.

2. Catalogue of Fish

The Herring and Its Relations

The Order *Clupeiformes*, which comprises the herring family and its relations, constitutes what is probably the most important group of food fish in the world.

The clupeoid or herring-like fish all have a single dorsal fin, placed near the middle of the body. They have no lateral line, but a network of sensory canals just under the skin of the head, which seems to fulfil a similar function. Most of them travel in huge shoals.

The family includes some species which spawn in, and are usually taken in, fresh water. These are the shad and their relations. Their abundance, indeed survival, depends on the state of the rivers in which they reproduce themselves. There are now far fewer shad to be had in Europe; but on the American side of the Atlantic they continue to be numerous and important as food.

I should also mention here three fish which are related to the herring and which stray north as far as Cape Cod from the warmer waters where they really belong. These are *Megalops atlantica* Valenciennes, the TARPON, a magnificent sporting fish which is illustrated at the foot of the page; *Elops saurus* Linnaeus, the ten-pounder; and *Albula vulpes* (Linnaeus), the bonefish. The first two belong to the family *Elopidae*, the last to the family *Albulidae*. None of them is important as a food fish in our area, but North American anglers take them from time to time, especially in the summer months.

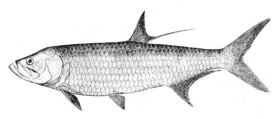

HERRING   Family *Clupeidae*

Clupea harengus Linnaeus

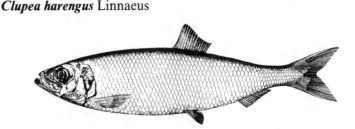

REMARKS   Maximum length 40 cm, but the usual adult length is about 20 to 25 cm. The back is dark blue, shading to silvery white below, sometimes with golden or reddish tints.

The species is distributed right across the North Atlantic, down to the north of France on one side and Chesapeake Bay on the other, but may be divided into different races or populations which belong to different areas and exhibit minor variations. One such race, the Baltic herring, seems to me to deserve separate treatment and is described on page 29.

Supplies of herring, the most important clupeoid fish in European waters, have fluctuated in a bewildering way for as far back
as any records exist, for example in the era of the Hanseatic League. This is a biological phenomenon. But herring have also been affected in this century by over-exploitation; and this seems to be the primary cause of the dramatic decline of the herring fishery in many countries. The North Sea herring stock is the most severely affected. The herring catch fell by half from the 1950s to the 1960s. Boats had to be laid up, or used for other purposes (like many of the vessels belonging to the great Scheveningen fleet, which now take tourists out for a day's sport fishing), or they had to find new fishing grounds. Mallaig, on the west coast of Scotland, has proved to be a good base for catching herring in quantities which the fishermen there had never dreamed of before. But the general picture is one of dwindling stocks being pursued by fewer and fewer boats with more and more sophisticated equipment; and of an increasing tendency to inhibit their activities by governmental restrictions, unilateral or internationally agreed, in an attempt to restore stocks to something like their former level.

There are important commercial fisheries for the herring in Canada and New England. In New Brunswick and Maine immature herring are canned as 'sardines'. The pioneer of this industry was a Mr George Burnham of Portland, who observed that myriads of small herring were caught annually at Eastport, Maine, and who

French: Hareng
Dutch: Haring
German: Hering
Polish: Sledź
Russian: Sel'd'
Finnish: Silli, Silakka
Swedish: Sill, Strömming
Norwegian: Sild
Danish: Sild
Icelandic: Sild, Hafsild
Other: Scadán (Irish);
    Ysgadenyn, Pennog (Welsh);
    Angmagssagssuaq
    (Greenlandic)

made the first experiments in canning them, using French techniques, in the 1860s. However, the so-called 'Russian sardines', which were young herring canned in and imported from Germany, continued to hold the New York market until, in the following decade, German ports were blockaded by the French Navy and the traffic was halted. Eastport 'sardines' were then canned in a more successful way and captured the market.

One odd thing about the herring was described thus by Francis Day (*The Fishes of Great Britain and Ireland*, 1880–84): 'The noise made by herrings when captured is peculiar, and has been likened to various things – to the cry of a mouse, to the word "cheese", a sneeze, or a squeak . . .' This noise is thought to be the result of air being expelled from the air bladder.

Day, whose lengthy and serious work is pleasantly spiced with material of an entertaining nature, also tells us that a Manxman going to fish for herring would always take a dead wren with him. The logic behind this was that there had been a sea-spirit which haunted herring tackle and brought on storms, but which had finally changed itself into a wren and flown off; wherefore the presence of a dead wren signified that all would be well.

CUISINE   The flesh of the herring is relatively fat and lends itself well to pickling. But it is not unduly fat, and it is perfectly in order to fry herrings. Coating them with oatmeal first, in the Scots fashion, seems to me to produce the best results. Serve boiled, not fried potatoes with them.

Herrings may also be grilled and baked; but they are not suitable for poaching or steaming. Kippers, however, can be cooked by pouring boiling water over them and letting them stand for a few minutes, with a weight or grid holding them down flat. It is well to place a pat of butter or margarine on each kipper fillet when serving them after they have been cooked in this way, or grilled, or baked. Ambrose Heath gives over two dozen recipes for kippers in his useful little book on *Herrings, Bloaters and Kippers*, including good instructions for making a kipper mousse. Since his book came out (in 1954) kipper pâté has become more popular, and deservedly so; but kippers have, alas, become more expensive.

RECIPES   (see also recipes for Baltic herring listed on page 29)

Shetland Herring Girls in the First World War – A Portrait

'Jackie and Lizzie lived at The Ark, Haroldswick, and during the summer season, i.e., mid-May to end September would work as gutter girls at the herring stations at Baltasound. A typical week during the busiest time would cause a riot nowadays. They would get up at 4 a.m., dress and take baked bread and fresh milk with them to Baltasound, about an hour's walk, to their station below Uregarth. Here they shared a room with six girls in one of the wooden blocks of houses; 16 rooms in a block so they could hold 96 girls. Here they changed into their working clothes: Baltic boots (leather up to the thighs), cut-off stockings to protect legs above boots to as high as they would go, a short skirt above the knees, covered with a black oilskin coat with bib, straps and a gathered skirt to cover the tops of their boots. A red ribbed jersey with short sleeves and head scarf tied at the back with no hair showing. Their rig was now complete except for the bandages covering their hands for protection and made from flour bags. There was normally no time to take these off for meals and [they] might be on till they finished work at midnight.

'While Gutting the girls worked in pairs with another one packing. The fish were emptied into farlings – big boxes on stands about three feet wide and about four farlings to a station. Each girl would take a fish and with one movement slit and remove the guts and put it in which ever tub it was graded for – Fulls, Mediums, Madjes (empty herring), Matties (the smallest) and Spent (no good). If the heads were not intact, the eyes not right or anything else they were no good for salting. They were then packed into the appropriate barrels.

'The crew of three got paid 1s. for each barrel of herring gutted and packed – or fourpence each girl. A good crew could work three barrels per hour – there would be approximately 900 herring in a barrel. Some girls could gut at the rate of 40 herring a minute . . . At the end of each week – usually midnight on Saturday, the girls would finish and go home for Sunday. Walking back down the Setter road they would be practically walking in their sleep, and in bed instead of counting sheep to go to sleep it would be herring . . .'

(Charles Sandison, *Unst: my island home and its story*, Shetland Times, Lerwick, 1968.)

These drawings show a selection of the brand marks which used to appear on the tops of herring barrels. The left-hand brand was, of course, the best.

BALTIC HERRING

REMARKS   As I explained on page 26, the Baltic herring is merely a sub-species. Common names used in the Baltic countries generally are given on that page. Names used in particular of the Baltic variety are: Lithuanian, silkē; Latvian, reņģe; Estonian, silk or räim; Russian, salaka.

The distinguishing features of the Baltic herring are that it is smaller than the Atlantic herring and has a lower fat content. Even within the Baltic, different populations can be distinguished; but this general statement is true of them all.

CUISINE   In the past, the Baltic herring was a staple food of the Baltic peoples and numerous different ways of curing it, so that it could be eaten inland, and all round the year, were devised. It is still a staple food, although no longer so dominant a feature of the diet, and most of the cures have survived because people have become used to the distinctive tastes which they impart. Salted Baltic herring is widely available. A good way of desalting it, practised in Finland, is to soak it in milk overnight. It may then be fried or grilled and served with small new potatoes in a cream and dill sauce – delicious!

Pickled herring is also very popular, in scores of different preparations. Perhaps the most remarkable of the cures, however, is the fermentation which produces the Swedish Surströmming (page 368).

The list of recipes below looks formidably long, but constitutes no more than a tiny proportion of those practised. I was told in Finland that in certain villages on the Bothnian coast a girl is judged ready for marriage when she is capable of preparing Baltic herring in twenty-five different ways. Apparently she is likely to attain this degree of prowess at about the age of twenty. But she can go much further. I have several books which contain more than 150 recipes each for Baltic herring.

RECIPES   (see also recipes for Atlantic herring listed on page 27)

Salt herring with sour cream, 331	Grilled, Finnish style, 362
Herring toasts for breakfast, 342	Finnish herring 'steaks', 363
Selga appetizer, 354	Fried to look like flounder, 367
Rosolje (Estonian salad), 357	Like chimney-sweeps, 369
Herring with pork fat sauce, 357	Sol over Gudhjelm, 387

WHITEBAIT

What is whitebait? People still ask the question. So far as Britain is concerned, it can be answered in two lines by saying that the name applies to the fry of *various* clupeoid fish, notably the herring and the sprat, and often mixed together. But the question used to cause great perplexity.

Whitebait are tiny fish, transparent or silver-white, which used to be fished in huge quantities in the tidal waters of the Thames, and elsewhere. Their size varies now, as it did in the past; but the figure of 180 to the pound weight may be taken as typical. Dr James Murie, in his *Report on the Sea Fisheries and Fishing Industries of the Thames Estuary* (1903), gave painstaking analyses of the contents of boxes of whitebait, and showed that as many as thirty-two different species might be found therein. The fry of twenty-one different fish, including eels, plaice and lumpfish, turned up from time to time, together with various shrimps, crabs, octopus and even jellyfish! But these intruders were few in number, compared with the tiny herrings and sprats.

Whitebait appeared on an English menu as long ago as 1612, although Buckland (*The Natural History of British Fishes*, 1883) records a claim that it was Richard Cannon of Blackwall who, in 1780, first persuaded the local tavern keepers to serve whitebait dinners regularly. Cannon had problems with the Thames authorities, who argued, correctly, that the practice involved the consumption of the fry of herrings and sprats. But he convinced the Lord Mayor of London that whitebait were a distinct species; and many natural historians shared this view, while arguing spiritedly among themselves about how to classify it. The Frenchman Valenciennes even instituted a new genus, *Rogenia*, to accommodate the species.

While the controversy raged, whitebait became more and more popular, so much so that Buckland could describe it as being an essential food for Londoners. The season ran from about February until August and not only engaged the attention of the wealthy and fashionable but would also provoke what one author called 'a vast resort of the lower order of epicures' to the taverns at which freshly caught whitebait were served.

In the United States, especially in New England and Long Island, whitebait are usually silversides (page 79) or sand-eels (page 122).

Parnell (*Fishes of the Firth of Forth*, 1838) was among those who regarded whitebait as a distinct species. This is the drawing which he published in support of his view.

SPRAT
Family *Clupeidae*

Sprattus sprattus (Linnaeus)

REMARKS   Maximum length 14 cm. The back is blue or bluish green, the sides and belly silvery. The lower jaw projects beyond the upper, giving the mouth an upwards tilt. The belly is sharply keeled, with a line of spiny scales running from throat to vent.

This small fish is a coastal species which can survive in waters of low salinity such as those of the Baltic (where it occurs in the form of a sub-species, *Sprattus sprattus balticus*). Its range is from the north of Norway down to the Mediterranean.

As Wheeler (*The Fishes of the British Isles and North West Europe*, 1969) points out: 'In Norway conditions are ideal for a special sprat fishery where the fish are trapped in the long, narrow fjords by means of nets, then driven into keeping pens until required for the canning factories. The resultant sprats, seasoned and canned in oil, are sold as "brisling".' In Sweden they are sold as 'Swedish anchovies'.

Portuguese: Espadilha, Lavadilha
Spanish: Espadin
French: Sprat, Esprot
Dutch: Sprot
German: Sprotte, Sprot
Polish: Szprot
Russian: Shprot
Finnish: Kilohaili
Swedish: Skarpsill, Vassbuk
Norwegian: Brisling
Danish: Brisling
Other: Silkele (Lithuanian); Kilu (Estonian); Garvie (Scottish); Coog pennog (Welsh)

CUISINE AND RECIPE   As for the sardine/pilchard (page 39). Very small sprats are 'whitebait', as explained on page 30.

In Holland and Belgium small bundles of lightly smoked sprats are offered for sale at a low price. They are to be skinned before being eaten.

In Germany the sprats smoked at Kiel, known as Kieler Sprotten (or echte Kieler Sprotten if care has been taken to ensure that they do not include any small herring), are an established delicacy. They are hot-smoked, whole, and are consumed like Bucklinge (page 324).

A recipe for an Estonian sprat pâté is given on page 356. I have also come across a Polish one, quite similar but incorporating chopped black olives.

SHAD, ALLIS (or ALLICE) SHAD   Family *Clupeidae*

Alosa alosa (Linnaeus)

REMARKS Maximum length 60 cm. The back is deep blue, the sides silvery white. There may or may not be a single dark spot behind the gill cover.

This large shad is rare in northern European waters and is not found in the Baltic. But from southern Ireland southwards it is fairly common. The adults enter rivers during the spring (hence names meaning May fish) to spawn; but the number of rivers not blocked by man-made obstacles is smaller than it used to be.

Portuguese: Sável
Spanish: Sábalo
French: Alose
Dutch: Elft
German: Alse, Maifisch
Swedish: Majfisk, Majsill
Norwegian: Maisild
Danish: Majsild
Other: Gwangen (Welsh, also of twaite shad)

CUISINE Francis Day took pains, when writing *The Fishes of Great Britain and Ireland* (1880–84), not only to describe the fish but to comment on their edibility. On the shad he observed that: 'Opinions vary, and for several reasons. Being full of bones it is more troublesome to eat without being choked (unless properly carved) than most persons approve of, but if carved properly this unpleasantness is avoided. Taken from the sea during the winter it is poor and dry, but after sojourning in fresh water it becomes plump and delicate, while the higher it ascends the streams the better it is.'

The bones certainly are a snag. One solution is so to soften them, in the cooking, that they can be eaten or, at least, will not cause pain if swallowed by mistake. Prolonged cooking will have this effect, as in the second recipe listed below. Sorrel is also supposed to have a softening effect and some French recipes use it in a stuffing for shad. But Alose à l'oseille is just as likely to mean shad served with sorrel as a separate accompaniment. Both versions are met in the Gironde, where shad is regarded as a speciality.

I should add that the bones *can* be removed, if you know how. The Portuguese book cited under Olleboma in the Bibliography gives instructions in eight stages, with four illustrations, attributing the technique to the family Vanzeller Guedes da Quinta de Avelêda of Penafiel. Vic Dunaway (*From Hook to Table*, 1974) says that boning shad is 'simple'. His explanation has six stages and seven photographs.

RECIPES   (see also North American recipes listed on page 35)
Alose grillée, sauce béarnaise, 288   Alose au four, 294

TWAITE SHAD

Family *Clupeidae*

Alosa fallax (Lacépède)
Alosa finta

REMARKS Maximum length 50 cm. The back is a brilliant blue-black, the flanks and belly silver to white and the sides of the head golden. Note the row of spots, which may number six or seven on each side.

This slightly smaller shad has a more extensive northward range than the allis shad, and is present in the Baltic, although not common there.

'We are told that in Germany this fish is believed to be terrified at storms and troubled waters, delighting in quiet and musical sounds. Therefore to the nets are fastened bows of wood, to which are suspended a number of small bells which chime in harmony together on the nets being moved: the fish are thought to be thus attracted to their destruction, and as long as the alluring sounds continue they cease all efforts at escape.' (Day)

Some authorities recognize various sub-species, of which an interesting one is *Alosa fallax killarnensis* Regan. This is a landlocked shad of small size, found in the lakes of Killarney and locally known as the goureen.

CUISINE AND RECIPES   As for the preceding species.

Portuguese: Saboga
Spanish: Saboga
French: Alose finte
Dutch: Fint
German: Finte, Maifisch
Polish: Parposz
Russian: Finta
Finnish: Täpläsilli
Swedish: Staksill
Norwegian: Stamsild
Danish: Stavsild, Stamsild
Icelandic: Augnasíld

SHAD, AMERICAN SHAD

Family *Clupeidae*

Alosa sapidissima (Wilson)

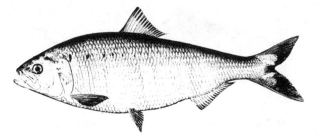

REMARKS   Maximum length 60 cm, usual length 40 to 50 cm. The colour is dark blue above, shading to a silvery white below; whence the names white shad and poplarback shad. There is a golden tinge over the fish, especially the head, when it is in fat condition and at sea. Males have a reddish tinge on head and mouth in the spawning season. Note the depth of the body.

This important species has a range from Labrador to Florida; and also occurs on the Pacific coast, where it was introduced in the nineteenth century. Young shad are born in rivers in the summer and move out into the sea by the autumn. They usually remain there until they are five years old, when they re-enter the rivers to spawn. That is when they are caught.

The favourite spawning grounds of the Shad, or 'Shad Wallows', as they are termed by the fishermen, are on the sandy flats which border the streams, and the sand-bars which are found at intervals higher up the river. When the fish have reached suitable spawning grounds and are ready to cast their eggs, they move up to the flats seemingly in pairs. The time of this movement is usually between sundown and 11 p.m. When in the act of coition they swim close together and near the surface, their back fins projecting above the water. The rapid, vigorous, spasmodic movements which accompany this operation produce a splashing in the water which can be plainly heard from the shore, and which the fishermen characterize as 'washing'. (Marshall McDonald.) *

CUISINE   'This well-known fish is a general favorite among all classes of persons, as its flesh is considered among the best, sweetest, the most delicate, as well as being the most plentiful when in season. Nothing but its numerous bones can be said against it . . . The roes of the female shad are considered a delicacy, and by some superior to the fish itself. The male shad has also roes, or rather a melt; but they are much smaller and not so seedy-looking or red, but which many prefer, as they think it more delicate eating.' Thus De Voe,† who also points out that shad which are

---

* In his contribution about the American shad to Goode's great work *The Food Fishes of the United States* (1885–7).

† Thomas De Voe published at New York in 1866 a book entitled *The Market Assistant*, 'containing a brief description of every article of human food sold in the public markets of New York, Boston, Philadelphia and Brooklyn . . . with many curious incidents and anecdotes'. De

'spent' after spawning are not worth eating; 'in fact, no orthodox sportsman will permit a shad upon his table after the 1st of June, as they are usually nothing but head, fins and bones.'

There are some long and slow methods of cooking shad which soften the small bones to the point at which they can be eaten. And there are people (as explained on page 32) who are able to get rid of them when filleting the fish. But they are generally regarded as a great nuisance. The *Canadian Fisheries Manual* for 1942, while praising the delicate flavour of the shad, remarks on 'the drawback that its flesh is cursed with a superfluity of small bones' and attributes to the Micmac Indians a legend which explains the phenomenon. According to this, the shad was originally a discontented porcupine, which asked the Great Spirit Manitou to change it into something else. In response, the spirit 'seized the animal, turned it inside out, and tossed it into the river to begin a new existence as a shad . . .'

RECIPES
Baked Connecticut shad, 419
Planked shad, 419
Maryland stuffed shad roe, 426

HICKORY SHAD

Family *Clupeidae*

Pomolobus mediocris (Mitchill)

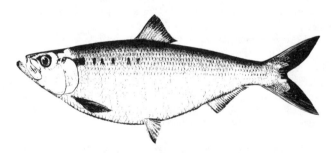

REMARKS   Maximum length 60 cm, usual length 35 to 40 cm. Greyish green above, silvery below. The range of the species is from Maine down to Florida. It is of some commercial importance, for example in the Chesapeake Bay area. It may be prepared like the other shad described in the preceding entries.

Voe was a butcher, but he gives a very full account of the fish on sale. He was as insatiable in acquiring information as he was adept at conveying it in a lively way.

ALEWIFE (U.S.A.), GASPAREAU (Canada)   Family *Clupeidae*

Alosa pseudoharengus (Wilson)

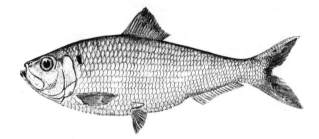

REMARKS   Maximum length 38 cm, usual length 25 to 30 cm. The back is greyish green, the sides and belly silvery. The sides of freshly caught specimens are iridescent; and sea-run fish have a golden tinge to the head. The range of the species is from Newfoundland down to North Carolina.

Josselyn, in his *Account of Two Voyages to New England* (1765), says that 'The *Alewife* is like a *Herrin*, but has a bigger bellie; therefore, called an *Alewife*; they come in the end of April into fresh Rivers and Ponds . . .' Well put. The alewives ascend rivers to spawn, and constitute during the summer a large proportion of the fish in the rivers of the eastern seaboard. They are, by the way, sometimes called sawbellies.

The alewife can be distinguished from the herring by its greater body depth, and from the shad by its single spot on each side. It is less easy to distinguish it from its very close relation *Alosa aestivalis* (Mitchill), the blueback or glut herring (not shown, because the only difference visible to the layman is that the back is bluish grey instead of greyish green). The blueback has a range which is more southerly than that of the alewife, although they overlap extensively, and its 'runs' occur in the summer (hence *aestivalis*) rather than the spring.

CUISINE   Douglass, in his *North America* (1740), described the alewives as 'very mean, dry and insipid fish. Some of them are cured . . . and sent to the sugar islands for the slaves, but because of their bad quality they are not much in request . . .' A severe judgment. In fact, they are good enough to be marketed fresh as well as in salted or marinated form. Treat them like herring (page 27), but grill or bake them rather than frying them, and have lemon juice or vinegar to hand. The roe and milt are not merely edible, but good. However, most of the catch is turned into pet food or used as lobster bait.

MENHADEN, POGY, MOSSBUNKER   Family *Clupeidae*

Brevoortia tyrannus (Latrobe)

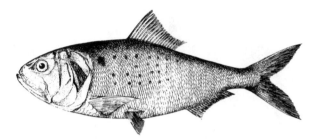

REMARKS Maximum length 50 cm, common length around 35 cm. The back is bluish, greenish or brownish, the sides silvery with a brassy lustre. Note the large scaleless head, the conspicuous blotch on the side and the irregularly arranged spots behind it.

Menhaden occur from the Gulf of Maine, and western Nova Scotia, south to Florida. They travel in large schools, feeding on plankton, especially the small planktonic plants known as diatoms.

Common names for the menhaden are numerous. Of those at the top of the page, the first two are derived from Indian words meaning fertilizer; while mossbunker, long used at New York, comes from a Dutch name for shad which the early settlers applied. Around the Potomac and Chesapeake, alewife is used; while Virginia gives us bug-head or bug fish, in allusion to the parasitic crustacean found in the mouths of southern menhaden. The menhaden has also been canned as American sardine, American club-fish, shadine and even ocean trout!

CUISINE The main commercial use of menhaden is as a fertilizer. They are edible, but too oily for most people. The oiliness may, however, be attenuated by mixing the grilled flesh with plenty of potato to make croquettes.

The roe is good. Elizabeth Hedgecock Sparks, in her excellent book on *North Carolina and Old Salem Cookery* (1955), points out that it is a speciality of North Carolina 'because menhaden, like the birds, moves from cold weather to warm, and as it moves south the roe develops. A roe is ready for eating or "ripe" just about the time the fish reaches Cape Hatteras . . . The flavour of the roe is regarded by many as just as good as that of the shad. Some call it mammy shad roe. It is smaller in size than shad roe and yellow in colour.' The same authoress observes that people in Morehead preserve grey mullet roe, and also menhaden roe, by soaking it in salt water, squeezing it between boards, sun-drying it and then coating it with wax. (This is the same procedure which produces the delicious boutargue of the Mediterranean.)

SARDINE (young), PILCHARD (adult)   Family *Clupeidae*

Sardina pilchardus (Walbaum)

REMARKS   The maximum length of a pilchard is 25 cm. A sardine is an immature pilchard.*

The sardine or pilchard has a green back, yellow sides and a silver belly. Its range is from the Mediterranean to the southern coasts of England and Ireland; and sometimes further north, in warm weather. The northern populations seem to mature later, grow larger and live longer than the southern ones. This helps to explain why the fishery for the sardine, the young of this species, is important in Portugal, Spain and France, but not in Britain, where there is, however, a small fishery for the adult pilchard.

Portuguese: Sardina, Sardinopa
Spanish: Sardina
French: Sardine
Dutch: Pelser, Sardien
German: Sardine
Swedish: Sardiner
Norwegian: Sardin
Danish: Sardin
Icelandic: Sardina
Other: Pennog mair (Welsh); Royan (Charentes); Celan (Boulogne)

They are shoaling fish, swimming around at about 40 metres below the surface by day and 25 metres down by night. They have a reputation for timidity. In *The Natural History of Ireland* (1755), the then Archbishop of Dublin stated that 'there was a good fishery of pilchards on the south coast of Ireland before the year 1688, but since the fight in Bantry Bay between some of the English fleet under Sir George Rook and the French in 1689, the pilchards, I understand, have not been on that coast; the reason of their leaving it is supposed to be the shock given by the firing of guns...'

The pilchard fishery in Cornwall, to which I referred above, used to be an important one. Frank Buckland (in *The Natural History of British Fishes*, 1883) records that a single boat once took 80,000 pilchards in one night. The fishermen would find the shoals by hammering or stamping on the bottom of the boat, 'the concussion arising therefrom causing any pilchards in the neighbourhood to jump

*The second of these statements is correct in Britain, but not on the other side of the Atlantic, where the term sardine is applied to other members of the clupeoid family, when canned; no doubt on the basis that they resemble the true sardines in their familiar canned form. The name sardine is also used on the European continent for related small fish, canned.

and discover themselves by "briming", that is to say, causing a brilliant phosphorescent appearance in the water.' This night fishing was done with driving-nets. But there was also a daytime fishery with seine nets. This involved a man called a 'huer', stationed on the top of the nearest cliff, whence he had a clear sight of the shoals. Holding a furze bush in each hand, he would signal guidance to the seine boats below. Buckland adds that when fish were located the inhabitants would rush round shouting 'Hev'ah, hev'ah', repeatedly. What with these shouts and the waving of furze bushes, the whole scene must have been baffling for stray visitors.

CUISINE Fresh sardines are excellent when grilled and are standard fare in Portugal and Spain. The Spanish humorist Julio Camba suggested that one should never eat fewer than a dozen at a time, and that one should choose one's company carefully. He was thinking in male terms, and of female company; and his advice was not to eat sardines with the virtuous mother of one's children, but with a woman who is '*golfa e escandalosa*'. By this, a Spanish friend tells me, he meant a woman who is light-hearted and unselfconscious, laughing frequently and enjoying life. I commend the positive part of this advice, but do not see why such virtuous mothers as are capable of light-hearted laughter should not also be allowed to attend sardine-feasts on the beach.

Frozen sardines are now generally available and are almost as good as fresh ones. However, many of the traditional methods of preserving sardines for a while continue to be used, especially in France, where the 'demi-sels', sardines lightly sprinkled with salt, are a delicacy at La Rochelle. Exceptionally good sea salt comes from l'Île de Ré in this region.

For most people, of course, sardines are canned sardines; quite different from the fresh product and a delicacy in their own right. Elizabeth David (in the *Spectator*, 12 October 1962) gives fascinating details of the birth of the canned sardine industry at Nantes in the 1820s. And she recalls some stern words from a director of Philippe et Canaud, the largest and oldest sardine-canning firm of that city. ' "Our fine sardines," he said, "should not be cooked. At an English meal I was given *hot* sardines, on cold toast. It was most strange. They were my sardines and I could not recognise them. The taste had become coarse. Perhaps for inferior sardines . . . but ours are best just as they are. A little cayenne or lemon if you like, and butter with sardines is traditional in France, although they are fat and do not really need it. But, please, no shock treatment." '

Fresh pilchards, like fresh sardines, may be simply scaled, gutted and grilled. Or one may follow the old Cornish practice, described as follows by Mr Howard Fox of Falmouth in *Land and Water*. 'The approved method of cooking them is to split and pepper, place one fish flat on another, backs outside, and roast on a gridiron. This is the process provincially termed "scrowling".' One might also revive another Cornish tradition, the dish called Dippie. This is made by cooking potatoes and fresh pilchards in thin cream, a commodity which used to be in surplus at Penzance and elsewhere.

ANCHOVY

Family *Engraulidae*

Engraulis encrasicolus (Linnaeus)

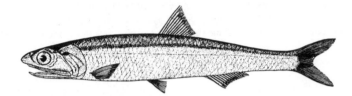

REMARKS   Maximum length 20 cm. The back is green, sometimes with a blue tinge, the sides and belly a bright silver.

This little fish, which favours the warmer waters of the Mediterranean, the Iberian Peninsula and the Bay of Biscay, is not uncommon as far north as the English Channel, and even reaches Danish waters. It has its counterparts on the American side of the North Atlantic, notably *Anchoa hepsetus* (Mitchill), the STRIPED ANCHOVY, which is shown below. The band along its side is silver.

Portuguese: Anchova, Biqueirão
Spanish: Anchoa, Boquerón
French: Anchois
Dutch: Ansjovis
German: Sardelle
Danish: Ansjos
Other: Brwyniad (Welsh)

CUISINE   The anchovy, of which there are various species all round the world, is unique among the important food fishes in that it is not normally eaten fresh – although it can be – but is marketed in almost every other form: salted; canned whole or filleted, in oil or sauce; hot-smoked (in the Soviet Union); dried (in the Orient); reduced to fish sauce (in South-East Asia) or to a pâté or to anchovy essence. Its highly characteristic flavour survives all these processes and is of great value to the cook. It may be a dominant flavour at table, as when a salade niçoise is served; or one main theme in a selection of hors d'oeuvres; or an auxiliary element, as when an unexciting fish is served with an anchovy sauce.

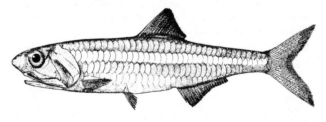

The Salmon Family and Close Relations

This is a puzzling group of fish; puzzling, at least, for someone who has set himself the task of writing about sea fish and not about freshwater fish. The salmon starts life in fresh water and comes back to be caught or to spawn, but spends half or more of its life in the sea. The sea or salmon trout, which behaves similarly, is the same species as the brown trout, which stays in fresh water all the time. And fish which we know in Britain from lakes and lochs are caught by sea fishermen in the Baltic. The result is that in this part of the catalogue, which deals with the Order *Salmoniformes*, I have to make interesting excursions among what are usually regarded as freshwater species.

Salmon used to be plentiful in almost all the rivers of western Europe and North America. In past centuries they counted as a common food fish, and everyone has heard the tale of the apprentices at this or that city who stipulated that they should not be fed salmon more than twice a week by their masters. However, the works of nineteenth- and twentieth-century man, in the form of dams which obstruct the salmon in their attempts to return to their spawning grounds, and pollution which has affected many river systems, have greatly reduced the number of rivers in which salmon are found. Netboy, in *The Atlantic Salmon – A Vanishing Species?* (1968), has compared the situation in various countries. Some have been successful in maintaining stocks, by various techniques; for example, the construction of 'ladders' up which the salmon can pass in circumventing dams, the control of pollution, or the establishment of breeding programmes in usable rivers. Sweden, Norway, Iceland, Ireland and Canada have done well. The United States, on their eastern seaboard, Spain, France, Germany and Poland have not.

Meanwhile, a new dimension has been added to the problem. It has been found that the salmon have an important feeding ground off the coast of Greenland; and Greenlanders have therefore started to catch them at sea. In countries where salmon have traditionally been caught in the rivers, often with very strict control over the numbers taken, so that stocks can be maintained, this seems like unsporting, even unscrupulous behaviour. However, the matter looks rather different to a Greenlander, who may not be disposed to leave this important resource unexploited, in response to the plaints of, say, a wealthy salmon-fishing syndicate in Scotland. It certainly seems difficult to justify a complete ban on the catching of salmon at sea; but reasonable to insist that such catches should not become one more factor to threaten the survival of the species.

SALMON

Family *Salmonidae*

Salmo salar Linnaeus

REMARKS   Almost any remarks which can be made about the salmon have to be related to one or another stage in its life-cycle, which I therefore describe first.

LIFE-CYCLE   As Netboy puts it: 'Every salmon that finds its way to the sea starts life as a pink blob, not much larger than buckshot, buried in the deep gravel of a cold stream.' The eggs remain buried in the gravel for about eighty to ninety days in Britain (but up to twice as long in colder climates) and then hatch. What emerge are ALEVINS, less than 1½ cm long, each with a yolk-sac protruding from its belly. When this has been digested, the alevins come out of the gravel, and they are then referred to as FRY. As they gain in size, they become PARR. The parr stage lasts until the fish migrate to sea. In Britain they usually do this in their second year; but further north it is more likely to be in their third year. While they are in the parr stage (and still no bigger than a man's finger) they develop brown backs with black spots along their sides, and a few red ones; and they have nine to thirteen dark bars, called parr marks, on their sides. See the drawing below.

Portuguese: Salmão
Spanish: Salmón
French: Saumon
Dutch: Zalm
German: Lachs
Polish: Losós
Russian: Sëmga, Losos'
Finnish: Lohi
Swedish: Lax
Norwegian: Laks
Danish: Laks
Icelandic: Lax
Other: Laksur (Faroese);
    Bradán (Irish); Eog (Welsh)

'The first spate in May takes the smolts away.' Thus an old English saying, which refers to the departure seawards of the young salmon. This is when they enter the SMOLT stage, which is marked by noticeable physical changes. Parr marks and spots disappear. Tails become longer and more deeply forked. The fish assume a silvery colour, suitable for ocean travel; and internal changes take place, especially in the respiratory system and the bloodstream, which fit them for life in salt water.

And so to sea – and usually out of man's ken until they come back to their native rivers to spawn. Salmon which come back after one year at sea are known as GRILSE. They will measure about 50 cm and weigh anything from under 1 to over 4 kilos. If they come back after two, three or four years at sea they are adult SALMON. Their size then will depend on how long they have been at sea (and in what sea – Baltic salmon are smaller than Atlantic salmon). They are likely to be from 80 cm to 1 metre in length and to weigh from 4 to 12 kilos; but salmon of even greater size are sometimes taken.

It is on their journey back to spawn, when they are big and healthy after feeding in the sea, that salmon are normally caught. Those which are not caught on the way upstream to the spawning grounds mostly perish after spawning. But while they survive they are known as KELTS; and if they make it back to the sea, as some do, they are quaintly known as MENDED KELTS.

THE MIGRATORY INSTINCT Salmon make long journeys from their native rivers to their feeding grounds in the ocean. 1000 miles is commonplace, and distances of 2500 miles are known to have been covered by some salmon, making a round trip of 5000. Baltic salmon, on the whole, stay inside the Baltic, but salmon from western Europe mostly go to feeding grounds around Greenland. So do Canadian and American Atlantic salmon. Yet the fish find their way back unerringly to their native rivers. How do they do this? Nobody seems to know for sure, but it may be that they are guided by what one might call the taste of the water, especially when it comes to selecting the right river and then the right tributary stream of it. If fry are collected from one stream and deposited in another, it is to the second that they will return and in which they will spawn.

SPAWNING If the salmon succeed in negotiating all obstacles and evading capture on their way upstream and finally reach the right spot, this is what they do:

The female digs and shapes a nest (redd) in the gravel of the river bed by alternately bending and straightening her body, thus forcefully moving her tail and dislodging the gravel from beneath her. The smaller stones and silt are swept away by the current, the larger ones moving only slightly to the rear of the redd . . . When the redd is between 6 and 12 inches deep, depending on the size of the female, the male joins her at the redd. Spawning follows, the female adopting a 'crouched' position with open mouth when she is joined by the male, who adopts a similar attitude. The spawn and milt are ejected simultaneously and fall into the interstices of the gravel. Immediately after the eggs are laid the male returns to the resting pool downstream; meanwhile the female begins cutting another redd above the first, which has the effect of deeply burying the eggs.

The quotation is from Wheeler, who goes on to explain that the adult salmon are often joined in the redd by small male parr which eject their little contribution of milt too; a pleasant and unusual example of cooperation between the generations in reproduction, and also a form of biological insurance, since the milt of the parr is likely to go deeper into the gravel than that of the adult male and is less apt to be swept away by the current.

BALTIC SALMON I mentioned above that Baltic salmon usually stay in the Baltic. They are not a separate sub-species, but they do have certain distinguishing characteristics. Their flesh is usually of a paler pink than that of the Atlantic salmon, no doubt because their diet includes a smaller proportion of the caryatid pigment which salmon absorb when eating crustaceans. The flesh also has a higher fat content. I could see this for myself in looking at salmon in the market at Helsinki. The pale orange meat is heavily streaked with white.

CUISINE   It is usual to poach a whole salmon in a court-bouillon and serve it either hot or cold, with simple accompaniments which will not compete with its own excellent flavour. New potatoes, sliced cucumber, lemon wedges and mayonnaise are favoured. Salmon steaks can be dealt with in the same way, but they can also be grilled or fried. The flesh of the salmon is remarkably compact, and it is not necessary to provide helpings as large as those which would be suitable for, say, cod; although the taste is so good that the demand may be for larger rather than smaller helpings!

RECIPES   (See also the Welsh recipe for salmon trout on page 461)

SALMON TROUT, SEA TROUT, BROWN TROUT

Family *Salmonidae*

Salmo trutta Linnaeus

REMARKS The maximum length of sea-run trout seems to be over 1 metre, but this is exceptional. The freshwater varieties of the species are smaller. The colour is variable. Sea trout are usually grey or silvery with black or reddish spots.

This is a confusing species, which embraces the brown trout of rivers; the bull or lake trout of larger inland waters; and the sea trout, which is a migratory fish with a natural range from North Africa to Norway and Iceland. It has been introduced into North American waters and has become an important species there. But see pages 106 and 108 for another use of the name sea trout.

The life and habits of the sea trout are similar to those of the salmon. So is its diet, and its flesh is therefore usually pink, as a result of absorbing caryatid pigment from the crustaceans which form part of this diet. (The same pigment, by the way, occurs in paprika; so that hatchery trout which are fed paprika come out with pink flesh too.)

Portuguese: Truta marisca
Spanish: Trucha marina
French: Truite de mer
Dutch: Zeeforel, Schotje
German: Meerforel
Polish: Troć
Russian: Kumzha, Taïmen'
Finnish: Meritaimen
Swedish: Öring, Laxöring
Norwegian: Sjøaure, Sjøørret
Danish: Havørred
Icelandic: Urriði
Other: Sewin (Welsh); Breac geal (Irish); Síl (Faroese)

CUISINE AND RECIPES As for the salmon. There are those, and my mother was one of them, who think that a really good salmon trout is even better than a salmon. This is debatable; but all agree that salmon trout of medium size are usually better than the very big ones.

The Norwegian speciality Rakørret is fermented salmon trout. See page 377. A Welsh recipe for salmon trout is given on page 461. A recipe for Sea Trout jelly, from the Canadian Micmac Indians, is given on page 405.

ARCTIC CHAR, CHARR

Family *Salmonidae*

Salvelinus alpinus (Linnaeus)

REMARKS Maximum length 1 metre (sea-run fish) or 40 cm (freshwater populations). The sea-run fish have metallic blue or green backs and yellowish sides, marked with a pattern of small spots. The colour of the freshwater races is highly variable.

Russian: Golec
Swedish: Röding
Norwegian: Røye
Danish: Fjaeldørred
Faroese: Bleikja
Greenlandic: Eqaluc
Other: Hudson Bay salmon, Sea trout

The distribution of the Arctic char at sea is circumpolar. In the North Atlantic area it descends as far as northern Newfoundland, Iceland and northern Norway; but landlocked freshwater populations are found further south (for example, Lake Windermere in England and Lac Leman in France/Switzerland, where it is the omble chevalier). To confuse matters further, the species has a close relation, ***Salvelinus fontinalis*** (Mitchill), the brook trout or speckled trout, which is a freshwater fish but sometimes descends into the sea, and, indeed, reaches a larger size there than in the rivers and lakes. Sea-run brook trout have steel-blue or green backs and silvery sides.

Incidentally, the use of the names char and trout do not correspond to the biological facts. The brook trout belongs to the same genus as the Arctic char, and would more appropriately be called a char. The chief distinction between trout proper and char is that the latter are more brightly coloured – their spots are grey, yellow, orange or red, never black or dark brown like those of the true trout. They also have finer scales.

Eskimos have for long eaten the Arctic char with appreciation. More recently it has become a kind of official banquet fish for Canadians and has graduated from the igloo and the log cabin to the governmental or diplomatic dining table, which it graces well so long as the chef can be persuaded not to mask it too heavily with fancy sauces and excessive garnishings.

CUISINE The arctic char is an excellent fish, to be treated like salmon trout (page 45). Its flesh may be white or pink. The *Northern Cookbook*, published under the aegis of the Canadian Minister of Indian Affairs and Northern Development, recommends steaming or frying fillets, broiling cubes of the meat, and stuffing and baking whole fish.

WHITEFISH

Family *Coregonidae*

Coregonus spp.

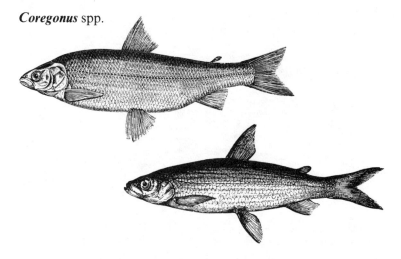

REMARKS The family *Coregonidae* is essentially a family of freshwater fish. But two of the species come out into the Baltic and are taken there as part of the sea fisheries; and to the north of the Arctic circle, especially in Canadian waters, this pattern of migration to and from the sea is common.

The larger of the two Baltic species is ***Coregonus lavaretus*** (Linnaeus), shown in the upper drawing. It is the same as the freshwater houting which goes under such local names as powan (Loch Lomond), skelly (the English Lake District) and gwyniad (Wales). Its usual adult length in the Baltic is 40 to 55 cm. It is silvery in colour with a greenish-brown back. The Finns call it siika, the Swedes sik and the Danes helt. It is an excellent fish; and smoked whitefish, for which a recipe is given on page 361, is particularly good. Whitefish roe is used, in Finland for example, to make a sort of orange caviar; salty but quite good.

The smaller species is ***Coregonus albula*** (Linnaeus), shown in the lower drawing. It occurs as a purely freshwater fish in many other places, including Britain, where it is known as the vendace or pollan. Its usual adult size is from 10 to 20 cm. It has silvery sides and a bluish-green back. In Finland it is called muikku, and in Sweden siklöja or mujka.

The vendace is a rich little fish, with a distinctive flavour; at its best when deep-fried, in vegetable oil. Its roe produces an acceptable caviar, again rather salty but good if served with sour cream – which diminishes the saltiness – and a discreet sprinkling of black pepper.

Very small vendace are called naiolamuikku (nail vendace) in Finland. Only their heads are removed before they are deep-fried.

The Soviet Union has a very large number of species of whitefish. The general Russian name for them is sig.

SMELT, RAINBOW SMELT, SPARLING

Family *Osmeridae*

Osmerus eperlanus (Linnaeus)

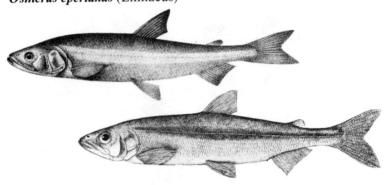

REMARKS Maximum length 35 cm, usual length about 20 cm. The back is a light olive-green. A silvery stripe runs along the side and the belly is creamy white. The species occurs in the Baltic, round the British Isles and in the Bay of Biscay. It tolerates water of low salinity; indeed there are some landlocked freshwater populations.

French: Eperlan
Dutch: Spiering
German: Stint
Polish: Stynka
Russian: Korjuszka
Finnish: Kuore
Swedish: Nors
Danish: Smelt

The smelt is well known in parts of France. Barberousse, whose book on the cuisine of Normandy contains a fine chapter on fish, refers to it as the pearl of the sea and remarks that three smelt are to be seen on the coat of arms of Caudebec on the Seine. The smelt appear off the Normandy coast in February and go up the rivers as far as they can without leaving brackish waters. Caudebec is their limit in the Seine.

On the other side of the Atlantic a close relation, *Osmerus mordax* (Mitchill), is found from the Gulf of St Lawrence down to Virginia. It is shown in the lower drawing. In the nineteenth century New Yorkers enthused especially over the 'green' ones from Raritan Bay. These were caught swimming, whereas many of the smelt marketed had been naturally frozen in the winter ice. The smelt is still the object of an important commercial fishery in North America.

CUISINE AND RECIPES Smelt have an unusual taste, and smell strongly of cucumber (or of violets, say some); but most people find them delicious when really fresh. They are usually fried. (Scale and gut them, thread them through the eyes in batches of four or six on thin skewers, dip them in milk, flour them and deep-fry them briefly in very hot oil so that they come out '*craquants et croquants*'.) But they may also be poached or steamed. A Dutch recipe is given on page 315 and a Canadian one on page 408.

CAPELIN; CAPELAN (French Canadian)   Family *Osmeridae*

Mallotus villosus (Müller)

REMARKS   Maximum length just under 25 cm. The colour of the back is a sort of transparent olive or bottle-green, suited to the Arctic waters in which this species thrives.

Norwegian: Lodde
Icelandic: Loona
Greenlandic: Angmagssaq
Faroese: Loðna

The capelin's chief importance in the scheme of things is as food for the cod. An observer thus described the scene in Conception Bay round 1818:

> It is impossible to conceive, much more to describe, the splendid appearance of Conception Bay and its harbors on such a night, at the time of what is there called the Capelin Skull. Then its vast surface is completely covered with myriads of fishes of various kinds and sizes, all actively engaged either in pursuing or avoiding each other; the whales alternately rising and plunging, throwing into the air spouts of water; the codfish bounding above the waves and reflecting the light of the moon from their silvery surface; the Capelins hurrying away in immense shoals to seek a refuge on the shore, where each retiring wave leaves countless multitudes skipping upon the sand, an easy prey to the women and children who stand there with barrows and baskets ready to seize upon the precious and plentiful booty . . .

Thus harried and pursued, the capelin emerge from the water to indulge in sexual activities, which also sound to be of a trying nature:

> The manner in which the Capelin deposits its spawn is one of the most curious . . . The male fishes are somewhat larger than the female, and are provided with a sort of ridge projecting on each side of their backbones, similar to the eaves of a house, in which the female Capelin is deficient. The latter, on approaching the beach to deposit its spawn, is attended by two male fishes, who huddle the female between them, until the whole body is concealed under the projecting ridges, and her head only is visible. In this position all three run together, with great swiftness, upon the sands, when the males, by some inherent imperceptible power, compress the body of the female between their own, so as to expel the spawn from the orifice and the tail. Having thus accomplished its delivery, the three Capelins separate, and, paddling with their whole force through the shallow water of the beach, generally succeed in regaining once more the bosom of the deep, although many fail to do so . . . (Charles Lanman, in a *Report to the U.S. Commissioners for Fish and Fisheries*, 1872–3.)

CUISINE   As for the smelt (see preceding entry). The capelin also has a cucumber smell. It is a well-loved food in Greenland.

ARGENTINE, SILVER SMELT

Family *Argentinidae*

Argentina silus Ascanius

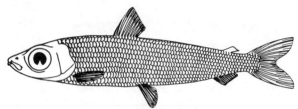

REMARKS   Maximum length 55 cm. A yellowish fish with an underlying silvery sheen, which is distributed right across the northerly waters of the North Atlantic, down to the latitude of Ireland in the east and Maine in the west.

Portuguese: Biqueirão branco
Spanish: Pejerrey, Pez de plata
French: Argentine
Dutch: Zilvervis
German: Glasauge
Swedish: Guldlax
Norwegian: Berglax, Stavsild
Danish: Guldlaks
Icelandic: Gulllax

On the European side there is another, more southerly, species *Argentina sphyraena* Linnaeus. This fish, which is shown in the lower drawing, only grows to half the size of its brother and frequents the edge of the continental shelf. Its range extends down to the Mediterranean; and the Portuguese, Spanish and French names cited above apply to it. Its Danish name is strømsild.

Argentina silus is sometimes marketed; but *Argentina sphyraena* only appears in Mediterranean markets. The silver pigment from the scales and swim bladder of these fish is used to produce 'pearl essence', used in the manufacture of artificial pearls.

CUISINE   These fish are worth frying.

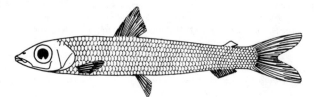

The Cod and Its Relations

The Order *Gadiformes* contains a number of species which are of great importance as food and which are found only in the North Atlantic. Some of the species occur in the Mediterranean; but, viewed collectively, they are a group of cold-water fish. This is certainly true of the cod, haddock and saithe, which are the three principal species.

The cod, for all its popularity, has had a lack-lustre image in England, seeming to typify 'the ordinary fish'. This is strange. Whether one looks at it with the eyes of a cook or those of a biologist, it is of outstanding interest; and for historians it has even more fascination than the herring.

There are grounds for thinking that the European colonization of North America was prompted to a large extent by the existence of large stocks of cod on that side of the Atlantic. Cape Cod was of course named for the cod; and Boston, 'the home of the bean and the cod', has an effigy of the 'sacred cod', from which the city derived much of its wealth, hanging in the State House. The trade in dried cod and salted cod, to which I refer on page 54, was so important in previous centuries as to be comparable with some international staple such as rice today. And in the last few decades the vexed question, happily now unvexed, of fishing for cod in Icelandic waters has had international and legal repercussions of which the full effects are yet to be seen.

Shed, therefore, any idea that the cod is an ordinary fish and invest the next piece of cod which you buy with the exciting qualities which are its by right. If you find this difficult, read Rudyard Kipling's *Captains Courageous*, or take a trip to Bergen in Norway. This trip is almost obligatory for anyone who would like to taste really fresh cod, which is cod at its best; a statement substantiated in the Norwegian recipe section, especially on page 382.

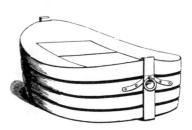

It is sad to think that live cod used to be landed in England too, and indeed in many places, during previous centuries. The drawing on the right shows one of the cod chests which were used to keep cod alive for the market in the English port of Harwich a hundred years ago.

COD; ATLANTIC COD (U.S.A.)   Family *Gadidae*

Gadus morhua Linnaeus
Gadus callarias

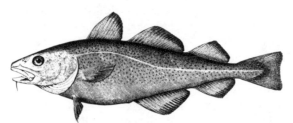

REMARKS   Maximum length 150 cm (which corresponds to a weight of 40 kilos); but a cod of anything like this size is a rarity. In the United States cod are classified as scrod* up to 50 cm; market cod from 50 to 75 cm; large cod from 75 to 100 cm; and whole cod if bigger than that.

Portuguese: Bacalhau
Spanish: Bacalao
French: Cabillaud, Morue
Dutch: Kabeljauw, Cul (small)
German: Kabeljau, Dorsch
Polish: Dorsz, Watlusz
Russian: Treska, Pertui
Finnish: Turska
Swedish: Torsk
Norwegian: Torsk, Skrei
Danish: Torsk
Icelandic: Þorskur
Other: Torskur (Faroese);
   Sârugdlik (Greenlandic);
   Trosc (Irish); Bodach
   (Scottish); Penfras (Welsh)

An Irish fishery pamphlet compares the coloration of the cod to that of Connemara marble, an apt and pleasing analogy. The back is usually sandy in colour, but with a green tinge and brown mottling. The lateral line and the belly are white.

There are, however, various 'races' or 'stocks' of cod, such as the Icelandic, the Arcto–Norwegian and the Baltic, which exhibit minor variations, not least in their growth rates. Within these races, fishermen distinguish further categories, according to the time of year at which the fish appear, the grounds on which they are taken, their preferred food, and so forth. As for food, the cod 'is indiscriminate in its choice, consuming what ever inhabitants of the deep it is able to master'. It will also consume inanimate objects: a 'book in three treatises' was taken from one captured on Midsummer's Eve in 1626 and presented, fittingly, to the Vice-Chancellor of Cambridge University (Day, *The Fishes of Great Britain and Ireland*, 1880–84).

Some but not all authorities count the Greenland cod as a separate species,

---

* The name scrod has an interesting history. The story goes that the Parker House, a famous old restaurant in Boston, always had the freshest fish of the day on its menu. But the manager never knew which this would be on a given day. So he invented the word scrod as a catch-all name for it. Thus, although scrod now officially means young cod, it is historically correct to use it for, e.g., young haddock too.

Gadus ogac Richardson. It does differ visibly from the common cod in not having its lateral line picked out in white; and has a northerly range, centred on Greenland, where it is known as ugaq. It is not to be confused with the Polar cod, *Boreogadus saida* (Lépèchin), which is even more northerly in its range and has the name eqalúgaq in Greenland.

CUISINE Cod steaks or fillets may be fried, poached, steamed, baked or (perhaps less successfully) grilled. They are fine material for all the any-fish-will-do recipes.

The cod which most people, other than coastal Norwegians and Newfoundlanders, buy is in good shape, but not exactly fresh from the sea. I was once told by a major merchant in cod at Grimsby that really fresh cod is uneatable. I am sure he believed this; and it is true that many fishermen prefer cod which is a day old, or rather a day dead, to one which has just been caught. But I fully support the Norwegian view (see page 382) that really fresh cod is marvellously good and much better than any other kind.

Cod roe is well-known and easy to obtain. But most fishermen will tell you that the best parts of the cod are in the head, namely the cheeks and the 'tongues' (more properly, throat muscles). Cheeks and tongues can be had in places like Grimsby, where they are sold cheaply, although in strong demand. Cod sounds, which are the air bladders which run alongside the spines of these fish, are also good eating. I have listed recipes for some of these specialities below, but add here two notes about ways of cooking the throat muscles.

The Bergen way is to put them in a baking dish in a white sauce into which grated cheese and a whole egg plus an egg yolk have been mixed, and bake them thus in a moderate oven (355° F. gas 4) for 30 minutes.

In Iceland the throat muscles are known as gellur. Whether fresh or salted, they are poached and eaten with boiled potatoes.

RECIPES FOR COD

RECIPES FOR COD ROE, HEAD, CHEEKS, 'TONGUES', LIVER, ETC.

DRIED AND SALTED COD

Cod and similar fish can be preserved by being dried until their water content is reduced to about 16 per cent. Or they can be salted, and then dried to a lesser extent. The former method is the older method, and the product has been known from early medieval times as stockfish. However, when it became feasible to salt fish on a large scale, the latter method became the more popular of the two. Cod which has been both salted and partially dried goes under various names, such as klippfisk in Norway (cf. page 383).

The trade in cod and related species which have been preserved in these ways continues to be of great importance. Stockfish is preferred in Africa, and by some Italians. Italy also imports salt cod; and salt cod is what the French eat as morue, the Spaniards as bacalao, and the Portuguese as bacalhau. Salt cod is equivalent in nutritional value to $3\frac{1}{2}$ times its own weight of fresh fish. The ratio for stockfish, from which more water has been extracted, is 5 to 1.

The principal exporting countries are Canada, Iceland and Norway. Newfoundland is the largest single source.

CUISINE   Stockfish need only be soaked to prepare it for cooking. Salt cod must also be desalted. Here is what José Castillo, a Basque expert, has to say. 'I regard bacalao as though it were steel. If you do not give it the necessary "tempering", it will not be in the right state; while, on the other hand, even an inferior steel, well tempered, can give a much better result.' His advice, in detail, is as follows.

First, remove the bones from the middle part, the sides and the tail, reserving them for the subsequent confection of a salt-cod soup. Then cut the bacalao into squares of about 7 cm. Soak these, with the irregular off-cuts, in twice as much water as is needed to cover them. After 11 hours, stir them around with your hand, then transfer them to a new lot of fresh water for a second period of 11 hours. After this, scale the pieces, place them in an earthenware casserole in a third lot of fresh water, and let this warm slowly by the side of the fire for 2 hours. The water should never become hotter than your hand can bear.

Finally, remove the casserole from the side of the fire, let the water cool, and then remove the pieces of bacalao to a cloth-covered platter. They are then ready for whatever recipe you wish to use.

RECIPES

Salt cod scrambled with eggs and potato (Portuguese), 267
Dried cod in the Basque manner, 278
Morue à la Bordelaise, 287

Stokvis (Netherlands), 317
Klipfisk (Danish), 390
New England salt cod dinner, 412

TOMCOD

Family *Gadidae*

Microgadus tomcod (Walbaum)

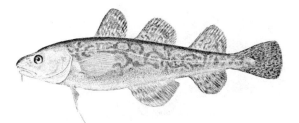

REMARKS   Maximum length 40 cm, but specimens longer than 30 or 35 cm are rare. The colour varies, but is usually olive-brown above, with green or yellow tinges and darker mottling.

This small edition of cod (to be distinguished from codling by the long filaments of the ventral fins and the more rounded tail fin) is found only in the north-western Atlantic, where its range is from Labrador to Virginia. It frequents coastal waters and estuaries, subsisting on a healthy diet of small crustaceans and molluscs and baby fish.

Some fishing for this species is carried out in Canada, including a remarkable winter ice fishery in the St Lawrence River, where gaily painted fishing cabins are erected on the ice, especially at Sainte Anne de la Perade.

As the season progresses and winter's rigours thicken the ice up to two feet, it can then support a veritable village of fishing cabins . . . In each cabin a rectangular hole is cut in the ice, some 6 feet long by 16 inches wide, which is kept covered by a wooden board outside the hours of fishing to prevent freezing. In these comfortably heated cabins, each fisherman usually uses two lines. Each line, provided in the middle with a matchstick, has two hooks baited with a small piece of frozen pork liver . . . A jiggling movement of the match indicates that there is a bite. With a single jerk the fisherman brings up the Tomcod, and then throws it out through the window. The fish freeze instantly, thus conserving their flavour. (Vladykov, albums of the *Fishes of Quebec*, 1955.)

Among the names cited by Leim and Scott for this species in Canada are poulamon atlantique, frostfish, petite morue, loche and snig. This last name is apparently an old English or Scottish one, meaning a small eel.

CUISINE   Fry, poach or bake. A good fish, which used to be regarded as a delicacy in the United States. It still is in New York. But in Canada much of the catch nowadays goes to feed silver foxes and other objects of animal husbandry.

POOR COD

Family *Gadidae*

Trisopterus minutus (Linnaeus)

REMARKS Maximum length just under 25 cm. The back is brownish yellow, the flanks silvery brown. These little fish provide abundant food for commercially important species such as cod, hake and turbot. When they are themselves taken in trawls they are most often used for fish meal; but they are found in French markets and they have been fished with some enthusiasm in Cornwall,

Portuguese: Fanecào
Spanish: Mollera
French: Capelan
Dutch: Dwergbolk
German: Zwergdorsch
Swedish: Glyskolja
Norwegian: Sypike
Danish: Glyse

where they may be called blens or blinds. Day remarks that: '. . . these last names are doubtless due to a sort of loose bag capable of inflation existing in front of the eye . . . well designated by the local words bleb or blain, terms for a bubble in the water, or a blister.'

In the same genus two other small species deserve mention. *Trisopterus luscus* (Linnaeus), the BIB or POUT, has a coppery-coloured back and a black spot at the base of the pectoral fin, shown in the drawing below. Its range is from the Mediterranean to the North Sea. It is faneca in Spain and tacaud in France, but p'louse at Boulogne. Further north, this species is replaced by *Trisopterus esmarckii* (Nilsson), the Norway pout, known as augepål in Norway, spærling in Denmark and spærlingur in Iceland.

CUISINE   Bony fish, which spoil quickly; but the larger ones are worth frying.

POLLACK

Family *Gadidae*

Pollachius pollachius (Linnaeus)

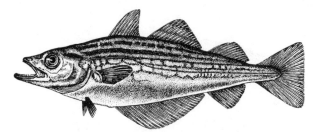

REMARKS Maximum length may be over
1 metre, but the normal maximum is about
75 cm and the common market length 40 to
50 cm. The colour varies with the habitat,
but the back is usually brown, or 'dark rifle
green' as Day describes it, shading to yellow
and a lighter colour on the belly. Note the
arched lateral line.

Portuguese: Badejo, Juliana
Spanish: Abadejo
French: Lieu jaune
Dutch: Witte koolvis, Pollak
German: Pollack
Swedish: Lyrtorsk, Bleka
Norwegian: Lyr
Danish: Lubbe
Icelandic: Lýr
Other: Lýri (Faroese);
Colin (N. France)

The pollack has an extensive range, from
Iceland and Norway down to the Iberian
Peninsula, but it is not an important commer-
cial fish, since only limited quantities are taken.

Pollack frequent rocky coastal waters and like to feed on sand eels and small cod
and herring. 'Sars observed off the coast of Norway that the pollack systematically
chased the young codfish. Schools of the former appeared to surround the little
codfishes on all sides, making the circle narrower and narrower, till all the codfish
were gathered into one lump, which they then by a quick movement chased up to
the surface of the water. They were now attacked on two sides, below by the
pollack, above by the sea-gulls.' (Day.)

There is a wealth of Irish names for pollack and coalfish (see next entry) of
different sizes. Mágach and mongach seem to be the best known. In Scotland and
the north of England, lythe is used, 'perhaps signifying its pliancy and rapidity of
movements', as Day observes.

CUISINE A fish of satisfactory quality which may be treated like cod or haddock.
Most of the recipes listed on pages 53 and 61 for these other species may be applied
to the pollack.

SAITHE, COALFISH, COLEY (U.K.), POLLOCK (U.S.A.)

Family *Gadidae*

Pollachius virens (Linnaeus)

REMARKS   Maximum length 120 cm, usual adult length 60 to 90 cm. The back is usually greenish brown although sometimes of a charcoal colour (hence coalfish, from col, charcoal). This species spans the Atlantic in northern waters, descending as far as New Jersey in the west and the English Channel in the east.

French: Lieu noir
Dutch: Koolvis
German: Kohler, Seelachs
Swedish: Sej, Gråsej
Norwegian: Sei, Pale (small)
Danish: Sej
Icelandic: Ufsi
Other: Seiður (Faroese);
   Goberge (Fr. Can.); Boston
   bluefish

The importance of the saithe is attested by the extraordinary number of vernacular names for it. Day listed fifty-seven for Britain. In any community where it is well known, one is likely to find several names, corresponding to the different sizes. In Shetland, for example, the small ones, about 10 cm long, are sillock or sillack; while year-old specimens, about 20 to 25 cm long, are piltock. In Orkney the latter are cuithe and the next size up (40 cm) are harben. In both places the full-grown fish are saithe. One of the many similar progressions in Ireland is from gilpin to blockan to greylord to glashan.

Eliza Edmonston wrote pleasantly, in her *Sketches and Tales of Shetland* (1856), about sillock and piltock. 'The small fish called sillack and piltack, which so largely enters into the diet of the Shetland peasantry, is brought to their very doors by the waters of every bay and creek, so that even the aged females and children may in moderate weather obtain a supply each morning and evening throughout the year.' She explains that in May in Shetland everyone is on the look-out for the first small sillack, and also for the first of the season's piltack, at its best in the early summer. 'As summer advances, when the men are all engaged in the more important deep sea, or "haff" fishing, the sillacks are growing apace. The old men and boys, too old or too young for "rowing to the haff", may be seen in their little "whilly" boats, during the long twilight, while females and others of the boys, without leaving the shore, wield their light rods over the crags ...' This is the 'craig-fishing' which was such a feature of Shetland life and which had its parallel in Maine, where the capture of young pollock from the rocks was a 'favourite amusement', according to Goode. Idyllic scenes; although on closer inspection the Shetlanders in their boats would have been seen to engage in non-idyllic techniques to 'so', which is to say lure, the sillacks. 'The fisherman in a small boat fishing with a rod and line had a large supply of half boiled limpets which he chewed to an oily pulp before spitting them out in a rapid series of blobs on the sea immediately around the boat. As the oily "vam" spread, sillacks were attracted to the area and as soon as the lust grew the fisherman no longer had to bait his hook but just kept "soing" and taking the fish aboard on a bare hook.' (Goodlaa, *Shetland Fishing Saga*, 1971.)

The saithe is fished on both sides of the Atlantic, but the catch on the eastern side is by far the greater. It is marketed fresh, cured and canned.

CUISINE AND RECIPES   The adult saithe is rather a coarse fish. 'That's one that needs jumping up,' commented a Shetland housewife. The most jumped-up effect is produced by the Germans and Danes, who salt and smoke slices of it, producing something which looks like smoked salmon. The German name Seelachs, meaning sea salmon, helps the effect. Moreover, during the process a salmon-like colour is imparted to the flesh, which is normally grey (and none the worse for that, but it puts off those who like their fish white).

Young saithe, freshly caught, are excellent fare. In Scotland it is usual to fry them, 'breaded' with oatmeal; or to poach them, preferably in sea water. Mrs M. Sinclair of Lerwick told me that piltocks 'should be boiled at once, when the men bring them in' and that they can then be left overnight in the cooking liquid and eaten cold. Another Shetland method is to clean the piltocks through the gill openings, without cutting the fish, stuff them with livers, put a small potato as a stopper in the gullet of each and grill or bake them thus. This dish is called Liver cuids; it used to be done on an iron grid called a brand-iron, over glowing peat embers.

The traditional practice in Orkney was to split the fresh cuithes, salt them and dry them over the peat 'reek' of the open hearth. This is still done, although there are not many open hearths burning peat nowadays. Once dried, cuithes are like wood and slightly phosphorescent. In some houses so many might be hanging from the rafters that you could read by their light.

However, young saithe are not generally available. Readers are more likely to encounter fillets of the adult fish. In this event, recipes for cod or haddock may be used. See also the important recipe for Bergen fish soup on page 378, and other remarks about saithe in Norway on pages 380 and 381.

HADDOCK
Family *Gadidae*

Melanogrammus aeglefinus (Linnaeus)

REMARKS   Maximum length 80 cm, although giants over a metre long have been taken; market length 40 to 60 cm. The back is of a dark greenish-brown or purplish-grey. The lateral line is black and there is a 'thumbprint' on the side, as shown in the drawing. In this the haddock resembles the John Dory, and fishermen at Boulogne therefore call it faux Saint-Pierre, or by the curious name calevés, which may be of Spanish origin, as some survivors of the Armada settled there.

French: Eglefin
Dutch: Schelvis
German: Schellfisch
Russian: Piksha
Swedish: Kolja
Norwegian: Hyse
Danish: Kuller
Icelandic: Ýsa
Other: Cadóg (Irish);
   Corbenfras (Welsh);
   Hýsa (Faroese);
   Anon (French)

The haddock spans the North Atlantic, descending as far as New England in the west and the northern parts of the Bay of Biscay in the east. It is an important commercial fish, of which there are various local populations with their own characteristics, but these are rarely as noticeable as the canary colour of a haddock which a certain Dr Ball once obtained at Dublin. One feature which seems to apply to all the populations is that the success of their spawning varies considerably from year to year. After a particularly good year, and after the numerous fry have had time to grow up, the fishing will be more profitable than usual for a while and haddock may be taken in areas where they are not normally present. The catches fluctuate in quality as well as in quantity. The fish from certain grounds are better than those from others. Dublin Bay haddock used to be famous.

Haddock which have been taken by line fishing are in much better shape than those which have been trawled. This is, of course, true of many species, but the difference is especially noticeable in haddock catches.

Haddock does not take salt as well as cod. The traditional ways of curing haddock were therefore by drying and smoking. 'Rizzared' haddock in Scotland were simply sun-dried. Those which were dried thus on the rocks at Collieston, a former fishing village, were known as Collieston speldings. They could be eaten raw. The same fate no doubt befell the 'hazel haddocks', which were small ones hung up to dry in the rigging of fishing boats as the 'perks' of the apprentices. But greater fame was achieved by a product of the fishing village of Finnan, near Aberdeen, where haddocks were smoked over a peat-reek and sold as Finnan haddocks. Although peat is no longer used, and large quantities of haddock are smoked elsewhere, the Finnan haddies have maintained their reputation for an excellent and distinctive flavour. The taste for them spread to the United States, where they were 'manufactured in enormous quantities in Portland and Boston' (Goode, who called them Finland haddocks, whether by his error or that of the manufacturers I do not know).

Smoked haddock has also become popular in France. When the French talk of 'haddock', which has become a French word, they mean smoked haddock.

In fact, the process does not consist simply in smoking. After being cleaned and split open the fish are brined for a while and then hung up to drain. The swelling of the protein, which results from the brining, and the drying of the surface combine to give the fish a good gloss at this stage. The smoking comes next and is continued until the fish develop a straw colour. They are then taken out, after which the colour will darken further.

What are called 'Glasgow pales' are small haddock which have been given this sort of treatment but removed from the smoke when they have barely acquired a pale straw colour. Their final appearance is therefore paler than that of the Finnan haddies.

At Provincetown on Cape Cod, haddock used to be split, salted and dried; after which treatment they bore the curious name of 'scoodled skulljoe'.

Very light salting is also practised on haddocks. The 'Green-salted' haddock of Denmark, listed among the recipes below, is matched by a similar technique in Iceland. There the product is known as Nætursaltaður fiskur, or 'night-salted' fish. Haddock is the preferred fish, although cod can also be treated in this way. The procedure is to clean and fillet the fish and to leave the fillets covered with fine salt for 48 hours, or longer in very cold weather. They are then washed free of salt, cut up and poached. I have not tasted the result, but am assured that it is particularly good.

In commenting on the use of haddock in the fried fish trade in Britain some fifty years ago, 'Chatchip', who was a former president of the National Association of Fish Caterers, observed that young haddocks were known in the trade as 'chats' and that very small haddocks bore the peculiar trade name of 'ping-pongs'.

CUISINE   The haddock is held by many, including the knowledgeable Icelanders, to be superior to the cod. At its best it is very good indeed. It may be prepared in any of the ways suited to cod; and its roe is a delicacy.

RECIPES

HAKE

Family *Gadidae*

Merluccius merluccius (Linnaeus)

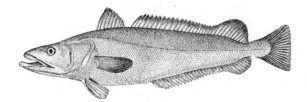

REMARKS   Maximum length of females 1 metre. Males are smaller. The usual market size is from 30 to 70 cm. The back is slate grey or bluish. The large mouth is grey-black inside, which accounts for, e.g., the Danish name, from which the Irish name colmoír is probably derived. The hake has no barbel.

Portuguese: Pescada, or
   (young ones) Pescadinha
Spanish: Merluza
French: Merlu, Merluche
Dutch: Heek
German: Seehechte
Swedish: Kummel
Norwegian: Lysing, Haeg,
   Kolkjeft'
Danish: Kolmuler
Icelandic: Lýsingur
Other: Ceggdu (Welsh);
   Legatza (Basque);
   Canapé (Boulogne)

This species is most abundant off Portugal and Spain, in the Bay of Biscay and off the Irish coast. Supplies have been dwindling in northern waters. But they remain quite healthy in the south, to judge by my last visit to the fish market at Cascais, near Lisbon, where nine tenths of the floor was taken up by boxes of hake, many of them with their livers hanging out of the otherwise empty gut cavity. Gutting hake, by the way, can produce surprising revelations, for they are very voracious fish. Jonathan Couch (in his lavishly illustrated *A History of the Fishes of the British Islands*, 1877) observes that: 'When a school of pilchards is enclosed within a sean, it will commonly happen that several Hakes are cooped up with them; and when the tucking of the sean is in progress, for the purpose of taking up the imprisoned fish, the Hakes are often found so filled with the smaller fish as to be utterly helpless. Seventeen Pilchards have been found in the stomach of a Hake . . .'

CUISINE   A good fish, which may be poached, steamed, baked or fried. The Portuguese and the Spaniards are perhaps the greatest experts in cooking it; and they also consume large quantities of dried hake.

The expression 'milky hake' is used by fishmongers on Merseyside, presumably to indicate good quality.

In the Basque country the arrowhead-shaped flesh of the lower jaw is greatly prized under the name Kokotxes. I once ate a whole dish of these succulent morsels, served in a bubbling garlic and olive oil sauce.

RECIPES

Hake in aspic (Portuguese), 269

Hake baked with potatoes,
Portuguese style, 270

Hake in a green sauce, 281

Hake, Irish style, 472

SILVER HAKE
Family *Gadidae*

Merluccius bilinearis (Mitchill)

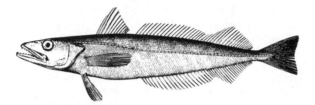

REMARKS   Maximum length about 80 cm, usual length from 30 to 45 cm. Fresh from the water, this fish has the silvery iridescent sheen to which it owes its common name. In death the back turns brownish or grey, but the lower sides and belly remain silvery. The inside of the mouth is dusky blue.

This species ranges from the Gulf of St Lawrence and the southern shores of Newfoundland to North Carolina; it is common from Nova Scotia to Virginia. A common market name for it is whiting (but cf. page 64). The French Canadian name for it is merlan argenté. In New England it may be called frostfish, because it abounds round piers and beaches during the late autumn. In fact, however, it shuns frosty temperatures and moves from inshore to deeper waters at the onset of winter, returning again in the spring.

Gloucester, Mass., has been the traditional silver hake port, although the fish is landed at many others. It was not appreciated during the nineteenth century and much of the catch during the present century has gone to produce animal food and fish meal. However, even in the 1920s about a quarter of the catch was used in the 'hot-fish shops' of the Midwest; and consumer acceptance has increased noticeably since then.

CUISINE AND RECIPES   As for the European hake (above), but see also the recipe for Gloucester corned hake on page 413.

WHITING

Family *Gadidae*

Merlangius merlangus (Linnaeus)

REMARKS   Maximum length about 70 cm (of the female; the male is smaller); market length 20 to 35 cm. The back may be dark blue or green, or sandy, but the sides and belly are always silvery or white. Note the dark spot at the base of the pectoral fin. There is no barbel.

The whiting ranges from Iceland and Norway to the Mediterranean, but over half the European landings are made from the North Sea. It likes shallow, sandy waters and is often taken close inshore.

Portuguese: Badejo *
Spanish: Merlán
French: Merlan
Dutch: Wijting
German: Wittling
Polish: Witlinek
Swedish: Vitling
Norwegian: Kviting
Danish: Hvitting
Icelandic: Lýsa
Other: Faoitín (Irish);
   Gwyniad y môr (Welsh)

CUISINE   It is a commonplace that the flesh of the whiting, steamed, is good for invalids. So it is. But the delicacy of the flesh also gives it a special interest for the healthy. Cooked when fresh, it makes a delicious and light dish. Poaching and frying are recommended, as well as steaming. Merlans en colère (biting their own tails) look well, think some. Ready-fried fillets of whiting are sold in Holland as Lekkerbekjes, the idea being that customers will be attracted by the implication that he who eats a lekkerbekje must be a lekkerbek, or gourmet.

The whiting dries well in the wind and was often used for 'blawn', i.e. wind-dried, fish in Scotland. The same product is still popular in Ostend.

RECIPES
Whiting in a parsley sauce, 441
Fish with samphire sauce, 454

Fillets of whiting poached
   in cider, 472

* The whiting is uncommon in Portuguese waters. Several dictionaries mis-translate pescada (Portuguese for hake) as whiting.

BLUE WHITING

Family *Gadidae*

Micromesistius poutassou (Risso)

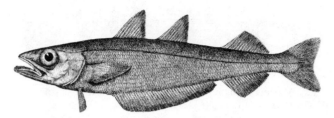

REMARKS Maximum length just over 40 cm. This species has a blue back and silvery sides and belly. Note the length and position of the first anal fin.

The blue whiting is an oceanic fish, which occurs on both sides of the Atlantic, often in huge shoals on the eastern side. Trawlers fishing in deep water for other species have taken large quantities, inadvertently. So far, the species has not been exploited commercially, but the possibility is being considered. British fishermen, for example, if they had the necessary equipment and could gear themselves to what would be a major but seasonal fishery, could take a million tons annually from waters within 200 miles of the British coasts. This is a tempting prospect, but the success of the operation would depend on the development of suitable machinery for processing what are rather small fish, and on the acceptability of the product to the consumer. This catalogue entry is therefore an anticipatory one.

Portuguese: Pichelim
Spanish: Bacaladilla
French: Poutassou
Dutch: Blauwe wijting
German: Blauer Wittling
Swedish: Kolmule, Blagunnar
Norwegian: Blågunnar, Kolmule
Danish: Kulmule
Icelandic: Kolmunni

CUISINE The quality of the blue whiting is satisfactory and numerous experiments are being made to determine the best methods of preparing and cooking it. It would be premature to recommend particular recipes before it becomes clear whether it will be marketed in fillets, or in minced form, or only in products like fish sticks. But anyone who acquires one could follow the advice given for the ordinary whiting (page 64).

LING, COMMON LING

Family *Gadidae*

Molva molva (Linnaeus)

REMARKS   Maximum length 2 metres, usual market length 75 cm to 1 metre. The back is bronze-green or brown, and often marbled. Note the dark spot at the rear of the first dorsal fin. The dorsal and anal fins have white edges.

This species, which is commercially valuable, is mainly taken around Iceland, in the Norwegian Sea and on the west coasts of the British Isles.

Two other ling have to be mentioned. *Molva macrophthalma* (Rafinesque), the Spanish or Mediterranean ling, has a much more elongated body. It comes as far north as the south-western coasts of Britain. In that area it might meet a southward-roaming member of the third species, which is *Molva dypterygia* (Pennant), the blue ling (French lingue bleu or lingue bâtarde, German blauer Leng, etc.). This is a northerly, deep-water species and is probably taken in larger quantity than the common ling, which it closely resembles, but from which it may be distinguished by its protruding lower jaw. It is not blue, but has a coppery back.

Ling take well to being dried or salted and dried, and used to be cured in these ways on a big scale. Scilly was famous for its dried ling, and I have even seen it suggested that the name Scilly comes from a Cornish name for ling, zilli. Dried ling can still be had on the west coast of Ireland.

Portuguese: Juliana
Spanish: Maruca
French: Lingue, Julienne
Dutch: Leng
German: Leng
Swedish: Långa
Norwegian: Lange
Danish: Lange
Icelandic: Langa
Other: Longa (Faroese and Irish); Honos (Welsh)

CUISINE AND RECIPE   A good fish, which may be treated like cod. The liver is firm and used to be eaten in Shetland. An Irish recipe for Salt ling with colcannon is given on page 470.

TORSK, TUSK, CUSK

Family *Gadidae*

Brosme brosme (Ascanius)

REMARKS Maximum length 110 cm, market length 45 to 60 cm. The colour may be reddish brown or greenish brown or yellowish grey, shading to cream below. The dorsal, tail and anal fins have white edges, and are joined together at their bases. Note the single dorsal fin and the single barbel.

French: Brosme, Loquette
Dutch: Lom
German: Lumb
Swedish: Lubb, Brosme
Norwegian: Brosme, Lubb
Danish: Brosme
Icelandic: Keila

The torsk, which ranges right across the Atlantic, but only in northerly waters, may be regarded as the odd fish out in the gadoid family. It is of a sedentary and solitary nature, never massing in large shoals like its relations. It grows slowly, since the cold Arctic waters induce a lower rate of metabolism and are anyway poor in food.

There is some commercial fishing for the torsk, which is marketed in both fresh and salted form.

CUISINE AND RECIPE The flesh of the torsk (or cusk, as it is usually known in America) contains a moderate amount of oil and is well suited to grilling or baking. Marion H. Neil, who deals with several relatively obscure fish in *The Thrift Cook Book*, recommends eating broiled cusk for breakfast and also gives a recipe for Stuffed cusk. The fish is cleaned, washed, split and boned; they stuffed with a mixture of 2 tbs margarine, ¾ cup corn meal or soft breadcrumbs, a beaten egg, chopped fresh parsley and dried herbs to choice; and then sewn up. Incisions are made in the sides, into which strips of salt pork are inserted. Other such strips are placed in the bottom of an oven dish, the fish on top of them, and the dish baked in a hot oven (430° F, gas 7) for 30 minutes or until cooked through and browned; whereupon it is served with a parsley sauce.

ROCKLING,
THREE-BEARDED ROCKLING

Family *Gadidae*

Gaidropsarus vulgaris (Cloquet)
Motella tricirrata

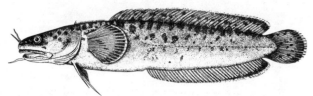

REMARKS   Maximum length just over 50 cm. In life, the upper part of this fish is of a red or salmon colour, marked with brown blotches (as shown in the drawing, together with the three barbels, misnamed 'beards'). So it is easy to identify. But it and its close relations (of which I mention only *Rhinonemus cimbrius* (Linnaeus), since it occurs on both sides of the Atlantic) have constituted an intractable, albeit trivial, problem for taxonomists, who have all but buried the small creatures under a mass of competing scientific names. All the layman need know is that the rocklings all have a very low first dorsal fin (just visible in the drawing) that they may have three, four or five barbels and that they have no commercial importance on either side of the North Atlantic.

Portuguese: Laibeque
Spanish: Lota, Mollareta
French: Motelle à trois
  barbillons
Dutch: Driedradige meun
German: Dreibärtelige
  Seequappe
Swedish: Tretömmad
  skårlånga
Norwegian: Treskjegget
  tangbrosme
Danish: Tretrådet havkvabbe
Other: Whistler

CUISINE   As the Belgian authority Max Poll observed, the rockling tribe have quite delicate flesh but are rarely seen in the markets. If you catch one, treat it like whiting (page 64). It is worth adding that rocklings should not be packed in numbers in fish boxes or in polythene wrappings, since in these conditions, even when they are very fresh, they will produce a pungent and unpleasant odour.

FORKBEARD, GREATER FORKBEARD

Family *Gadidae*

Phycis blennoides (Brünnich)

REMARKS Maximum length 75 cm. A brownish fish. The dorsal, tail and anal fins are edged with black.

This fish is called forkbeard because the pelvic fins are long and forked and look faintly like a beard. The characteristic is shared by a number of related species. Two of these which occur in North American waters are shown on the next page.

Portuguese: Abrótia do alto
Spanish: Brótola de fango
French: Mostelle de roche
Dutch: Sluismeester
German: Gabeldorsch
Swedish: Fjällbrosme
Norwegian: Skjellbrosme
Danish: Skælbrosme
Icelandic: Litla brosma

The forkbeards have one relation which is sufficiently amusing to warrant being mentioned. This is the TADPOLE-FISH, shown below. Its scientific name is ***Raniceps raninus*** (Linnaeus). It only attains a length of 30 cm and is tadpole-coloured as well as tadpole-shaped. It is widespread but uncommon around the British coasts; but quite common in Norwegian waters. The Norwegians call it paddetorsk.

CUISINE   To be treated like the hake (page 62); but it is less good.

WHITE HAKE, BOSTON LING

Family *Gadidae*

Urophycis tenuis (Mitchill)

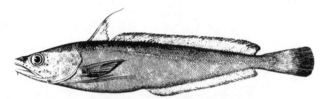

REMARKS   Maximum length just over 1 metre. This species, of which the French Canadian name is merluche blanche, occurs from Newfoundland to Cape Hatteras. It is not a true hake, but it does resemble the hake (page 62) in having two dorsal fins and one anal fin; so the name white hake is less inappropriate than Boston ling. Although edible, it is not fished or eaten extensively.

SQUIRREL HAKE

Family *Gadidae*

Urophycis chuss (Walbaum)

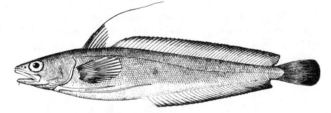

REMARKS   Maximum length rather less than a metre. This species is also called red hake and squirrel ling. Some authorities believe that it cannot really be distinguished from the preceding species; others point to the longer filamentous ray of the first dorsal fin and other differences which they think sufficient, and sufficiently constant, to justify the maintenance of two species. There certainly seems to be nothing to choose between them from the gastronomic point of view.

EEL-POUT (U.K.), OCEAN POUT, MUTTON-FISH (U.S.A.)

Family *Zoarcidae*

Zoarces viviparus (Linnaeus)

REMARKS Maximum length about 45 cm, common length 30 cm. A yellowish-brown or greyish fish, which is a northern species, common in Scandinavian and Scottish waters. It is viviparous and may give birth to several hundred young.

Its American counterpart is **Macrozoarces americanus** (B. and S.), shown below, which occurs from Labrador to Delaware and may reach a length of over 1 metre.

French: Loquette (?)
Dutch: Puitaal
German: Aalmutter
Polish: Wegorzyca
Russian: Bel'dyuga
Finnish: Kivinilkka
Swedish: Tånglake, Ålkusa
Norwegian: Ålekone, Ålekvabbe
Danish: Ålekvabbe

CUISINE Goode remarks that the mutton-fish 'is one of those species which, while possessing excellent qualities as a food-fish, is not generally eaten'. Its flesh is indeed lean and wholesome; it was apparently fishermen of Cape Ann who remarked on the mutton-like flavour and named the fish accordingly. But others gave it the unprepossessing name yellow eel. A move is now afoot in the United States to market it as 'ocean sole', in defiance of biology and on the ground that its fillets are shaped like those of that utterly different fish, the sole.

On the European side the eel-pout used to be marketed in Edinburgh, for example, and Day records being told at St Andrews by 'a most intelligent mechanic' that no better fish was obtainable. I think that the mechanic went too far; but it is a wholesome and satisfactory fish and may be eaten more widely in the future. Fry, bake, poach, or use in chowders.

GRENADIER, RAT-TAIL

Family *Macrouridae*

Macrourus berglax Lacépède

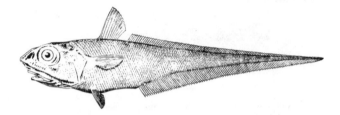

REMARKS Maximum length 90 cm, or even a little more. The colour is ash-grey.

This species is catalogued as the representative of the macrourid group of fishes, of which there are several species in the North Atlantic. They are bottom-dwelling, deep-water fish, abundant but difficult to catch, unattractive in appearance and not easy to skin and fillet by mechanical means. Even so, they constitute a considerable resource which is likely to be exploited more fully in the future; although their growth rate is so slow that they might not withstand really heavy exploitation.

German: Grenadierfisch
Russian: Siewiernyj
Swedish: Långstjärt
Norwegian: Isgalt
Danish: Langhale
Icelandic: Snarpi langhali, Snarphali

Leim and Scott, noting the presence of the species in Canadian waters, cite the names rough-head grenadier, smooth-spined rat-tail and onion-eye, none of which seems likely to have much market appeal. However, the related species *Nezumia bairdi* (Goode and Bean) is already being fished by Soviet and other foreign fleets off the Canadian continental shelf; and this one has the excellent common name MARLIN-SPIKE. It is shown below.

CUISINE AND RECIPE The grenadier's tapering shape is inconvenient; but it has firm flesh with quite a good texture and flavour. I record on page 408 a recipe for Grenadier chowder from an experimental kitchen in Canada.

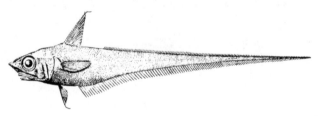

A Mixed Bag: Eels, Garfish and the Like, Silversides, the John Dory, the Red 'Bream' and the Opah

The Order *Anguilliformes* is the order of eels. The three most important are the common eel, the moray eel and the conger. The first of these can be counted as a marine fish, since the sea is where it begins and ends its life, although most of its years are spent in fresh water. The other two are purely marine; but the moray eel belongs to warmer waters than those of the North Atlantic and is not catalogued here.

Eels possess great tenacity of life. This applies especially to the common eel. It will remain alive out of water for a surprisingly long time. The conger also exhibits considerable staying power, and keeps very well after death. 'Yes, it's very rare that we condemn a box of conger,' said an inspector at Billingsgate to me once.

The Order *Atheriniformes* includes the flying fish of tropical and near-tropical waters and several other species which can plane along the surface of the sea. All these have extended jaws. They are represented in the catalogue by the garfish and the skipper, and followed by the silverside or sand smelt, of the family *Atherinidae*.

The Order *Zeiformes*, which comes next, provides the quaint and admirable John Dory. The Order *Beryciformes* offers the unexciting red 'bream', so-called. Finally, the Order *Lampridiformes* includes the remarkable opah.

The opah is very beautiful as well as rare. Since most of the catalogue entry for it (page 82) is taken up with comments on its quality as food, I shall here whet the reader's appetite by quoting Jane Grigson's description of its appearance in her book *Fish Cookery*.

A large fish, of curves and perfect beauty of colour. The aspect of its rounded eyes and rounded head is mild, almost dolphin-like. The huge, plump body, a taut oval up to 6 feet long, is softly spotted with white. The main blue-grey and green of its skin reflects an iridescence of rose, purple and gold. The fins are a brilliant red. The sickle tail has reminded people of the moon's shape; the ribs of its fins have seemed like the scarlet rays of the sun.

Others, of course, have sought to convey, whether in prose or paint, the striking beauty of the fish. The illustration in Couch's *British Fishes* is almost too bright to view without the protection of sunglasses! Many writers have also drawn attention to the magical quality of its common names in many languages. (I particularly like 'mariposa moonfish', cited by Artemas Ward as an American name; although, since mariposa is Spanish for butterfly, the name does risk making this very large fish sound less substantial than it is.)

EEL

Family *Anguillidae*

Anguilla anguilla (Linnaeus)

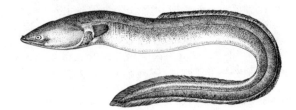

REMARKS Maximum length 135 cm. A specimen of this size would weigh 9 kilos. But this is exceptional. The usual adult size is much less and the British record for an eel caught by rod is less than 4 kilos.

Colour varies. Adults are usually black, greenish black or grey-brown on back and sides and yellowish below. Sides and belly become bright silver when the eel approaches sexual maturity and sets off to spawn (see below).

The eel is born at sea, spends most of its life in rivers or lakes and returns to the sea to spawn and die. It is present throughout western Europe. The American species *Anguilla rostrata* (Lesueur) ranges from Newfoundland to the West Indies and beyond.

Portuguese: Enguia, Eiró
Spanish: Anguila
French: Anguille
Dutch: Aal, Paling
German: Aal, Flussaal
Polish: Wegorz
Russian: Ugor'
Finnish: Ankerias
Swedish: Ål
Norwegian: Ål
Danish: Ål
Icelandic: Áll
Other: Eascú (Irish);
   Llysywen (Welsh);
   Anweye (Walloon)

Its eyes are smaller than those of the European eel and its maximum length is less (only 65 cm for the males).

The spawning grounds for both European and American eels are in the vicinity of the Sargasso Sea, and probably overlap. There the eggs hatch into larvae, which soon develop into the 'leptocephalus' stage – tiny, transparent, ribbon-like creatures which are carried by the currents or actively swim towards the shores which are their destination. The European species takes three years for the journey, the American only one. When they arrive in estuaries on their respective sides of the Atlantic they are still transparent but cylindrical in shape. They are now known as elvers. At certain places in Europe, especially in Spain and Italy, their arrival is welcomed and they are caught and eaten. But most pass unscathed up the rivers, turning dark in colour as they do so, and then live and grow in fresh water for an average period of nine years (males) or twelve (females, both averages being based on English data) before returning to the ocean to spawn. When they leave the rivers they are known as silver eels because of the colour change referred to above.

The fishery for eels is important in many countries. Although I am counting the eel as a marine fish, since it comes from the sea and goes back to the sea, it is of course in fresh or brackish waters that it is usually caught. The French think that those taken from brackish waters are the best.

CUISINE   The eel is relatively fat and makes a rich dish if cooked fresh. The best way to do this is to buy eels alive; have them killed, bled, skinned, cleaned and cut into sections; then grill these, or smoke them yourself in a small Scandinavian-type smoking box (page 262), or use them for a soup, or stew or braise them.

Smoked eel is still rich, but seems meatier and less fat. If the smoking has been well done, the texture and flavour are excellent.

The Dutch and their neighbours to the north are particularly partial to smoked eel. This is very good in Scandinavia, but superlative in the Netherlands. I asked an expert at IJmuiden why the Dutch version is best, given that some of the eels smoked there are imported for the purpose. He replied that Dutch smoked eel is best because the Dutch love it more than any other people and are therefore more discriminating about its quality. The Dutch smokers, who constitute an artisan industry centred on the village of Sparendam, respond to this discriminating demand. One secret of their success lies in the careful selection of suitably fat eels for the smoking process.

In Denmark there are interesting recipes for baking eel on top of a loaf of bread; no bad idea as the bread balances the rather fat meat of the eel. A similar tradition exists in Zeeland, where bread rolls are baked with eel inside. These are called paling broodjes and are delicious.

Eels are eaten with enthusiasm in the Province of Quebec and make a popular winter dish in Prince Edward Island. I have also found traces of eel-eating in the eastern United States. But most of the North American catch is exported to Europe or used as bait.

RECIPES

Anguille médocaine, 287

Paling in't groen, 307

Fried fillets of eel, Dutch
   style, 316

Eel cooked with apples
   (Dutch), 316

Hamburg eel soup, 323

Danish ways with fresh eel, 392

Danish ways with smoked eel, 392

Anguille au vin blanc
   (French Canadian), 404

(and see also Lamprey pie, 450)

This is what an elver (see previous page) looks like. It is about 6 or 7 cm in length.

CONGER EEL

Conger conger (Linnaeus)

Family *Congridae*

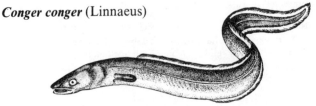

REMARKS   Maximum length 275 cm (exceptionally, normal maximum 175 cm, market length around 1 metre). Colour varies according to habitat.

Portuguese: Congro, Safio
Spanish: Congrio
French: Congre
Dutch: Zeepaling, Kommeraal
German: Meeraal
Swedish: Havsål
Norwegian: Havål
Danish: Havål
Icelandic: Hafáll
Other: Eascú (Irish):
Môr-lysywen (Welsh)

The conger ranges from the Mediterranean to the south and west coasts of Britain and, in smaller numbers, up to Norway and Iceland. On the American side of the North Atlantic there is a close relation, *Conger oceanicus* (Mitchill), which is found south from Cape Cod. It is not, however, fished or eaten to any great extent by North Americans.

The conger is a fierce creature, which used to be called evil-eye at Aberdeen. It lurks in rocky crevices and wrecks, emerging at night to prey on various fish, crustaceans and molluscs. It is willing to do battle with the octopus, whose principal enemy it is.

CUISINE AND RECIPES   Avoid the bony tail end, except for making soup. A middle cut of conger, poached or braised, can be good; and it is also possible to roast such a piece as though it were meat.

A recipe for Conger eel stew from Bragança is given on page 268, and a recipe from the north of Wales on page 462.

Spaniards also eat a lot of conger, which is the subject of a traditional recipe called Congrio al ajo arriero. Arriero means muleteer, one of those who would journey from the coast to the interior with a load of fish packed in salt, ice and straw. If, despite these precautions, the fish began to spoil, the muleteers would overwhelm the disagreeable taste with a massive quantity of the ajo (garlic) which also figures in the title of the recipe.

A more practical recipe is Congre au lait, from south-western France. Skin and bone a centre cut of conger weighing ¾ kilo (1½ lb), slice it and cut the slices into small squares or rounds. Put these in a buttered oven dish, cover them with ½ kilo (1 lb) potatoes and a medium onion, all peeled and thinly sliced, season generously, pour a litre (2 pints) of milk over all and cook for 1½ hours in a slow oven (330° F, gas 3). A Cornish touch may be added by putting in some marigold petals.

The conger is esteemed in Brittany and even enjoys the name of 'boeuf bellilois' in Belle-Île.

GARFISH

Family *Belonidae*

Belone belone (Linnaeus)

REMARKS Maximum length 75 cm, market length 35 to 60 cm. The back is a brilliant green or dark blue, the flanks silver, with a yellow tinge to the belly. The lateral line runs very low along the body. This is an oceanic fish, which enters coastal waters and spawns there. It occurs from the Mediterranean to the Baltic, Norway and Iceland.

Portuguese: Agulha
Spanish: Aguja
French: Orphie, Aiguille
Dutch: Geep
German: Hornhecht
Polish: Belona
Russian: Sargan
Finnish: Nokkakala
Swedish: Horngädda, Hornfisk
Norwegian: Horngjel, Nebbesild
Danish: Hornfisk
Icelandic: Hornfiskur
Other: Môr nodwydd (Welsh); Orratza (Basque)

The garfish has been given many vernacular names, such as sea-needle and gore-bill. Names such as green-bone refer to its green bones (not just greenish, but a good strong viridian); while names like mackerel-scout were given because the garfish often arrives in coastal waters ahead of the mackerel. The Irish misguidedly call it Spanish mackerel.

The garfish is capable of planing along the surface of the water and leaping over low rocks. It strikes upwards at a bait, so that the first the fisherman knows of the capture is the sight of the fish beating itself about on the surface to get rid of the hook. Jonathan Couch (in his *History of the Fishes of the British Islands*, 1877) observed that 'in doing this it always emits a very strong and peculiar odour.' Newly caught garfish sometimes have a strange smell, which may be the same one.

CUISINE AND RECIPES Day put it well. 'Pretty good, but owing to the green colour of the bones of this fish, both before and after boiling, a prejudice against eating it is entertained in some localities.' In fact, the greenness of the bones need not put people off. The flesh of the garfish is perfectly wholesome and has a good taste, although it is sometimes rather dry. Poach or fry, whole or in fillets. A French recipe is given on page 295; and one from Denmark, where garfish is popular, on page 388.

SKIPPER, SAURY, NEEDLEFISH

Family *Scomberesocidae*

Scomberesox saurus (Walbaum)

REMARKS   Maximum length nearly 50 cm. A silver band running from the eye to near the tail separates the darker (olive-green or blue) back from the golden or silvery underside. Note the presence of finlets near the tail; that the lateral line is the one shown very low on the body; and that the lower jaw projects slightly beyond the upper one, although not at all stages of growth.

The home waters of this species are in the ocean, around the latitude of Madeira, but they migrate northwards in the summer, as far as Norway, Iceland and Newfoundland.

Portuguese: Agulhão
Spanish: Paparda
French: Balaou, Aiguille de mer
Dutch: Makreelgeep
German: Makrelenhechte
Swedish: Makrillgädda
Norwegian: Makrellgjedde
Danish: Makrelgedde
Icelandic: Geirnefur

The names skipper and the like are given because these fish, which swim in schools, jump out of the water to escape predators or nets. They used to be canned in Canada and were considered to be very good. Irregularity of supply put an end to the practice, but a minor commercial fishery for these fish is growing up again in North America, using the Japanese technique of attracting the fish by lights and then scoop-netting them.

CUISINE   As for the garfish. Worth eating.

SILVERSIDE, ATLANTIC SILVERSIDE

Family *Atherinidae*

Menidia menidia (Linnaeus)

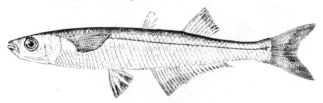

REMARKS Maximum length 14 cm. The back and upper sides of this pretty little fish are transparent green. A silver band, marked above by a dark line, runs along the side. The belly is white.

This north American species covers the waterfront up to the Gulf of St Lawrence. Its common names include green smelt, shiner, whitebait, spearing and sperling. These fish congregate in shoals, close inshore, and willingly enter brackish waters. They have been described, when spawning in sedge grass at the head of a bay, as rolling about and jumping out of the water in such numbers that the water was 'whitened with the milt, and the grass so full of eggs that they could be taken out by the handful'. Cheerful, fecund little creatures.

The corresponding European species is ***Atherina presbyter*** Cuvier, the SAND SMELT or SILVERSIDE, of which a drawing is shown below. It is similar in appearance and size to the American species, and has a range from the Mediterranean to Britain and even further north. There is a commercial fishery for it in the Mediterranean, but not, so far as I can discover, in the Atlantic. It is known as peixe-rei or camarâo bruxo in Portugal, as abichón in Spain, and as prêtre in France.

CUISINE Silversides are delicious. If you can obtain small ones, treat them like whitebait. Large ones are good fried, following the recipe for Lançons en friture (page 297).

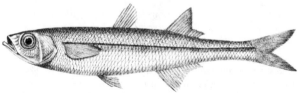

JOHN DORY, DORY

Family *Zeidae*

Zeus faber Linnaeus

REMARKS Maximum length of females over 65 cm; of males about 45 cm. This is a yellowish-brown or greyish fish with a highly compressed body and characteristic 'thumbprints' on its sides, which have been attributed by most to St Peter but by some to St Christopher. (The touch of whichever saint may have imparted to the species its solitary habits, but not an ascetic attitude, for the John Dory uses its extendable mouth to engulf other fish voraciously.)

Portuguese: Peixe galo, Peixe São Pedro
Spanish: Pez de San Pedro
French: Saint-Pierre
Dutch: Zonnevis
German: Heringskönig
Swedish: Sankt Pers fisk
Norwegian: St Petersfisk
Danish: Sankt Peters-fisk

The origin of the name John Dory is unclear. Dory seems to be derived from dorée, a name by which the fish has been known in some parts of France. Macleod, in his learned *Key to the Names of British Fishes, Mammals, Amphibians and Reptiles* (1956), inclines to the view that John is a nickname, like Jack in jackdaw. Earlier authors, however, suggest that the eighteenth-century actor John Quin was responsible for giving the fish a good reputation in England and that it was therefore called John's or John Dory. Parnell (in *Fishes of the Firth of Forth*, 1838) asserts that this name acquired currency in Bath, 'where Quin's celebrity as the prince of epicures was well-known, and where his palate finished its voluptuous career'.

The species is well known in the Mediterranean and the Bay of Biscay. It occurs as far north as Norway but is not found in abundance north of the English Channel and Ireland. Its American counterpart, **Zenopsis ocellata** (Storer), is found mainly between Nova Scotia and North Carolina, but not in quantities sufficient to excite commercial interest.

CUISINE AND RECIPES The uncouth appearance of this fish, which used to be called l'horrible in parts of France (although also known, more kindly, as poulet de mer), has deterred some from eating it, which is a pity.

In fact, the John Dory yields good, bone-free fillets of white flesh, which can in general be treated like fillets of sole or flounder. Remember, however, if you buy a whole John Dory, that the proportion of fillets to the whole fish is unusually low. On the other hand, most of the rest of the fish can be used for making a particularly good fish fumet.

Quin, he of the voluptuous palate, recommended poaching the fish in sea water and serving it with a lobster or shrimp sauce, or with no sauce. The fillets are also suitable for frying; and for baking, but with added liquid, so that the flesh does not dry out. The recipe on page 455, from Devonshire, calls for both cider and cream; a good combination which I have also met in Normandy. A Dutch recipe for fillets in cheese sauce is given on page 315.

RED 'BREAM' Family *Berycidae*

Beryx decadactylus Cuvier

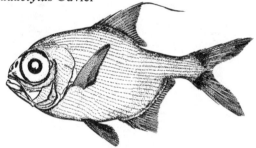

REMARKS Maximum length 60 cm. This fish is orange or red all over, so the first word in the English name is justified; but it is not a bream, which is why I put the second one in quotation marks. It is a deep-water fish, found from the Bay of Biscay northwards and occasionally marketed.

French: Beryx, Dorade rouge
German: Kaiserbarsch
Swedish: Nordiska beryxen
Norwegian: Brudefisk
Danish: Nordisk beryx

Further south, the species ***Beryx splendens*** Lowe is to be found. It is less deep in the body and has a maximum length of 45 cm. Its Spanish name, oddly, is besugo americano, meaning American bream.

CUISINE The flesh is of good quality and may be prepared like that of the true breams (pages 98 to 100).

OPAH, MOONFISH (but cf. page 97)   Family *Lamprididae*

Lampris guttatus (Brünnich)
Lampris regius

REMARKS   Maximum length 150 cm (corresponding to a weight of 50 kilos). This beautiful fish is not uncommon in the central and southern parts of the Atlantic and may swim as far north as Iceland and Norway; but it is a rarity in the North Atlantic. There can surely have been only one occasion (Swindon, A.D. 1971) when a famous poet and a famous cook (Geoffrey and Jane Grigson) have entered a British fish shop and been confronted by a whole opah. For the resulting, lyrical description of the fish, see page 73.

Portuguese: Peixe cravo
Spanish: Luna real
French: Poisson lune, Poisson royal
Dutch: Koningsvis
German: Gotteslachs
Swedish: Glansfisk
Norwegian: Laksestørje
Danish: Glansfisk
Icelandic: Guðlax
Other: Sunfish, Jerusalem haddock

CUISINE AND RECIPE   Thanks to the vigilance of Jack Shiells at Billingsgate, he and I recently shared an opah of 25 kilos. He reported that the flesh, especially the darker parts, is delicious if sliced thinly and eaten raw, Japanese style; that fried escalopes are a great success; and that the same applies to Jane Grigson's recipe for Sunfish in cream (*Fish Cookery*, page 150). Our own family conclusions were that nothing could be better than steaks from the upper rear part of the fish, simply grilled; but that a 'shoulder' can be very successfully roasted. The flesh is pink and firm. Flavour and texture are excellent, with hints of salmon, of tuna, of Ray's bream (page 104) and of veal. The skin, which is relatively thin for such a big fish, should certainly be eaten.

A recipe for curried opah, from Denmark, is given on page 387.

Bass, Groupers and the Tilefish

At this point in the catalogue we move into the large and important Order *Perciformes*, the order of perch-like fish, from which we shall not emerge until more than sixty pages hence.

Surveying the wide variety of the fish exhibited in these next sixty or so pages, the reader may wonder what 'perch-like' means. The answer is that the fish of this order all have some spiny fins. Some of the leading rays of the dorsal and anal fins are always thickened and unjointed, and are in most instances sharp. The pelvic fins usually have one spiny ray each and are well forward on the body, beneath the pectoral fins. The pectoral fins themselves are high up on the body; whereas the more primitive fish in other orders have low-slung pectorals.

Our first batch of perciform fish contains the sizeable sea bass and groupers of the important families *Percichthyidae* and *Serranidae*, followed by the polychrome tilefish.

Mention of the groupers prompts a little excursion into zoogeography. I said in the Introduction that, for the purposes of this book, the southern boundary of the North Atlantic on the American side would be the state line between Georgia and Florida; and that the marine fauna of Florida were, broadly speaking, those of the Caribbean and the Gulf of Mexico. This is true, but it is also true that in *offshore waters*, which are warmed by the Gulf Stream, the range of these tropical and semi-tropical species extends further north, usually as far as Cape Hatteras.

This fact has become better known in recent decades because of the development of 'headboat' fishing from the Carolinas. (Headboats are so-called because anglers pay so much per head for a day's fishing from them; and they range 30 to 60 nautical miles out to sea, to the edge of the continental shelf.) This fishery now results in about a million and a half pounds of tropical, deep-water fish being landed annually in ports north of Florida. The species in question and their relative abundance were well described by Gene R. Huntsman in an article in *The Marine Fisheries Review* (Vol. 38, No. 3, March 1976). They include a large number of groupers. To catalogue them all here, together with various grunts, snappers, porgies and other species which have similar ranges, would involve straying into another domain. Yet to ignore them completely would be unrealistic. The solution I have adopted is to list a few only, choosing those which are most often marketed as representatives of the whole group.

BASS, SEA BASS

Family *Percichthyidae*

Dicentrarchus labrax (Linnaeus)

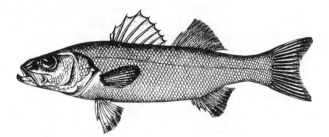

REMARKS   Maximum length 80 cm or even, rarely, up to 1 metre. The back is grey or blue, the flanks silvery and the belly yellowish or white. Living bass seem predominantly bright silver. Young fish may be spotted, but large spotted specimens will belong to the related species *Dicentrarchus punctatus* (Bloch), the spotted sea bass, which only comes as far north as the southern

Portuguese: Robalo
Spanish: Lubina
French: Bar, Loup
Dutch: Zeebaars
German: Seebarsch
Swedish: Havsabborre
Norwegian: Hav-åbor
Danish: Bars

Bay of Biscay. *Dicentrarchus labrax* has been plentiful off the south and west coasts of Britain and Ireland, and is taken as far north as Norway. But stocks have suffered from overfishing.

This handsome and voracious fish comes into coastal waters in the summer and is a favourite of anglers, especially in the south of Ireland. Of the various Irish names, bairs (Waterford) is interesting as it is closer to the Danish bars and the Anglo-Saxon root baers than the English bass.

CUISINE   Piscator remarked that the bass 'resembles a salmon in colour, and somewhat in form; on which account the fishwomen of the west of England have dignified it with the title of "salmon-bass", although it is in no way whatever connected with the salmon family. Still, for all this, the bass is a very good fish and a very useful one, as it is capable of being cooked in a great variety of ways, – boiled, broiled, fried, stewed, baked, or made up into pie.' True, but a bewildering choice. The simpler advice of Ambrose Heath is to cook it, according to size, in any way applicable to the salmon (page 44).

RECIPE
Lubina a la Santanderina, 277   Bar au beurre blanc nantais, 295

WHITE PERCH, SEA PERCH   Family *Percichthyidae*

Morone americanus (Gmelin)
Roccus americanus

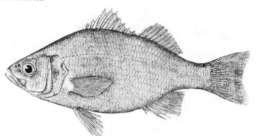

REMARKS Maximum length 35 cm, but the common length is only 20 to 25 cm. This light-coloured fish, which has a range from Nova Scotia to South Carolina, is found in fresh and brackish water as well as in the sea. It is often associated with its larger relation the striped bass, which I describe on the following page, and has similar habits. It has been accused of eating the spawn of other fish. 'Swarms of young perch . . . have been seen following the alewives around the shores of ponds on Martha's Vineyard, eating their spawn as it was deposited.' (Bigelow and Schroeder, writing in their classic work *Fishes of the Gulf of Maine*, 1953.)

CUISINE In his report on *The Food Fishes of the United States* (1884–7). Goode took the occasion to try to influence public taste. Earlier nineteenth-century writers on American fish had spoken slightingly of the white perch. In seeking to improve its reputation, Goode recalled with approval that: 'It found an earnest advocate in Mr Thaddeus Norris, who, after protesting strenuously against the statement of various writers that it is rarely brought to market for food, that it is only fit for chowder, that it is not of sufficient importance to merit particular notice, and so on, goes on to state, what is undoubtedly true, that in season the White Perch is *the* pan-fish, excelled by none of the Philadelphia, Baltimore, Washington, Norfolk and Richmond markets; and, he might have added, had he been writing at the present time, of the New York market also . . .'

The reader will find that the advice to pan-fry these fish is indeed well founded; but one may of course fillet the larger specimens and do as one pleases with the fillets.

STRIPED BASS

Family *Percichthyidae*

Morone saxatilis (Walbaum)
Roccus saxatilis

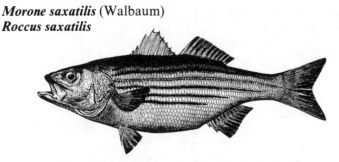

REMARKS This species, which has a maximum length of well over 1 metre, but a market length of 25 to 45 cm, is closely related to the European sea bass (page 84), but differs from it in bearing conspicuous stripes on its olive-green back. It ranges from the Gulf of St Lawrence to the Gulf of Mexico.

Goode provides interesting information about its name. 'In the North it is called the "Striped Bass", in the South the "Rock-fish" or the "Rock". The neutral territory where both these names are in use appears to be New Jersey. Large sea-going individuals are sometimes known in New England by the names "Green-head" and "Squid-hound".'

Like the European sea bass, this is a favourite of sportsmen; but it is also the object of a commercial fishery. In Chesapeake Bay, for example, it is the most important and valuable fish. A study of its behaviour there shows that its year falls into three seasons. In the winter the striped bass move out into deeper waters, to avoid the cold. Between April and June they come back up the bay and its tributaries to their spawning grounds. In the summer the schools spread out and feed in the bay proper. However, it seems that populations in other areas choose to winter in estuaries or rivers.

The striped bass is very definitely an inshore fish and is rarely taken more than four or five miles from the coast. It was successfully introduced to the Pacific coast in the nineteenth century, and now provides sport for anglers there as well as on the eastern seaboard. It is a voracious fish and a remarkable variety of prey may be discovered in its stomach, including other fish such as alewives, croakers, eels, flounders and sculpins, as well as a wide variety of invertebrates. In estuarine haunts it seems to have a particular taste for sea worms (*Nereis* spp.). Jordan and Evermann observe that despite its catholic tastes the striped bass tends to gorge on one particular food at a time, and then rest to digest. Schools of striped bass show a tendency to do this in unison.

The striped bass has a limited distribution in Canada, but migrates up various rivers, such as the St John, Shubenacadie and St Lawrence, for spawning purposes. Because of the way they behave when spawning they are sometimes referred to as 'rollers'.

CUISINE An excellent fish, well described by Wood (*New Englands Prospect*, 1634): 'The basse is one of the best fishes in the country, and though men are soon wearied with other fish, yet are they never with basse. It is a delicate, fine, fat, fast fish, having a bone in his head which contains a saucerfull of marrow sweet and good, pleasant to the pallat and wholesome to the stomach . . .'

Cap'n Phil Schwind, author of the salt-breezy *Clam Shack Cookery*, devotes almost a page to describing how 'stripers' should be filleted in preparation for being fried, which he recommends; or broiled, on which he remarks that they are slightly oily fish and do not need to be basted. This is good advice; but the striped bass is a versatile fish and will respond equally well to being poached in a court-bouillon. The flaky white flesh makes a good fish salad. Specimens of moderate size can also be stuffed.

RECIPES
Stuffed striped bass Rothschild, 419   To boil rockfish (Mrs Mary Randolph), 427

BLACK SEA-BASS

Family *Percichthyidae*

Centropristes striatus (Linnaeus)

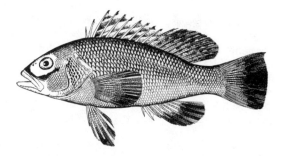

REMARKS Maximum length nearly 50 cm. The back is grey, dark brown or blackish, the lower part of the body lighter. Pale streaks run along the dorsal fin and the sides of the fish. Males develop a blue bump on their heads during the spawning season.

This bottom-feeding fish has a range from Florida to Cape Ann and is most common between Cape Hatteras and Cape Cod. Unlike the striped bass and white perch, it is a purely marine species. It is sometimes called blackfish; a name also applied to the tautog (page 119).

CUISINE A fish of very good quality. The flesh is firm and white. Frying and baking are recommended.

WRECKFISH, STONE BASS

Family *Percichthyidae*

Polyprion americanus (B. and S.)

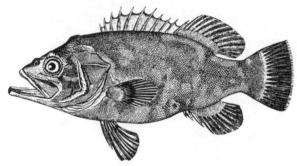

REMARKS   Maximum length about 2 metres. A greyish or dark brown fish, whose tail fin is edged with white. Its range includes the southern Atlantic and the Mediterranean and both sides of the northern Atlantic. It occurs as far north as Norway and Newfoundland, but is rare in those latitudes and indeed not common anywhere.

Portuguese: Cherne
Spanish: Cherna
French: Cernier
Dutch: Wrakbaars
German: Wrackbarsch
Swedish: Vrakfisk
Danish: Vragfisk

The wreckfish is so called because of its habit of following bits of floating wood or seaweed, usually on the high seas but sometimes into inshore waters. This habit may account for the northward journeys of some of these fish; if they find an attractive piece of wreckage which is being carried north by the currents they go along with it.

Passing on to the family *Serranidae*. I show below ***Serranus cabrilla*** (Linnaeus), the COMBER (Portuguese alecrim. Spanish cabrilla and French serran), which is like a small version of the groupers shown on the next page and is quite common in Portuguese waters and the Bay of Biscay. It is appreciated by the Portuguese.

CUISINE   The wreckfish is of good quality. Treat it like the groupers on the next page. The same applies to the comber, which, being smaller, is usually cooked whole.

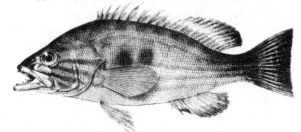

RED GROUPER   Family *Serranidae*

Epinephelus morio (C. and V.)

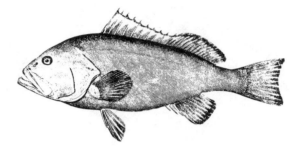

REMARKS   Maximum length about 90 cm. Despite its name, this fish is usually brown in colour, with some mottling. It provides a good example of the groupers which are found in offshore waters on the eastern seaboard, up to or even beyond Cape Hatteras, as explained on page 83. Others are the smaller *Epinephelus adscensionis* (Osbeck), the rock hind; *Epinephelus drummondhayi* Goode and Bean, the speckled hind or strawberry grouper; and some larger species, including the giant Warsaw grouper, *Epinephelus nigritus* (Holbrook).

The situation on the European side of the Atlantic is similar. The Mediterranean harbours four fine groupers and the waters up to Biscay are warm enough for most of them; but only one. *Epinephelus guaza* (Linnaeus), strays further north. This is the species shown at the foot of the page. European names for the groupers are mérou (French), mero (Spanish) and mero or mera (Portuguese).

The groupers are solitary fish, which establish their individual territories in rocky waters. They constitute a favourite prey for underwater fishermen; but are capable, at least in the Indian Ocean, of showing amiability towards the human species, for I know a man who made friends with two.

CUISINE AND RECIPES   The groupers provide excellent, firm steaks which may be grilled or baked. Smaller groupers may be cooked whole.

TILEFISH   Family *Branchiostegidae*

Lopholatilus chamaeleonticeps Goode and Bean

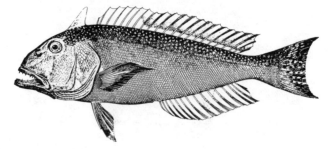

REMARKS   Maximum length about 115 cm (when the weight would be over 15 kilos); usual adult length around 80 cm. This is one of the most brilliantly coloured fish known outside the tropics. No doubt that is why it was given the name *chamaeleonticeps*, although it only resembles the chameleon in exhibiting a whole spectrum of colours, not in changing them at will. Leim and Scott describe it as 'bluish to olive-green on back and upper part of sides, changing to yellow and rose on lower sides and belly, latter with white midline. Head reddish on sides, white below. Back and sides above lateral line thickly dotted with irregular yellow spots. Dorsal fin dusky with larger yellowish spots, its soft-rayed portion pale edged; adipose flap greenish-yellow; anal fin pinkish with purple to blue iridescence; pectoral pale sooty-brown with purplish reflections.' Its range is from the vicinity of Nova Scotia to Chesapeake Bay; but it also occurs in the waters of southern Florida and the Gulf of Mexico. It is a deep-water fish.

The abundance of the tilefish in northern waters has fluctuated considerably. There were lots of them in about 1880. Then an influx of cold water into their haunts killed millions of them. During the First World War they were again so plentiful that the United States catch for 1916–17 was over 5 million kilos.

CUISINE   Recording the 'discovery' of the species off Massachusetts in the late 1870s, Goode describes how specimens were collected by a Fish Commission steamer. 'They were tasted at the ward-room table and the flesh was found to be fine-grained and delicate in flavor, resembling in some respects that of the cod, in others, that of the striped bass.' Evelene Spencer and John Cobb (whose expert and comprehensive book *Fish Cookery* was published at Boston in 1922) say that it is 'a superior food fish in every way. It is best when boiled or baked like the cod.' Smoked tilefish are said to be good; but so far as I know there has been no commercial smoking of them in recent times. Thin, raw slices of tilefish, sashimi-style, are excellent.

Bluefish, Scad, Jacks, the Pompano, etc.

This section of the catalogue is almost entirely devoted to what are called the carangid fish. The first species listed, the bluefish, is not one of them but resembles them. So does the COBIA or SERGEANT-FISH, *Rachycentron canadum* (Linnaeus), a species which I have not listed, since it really belongs to the warmer waters further south. However, it is found as far north as Chesapeake Bay and even beyond, and deserves to be mentioned as a fine game fish which provides good eating for anglers in the Carolinas. It has also been called crab-eater and black bonito. I show it below, illustrating the stripe which accounts for the name sergeant-fish.

Which said, the rest of this section is about members of the family *Carangidae*. They vary considerably in quality. The pompano is first-class. The horse mackerel is distinctly less good.

The section ends with the moonfish and the lookdown, which are thin, grave-looking fish whose appearance would suggest that they should be engaged in philosophical discussion rather than cooked and eaten. Nor is there much of them to eat. But they have a certain gastronomic interest; and they possess one useful quality, which is that they can be dried quickly without the aid of any special device, and may be kept thus, hanging in the kitchen and introducing a note of solemnity thereto.

One more carangid fish deserves a mention here and is illustrated below. This is *Seriola dumerili* (Risso), the AMBERJACK (U.K.) or RUDDERFISH (U.S.A.), which ranges right across the warmer waters of the Atlantic. It does not come far north of the Mediterranean on the European side, but is found up to Chesapeake Bay and beyond on the American side. It is good to eat, but not of commercial importance in our region.

BLUEFISH   Family *Pomatomidae*

Pomatomus saltatrix (Linnaeus)

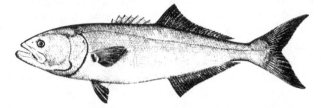

REMARKS   Maximum length about 110 cm, common length 60 to 80 cm. Sea-green above, silvery below. In the western waters of the North Atlantic this species travels up to Cape Cod and even beyond; but on the eastern side it is uncommon north of the Mediterranean and Morocco.

Portuguese: Anchova
Spanish: Anjova
French: Tassergal
Other: Snapper (small ones, New England to Chesapeake)

I cannot better the prose of Jordan and Evermann (*American Food and Game Fishes*, 1902), who support with great verve their assertion that the bluefish is:

a carnivorous animal of the most pronounced type ... It has been likened to an animated chopping-machine the business of which is to cut to pieces and otherwise destroy as many fish as possible in a given space of time. Going in large schools, in pursuit of fish not much inferior to themselves in size, they move along like a pack of hungry wolves, destroying everything before them. Their trail is marked by fragments of fish and by the stain of blood in the sea, as, when the fish is too large to be swallowed entire, the hinder portion will be bitten off and the anterior part allowed to float or sink. It has been even maintained that such is the gluttony of this fish, that when the stomach becomes full the contents are disgorged and then again filled! It is certain that it kills more fish than it needs or can use. The amount of food they consume or destroy is incredibly great. It has been estimated at twice the weight of the fish in a day, and one observer says that a bluefish will destroy daily a thousand other fish. It has been estimated that there are annually on our coast from New Jersey to Mononomy a thousand million bluefish averaging 5 or 6 pounds each in weight, and that these eat or destroy at the lowest estimate 10 fish each every day, or a total of ten thousand millions of fish destroyed every day.

The same authors go on to quote a gentleman called Nimrod Wildfire, whose eloquence matches their own when he speaks of the power and energy of the bluefish. 'It can jump higher and come down quicker, dive deeper, and stay under longer' than any other salt-water fish of its size. 'Look at his clean build, and it is accounted for; his narrow waist and depth of hull, falling off sharply as it approaches the keel, enabling him to keep well to windward, as if he had his centre-board always down. See his immense propeller behind! No fish of his size is more wicked or wild when hooked. I have sometimes struck a 3-pound bluefish, and thought I had a 6-pound weakfish, until he commenced jumping, and after giving him considerable play, have at last drawn him in by sheer force, with his pluck not the least abated.'

Bluefish seem to stimulate a lot of vivid prose and activity. In his book *Salt Water Fishing* (1946), Van Campen Heiler explains how he used model T Fords in fishing for them, for example near Cape Hatteras.

One day in September a bunch of us, eight cars to be exact, were cruising slowly along the surf ... looking for blues. Each 'beach buggy' was equipped according to its owner's particular fancy; some with no tops, others with seats like a jaunting car, painted the colors of the rainbow, but mostly aluminium or metalicote, bait boxes on the rear, rods in sockets on the sides, all with huge oversize tires and all stripped for action.

Suddenly, as if in unison, the cry burst above the roaring surf, 'There they are! Blues!' Eight exhausts burst into a staccato roar and eight ancient vehicles rushed headlong over the dunes towards the dipping gulls a mile away. We ... reached the fish first, and without stopping to shut off the engine, leaped into the surf with rods already swinging. In clouds of sand the other buggies quickly arrived and their occupants rushed to the water's edge. For a few minutes the air was full of singing lines and flashing squids and the big blues commenced to dot the sand in all directions. Then as suddenly as they had risen, the school sank, and gathering up our fish we commenced our slow promenade once more.

CUISINE This fish is well regarded in the Mediterranean, hardly known in northern Europe and highly esteemed in North America. Its quality is comparable to that of the pompano and the Spanish mackerel; it is marketed in large quantities and bought with enthusiasm. It does not keep very well, but, if bought and cooked with dispatch, offers firm flesh of an excellent taste.

Since bluefish are naturally oily, it is not a good plan to fry them. This rule does not, however, apply to the small specimens known as snapper blues or snappers. These little fish, 10 to 15 cm long, are delicious when simply beheaded, gutted and pan-fried. 'Harbour blues' are the next size up, and may qualify for similar treatment, although I would prefer to have them grilled.

As for the larger bluefish, they may be prepared in any way which suits mackerel, including the recipes listed on page 127. Mackerel are in fact slightly oilier than bluefish, but the difference is not great. Bluefish are often baked, and a good recipe for this is listed below. But they may also be grilled or poached in a court-bouillon. I suggest serving a tart sauce with them; or perhaps the royal grey sauce of Poland (page 334) which deserves to have a wider application.

One good way of coping with bluefish which you do not wish to eat at once is to borrow from the Portuguese of Provincetown the use of what they call vinha d'alhos. For 1 kg (2 lb) of fillets of bluefish, combine the following: 1 cup each of wine vinegar and dry red wine; 4 crushed cloves of garlic; 1 tsp cumin seed; 1 tsp salt; and a dash of cayenne pepper. Coat the inside of a glass or earthenware casserole with olive oil, lay the fish fillets in it and pour the vinha d'alhos over them. Leave it in a cool place, or the refrigerator, for 6 to 24 hours, turning the fillets occasionally. Then drain them and pan-fry them in olive oil.

RECIPES
Fillets of bluefish flambé with
    gin, 414

Baked bluefish, with herbs, 420

SCAD, HORSE MACKEREL — Family *Carangidae*

Trachurus trachurus (Linnaeus)

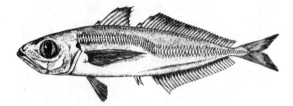

REMARKS Maximum length over 30 cm. The scad has a grey-blue back with greenish tints, silvery sides and a white belly. Its head is large and its sides are adorned (if that is the right word for what I regard as an unattractive feature) by a row of bony plates (scutes) along the lateral line.

The scad is common enough in Portuguese and Spanish waters and is found as far north as Norway. It penetrates the Baltic to a short distance. It is also known, but as an uncommon fish, on the American Atlantic coast, where *Selar crumenophthalmus* (Bloch), the goggled-eyed scad, is also an occasional visitor.

Portuguese: Carapau, Chicharro
Spanish: Chicharro
French: Chinchard
Dutch: Horsmakreel
German: Stöcker, Bastardmakrele
Polish: Ostrobok
Swedish: Taggmakrill, Taggsill
Norwegian: Taggmakrell, Hestemakrell
Danish: Støkker, Hestemakrel
Other: Crake-herring (N. Ireland)

The name horse mackerel is said to have been given in indication of its inferior quality. Perhaps; but Sir Thomas Browne, writing in the seventeenth century,* said that Norfolk fishermen called them simply Horse, and I have a hunch that if one looked at a horse mackerel with sufficient attention one would eventually perceive something visually horselike about it. (I make no corresponding prophecy about the name Jenny Lind, used in Chesapeake Bay.)

CUISINE AND RECIPE This fish is of moderate quality, quite edible when grilled, but uninspiring. However, the Portuguese do interesting things with it. Only one of their recipes is given, that for Carapau de escabeche (page 270), but others exist in the Algarve and the Berlenga Islands.

In France the scad is counted as good material for making a fish fumet; but may also be prepared au beurre, in much the same way as Lançons en friture (page 297).

---

* Sir Thomas Browne (1605–82), *Notes and Letters on the Natural History of Norfolk*, being manuscript notes by him, edited with notes by Thomas Southwell, London, 1902.

JACK, COMMON JACK, CREVALLE

Family *Carangidae*

Caranx hippos (Linnaeus)

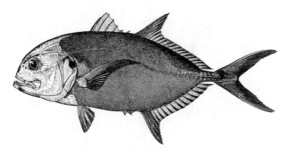

REMARKS Maximum length 75 cm. A glance at the drawing will show that this species has many distinctive features, including a sickle-shaped pectoral fin, a naked breast and a large dark spot on the gill cover. Its back is bluish green or greenish bronze. It is common as far north as Wood's Hole on the North American Atlantic coast; but does not appear at all in European waters. The same is true of *Caranx crysos* (Mitchill), the BLUE RUNNER or HARDTAIL, shown in the lower drawing. It may reach a length of 60 cm, but northern examples are rarely more than 30 or 35 cm long. The back is greenish bronze, the lower parts of the body golden or silvery.

CUISINE The jack is large enough to be interesting, and of fair quality. It may be grilled whole (a technique which I have seen applied in Thailand – with remarkably good results – to a closely related Indo-Pacific species). Alternatively, it will yield good fillets which can be dealt with in any of the standard ways.

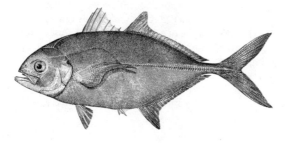

POMPANO

Family *Carangidae*

Trachinotus carolinus (Linnaeus)

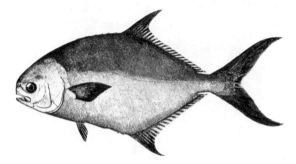

REMARKS   Maximum length 45 cm. This aristocratic-looking fish has the coloration which is typical of the carangid family, blue-green above shading to silver below. It is unknown in European waters. On the American side it has a range up to Chesapeake Bay, and small specimens may be taken further north.

The name pompano seems to be derived from the Spanish pámpana, meaning vine leaf, which in the slightly different form pámpano is the name of various fish in Spain, including a couple which bear some resemblance to the pompano.

Two other pompano may be taken on the American Atlantic coast. One is *Trachinotus ovatus* (Linnaeus), a cosmopolitan fish which is well known in the Mediterranean and parts of the Indian Ocean. It is called the round pompano. Another species, more of a West Indian fish and less esteemed, is *Trachinotus glaucus* (Bloch), the curiously named gaff-topsail pompano. ('May I have a pound and a half of gaff-topsail pompano, please?' No, it can't be a name in real use.)

CUISINE   'As a food fish there is none better than the pompano, either in the fresh waters or in the seas. This is practically the unanimous verdict of epicures and all others who have had the pleasure of eating the pompano, fresh from the water. The flesh is firm and rich, and possesses a delicacy of flavour peculiarly pleasing to the palate.' Thus Jordan and Evermann. Perhaps they exaggerate; but the pompano is indeed excellent. It may be grilled, baked or cooked à la meunière. Its flavour being so good, it does not benefit from the addition of a strong sauce; and there is absolutely no need to embellish it with bits of lobster or otherwise obscure its own merits.

RECIPES   I suggest Pescada en geleia (page 269), Saumon en pain de Caudebec (page 294), Bar au beurre blanc nantais (page 295), Baked bluefish (page 420) or the Welsh recipe for sewin on page 461, all of which may be applied to the pompano.

MOONFISH (but cf. page 82)   Family *Carangidae*

Vomer setapinnis (Mitchill)

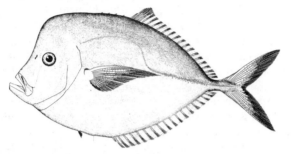

REMARKS   Maximum length about 30 cm. This thin, silvery fish, which reminds me by its facial expression of the chairman of a Whitehall committee in which I once sat, belongs to tropical waters but is a summer visitor on the American Atlantic coast as far north as Wood's Hole.

Even thinner, and like the same chairman at the end of a long meeting, is **Selene vomer** (Linnaeus), the LOOKDOWN. This is shown below, more as a decoration than because it can be taken seriously as food, although it has been marketed in Florida.

CUISINE   The moonfish is too thin to rank high as a food fish. But it was at one time esteemed in New York, where it was apparently known as the blunt-nosed shiner; and it has also been consumed in Massachusetts, under the equally strange name hump-backed butterfish. Fry or bake.

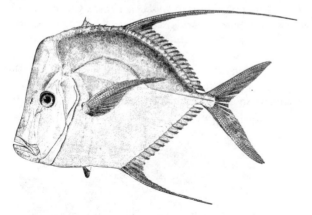

Bream, Porgies and Others

Most of the species which fall under this heading are fish which belong to tropical or near-tropical waters and only occasionally stray into colder regions such as the North Atlantic. Thus the Mediterranean contains many species of bream, of which quite a few occur in the Atlantic also; but only as far north as the Bay of Biscay or the English Channel. I have dealt summarily with such species on pages 99 and 100.

On the American side of the North Atlantic there are some excellent porgies (which is the general name corresponding to sea bream) with a range extending to New England or even further north. However, many members of this family (like the groupers – cf. page 83) belong essentially to the warmer waters of the Caribbean or Florida and are rarely taken north of the Carolinas, and only in the offshore waters there. Among such species are **Calamus leucosteus** Jordan and Gilbert, the whitebone porgy, and **Calamus nodosus** Randall and Caldwell, the knobbed porgy.

The famous RED SNAPPER is not a porgy, but a member of the family *Lutjanidae*. All the members of this family are tropical or semi-tropical fish, but several of them swim as far north as Cape Hatteras in the offshore waters and the red snapper in particular often travels further north in trucks or boxcars, since its excellence has caused it to be in strong demand. The name red snapper, strictly speaking, should be applied only to **Lutjanus campechanus** (Poey), the species illustrated below, but is often applied also to **Lutjanus vivanus** Cuvier, the silk snapper, and to **Rhomboplites aurorubens** (Cuvier), the vermilion snapper.

The last two pages of this section are occupied by species which are not members of the bream family. Ray's bream, so called after the naturalist Ray, belongs to the separate family *Bramidae*. The Butterfish and Harvest-fish belong to the quite different family *Stromateidae*. But it is convenient to locate them here, since they share a bream-like characteristic which is important to the cook, namely having a compressed body.

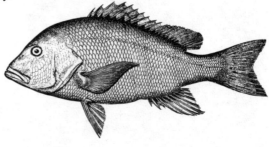

RED SEA-BREAM

Family *Sparidae*

Pagellus bogaraveo (Brünnich)
Pagellus centrodontus

REMARKS Maximum length 50 cm. Adult fish are rose or grey-red in colour. Note the dark spot on the shoulder, the depth of the body and the size of the eye.

Portuguese: Goraz
Spanish: Besugo
French: Dorade commune
Dutch: Roode zeebrasen
German: Nordischer Meerbrassen
Other: Bishigua (Basque)

This species is the only member of the family which is common in European Atlantic waters. It is found in the English Channel and off the south-west and west coasts of the British Isles; and it goes further north in warm weather. It is the subject of a small commercial fishery, mainly by French and Spanish boats.

A less common species, which has a similar range, deserves mention. It is **Spondyliosoma cantharus** (Linnaeus), the black sea bream or old wife (Portuguese choupa, Spanish chopa, French dorade grise or brème (de rochers), Dutch zeekarper, German Seekarpfen, Danish havrude). It is grey to black in colour and attains a length of 30 cm or, exceptionally, 40 to 50 cm. Other sea bream which come up as far as the Bay of Biscay include **Boops boops** (Linnaeus), the bogue (Portuguese and Spanish boga, French bogue); **Pagellus erythrinus** (Linnaeus), the pandora (bica in Portugal, breca in Spain and pageot or pageau in France); and the two species which are catalogued overleaf.

Readers in Portugal, Spain and France who would find it useful to have fuller details of the European sea breams than are supplied on this and the following page will find these in my *Mediterranean Seafood*.

CUISINE The red sea-bream is a fish of good quality, which may be poached or stuffed and baked. The black sea-bream is considered to be less good.

SEA BREAM (U.K.), RED PORGY (U.S.A.)

Family *Sparidae*

Pagrus pagrus (Linnaeus)

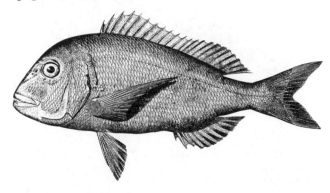

REMARKS   This species, which has a maximum length of about 75 cm, is the only member of its family to be found on both sides of the North Atlantic. It is pargo in Portugal and Spain, and pagre in France.

The species, which ranges well up the eastern seaboard of the United States, was for many years treated by American ichthyologists as a separate species, *Pagrus sedecim*. However, a recent study by Manooch and others has demonstrated its synonymy with *Pagrus pagrus*; and has also produced the interesting suggestion that the species first crossed the Atlantic in the form of eggs borne by the east-to-west current, and that the continuation of this traffic has sufficed to prevent the American colony from acquiring new characteristics which would warrant treating them as a separate species.

This fish makes good eating, but is surpassed by the species shown below, **Sparus auratus** Linnaeus, which ranges from the Mediterranean to the Bay of Biscay. It is the famous daurade of France; and bears the names dourada in Portugal, dorada in Spain and GILT-HEAD BREAM in England.

CUISINE   Smaller specimens may be grilled whole. Larger ones may be poached or baked. Try the recipe for Poisson aux tomates, gratiné, on page 296; or that for Bar au beurre blanc on page 295.

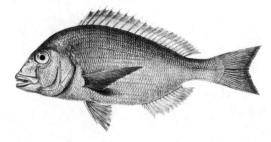

PORGY, NORTHERN PORGY, SCUP, SCUPPAUG

Family *Sparidae*

Stenotomus chrysops (Linnaeus)

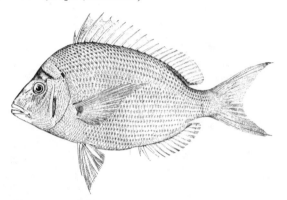

REMARKS   Maximum length 45 cm (weighing nearly 2 kilos); common length 20 to 30 cm. The colour is brownish above and silvery below.

The Narragansett Indians called it mishcuppauog, pauog being their name for fertilizer. This was shortened by the early settlers in New England to scuppaug; and afterwards to scup, a better name than porgy (or paugy, as it used to be spelled at New York).

The species ranges from Cape Cod to the Carolinas. Further south, the Southern porgy, *Stenotomus aculeatus* (C. and V.). takes over.

Various nineteenth-century reports record an amazing abundance of scup in New England waters. Goode quotes a description by Professor Baird (an ichthyologist with a military background?) of how the advance-guard of scup would descend on the New England coast in May, followed successively by other detachments. 'The western division of this arm appears to strike first at Watch Hill, to the west of Point Judith, and to make its way slowly along eastward, the smaller or eastern division moving through Vineyard Sound.' Their abundance was so great that any number of fishermen 'could take five hundred to one thousand pounds a day without the slightest difficulty'. Moreover, they could be outmanoeuvred by one man and his dog. A Mr Dunham of Nantucket, out in his boat, would sometimes throw a stone overboard so as to give the scup a start toward the shore; 'and then following and throwing his dog overboard, he has driven the fish clear out of the water upon the beach and has taken as many as five hundred in this way at one time.'

CUISINE   This is a good fish, with firm and flaky flesh. The fishery for it is again becoming important. In general, it may be treated like the sheepshead (see the next page), but I have one other suggestion to offer. An ichthyologist at the complex of fishery and oceanographic institutions at Wood's Hole, Mass., told me that he had eaten it aboard a Soviet fishing vessel, 'barbecued and with a tomato sauce – quite delicious'.

SHEEPSHEAD

Family *Sparidae*

Archosargus probatocephalus (Walbaum).

REMARKS   Maximum length about 75 cm, corresponding to a weight of 9 kilos or so; market size usually much less than this. This admirable fish is silvery or greenish-yellow in colour, with seven dark bars as shown in the drawing. It owes its name to the resemblance of its profile and teeth to those of a sheep, and also to its browsing habits. What it browses on are oysters, mussels, barnacles and the like, the shells of which are readily crushed by its strong jaws and teeth.

The sheepshead is remarkable for having only the one vernacular name throughout its range, which is traditionally given as 'Cape Cod to Texas'. The species has, however, become progressively rarer in the north. At the beginning of the nineteenth century, sheepshead were abundant in the vicinity of Long Island; indeed, Sheepshead Bay in Brooklyn was named for them. But nowadays they seem to be rare anywhere north of Virginia.

The sheepshead has always been highly prized as food. The natural historian Mitchill, who published his survey *The Fishes of New York* ... in 1815, said that: 'The outfitting of a Sheepshead party is always an occasion of considerable excitement and high expectation, as I have often experienced. Whenever a Sheepshead is brought on board the boat more joy is manifested than by the possession of any other kind of fish. The sportsmen view the exercises so much above common fishing that the capture of the Sheepshead is the most desirable combination of luck and skill; and the feats of hooking and landing him safely in the boat furnish abundant materials for the most pleasing and hyperbolical stories.'

In the southern states the sheepshead used to be taken among the roots of mangrove trees, where there were lots of barnacles. However, as William Elliott wrote (in *Carolina Sports by Land and Water*, New York, 1859): 'as these lands have been cleared for the culture of sea-island cotton, the trees have disappeared, and with them the fish; and it has been found necessary to renew their feeding-grounds by artificial means. Logs of pine or oak are cut and framed into a sort of hut without a roof. It is floored and built up five or six feet high, then floated to the place desired, and sunk in eight feet of water ... As soon as the barnacles are formed, which will happen in a few weeks, the fish will begin to resort to the ground.'

Another fish which is related to and often found with the sheepshead is **Lagodon rhomboides** (Linnaeus), the dark green PINFISH or SAILOR'S CHOICE, which is shown at the foot of this page. It only reaches a length of 15 to 25 cm, but it is an excellent pan fish.

CUISINE 'There are many that think it the very best fish for a boil that swims,' wrote Thomas De Voe. In the north it was indeed the custom to boil the sheeps-head; but the smaller specimens found further south were more often pan-fried. Either technique is suitable; but for 'boil' read, as always, 'simmer in a court-bouillon'. The sheepshead may also be grilled, or filleted and fried, or baked.

Small sheepshead, because they are 'firm boiling fish', were the preferred sea fish for use in Pine bark stew, a southern concoction involving a vat full of layers of fish, sliced potatoes and sliced onions, with a rich gravy as dark as pine bark. An authentic and vivid description of this is given in *200 Years of Charleston Cooking*; but there are certainly many easier ways of enjoying sheepshead, large or small.

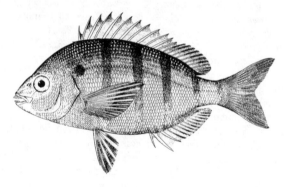

RAY'S BREAM

Family *Bramidae*

Brama brama (Bonnaterre)

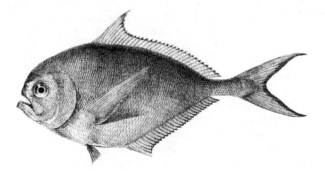

REMARKS   Maximum length over 70 cm (but the experts disagree). A solitary fish of engaging appearance. The back is dark, usually brown or bluish or greenish-brown and the sides silvery.

Portuguese: Chaputa, Freira
Spanish: Palometa, Japuta
French: Castagnole
Dutch: Braam
German: Braschsenmakrele
Swedish: Rays havbrax
Norwegian: Havbrasme
Danish: Havbrasen
Icelandic: Brámafiskur

This species is common in the deep waters off the Spanish coasts and spreads northwards in the spring and summer. The extent of this migration varies. In some years Ray's bream is almost common in northern European waters. It seems also to be present on the American side of the Atlantic; although to judge by the literature, for example Breder's reference (in the *Field Book of Marine Fishes of the Atlantic Coast*, 1929) to a single specimen caught at a place called No Man's Land in Massachusetts and measuring only 6 inches, the presence is discreet. Its 'official' common name in the U.S.A. is pomfret; but this nomenclature seems to rest on Bermudan usage in the nineteenth century.

CUISINE AND RECIPES   I am a great enthusiast for this fish, which seems to me to have unique characteristics and to be of very fine quality. The flesh is faintly tinged with pink and is formed of long strands, rather like that of the skate or ray. The flavour is delicious.

I recommend poaching the fish in a court-bouillon which incorporates white wine, coating it with a rich sauce made therefrom and then browning the dish briefly under the grill. Or follow the recipe for Palometa con salsa de tomate on page 282. (Palometa, by the way, is the respectable Spanish name for this fish. Japuta, the more common name, means son of a bitch. Why it should be applied to the blameless creature is a mystery.)

BUTTERFISH

Family *Stromateidae*

Peprilus triacanthus (Peck)

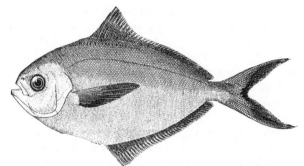

REMARKS   Maximum length 30 cm. Common length about 20 cm. The back is of a leaden bluish colour, the sides paler and the belly silvery. The body is thin as well as deep. The species has a range from South Carolina to the Gulf of St Lawrence and the southern and eastern coasts of Newfoundland.

Other common names for this fish are dollarfish, shiner and pumpkin-seed. It may also be called harvest-fish and star-fish, but these names are better used for the closely related but smaller *Peprilus alepidotus* Linnaeus. This is a fish with a greenish-silvery back, often found in company with the butterfish but rarely going north of New Jersey. *Peprilus paru* (Linnaeus) is similar but has a northerly range.

CUISINE   A good pan fish. Market supplies fluctuate considerably, but this is definitely a fish to buy when it is available.

Howard Mitcham, in his *Provincetown Seafood Cookbook* (1975), describes baby butterfish as 'one of the most delicious treats which Mother Ocean provides, and one of the rarest'. They only appear at Provincetown in October, and not in every October. Although they are often regarded as trash fish, the fishermen do not throw them back. 'They save every one of them and pass them out to their relatives and friends. Sometimes a fisherman will bring a bucket of baby butterfish into Cookie's, and Joe and Wilbur will put on a fish fry. They'll fry these babies and the customers will sit there all afternoon nibbling the fish and washing them down with beer.'

Joe and Wilbur have a simple task. 'Baby butterfish are about the size of your little finger. You don't have to clean them. You just drop them whole in flour, then fry in deep hot fat until they are crisp, and drain on paper towels.'

Weakfish, Drums, etc. and the Red Mullet

Most of the species in this section belong to the family *Sciaenidae*, of which a general characteristic is the ability to make a loud drumming noise in the water. This is done by a snapping of the muscles attached to the air bladder, which acts as a resonance chamber. Hence names such as drum and croaker, which are also used for related species in the Indo-Pacific regions. A Chinese author wrote about the croakers coming in from the deep, in file, making a 'thundering noise'. This may be an exaggeration, but the family impulse to make a noise is certainly very strong. Sciaenid fish which lack an air bladder, such as the members of the genus *Menticirrhus*, have been known to make themselves audible by grinding their teeth together.

One problem of nomenclature needs to be mentioned. The species catalogued on page 108, of the genus *Cynoscion*, are often called trout in the southern states of the U.S.A. On one occasion I naïvely ordered a 'trout dinner' in South Carolina, thinking that I would have a change from sea fish. The plate brought to me contained really large pieces of a fish which must have measured nearly a metre long and plainly could not have been the sort of trout I was expecting. In fact it was *Cynoscion regalis*, not a trout at all.

These weakfish or 'trout' are apparently very susceptible to cold. Smith, in *The Fishes of North Carolina*, explains that *Cynoscion nebulosus* is the most important member of the drum family in that state, and that in very cold weather the species is afflicted by something called a 'trout numb'. What happens is that the 'trout' are found floating on the surface of the water, more or less unable to move. More exactly, they are numbed during the cold weather and rise to the surface in this condition on the first sunny day thereafter. They will then, after another day or two, die and sink to the bottom or be washed ashore. But, once it is known that a trout numb is happening, many people come down with nets or even just their bare hands to pick up the fish.

The red mullet was well known in classical times. There are many familiar anecdotes about it – especially about the exaggerated enthusiasm of Romans for large specimens – in Latin literature. It is not uncommon as far north as southern England; but one thinks of it as a Mediterranean fish, and it is in the Mediterranean that it tastes best.

ATLANTIC CROAKER, HARDHEAD   Family *Sciaenidae*

Micropogon undulatus (Linnaeus)

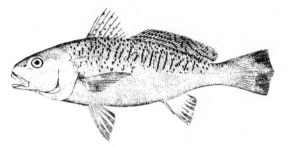

REMARKS   Maximum length just over 50 cm, common length about half this. This croaker is grey or silvery green above and white below. Back and sides bear brownish, wavy, diagonal bars (hence *undulatus* in the scientific name). The species has a range from Texas to Cape Cod. It has been an important commercial fish in the Chesapeake Bay region. Back in 1920. it ranked second in quantity and third in value of the fishes taken in the Bay. The spring run of croakers was particularly abundant and sometimes produced an unmanageable glut. However, supplies have dwindled in recent years. Whether the species will become more common again, and resume its former importance on the eastern seaboard, remains to be seen. Meanwhile, I am told that an extensive fishery for it has developed further south, in the Gulf States, and that its attraction to the consumer has been enhanced by use of the name golden croaker.

CUISINE   This is a good pan fish. Bigelow and Schroeder (in their survey *Fishes of the Gulf of Maine*, 1953) observed that it was popular because of its abundance and low price, but was generally held to be inferior to the spot (page 112) and the squeteague (page 108). However, they added, some people preferred it to almost any other fish.

WEAKFISH, SQUETEAGUE

Family *Sciaenidae*

Cynoscion regalis (B. and S.)

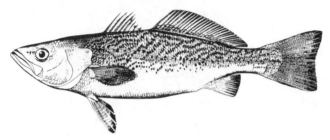

REMARKS   Maximum length almost 1 metre (corresponding to a weight of about 5 kilos) or (very exceptionally) more. The colour of the body is complicated. 'Dark olive green above with the back and sides variously burnished with purple, lavender, green, blue, golden, or coppery, and marked with a large number of small black, dark green, or bronze spots, vaguely outlined and running together more or less, especially on the back; thus forming irregular lines that run downward and forward.' (Bigelow and Schroeder.) The name weakfish does not refer to its general physique, which is robust, but to its tender mouth, which is easily torn by a hook.

This is the most important sciaenid fish in American waters. It swims in schools, from Massachusetts (as a summer visitor) to Florida.

The females of the species are mute, but the males have strong croaking muscles. The general names croaker and drum therefore apply to this fish, in addition to the misnomers trout, sea trout and grey trout, on which see page 106. The related species *Cynoscion nebulosus* (Cuvier), the SPOTTED SQUETEAGUE, is shown below. It may be called spotted trout or salmon trout in the southern states. It is abundant in North Carolina, but generally less common than the ordinary squeteague. Its quality is better.

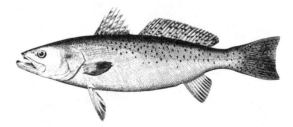

CUISINEANDRECIPE A good fish, when fresh-caught; a bit flabby later on. The flesh is lean and flaky. 'Weaks' may be grilled whole or pan-fried or used in fish chowders. Cora, Rose and Bob Brown recommend generous seasoning and tasty sauces, and suggest this recipe. 'Dredge well with seasoned flour well reddened with paprika, and fry in just enough butter, or butter mixed with bacon fat, to brown nicely. After taking up fish toss 1–2 tablespoonfuls shredded almonds or hazel nuts in pan until crisped, add 2 tablespoonfuls lemon juice, stir together quickly and pour at once over fried fish.' (*The Fish and Sea Food Cook Book*, 1940.) See also Fried fish southern style (page 432).

SEA DRUM, BLACK DRUM   Family *Sciaenidae*

Pogonias cromis (Linnaeus)

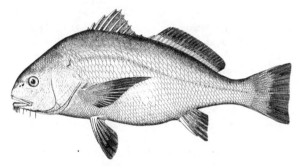

REMARKS Maximum length about 140 cm, but an adult length of about 1 metre is more common. A silvery fish with a brassy lustre, turning grey after death. It has very strong jaws, for crushing oyster-shells and so forth, and has the most powerful noise-producing equipment of any of the drums.

Its scales are also remarkable. They are large and silvery and very firmly attached, so that a really heavy blade (or even an axe) is needed to get them off. They have been used extensively in Florida for the sort of fancy-work known as 'fish-scale jewellery'.

This drum is abundant from the Carolinas southwards, but common as far north as New York.

CUISINE So-so. Young drum make good pan fish. Larger specimens may be treated like, say, cod, but are of less good quality.

Goode was told that in the Carolinas 'the roe is considered very delicious, and it is customary for the residents of the coast to salt and dry them and send them "up-country" to their friends.' However, I found no trace of this beneficent traffic when I last visited the Carolinas.

RED DRUM, CHANNEL BASS

Family *Sciaenidae*

Sciaenops ocellata (Linnaeus)

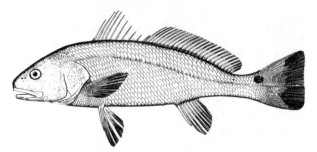

REMARKS This is a large drum, with maximum length of about 150 cm. However, the large specimens have coarse flesh; and, although they excite the angler (see adjoining 'Song of the Old-timers', to be sung to the tune of 'Watermelon Hanging on

'Oh, the weakfish am good,
    And the kingfish am great,
The striped bass am very, very fine;
    But give me, oh, give me.
Oh, how I wish you would!
    A channel bass a-hangin' on my line!'

the Vine'), it is the smaller fish, known as puppy drum, which are good to eat.

The red drum is a well-known fish from Chesapeake Bay southwards. It is not really red in life, although Goode concedes that in adults one may observe 'a tint, an evanescent, metallic reflection of claret from the scales'. But the name channel bass does not seem very appropriate either.

The red drum is generally considered to resemble the striped bass in eating qualities, but to be slightly less good. It may be prepared according to the advice given for the striped bass on page 86.

A short entry is required for the MEAGRE, *Argyrosomum regius* (Asso), a sciaenid fish of the Mediterranean which occasionally ranges up to the English Channel. Its usual adult length is about 1 metre; back silvery brown, fins reddish brown. It is corvina in Portugal, corbina in Spain and maigre in France. Its quality is good, and it too may be prepared like the striped bass.

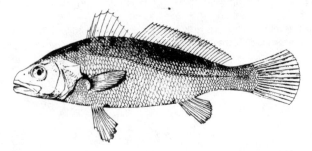

NORTHERN KINGFISH

Family *Sciaenidae*

Menticirrhus saxatilis (B. and S.)

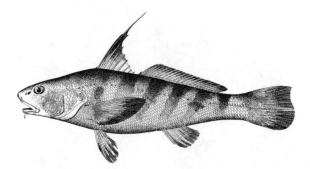

REMARKS   Maximum length just over 40 cm. The back is leaden in colour or grey, sometimes almost black; the sides are marked irregularly with dark bars; and the underside is whitish. Note the small barbel. The kingfish, by the way, has no air bladder, so cannot make the drumming or croaking noises which other members of the family produce.

This species is most common between Chesapeake Bay and New York, but it occurs up to Cape Cod and down to Florida. In the north it is a summer visitor. In the southern part of its range it is largely replaced by *Menticirrhus americanus* (Linnaeus), the SOUTHERN KINGFISH, shown below, which closely resembles it.

A fantastic wreath of inappropriate common names gathered over the kingfish in the nineteenth century. They were called hake or barb (New Jersey and Delaware), tom-cod (Connecticut), black mullet (Chesapeake), whiting (in the south) and sea-mink (N. Carolina).

CUISINE   An excellent table fish. At the beginning of the century it was almost entirely neglected, but then rose swiftly to popularity. It has a low fat content and responds well to being fried, poached or steamed and served with a rich sauce. The flesh is pure white and of a fine texture, which makes it a good fish for salads. One could, for example, use it in making the Swedish Skärhamnsallad (page 374).

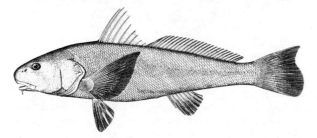

SPOT, LAFAYETTE

Family *Sciaenidae*

Leiostomus xanthurus Lacépède

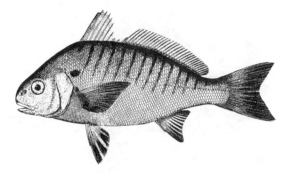

REMARKS   Maximum length about 35 cm; common length 15 to 25 cm. This fish is blue-grey above, with golden gleams, and silvery below. Its range is from Texas to Cape Cod. It frequents sheltered bays and estuaries and is of some commercial importance in the Chesapeake Bay area.

CUISINE   A good pan fish. The same applies to the smaller species shown below.

SILVER PERCH, YELLOW-TAIL

Family *Sciaenidae*

Bairdiella chrysura (Lacépède)

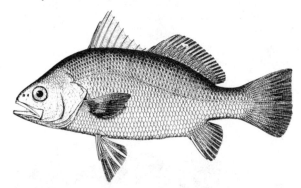

REMARKS   Maximum length 30 cm; usual adult length not more than 20 cm. This little fish is olive, greenish or bluish-grey on the back, silvery on the sides and white below. It has mostly yellow fins (including the tail fin). It belongs to a genus of tropical waters, but its range extends from Texas to New York, although it is less common in the northern part of this range, where it is a summer visitor.

RED MULLET

Family *Mullidae*

Mullus surmuletus Linnaeus

REMARKS   Maximum length 40 cm. Back and sides are reddish, with yellow stripes. Note the striped dorsal fin and twin barbels.

Of the two red mullet commonly found in the Mediterranean this is the one which adventures as far north as Britain and Ireland (especially the south and west coasts) and even to southern Norway. It is. however. only a summer visitor in British waters.

On the western side of the Atlantic (as in the Indo-Pacific region), these fish are

Portuguese: Salmonete
Spanish: Salmonete de roca
French: Rouget de roche
Dutch: Mul
German: Meerbarbe
Swedish: Mulle
Norwegian: Mulle
Danish: Mulle
Other: Belberiña (Basque);
   Mallette (Boulogne)

generally called goatfish. There are many of them in the West Indies. One species, *Mullus auratus* Jordan and Gilbert, is found as far north as Cape Cod and is therefore known as the NORTHERN GOATFISH. It is shown below. It only reaches a length of 20 cm.

CUISINE AND RECIPES   The red mullet is famous in the Mediterranean for its delicate flavour. Small specimens are to be fried. Larger ones may be grilled. They are often cooked whole (not gutted) in the Mediterranean; but not poached or steamed. (Asians, on the other hand, do cook them thus with good results.) Recipes from Portugal and France are given on pages 270 and 288 respectively.

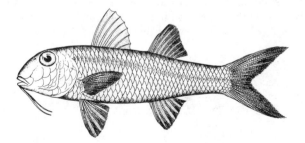

Miscellaneous Perciform Fish

This section of the catalogue looks like a real miscellany, and is, although we are still progressing through the Order *Perciformes*, to which all these species belong.

Only some of these species are of current importance as food, but several of them could and may be exploited more fully in the future. This is also true of a species which I have not catalogued **Centrolophus niger** (Gmelin), the blackfish (or black ruff, as it is known in America). It is a deep-water fish, of which not much is known. It is dull black in colour, may measure as much as 85 cm and has rather flabby flesh which is used in some places for making fish balls.

It is here also that I would catalogue gobies and blennies if they found a place in the book. However, the Atlantic species of both tribes are hardly eaten at all and the day seems distant when they will be.

It is a curious fact about gobies that of all the peoples in the world only the Turks and certain Spaniards, for example at Málaga, have a really lively interest in them. They are eaten on a small scale and without great enthusiasm in some other parts of the world; but their small size is discouraging. In the Atlantic and the Baltic **Gobius niger** (Linnaeus), the BLACK GOBY, attains respectable dimensions (maximum length 17 cm) and has a wide distribution. Since it is one of the gobies which the Turks hold in particular esteem, I may as well enter here a rather wan plea that others try it, and to this end show a drawing of it at the foot of the page.

The blennies are negligible from the cook's point of view, but may, none the less, find a place in fish soups. They are so used in the Mediterranean.

To end this introductory page on a more positive note, I draw attention to the obscure sand-eel (page 122). Elizabeth David once told me that she made a point of stopping at a certain place in Normandy to enjoy fried sand-eels – 'better than any whitebait'. Lançons, as they are known, are a speciality of more than one town in the region, including Granville; but the taste for them in Britain, once strong, seems now to be in abeyance.

GREY MULLET; STRIPED MULLET (U.S.A.)

Family *Mugilidae*

Mugil cephalus Linnaeus

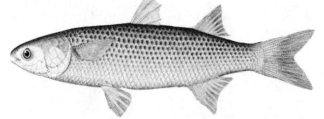

REMARKS Maximum length 60 cm. The tribe of grey mullet is a large one, but *Mugil cephalus* may fairly claim to be its head, since it is a species of world-wide distribution and occurs on both sides of the Atlantic, as far north as Cape Cod in the west and the Bay of Biscay in the east.

Portuguese: Fataca, Mugem
Spanish: Pardete, Cabejudo, Lisa
French: Muge, Mulet
Dutch: Harder
Other: Meuille (Charentes)

On the American side it has become important as a source of frozen fillets and frozen breaded fish. On the European side it is usually marketed fresh and whole.

Two other European grey mullet are listed on page 117. I should also mention a species found only in American waters, *Mugil curema* C. and V., usually known as the white mullet. Its length is around 30 cm and it ventures out into the sea more than *Mugil cephalus*, which is a bay fish. The name silverside mullet is applied to *Mugil curema* at Beaufort, North Carolina, and in some other places it is known as the blue-back mullet. Its range extends as far north as Cape Cod, but it is most abundant in tropical waters.

What follows applies to the grey mullet generally, for the various species are markedly similar in appearance and habits.

The grey mullet are beautifully streamlined, but are not narrow fish – indeed, they remind me of wide-bodied jets. They have grey backs and silvery sides, with stripes along the scale rows. They are all inshore fish, often found in brackish or even fresh water. And they are all herbivorous.

The mullet is a bottom-feeder and prefers still, shoal water with grassy and sandy or muddy bottom. It swims along the bottom, head down, now and then taking a mouthful of mud, which is partially culled over in the mouth, the microscopic particles of animal or vegetable matter retained, and the refuse expelled. When one fish finds a spot rich in the desired food, its companions immediately flock around in a manner reminding one of barn-yard fowls feeding from a dish. The mullet eats no fish or anything of any size, but is preyed upon by all other common fishes larger than itself. (Jordan and Evermann.)

The inoffensive behaviour of the mullet earned it praise from Roman moralists, and would earn it praise today from the ecologically-minded, for it is an admirable thing, we now realize, to extract one's food from mud, close to the bottom of the food chain. However, the quality and cleanliness of the mud must then be of interest not only to the mullet but also to anyone subsequently eating the mullet. It is a fish which can smack of mud in a highly displeasing way, a characteristic which it shares with other herbivorous fish such as carp, roach and tench, but from which carnivorous fish are free. Anyway, it is advisable to buy mullet taken from clean waters, as we were able to do when living near the Lake of Tunis, and to clean them thoroughly and without delay. In doing so you will have the opportunity to observe the gizzard-like stomach, of which a charming drawing from Day is shown on the right, and the enormously long intestine – seven feet of it for a fish one foot long. The herbivorous fish all have long guts, whereas the carnivorous ones have short guts.

However, these generalizations may not be universally valid. I pause when I think of one of the herbivorous fish of South-East Asia, namely *Pangasianodon gigas* Chevey, the Giant Catfish of the Mekong, which never, never tastes of mud, at least not in Laos, which is where I met it, and which is indeed one of the most delicious fish which I have ever eaten anywhere. See my *Fish and Fish Dishes of Laos*, the least practical cookery book of the century for anyone not resident in Laos. I realize now, too late, that when I was attending the dismemberment of one of these almost holy fish in Vientiane market and photographing its fins and buying some of its bones for the British Museum I should have competed also for possession of its gut.

CUISINE AND RECIPES   Taken from suitable waters, this is a good fish. It may be poached, fried or grilled. It is well suited to stuffing and baking. A French recipe is given on page 289. Since there are rather few specific recipes for grey mullet, let me add the two recommendations of Mme Millet-Robinet, the domestic encyclopaedist who wrote *Maison rustique des Dames* (1844–45). The first is to gut the fish through the gills and then to stuff it with a mixture of breadcrumbs, chopped spring onions and parsley, olive oil or butter, and seasoning; to envelop the stuffed fish tightly in buttered cooking paper; and to grill the package over a gentle heat. The second is to cook the fish in milk. Either way, the cooked mullet may be served with either a white caper sauce or a tomato sauce.

The roe of the grey mullet can be made into the famous Mediterranean delicacy, Boutargue. Smoked grey mullet is becoming popular in the U.S.A.

Chelon labrosus (Risso), the THICK-LIPPED GREY MULLET, is common on north European coastlines. It is muge noir in French, herder in Dutch, Meerasche in German and multe in Danish. It is a species with a good reputation. The county of Sussex in England, where I once lived, was famed for five marine delicacies: a Chichester lobster, a Selsey cockle, an Arundel mullet, a Pulborough eel and a Rye herring – the Arundel mullet being of this species, according to Yarrell. And, across the North Sea, Dutch fishmongers, who have the delightful title visboer, will call it witte zalm, i.e. white salmon.

Liza ramada (Risso), the THIN-LIPPED GREY MULLET, is also fairly common as far north as the English Channel and the Irish Sea. In Portugal it is taínha, a name also applied to other grey mullet, especially *Liza aurata* Risso, the attractive golden grey mullet, so called because it has gold spots beside its eyes and a golden tint to its body. This last species is common in the Mediterranean and abundant around Madeira but also ranges north to the English Channel and even beyond.

WRASSE, BALLAN WRASSE

Family *Labridae*

Labrus bergylta Ascanius

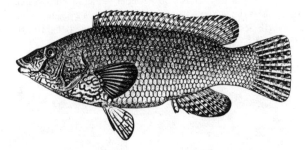

REMARKS   Maximum length 50 cm. This species, like most other wrasses, has a very variable coloration, in which green or greeny brown is usually dominant. It is the most common wrasse in British inshore waters, and has a range from the Mediterranean to Norway. The scientific name is derived from the Norwegian and Danish names, which are in turn echoed in Orkney by the name bergle.

Another English name which keeps turning up is old wife (cf. the French and Welsh names). The point of this escapes me. The Yorkshire name sweetlips is more easily explicable.

Portuguese: Margota
Spanish: Maragota, Durdo
French: Vieille, Labre
Dutch: Lipvis
German: Lippfisch
Polish: Kniazik
Swedish: Berggylta
Norwegian: Berggylte
Danish: Berggylt
Other: Gwrach (Welsh, meaning old woman); Ballach (Irish)

CUISINE   Opinions vary. The flesh has been condemned by some as insipid or coarse. Others (including, traditionally, the people of Orkney and of Galway) seem to have inherited something of the Roman enthusiasm for fish of this family. The flavour may depend on what the fish has been eating.

Having looked at the question from the other side of the world, where the Chinese, for example, esteem similar fish, I think that the best plan is not to grill them, but to steam or poach them, or to serve them sweet and sour.

Frying is also possible. Wrasses are fairly common in the markets of le Cotentin in Normandy, and they are often fried there. Another alternative, which sounds good, is Vras à la cherbourgeoise. You need one big and one small wrasse for each person. Combine the flesh of the small one with soft breadcrumbs which have been soaked in milk and squeezed, and with fines herbes. Use this as a stuffing for the large one, which has been cleaned, and split open on one side to permit deboning. The stuffed wrasse is then baked in a hot oven for about 15 minutes. Baste generously with cider and butter after the first 5 minutes; and use the cooking juices as a sauce.

TAUTOG, BLACKFISH

Family *Labridae*

Tautoga onitis (Linnaeus)

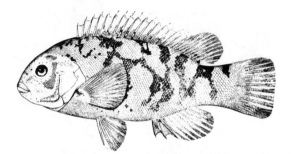

REMARKS Maximum length about 1 metre, but the common length is 35 to 50 cm. This is a dark wrasse, often mottled like the specimen in the drawing. It has a range

Other names: Tautogue noir (Fr. Can.); Black porgy; Chub; Oyster-fish (N. Carolina)

from Nova Scotia to South Carolina; and is most abundant between Cape Cod and Delaware Bay.

The name tautog is a version of tautauog, the name used by Indians. It is fortunate that this attractive name has prevailed. The last three of those listed above right are less suitable and belong to other species.

The tautog feeds on clams, mussels and crustaceans. Its own reputation as food has been consistently high. It is related that in the early nineteenth century a certain General Pinckney was so impressed by its merits that he imported a smack-load of tautog from Rhode Island and let them loose in the harbour of Charleston, South Carolina, where their descendants were still swimming about fifty years later. Whether true or not, it is an agreeable story, reminiscent of (indeed possibly inspired by, for the General may have been a classical scholar) the efforts which powerful Roman gourmets made to establish fish stocks, notably of another species of wrasse, where they wanted them.

CUISINE AND RECIPE I allow Goode to speak first. 'The Tautog has always been a favorite table fish, especially in New York, its flesh being white, dry, and of a delicate flavor.' It may be grilled or baked. And its firm flesh makes it especially suitable for fish chowder, a dish in which it is often used on Cape Cod.

CUNNER, BERGALL

Family *Labridae*

Tautogolabrus adspersus (Walbaum)

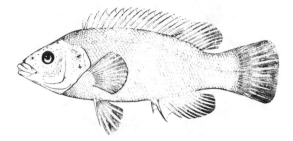

REMARKS   Maximum length about 40 cm, common length up to 30 cm. The colour is variable, usually brown, red or blue and mottled. This fish may be distinguished from its larger relation, the tautog (see preceding page), by the profile of its head and the shape of its tail. Its distribution is similar but more southerly.

The names of this species are interesting. Cunner was applied by British settlers, who recalled the species of that name in their home waters (conner or connor was used of various wrasses, especially in Cornwall). Bergall or burgall is a version of berggylt (cf. page 118). The name chogset, or cachogset, was taken over from the Indians. Some tiresomely vague names like bluefish and sea perch were in vogue among the undiscriminating; but the people of Salem showed powers of observation and originality when they named the fish nipper or bait-stealer, since it is in the habit of doing that and of scavenging in harbours. French Canadian names which are used include vieille (the general French name for the wrasses), achigan de mer and tanche-tautogue.

CUISINE   The cunner is not as popular and important as the tautog, but it offers good eating. It used to be very well liked from Eastport, Maine, to the Boston area, although despised further north and further south. It may be grilled or baked, or filleted and the fillets used as you will.

WOLF-FISH, CATFISH

Family *Anarhichadidae*

Anarhichas lupus Linnaeus

REMARKS An adult wolf-fish may measure well over 1 metre; and the spotted wolf-fish (*Anarhichas minor* Olafsen) is even larger. The colour is dark, blue-grey or greenish.

French: Loup marin
Dutch: Zeewolf
German: Katfisch, Seewolf
Polish: Zebacz smugowy
Russian: Zubatka
Finnish: Merikissa
Swedish: Havkatt
Norwegian: Havkat, Steinbit
Danish: Havkat
Icelandic: Steinbítur

The wolf-fish ranges down from Greenland and Spitzbergen as far as Cape Cod to the west and France to the east. Its lupine characteristics greatly impressed Goode. 'It is impossible to imagine a more voracious-looking animal,' he wrote, describing its 'great pavements of teeth', those in front pointed like those of a tiger and those behind adapted for crushing. Since the wolf-fish gobbles spiny sea urchins and crabs and clams, among other foods, it needs this formidable apparatus, to which the Icelandic name, meaning stone-biter, pays tribute.

Anarhichas in the scientific name means climber, in reference to a belief held in the Baltic that the wolf-fish climbs up on to rocks.

CUISINE AND RECIPE The wolf-fish was not widely consumed in earlier centuries, probably because it was not caught in quantity. It was sufficiently unfamiliar in the late nineteenth century for Day to think it worth while to quote comments from those who had tasted it. He said that Yorkshire fishermen loved it, Frank Buckland (see page 20) thought it like a veal chop and De Kay (the natural historian of New York) found that smoked wolf-fish resembled salmon.

Nowadays the wolf-fish is commercially exploited; and it is a much better fish than it looks. Its diet of fruits de mer may account for the good flavour of its flesh. I find that fillets which have been deep-fried are excellent. I also recommend the recipe for Zeewolf op zijn Brabants on page 307.

SAND-EEL, SAND-LANCE

Family *Ammodytidae*

Ammodytes tobianus Linnaeus

REMARKS　Maximum length 20 cm. There are several species of these silvery little fish. *Ammodytes tobianus* is the common inshore version of European waters: ***Ammodytes marinus*** Raitt its offshore counterpart. Most authorities distinguish ***Ammodytes americanus*** De Kay as the North American sand-eel, and it is often called, and treated like, whitebait in America.

It used to be the practice to call the smaller ones sand-lances (or sand-launces, a pleasantly archaic touch) and the bigger ones sand-eels. Whatever their size, these fish have one habit in common, which is to bury themselves in the sand for protection. Their lance-like form enables them to burrow rapidly downwards to a depth of a foot or more, often in the intertidal zone, and there they will stay for hours on end, unless a human being (or, occasionally, a porpoise) comes to dig them up. The drawing below shows the kind of rake which used to be used on the beaches at Portobello near Edinburgh and in the west country, where sand-eels abounded and a taste for them had developed, especially at Teignmouth. However, sand-eels are most often caught when swimming.

Spanish: Barrinaire
French: Lançon, Equille
Dutch: Smelt, Zandspiering
German: Sandaal, Sandspierling
Polish: Dobijak
Russian: Peschanka
Finnish: Pikkutuulenkala
Swedish: Tobis, Sandål
Norwegian: Småsil, Sandgrevling
Danish: Tobis
Icelandic: Sandsíli
Other: Riggle (Sussex); Gibbin (Isle of Man)

CUISINE AND RECIPE　Eliza Acton observes that: 'The common mode of dressing the fish, which is considered by many a great delicacy, is to divest them of their heads, and to remove the insides with the gills, to dry them well in a cloth with flour, and to fry them until crisp. They are sometimes also dipped in batter like smelts.' The first of her sentences is nicely echoed in the recipe for Lançons en friture, given on page 297.

WEEVER, GREATER WEEVER

Family *Trachinidae*

Trachinus draco Linnaeus

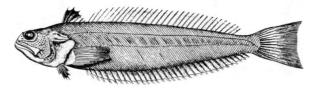

REMARKS Maximum length 40 cm, common length 25 to 30 cm. The back is grey-brown, the lower sides and belly creamy or yellowish. The range of the species extends from the Mediterranean to the southern coast of Norway.

Portuguese: Aranha,
Spanish: Escorpión
French: Vive, Grande vive
Dutch: Pieterman
German: Petermann
Swedish: Fjärsing
Norwegian: Fjesing
Danish: Fjaesing
Other: Mor wiber fawr (Welsh)

The weevers have venomous spines on their gill covers. In some countries it is illegal to sell them before removing these spines, which are capable of inflicting troublesome wounds. The first spine of the dorsal fin also contains poisonous tissue.

The greater weever (which has a smaller relation, the lesser weever) is a fish which lives on the bottom and likes to bury itself in the sand. It enjoys a healthy diet of small crustaceans and fish. The French name vive probably refers to its ability to remain alive for a long time after being taken out of the water.

CUISINE Smaller specimens are good material for fish soups. Larger ones may be filleted and cooked as you please. The flesh is firm and has a good flavour. Although weevers have rarely been offered for sale in Britain, they are marketed in various European countries.

SCABBARD FISH, BLACK SCABBARD FISH

Family *Trichiuridae*

Aphanopus carbo Lowe

REMARKS   Maximum length 150 cm. This thin, blackish fish is most frequently taken at Madeira, where it is the dominant commercial species, but it merits inclusion in the catalogue because it seems to be available in deep water as far north as Norway, and has also been reported from Greenland and

Portuguese: Peixe espada preta
Spanish: Pez cinto
French: Sabre
German: Degenfisch
Norwegian: Dolkfisk
Other: Cutlass fish, Hairtail

northern Canadian waters; and because it is, in my opinion, a fish which is well worth eating and which could be landed in greater quantities in future, despite the villainous appearance of its heavily toothed head.

Another species of scabbard fish, **Lepidotus caudatus** (Euphrasen), occurs on both sides of the Atlantic. It is silvery in colour and is shown in the lower drawing. Its range on the American side extends north of Cape Cod.

CUISINE AND RECIPE   The rear end of these fish does not offer much to eat, but the forward and central parts can be cut into pieces about 6 cm long, after the fish has been cleaned, and are good when fried, grilled or baked. Portuguese cooks often prepare it de escabeche (page 270), after which it may be kept for two weeks. However, culinary study of this fish is less far advanced in the Atlantic area than in the Orient, where the Chinese consume scabbard fish, of another species, on a large scale.

Mackerel and Tuna: the Family Scombridae

Some families of fish are defined by characteristics which the layman might fail to discern; but this family looks like a family even to the least tutored eye. All its members are powerful swimmers, with muscular and beautifully streamlined bodies. Day put it well. 'Carnivorous and exceedingly active, their shapes are well adapted to enable them to glide rapidly through the water: while to obviate the least impediment, we even find in some depressions for the reception of the pectoral fins.' They all perform migrations of considerable extent. They all have deeply forked or crescent-shaped tail fins; and a row of dorsal and anal finlets to the rear of the dorsal and anal fins. Their scales are small (and those of the tunas cover only part of the body, in what is called a corselet) and their coloration is like a uniform with only minor variations – blue or blue-green back, silvery sides and belly.

The ability of these fish to make long migratory journeys has resulted in many of them being represented right round the world, or at least on both sides of the Atlantic.

The mackerel and tuna catalogued in the following pages are those which are most common in North Atlantic waters. But others, which only live in the warmer waters further south, sometimes stray north as far as the Bay of Biscay or the English Channel and up to New England. These include the so-called frigate mackerel, *Auxis thazard* (Lacépède), a small fish of no particular merit; the little tunny or false albacore, *Euthynnus alletteratus* (Rafinesque), of which the specific name alludes to the scribble-like markings on its back; and the yellowfin tuna, *Thunnus albacares* (Bonnaterre). Any of these may leap out of the water, a favourite piece of behaviour on the part of mackerel and tuna, in waters far to the north of their usual haunts; but they cannot be counted as North Atlantic species.

The same applies, with a qualification, to *Scomber colias* Gmelin, the chub mackerel. It is common in the Mediterranean, but may be found off the Iberian and French Atlantic coasts. On the other side of the Atlantic, however, it occurs every now and then off the New England coast, but is virtually unknown from New Jersey southwards. It is a smaller fish than the Atlantic mackerel (see overleaf) and has more delicate markings on its back; but fishmongers have no reason to distinguish between the two. It is cavala in Portugal, estornino in Spain, maquereau espagnol in France and, sometimes, Spanish mackerel in Britain; but the name Spanish mackerel is better reserved for the species on pages 128 and 129.

MACKEREL, ATLANTIC MACKEREL

Family *Scombridae*

Scomber scombrus Linnaeus

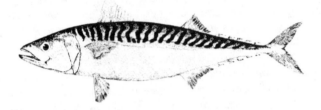

REMARKS   Maximum length 55 cm or even more ('giants' of exceptional dimensions are sometimes taken in the western Atlantic); market length 30 to 35 cm.

Portuguese: Sarda, Cavala
Spanish: Caballa
French: Maquereau
Dutch: Makreel
German: Makrele
Polish: Makrela
Russian: Makrel, Skumbriya
Finnish: Makrilli
Swedish: Mackrill
Norwegian: Makrell
Danish: Makrel
Icelandic: Makrill
Other: Ronnach (Irish)

I suppose that everyone is familiar with the appearance of this handsome fish, with its brilliant greeny-blue back marked with dark curving lines, its metallic sides and its white belly. The French name maquereau also means pimp, no doubt in allusion to the brilliance of the colours. Lemery, however, observes that 'some pretend' that the name was given to it 'because as soon as the Spring comes, he follows the young Shad, that are commonly call'd Virgins, and brings them to their Males, and so they make a Bawd of this Fish.' This would be a highly satisfactory, because so precise, explanation, but it does not seem to be true, at least not of modern mackerel.

The mackerel has an extensive range, from the Mediterranean to Iceland and the north of Norway, and from Cape Hatteras to Labrador on the American side. They are ocean fish, which swim in very large shoals. The long spawning season (spring and early and even late summer) brings them to the shallow waters of the continental shelf. During the winter they retreat to deeper water and go into a state of near-hibernation, fasting and waiting for the spring, when they can resume gobbling copepods (what the fishermen call 'red seed', the subject of the note on the next page) and sporting about in laying their numerous eggs (up to half a million from one female). Sometimes they can be too playful: 'Pontoppidan relates how a Norwegian sailor was destroyed by a shoal of mackerel who surrounded him while bathing, carried him out to sea, and managed, while pushing him along, to so bite and nibble at their victim that his friends, with all their exertions, were scarcely able to get him alive into their boat, where he soon expired from exhaustion and loss of blood.' (Day.)

Frank Buçkland recorded that at Rye in Sussex there used to be an important mackerel fishery; and that the fish were caught there in large fixed nets, called kettle nets. He suggests that this may be the origin of the phrase: 'What a pretty kettle of fish!' I find this idea plausible, although the *Oxford English Dictionary* prefers a rival explanation, that persons picnicking on the banks of the River Tweed, for example, were wont to cook fish in a large kettle and eat it al fresco, uttering the familiar exclamation as they did so.

CUISINE The qualities of the mackerel were well described by Day. 'Mackerel are much esteemed, the moderately sized more than the very large ones, but they taint very rapidly, as well as lose flavour when kept ... Owing to the rapidity with which these fish decompose in hot weather, and the consequent deleterious results to consumers, vendors were permitted as early as 1698 to cry them through the streets of London on Sundays, an enactment which does not seem to have ever been repealed.' (Nor will it be, now that Sunday trading in Britain is allowed, a development which has robbed the mackerel of its sabbatical advantage in the market.)

The meat of mackerel is fairly oily, which is why it spoils fast. But it is firm and free of tiresome bones and has an excellent flavour. The best thing to do with it is to grill or bake it, or poach it in a court-bouillon, and to serve it with a sharp sauce. Almost every cookery book extols the combination of mackerel with the traditional (in England and Normandy) gooseberry sauce. Jane Grigson devotes a whole page in her *Fish Cookery* to describing three different versions of gooseberry sauce; *quod vide*, as authors used to say. But a cranberry sauce, unsweetened, is equally good; and inexpensive rhubarb will also provide the necessary touch of acerbity.

Hot-smoked mackerel, which needs no further cooking, is becoming more and more popular in Europe. It can be eaten as it is or turned into a delicious pâté. Remember, however, that mackerel is rich. Do not eat too much of it.

RECIPES

Maquereaux à la façon de Quimper, 298
Mackerel soup (Swedish), 367
Gravad makrel (Danish), 391
Dried and fried mackerel, 391
East Riding mackerel, 455
Mackerel with rhubarb (Irish), 473

NOTE 'Red seed', referred to on the previous page and sometimes also known as 'cayenne', consists in planktonic crustacea, minute in size and red in colour. Goode recalls that an aged skipper in Maine, Cap'n Gorham Babson – a name crying out to be used in a novel – referred to them as 'Rhode Island bed-bugs' and advised a younger skipper that whenever he saw these creatures he should stay with them, for fish would certainly arrive before long.

SPANISH MACKEREL   Family *Scombridae*

Scomberomorus maculatus (Mitchill)

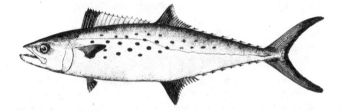

REMARKS   Maximum length about 70 cm, common length about 50 cm. The back is dark blue or blue-green, the sides marked with many oval spots, which are orange or yellowish in colour. The specific name *maculatus* means spotted.

This is the most important of the three species of Spanish mackerel which are found on the eastern coasts of North America. (The other two are shown on the facing page.) The range of *Scomberomorus maculatus* is from the Gulf of Mexico to Cape Cod.

Figures for the size of Spanish mackerel provide an interesting example of the perils of drawing on earlier books without adequate verification, or at least a critical scrutiny. Jordan and Evermann (in *The Fishes of North and Middle America*, 1896) said that *Scomberomorus regalis* reached a length of 6 feet and a weight of 20 pounds, and that the corresponding figures for *Scomberomorus cavalla* were 5 feet and 100 pounds. The discrepancy should jump to the eye. But the figures are repeated by Breder and other later authors without any apparent batting of the eyelids. The correct figures are, as it happens, elusive but seem to be roughly as follows: *Scomberomorus regalis* up to just over 1 metre and about 35 pounds, *Scomberomorus cavalla* up to 180 cm and close to 100 pounds. It is of course rare to meet specimens of anything like these dimensions.

CUISINE   A fish of high quality, which may be treated like the Atlantic mackerel (page 127). Being larger, it offers more possibilities in the way of presentation. Related species are among the most highly esteemed fish of South-East Asian waters and are often served in curried dishes, for which their firm flesh is well adapted.

These remarks apply equally to the two species on the next page.

CERO, PAINTED MACKEREL   Family *Scombridae*

Scomberomorus regalis (Bloch)

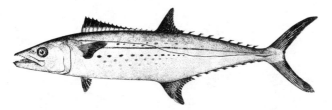

REMARKS   This species may reach a length of just over 1 metre. It is marked by a narrow brownish strip which runs, as shown in the drawing, from behind the pectoral fin to the base of the tail, crossing the lateral line where the latter curves downwards. This fish is abundant in the West Indies and the Florida Keys, where it may be called king cero; and much less common in the waters up to Cape Cod.

KING MACKEREL, CAVALLA   Family *Scombridae*

Scomberomorus cavalla (Cuvier)

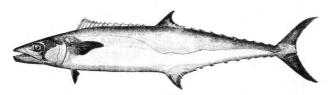

REMARKS   Said to reach a maximum length of over 1½ metres. The spots on the side tend to disappear in larger specimens and are not shown in the drawing. Note that the lateral line curves down much more sharply than that of the preceding species. This fish does not often come further north than North Carolina, where it may be taken in the summer.

TUNA, BLUEFIN TUNA, TUNNY   Family *Scombridae*

Thunnus thynnus (Linnaeus)

REMARKS Maximum length 4 metres or more, maximum weight about 900 kilos. But dimensions of this order are exceptional. The common length is 1 to 2 metres. The back is dark blue, the sides and belly silvery grey.

This large and splendid fish roams northwards to Norway, Iceland and Newfoundland, devouring great quantities of smaller fishes but falling prey itself to the huge killer whale, and also to man, especially *Homo japonicus*, who will pay very high prices for this fish.

The tuna is a schooling fish, but the size of the school is in inverse ratio to the size of the individual fish in the school. So the very largest tuna of all may swim in solitary state.

Portuguese: Atum
Spanish: Atún
French: Thon rouge
Dutch: Tonijn
German: Thunfisch, Roter Thun
Polish: Tunczyk
Russian: Tunets
Finnish: Tonnikala
Swedish: Tonfisk
Norwegian: Makrellstørje
Danish: Tunfisk
Icelandic: Túnfiskur
Other: Horse mackerel
    (U.S.A., a misnomer which
    formerly had wide currency)

CUISINE Everyone is familiar with canned tuna (of various species). Fresh tuna is less easily acquired, but makes good eating. The flesh is very compact and much more 'heavy' than the flesh of most fish. It resembles meat, and may be cooked in similar ways, for example by braising a large piece of it. Steaks or slices may be grilled or cooked en papillote, with a few drops of olive oil and some herbs. The best part is the cut from the belly known as 'ventresca' in Italy, where the cooking of fresh tuna is at its best. Fresh tuna is also suitable for eating raw, in thin slices, sashimi-style.

Although tuna is now a staple food in North America, in canned form, it was not always popular there. Writing at the end of the nineteenth century, Goode observed that, despite their reputation in the Old World and their abundance in American waters, tuna were hardly ever eaten by human beings, although sometimes used as chicken food. 'Some chicken food!' as Sir Winston Churchill might have said.

It is worth recalling that Mme Recamier, who, as David's painting and Brillat-Savarin's prose both tell us, was for twenty years the most beautiful woman in Paris, was also devoted to charitable work. Visiting a certain Curé one afternoon in this connection, she received an unexpected reward. The Curé was dining early, and invited her to share his Omelette au thon, of which Brillat-Savarin gives a description. It was 'round, sufficiently thick, and cooked, so to speak, to a hair's breadth. As the spoon entered it, a thick rich juice issued from it, pleasant to the eyes as well as to the smell; the dish became full of it; and our fair friend owns that, between the perfume and the sight, it made her mouth water.' Indeed, the beautiful visitor observed that she had never seen an omelette so enticing at a lay table.

To recreate the culinary part of this experience, it is enough to take some fresh tuna, the size of a hen's egg, and to mince it with a small shallot. All this is incorporated in 10 beaten eggs, prepared as usual for making an omelette. Some would add the blanched roes of a carp, but there is no evidence that the Curé's omelette had this addition.

RECIPES

Thon de Saint-Jean, 289   See also Créat mariné, 290
Thon froid, sauce bretonne, 298

LONG-FIN TUNA, ALBACORE   Family *Scombridae*

Thunnus alalunga (Bonnaterre)

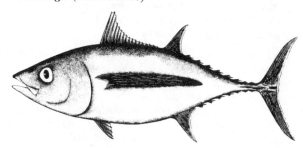

REMARKS Maximum length just over 1 metre. This smaller tuna (albacora in Portugal and Spain, germon or thon blanc in France) has the usual tuna coloration and may be distinguished from its brethren by the long pectoral fins. It is common as far north as the Bay of Biscay on the European side; and is present, but sparsely, on the Atlantic coast of the United States. It is prepared like the bluefin tuna (see above), but the meat is less heavy.

BONITO

Family *Scombridae*

Sarda sarda (Bloch)

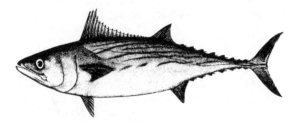

REMARKS Maximum length 90 cm, although never of this size in European waters. Sides and belly are silvery, the back steel-blue with dark blue slanting stripes. Note how far back, in relation to the eye, the upper jaw extends; this is a good recognition point, as is the straight upper edge of the first dorsal fin.

Portuguese: Bonito, Sarda, Serrajão
Spanish: Bonito
French: Pélamide, Bonite à dos rayé
Dutch: Boniter
Other: Egalushe (Basque)

The bonito is found on both sides of the Atlantic, as far north as Cape Cod and the southern coast of Britain (and sometimes further, but it is not common north of the Bay of Biscay). Bonito swim around in shoals, often about fifteen to twenty miles from shore, and frequently leap out of the water while feeding.

The striped bonito or skipjack, **Euthynnus pelamis** (Linnaeus), is found in the warmer waters of all the great oceans, but is uncommon in the North Atlantic. It may be recognized by the stripes on its belly.

CUISINE The bonito is comparable with the bluefish (page 92) and the Spanish mackerel (pages 128 and 129), and may be treated in similar ways. It is highly prized in the north of Spain and is prominent in the cuisines of Galicia, Santander and the Basque country. Two Spanish recipes are listed below, but I should also mention that the bonito is suitable for preparing de escabeche (page 270), and that Leonora Ramírez (in *El pescado en mi cocina*) recommends a very simple recipe for Bonito asado. The underneath part of the fish, sometimes called 'chaleco', is washed, dried, lightly salted, sprinkled with olive oil, breadcrumbs, finely chopped garlic and chopped parsley, and baked in the oven until golden brown.

RECIPES
Bonito in the Asturian style, 280   Marmite, 280

Swordfish and Marlin (or Spearfish)

The fish in this section of the catalogue are all large and equipped with swords. The swordfish itself is found in all the great oceans and has a wide range from south to north on both sides of the Atlantic. The others, however, are fish of warm waters and only move up into the North Atlantic during the summer. Indeed, the sailfishes, whose dorsal fins are so lofty as to resemble sails, are such rare visitors that I have not catalogued any of them here. A pair of marlins are catalogued, but briefly as befits their non-resident status.

The sword of the swordfish is a powerful weapon and has often been embedded in the wooden hulls of ships. The creature seems to have an overwhelming impulse to attack objects larger than itself. Oppian thought that the explanation was plain silliness: 'Nature her bounty to his mouth confined, Gave him a sword, but left unarmed his mind.' It may be, however, that boats or small ships look like whales to the swordfish. What is certain is that it does the swordfish no good to carry out such attacks. An interesting court case took place in 1868 to determine whether the ship *Dreadnought* had been holed by a swordfish (which was an insurable risk) or by some other means. She indisputably had an (empty) hole, about an inch in diameter, and there was strong circumstantial evidence pointing to a swordfish as the culprit. But it emerged that the expert witnesses could not recall any other instance, among the hundreds of incidents on record, of a swordfish driving its sword into a ship's hull and then managing to extricate it. (In testifying to the court, Professor Richard Owen said that the fish would have struck with the force of fifteen two-handed hammers.)

Altogether, the swordfish remains a mysterious creature. Its methods of reproduction are still not understood; and it is oddly difficult, except in the Mediterranean, to locate baby swordfish.

There is also the strange affair of its mercury content. It came to light some years ago that swordfish had far more mercury in them than the amount laid down as acceptable for human consumption. Sales in the United States almost stopped as a result. In fact, the swordfish had probably been like that for a long time; and it is unlikely that eating it holds any dangers for us. The acceptable level had been set too low.

SWORDFISH

Family *Xiphiidae*

Xiphias gladius Linnaeus

REMARKS   Maximum length (including the sword, which accounts for a third of it) 5 metres or so. The maximum weight is close to 500 kilos. However, the specimens landed are usually much smaller – perhaps 2 to 3 metres in length. The swordfish is dark above and white with a silvery sheen below; but it is most easily recognized by its flat, sharp-edged and pointed sword.

The range of the swordfish in the Atlantic extends to northern Norway and to New-foundland. It is an oceanic fish; and is usually taken by harpoon.

Portuguese: Espadarte, Agulha
Spanish: Pez espada
French: Espadon
Dutch: Zwaardvis
German: Schwertfisch
Polish: Wlocznik
Russian: Mech-rȳba
Finnish: Miekkakala
Swedish: Svärdfisk
Norwegian: Svaerdfisk
Danish: Svaerdfisk
Icelandic: Sverðfiskur

CUISINE   Linnaeus compared the flesh of the swordfish to that of salmon, by way of compliment. The compliment is deserved, but the comparison does not seem entirely apt. The flesh of the swordfish is notably white and firm, and has a fine grain. It is admirably well suited to being cut into steaks, which may be grilled and served with a thread of lemon juice or of good vinegar. They may also be baked, with added liquid.

Smoked swordfish is produced in the vicinity of Lisbon. It is served in very thin slices and rivals smoked salmon in quality, although it has a stronger and saltier taste.

In the United States the swordfish was for long despised, but has now won great esteem (diminished temporarily by the mercury affair discussed on the preceding page). In Europe it is less familiar but equally prized.

RECIPE
Broiled Martha's Vineyard swordfish, 414

BLUE MARLIN

Family *Istiophoridae*

Makaira nigricans Lacépède

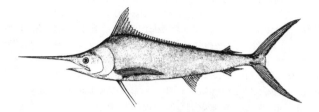

REMARKS Maximum length uncertain, but probably about 4½ metres. The normal adult length is more like 3 to 3½ metres. The back is of a dark and dull blue and the flanks and belly are also darkish.

This species is at home in the warmer waters of Cuba and the Straits of Florida, but it does stray northwards to the Gulf of Maine.

CUISINE As for the swordfish (page 134), but less good. This and the white marlin are available smoked, usually from Florida.

WHITE MARLIN

Family *Istiophoridae*

Makaira albida (Poey)
Tetrapturus albidus

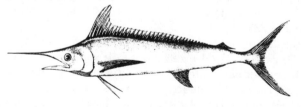

REMARKS Maximum length about 3 metres. This species has paler flanks than the blue marlin, and a white belly. It comes north as far as New York waters and southern Massachusetts during the summer, in fairly large numbers.

CUISINE As for the swordfish (page 134). Slightly better than the blue marlin.

Bony-cheeked Fish

This group of fish brings us to the end of the long list of species in the Order *Perciformes*. There are indeed some systems of classification under which they would be outside this order and in an order of their own, to which names such as *Scleroparei* have been given. This name means 'mail-cheeked', but the characteristic which it denotes is not always obvious. In technical terms: 'The second suborbital bone is elongated and enlarged across the cheek to articulate with the pre-operculum. This bony stay across the cheek is obvious externally in some fish (for instance the scorpion fishes) but can only be confirmed by dissection in others.' (Wheeler.)

One such fish, the rascasse rouge of the Mediterranean, is of outstanding quality; but it, unfortunately, does not travel far north in the Atlantic. The others are wholesome and, in some instances, important food fishes, but not such as to cause any real excitement in the kitchen or at table.

The lumpfish, however, causes puzzlement, at least in countries where it is not familiar. An agreeable perplexity is induced by studying opinions of it expressed by British authors in the past. Sir Thomas Browne, in 1662, recorded it as 'esteemed by some as a festival dish, though it affords but a glutinous jelly, and the skin is beset with stony knobs after no certain order'. Parnell said that: 'The flesh, when cooked, is soft and very rich, and is considered by some of the inhabitants of Edinburgh as a luxury.' The force of the word 'some' is revealed by the additional comment that 'there are few stomachs with which it agrees, in consequence of its oily nature.' Buckland is more critical: 'I do not like the flesh at all myself; it is like a glue pudding.'

Festival dish or glue pudding? The answer is both. There is a considerable difference between the edibility of male and female; which is why there are separate names for them in countries where the lumpfish is well known, such as Sweden and Iceland. And the female is edible at certain seasons, but not at others. An Icelander told me that when females with roe were taken and the roe had been extracted, to make lumpfish caviar, what was left was really no more than a glutinous mass, unsuitable even for making fish meal. It goes over the side. The male, on the other hand, provides good eating.

I believe that the lumpfish is almost unique in covering such a wide spectrum of edibility and inedibility; and that, if only for this reason, it is a particularly interesting fish.

SCULPIN, SHORTHORN SCULPIN (U.S.A.), SEA SCORPION (U.K.)

Family *Cottidae*

Myoxocephalus scorpius (Linnaeus)

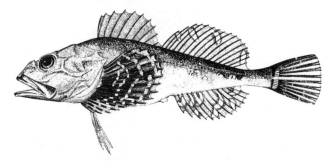

REMARKS A maximum length of over 90 cm has been reported, but the normal maximum is about 45 to 50 cm. Colour, mottling and spots are variable, but the basic colour is usually dark greenish above and yellowish below.

This species occurs on both sides of the North Atlantic, not to mention Siberia and Alaska. Its range extends down to New York in the west and the Bay of Biscay in the east.

A related species which is very common on the American side is *Myoxocephalus octodecemspinosus* (Mitchill), the longhorn sculpin. The French Canadian name for both species is chaboisseau.

Myoxocephalus quadricornis (Linnaeus) occurs on both sides of the Atlantic and in the Baltic. Some Finns eat it. Indeed, it appears on the menu of the leading fish restaurant in Helsinki, under its scientific name as well as under the Finnish name härkäsimppu and the Swedish name hornsimpa, as being an excellent basis for a fish soup.

These uncouth little fish, with reputedly venomous spines on their heads, have some interesting English names. Lasher refers to the manner in which they will attack larger fish, lashing out with these same spines. I have seen a reference to an old Cornish name, poison-pate, which I like; and Day cites the improbable name rock dolphin from Brighton.

CUISINE Not many people regard the sculpins as worth eating. They may, however, be used for fish soups, as mentioned above; and it is possible to obtain respectable fillets from the larger specimens. Greenlanders eat them with pleasure, and are advised in the *Kogebog for Grønland* to cook them like cod and not to neglect the liver. The Greenlandic name for the sculpin, by the way, is kanajok.

Although sculpin are not normally eaten on the eastern seaboard of North America, James Beard, in *James Beard's Fish Cookery*, reminds his readers that some sculpin are sold commercially in the California markets, and adds optimistically: 'I am sure that if you try it you will find it an excellent food fish.'

BLUE-MOUTH

Family *Scorpaenidae*

Helicolenus dactylopterus (Delaroche)

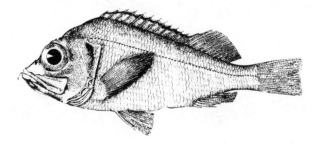

REMARKS Maximum length 45 cm. The colour shades from red above to rose-pink below; but the mouth and pharynx are lead-blue.

This is a deep-water fish, which ranges from the Mediterranean to Norway and is also known in North American waters.

CUISINE The blue-mouth is not often found in the markets and only deserves a place in the catalogue on the dubious basis that it is closely related to the famous RASCASSE of the Mediterranean, *Scorpaena scrofa* Linnaeus, pictured below. The rascasse does inhabit Atlantic waters up to Brittany, but Europeans further north and any North Americans who wish to make a reasonably authentic bouillabaisse (in which it is an essential ingredient) have to make do with a blue-mouth prepared for the purpose by being marinated in thyme-scented olive oil.

Portuguese: Cantarilho
Spanish: Gallineta
French: Sébaste chèvre, Rascasse du nord
German: Blaumaul
Polish: Sebdak
Russian: Sinerotyĭ okun'
Finnish: Merikonna
Swedish: Blåkaft
Norwegian: Blåkjeft
Danish: Blåkaeft
Other: Boca negra (Madeira)

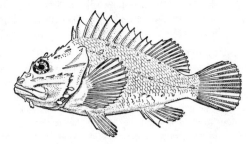

REDFISH; OCEAN PERCH (U.S.A.) Family *Scorpaenidae*

Sebastes marinus (Linnaeus)

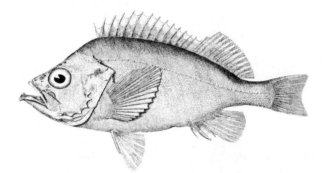

REMARKS Maximum length about 1 metre, usual market length 25 to 50 cm. The colour is bright red, or orange-red.

This species frequents the cold, northerly waters on both sides of the Atlantic, down to the Gulf of Maine and the North Sea. It grows slowly (over twenty years) and is found at depths of 100 to 500 metres (or even deeper). It has a close relation in shallower waters, **Sebastes viviparus** Krøyer, which only attains a length of 25 cm. This last species, not shown, is berggalt in Norway and Norway haddock in Britain (although this name and redfish tend to be used indiscriminately).

Sebastes marinus has become the object of an important commercial fishery in the last few decades. It is eaten in Norway and Sweden, for example; also in Germany, where it may appear on the menu as Island Rotbarsch, since most of the supply comes from Icelandic waters.

Dutch: Roodbaars
German: Rotbarsch
Polish: Karmazyn
Russian: Morskoï okun'
Finnish: Iso kuninkaankala
Swedish: Rødfisk, Stor rødfisk
Norwegian: Uer, Raudfisk
Danish: Stor rødfisk
Icelandic: Karfi, Stóri karfi
Other: Rose-fish; Red perch
  (U.S.A.); Sulugpâgaq
  (Greenland); Rascasse
  (Boulogne, but see page
  138).

CUISINE The redfish may be poached, or filleted and fried; but it is perhaps even better when baked.

RECIPES
Redfish loaf (German), 326
Polish cold fish soup, 332

Fish à la Nelson (Polish), 335
Fish, Lithuanian style, 352

GREY GURNARD

Family *Triglidae*

Eutrigla gurnardus (Linnaeus)

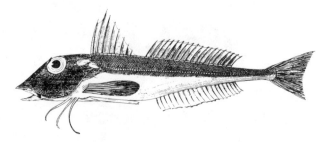

REMARKS   Maximum length around 40 cm. Back and sides are usually grey or greyish brown, with lots of small pale spots, but may have a red tinge (which would account for the first Spanish name, meaning drunkard). Note the black mark on the first dorsal fin.

Distribution extends from Norway and Iceland down to the Mediterranean. This is the most common gurnard in British waters.

All gurnards make croaking noises (like snoring, said one observer) both to themselves in the water and by way of complaint when caught. The Scots name crooner was thought by Dr Johnson to refer to this habit.

Portuguese: Ruivo
Spanish: Borracho, Perla
French: Grondin gris
Dutch: Grauwe poon
German: Grauer Knurrhahn
Polish: Kurek
Russian: Morskoï petukh
Swedish: Knorrhane, Knot
Norwegian: Knurr
Danish: Grå knurhane
Icelandic: Urrari
Other: Crúdán or Cnúdán
    (Irish, of all gurnards)

As the drawings show, the lower three rays of the pectoral fins of gurnards extend separately downwards. They are used to feel for food in the sea-bed.

CUISINE   Grey gurnards are marketed and are worth eating. The flesh tends to be dry, but is firm and white. I recommend baking these fish whole; but fillets may be lifted and poached or fried. Fried gurnard fillets are a popular dish in the Netherlands. And in times gone by it was the practice in various places to souse fried fillets in vinegar and thus preserve them. Some Neapolitan cooks still do this, but the habit has died in England, perhaps discouraged by Shakespeare, who implied an adverse judgment on the dish when he made Falstaff say: 'If I be not ashamed of my soldiers, I am a soused gurnet.'

RECIPES
Farci à la boulonnaise, 297
Au vin blanc et à la crême, 301

Fish fillets with cheese sauce, 315
Fish and leek pie, 464

Aspitrigla cuculus (Linnaeus), the RED GURNARD, reaches a length of 30 cm and is red in colour. It ranges from the Mediterranean to Britain, but is not common in the North Sea. It is known as the grondin rouge in France. The Dutch have called it Engelse soldaat, thinking no doubt of the redcoats against whom they once did battle. It is of good quality.

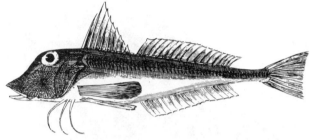

Trigla lucerna Linnaeus may reach a length of more than 60 cm and is thus the largest gurnard in the north-east Atlantic. It is known as the TUB GURNARD and may be recognized by its bright colours when alive. The body is red. The pectoral fins are bright red with peacock-blue and green spots and edges. In most languages it has names which refer to the red colour (for example, Roter Knurrhahn in German, rødknurr in Norwegian). The approved French name is perlon, but tombe and moelleux are used at Boulogne.

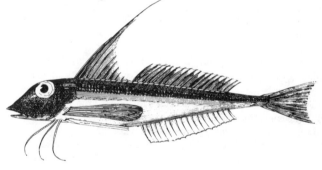

Prionotus carolinus (Linnaeus) is the best-known gurnard of the American Atlantic coast, where it and its relations are known as SEA-ROBINS. This one reaches a length of nearly 50 cm.

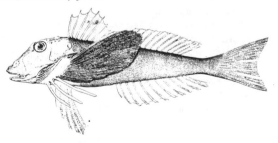

LUMPFISH

Family *Cyclopteridae*

Cyclopterus lumpus Linnaeus

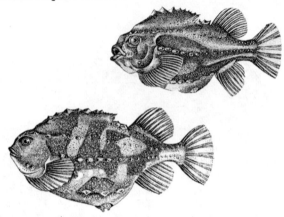

REMARKS Maximum length of females 60 cm, of males 50 cm. The colour varies, but is usually grey, or translucent green. During the spawning season the underside of the male becomes temporarily a brilliant red or orange, and its upper parts blue.

The lumpfish is found on both sides of the Atlantic, down to New Jersey and to Brittany. It is present in the Baltic.

The lumpy form of the fish accounts for its English name; and its suctorial disc for the various names which incorporate sucker. The Scots name paddle-cock or cock-paidle refers to its cock-like crest.

CUISINE AND RECIPES I have already said something about this on page 136. The chief value of the lumpfish is in the roe of the female, which is made into lumpfish caviar, coloured red or black. This is quite good. Otherwise, the flesh of the male is palatable. It is usual to take off the fillets and poach them. The flesh of the female is quite inedible during the spawning season; but earlier in the year it is turned by the Icelanders into a delicacy known as Sigin grásleppa (page 400, where instructions are also given for Soðinn rauðmagi, poached Icelandic male lumpfish).

A Swedish recipe for lumpfish in aspic is given on page 373.

French: Gros mollet, Lompe, Lièvre de mer
Dutch: Snotdolf
German: Seehase
Polish: Tasza
Russian: Pinagor
Finnish: Rasvakala, Vilukala
Swedish: Stenbit (male), Kvabbso (meaning sow, of the female), Sjurygg (both sexes)
Norwegian: Rognkall, Rognkjekse
Danish: Stenbider
Icelandic: Rauðmagi (male), Grásleppa (female), Hrognkelsi (both sexes)
Other: Lumpsucker, Henfish

Flatfish

As a general rule, the fish in this book are shown swimming from right to left across the page. But it would be a solecism to show soles so doing. The reason is that flatfish, which belong to the Order *Pleuronectiformes*, have both eyes on the same side of the head; some (the sinistral flatfish) on the left side and some (the dextral flatfish) on the right. Dextral flatfish, for example soles, must therefore be portrayed swimming from left to right.

The reason for this strange arrangement of the eyes is that the flatfish are adapted to lurking on the sea bed on their sides and need to have both their eyes on top. They like to half-bury themselves in the sand and have a coloration which renders them almost invisible when they do so. They can 'disappear' in this way with remarkable speed. Buckland describes an incident on the coast of Kent when a seine net full of plaice rolled over, and the plaice started to escape.

A fisherman cried, 'Look out, they'll sand!' a capital expression for I found that the fish sunk into the sand with such rapidity that the operation must be seen to be believed. The plaice lifts up its head and the upper third of its body and then brings it down on the sand three or four times with sharp, quick raps; a small cavity is thus made in the soft, wet sand, which at once fills with water; the fish then works its fins on each side of its body with such a rapid motion that they seem almost to vibrate. These combined efforts enable the fish to conceal itself almost quicker than the eye can follow, and nothing can be seen but its eye, which is of a lovely emerald colour.

From the cook's point of view, flatfish have several advantages. They cook quickly and evenly, being thin-bodied. They are simple to fillet. And their bone structure is such that the bones are not a nuisance at all.

It is unfortunate for Americans that *Solea solea*, which is *the* sole, is only found on the eastern side of the Atlantic. Indeed, American waters harbour no true soles, although several of the flatfish found there have been called soles. Bigelow and Schroeder consider that **Achirus fasciatus** Lacépède is the American species most closely related to the sole. This is a small flatfish with the unpromising name of hogchoker (bestowed, it seems, because hogs which try to eat specimens discarded on the beach find their scales so hard and rough that they choke). Yet it has a delicious flavour. It is a pity that it does not reach a length greater than about 15 cm.

However, there are good American flounders; and the halibut, king of flatfish, is common property to both sides of the Atlantic.

TURBOT

Family *Bothidae*

Psetta maxima (Linnaeus)
Scophthalmus maximus
Rhombus maximus

REMARKS Maximum length about 1 metre; common length 40 to 50 cm. The colour of the back matches the sea bed; sandy brown is therefore usual. The turbot has no scales, but sports bony tubercles on its body. The great breadth of the body accounts for the old Scots name Bannock-fluke (bannock being a round oatcake).

An inshore fish of European waters only, the turbot is found from the Mediterranean to Iceland and Norway; but the main fishery for it is on sandbanks in the North Sea. The numbers taken are not great, but this is no fault of the turbot – Buckland calculated that the roe of a 23-pounder contained 14,311,200 eggs.

Portuguese: Rodovalho, Pregado
Spanish: Rodaballo
French: Turbot
Dutch: Tarbot
German: Steinbutt
Polish: Skarp
Russian: Tyurbo
Finnish: Piikkikampela
Swedish: Piggvar
Norwegian: Piggvar
Danish: Pighvarre
Icelandic: Sandhverfa

CUISINE The turbot is greatly prized for its firm and delicious white flesh. It is a venial extravagance to acquire a turbotière (a turbot-shaped fish-kettle), as I did even before I owned a frying pan, with which to do it honour. Poach it whole therein and serve it with a lobster sauce if the makings are to hand. Jenny Wren (the charming and dogmatic authoress of *Modern Domestic Cookery*, Paisley, 1880) suggests a caper sauce and insists that the cook should not 'tamper with the fins, which are the *tid-bit* of the turbot'.

RECIPES
Brillat-Savarin's steamed turbot, 299   Turbot with Hollandaise sauce, 319

BRILL

Family *Bothidae*

Scophthalmus rhombus (Linnaeus)
Rhombus laevis

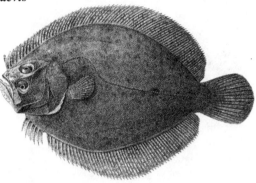

REMARKS Maximum length 60 cm, common length 30 cm. The back is sandy-brown or grey, with freckles. Unlike the turbot, the brill has scales and lacks tubercles. The shape is also different. But otherwise the two species resemble each other, and one could describe the brill as a smaller, shallow-water version of the turbot. Hybrids, between the two species, are not unknown.

Like the turbot, the brill does not occur on the American side of the Atlantic; but I mention here **Scophthalmus aquosus** (Mitchill), the windowpane, which does. It reaches a length of 50 cm, but is a thin-bodied fish with little flesh. It has been marketed in the past (sometimes as New York plaice, a misnomer), but has no commercial importance at present, although it is worth eating if you catch one.

Portuguese: Rodovalho, Patrúcia
Spanish: Rémol
French: Barbue
Dutch: Griet
German: Kleist, Glattbutt
Polish: Naglad
Russian: Kalkas
Swedish: Slätvar
Norwegian: Slettvar
Danish: Slethvarre
Other: Kite (SW. England); Broit (Irish)

CUISINE The brill is inferior to the turbot, but still a good fish. It should be prepared in similar fashion; but with less pomp (i.e. no lobster sauce, a parsley sauce will do).

RECIPE
Brill with chanterelles (Swedish), 374

MEGRIM, SAIL-FLUKE, WHIFF

Family *Bothidae*

Lepidorhombus whiffiagonis (Walbaum)
Pleuronectes megastoma

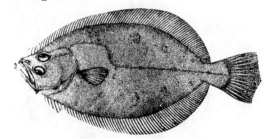

REMARKS Maximum length 60 cm. Another flatfish with a yellowish-brown or grey back, which bears vague dark spots.

The megrim is a deep-water fish, with a range from the Mediterranean to Iceland. It is fished commercially, for example in the Biscay area and to the west and south of Ireland. The related **Lepidorhombus boscii** (Risso) is often taken with it, but may be distinguished by a pair of distinct black spots on both dorsal and anal fins, at the rear.

Portuguese: Areeiro, Pregado
Spanish: Lliseria, Gallo
French: Cardine
Dutch: Scharretong
Polish: Smuklica
Finnish: Silokampela
Swedish: Glasvar
Norwegian: Glasvar
Danish: Glashvarre
Icelandic: Stórkjafta
Other: Ollarra (Basque)

CUISINE AND RECIPE Of medium quality. The flesh tends to be dry and lacks the exquisite flavour which the best flatfish have. It is therefore well to cook megrim with plenty of fat or liquid and with added flavours. The fishermen of Boulogne would use megrim in their shipboard fish stews, but gave it the highly uncomplimentary name of salope.

Devilled witches is really a recipe for the witch (page 150), but also serves to enliven megrim. Lift the fillets from four fish. Spread on them a paste made with 2 egg yolks, ½ tbs dry mustard, salt and pepper to taste, ½ tsp sugar, ½ tsp lemon juice, 1 tbs single cream and 15 g (½ oz) butter. Make a light batter by combining 3 tbs plain flour with 1½ dl (¼ pint) tepid water and 1 tbs salad oil, with an egg white, beaten stiff, folded into it. Dip the fillets in the batter and set them to fry in a pan of hot fat. Before the batter has quite set, sprinkle dry breadcrumbs over them. Then finish the frying. Serve with a garnish of parsley and lemon slices.

SCALDFISH
Family *Bothidae*

Arnoglossus laterna (Walbaum)

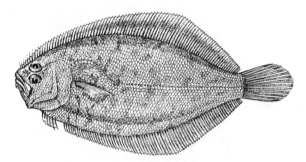

REMARKS Maximum length nearly 20 cm. A brown or grey fish with diffuse darker marks. Its range is from the Mediterranean to Norway; its habitat inshore waters.

The name scaldfish refers to the fact that its scales come off very easily, so that captured specimens have a 'scalded' appearance.

CUISINE One of the less good flatfish, as the alternative French name sole maudite would suggest. But it may be met in the markets and is worth eating. Fry, poach or steam.

Portuguese: Areeiro, Carta
Spanish: Serrandell
French: Fausse limande
Dutch: Schurftvis
German: Lammzunge, Schorrfisch
Swedish: Tungevar
Norwegian: Tungevar
Danish: Tungehvarre

TOPKNOT
Family *Bothidae*

Zeugopterus punctatus (Bloch)

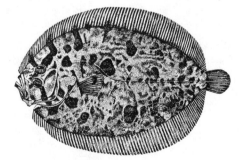

The small drawing to the right shows this other small (to 25 cm) member of the family *Bothidae*. It is targeur or sole des rochers in France; not common but worth eating if you come across it.

PLAICE

Family *Pleuronectidae*

Pleuronectes platessa Linnaeus

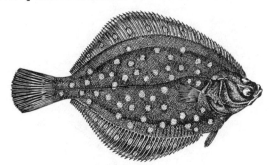

REMARKS The absolute maximum length of the plaice is about 90 cm, but the usual length of a fully grown fish does not exceed 50 cm. The coloration of the eyed side is a warm brown with the familiar orange or red spots. The blind side is pearly white.

The plaice ranges from the western Mediterranean to Iceland and Norway, living in the waters of the continental shelf. It is an abundant and important species – the most important flatfish of the European fisheries. The best plaice are those taken from sandy bottoms; and it is perhaps these which merit the complimentary Flemish name mooie meid (beautiful maiden).

Portuguese: Solha
Spanish: Platija
French: Plie, Carrelet
Dutch: Schol
German: Scholle
Polish: Gladzica
Russian: Morskaya kambala
Finnish: Punakampela
Swedish: Rödspotta, Skadda
Norwegian: Gullflyndre, Rødspette
Danish: Rødspætte
Icelandic: Skarkoli
Other: Leathóg (Irish); Lleden (Welsh); Pladijs (Belgian Flemish)

CUISINE This is a good flatfish, although how good is a matter of opinion. Danes and Swedes are among the greatest enthusiasts. I find that fried fillets of plaice, if the frying be skilfully done, are delicious. Small plaice may be grilled whole and plaice of any size may be poached.

RECIPES
Plaice with a purée of potato and sorrel (Flemish), 308
Plaice in the Harlingen style, 320

Plaice with smoked bacon in the style of Finkenwerder, 328
Plaice with cranberry sauce, (Danish), 390
Fishermen's plaice, 390
Fish and chips, 449

FLOUNDER

Family *Pleuronectidae*

(but see pages 150 and 151 for American flounders)

Platichthys flesus (Linnaeus)

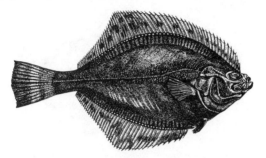

REMARKS Maximum length about 50 cm. This is a dextral fish, but reversed examples are common. The eyed side is dull brown, greyish or dull green. It may bear orange speckles (not as bright as the orange spots of the plaice). The blind side is dead white. Freak specimens which have been recorded include an albino taken in Norfolk which must have been a pretty sight – white on both sides, with pink eyes and fins.

The flounder, which ranges from the Mediterranean to the White Sea, is common in estuaries and especially abundant in the Baltic Sea. It is much more important as a food fish in northern Europe than in Britain. Its own diet features bivalves. It likes to come in with the tide and browse on cockle beds during the period of high tide. The flounder will also penetrate fresh waters. Frieslanders were able to culture it in ponds. Even today the species can be found in the Thames as far upstream as Teddington.

Portuguese: Patruça, Solha das pedras
Spanish: Platija
French: Flet
Dutch: Bot
German: Flunder
Polish: Stornia
Russian: Rechnaya kambala
Finnish: Kampela
Swedish: Skrubba
Norwegian: Skrubbe, Harbakke, Kvasse, Vassflyndre
Danish: Skrubbe
Other: Fluke (e.g. in Ireland); Lleden fach (Welsh)

CUISINE The flounder is inferior to the plaice and has even been condemned as 'watery, poor eating'. At its worst it may be; but its quality varies and a good flounder is not at all to be despised. Fry or steam.

WINTER FLOUNDER, COMMON FLOUNDER

Family *Pleuronectidae*

Pseudopleuronectes americanus (Walbaum)

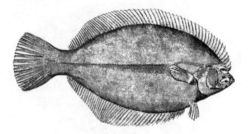

REMARKS   Maximum length over 60 cm, usual length up to 45 cm. The eyed side varies in colour according to the bottom on which the fish lie, but is often reddish brown; whence the French Canadian name plie rouge. Note the straight lateral line. The range of the species is from Labrador to Georgia. It is especially abundant in New England waters. The largest specimens are fished from the Georges Bank; the largest on record weighed 8 lb.

In New England it is usual to call specimens weighing up to 3 lb blackbacks; and those which exceed that weight lemon sole (not to be confused with the lemon sole of European waters, page 156).

In the southern part of its range this fish comes inshore in search of warmer waters during the winter, and this accounts for the name winter flounder.

CUISINE   This is the thickest and meatiest flatfish of the eastern seaboard, except for the halibut. Its flesh is white and firm and well suited to grilling or pan-frying. Fillets may be treated like fillets of sole (page 158).

WITCH FLOUNDER, WITCH, POLE DAB

Family *Pleuronectidae*

Glyptocephalus cynoglossus (Linnaeus)

REMARKS   This species, shown at the top of the next page, occurs on both sides of the Atlantic. On the American side it may reach a length of 60 cm. It resembles the winter flounder (see above), but may be distinguished from it by the presence of deep pits on the blind side of its head and by the greater number of rays in its dorsal and anal fins. Its names include plie grise and flet (Canada), smørflyndre (Norway), mareflundra (Sweden), skærising (Denmark) and langlúra (Iceland). The body is thin, but the flavour good. Fry, poach or steam.

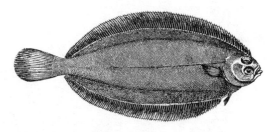

SUMMER FLOUNDER, NORTHERN FLUKE

Family *Pleuronectidae*

Paralichthys dentatus (Linnaeus)

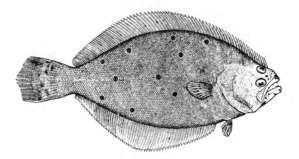

REMARKS   Maximum length almost 1 metre. The back is usually brown or grey, but may be green or nearly black. It normally bears a number of dark spots, but these may not be conspicuous. This is an important species in the U.S.A. Its range is from South Carolina to Maine. Further south it is replaced by *Paralichthys lethostigmus* Jordan and Gilbert, the southern fluke.

The name summer flounder was bestowed because the species comes inshore during the summer and in most areas retreats to deeper and warmer waters for the winter.

Goode says that when the first specimen of this fish was sent to Linnaeus by Dr Garden in South Carolina in 1766 it was locally known as plaice, and that this name was still current on various parts of the Atlantic seaboard at the end of the nineteenth century.

A smaller species, *Paralichthys oblongus* (Mitchill), is also common in New England waters. It may be distinguished by the four elliptical dark spots on its back, which give it the name four-spotted flounder.

CUISINE   An excellent fish. Fry, grill, bake.

DAB

Family *Pleuronectidae*

Limanda limanda (Linnaeus)

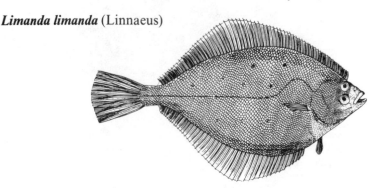

REMARKS   Maximum length just under 40 cm, common length 20 to 25 cm. The back is brown, often freckled. This dab, which occurs only on the European side, ranges from the White Sea down to the French coast. It is abundant in inshore waters and is fished for commercially, but with more interest on the continent than in Britain. The very name dab used to be a term of contempt in Lincolnshire.

French: Limande
Dutch: Schar
German: Kliesche
Polish: Zimnica
Russian: Ërshevatka
Finnish: Hietakampela
Swedish: Sandskädda,
   Sandflundra
Norwegian: Sandflyndre
Danish: Ising, Slette
Icelandic: Sandkoli

A related species occurs in North American waters. This is *Limanda ferruginea* (Storer), the YELLOWTAIL DAB or RUSTY FLOUNDER, which is shown below. It reaches a length of 60 cm and ranges from Labrador to Chesapeake Bay.

CUISINE   Both the dab and the yellowtail flounder are good fish, with a pleasing flavour. Small ones may be fried whole, after being skinned. Larger ones may be filleted and the fillets dealt with as you please.

In Jutland dabs are salted and dried and sold as Tøerrede Jyde (meaning dried Jutlanders); and a similar product is available on the Belgian coast. Dabs may also be smoked.

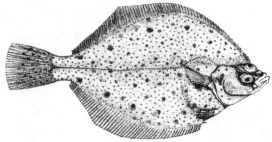

AMERICAN or CANADIAN PLAICE, SAND-DAB, LONG ROUGH DAB

Family *Pleuronectidae*

Hippoglossoides platessoides (Fabricius)

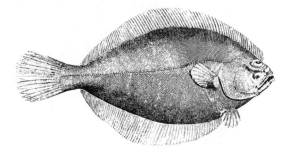

REMARKS Maximum length about 60 cm (or, exceptionally, up to 80 cm) in North American waters, but only just over 30 cm in European waters. In fact, the authorities recognize two sub-species, one on each side of the Atlantic. (The drawing is of the American variety, ***Hippoglossoides platessoides platessoides***.)

The colour of the eyed side is greyish to reddish brown. The tips of the dorsal and anal fins are white. The scales are rough to the touch. Note that the lateral line is almost straight.

French: Fausse sole, Sole d'Ecosse
Dutch: Lange schar
German: Scharbenzunge
Polish: Niegl-adzica
Russian: Kambala-ёrsh
Finnish: Liejukampela
Swedish: Lerskadda, Storgap
Norwegian: Gapeflyndre
Danish: Håising
Icelandic: Skrápflúra

The European version, ***Hippoglossoides platessoides limandoides***, is abundant in northern waters (Iceland, Norway, Scotland) but is not yet in great demand, partly, no doubt, because of its relatively small size. The American version is the object of an important fishery, for example in Canada, and is found as far south as Rhode Island.

The confusion which pervades the English nomenclature of flatfish is almost total for this species. It is not only called a plaice and a dab, but also a flounder and a sole. It only remains for someone to take the hint offered by the scientific name and dub it some sort of halibut.

CUISINE These are fish of quite good quality, which may be treated like the flounders.

HALIBUT
Family *Pleuronectidae*

Hippoglossus hippoglossus (Linnaeus)

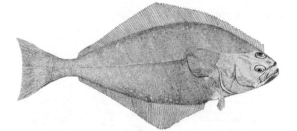

REMARKS   The maximum length of this great fish is 2½ metres and it may weigh over 300 kilos. Although such measurements are quite exceptional, the halibut is by far the greatest of the flatfish. Its back is dark olive-green, the blind side pearly white.

The halibut is a northern fish, not common south of Scotland or below New Jersey. It is a deep-water fish and is sometimes taken by trawlers fishing for cod in Arctic waters, but the directed fishery for it, by line or

French: Flétan
Dutch: Heilbot
German: Heilbutt
Polish: Halibut, Kulbak
Russian: Paltus
Swedish: Hälleflundra
Norwegian: Kveite
Danish: Helleflynder
Icelandic: Lúða, Flyðra, Heilagfiski

trawl, is a specialized business. The drawing on the next page shows the crew of a small dory from a halibut schooner 'hauling the trawl, gaffing and clubbing the halibut', some eighty years ago. This was no easy task, since the halibut has enormous vitality and is a strong fighter. In his autobiography *Roving Fisherman*, the Canadian author F. W. Wallace wrote: 'It will spin around like a whirling top, thereby making the job of giving him his quietus with the "killer" an exceedingly difficult one. For perhaps a minute or two, there is spray and profanity flying, punctuated by dull thuds of the club on the halibut's snout . . .' He had seen men's wrists broken in such a mêlée.

CUISINE AND RECIPES   The halibut is now highly esteemed almost everywhere; but in the nineteenth century it was rated a poor fish in England. A certain Mr Rowell was ahead of his time when he wrote in *Land and Water* in 1818: 'Let anyone get a piece of halibut from a small one, season it with nutmeg, pepper and salt, and bake it in the oven, and I know nothing so fine . . .' Halibut steaks may also be grilled or poached. They have a fine, close texture. See also the recipes for Halibut salad (Sweden) on page 374 and Halibut soup (Iceland) on page 396.

GREENLAND HALIBUT

Family *Pleuronectidae*

Reinhardtius hippoglossoides (Walbaum)

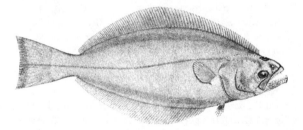

REMARKS Maximum length 1 metre. This species of Arctic and sub-Arctic waters is like the true halibut in many respects, but smaller. It is therefore sometimes called little halibut; a name not to be confused with the term chicken halibut, which refers to a small true halibut.

Note the almost straight lateral line. The colour of the eyed side is blackish grey or brown, and the underside is almost as dark. Common names in other languages mostly mean black halibut, for example svartkeite (Norway).

Goode remarked that the Greenlanders, who call it kalleraglik, preferred it to any other fish and eagerly fished for it through holes in the ice. They still pursue it, and maintain their liking for marinated halibut fins (page 401).

The smoked Greenland halibut which is available in Denmark and elsewhere is delicious. It is a fish with a high fat content, and smoking seems to be the best treatment for it.

LEMON SOLE

Family *Pleuronectidae*

Microstomus kitt (Walbaum)

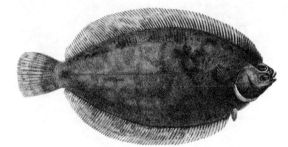

REMARKS   Maximum length 65 cm. The colour is 'generally dull brown, but with varied and irregular rounded markings of mahogany, orange, yellow and even green blended into the background colour' (Wheeler). The skin is slimy and smooth. Note the small head and mouth.

Spanish: Mendo limón
French: Sole limande
Dutch: Tongschar
German: Rotzunge
Swedish: Bergtunga, Bergskädda
Norwegian: Lomre, Bergflyndre
Danish: Rødtunge
Icelandic: Þykkvalúra

The lemon sole (which is not, strictly speaking, a sole, but never mind) is an important food fish which is widespread on the coastal banks of Europe from Iceland and Norway to France. It is mainly exploited by British and French fishermen, using trawls or seine nets. It is not, of course, the same fish as the American winter flounder (page 150), although the latter may also be called lemon sole.

CUISINE   This is a good flatfish, not quite up to the standard of the true sole (page 158) but suitable for whatever treatment you would give to the more favoured species, grilling included.

The lemon sole is available in salted and dried form on the Belgian coast, where it is known as Schotse schol (Scottish sole) and regarded as a delicacy. What you do with it is to cut off the head and trim off the fins, then cut the body in two lengthways and make transverse cuts in each half from the outside almost to the centre line. The cuts are made at intervals of about 2 cm, so as to form a series of morsel-sized pieces which can be plucked off one by one, and eaten as they are, without any further preparation.

SAND SOLE, FRENCH SOLE

Family *Soleidae*

Pegusa lascaris (Risso)

REMARKS Maximum length 35 cm. The sand sole has a freckled, grey-brown or yellow-brown back and is found on sandy bottoms in inshore waters from the Mediterranean to the English Channel.

Portuguese: Linguado da areia
Spanish: Sortija
French: Sole pôle, Sole pelouse
Dutch: Franse tong

Another smaller sole, which deserves a mention and is shown below, is **Microchirus variegatus** (Donovan), the THICKBACK SOLE, which has a similar range and reaches a length of 25 cm. It is known as the sole panachée in France. It is proportionately thicker in the body than the Dover sole.

CUISINE Both the above soles are of good quality. What is said about the Dover sole on the following page applies to them too, with a little less enthusiasm. The thickback sole has a better flavour than the sand sole, and is traditionally relished in Devon and Cornwall.

SOLE, DOVER SOLE   Family *Soleidae*

Solea solea (Linnaeus)

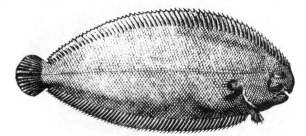

REMARKS   Maximum length 50 cm. This is a fish of superb quality, so it is worth while to know for sure how to identify it. Note that the pectoral fins on both sides are well developed; that the dorsal and anal fins are joined to the tail fin by membranes; and that the upper pectoral fin has an elliptical black spot on its rear margin. The colour of the eyed side is sepia, marked in life (but not after death) by irregular darker blotches.

Portuguese: Linguado
Spanish: Lenguado
French: Sole
Dutch: Tong
German: Zunge
Polish: Sola
Russian: Morskoï yazyk
Finnish: Kielikampala
Swedish: Tunga
Norwegian: Tunge
Danish: Tunge
Other: Slip (young ones)

The name *Solea* is from the Greek, 'as the Greeks considered it would form a fit sandal for an ocean nymph' (Day).

The range of this super-fish is from the Mediterranean to the north of Scotland and the south of Norway. It is not present in the Baltic, except around the mouth of that sea. The best fishing grounds for it are in the North Sea and the Bay of Biscay. Dover is not its home in any exclusive sense, but was the best source of supply to the London market of freshly caught soles.

It is, of course, desirable to have your sole fresh; but I should add that it keeps relatively well and that many authorities hold that it is at its peak of perfection about a day after death. There is some evidence that its flavour develops during this time, whereas that of most flatfish merely deteriorates.

CUISINE   Everyone knows how good the sole is; and it is never better than when plainly grilled and served with a simple garnish of lemon wedges. However, it is also very good when cooked à la meunière; and the fillets, which can be lifted off easily, may be used for a great variety of culinary feats. Most of these involve poaching them in a court-bouillon or wine and then dressing them with a sauce. Do so by all means; but do not complicate your dish unduly or risk masking the delicious flavour of the sole itself.

In pursuance of this last thought, I quote Wyvern (*Common Sense Cookery*, 1894):

The tendency of the modern French school is certainly to overdo the cooking of fish. No variety can escape. At establishments renowned for the highest culinary proficiency you are regaled with compositions so elaborate and *travaillés*, that you cannot recognise the fish which, according to the *menu*, is supposed to exist somewhere in a rich creamy bath, or amid a hotchpotch of mushrooms, truffles, and divers kinds of shellfish. The sole is often the victim chosen for these exaggerations.

It is indeed. *Le Répertoire de la Cuisine* by Saulnier (1914) lists over 340 sole dishes, among which we find entries such as: 'Moulin d'Or – Prepared as for Colbert, stuffed with foie gras purée mixed with truffles, treated same as au gratin with cèpes instead of mushrooms, roundels of foie gras surmounted with sliced truffles on top of cèpes, lemon juice and chopped parsley.'

Pooh to all that. One may derive a certain pleasure and amusement from the contemplation of such antics, especially when they are beautifully illustrated, as in the engraving below, reproduced from Urbain Dubois; but this is not how to cook fish of any kind, and it is plain wasteful to convert what would have been a delicious sole into a mere plinth for such a mound of 100 franc notes.

My own list of recipes for sole is short. I supplement it by inviting attention to Sole en matelote à la normande, in *French Provincial Cooking* by Elizabeth David, who deftly transports us back through the age of culinary ostentation to a simple dish which was made by normal people, and which both reflects a proper respect for the sole itself and demonstrates the appropriate use of other ingredients.

RECIPES

Filets de sole aux morilles,
gratinés, 300
Sole au glui, 300

With cheese sauce (Dutch), 315
With samphire sauce, 454
Eliza Acton's baked soles, 458

NOT RECOMMENDED
Timbales de sole à
l'ambassadrice, from
Urbain Dubois, *Cuisine
artistique* (1872–74)
splendid book though
this is, of its kind.

Miscellaneous Uncouth Fish

Of the three fish listed under this uncomplimentary title, the first belongs to the Order *Lophiiformes* and the others to the Order *Tetraodontiformes*. All three have extraordinary characteristics, which cannot be said to affect their flavour but which may still invest the act of eating them with additional pleasure and interest.

The angler-fish is a master of camouflage, concealing itself on the sea bed in a manner well described by the Duke of Argyll (quoted by Goode, who omits to say which Duke):

> The whole upper surface is tinted and mottled in such close resemblance to stones and gravel and seaweeds that it becomes quite indistinguishable among them. In order to complete the method of concealment, the whole margins of the fish, and the very edge of the lips and jaws, have loose tags and fringes which wave and sway about amid the currents of water so as to look exactly like the smaller algae which move around them and along with them. Even the very ventral fins of this devouring deception, which are thick, strong and fleshy, almost like hands, and which evidently help in a sudden leap, are made like two great clam-shells, while the iris of the eyes is so coloured in lines radiating from the pupil as to look precisely like some species of *Patella* or limpet.

Thus disguised, the angler agitates the 'fishing-rod' above its head and prepares to engulf with its hinged teeth the smaller fish which have come to investigate.

It even has a spare fishing rod. The one which one notices projects forward and has a piece of tissue on the end as 'bait'. But in case this is bitten off, there is another behind which can be brought forward. This one bears no bait, but I am told that bait will grow on it if it has to be used.

It is not only little fish which are devoured by the angler. The size of its mouth and the capacity of its stomach allow it to ingest quite large victims. Bigelow and Schroeder report that an angler $3\frac{1}{2}$ feet long has a mouth which gapes 9 inches horizontally and 8 inches vertically; and that an angler 26 inches long was found to contain a codling 23 inches long. They assert that it is not at all unusual for one of these fish to contain a mass of food half as heavy as itself.

The tail of the angler-fish, or rather the tail end of its body, is the part which is marketed, after being skinned and trimmed. In the Netherlands it is sold as 'ham' or hozemondham. In Sweden it is called kotlettfisk, a name also applied to cleaned and skinned wolf-fish. The merits of the angler-fish are now widely acknowledged in Europe, but it still has to win acceptance as a food for humans on the other side of the Atlantic.

ANGLER-FISH, MONKFISH (U.K.), GOOSEFISH (U.S.A.)

Family *Lophiidae*

Lophius piscatorius Linnaeus

REMARKS Maximum length 2 metres. The species occurs from the Mediterranean to Iceland. A close relation, ***Lophius americanus*** Valenciennes, is found in American waters.

Many remarkable features of the angler-fish have been described on the preceding page. A creature of such bizarre appearance and so superbly equipped for the practice of gluttony has naturally attracted some interesting vernacular names, such as bellyfish and goosefish (because it stuffs itself), allmouth (North Carolina), and the cognate 'lawyer' (parts of New England), and bellows fish.

Portuguese: Peixe sapo, Ra do mar
Spanish: Rape
French: Baudroie, Lotte
Dutch: Zeeduivel, Hozemond
German: Seeteufel
Swedish: Marulk, Havspadda
Norwegian: Bredflab, Havtask
Danish: Bredflab, Havtask
Icelandic: Skotuselur
Other: Pejesapo (Basque); Seyot (Boulogne)

The Scots name Molly Gowan has no obvious explanation, but the Irish name frogish is understandable. Another Irish name, láimhíneach, alludes to the resemblance between the pectoral fins and human hands. (See the lower drawing.)

CUISINE AND RECIPES The tail end of the angler has long been prized by knowing people like the Venetians. It is white and so firm in texture that it invites comparison with the lobster. A friend at Billingsgate once said to me. 'If Mr X comes down and orders two whole lobsters and forty pounds of angler tail, I know what's on the menu that evening and it isn't angler.'

The dressed tail can be poached or steamed; cut into steaks and fried; or opened out butterfly fashion and grilled. The head, by the way, makes a good soup.

A French Canadian recipe for Ragoût de lotte is given on page 405.

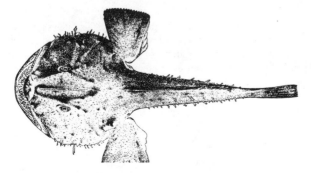

TRIGGER-FISH

Family *Balistidae*

Balistes carolinensis Gmelin

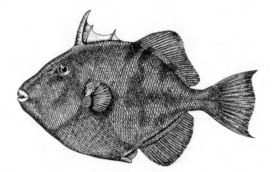

REMARKS   Maximum length 40 cm. A dark fish, usually greenish- or greyish-brown. The 'trigger' is the third spine of the front dorsal fin, which has to be depressed before the first spine can be folded down.

Portuguese: Peixe
   porco. Cangulo
Spanish: Pez ballesta
French: Baliste
Dutch: Trekkervis
Other: Leather-jacket; Grey
   trigger-fish; Turbot
   (Bermuda, Florida,
   Bahamas)

This is really a species of tropical or near-tropical waters, but its range on the European side of the Atlantic extends to the English Channel and SW. Ireland; and on the American side it sometimes strays as far north as Massachusetts. There are various kindred species, such as those called queen trigger-fish and ocean trigger-fish on the American side.

The trigger-fish often outwits fishermen by 'stealing' bait from their hooks.

Its manner of taking the bait is rather peculiar, I think, for instead of pulling the line backward or to one side it raises it upward so quietly that the fisherman does not perceive the motion, and then, by careful nibbling, cleans the hook without injury to itself. Expert fishermen, however, can tell by the 'lifting of the lead', as it is called, what is going on below, and know what they have to contend against. The usual remedy is to seek other fishing grounds ... When one of these crafty fish has been hooked there is not much probability that it can be landed, for its sharp, powerful teeth are almost sure to cut some part of the gear, enabling it to escape. (Goode.)

CUISINE   Remove the 'leather jacket', that is to say, the tough skin, before trying to cook this fish. The results are rewarding, since the flesh is good and firm. Use a turbotière if you have a large specimen; or cut it into pieces. Poaching is the best technique, and provision of a sauce is recommended.

PUFFER, NORTHERN
SWELLFISH, BLOWFISH

Family *Tetraodontidae*

Spheroides maculatus (B. and S.)

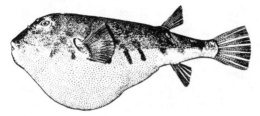

REMARKS   Maximum length about 35 cm. The puffers are essentially warm-water species, but this one is found as far north as New York and even the south of Newfoundland. It has no counterpart in European waters.

Puffers have two unusual protective devices. They can inflate their abdomens to a remarkable extent, thus making themselves too much of a mouthful for predators. Moreover, their scales have been modified into small prickles which stand out when the abdomen is inflated, so that the prospective mouthful is not only too big but also too prickly.

They are themselves predators of crustaceans and molluscs. 'It is not an uncommon sight to see a group of them "mob" a solitary blue crab and in an exceedingly short time dispatch him, for their hard cutting jaws are well able to bite through the resistant shell, although they are not fond of being nipped by the sharp chaela of the crab and will seldom tackle one alone. The spectacle always suggests concerted action and the possession of more reasoning power than we have any right to assign to such a fish.' (Breder.)

CUISINE AND RECIPE   These fish are eaten in New Jersey and on Long Island, for example. They are sometimes dressed and marketed as 'sea squab'. I have not tasted the species myself, but it ought to be good, since it is related to the famous puffer fish of Japan. One has to take special precautions in eating the Japanese species, but the American one is less of a problem. Do, however, wear gloves when cleaning it. The first step is to cut off the head. Then peel back the skin like a glove, from neck to tail. The innards will drop out, leaving in your hands the backbone with all the meat on it. This can be fried or baked whole, rather like a chicken's leg or frog's leg. Or you can slice off small fillets of meat and pan-fry them. Euell Gibbons enthuses persuasively over the results of this treatment. However, even he is outdone by Bunny Day, who devotes nine recipes to blowfish in her slim volume *Hook'em and Cook'em* (1962).

Non-bony Fish: Sharks, Rays or Skates, and the Sea Lamprey

The fish to which we now come are non-bony in two senses. First, they have a skeleton which is cartilaginous, not of real bone. Secondly, they are thus free of those tiresome little bones which discourage people from eating some species. This is an advantage; and the corresponding disadvantages are more apparent than real.

The repellent aspect of sharks and rays is of little practical consequence; the less so since they are rarely marketed whole. Pieces of shark, usually the small ones called dogfish, look quite respectable on the fishmonger's slab. Wings of ray or skate, dressed for sale, look positively attractive.

What matters more, and needs to be understood, is that these fish tend to have an ammoniac smell. The reason is this: all sea fish have a problem in that they themselves, their bloodstreams and tissues, are less salty than the waters in which they swim; and there is therefore a natural tendency for them to lose water, by osmosis, to the sea. If they did nothing about this their blood would quickly become too salty. Bony fish solve the problem by means of special chloride cells on their gills, which get rid of excess salt. But the non-bony fish use a different technique. They make and maintain in their blood and tissues a supply of urea, a constituent of urine, which reverses the tendency to lose water to the sea and enables them to keep what is called an osmotic balance. These fish, when alive, contain only a little ammonia; but after death the urea breaks up and produces much more. Hence the strong ammoniac smell.

What the consumer needs to remember is that some smell of ammonia is natural and serves to indicate the welcome disappearance of the urea; and that the smell, indeed the ammonia itself, will disappear in cooking and is nothing to worry about. The reader will also realize why ray or skate is better when it is not fresh-caught but a day or two old. After about forty-eight hours the beneficial chemical changes have occurred, but undesirable ones have not yet set in. This has long been known. 'The Thornback, in order to the producing of good Effects, and to be made more agreeable to the Taste, should not be too fresh. It must be kept for some time, during which there is a little Fermentation wrought in it, whereby some dull and viscous Matters, which make it hard and tough, are insensibly attenuated and destroyed; and therefore those that live at *Paris*, and other Parts, eat the Thornback in a better Condition than those near the Sea-side, because it has more time to lie by.' (Lemery, *A Treatise of All Sorts of Foods*, 1745.)

The thornback is usually considered to be the best of the rays. Their quality certainly varies and fishermen have clear preferences among them; but their capacity for discrimination tends to disappear in the wholesale markets and in fish shops. It is, admittedly, difficult to make any systematic comparison of the quality of the various different rays, because of the lack of generally accepted common names. Ray or skate? In North America all fish of the family *Rajidae* have been known as skates (although the name rajafish has now gained currency). In Britain the two terms have become almost interchangeable. It seems to me worth preserving the old distinction whereby the skates were the bigger ones with long snouts, and the rays were the smaller ones with rounded heads.

I have seen a suggestion that the name ray, which comes from the French raie, refers to the long fibres of flesh in the wings of these fish. I am not sure about this, but at least there is no doubt about the origin of the various names given to *Squatina squatina* (page 171), which represents a sort of intermediate stage between ray and shark. McCormick, Allen and Young, in *Shadows in the Sea*, remark that pious medieval observers 'saw its pectorals as wings and its tapering body and tail as angelic robes. They named it an Angel. Later, it become a Monk. And finally it was dubbed a Bishop. (An Australian species, ornately dappled with denticles, managed to become an Archbishop.)' They go on to quote Rondelet, writing in 1588: 'In our time in Norway a sea-monster has been taken after a great storm, to which all who saw it at once gave the name of monk, for it had a man's face, rude and ungracious, the head smooth and shorn. On the shoulders, like the cloak of a monk, were two long fins in place of arms...'

The drawing is a medieval wood-cut intended to show the angel fish in episcopal guise. This tradition has continued into modern times. In a certain side street in Ostend is a shop which sells dried angel fish, cleverly cut and carved so as to look like parchment-coloured ghosts. This is done elsewhere, but I feel sure that it is in the land of Breugel and Bosch that the art is pursued most seriously.

PORBEAGLE SHARK, MACKEREL SHARK

Family *Isuridae*

Lamna nasus (Bonnaterre)

REMARKS   Maximum length 3 to 4 metres. This shark, bluish grey above and white below, is found on both sides of the Atlantic, from the Carolinas to Newfoundland in the west and from the Mediterranean to the waters between Orkney and Iceland in the east.

Portuguese: Anequim
Spanish: Marrajo
French: Taupe, Lamie, Latour
Dutch: Neushaai
German: Heringshai
Swedish: Sillhaj, Håbrand
Norwegian: Håbrann
Danish: Sildehaj
Icelandic: Hámeri
Other: Morgi mawr (Welsh); Maraiche (Fr. Can.)

The name mackerel shark is given because of the shape of the tail. The name porbeagle seems to be a compound of porpoise and beagle (or hunting dog).

For all its broad shoulders and fierce teeth, this shark behaves rather feebly when caught, although Couch reported one atypical instance of a porbeagle springing at a fisherman and tearing his clothes. Sport fishermen are much more interested in its relation, *Isurus oxyrinchus* Rafinesque, the mako or sharp-nosed mackerel shark, which is a vigorous fighter. It ranges north to Norway and to the Gulf of Maine and is almost as long as the porbeagle, despite its shorter nose, but less deep in the body.

CUISINE   Couch speaks with irony. 'According to Risso it is an article of food in the Mediterranean, and he goes so far as to say that it is much esteemed. This is a piece of luxury to which our fishermen and the public have not yet attained; and consequently with us it is only employed as manure.' A similar view, expressed in more general terms, was put forward by Jordan and Evermann on the other side of the Atlantic at the beginning of the century: 'Our people are too well fed to care for the coarse rank flesh of sharks, however much its flavour may be disguised by ingenious cooks.'

More recently the porbeagle has been marketed in Britain, Europe and the United States. The Germans are particularly partial to it, and it is not unusual to find items like Heringshai von der Murmanküste on the menu of a German restaurant. In the United States there is quite a keen demand for the mako, whose flesh, like that of the porbeagle, may be compared to swordfish but costs much less.

My advice for both the porbeagle and the mako is to grill steaks and serve them with a simple dressing of lemon juice.

HAMMERHEAD, HAMMERHEAD SHARK

Family *Sphyrnidae*

Sphyrna zygaena (Linnaeus)

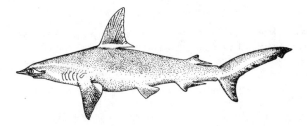

REMARKS Maximum length 4 metres. This shark has an olive-brown or brownish-grey back. Its (literally) salient characteristic is the extraordinary head, shaped like a hammer, with the eyes set in the projections. The scientific name *zygaena* means balance, another interpretation of the shape of the head.

Portuguese: Cornuda
Spanish: Pez martillo
French: Requin marteau
Dutch: Hamerhaai
Other: Shovelhead shark

The hammerhead belongs to the tropical and warm temperate waters of both sides of the Atlantic. Small schools of the species go up as far as Cape Cod in the summer, and stray specimens reach the southern coast of England. A specimen netted at Long Island in 1805 contained parts of a man in its stomach, an incident which darkened the American reputation of the species.

CUISINE I and my wife once cooked a whole hammerhead, of small size, by poaching it in a court-bouillon. Although our audience consisted mostly of ladies who had not knowingly eaten shark before, they consumed every morsel. The flesh has a good consistency and a pleasant taste.

DOGFISH,
LESSER-SPOTTED DOGFISH,
ROUGH HOUND

Family *Scyliorhinidae*

Scyliorhinus canicula (Linnaeus)

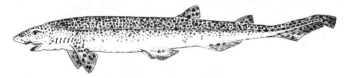

REMARKS   Maximum length about 75 cm. A sandy or brown fish with lots of little brown spots on the back and sides.

This is a common dogfish in European Atlantic waters. *Scyliorhinus stellaris* (Linnaeus), the larger-spotted dogfish, may be twice the size and has relatively larger spots, but is much less common.

These dogfish deposit their eggs in little containers (pixy cases or mermaids' purses) of a pleasing design (see the drawing below). Their own skins, especially that of *Scyliorhinus stellaris*, are so rough that they were used in the past for such tasks as polishing wood and alabaster and raising the hair of beaver hats.

Portuguese: Pataroxa
Spanish: Gato
French: Petite roussette
Dutch: Hondshaai
German: Kleingefleckter
   Kaltenhai
Polish: Rekinek
Russian: Morskoï kot
Swedish: Småflackig rödhaj
Norwegian: Raudhå
Danish: Smaplettet rødhaj
Other: Morgay (Scotland and
   Cornwall); Morgi meiaf
   (Welsh)

The name catfish is sometimes given to the larger of the two species; also the baffling name nurse-hound (in which nurse may be a corruption of huss or hurse, an old dialect name which may itself be a version of hound-fish, which leaves nurse-hound meaning hound-fish-hound!).

CUISINE   This is one of the species which has been sold as rock eel or rock salmon in the U.K. It is satisfactory material for the fish fryer and may also be baked with good results, preferably with the addition of tomatoes.

RECIPES
Dogfish in the Basque style, 279
Saumonette au vin blanc et à la
   crème, 301

SMOOTH HOUND

Family *Triakidae*

Mustelus mustelus (Linnaeus)

REMARKS Maximum length 120 cm. This shark has a dull-grey back. A close relation with which it has often been confused, *Mustelus asterias* Cloquet, has small white spots on its back and sides.

These sharks have a range from the Mediterranean to the North Sea. They have a relation on the American side of the Atlantic, *Mustelus canis* (Mitchill).

The smooth hounds have smooth skins and

Portuguese: Cação, Cachuco
Spanish: Musola, Cazón
French: Emissole
Dutch: Gladde haai
German: Glatthai
Swedish: Glatthaj
Norwegian: Glatthai
Danish: Glathaj
Other: Tolla (Basque)

a rather noticeable ammoniac smell, wherefore the Irish have called it stinkard and the sly folk of Devon, chuckling to themselves, sweet william. The smooth hounds share this last name with another smelly shark, which is better known as the TOPE (French milandre). This is *Galeorhinus galeus* (Linnaeus), a solitary shark which affords sport for the angler from the Mediterranean to Norway and may reach a length of 1½ metres. Its skin is not smooth, but like sandpaper. A drawing of it appears below.

CUISINE The smooth hounds make good eating. They are generally more appreciated in the Mediterranean than elsewhere. What was said about the dogfish on page 168 applies equally to them.

SPUR-DOG

Family *Squalidae*

Squalus acanthias (Linnaeus)

REMARKS Maximum length 120 cm. The spur-dog takes its name from the strong spine in its dorsal fin. It is by far the most common of such spiny sharks in European waters (from the Mediterranean to Norway and Iceland) and in the American Atlantic.

The spur-dog, which grows slowly and may live for a quarter of a century, preys on many fish, crustaceans and molluscs which human beings could otherwise eat. But it is itself marketed on a large scale in Europe. As for American waters, Bigelow and Schroeder allude severely to its 'obnoxious abundance' in the Gulf of Maine and to the

Portuguese: Galhudo
Spanish: Agulat
French: Aiguillat
Dutch: Doornhaai
German: Gemeiner Dornhai
Swedish: Hå, Pigghaj
Norwegian: Pigghå
Danish: Pighaj
Icelandic: Hafur
Other: Picked or Picky dog
(? = spiked dog); Cu-maire
(Scottish); Ci pigog (Welsh);
Fiógach (Irish)

the great damage which it does to stocks of table fish and to fishing gear; and express regret that no way has yet been found of consuming it on a substantial scale in the United States.

The spur-dog is viviparous. The young are born, four to six at a time, in a thin amber-coloured capsule which breaks up and releases them into the mother's oviduct. The doggy nomenclature which applies to all these dogfish is extended to the younglings, who constitute a 'litter' of 'pups'.

CUISINE This particular dogfish is highly rated in some parts of the Mediterranean. It used to be dried on parts of the British coast. Day observes that it was largely eaten by the poor in the Hebrides, where the name Darwin salmon, which must have been the invention of some local wag, was used. In Scandinavia and Holland the spur-dog is still sold in smoked form.

This is certainly one of the better dogfish and may be prepared according to any of the recipes indicated on page 168. It tends to have a strong flavour, which some like to attenuate by provision of a highly flavoured sauce.

ANGEL SHARK, ANGEL FISH, MONKFISH

Family *Squatinidae*

Squatina squatina (Linnaeus)

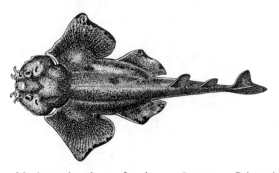

REMARKS Maximum length not far short of 2 metres. The body, which is greyish or sandy above and white below, has a distinctive shape, open to different interpretations. The name monkfish* refers to the fancied appearance of a cowl on its head. Names with angel in them were bestowed because the large pectoral fins were thought to resemble wings, although the Dutch, for example, seem just as ready to call the fish a sea devil as a sea angel, and sea devil occurs in Cornwall also. My own preference is for puppy-fish, another Cornish name. Mongrel skate (cited from the Firth of Forth) is too derogatory.

Portuguese: Peixe anjo, Anjo
Spanish: Angelote
French: Ange de mer
Dutch: Zeeëngel
German: Meerengel
Danish: Havengel

As its flat shape suggests, this shark lives on the bottom. Its range extends from the Mediterranean to Scotland and Denmark (just). On the American side of the Atlantic, another angel shark, *Squatina dumerili* Lesueur, occasionally ascends as far as Cape Cod.

Scientists count the species as a shark, but see it as an evolutionary link between the sharks and the rays.

CUISINE AND RECIPE We often ate this fish in the Mediterranean and found it good. The flesh has a pleasant consistency and taste, and there are no tiresome bones. It is best poached; but pieces may also be fried or baked.

I notice that very few of the fish cookery books in my collection even mention the monkfish. A shining exception is the (undated, ? *c.* 1930) *Daily Express Prize Recipes for Fish Cookery*, which gives seven, including Monkfish and fried apples, which I reproduce on page 457.

---

* The name is also applied to the angler-fish (page 161).

THORNBACK RAY

Family *Rajidae*

Raja clavata Linnaeus

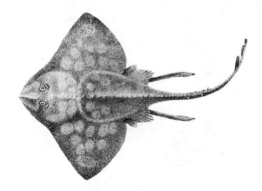

REMARKS   Maximum length 85 cm. The colour of the back is usually a mottled grey or fawn. The back also bears coarse prickles which, in adults, develop into spines with swollen, bony bases (or bucklers). Females have these on their bellies also.

This, the most abundant ray in British waters, has a range from the Mediterranean to Norway and Iceland. It is essentially a sedentary species, but makes local migrations at certain seasons, in unisexual shoals; thus fishermen will catch large numbers of either males or females but not both.

Like the dogfish, rays lay their eggs in little capsules which are often seen cast up on the beach and are called mermaids' purses.

The thornback is an important fish com-

Portuguese: Raia pregada, Lenga
Spanish: Raya de clavos
French: Raie bouclée
Dutch: Stekelrog
German: Keulenrochen, Nagelrochen
Polish: Raja nabijana
Russian: Shipovatÿi skat
Swedish: Knaggrocka
Norwegian: Piggskate
Danish: Sømrokke
Icelandic: Drøfnuskata
Other: Roker (East Anglia); Cath fôr (Welsh); Bastanga (Basque)

mercially. It is taken in large quantities and is generally held to be among the best rays for eating. The learned Piscator gives top marks jointly to it and to the spotted ray, which appears on the next page.

CUISINE   The best of the rays and skates make excellent eating. I have explained on page 164 why they have an ammoniac smell and why this need not put off the cook.

When you have bought a wing of ray or skate cut it across into strips about an inch wide and keep these for a while in cold water with lots of salt 'which will extract every rank taint, and impart a more white and delicate appearance to the flesh' (Piscator). This is not necessary, but it does help. You may then choose between a wide variety of preparations, of which the most famous is Raie au beurre noir. This is not among the recipes listed below, for it has been described as well as it ever will be by Elizabeth David in *French Provincial Cooking*, and I can hardly reproduce her account of it *again*, having already done so in a Mediterranean context. I do, however, strongly recommend the last two of the recipes listed.

Spencer and Cobb, who, despite the general neglect of rays in the United States, devote seven pages of recipes to them (in *Fish Cookery*, Boston, 1922), point out that advantage may be taken of the resemblance in texture between the flesh of the ray and crabmeat, as in their recipe on page 428. Others see a resemblance to lobster. 'This fish used to be esteemed, when eaten *cold* with mustard and vinegar, quite a grande régale by those sober citizens of Edinburgh who repaired on holidays to the fishing hamlets round the city. It is thought to eat like lobster – by persons of lively imagination.' (Meg Dods.)

Small rays (raitons in France, maids in England) may be simply cleaned, skinned, floured and fried. Their 'bones' will be tender enough to eat.

RECIPES

Pickled ray (Belgian), 309
Skate livers on toast, 309
Crab and skate salad, 428

Fricasseed skate, 456
Picnic skate pie, 456

SPOTTED RAY, HOMELYN RAY   Family *Rajidae*

Raja montagui Fowler

Portuguese: Raia pintada
Spanish: Raya pintada
French: Raie douce
Dutch: Gladde rog

REMARKS   Maximum length 75 cm. The back is brownish with small black spots.

The range of this ray is from the Mediterranean to Shetland.

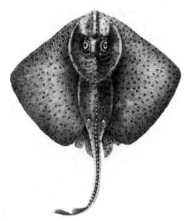

STARRY RAY; THORNY SKATE (U.S.A.)

Family *Rajidae*

Raja radiata Donovan

REMARKS Maximum length 1 metre in American waters, but only 50 cm in European waters. This is a ray of the Arctic Sea and of northern waters on both sides of the Atlantic. It usually has a light brown back, with cream marbling, black spots and noticeable thorns or prickles.

Dutch: Keilrog
German: Sternroche
Swedish: Klorocka
Norwegian: Kloskate
Danish: Tærbe
Icelandic: Tindaskata

CUISINE The starry ray is eaten in northern Europe, where it has some commercial importance, but is only used for the production of fish meal on the American side. However, not all Americans neglect the rays and skates. Euell Gibbons, in *Stalking the Blue-eyed Scallop*, drew the attention of his readers to *Raja erinacea* Mitchill, the LITTLE or COMMON SKATE, the species which North American anglers are most likely to capture. I show a drawing of this species on the right. Its French Canadian name is raie hérisson. It grows to a length of 60 to 70 cm only, but Gibbons, ever alert to unused foodstuffs, pointed out that it is not merely edible but good, and that in his experience its wings, suitably cut up, could be treated like scallops. I have been told, however, that this practice is more often carried out on *Raja ocellata* (Mitchill), the winter skate, or *Symnura micrura* (B. and S.), the smooth butterfly ray.

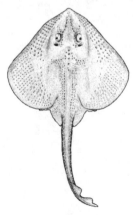

SKATE

Family *Rajidae*

Raja batis Linnaeus

REMARKS This deep-water species grows to a length of about 2 metres. It has a grey or brown back with lighter spots and black dots; the underside is blue-grey or ash, with spots. It is shown in the upper drawing.

Note the long snout. That of **Raja oxyrhynchus** Linnaeus, shown in the lower drawing, is even longer; so it is called the LONG-NOSE SKATE. This is known in France as pocheteau noir, or as raie capucin, after the hood of a Capucin friar, or by the mysterious name tyre, at Boulogne.

Raja batis ranges from the Mediterranean to northern Norway and Iceland. Its counterpart in North American waters is **Raja laevis** Mitchill, the barndoor skate.

Portuguese: Airoga, Raia
Spanish: Noriega
French: Pocheteau (blanc)
Dutch: Vleet
German: Glattroche
Polish: Raja gladka
Russian: Serȳi skat
Swedish: Slatrokka
Norwegian: Storskate, Glattskate
Danish: Skade
Icelandic: Skata
Other: Scat (Ireland); Blue skate (Scotland) and Dinnan (Aberdeen)

Day has an interesting passage about this fish. 'The skate is frequently taken off the Irish coast having a hook in one of its fins, for the natives of Ireland, when they find them on their lines, cut them off close to the hook sooner than be troubled with unhooking the fish. These hooks are so common near the end of the fin that it has been inferred that the skate has used the waving motion of the fin to bring the bait near its mouth, and so doing has got the hook into its body.'

CUISINE As for the other rays, page 173. Quite good in quality. St John's College, Cambridge, once served one weighing 200 pounds, which fed 120 persons.

LAMPREY, SEA LAMPREY   Family *Petromyzonidae*

Petromyzon marinus (Linnaeus)

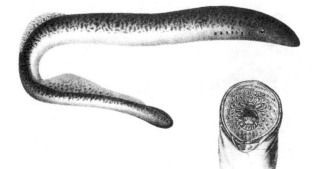

REMARKS   This slimy and antique creature may reach a length of 90 cm. It has a greenish-grey, bluish-brown or olive-brown back.

The class *Marsipobranchii*, to which the lamprey belongs, is a small one, and its members have the distinction of being the most primitive of living vertebrates.

The lamprey has no proper bones or jaw. Its head is adorned by a single nostril on top, seven little gill openings on each side, and a suctorial 'mouth' or pad armed with teeth underneath. Hieronymus Bosch might well have invented this creature if it had not existed already.

Portuguese: Lampreia do mar
Spanish: Lamprea de mar
French: Lamproie marine
Dutch: Zeeprik
German: Meerneunauge, Seelamprete
Polish: Minog morski
Russian: Morskaya minoga
Finnish: Merinahkiainen
Swedish: Havsnejonoga
Norwegian: Hav-niauge, Havlamprett
Danish: Havlampret

The lamprey is anadromous like the salmon, and is more often met in rivers than at sea. It also has a freshwater relation, the river lamprey or lampern.

On the American side of the Atlantic, the lamprey used to be eaten in Massachusetts and Connecticut, for example. The note on the next page gives a pleasing vignette of lamprey fishing in those days. And some Canadians still eat lamprey. But Americans no longer do, regarding it instead as a pure nuisance for the havoc which it causes among stocks of other and more desirable fish, such as whitefish and trout in fresh waters, and salmon, cod and many other fish which the lamprey attacks at sea.

The lamprey, Boschian in behaviour as in construction, attaches itself to its victim by means of the suctorial pad, and then rasps and sucks away until it has made a meal of the victim's blood. Such attacks are fatal when the victim is small; and they do no good at all to larger fish, such as salmon.

On the European side, however, the depredations of the lamprey are less noticeable and there are various places where the lamprey itself is still eaten. One such is Portugal, where the village of Moncao on the Minho River is the centre of a busy lamprey-fishing season from early in the year until late April. Another is the Bordeaux region of France, where one firm produces tins of an excellent conserve de lamproie à la bordelaise. Further north, smoked lamprey is a speciality of Pori and Rauma in Finland.

However, consumption of lampreys has diminished, especially in England. One hears no more of potted Severn lamprey, although this was famous in its day. Old English cookery books contain many recipes for the lamprey. To take a random example from my shelves, Richard Briggs (*The English Art of Cookery*, 1788) gives recipes for frying, stewing, roasting and baking lampreys. But sixty years later there is but a single recipe in Soyer's *Gastronomic Regenerator*; and in the present century it is rare to find even a mention of the lamprey.

CUISINE AND RECIPES   The lamprey looks rather like an eel, and recipes for eel, listed on page 75, may in general be applied to the lamprey too. I suggest, however, that you do not try to do anything with smoked lamprey, and that you marinate fresh lamprey for a while before cooking it. The advantages of marination became very clear to those who made the Queen's Jubilee lamprey pie, for which the recipe is given on page 450. A marinade also plays a part in the famous Portuguese recipe for lamprey, given on page 268.*

NOTE   The Hartford (Connecticut) *Post* of June 1876 carried a piece headed 'Curious Habits of Lamprey Eels', about two gentlemen from Granby who had caught 110 lampreys near Hartford.

The method of taking these eels is quite novel. They are found only in shallow water, with stony or gravelly bottom, and the fisherman goes provided with a large bag of netting, the mouth of the bag being distended with a hoop, and an instrument of iron about eighteen inches long terminating in a hook.

The Eels have what are called nests, made by heaping up stones in a circle of about eighteen inches in diameter. These stones they place in this position by fastening their sucker mouths thereon and moving themselves laterally, drawing the stones along with them. Inside this circle of stones lie usually from three to five Eels, parallel with one another, their heads all in one direction and each Eel made fast by suction to a stone. The bold fisherman approaches them from behind, and, skilfully putting his hook under an Eel, he suddenly brings it up with such force that it penetrates the hide, and brings out the fish, when, after two or three flourishes in the air to get him in the right position, he is deposited in the bag. Each Eel in the nest is in turn made the subject of a similar operation, the creatures often holding on to the stone with such tenacity as to bring it out of the water with them . . .

These Eels, it is said, are wholly free from bones save the backbone, which is removed in dressing, and when salted for a few weeks and fried make an article of food second to none in the way of fish.

* It is, incidentally, interesting to note that the very earliest Portuguese cookery book contains only one fish recipe, and that is for lampreys. The book in question is the *Livro de Cozinha* of the Infanta D. Maria de Portugal, a fifteenth-century codex which recently came to light in the National Library at Naples.

In a Class by Itself: the Sturgeon

To be exact, I should have headed this: 'In a Sub-class by Itself'. We have just been surveying the non-bony fish. Previously we had looked at the more numerous bony fish. Now we come to the sturgeon, of which the skeleton is only bony in part, and which some authorities have therefore placed in a special sub-class of bony fish. One might call it a semi-bony fish.

The sturgeon which swim around today are remarkably similar to the sturgeon of 100 million years ago, as we can tell from the fossilized remains of the latter. Their backbone is cartilaginous; but they have five rows of bony scutes along their bodies and the head is covered with hard bony plates. This same head has a snout, underneath which sprout four barbels. By burrowing with the snout and feeling with the barbels the sturgeon can find its food on the sea or river bottom.

In previous centuries this valuable fish was fairly common in European waters. Quite large numbers were taken, especially when they entered rivers to spawn. Now, however, there are few. The only surviving eastern Atlantic populations are based on the rivers Gironde in France and Guadalquivir in Spain and at Lake Ladoga in the Soviet Union. The sturgeon fishery in the Gironde estuary is of some importance. Since Monsieur Prunier (of the famous Paris restaurant) took a holiday there after the First World War, perceived the neglected opportunity and dispatched a knowledgeable Russian émigré to the region, caviar has been produced there. French regulations about adding preservatives differ from Russian and Iranian ones and this French caviar is therefore sold after only a light salting. It is best eaten fresh in the region (during June and July at Talmont and Saint-Neurin), but it does travel under refrigeration and accounts for over a quarter of the twenty-five tons of caviar consumed annually in France.

The scarcity of the sturgeon on the European side of the Atlantic makes eating it a rare treat. However, the position on the American side is rather more favourable. It gave me quite a start when visiting the fish market at Washington D.C. in 1975 (a picturesque floating market, mounted on decommissioned fishing boats in the Potomac, the purpose being partly no doubt aesthetic but also to remove the fishmongers from the jurisdiction of the District of Columbia authorities) and beheld three sturgeon lying side by side, for sale at a most reasonable price. They were less than a metre long and were said to have been taken on the southern shore of Chesapeake Bay, in Maryland.

The sturgeon fishery in the United States was formerly an important one, producing caviar as well as sturgeon meat. ('Meat' seems a particularly appropriate term for pink flesh which resembles veal in taste and which was once known as 'Albany beef' in New York State, a name derived, according to De Voe, who took a particular interest in this piece of nomenclature as he was himself a butcher, 'from its great plentifulness, cheapness and peculiar colour of the flesh'.) *A Report on the Sturgeon Fishery of Delaware River and Bay* by John N. Cobb (1899) recalls that: 'The earliest settlers to this country were especially struck at the immense numbers of sturgeon seen in the Delaware, and their letters to the home folk in England and Germany contain frequent references testifying to their wonderment.' William Penn himself made a special note of the fish; and there were times when a man could speak of having seen several thousand of them together. By the end of the nineteenth century the catch had declined, but the fishery itself was still quite elaborate. Legislation had been passed to prevent other fishermen catching or harming young sturgeon (known as mammoses). Over 1000 men were engaged in the sturgeon fishery in Delaware and Pennsylvania. Fishing was done by gill net; and the catch was classified as 'cows' (females with hard roe), 'runners' (females with soft spawn running out of them), 'slunkers' (females which had already spawned) and 'bucks' (males). The last three categories were valued only for the meat. The caviar from the 'cows' amounted to a quarter of a million pounds or more, by weight, in a season and was mostly shipped to Germany.

The catalogue entry which follows is devoted to the European Sturgeon, *Acipenser sturio*. The American Atlantic species is a different one, **Acipenser oxyrhynchus** Mitchill. I show a drawing of it below, together with the smaller SHORTNOSE STURGEON, **Acipenser brevirostrum** Lesueur, which is found in limited numbers in northern waters; for example in New Brunswick in Canada. There seems to be no organized fishery for the shortnose sturgeon, but I know one marine biologist at St Andrews, N.B., who manages to keep himself and his friends supplied with caviar from this source.

STURGEON

Family *Acipenseridae*

Acipenser sturio Linnaeus

REMARKS   Maximum length about 4 metres. I have already given some description of this antique creature on the preceding pages. Here I point out that the German name Stör is the root of many other names, including the English and French ones; and that it is probably derived from the verb störer, to root about, which is what the sturgeon does when seeking food.

Portuguese: Esturjão
Spanish: Esturión
French: Esturgeon
Dutch: Steur
German: Stör
Polish: Jesiotr
Russian: Osëtr Baltiĭskiĭ
Finnish: Sampi
Swedish: Stör
Norwegian: Stør
Danish: Stør
Icelandic: Styrja
Other: Créat (Gironde)

CUISINE   It is commonly said that the flesh of the sturgeon is like veal and that it may be accommodated in similar ways, e.g. by roasting it. This is so. (cf. my *Mediterranean Seafood*.) Here I offer the two recipes listed below and this admirably succinct one from Piscator, writing in the mid nineteenth century, when sturgeon was fairly common in England. 'Sturgeon should be cut up in slices of about an inch, or a little more, in thickness, which, being half-fried, should be placed in a stewpan with some good veal broth, an onion, and a bundle of sweet herbs, and be allowed to stew until it becomes perfectly tender. Having then fried an onion or two in the butter in which the fish was previously fried, pour this, and also the gravy in which the fish was stewed, into a saucepan, adding to it a glass or two of wine, some butter rolled in flour ... and a spoonful of ketchup ... As soon as the whole has boiled up well together, strain it through a sieve ... and pour it over the fish. Garnish with sliced lemon.'

I also recommend smoked sturgeon, if you can get it.

RECIPES

3. Catalogue of Crustaceans

Shrimps, Prawns and Lobsters

Most Americans use the name shrimp to include what are, in British usage, both shrimp and prawns. I say most, because I am told that at San Francisco, for example, something close to the British terminology is employed. The confusion here seems to be inevitable, since these names cut across the scientific classifications and cannot be reconciled with them or with each other. The difficulty, and the subsidiary question whether the plural of shrimp is shrimp or shrimps, can only be acknowledged, popular usage being too well established to permit any remedy.

European travellers will wish to know that most Mediterranean prawns have a range which extends into Portuguese and Spanish waters in the Atlantic. These species are described in my *Mediterranean Seafood.**

So far, in most parts of the world, man has not attempted or bothered to eat anything shrimp-like smaller than the common shrimp. However, the oceans abound in much smaller crustaceans such as amphipods and copepods; and these are edible. In South-East Asia they enter into the composition of certain shrimp pastes. The Russians have recently been using them for a similar purpose. And Dr Schmitt, in his highly readable book *Crustaceans*, reminds us that the few survivors of the Greely Expedition to the Arctic, who were rescued in June 1884, owed their lives to amphipods which they caught in nets made from pieces of sacking and baited with bones and scraps of meat or seal skin. As their journal for 25 March 1884 records: 'the shrimps are now mixed with our stews, and are quite palatable. The minute animals have opened up to us a new avenue of escape.' Looking to the future, when these resources may be exploited on a large scale, I have begun to collect recipes for krill, the collective noun which applies to them, but some time is likely to pass before they have practical application for private persons.

---

* For convenience I mention here that in Portugal the common prawn is **Parapenaeus longirostris** (Lucas), known as gamba in both Portugal and Spain. One might also meet **Aristeus antennatus** (Risso) as gamba rosada in Portugal or carabinero in Spain; and the dark red **Aristeomorphus foliacea** (Risso) as gamba vermelho in Portugal and langostino moruno in Spain. Both these last two species may be called carabineiro in Portugal.

SHRIMP; BROWN SHRIMP (U.K.) Family *Crangonidae*

Crangon crangon (Linnaeus)

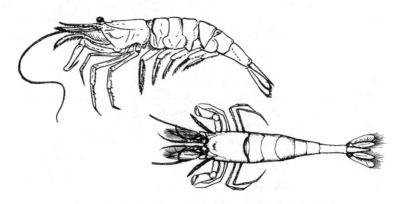

REMARKS Maximum length only 6 cm. This little creature, shown on the left in side view, is greyish or brownish in life, and translucent. It lives on sandy ground and has the ability to change its colour to match whatever sand it is on (or in, since it often burrows into the sand, leaving only the antennae projecting). Its range is from the Mediterranean to Norway.

Portuguese: Camarão negro
Spanish: Qúisquilla
French: Crevette grise
Dutch: Garnaal
German: Garnele, Krabbe
Polish: Garnela
Russian: Seraya krevetka
Finnish: Hietakatkarapu
Swedish: Sandräka
Norwegian: Hestereke
Danish: Hestereje, Sandhest
Other: Perdysen (Welsh);
  Sauterelle (Boulogne)

Crangon septemspinosa Say, its American equivalent, is found from Baffin Bay to Florida. It is shown on the right, viewed from above.

The shrimp fishery in England used to be very extensive. Large harvests were collected from rich grounds in the Severn estuary and, best of all, Morecambe Bay. But the cost of labour has caused the fishery to decline.

In Morecambe Bay one used to be able to see shrimp fishermen at work on horseback. Nowadays, however, I believe that it is only on the Belgian coast, near Oostduinkerke, that one can still see the sight; and even there the practice has almost died out. Fortunately, it has been recorded both in a book (*Garnalenvissers te paard*, by Frans van Immerseel) and in tiles on the walls of the restaurant Chez Vincent in Brussels.

CUISINE Shrimp are to be boiled for a few minutes, just long enough to cook them and turn them brown. Many French people are then willing to eat them whole, but the custom in most countries is to pick out the meat from the tiny tail. This is tedious, but children may enjoy the work if they have the prospect of a shrimp tea to follow.

The best thing to do with the cooked and picked shrimps is to pot them in butter. It is traditional in England to add a very little mace and nutmeg. Other flavours could be added. Lady Clark of Tillypronie used one pounded anchovy for each ¼ kg (½ lb) pot. But I think it better to use just one drop of anchovy essence, as in Betsy Tatterstall's shrimp paste.

RECIPES

Potatoes stuffed with shrimps, 309
Horseback fishermen's scallop dish
  of shrimps (Belgian), 310
Shrimp croquettes (Belgian), 310
Shrimp sauce (Dutch), 319

Pea soup with shrimps, 329
Shrimps on rye bread with a fried egg
  (German), 329
Betsy Tatterstall's shrimp paste, 459

PRAWN, COMMON PRAWN   Family *Palaemonidae*

Palaemon serratus (Pennant)

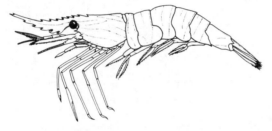

REMARKS Maximum length 10 cm, market length from 7 or 8 cm. Alive, these prawns are almost colourless; after being cooked, a fine orange-red.

This is a prawn of inshore waters. It walks forward, searching for food: looking with its stalked eyes, feeling with its antennae and sweeping the bottom with its second pair of legs. If disturbed, it will shoot backwards by a rapid flexing and straightening of its abdomen. It has an extensive range, from Norway to the Mediterranean.

Portuguese: Camarão branco
Spanish: Camarón, Gamba
French: Crevette rose, Bouquet
Dutch: Steurgarnaal
German: Sägegarnele
Swedish: Tångräka
Norwegian: Strandreke
Danish: Roskildereje
Other: Corgimwch (Welsh)

CUISINE For small specimens, see under shrimp above; for larger ones, see page 185.

BROWN SHRIMP (U.S.A.)   Family *Penaeidae*
Penaeus aztecus aztecus Ives

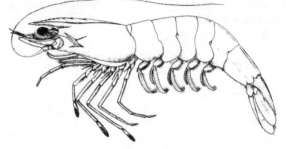

REMARKS   Maximum length of females, which grow larger than the males, is over 20 cm; usual market length 5 to 16 cm. The body is normally brownish in colour, but red, orange and green individuals occur. This species is fished from North Carolina southwards. In most years it is taken in larger quantities than any other American shrimp.

The closely related *Penaeus duorarum duorarum* Burkenroad, not shown because it is a more southerly species, is the pink shrimp, although it is not always pink.

WHITE SHRIMP (U.S.A.)   Family *Penaeidae*
Penaeus setiferus (Linnaeus)

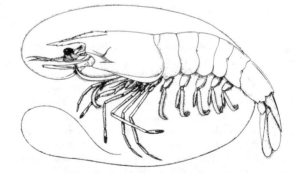

REMARKS   Maximum length of females 20 cm, of males 17 cm; usual market length 5 to 15 cm. Note the very long antennae. The body is usually translucent white, but may have tinges of colour sufficient to warrant the names grey shrimp and green shrimp, or may be tinged with blue.

The white shrimp is most abundant from the Carolinas southwards. It comes into season later than the brown shrimp.

DEEP-WATER PRAWN, NORTHERN PRAWN

Family *Pandalidae*

Pandalus borealis Krøyer

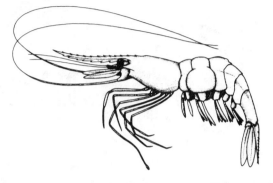

REMARKS Maximum length 12 cm. The colour of this prawn in life is red, but, since it is a deep-water species and usually cooked at sea after capture, few people ever see it alive. Its range extends from Greenland (where it is called kingugssvaq) down to Martha's Vineyard in the west and Britain in the east. It is fished in large quantities, by otter-trawl, in Norwegian waters.

French: Crevette nordique
Dutch: Noorse steurgarnaal
German: Tiefseegarnele
Russian: Glubokovodnaya krevetka
Swedish: Nordhavsräka
Danish: Dybhavsreje
Icelandic: Kampalampi

The smaller species ***Pandalus montagui*** Leach also occurs in British waters. It may be distinguished by the red and white stripes on the antennae, rather like a barber's pole. It is often referred to as the pink shrimp.

CUISINE FOR PRAWNS (AMERICAN SHRIMP) IN GENERAL, AND RECIPES
What you eat are the tails. These are easily peeled if you buy ready-cooked prawns. Uncooked prawns can be peeled, but it is easier to do so after cooking them for 3 to 10 minutes, according to size, in lightly salted boiling water. Although only the tails are eaten, the other parts yield flavour, so there is some advantage in buying whole prawns.

A dark thread-like gut runs along the back of the tail, just below the surface. This should be removed from all but the smaller specimens.

Once you have your cooked tail meats you can serve them with rice, a happy combination; or make them into a soup; or batter and deep-fry them; or sauté them; or use them in a salad or as a garnish for other fish dishes. Recipes given in this book include Belgian shrimp croquettes (page 310) and a bevy of American recipes which are grouped together on pages 432 to 434.

DUBLIN BAY PRAWN, NORWAY LOBSTER

Family *Nephropsidae*

Nephrops norvegicus (Linnaeus)

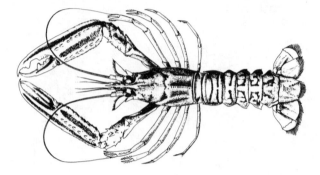

REMARKS Maximum length, not counting the claws, 24 cm. The carapace is pale pink, rose or orange-red; the claws are banded in red and white.

The Norway lobster lives on a muddy sea bottom, in burrows, from which it emerges at night to seek food. Its range is from Iceland down to Morocco and the west and central Mediterranean. There is a numerous colony in the Adriatic, which has for long been exploited by the Italians.

Portuguese: Lagostim
Spanish: Cigala *
French: Langoustine
Dutch: Noorse kreeft
German: Kaisergranat
Swedish: Havskräfta
Norwegian: Sjøkreps, Bokstavhummer
Danish: Jomfruhummer
Icelandic: Leturhumar

The penny dropped more slowly in some of the Atlantic countries. Until the 1950s British fishermen usually discarded any Norway lobsters which they caught. But the species has gained enormously in popularity, to such an extent that 'scampi' (the plural of the Italian name) are almost an obligatory feature of restaurant menus in Britain, and it is now the most valuable crustacean catch off the Scottish coasts. French and Danish fishermen also take large quantities. The continental practice is to sell the creatures whole, alive or cooked. A common British practice is to separate the tails and freeze them (this breaks down the membrane which holds the meat to the carapace); thaw, shell, clean and refreeze them. This procedure provides firm meat with a sweet shellfish taste, although it leaves one without the delicious little pieces of meat in the claws.

But I have still to explain the name Dublin Bay prawn and to give the Irish their due for perceiving long ago the merits of this crustacean. It is not, in fact, an inhabitant of Dublin Bay. The name was bestowed because the fishing boats coming into Dublin Bay often had these prawns on board, having caught them

* Confusing (see page 191); but the name langostina is also used.

incidentally. Since they were not fish, the fishermen could dispose of them on the side to the Dublin street-vendors, of whom Molly Malone of the well-known song became the archetype. So the prawns were called Dublin Bay prawns, because out in the bay was where the vendors got them.

Another pleasant name for these prawns is demoiselles de Cherbourg.

CUISINE AND RECIPES As for prawns (page 185), but these are larger creatures and will need a longer cooking time if you do the cooking yourself. The tails are particularly good when deep-fried or served cold with a mayonnaise. They can also be brushed with olive oil and grilled; and other suitable recipes will be found in books on Mediterranean cookery. The recipes given in this book are for Dublin Bay prawn cocktail, page 474, and Dublin Bay prawns in carragheen aspic, page 476.

MANTIS SHRIMP   Family *Squillidae*

Squilla empusa Say

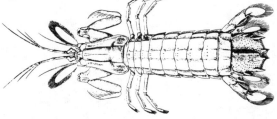

REMARKS This unusual creature belongs to the Order *Stomatopoda* and might be better grouped with the crabs; but it looks like a prawn and bears names like shrimp, so is presented here. It has a maximum length of about 25 cm and is of a yellowish-green colour; each segment of the carapace being bordered with darker green and edged with yellow. Of its five pairs of legs, those at the front are extensions of the mouth, while the next pair are large ones used for grasping food; an arrangement reminiscent of the praying mantis. The creature lives in holes in the mud below low-water mark on the eastern seaboard of the U.S.A.

Its European counterpart, **Squilla mantis** (Linnaeus), is brown-grey in colour. It is zagaia in Portugal (although the names castanheta, galera and lagostim may also be used), galera in Spain, and squille in France. It does not seem to be found further north.

CUISINE Mantis shrimp are not often seen in European or American markets (except in the Mediterranean and at Hawaii), which is a pity. They are good in fish soups and may even be used to make a special mantis shrimp soup; or may be steamed with herbs, or boiled, and subsequently treated like prawns.

LOBSTER (both EUROPEAN and AMERICAN)

Family *Nephropsidae*

Homarus gammarus (Linnaeus) and *Homarus americanus* Milne Edwards

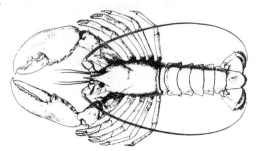

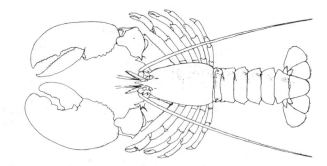

REMARKS The European and American lobsters resemble each other closely, but the American is the larger. It is difficult to give maximum dimensions. In the past, before the lobster fisheries were as intensive as they now are, some lobsters lived to a great age and a great size. One taken off the coast of Virginia in the 1930s weighed about 20 kg (44 lb) and was well over a metre long. But nowadays a lobster of half this size would be considered a giant.

The colour of the live lobster varies according to its habitat, but is usually dark blue or greenish. After being cooked, it is red; 'like a cardinal's hat', as one French writer put it.

Portuguese: Lavagante
Spanish: Bogavante
French: Homard
Dutch: Kreeft, Zeekreeft
German: Hummer
Polish: Homar
Russian: Omar
Finnish: Hummeri
Swedish: Hummer
Norwegian: Hummer
Danish: Hummer
Icelandic: Humar
Other: Legrest (Brittany); Cimwch (Welsh)

The range of the European lobster is from the far north down to the Mediterranean. The American lobster occurs as far south as South Carolina. Their habits are such that they can only be caught in special lobster pots, and the fishery for them is a relatively expensive and arduous one. Partly for this reason, the lobster has become one of the most costly seafoods in the world. In North America it is the Maine lobster which is most famous; but this fact merely reflects the hard work put in by Maine publicists. The Canadian catch is more than twice the size of the United States one, and the southern part of the Gulf of St Lawrence is the richest lobster-breeding ground in the world.

Most sea creatures have worse enemies than man. Whales are an exception; so are adult lobsters. Baby and small lobsters fall prey to predators of their own element; but those which reach a respectable size are able to defend themselves very well. The stalked eyes give the lobster good warning of impending danger. The powerful abdomen, snapped down, will propel it backwards at an astonishing speed into a rocky crevice. The claws are formidable weapons in combat; and the shell (properly, the exo-skeleton) is an effective armour. However, since the shell is rigid, it has to be shed periodically as the lobster grows (cf. pages 200 and 201 on the 'moulting' of crabs). Immediately after moulting, the lobster is a sorry sight, and as defenceless as a medieval knight who has doffed his armour. The body is soft and the claws shrunken and shapeless. Although the lobster quickly swells to its new size and starts to develop a new exo-skeleton, it is not good to eat at the time. The swelling up to the new size is largely accomplished by absorbing a lot of water; the meat is therefore watery and not at all like the firm flesh which lobster-eaters expect.

CUISINE   Lobsters are often bought ready-cooked. All that is then necessary is to open them up and extract the meat. To do this, lay the lobster on its back and insert the point of a strong kitchen knife into the joint between body and tail. Bring the handle of the knife firmly down towards the tail fin, thus splitting the tail end in two. Replace the point of the knife where you had it before and split the body in the same way. Crack the claws. Everything which you have now exposed is edible, except for the dark gut which runs along the tail section and the little pouch of grit at the top of the head. Some people only eat the white meat, after cutting it into neat slices and lavishing a few more expensive ingredients on it; but it is a great mistake to waste the creamy substance and the green liver (tomalley) in the body, or of course the coral (roe) of a hen lobster.

If you have a live lobster, you can follow the directions from Heligoland or Maine, listed below. You may wish to know that, according to the Universities Federation for Animal Welfare in Britain, the most humane method of killing a lobster is to plunge it into water which is already boiling.

RECIPES

SPINY LOBSTER, CRAYFISH, CRAWFISH

Family *Palinuridae*

Palinurus elephas (Fabricius)
Palinurus vulgaris

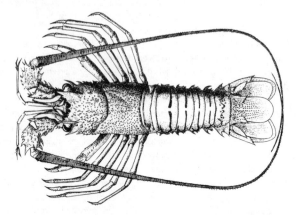

REMARKS Maximum length 50 cm. The most obvious difference between the spiny lobster and the true lobster is that the former does not have the huge claws which are such a noticeable feature of the latter.

This species of spiny lobster is reddish brown or brown in colour, with yellow and white markings. It has a range extending from the Mediterranean to south-western England, and is rare in waters further north. The Gulf Stream may, however, carry young spiny lobsters as far as the west coast of Norway, where conditions permit them to survive and grow but not to reproduce. The marine biological station at Espegrend made a pet of one such and preserved in glass jars the exo-skeletons which it shed annually. The pigments which give the spiny lobster its colours lie below, not in, the exo-skeleton. So there are six successive jars containing ghostly and colourless carapaces, each bigger than the last. The seventh jar contains the spiny lobster itself, all of it with all its colour. It had been misguided enough to pull the plug out of its own tank one day, and had expired before its plight was noticed. The sight startled me, for I happened to have been musing on the seven stages of the life of man, and on the extent to which the earlier stages in one's life may be said still to exist in whatever is one's current stage, these being the sort of questions which

Portuguese: Lagosta *
Spanish: Langosta
French: Langouste
Dutch: Langoest
German: Languste
Swedish: Languster
Norwegian: Languster
Danish: Languster
Icelandic: Humrar
Other: Otarraina (Basque)

* Specifically, lagosta castanha; *Palinurus mauritanicus* Gruvel also occurs in Portuguese waters and is known as lagosta rósea.

spontaneously occur to anyone stranded for an evening in the main railway station of Oslo; and here in these glass jars, so it seemed, some kind of answer was being displayed.

Spiny lobsters hardly occur at all on the American side of the North Atlantic, although *Panulirus argus* (Latreille) may occasionally be found as far north as the Carolinas. The supply of spiny lobsters on the European side is limited. Where demand is highest, notably in Paris, consignments will be brought to the markets from surprisingly remote places, such as North Africa and even South America. Elsewhere, local catches tend to be sold at the port of landing.

Although the spiny lobster is often called crawfish or crayfish, it is, of course, quite different from the small freshwater crayfish.

CUISINE AND RECIPES As for the lobster.

FLAT LOBSTER, SLIPPER LOBSTER Family *Scyllaridae*

Scyllarus arctus (Linnaeus)

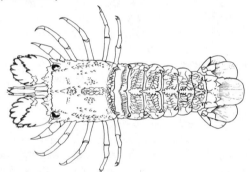

REMARKS Maximum length 14 cm. This creature is like a lobster without claws. Its larger relation, *Scyllarides latus* (Latreille), reaches a length of over 40 cm, but is not found north of the Mediterranean and the Iberian Peninsula. They both make cricket-like noises in the water, which accounts for most of their common names; while a supposed resemblance to a slipper accounts for others.

Portuguese: Cigarra do mar, Lagosta da pedra
Spanish: Cigarra de mar
French: Cigale, Petite cigale
German: Barenkrebs
Danish: Bjornekrebs

The corresponding American species, *Scyllarides nodifer* Stimpson and *Scyllarus depressus* Smith, are both found in North Carolina, for example, but seem to be ignored. (Americans import a related species from Australia as slipper lobster; and use the name rock lobster for imported spiny lobsters.)

CUISINE The meat of the tail is good; but there is not much of it in this particular species, which is therefore often condemned to the soup-pot.

Crabs and the Goose-necked Barnacle

The catalogue of crustaceans continues with the horseshoe crab, a member of the sub-phylum of arachnids, not a real crustacean; the crabs proper, which belong to the Order *Decapoda reptantia* or ten-footed crawlers, not the best of names since many of them are swimming crabs; and the goose-necked barnacle, a creature which belongs to the Order *Cirripedia*. There is good material here, on both sides of the Atlantic. The submarine palm for excellence should perhaps be awarded to the blue crab for which Chesapeake Bay is famous, but the edible crab of Europe is just about as good.

Crabs are reasonably cheap. Sometimes they are very cheap. I was startled when staying in Orkney to find a small boy at my host's door with a bucketful of large 'partans', as the edible crab is known there, which he wished to sell at 3p each. I suppose that the partans tasted particularly good to me because they were so cheap and so freshly caught. I certainly had the impression that no lobster or other more expensive fare could have been better. But many people do tend to relate desirability to price, and therefore pine constantly for lobsters and scampi, without realizing that price depends on abundance and that it is manifestly absurd to suppose that there is a necessary relationship between abundance and excellence.

Anyway, my view is that crabs are first-class food and that any cook will do well to learn about them, both large and small. It is true that the smaller ones are finicky to prepare, but they can always be used for a crab soup.

I conclude by displaying another small crustacean which can be eaten almost whole. It is **Hippa talpoida** Say, the SAND-BUG, which has a range from Cape Cod to Florida. It is thoroughly neglected there, except by Americans who have shared with the royal family of Thailand (and with me) the experience of eating these little creatures (*Hippa asiatica* in that part of the world) deep-fried and dunked in jungle honey. They are delicious in flavour and admirably crunchy; and one can eat them by the score.

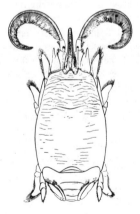

HORSESHOE CRAB

Family *Limulidae*

Limulus polyphemus (Linnaeus)

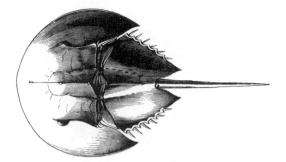

REMARKS   The full length of this strange creature is about 30 cm. It is often referred to as a 'living fossil', since it has been around for something like 200 million years. There are now only two populations of horseshoe crabs, *Limulus polyphemus* on the American coast from Maine to Mexico and two related species in South-East Asia, one of which is much bigger. All of these creatures are nowadays classified as arachnids, but to the layman they are of course crabs and it is as crabs that I present them in this catalogue.

The horseshoe crab has blood, bluish in colour, which Asians take care to use in cooking it (see my *Seafood of South-East Asia*). It also has other peculiarities. For example, it cannot eat unless it is moving. As it travels along the sea bed, like a little bulldozer, with the rim of its shell under the mud, the front pincers gather edible organisms, which the legs then grind and pass into the abdominal mouth. The telson or tail is on a jointed socket and can be used to right the crab if it is turned on its back. (In the Singapore aquarium I once witnessed the poignant sight of a horseshoe crab which had only the stump of its telson and was on its back; a situation which could only be relieved, eventually, by death.)

When the females come out of the water to lay their eggs, males (sometimes several in a string) ride on their backs. This has caused people in Thailand to dub these crabs, or the males at least, pimps.

Horseshoe crabs have been remarkably abundant on the New Jersey coast. Richard Rathbun (see Bibliography) tells an amusing tale of a ship's master who collected a cargo of sand there, put out to sea and then found that most of the grains of 'sand' hatched into baby horseshoe crabs, so that the whole cargo had to be jettisoned.

CUISINE   The proportion of meat to shell is small, but what meat there is is edible, and has sometimes been eaten in the Middle Atlantic States. The crab itself should be detached from the huge carapace before being prepared. I feel sure that the South-East Asian preference for 'berried', i.e. egg-carrying, females would turn out to be justified in America too.

EDIBLE CRAB, COMMON CRAB   Family *Cancridae*

Cancer pagurus Linnaeus

REMARKS Maximum width over 20 cm. This is the familiar large crab to be found on sale by British and other European fishmongers. The species is found as far north as Norway, but does not occur on the American side of the Atlantic.

The crab is encased in a hard, rigid shell, which, like that of other crustaceans, has to be shed at intervals to permit growth. There is more about this on page 200. Moulting takes place at frequent intervals during the first years of a crab's life, but only every two years after it is fully grown. In Britain crabs must not be landed for sale if they are below adult size (roughly 12 cm across) or if they are females carrying eggs ('berried').

Portuguese: Sapateira
Spanish: Buey
French: Tourteau, Dormeur
Dutch: Noordzeekrab
German: Taschenkrebs
Russian: Oval'nyӯï krab
Swedish: Krabba, Krabbtaska
Norwegian: Krabbe, Taskekrabbe
Danish: Taskekrabbe
Icelandic: Töskukrabbi
Other: Partan (Ireland and Scotland); Hoofdkrab (Zeeland); Poingclos (Brittany)

CUISINE Crab meat may not be quite as good as that of the lobster; but the difference, in my view, is not nearly so marked as the difference in price. It is well worth while to know about crabs and to this end I have devoted part of the page opposite to explanatory drawings.

Crabs should be bought alive, or ready-cooked. If you have a live crab, kill it humanely by the method shown. (Drowning it in fresh water is an inhumane alternative. Plunging it into boiling water will not do, since it will then be likely to shed claws.) Then cook it whole in boiling salted water for 20 to 25 minutes, depending on its size. Make sure that the water is really boiling throughout. Once the crab is cooked, remove it, give it a shower of cold water and leave it to cool at room temperature for 3 to 4 hours. Then dismember it and remove the meat. The white meat comes principally from the claws, but some may also be had from the body and small legs. The brown meat, which has a different flavour and texture, consists mainly of the digestive gland or 'liver' and reproductive organs; and it all comes from within the carapace or 'cart'. What you do not eat are the gills, or 'dead men's fingers'. On average the yield of meat from a crab will be one third of the body weight; and about two thirds of this yield will be brown meat. The proportion of white meat taken from a male, with its larger claws, is higher than that from a female.

Having got your cooked crab-meat, you may proceed to do what you wish with it, using it for a crab salad, or a scalloped crab dish, or crab cakes or whatever.

RECIPES (see also American recipes listed on page 199)
Portuguese crab au gratin, 273   Donegal crab pie, 474
Partan dressed hot, 446

TO KILL A CRAB HUMANELY, use an awl such as UFAW (Universities Federation for Animal Welfare in Britain) sell for the purpose.

The drawing shows the points on the underside of the crab into which the awl is driven. Point 1, revealed by folding back the tail flap, covers the ventral nervous centre. Point 2 is above the brain. Stab each at several slightly different angles.

TO REMOVE THE INEDIBLE PARTS, turn the cooked crab on its back. Grip it as shown, then press forward and up with the thumbs to separate body (with legs) from carapace.

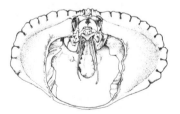

The stomach and attached organs are now seen, attached to the carapace. Press down on the mouth part of the carapace until it cracks off, bringing with it the stomach complex. Discard this.

The gills come away with the body (here shown minus the legs) and are also discarded. The tail contains no edible matter. Otherwise you can eat everything you can pick out.

ROCK CRAB

Family *Cancridae*

Cancer irroratus Say

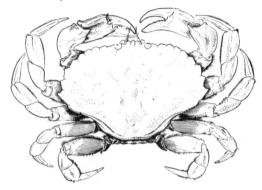

REMARKS   Maximum width 10 or 11 cm. This crab, shown above, has a yellowish back, dotted with brown or purple spots. It ranges from Labrador to Florida.

Its close relation, ***Cancer borealis*** Stimpson, the JONAH CRAB, is shown below. The Jonah has a brick-red back and is a little bigger. It may weigh up to 1½ pounds in deep water and averages 1 pound; and its claws are large. It is found in certain localities only from Nova Scotia to Florida.

CUISINE AND RECIPES   These crabs do not enjoy, or indeed deserve, the esteem which attaches to the blue crab, but they are well worth eating. The first joints of the large walking legs hold a lot of meat. Boil the crabs for 10 minutes, then extract the meat and use it, for example, to make crab cakes (adding only salt and beaten egg). The cakes may be baked or fried. See recipes on pages 428 and 429.

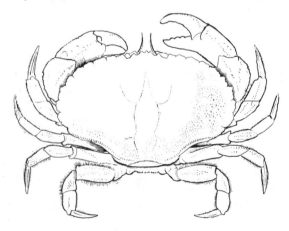

SOUTHERN STONE CRAB

Family *Xanthidae*

Menippe mercenaria (Say)

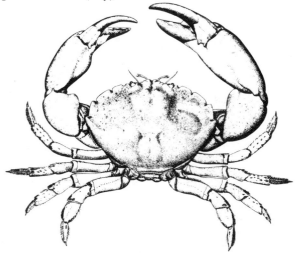

REMARKS Maximum width just over 12 cm. The colour of the stone crab is greyish and its huge claws, one of which is usually larger than the other, are tipped with black. The four pairs of feet have hairy spiked ends.

These crabs live in deep holes in mud or in heaps of rock in tidal creeks and estuaries. Their range extends from the Gulf of Texas round Florida and up to the Carolinas, but no further north; so their credentials as North Atlantic seafood are not beyond question and their inclusion in this catalogue must be partly justified by their penetration of markets further north than their habitat. This penetration would have exercised Damon Runyon, who regarded the stone crab as the property of Florida and too good for visitors or outsiders, while acknowledging that it was an 'ornery-looking critter'.

CUISINE 'The stone crab is much larger than the northern crab and has a shell harder than a landlord's heart. In places in Dade County where stone crabs are served, the shell is cracked with a large wooden mallet before being set before the customer. Only the huge claws of the stone crab contain the edible meat. The body is waste . . . The stone crab is cooked by boiling. A lot of people have tried to think up better ways, but boiling is best. It is served cold with hot melted butter with a dash of lemon in it on the side. Probably the right place in which to eat stone crabs would be the bath-tub. The fingers are used in toying with them. Some high-toned folks use those little dinky oyster forks, but the fingers are far speedier and more efficient.' Thus Damon Runyon, quoted in the *Miami Daily News* of 28 December 1954. I need only add that the body is not entirely waste, since the back-fin meat, as one would expect, is good – although not as good as the meat of the huge claws.

BLUE CRAB, ATLANTIC BLUE CRAB

Family *Portunidae*

Callinectes sapidus Rathbun

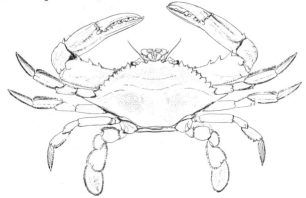

REMARKS   Maximum body width over 20 cm (8 inches). The marketing authorities in the State of Maryland define the sizes of the blue crab (in its 'soft' state) thus: 'whales' or 'slabs' are over 5 inches in width; 'jumbos' $4\frac{1}{2}$ to 5 inches; 'primes' 4 to $4\frac{1}{2}$; 'hotels' $3\frac{1}{2}$ to 4; and 'mediums' 3 to $3\frac{1}{2}$.

This information and almost everything else one could wish to know about the blue crab, its habitat and habits, the fishery for it, and the fishermen is to be found in *Beautiful Swimmers – Watermen, Crabs and the Chesapeake Bay* by William W. Warner, a book which is wholly devoted to this subject and which can only be described as perfect of its kind.

Warner begins Chapter Five of his book by remarking that the scientific name of the blue crab was well chosen. '*Callinectes* is Greek for beautiful swimmer. *Sapidus*, of course, means tasty or savory in Latin. Rathbun is the late Dr Mary J. Rathbun of the Smithsonian Institution, who first gave the crab its specific name. Dr Rathbun, known as Mary Jane to her Smithsonian colleagues . . . identified and described over 998 new species of crabs, an absolute record in the annals of carcinology. In only one case did she choose to honor culinary qualities. History has borne out the wisdom of her choice. No crab in the world has been as much caught or eagerly consumed as *sapidus*.'

Contrary to popular belief, the blue crab is not exclusively north American. It was in Mary Jane's time. But it has since been introduced into the eastern Mediterranean and is now part of the fauna there.

However, despite its Mediterranean colony, the blue crab is as American as the stars and stripes. The fishery for it extends from Delaware Bay down to Florida and the Gulf States; but the biggest catch comes from Chesapeake Bay. Something like 200 million blue crabs are taken from the bay each year, and almost the whole of the national catch of soft-shelled crabs (see pages 200 and 201) comes from there.

The fishermen of Chesapeake Bay, as I discovered for myself when there, have an extensive vocabulary of terms for the blue crab. A 'sook' is a sexually mature female. A 'jimmy' is a mature male. Berried females are known as 'sponges', 'busted sooks', 'lemon bellies' or 'punks'. A crab which is about to moult is a 'peeler'. There are many other such terms; the Chesapeake watermen have a real gift for vivid description. Two old-timers are quoted thus, by William Warner, on crab court-ship:

'My friend, you never seen crabs making love?'
'Act real horny, they do. Males get way up on their tippy toes.'
'Do I think so? I don't think so, I *know* so!'
'That's right, the Jimmies on their toes and the females rocking side to side, contented like.'

CUISINE The blue crab is of excellent quality. It yields very good white meat (mostly from the claws, but the back-fin meat, also known as 'jumbo lump', is important) and the usual brown meat too.

Most blue crabs are taken in the hard state and are immediately processed at the 'crab house' or 'picking plant'. Until the meat has been made firm by cooking, it cannot conveniently be taken out of the shell. So the first step, whether at the crab house, or in your own kitchen, is to steam or boil the crab until it is cooked through and the top of the shell and the claws have turned red. (Americans who cook crabs at home often use a convenient product known as 'crab boil' or 'crab boil spices'. This is usually a mixture of mustard seed, coriander seed, dill seed, cayenne pepper, allspice and cloves. It can also be used to good effect in cooking lobsters or prawns.) The second step, after the cooked crabs have cooled off a little, is to pick out the meat, which will take forty seconds per crab for the champions at Crisfield's annual National Hard Crab Derby, but takes me at least four minutes.

After these preliminaries, you can follow any of the dozens of good crab recipes, such as those listed below and the European ones on page 195.

I add here one short but valuable recipe from an expert on crabs, Bob Learson. He recommends, for any crab claws, a mustard sauce made thus. For 8 large crab claws, take ½ cup sour cream, 1½ tbs prepared mustard, a knob of butter (say, 20 g or ⅔ oz), 1 tsp chopped parsley (or ½ tsp dried parsley flakes) and a pinch of salt. Heat and stir this mixture, but do not let it boil. The result should be about ⅔ cup of sauce, which can be served either hot or cold with the claws.

RECIPES
Devilled crab, 427
Maryland crab meat cakes, 429
Crab meat Norfolk style, 429
She-crab soup, 436

TELLING THE SEXES APART

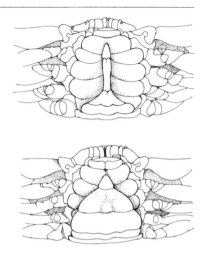

Males and females are easily recognized. All females have bright red tips to their claws. Males do not. The males have a distinctive inverted T-shape to their apron. This is shown above right. That of a mature female is shown below right. An immature female has an apron shaped like an inverted V.

A NOTE ON SOFT-SHELL CRABS

Since some people really do think that soft-shell crabs are a separate species, and since there is much of interest to be said about them, I provide this note. It is, however, essentially a footnote to the preceding entry, on the blue crab, since that is the species which is eaten in the soft state in the United States; and eaten on a scale which cannot be matched on the Atlantic coast of Europe, although in principle other crabs can be so treated (cf. the Venetian practice referred to on page 202).

Like other arthropods, crabs can only grow if they are able to cast off periodically their rigid exo-skeleton or shell, and grow a new and larger one in its stead. This is an uncomfortable process, and the creatures are for a short time bereft of their natural defences, after they have wriggled out of the old shells. The degree of softness varies from species to species. The blue crab is very soft indeed when it emerges, and will normally take refuge in some relatively safe nook for a day or so until the new shell is reasonably hard.

A crab which is just about ready to shed is called a 'comer' or 'peeler'. The condition can be recognized, at an advanced stage, by the appearance of a red line along the edge of the 'paddlers' at the rear of the crab. During the actual process of shedding, the crab is a 'buster', 'peeler' or 'shedder'. At the moment of emergence from the old shell it is a 'soft crab' in the full sense of the term. Soon afterwards, as a slight hardening becomes apparent, it is termed a 'paper shell'. Further hardening turns it into a 'buckram' or 'buckler'. At this stage the new shell is still flexible, but the crab is no longer soft enough to be treated as a soft-shell crab, and its muscles are thin and watery. Within twenty-four hours or so of the shedding the new shell will be hard and the crab can resume a normal life.

There is a further complication in all this. The female must mate with the male immediately after her own shedding. When she is almost ready, the male will pick her up, clasping her beneath him, and carry her to a suitable spot. She then sheds and mating takes place. Crabbers are of course very pleased if they catch a couple on this amorous journey, since they gain simultaneously a hard male and a female shedder. Such a pair are called 'hard doublers'. If, however, mating is successfully achieved, the female will become a 'sponge crab', carrying a large mass of eggs, of an orange-lemon colour, on her abdomen. It is illegal to have in your possession either a sponge crab or a buckram.

Catching and marketing the soft crabs is no easy business. They cannot in fact be caught while they are soft. They have to be caught in advance and kept in special 'floats' until they moult. These floats must be patrolled regularly so that damaged crabs can be removed and crabs which have just moulted be culled, i.e. gathered for market. The culling must be done swiftly, since the period of softness is so short, and conveyance to market must be rapid, too. The peak season for Chesapeake Bay crabbers comes in May.

CUISINE Soft crabs may be bought frozen. It is then only necessary to thaw them before they are fried or grilled.

If soft crabs are bought alive, they must first be dressed, thus: 'With a sharp knife, cut off the apron or flap that folds under the rear of the body. Turn the crab and cut off the face at a joint just back of the eyes. Lift each point at the sides with the fingers, clean out the gills, and wash the crabs in cold water. Pat dry with a paper towel.' (Seafood Marketing Authority, Annapolis.)

It is usual to fry the prepared soft-shell crabs in butter, after patting them dry and flouring them. It is best to use clarified butter, as advised by Anna Wetherill Reed (*The Philadelphia Cook Book of Town and Country*, 1940). She also recommends that when the fried crabs have been removed to a serving platter the cook should add some lemon juice to the butter remaining in the pan, and strain the combination over the crabs.

I find that the unusual texture of the soft-shell crab is enhanced by serving it on half of a soft roll, and eating it as a sort of open sandwich. I ate some prepared in this way at Tilghman, with tartare sauce, and found them excellent thus. (A tartare sauce can be made very easily by adding to mayonnaise some finely chopped gherkin and parsley, and perhaps a little minced onion. But a better procedure is to start by rubbing two hard-boiled egg-yolks into a paste, with seasoning. Turn this into a liquid by adding olive oil and tarragon vinegar. Then add also some very finely chopped chives, gherkin and capers, a little French mustard and a touch of cayenne pepper. Blend this mixture with a suitable quantity of home-made mayonnaise.)

SHORE CRAB, GREEN CRAB   Family *Portunidae*

Carcinus maenas Linnaeus

REMARKS Maximum width 7 cm. The carapace is green, often with yellow spots. This is the familiar shore crab of both sides of the North Atlantic. Its specific name *maenas* means frenzied, and the second French name cited also alludes to the reckless and fierce way in which this little creature will struggle and fight when brought to bay or captured. It has surprising strength. 'If you are so unfortunate as to be gripped by the crushing pincer of a green crab, try to forget the pain by musing over the fact that the creature probably is exerting a pull of about two kilograms, a force equivalent to nearly thirty times the weight of its own body. The average hand grip of a man is capable of a fifty-kilogram pull, about two thirds of his own weight . . .' (Professor Donald J. Zinn in *The Handbook for Beach Strollers from Maine to Cape Hatteras*, 1973; a fine example of writing by a scientist for laymen.)

Portuguese: Caranguejo (mouro)
Spanish: Cangrejo de mar
French: Crabe vert, Crabe enragé
Dutch: Strandkrab
German: Strandkrabbe
Russian: Pribrezhnÿi krab
Swedish: Strandkrabba
Norwegian: Strandkrabbe
Danish: Strandkrabbe
Icelandic: Krabbi

CUISINE The Mediterranean form of this crab, *Carcinus mediterraneus* Czerniavsky, is the very crab which Venetians and others so enjoy eating when it is in its soft state, immediately after it has shed its carapace. Such crabs are known as moleche in Venice. No one in the Atlantic area seems yet to have tried to exploit the possibilities indicated by Venetian practice. The shore crab is in many places used in soups and sometimes for its meat, but the general attitude echoes statements by nineteenth-century writers that it is food 'for the lower classes' or 'eaten by the poor'.

The soup-pot is also the usual destination of the other two small swimming crabs shown on page 203.

TWO OTHER SWIMMING CRABS

Ovalipes ocellatus (Herbst) is an American species, known as the LADY CRAB because of its attractive appearance. Its carapace is white, with rings of red or purple spots. Other names are calico crab and sand crab. Maximum width 7 cm.

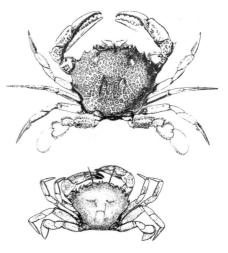

Macropipus puber (Linnaeus) is one of a whole tribe of small swimming crabs found in European waters. The French call it ÉTRILLE or nageur. It is usually dark brown in colour, with blue markings. Although small, it is a courageous fighter.

THE HERMIT CRABS

These strange creatures, which occur on both sides of the Atlantic, are edible, although rarely eaten outside France. ***Eupagurus bernhardus*** Linnaeus is the most common and is the subject of an amusing entry in Alexandre Dumas's *Grand Dictionnaire de Cuisine* (1873):

A species of crab whose meat is regarded as a delicious morsel. It is usually grilled in its shell before being eaten.

There is nothing more comical than this little crustacean. Nature has furnished him with armour as far as the waist – cuirass, gauntlets and visor of iron, this half of him has everything. But from the waist to the other end there is nothing, not even a nightshirt. The result of this is that the hermit crab stuffs this extremity of himself into whatever refuge he can find.

The Creator, who had begun to dress the creature as a lobster, was disturbed or distracted in the middle of the operation and finished him off as a slug. This part of the hermit crab, so poorly defended and so tempting to an enemy, is his great preoccupation; a preoccupation which can at times make him fierce. If he sees a shell which suits him, he eats the owner and takes his place while it is still warm – the history of the world in microscopic form. But since, when all is said and done, the house was not made for him, he staggers about like a drunkard instead of having the serious air of a snail . . .

RED CRAB

Family *Geryonidae*

Geryon quinquedens Smith

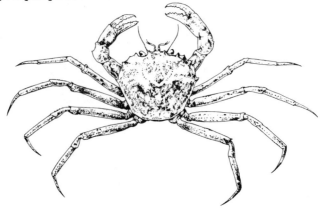

REMARKS   Maximum width about 15 cm. The colour of the carapace is red. This is a deep-sea crab, usually found at depths between 300 and 900 metres. It is an under-exploited species, with a range from Nova Scotia to Cuba. There is a small fishery for it in southern New England, which may be expanded in the light of research into its habits.

Another species of the same genus occurs in deep waters on the eastern side of the Atlantic, but seems not have been fished at all, so far.

Canada is fortunate in possessing the excellent QUEEN CRAB or SNOW CRAB. This is shown below. Its scientific name is *Chionoecetes opilio* (Fabricius) and it is found only in cold northerly waters.

CUISINE   I ate a quantity of red crab at Gloucester, Mass., and liked the flavour. The legs are thin, but the meat slips out of them readily. Indeed the whole creature is remarkably easy to dismantle and consume.

As for the snow crab, I have only eaten it canned, but found it to be of very high quality.

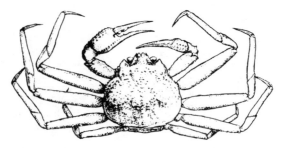

SPIDER CRAB, SPINY CRAB

Family *Maiidae*

Maia squinado (Herbst)

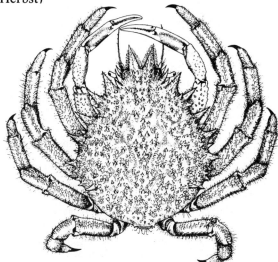

REMARKS Maximum width 20 cm. The colour of the carapace varies from reddish orange to brown. The arrangement of the legs makes one think of a spider. This species does not occur on the American Atlantic coast, although other spider crabs (not normally eaten) do. They all have a remarkable ability to disguise themselves.

Portuguese: Santola
Spanish: Centolla
French: Araignée (de mer)
Dutch: Augustinuskrab
German: Troldkrabbe
Swedish: Spindelkrabba
Danish: Troldkrabbe

Edward Step, in *A Naturalist's Holiday* (on the Cornish coast before the First World War), devotes a chapter to the spider crab, which was known locally as Gran'f'er Jenkin (or the gorwich or the gaber) and says that it usually emerges from winter retirement in May (hence *Maia*, the specific name *squinado* being taken from the common name of the species in Provence). He describes with charm how Gran'f'er uses his nippers to break off bits of podweed or other suitable camouflage and 'plants' these among the prickles and hooked hairs on his back, after 'kissing' the ends to coat them with gummy saliva. In this way, choosing always items which will bear transplanting and which blend with his surroundings, he makes himself all but invisible, looking like a small rock encrusted with natural growths.

CUISINE AND RECIPE A good crab, which is in particularly strong demand in France. It may be prepared according to any crab recipe. Or follow the recipe on page 282, from the Basque country, where this crab is known as txangurro.

OYSTER CRAB, PEA CRAB   Family *Pinnotheridae*

Pinnotheres ostreum Say

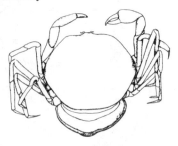

REMARKS   The maximum width of these tiny crabs is only about 1½ cm. At an early stage in their lives, both males and females invade the shells of oysters, mussels or other bivalves. The females stay put, but the males emerge in their first year and swim round looking for a female, snug in her bivalvular home, with which to copulate. The experience of sexual intercourse within the shell of a living oyster, which shakes the mind if translated into human dimensions, seems to be too much for it, since it then dies. However, the females may live for as long as three years.

Oyster crabs do not seem to perform any services for their host molluscs, although some ancient authors thought that they might operate a warning system, and indeed do not seem to do anything much at all, except slight damage to the oysters' gills. In their protected environment they remain permanently soft shelled, and lose the ability to make any but minor and sluggish movements. Their colour is pale pink, which is somehow suitable for such minuscule degenerates.

The crab which we have been discussing is a North American species. Its best-known counterpart in Europe is ***Pinnotheres pisum*** (Linnaeus), the pea crab in English, erwtekrabbetje in Dutch. It is often found in mussels, but is not itself eaten, so far as I can discover.

CUISINE AND RECIPES   The oyster crab used to be a delicacy in the United States, and an expensive one. The *Washington Evening Star* of 21 September 1900 stated that there had even been a proposal to call it the Washington crab, since the first President of the United States had liked it so well, and said that 'we often see it floating upon the surface of an oyster stew.'

It was usual to eat the little creatures whole, carapace and all, sautéed or deep-fried, with or without the oysters. They were also pickled. I am told, however, by a scientist at the Smithsonian that they ought to be eaten alive, that they provide a welcome change of texture in between oysters, and that they taste a little like celery.

Few books contain recipes for the oyster crab. An exception is *300 Ways to Cook and Serve Shell Fish* by H. Franklyn Hall, which was published at Philadelphia in 1901 and contains no fewer than sixteen. I reprint his Oyster crab omelette on page 430.

GOOSE-NECKED BARNACLE

Family *Pollicipidae*

Pollicipes cornucopia Leach

Portuguese: Perceve
Spanish: Percebe
French: Pouce-pied
Other: Lamperna
   (Basque)

REMARKS   Maximum length about 15 cm.

This creature, which belongs to the Order *Cirripedia*, is not like the other crustaceans. It consists of what might be called a tube, as thick as a finger, with a dark parchment-like skin bearing tiny scales. On this is mounted a sort of hoof – a pair of white bony pads, from between which emerge the creature's feet.

These barnacles are usually found in groups, attached to a rock; and are said to be most easily caught at full moon when the tide is low. In fact, the demand for them in Portugal and Spain is so great that they have become increasingly rare in accessible habitats; and the 'fishery' for them is nowadays quite perilous, since it involves diving in what are often rough seas to reach the rocks where they can still be found.

CUISINE   What one eats is, so to speak, the 'inner tube'. Pinch the outer skin near the hoofs and prise it off with your fingernails, revealing a stalk-like protuberance within, and bite this off entire. Eating the barnacles raw is perfectly possible, but those which are offered in bars and restaurants have been cooked briefly, and I think that they are better thus. I first ate them as a breakfast in a Lisbon seafood bar, with a Portuguese marine biologist as my host and tutor; and the exquisitely strong taste of the sea was, to use a cliché with accuracy, a real revelation. Spanish and Portuguese enthusiasm for the delicacy is fully understandable. (The French seem to be less enthusiastic.)

It is unlikely that the reader will have to cook these barnacles. But, if so, he may like to know that there is a recipe in verse in the old La Coruña cookery book by Sr Puga y Parga (*La Cocina Práctica* – an apt title, although it is highly poetical too). This tells you just to boil the barnacles briefly in salted water, but adds a lengthy injunction to use a large napkin, covering your whole chest, when eating them. (In fact, if the pinch-and-open technique is carefully executed, the risk of juices squirting about is small. But a napkin is certainly needed for wiping one's lips.)

4. Catalogue of Molluscs and Other Edible Sea Creatures

Single Shells

The single shells belong to the Order *Gastropoda*, in which there is a great variety of forms. Few of these need be considered here, since the Order is not rich in gastronomic interest. The creatures listed are, however, all eaten and most of them are quite good if properly selected and prepared.

I acknowledge that at least one in the list, the limpet, is not normally thought of as a delicacy. But it presents a stimulating challenge to the cook, and some of the ways in which it has traditionally been prepared in Britain and France are of interest. The traditions are very old. Visiting the beautifully kept Stone Age settlement at Skara Brae in Orkney, I was surprised to hear how important limpets had been in the diet of the inhabitants. Their middens still provide mute evidence of countless meals in which limpets must have been a main ingredient.

More recently, the tenacity of these creatures provided Wordsworth (or a pseudo-Wordsworth – see footnote) with one of many opportunities for marvelling at natural phenomena:

> And should the strongest arm endeavour
> The limpet from its rock to sever,
> 'Tis seen its loved support to clasp,
> With such tenacity of grasp,
> We wonder that such strength should dwell
> In such a small and simple shell.

However, limpets can be dislodged by strong men. 'At Eastbourne we have often seen the Irish reapers come down to the shore and eat the limpets raw which they have knocked off the rocks with their knives.' (Lovell, *The Edible Mollusca of Great Britain and Ireland.**) Nor was it only Irish reapers who relished the taste. Cornishmen liked them so well that they would pine for them from afar. Indeed Aflalo (in *The Sea-fishing Industry*

---

* I refer frequently to this book in my catalogue entries for the molluscs. Lovell was a writer after my own heart, whose book combined a properly scientific framework, beautiful illustrations, judiciously chosen classical allusions and a host of quaint facts and anecdotes from other parts of the world as well as from Britain. The book was first published in 1867. I confess, however, that the 'Wordsworth' quotation (which comes from Lovell's book, where it is simply attributed to Wordsworth's Poems) is of dubious authenticity. Most Wordsworth experts whom I have consulted opine that it is spurious; and the 'small literary prize' which I offered some time ago in *The Times Literary Supplement* for identification of its provenance remains unclaimed (and claimable!).

of England and Wales, 1904) records a curious traffic in limpets between a Mr Cregoe in Cornwall and the United States:

the idea owes its origin to the home-sickness of Cornishmen exiled in the United States. The limpet is hardly to be described as the most delicate of food, but distance lends enchantment even to tinned limpets and, some Cornish folk transplanted to the neighbourhood of Chicago having expressed a wish once again to taste limpets, a local storekeeper instituted inquiries, which eventually reached Mr. Cregoe. With characteristic enterprise he forthwith set lads to work picking limpets off the rocks at a fixed remuneration per basket, and these he pickled in vinegar and packed in small round tins for the American market. In this form does the lowly limpet carry memories of those lovely Cornish bays to men and women forced by circumstances to sweat out the remainder of their existence in the unpromising purlieus of Chicago.

However, enough by way of introduction. This part of the catalogue begins with a short entry for the benefit of travellers in the south-eastern part of our region.

MUREX

Murex spp.

Portuguese: Búzio
Spanish: Cañadilla
French: Rocher

Family *Muricidae*

REMARKS Maximum length about 10 cm. The gasteropods of this genus are southerly creatures, but worth a mention because they are deservedly popular in Portugal, Spain and France. The species illustrated is *Murex brandaris* (Linnaeus), which was the principal source of the Tyrian purple dye of antiquity. *Murex trunculus* (Linnaeus), the other common species, is less prickly.

CUISINE These are firm in texture, and delicious. Cook them in gently boiling water for about 15 minutes, then let them cool and pick the meat out entire with the slightly hooked instrument which can be bought for the purpose. (The tough disc which serves as a seal at the mouth of the shell is to be removed before the morsels are eaten.)

LIMPET

Family *Patellidae*

Patella vulgata Linnaeus

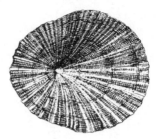

REMARKS   Maximum diameter 7 cm, usual size 5 cm. The colour of the shell is usually grey, yellowish or brown. This is a European species. Limpets on the eastern seaboard of North America are smaller. Even Euell Gibbons (see footnote on page 213) seems never to have managed to make a meal of them, despite his enthusiastic and optimistic approach to all natural foods.

CUISINE   Lovell gives an interesting survey of limpet-eating. The Scots used to mix limpet juice with their oatmeal. At Herm, 'limpets were placed on the ground, in their usual position, and cooked by being covered with a heap of straw, which had been set on fire, about twenty minutes before dinner.' At Eastbourne, people would put them upside down on the gridiron until their water had evaporated and would then eat them; and the same technique is recorded from Normandy.

Portuguese: Lapa
Spanish: Lapa, Lampa
French: Patelle, Bernique, Chapeau chinois
Dutch: Tepelhoidje
German: Schusselmuschel, Napfschnecke
Swedish: Skålsnäcka
Norwegian: Albuskjell
Danish: Albuskjael
Other: Venis (Brittany); Flie (French); Flia (Faroese); Flitter (Isle of Man); Crogan (Cornwall)

However, it is more usual to boil limpets, if they are small, or to fry them. I cannot claim that they are particularly good or tender; and think myself that they may best be used to flavour a soup or to make limpet sauce, thus, as advised by Hartland Reid in his *Practical Cookery*. Steep clean-shelled limpets in fresh water, then heat them in a pan until they part easily from their shells. They yield a rich brown liquor in which, after being shelled, they can be stewed for half an hour. The liquor is then thickened with butter and flour, strained, seasoned with salt and pepper and cayenne pepper and treated to a dash of lemon juice or vinegar before use. (The limpets are discarded.)

If, on the other hand, you wish to eat the limpets themselves, I recommend the Scottish recipe for Limpet stovies on page 447.

WINKLE, PERIWINKLE

Family *Lacunidae*

Littorina littorea (Linnaeus)

REMARKS Maximum length just over 2½ cm.

The shells are usually dark grey or brown, but many other colours occur, such as whitish green and even 'red or rufous-brown, with narrow bands of smoke colour' (Lovell, who thus reminds us of that useful but neglected word 'rufous').

The name for these little creatures in Zeeland is kruuk'ls. In the Pas de Calais they are pilots and I have heard that in some parts of France they are called sabots, meaning wooden shoes. The presence of large numbers of periwinkle shells in prehistoric mounds in Scotland, Denmark and elsewhere shows that the periwinkle has been a popular food for a very long time. Now, however, it is becoming grander and is often served as an '*amuse-gueule*' in luxury restaurants on the European continent. Ireland exports large quantities to Belgium and France.

Portuguese: Burriė, Burrelho
Spanish: Bígaro, Mincha
French: Bigorneau
Dutch: Alikruik
Swedish: Strandsnäcka
Norwegian: Strandsnile
Danish: Strandsnegl
Icelandic: Fjörudoppa
Other: Horse-winkle (Irish); Gwichiaid (Welsh)

The periwinkle occurs also on the American side of the Atlantic and its shells have been found in American Indian middens. But contemporary Americans ignore it almost completely.

CUISINE Periwinkles, or winkles as they are commonly called by their vendors, are usually cooked for about 10 minutes in boiling, salted water. They can then be picked out of their shells with a pin. However, their preparation does not always stop there. In Ireland, for example, they may end up in a sauce made by boiling carragheen moss in milk. In Nefyn and Bardsey Island in Wales, Minwel Tibbott (the author of *Welsh Fare*; see page 460) was told that the boiled winkles would be fried in bacon fat and then have an egg or two cracked over them, to be left to fry or else scrambled. In Zeeland, according to *Kezanse Kost*, a recent book by M. A. Aalbregtse on Zeeland cookery, the cooked winkles would be taken hot from their shells and turned in a thin mustard sauce with a little lemon juice and a crushed clove of garlic, then eaten with bread.

WHELK, WAVED WHELK   Family *Buccinidae*

Buccinum undatum Linnaeus

REMARKS   This, the principal species of whelk, reaches a length of 10 or even 15 cm. The colour of the shell is variable and it may or may not bear spiral bands or blotches.

A whelk is equipped with very strong lips, with which it applies a kiss of death to other molluscs, using them and its spiny tongue to bore through shells and extract the contents. It exhibits this ruthless behaviour on both sides of the North Atlantic. It also eats carrion.

The eggs of the whelk are contained in yellowish capsules about the size of split peas. The capsules occur in fist-sized conglomerations and may be found on the beach. Fishermen call them 'sea-wash balls', since they will lather if rubbed between the hands.

Portuguese: Búzio
Spanish: Bocina
French: Buccin
Dutch: Wulk
German: Wellhornschnecke
Swedish: Valthornssnäcka
Norwegian: Hvalolje
Danish: Konksnegl
Icelandic: Beitukongur
Other: Buckie (Scottish);
   Gwalc (Welsh);
   Pilot canteux (Boulogne)

Neptunea antiqua (Linnaeus) is another species, called almond whelk or red whelk. There may be some places where the large shells, which have been known to measure as much as 20 cm, are still used, as they once were in Shetland, for lamps. They were suspended from a nail in the wall or ceiling of the hut or croft, by means of a string fastened round the shell in a triangular form. The inside was filled with fish oil, and a wick of cotton or tow put into the canal at the extremity of the mouth.

Even larger whelks are found on the American side of the Atlantic. *Busycon carica* (Gmelin), the knobbed whelk, may reach a length of 30 cm. The knobs on its shell are used for striking and breaking open the shells of its prey, held helpless by the very large foot. *Busycon canaliculatum* (Linnaeus), the channeled whelk, is almost as large and may be distinguished by the deep, channeled grooves which follow the whorls of the shell.

CUISINE Whelks are too big for the sort of treatment given to the smaller gasteropods. The large muscular foot is the part usually eaten. When whelks are commercially processed in Canada, notably in Quebec Province, they are first washed and steamed, then shucked and trimmed down to this muscular part before being canned or packed in glass jars with a marinade of sugar and spiced vinegar. However, Dr Medcof, in a paper about the St Lawrence whelk fishery, records that some Canadians eat the whole whelk, except for the operculum, which is the hard disc – like a fingernail – which closes the aperture of the shell. Dr Medcof was told that the custom was to place whole, live whelks in a covered pot with a little water on a hot stove, and to cook them until the operculum separated from the meat. The whelks were then served piping hot. The diner would thrust a fork into the body, give the shell a twirl and thus bring the meat out of it. Whelks had a reputation for being very nutritious, 'as strengthening as a steak dinner'.

The giant whelks can indeed produce steaks, so big are they. Euell Gibbons recommends cutting steaks about 1 cm thick, enclosing them in muslin and flattening them with a mallet before cooking them.*

In certain climatic conditions whelks absorb toxin from the bivalves they eat; and may retain this for a long time. It is best to eat only whelks which have been professionally harvested, unless you are very knowledgeable.

SLIPPER LIMPET

Family *Calyptraeidae*

Crepidula fornicata (Linnaeus)

REMARKS A North American species which preys on the oyster. It is sometimes called boat-shell, since it has a 'half-deck' inside its shell. It was accidentally introduced to southern England along with some American oysters in about 1890 and is now firmly

established there. The pestilential character of this species would be mitigated if more people realized that slipper limpets are good to eat, either raw or cooked. Some were harvested and eaten in Britain and the Netherlands during the Second World War. But experiments at Gloucester, Mass., by Learson and others, have shown that there is no easy way of processing the creatures and producing an acceptably high yield of meat. A do-it-yourself seafood for the real enthusiast who wants to do the local oysters a good turn.

---

* Euell Gibbons, best known for his books *Stalking the Blue-Eyed Scallop* (1964) and *Stalking the Wild Asparagus* (1962) did much to open American eyes to the possibility of eating seafoods and plants which can be gathered for free but are rarely seen in the markets. He also gave useful advice on dealing to the best advantage with seafoods which are marketed, but from which many people shy away, through ignorance.

ORMER, ABALONE, EAR-SHELL   Family *Haliotidae*

Haliotis tuberculata Linnaeus

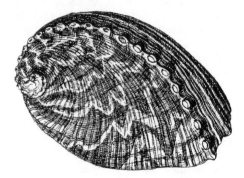

REMARKS   Maximum length 12 cm. This is the Atlantic representative of the abalones, which flourish in finer and larger forms in the Pacific.

Portuguese: Orelha
Spanish: Oreja de mar
French: Ormeau, Six-yeux, Oreille de mer
Dutch: Zee-oor

The range of the species extends as far north as the Channel Islands, where it is greatly prized. Ansted and Latham (in *The Channel Islands*, 1862) quoted someone who rhapsodized thus about the ormer (which he called Ormond): ' 'Tis much bigger than an oyster, and like that, good either fresh or pickled, but infinitely more pleasant to the gusto, so that an epicure would think his palate in paradise if he might but always gormandize on such delicious ambrosia.' Such paradise is nowadays denied to Jersey and Guernsey epicures, for the ormer is in short supply there; but it may still be had quite readily on the French coast and further south.

CUISINE AND RECIPES   Lovell provides, by courtesy of a Mr Morton of St Clement's in Jersey, a recipe boldly entitled 'To Dress Sea-ears to Perfection'. Mr Morton's advice is as follows: 'Take them out of the shells and well scrub them; then let them simmer for two or three hours, until they are quite tender, after which they may be scalloped as an oyster, or put into the pan to brown with butter.' This does work, but my own advice is to let 30 seconds' beating with a mallet replace the 3 hours of simmering, to cut the tenderized flesh into steaks, to dip these first in beaten egg and then seasoned flour, and to fry them lightly.

Simone Morand, in her *Gastronomie bretonne* (1965), gives an excellent range of Breton recipes for the ormer. A version of one of these appears on page 302.

Bivalves

Bivalves are creatures which live in double, hinged shells. They include some of the most delicious of all seafood – oysters, scallops and clams.

The name clam can be confusing, since it may be applied both in a general sense to whole groups of bivalves and in a more restricted way to certain species. The name mussel, in some other languages, has the same ambiguity.

The word clam is really a shortened form of clam-shell, a term which was derived from the verb clam, meaning shut. A clam-shell was a shell which could be closed tightly. On this basis almost all bivalves would be clams; although, paradoxically, the soft-shelled clam and the razor clam would not qualify, since they cannot close their shells completely. In practice the name clam is used as indicated in the catalogue entries which follow; and any confusion is inconsequential in everyday life. I mention the matter, however, because it is not uncommon to find people in Britain who suppose that the famous American clams are something quite apart from the European fauna, to be tasted only on the other side of the Atlantic or after opening a tin. The truth is that most of the American species exist in identical or similar form on the European side, but that they are rarely eaten in Britain or any of the countries to the north of France. The explanation of the greater enthusiasm shown by Canadians and Americans is perhaps partly to be sought in the experience of the early settlers in adopting some of the eating habits of the American Indians, who had not failed to take advantage of the rich harvest of clams on their shores.

The variety of edible bivalves is great. There are some which I have not catalogued because they are only eaten in certain localities or in one or two countries. Thus *Glycymeris glycymeris* (Linnaeus), the DOG COCKLE, which is shown below right, does not appear in the catalogue, although it can be eaten in France (amande de mer), Spain (almendra de mar) and Portugal (castanhola); and there are others. However, most small bivalves which are offered for sale can be eaten raw; or prepared for consumption by using recipes for better-known species.

MUSSEL; BLUE MUSSEL (U.S.A.)   Family *Mytilidae*

Mytilus edulis Linnaeus

REMARKS   Maximum length about 13 cm, usual market length 5 to 8 cm. Everyone is familiar with their dark-blue or blackish shells, but some varieties are paler or rayed with dark brown or purple. I show two varieties above.

This species has an extensive range, from the southern Arctic down to North Carolina and the Mediterranean. Until recently it was thought that the so-called Mediterranean mussel, which is found as far north as Britain, was a separate species, **Mytilus galloprovincialis** Lamarck. It has a less angular shell and the mantle-edge of live specimens is dark instead of white or pale. But it is now counted as a race or variety of the main species.

Portuguese: Mexilhão
Spanish: Mejillón
French: Moule
Dutch: Mossel
German: Miesmuschel
Polish: Omutek
Russian: Midiya
Swedish: Blåmussla
Norwegian: Blåskjell
Danish: Blåmusling
Icelandic: Kraeklingur
Other: Mojohon (Basque)

There are many places where mussels can be gathered in the wild state, if that term can be used of such a placid creature. But these are often meagre in body and may have suffered from pollution. The mussel seems to be particularly susceptible to maladies which make it unfit, or dangerous, for human consumption. Instances are reported from time to time of their causing paralytic shellfish poisoning (P.S.P.). This happens after there has been an abundance of a certain dinoflagellate planktonic organism in the water, an abundance which is often visible in the form of the so-called 'red tide'. The subject is highly complicated; and I do not wish to exaggerate what is normally a small risk. But it does seem to be preferable on both gastronomic and health grounds to eat only mussels which have been cultured and marketed under suitably strict conditions. Such mussels are plump, delicious and safe. They are also relatively cheap, since the culture of mussels requires less time and effort than that of oysters.

There are several methods of mussel cultivation. One, which is used most extensively in the Netherlands and Denmark, is to rear them in protected areas of the sea bed or in special mussel 'parks', which the Dutch can easily form in such places as the Wadden Zee. Dense colonies of baby mussels are formed, dredged up when they have grown a little, and spread out evenly in the parks. After two and a half or three years, during which special precautions are taken to protect them from predators such as starfish, they are ready to be marketed. Harvesting can be highly mechanized. Moreover, the mussels are able to feed and grow continuously, since they remain submerged all the time.

The oldest method of cultivation, which is still the principal method used in France, is to grow the mussels on poles, known as bouchots, fixed in the water. This method seems to have been the chance invention of an Irishman, as M. de Quatrefages tells us in his *Rambles of a Naturalist on the Coasts of France, Spain and Sicily* (English translation 1857). 'An Irishman of the name of Walton was shipwrecked on the coast in 1235, near the little village of Esnandes, in the Bay of Aiguillon, and was the only person saved out of all the crew of the ill-fated vessel.' He settled down and proceeded to invent a net to catch the birds which skimmed across the local mud flats at dusk; but 'in order to make these nets thoroughly effective, it was necessary to go to the centre of the immense bed of mud, where the birds sought their food, and to secure a number of poles to support the nets, which were between 300 and 400 yards in length. On examining these poles, Walton discovered that they were covered with mussel spawn.' The quick-witted man then switched from bird-catching to mussel-rearing by driving into the mud, at the level of the lowest tides, twin rows of stakes, which were the first bouchots. The procedure has since been refined, but remains essentially the same; and the Bay of l'Aiguillon is studded with bouchots to this day. Mussels reared in this way are protected from bottom-living predators. On the other hand, they are exposed at low tide and their feeding time is thus limited.

A third method, which has been developed with great success by the Spaniards, is to use large floating rafts with mussel ropes suspended from them. There are now about 3000 such rafts off the Galician coast, and Spain has become the world's leading producer of mussels.

Cultivated mussels vary in appearance, size and taste. In many a place one will be told that the locally grown ones are the best in the world. One such is Wimereux, just to the north of Boulogne, where the mussels are relatively small, with remarkably clean indigo shells and a flavour which must certainly be among the best.

Experimental steps towards the culture of mussels at a few places on the American Atlantic coast are being taken. Harvard University Press chose *The Mussel Cookbook* by Sarah Hurlburt as their first cook book.

CUISINE Mussels can be delicious when eaten raw, but all who are concerned with health and safety bid us to cook them first, since a certain risk attends the eating of any uncooked mussels. They must be scrubbed clean and 'bearded', by which is meant taking off the byssus, a tuft of fibres projecting from the shell, which serves to anchor the mussel to its perch. They should then be put in a pot with a little added liquid and steamed open; after which various things can be done with them, as indicated in the list of recipes.

RECIPES

Mouclade, 292

Moules à la Fécampoise, 303

Mussels and chips (Belgian), 311

Zeeland fried mussels, 321

HORSE MUSSEL   Family *Mytilidae*

Modiolus modiolus (Linnaeus)

REMARKS   Maximum length around 15 cm, although an exceptional specimen of 23 cm was once found.

Spanish: Mejillón barbado
French: Moule barbue
Swedish: Hästmussla
Norwegian: Oskjell
Other: Ova (Faroese); Yoag
  (Shetland)

This species has a wide range in the North Atlantic, from the White Sea down to Biscay and from Labrador to North Carolina; and is also present in the North Pacific.

The shells are purplish yellow in colour, but covered by a dark brown periostracum. The animal inside is orange, with a red foot. Like the fan mussel on the next page, this species often harbours a pea crab (see page 206) within its capacious shell.

In some places it forms extraordinarily dense beds. There is one of about 10 square miles near the Isle of Man, and many in Canadian waters. A density of 2030 horse mussels to the square metre was recorded in Passamaquoddy Bay.

CUISINE   The horse mussel is generally held to be inferior to the ordinary mussel. It is, however, one of the few bivalves which Norwegians eat. What they usually do is steam them open, shuck them, wrap them up in pieces of bacon and then fry the little parcels. The horse mussel has also been eaten in the north of Ireland, the Firth of Clyde and the Faroes. Glaswegians have known it by the name clabbydoo, from the Gaelic clab-dubh, meaning large black-mouth. (The Gaelic name for the common mussel is feusgan.)

Canadian authorities who are interested in marketing this large natural resource say that the startling colour of the orange female gonads may put consumers off, but that the problem is diminished if the meats are breaded in readiness for deep-frying. In the past, Canadians have steamed open these mussels, which they sometimes call red mussels, and eaten them like soft-shell clams.

Recipes for the ordinary mussel (see page 217) can usually be applied to horse mussels. Do not, however, try to make anything as delicate as Mouclade with them; they are rather coarse eating and call for a robust recipe.

FAN MUSSEL, PEN SHELL, SEA-WING

Family *Pinnidae*

Pinna fragilis Pennant
Pinna pectinata

Portuguese: Funil
Spanish: Nácar
French: Jambonneau
German: Steckmuschel

REMARKS This, the largest British bivalve, may measure over 35 cm in length. The shell is yellow-brown in colour. It lives in sand or mud, pointed end down, and attaches itself to its home by a silky byssus, from which an expensive kind of gold or cinnamon-coloured fabric used to be woven, notably at Tarentum. The nature and size of this byssus is indicated in the lower drawing, taken from Step (*British Shells*).

The *Pinna* . . . is always found in muddy places, but never without a companion, which they call *pinnoteres* or *pinnophylax*, and which is a little shrimp, or in some places a crab, a searcher for food. The *Pinna* first gapes open, and, being destitute of sight, exposes its body within to various little fishes, which come leaping by close to it, and being unmolested grow so bold as to skip into its shell and fill it full. The *Pinnoteres*, waiting for the opportunity, gives notice to the *Pinna* by a gentle pinch; upon which, shutting its mouth, it kills whatever is within the shell, and divides the spoil with its companion. (Pliny.)

The fan mussel is found as far north as Shetland. In parts of Ireland it used to be called powder horn; and at Plymouth caper-longer, a version of the Italian capa longa said to have been brought home by British bluejackets, who had evidently failed to notice that the Italian name applies rather to the razor-shell (page 240).

CUISINE As for the scallop (page 227). That is to say, the adductor muscle is eaten, and is delicious.

EUROPEAN OYSTER

Family *Ostreidae*

Ostrea edulis Linnaeus

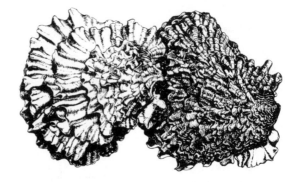

REMARKS   Maximum length about 11 cm, but larger specimens can be found. (All oysters tend to grow to fit their habitat and are likely to have distorted shapes, which may be exceptionally long.) The colour of the shells is variable; and they are covered by a thin, brownish periostracum.

Portuguese: Ostra plana
Spanish: Ostra
French: Huître, Huître plate
Dutch: Oester
German: Auster
Polish: Ostryga
Russian: Ustritsa
Finnish: Osteri
Swedish: Ostron
Norwegian: Østers
Danish: Østers
Icelandic: Ostra
Other: Llymarch (Welsh)

The natural range of this oyster is gratifyingly extensive; from the Norwegian Sea down to the Mediterranean and Morocco. It is cultured in many places, including: Britain, especially in Essex, Kent, Cornwall and the area of the Solent; France, where the district of Marennes-Oléron accounts for over 60 per cent of production, but there are many other famous names such as Arcachon, the Bay of l'Aiguillon, l'île de Ré, the Morbihan with Auray as its oyster capital, the Rade de Brest and the Channel coast from Saint-Brieuc to Cancale; Belgium, where the oysters of Ostend are renowned; the Netherlands, whose production is mainly in Zeeland; and Denmark, where Limfjord is the famous name.

The culture of oysters goes back to classical times. It is a field in which changes of a dramatic nature occur, either from accidental causes, such as the shipwreck mentioned on page 224, or as a result of natural disasters. Areas famed for their oysters may suddenly find themselves with none and have to undergo the apparent ignominy of purchasing seed oysters from rivals elsewhere. But the ignominy is not real, for oysters often benefit from being transferred and it is a characteristic of their culture that it involves moving them at intervals.

France is by far the largest producer of oysters in Europe. The culture of *Ostrea edulis* was first developed on a large scale in the Morbihan in the south of Brittany.

The story of ostreiculture in that region has been told in full and poetic detail by Eleanor Clark in *The Oysters of Locmariaquer*, a book to be recommended with the utmost warmth. Here I explain the procedures in more summary and prosaic style.

Oysters produce millions of larval oysters in the form of 'spat', which are at first free-swimming, but which soon anchor themselves to some support, to which in the ordinary course of events they would remain attached until death overtook them. Man, however, provides supports in the form of 'collectors', which in the south of Brittany are special hollow tiles treated with lime to afford a hold to the tiny oysters and to permit their easy removal. These are placed in the water at a carefully calculated time in June, when the fall of spat and the temperature are favourable. If all goes well, they are speedily encrusted with larval oysters, which are allowed to stay on them for eight to ten months. The tiles are then retrieved and the tiny oysters, each weighing about 1 gram, are stripped off so that they can be redisposed in parks or basins. There they will have some protection, while they grow, from their natural enemies such as starfish, whelks and various predatory fish. Each year they will be moved to a new park or basin. All this counts as the stage of 'élevage'.

The parks in which the oysters grow are of various kinds. Some are exposed at low tide, others are always submerged. The basins, or 'claires', which are used in many places are constructed so that they have a constant supply of the sea water from which the oysters draw their nutrition, each oyster filtering anything from 1 to 6 litres an hour – which in human terms would mean that each of us would work through the contents of a large public swimming-pool every day.

At the age of three or four years the oysters will be transferred for a few months to the best possible conditions for their 'affinage', or refinement of quality. Finally, they undergo 'l'expédition', which means preparing them to survive for ten days or so out of water and then packing them up.

CUISINE People for whom oysters are a rare treat will do well to eat them straight from the half-shell, with their own juices and a little lemon juice. Strong added tastes such as horseradish or tabasco are inappropriate.

However, there are places, even in Europe, where oysters can be gathered free or bought cheaply. It then becomes appropriate to use them in other ways, for variety. The main thing to remember, if you cook them, is that the cooking should be very brief, just enough to make their edges curl.

RECIPE (see also American recipes listed on page 225)
Huîtres farcies à la charentaise, 291

A diagram of an oyster of the species *Ostrea edulis*, adapted from the drawing by M. Boudarez and published by the Comité Interprofessionnel de la Conchyliculture (C.I.C.) in France.

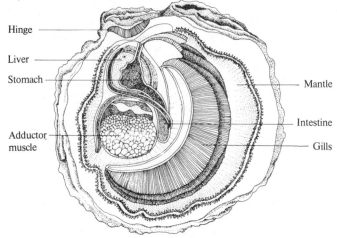

Hinge

Liver

Stomach

Mantle

Intestine

Adductor muscle

Gills

THE TERMINOLOGY OF OYSTERS IN BRITAIN AND FRANCE

Various terms are applied to oysters. Some refer to their species; some to their original provenance, that is to say, where the seed came from; some to the places in which they have been reared or readied for marketing; some to the manner in which they have been cultured; and some to their size.

Britain

The terms used in Britain of British oysters are as follows:

NATIVE OYSTERS are those which are reared from indigenous stock.

WHITSTABLE OYSTERS are from the vicinity of Whitstable in Kent. They are mostly relaid seed oysters from Brittany, and none the worse for that. However, ROYAL WHITSTABLES, an appellation controlled by the Company of Free Fishers and Dredgers of Whitstable, are genuine English natives.

HELFORD OYSTERS are from Helford in Cornwall.

COLCHESTER OYSTERS are from the vicinity of Colchester, and the most famous of these are PYEFLEETS, from the Pyefleet creek in the Colne fishery ground.

Those of the BLACKWATER river in Essex, which are fattened at West Mersea, are also well known.

The grading of British oysters by size is done more informally than in France. Precise measurements are not used. Those in the trade are practised in judging the size of the oyster itself by both the size of the shell and its weight. The largest oysters are grade 1; grade 2 oysters are big, grade 3 of medium size and grade 4 small. The very smallest are known as 'buttons'. One of the greatest experts in Britain tells me that in seeking value for money it is almost always best to buy grade 2 oysters.

France

The terms commonly used are as follows:

PLATES, often followed by a place name, as in Plates d'Arcachon, are simply oysters of the species *Ostrea edulis*, which are relatively flat in shape.

GRAVETTES D'ARCACHON are particularly flat and regular in shape and come, of course, from Arcachon.

BELONS and ARMORICAINES are other terms used for oysters of this species, indicating that they come from specific parts of Brittany.

HUÎTRES CREUSES is the name now used to denote either oyters of the species *Crassostrea angulata* (page 224), which have traditionally been called PORTUGAISES and still are, or those of the species *Crassostrea gigas* (page 224), which have gradually been supplanting the Portuguese oyster in the industry. Neither species is indigenous to France.

FINES DE CLAIRE is the name for oysters raised in special basins, such as those of Marennes-Oleron, many of which are former salt basins.

HUÎTRES SPÉCIALES is a name for Portuguese oysters of an exceptional quality, which is attained by placing them in strictly limited numbers in basins or parks of *Ostrea edulis*.

VERTES DE MARENNES, which may also be referred to simply as MARENNES, are oysters with a greenish tinge which they acquire naturally * through being reared in the important region of Marennes-Oléron, where over 60 per cent of French oysters are produced.

HUÎTRES DE BOUZIGUES, by the way, are from the Mediterranean; Bouzigues being a small place where ostreiculture was begun in the Bassin de Thau.

Finally, the grading by size, which is done differently according to the species, but always by weight.

HUÎTRES PLATES		HUÎTRES CREUSES	
grade number	weight of a hundred	grade number	weight of a thousand
000	11 kilos	1	100 kilos
00	9 kilos	2	80 kilos
0	8 kilos	3	60 kilos
1	7 kilos	4	40 kilos
2	6 kilos		
3	5 kilos		
4	4 kilos		

* The green colour is not produced by copper, as some people suppose, but is chlorophyll derived from a minute organism which turns blue-green in these (and some other) waters and which imparts its colour to the oysters when passing through the oysters' filtrage systems. The vertes de Marennes are my own favourite oysters; although I am not sure that I could match the feat of M. Progneaux, author of *Les spécialités et les recettes gastronomiques charentaises*, who was blindfolded and proceeded to eat a mixture of green and white oysters, every one of which he identified correctly.

PORTUGUESE OYSTER

Family *Ostreidae*

Crassostrea angulata (Lamarck)

REMARKS   Maximum length about 17 cm. The shell is usually whitish or a dirty brown.

The Portuguese oyster, as its name suggests, is a native of Portugal (and of Spain and Morocco), which has, however, been introduced into France and Britain. The story has often been told of how a ship called the *Morlaisien* had to shelter in the Gironde during stormy weather in the 1860s; how her cargo of Portuguese oysters, having spoiled, was thrown overboard; and how those oysters which were still alive found the 'eaux limoneuses' of the Gironde perfectly to their liking and multiplied. It is a characteristic of the Portuguese oyster to be adaptable. It also grows rapidly and is altogether more robust than *Ostrea edulis*.

Portuguese: Ostra (portuguesa)
Spanish: Ostra (portuguesa)
French: Portugaise

CUISINE   As for the European oyster (page 221); but it is generally less good.

GIANT OYSTER, PACIFIC OYSTER

Family *Ostreidae*

Crassostrea gigas (Thunberg)

This large oyster from the Orient is not a native of the North Atlantic area, but is being introduced successfully in some places. Its maximum size is dismaying: 25 cm! The drawing on the right shows what it looks like, although like all oysters it is of variable shape. Small specimens can be quite good.

AMERICAN OYSTER, EASTERN OYSTER

Family *Ostreidae*

Crassostrea virginica Gmelin

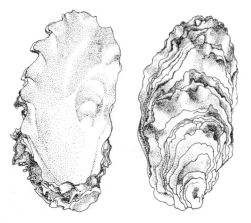

REMARKS   Maximum length about 17 cm. The shell is rough, heavy and usually greyish. These valuable creatures have a range from New Brunswick down to the Gulf of Mexico. Consumption of them was at its height in about 1895, when 170 million pounds were harvested. The annual total sank below 100 million in the late 1920s and has since fallen close to the 50 million mark.

These oysters are marketed under a variety of names, usually indicating whence they come. The most renowned are from Long Island (Blue Point, Robbins Island, Gardiners Bay, etc.) and the Chesapeake region (Chincoteague Bay etc.). Oysters are often transplanted to spend the last few months of their lives in these most favoured habitats, so as to acquire the special flavours associated with them.

I asked an expert at the Fisheries Laboratory at Gloucester, Mass., for a dispassionate opinion about the merits of the various types. He said without hesitation that the best were the 'Cape' oysters, from Cape Cod, whether they came from Wellfleet or Chatham or Wareham. This was because of their high salt content and slow growth-rate. It takes them five years to grow to full size in the cold waters of Cape Cod, whereas oysters in Chesapeake Bay only take three. Moreover, because they grow more slowly, they do not form such large clusters and keep a better shape, ideal for what is called the 'half-shell trade'.

CUISINE   As for the European oyster (page 221); but there is much more emphasis on cooking oysters on the American side of the Atlantic. This is because their relative abundance there has prompted Americans to seek a wide variety of ways of preparing them.

RECIPES

Oyster stew, 420

Oysters Kipling, 421

Eastern Shore oyster soup, 430

SCALLOP, GREAT SCALLOP

Family *Pectinidae*

Pecten maximus (Linnaeus)

Portuguese: Vieira
Spanish: Vieira, Concha de
   peregrino
French: Coquille Saint-Jacques
Dutch: St Jacobsschelp
German: Kammuschel
Russian: Grebeshok
Swedish: Kaḿmussla
Norwegian: Kamskjell
Danish: Kammusling
Icelandic: Hörpudiskor
Other: Escallop, Scollop;
   Godfiche (Normandy);
   Cragen gylchog (Welsh);
   Tanrogan (Isle of Man)

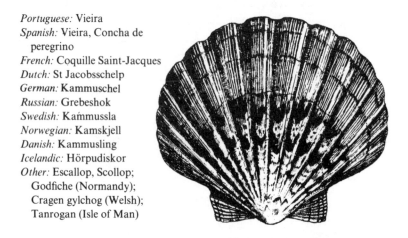

REMARKS   Maximum diameter about 15 cm. The shell is usually whitish, brown or pinkish. The species has a range from Norway to the Iberian Peninsula.

Pecten maximus is not the only large scallop in the North Atlantic. I show, below left. ***Placopecten magellicanus*** (Gmelin), the ATLANTIC DEEP-SEA SCALLOP, for which there is a growing North American fishery. The smaller ***Chlamys islandica*** (Müller), the ICELAND SCALLOP, is shown below right. It has been caught and marketed from both Iceland and Canada. It is of good quality, but its muscle is less white and somewhat firmer than those of the better-known scallops.

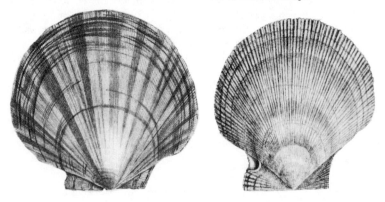

Scallops do not crawl or burrow, so do not have a large 'foot'. Instead they have a highly developed adductor muscle, by means of which they can open and close their shells and so propel themselves through the water.

Most scallops are hermaphrodites, each containing both an orange roe (or coral) and a whitish testis. It is the practice in Europe, but not in North America, to eat these as well as the adductor muscle.

The drawing shows these and other parts of the scallop, including the eyes. About fifty of these, green ringed with blue, are set in the frill, not to show the scallops where they are going, since they are always going in the other direction, but to warn them of danger approaching.

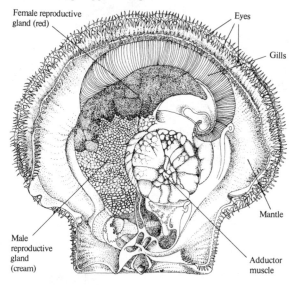

Female reproductive gland (red)

Eyes

Gills

Mantle

Male reproductive gland (cream)

Adductor muscle

CUISINE   Scallops are usually cleaned at sea, and only the muscle (or muscle and roe) are brought to market. In Canada, however, enterprising firms have sold canned 'scallop rings and roes' or 'rims and roes', incorporating the frill and providing good material for chowders.

Scallops may be baked in foil in the oven, with herbs; threaded on to skewers and grilled; cooked à la meunière; battered and deep-fried; or – a pleasing linguistic conceit, this – 'scalloped', i.e. baked in the oven, with a suitable dressing and breadcrumbs on top, in a scallop shell.

RECIPES

QUEEN, QUEEN SCALLOP, QUIN   Family *Pectinidae*

Chlamys opercularis (Linnaeus)

Portuguese: Vieira
Spanish: Volandeira
French: Vanneau
Dutch: Kammossel
German: Kammuschel
Swedish: Kammussla
Norwegian: Harpeskjell
Danish: Kammusling
Other: Cloisin (Irish)

REMARKS   Maximum diameter 10 cm, average size 6 cm. The shell is almost circular and has about twenty ribs. Its colour may be yellow, orange, pink, red, purple or brown; and it is often spotted or blotched.

The queen usually inhabits deeper waters than the great scallop, and the fishery for it in Britain is a recent development. For cuisine see below.

BAY SCALLOP   Family *Pectinidae*

Argopecten irradians (Lamarck)

REMARKS   Maximum diameter 8 cm. The colour of the shell is variable, from near-white to black through brown, red and purple. It has about twenty ribs.

This is the common commercial scallop of the American Atlantic coast and is found in several varieties, of which another is the southern scallop (New Jersey to Florida). 'On clear, calm days the immature individuals of this species may often be seen in shallow water disporting themselves most gaily, skipping about and snapping their valves in great glee.' (Augusta Foote Arnold.)

CUISINE   A great delicacy. It is usual to sell the muscle only. If this is really fresh, it may be eaten raw, flavoured only by its own juices. Otherwise, see page 227.

OCEAN QUAHOG

Family *Arcticidae*

Arctica islandica (Linnaeus)

REMARKS   The maximum diameter of this almost circular shell is about 11 cm. Its outer covering, or periostracum, is thick, coarse and wrinkled in texture and brown or blackish in colour; so it is sometimes known as the black or mahogany clam. The name ocean quahog is accounted for by its general resemblance to the quahog (page 232) and by the fact that it lives in fairly deep water (15 to 100 metres), in sandy mud. Its range is from Newfoundland to North Carolina. It may be found on beaches after an onshore gale, but has not been well known since it is inaccessible to the casual clam-gatherer. Now, however, large quantities of it are being landed in New England and the Middle Atlantic States, to be used for minced-clam products and stews. This is a result of a serious decline in the available stocks of surf clams (page 236).

The ocean quahog is also available in northern European waters, but is little known there. I learned in Orkney that the name given to it there is koo shell. Ku is the Norwegian word for cow, and this shell was formerly used as the 'cow' in Orkney children's farm games. The Norwegians call the ocean quahog kuskjell or kupeskjell or kuvskjell, presumably because they too, as children, employ the shell in farm games.

CUISINE   I have not had an opportunity to eat this clam myself, but have learned from technical studies by the National Marine Fisheries Service at Gloucester, Mass., that in many clam dishes it is just as good as the quahog (page 232). Some ocean quahogs have a very strong taste, described as being like iodine or seaweed; but this is greatly diminished by removal of the liver, and is anyway not present in ocean quahogs from certain fishing grounds. In general, quality seems to vary considerably according to habitat. Someone who ate some in Orkney declared them to be nothing better than 'watery, grey gristle'. These must have been specimens which had fed poorly and grown slowly. Specimens from good beds are of excellent quality. They do, however, all have dark meat, which makes them unsuitable for New England style clam chowders, which are white, and better for the Manhattan version, which is not.

COCKLE

Family *Cardiidae*

Cerastoderma edule (Linnaeus)
Cardium edule

REMARKS Maximum diameter about 6 cm, but there are said to be places in Orkney where giants of 8 cm have been found. 4 to 4½ cm is the usual size of full-grown specimens and cockles are considered to have reached marketable size at 2½ cm. The colour is brown, pale yellow or dirty white.

This species has a range from the Barents Sea and the Baltic to the Mediterranean and Senegal. In many places it is very abundant; indeed densities of over 10,000 specimens per square metre have been recorded.

Portuguese: Berbigão
Spanish: Berberecho
French: Coque, Bucarde
Dutch: Kokkel, Kokhaan
German: Herzmuschel
Swedish: Hjartmussla
Norwegian: Saueskjell,
    Hjerteskjell
Danish: Hjertemusling
Other: Sourdon (Charentes)

Acanthocardia aculeata (Linnaeus), the SPINY COCKLE (French coque épineuse), occurs as far north as the Channel Islands and Devon. It may reach a size of 10 cm. The creature inside the shell is red; hence the alternative name bloody cockle. *Acanthocardia echinata* (Linnaeus), the PRICKLY COCKLE (French coque rouge), has a range extending much further north, to Norway and the Baltic. These species are shown below, spiny on the left and prickly on the right.

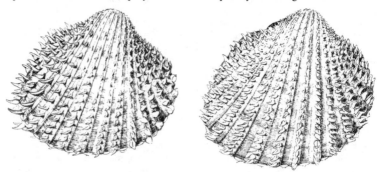

On the American side of the Atlantic the northern species ***Clinocardium ciliatum*** Fabricius ranges from Greenland down to Massachusetts. It is called the ICELAND COCKLE and reaches a size of 5 cm. (The giant Atlantic cockle, ***Dinocardium robustum*** Lightfoot is twice as big, but is rare north of Florida.)

CUISINE Cockles are a valuable and delicious food. They may be eaten raw, or cooked. Before either event they should be left for a few hours in a pail of clean sea water so that they can purge themselves.

RECIPES
Zeeland ways with cockles, 321   Cockles and eggs, 467
Welsh ways with cockles, 466

HEART SHELL, HEART COCKLE   Family *Glossidae*

Glossus humanus (Linnaeus)

REMARKS This species, which is not a true cockle but resembles them, has a range from Iceland and Norway to the Mediterranean. Viewed sideways, it is shaped like a heart; whence the English names and the French coeur de boeuf. It is good to eat, although uncommon in the markets. Lovell recorded great enthusiasm for the species among English fishermen, who used to call them Torbay-noses or oxhorn-cockles; and concludes their description with a recipe. 'The wife of a coastguardsman, who had lived many years at Brixham, and had often luxuriated in a dish of these delicious shellfish, gave me the following recipe for cooking them: *To dress Torbay noses.* Wash the shells well, then boil them till they open – about ten minutes or so; take the fish out of their shells and put them into a frying-pan with some butter, a little salt and pepper, and fry till they are of a good brown colour; then serve.'

QUAHOG, LITTLENECK, HARD CLAM, HARDSHELL CLAM

Family *Veneridae*

Mercenaria mercenaria (Linnaeus)

REMARKS   Maximum length about 13 cm. The more or less oval shell has a dull coloration outside – dirty white, brown or greyish, sometimes with zigzag red markings near the margins – and is purplish inside.

The quahog (pronounced co-hog) is a native of North America, but has established for itself (via the kitchens of ocean liners) English colonies in Southampton Water and Portsmouth harbour; a piece of private molluscan enterprise which has prompted human entrepreneurs to start the culture of quahogs in the Isle of Wight. The species has also been introduced to the basin of the River Seudre in France. The French call it 'clam'. It has also been introduced to certain harbours in the south of Ireland.

In America the range of the quahog extends from Canada down to Florida. It is of great commercial importance and may be met in the markets and restaurants under a variety of names. Quahog or quahaug is of Indian derivation. Hard clam is used in indication of the strength of the shell, in contrast to the thin shell of the soft-shelled clam (page 239). The drawing at the top of the next page shows the significance of the name littleneck. This refers to the short siphon of the species, which compels it to live near the surface of the muddy beds which are its favourite haunts. But names are also used to indicate different sizes. In New York the list runs thus: littlenecks, 450–650 to the bushel; cherrystones, 300–325 to the bushel; mediums, 180 to the bushel; and chowders, 125 to the bushel. A slightly different system operates at Boston, where the larger specimens are called sharps.

The name wampum clam may also be met. Wampum was Red Indian bead money and the purple interior of the quahog shell was used for high-denomination wampum.

CUISINE AND RECIPES   As Euell Gibbons remarks: 'How you eat a quahog depends largely on its size.' Those up to the size of cherrystones are best eaten raw. Mediums should be steamed open and served on the half-shell with melted butter, or used in a Rhode Island or Manhattan clam chowder (see page 423). The largest quahogs would be used for a New England clam chowder (page 416) or Stuffed clams (page 421). These are all American recipes. A French one suited to fairly small quahogs is that for Palourdes farcies on page 302.

A quahog or littleneck (page 232) meets a soft-shelled clam or long-neck (page 239), both with siphons extended.

WARTY VENUS

Family *Veneridae*

Venus verrucosa Linnaeus

REMARKS   Maximum length 7 cm. A plumpish shell which may be as wide as it is long. The colour is dirty white or brown, the periostracum chestnut-brown. The drawing, which is from the old-fashioned but ever-useful manual of Joubin and Le Danois, shows the 'praire vivante' and also brings out clearly the sculpture of concentric ridges on the shell, which develop into wart-like spines on the margins and account for the weird name warty venus.

Portuguese: Pé-de-burro (donkey's foot)
Spanish: Almeja
French: Praire

This is another southerly species, the range of which extends from the southern shores of Britain all the way down to and round the Cape of Good Hope.

A related clam which I met at Bilbao under the name almeja is *Venus gallina* Linnaeus, which has pretty zigzag stripes on its shell.

CUISINE   This species is highly appreciated in France. What is said on the next page about the palourde applies just as well to it.

CARPET-SHELL   Family *Veneridae*

Venerupis decussata (Linnaeus)

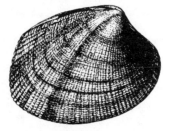

REMARKS   Maximum length 8 cm. The shell is white, yellow or light brown in colour, often with darker brown rays, streaks or other marks. The range of this species is from Britain to the Mediterranean.

Portuguese: Amêijoa
Spanish: Almeja fina
French: Palourde

Lovell states that this carpet-shell was called butter-fish in Hampshire. The name is presumably honorific (they melt in the mouth?), since Lovell also says that the 'butter-fish' were thought to be 'richer and better than cockles. They are found at low tide not far from high-water mark, and their locality is easily detected by *two* holes in the sand or gravel (unlike the cockle, which makes but one) about an inch or so apart . . . Butter-fish are considered very wholesome and I was assured by the cockle-gatherers that they might be eaten with impunity at all times of the year, and never disagreed with people as the mussels and cockles occasionally do.'

CUISINE AND RECIPES   Of excellent quality. The Portuguese and Spaniards consume large quantities and have many recipes for their preparation, such as those given on page 274. The French often eat them raw, like oysters, but also have numerous ways of cooking them. The recipe for Palourdes farcies (page 302) is well known in Brittany; and there are corresponding recipes in the Charentes region and elsewhere.

Venerupis aurea (Gmelin) is a smaller relation, known as the GOLDEN CARPET-SHELL (in French clovisse jaune). The shell is often, but not always, yellow and may measure up to $4\frac{1}{2}$ cm. It has an extensive range, from the Norwegian Sea to the Mediterranean. Like the true clovisse of the Mediterranean, it is excellent with pasta and makes a delicious soup.

VENUS SHELL (a generic name)   Family *Veneridae*

Callista chione (Linnaeus)
Meretrix chione

REMARKS Maximum length 9 cm, but 7 cm   *Portuguese:* Concha fina
is more usual. The shell is reddish brown or   *Spanish:* Saverina
pinkish brown in colour, with rays of a deeper   *French:* Verni
hue. The exterior has a highly distinctive
sheen, almost as though it had been varnished, which accounts for the French
name.

The range of the species is from the southern parts of Britain down to the
Mediterranean.

Lovell remarked that this was not a common bivalve, but that specimens had
been taken in Hayle, Cornwall, where the fishermen called them cocks, and that
they were fairly abundant at the mouth of the River Helford, where the name was
cram.

The shells are considered to be especially suitable for the delicate art of painting
miniatures on sea-shells.

CUISINE AND RECIPES In certain parts of France this clam is known as the
grosse palourde or grande palourde; and it may generally be treated like the
palourde (page 234). It is often eaten raw in the Mediterranean region; and I recall
having some magnificently handsome raw ones at La Rochelle, but finding that
their size made me wish that they had been cooked – for I have an instinct which
strives to restrain me from eating raw any bivalve larger than a grade ooo belon.
They certainly can be cooked, according to any of the standard recipes for clams of
middling size. Lovell quotes Poli (*Testacea utriusque Siciliae*) as opining that the
verni is at its best when simply cooked in oil or butter, with breadcrumbs, chopped
parsley and pepper and salt. No doubt Poli meant it to be cooked thus in the half-
shell; and his advice provides a simple version of Stuffed clams, for which a
transatlantic recipe will be found on page 421. The recipe for Palourdes farcies on
page 302 would also be suitable.

SURF CLAM, BAR CLAM, HEN CLAM (and sometimes SEA CLAM)

Family *Mactridae*

Spisula (*Hemimactra*) *solidissima* (Dillwyn)
Mactra solidissima

REMARKS   Maximum length about 16 cm. The shell is thick and smooth, creamy brown in colour with a periostracum of much the same hue. This is a species of the eastern coasts of North America and is particularly abundant off the New Jersey coast. It is of considerable commercial importance. Almost three quarters of the clams harvested in the whole of the United States are of this one species; but it is less important in Canada.

Although the species is known as surf clam, or bar clam, because the early settlers found them there, it really belongs to deeper offshore waters, whence it is often washed up on to beaches. A fisherman at Wellfleet on Cape Cod told me that after a recent hurricane large numbers of them had been washed up on the ocean side of the Cape; some as big as 20 cm across. He said that it was pathetic to see them gaping open and trying to manoeuvre themselves back into the sea. Meanwhile, the seagulls were 'having a ball'. They are accustomed to swooping down, picking a clam off the beach and flying over to the nearest parking-lot, where they drop the creature on to the 'black-top'. (I thought at first that he meant a motor-car with a black roof, but then realized that black-top means the surface of the parking-lot.) The effect of this is to shatter the shell of the clam, which the seagull proceeds to eat. However, on this occasion the seagulls found that they could just get the clams off the ground but could not then make it over to the parking-lot, since they were so heavy.

South of New Jersey, the size of this large clam diminishes. Around Cape Hatteras it is replaced by the southerly species *Spisula raveneli* (Conrad). Further north, in Canadian waters is *Spisula polynyma* (Stimpson), which has a flatter shell and a purple foot. The flesh turns red when cooked and has a superior flavour. The genus is also represented in European waters, for example by *Spisula solida* (Linnaeus), a smaller clam which does not seem to be eaten.

CUISINE AND RECIPES The surf clam is too big to be eaten whole like other clams. It is usually shucked raw and minced for use in clam chowders. Strips of the 'foot' are sometimes prepared for deep-frying. But if you are preparing the clams yourself remember that the 'foot' is rather tough and that the really delicious parts are the twin adductor muscles, which are found just below the apex of the shell. They are white and cylindrical, and about 2 cm in diameter and height. The juice of the surf clam is also good. Save it by opening the clams over a funnel inserted into a jug. Use some for washing the muscles free of any sand or grit. The rest can become a vehicle in which to freeze the muscles, or used in Clam chowder (page 423) or drunk as Clam nectar.

TROUGH-SHELLS AND OTTER SHELLS

Families *Mactridae* and *Lutrariidae*

The species catalogued on the previous page is by far the most important clam in this group. But *Spisula solida*, mentioned with it, is only one of a number of related clams which are found on the European side of the Atlantic and are worth eating. I describe two such species below and provide drawings of them at the foot of the page.

Mactra corallina (Linnaeus), the RAYED TROUGH-SHELL, is usually creamy in colour, with purplish tints and brown rays. It is of good quality and ranges from Norway down to the Mediterranean. It is called almeijóla in Portugal; and blanchet, flie, fausse palourde or fausse praire in France, the last two names implying an intent to deceive, of which the creature must surely be acquitted.

Lutraria lutraria (Linnaeus), the COMMON OTTER SHELL may be over 12 cm long. It is white, light yellow or fawn in colour, with a brown periostracum. Note the long shape (even more noticeable in some other members of the genus). These bivalves used to be known as clumps or horse-shoes in the Channel Islands. They are to be steamed open and then fried.

WEDGE SHELL, BEAN CLAM, COQUINA

Family *Donacidae*

Donax spp.

Portuguese: Cadelinha
Spanish: Coquina, Tellerina
French: Olive (or Haricot)
   de mer

REMARKS .There are many different species of these little wedge shells. The maximum length is generally under 4 cm. The colours of the shells vary greatly. Even within one species they may be white, yellow, brown or purple.

The species shown above, **Donax vittatus** (da Costa), belongs to the European side of the Atlantic, but has several close relations on the American side. They are all quite lively little creatures, compared with the general run of bivalves, and have even been described as 'agile'.

The wedge shells, which are found in the sand around low water mark, can be eaten raw, made into a soup, or steamed open and served with spaghetti.

TELLIN

Family *Scrobiculariidae*

Scrobicularia plana (da Costa)

REMARKS   Maximum width 6 to 7 cm. This species ranges from the Norwegian Sea down to the Mediterranean and beyond. It is abundant around the British Isles. Edward Step (*Shell Life*, 1902) observed that it was called the mud hen on parts of the British coast. The implication is that it was eaten. Nowadays, however, one only hears of it, so far as I can discover, in the Charente-Maritime, where it is known as the lavagnon and prized as a local speciality. The lavagnon has a slightly peppery taste. It is good eaten raw, especially as part of a seafood salad to which it contributes its own special flavour. A recipe for Lavagnons charentais is given on page 290.

SOFT-SHELLED CLAM, LONG-NECK, STEAMER

Family *Myacidae*

Mya (Arenomya) arenaria Linnaeus

REMARKS Maximum length about 15 cm; usual length much less. The shell, shown above left, is dirty white or fawn in colour; the periostracum fawn or light yellow. The shell is thin and brittle and has a permanent gape at each end. The double siphon is long, and accounts for the name long-neck. (In the drawing on page 233 this is shown horizontal, but its normal posture is vertical.)

French: Mye
Dutch: Strandgaper
German: Sandklaffmuschel
Swedish: Sandmussla
Norwegian: Sandskjell
Danish: Sandmusling
Other: Maninose, Nannynose
 (U.S.A.); Brallion (N. Ireland)

The distribution of the species extends from the White Sea down to North Carolina in the west and to Britain and France in the east. The smaller BLUNT GAPER, *Mya truncata* Linnaeus, shown above right, has a comparable range, but only down to Massachusetts in the west. Step, in his *British Shells*, says that the former species was commonly eaten under the name old maid, or clam, on some parts of the British coast at the beginning of the century; but the practice seems to have abated since then.

The soft-shelled clam will tolerate brackish or even fresh water. It will also survive for a long time out of water, and even without oxygen; so it can be marketed in good condition, despite its inability to close itself up completely.

CUISINE AND RECIPES Because they gape, these clams tend to be sandy and gritty. The first step is to purge them by keeping them alive in clean water for a day or two, preferably with a little cornmeal. Once clean, they may be used for any standard clam recipe. They are ideal for a Clambake (page 424), essential for Steamed soft-shelled clams (page 422), good in a Clam pie (page 422) and suitable for both the Canadian Micmac Indian clam chowder (page 406) and the Acadian recipe for Rappie pie with clams (also on page 406).

The reputation of *Mya arenaria* rests also on its excellence when battered and fried. It was the first clam to be so treated; an event said to have taken place at Essex, Mass., in the early part of this century. However, near-by Ipswich became the headquarters of the clam processors and soft-shelled clams therefore became known also as Ipswich clams. They remain the No. 1 clam in New England for battering and frying. See recipes on page 415.

RAZOR-SHELL

Family *Solenidae*

Ensis ensis (Linnaeus)

REMARKS The largest specimens may be over 12 cm long. The shells take their name from the shape of the old-fashioned cut-throat razor. They are very brittle and gape permanently open at both ends, which makes it impossible to market razor clams alive in their shells, as can be done with most other edible bivalves.

Portuguese: Faca, Longueirão
Spanish: Navaja
French: Couteau courbe
Dutch: Scheermes
German: Meerscheiden
Swedish: Knivmussla
Norwegian: Knivskjell
Danish: Knivmusling
Other: Spoot (Orkney)

There are several other closely related species in European waters, such as **Ensis arcuatus** (Jeffreys), which is curved and reaches a length of 15 cm, and **Solen marginatus** Pennant, which is straight in shape. On the American side there is **Ensis directus** Conrad, known as the EASTERN RAZOR CLAM or ATLANTIC JACKKNIFE. It is shown in the lower drawing. Its range is from Canada to South Carolina.

The razor-shells usually have a glossy brown exterior, the shell itself being white but the periostracum brown or yellowish brown or olive.

The razor clam has a long and powerful 'foot' which enables it to make its way through wet sand like a knife through butter, dodging danger by a swift descent downwards. Getting them out of the sand is difficult and may also be perilous, since the sharp edges of the shells can inflict nasty cuts. On some beaches it is possible to cause a razor-shell to pop up out of its hole by the simple expedient of pouring a teaspoonful of salt into the hole. But in other places this technique is dismissed with laughter by the locals, and rightly so for it does not work. One explanation which I have seen is that a razor-clam which has an unwanted dose of salt will if possible take evasive action by going deeper down; but that in places where this is not feasible, for example because there is hard clay under the sand, it will instead come

up. However, George Henry Lewes, who provides (in *Sea-side Studies*, 1858) the most thorough and most amusing discussion of the matter, does not find support for this view in his own experiments. 'There is,' as he says, 'something irresistibly ludicrous in grave men stooping over a hole – their coat-tails pendant in the water, their breath suspended, one hand holding salt, the other alert to clutch the victim – watching the perturbations of the sand, like hungry cats beside the holes of mice...' However, this is what he did, and the varying results convinced him that the procedure involves an intrinsic uncertainty 'which gives a relish to the sport'. He suggests indeed that often, when the razor-shell responds to the salt by letting the tip of his siphon appear momentarily, 'it is merely to see what is the matter, and to indulge in a not altogether frivolous curiosity as to the being who can illogically offer salt to *him* who lives in salt water...'

I have certainly had little success myself in hunting these creatures. 'Wanted: Spoots, Spoots and More Spoots' said a newspaper advertisement when I was last in Orkney, spoots being what they call razor-shells there. I went spooting, at the lowest of low tides and with an expert guide, but came back with nothing but mussels. At least the experience served to bring home to me the extent and depth of Orcadian enthusiasm for spoots; an enthusiasm which is shared by many such communities in which people still catch their own seafood.

CUISINE   For an appraisal of the merits of the razor clam, almost Orcadian in its combination of lyricism with practical detail, I invite the reader to turn to Chapter 5 (Razor Clams and Other Marine Cutlery) of Euell Gibbons's book *Stalking the Blue-Eyed Scallop*. He points out that the razor clam may be used in any recipe calling for clams, including fish soups and clambakes, and that they are delicious by themselves, steamed. 'To steam Razor Clams, put them into a covered kettle and add only ½ cup of water, and steam until all the clams are open, about 10 minutes after boiling starts.'

Razor clams, like oysters, may be eaten in their entirety. If they have a disadvantage, it is that their thin and narrow shells are unsuitable for being stuffed with the meat; but it is of course perfectly feasible to use the shells of other clams for this purpose.

RECIPES

Stuffed clams, 421   Spoots in Orkney, 447
Maryland clam fritters, 429

PIDDOCK

Family *Pholadidae*

Pholas dactylus Linnaeus

Portuguese: Taralhão
Spanish: Folado
French: Dail
German: Bohrmuschel,
   Steinbohrer
Swedish: Borr musslor
Danish: Knivmusling

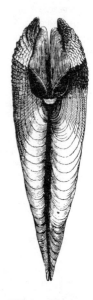

REMARKS A piddock shell may measure over 15 cm. It is whitish or pale grey in colour, but often discoloured by bits of whatever it has been boring into; for it is a most persistent and versatile borer. 'The common piddock bores into sand, peat, marl, wood, including submerged tree trunks, shale, slate, chalk, red sandstone and schists . . .' The purpose of this activity is to provide itself with a safe shelter, which it achieves at the cost of making itself a prisoner for life, communicating with the outside world and feeding by the sole means of its double siphon.

The piddock is remarkably luminous; so much so, according to one writer, that 'if the flesh is chewed and kept in the mouth, the breath becomes luminous and looks like a real flame.' Another found that a single piddock 'rendered seven ounces of milk so luminous that the faces of persons might be distinguished by it'.

The piddock has, or used to have, two interesting names at Brest: religieuse and bonne-soeur. Perhaps a resemblance was seen between its shape and that of the headgear of certain nuns.

CUISINE The piddock has a high reputation in some places. When the inhabitants of Weymouth called it the 'long oyster' they were not being ironic. Some Spaniards would echo the compliments; and the piddock has also been eaten with enthusiasm in Brittany and the Channel Islands. It can be eaten raw, after being cleaned, but is commonly boiled and dressed.

Cephalopods

Cephalopod means 'head-footed' and refers to the way in which the arms and tentacles of these creatures sprout directly from the head. The arrangement strikes many people as repulsive. Others find beauty, or at least fascination, in the extraordinary forms which an animal such as the octopus can assume. The convolutions of their tentacles, the 'wondrous curls' to which Athenaeus referred, are a frequent theme in classical art. Their excellence as food was also acknowledged by classical authors. These traditions have persisted in the Mediterranean area in a way which is only matched in Japan. (A study by the F.A.O. of the intensity of the exploitation of estimated cephalopod resources in the fifteen fishing areas of the world showed that it is only in the Mediterranean and the north-west Pacific that a level of about 50 per cent is attained, most areas recording less than 10 per cent.)

The heyday for cephalopods was far back in prehistoric times, when the waters swarmed with a multitude of species. They almost all had external shells then. Nowadays, only the nautilus and the argonaut possess these. The cuttlefish and squid have an internal shell, reduced in the squid to a chitinized 'pen'; and the octopus lacks even this. But contemporary cephalopods thrive, perhaps because of their superior intelligence. They are brainier than other molluscs; and the octopus is the brainiest of all.* The largest, however, and the only one to match the giant cephalopods of hundreds of millions of years ago, is the giant squid or kraken, which occurs in the North Atlantic as well as in other oceans and of which some famous specimens have been stranded on the shores of Norway and New-foundland. These occurrences are rare and such bits of these stranded giants as survived seem to have been given to biologists rather than cooks; so I do not know whether they are edible. If they are, they would feed a lot of people, since their total length (including the tentacles) may be over 20 metres.

---

* The squid is less impressive, having a tendency to be moon-struck, if Augusta Foote Arnold was correctly informed. 'On bright moonlight nights squids often go ashore in vast numbers, and perish within a few inches of their native element, which they seem to be unable to regain. These creatures usually swim backward, and the theory is that, dazzled by the bright light of the moon, they continue to gaze at it while swimming, and if there happens to be a shore in the direction of their movements, they suddenly find themselves beached. The fishermen of Canada and New England take advantage of this habit and capture great quantities of squids by placing bright lights in the bows of their boats and then rowing towards shore, thus driving the squids out of the water.'

The cephalopods all possess ink sacs, which secrete a black or brown ink. This can be ejected at will, to screen the creature's escape from a predator. (Some authorities believe that the ink is ejected, not to make a screen, but in such a way as to form a likeness of the cephalopod, which itself turns colourless and slips away while the predator attacks its inky ghost.)

Even more ingenious is the arrangement of chromatophores in the skin of a cephalopod. These are pigment cells which can be expanded and contracted by muscular action. The degree of expansion can be as much as 60 times, from pin-point to pinhead; and the change can be effected in less than a second. 'It is this speed which enables colour changes to sweep over the surface of a cephalopod with a rapidity and variety more like that of an animated electric sign than of an animal.' (Lane, in his superbly readable *Kingdom of the Octopus*.)

The edible cephalopods may be divided into the 'ten-footed' (cuttlefish and squid) and the 'eight-footed' (octopus). The quality of the species within each category varies; but in each the best is very good.

Cleaning cephalopods in preparation for cooking them is not difficult once one has learned how. To help my readers learn, I reproduce here, by kind permission of the New England Fisheries Development Program, versions of their drawings of how to clean squid, the cephalopod which is most widely consumed.

CUTTLEFISH

Family *Sepiidae*

Sepia officinalis (Linnaeus)

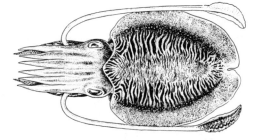

REMARKS Maximum body length about 25 cm. The colour is variable, but usually dark with markings such as those shown in the drawing.

The cuttlefish is unusual among the cephalopods in that it is confined to the eastern Atlantic (north and south) and the Mediterranean. It is also unusual in having an internal 'bone' or shell, which used to be ground by druggists into tooth-powder but is now mainly used for exercising the beaks

Portuguese: Choco
Spanish: Jibia
French: Seiche
Dutch: Zeekat
German: Tintenfische
Swedish: Bläckfiskar
Norwegian: Blekksprut
Danish: Blæksprutte
Icelandic: Smokkfiskur
Other: Casseron (Charentes)

of pet birds. The ink of the cuttlefish was formerly used for making the colour sepia. Its ink is certainly abundant and pervasive, and one should try not to break the ink sacs if discarding them. Otherwise one risks a repetition of the cry in a play of Antiphanes (echoed by me to wife in our own kitchen when I first tackled a cuttlefish):

> 'Give me some cuttlefish first. O Hercules,
> They've dirtied every place with ink; here, take them,
> And wash them clean.'

CUISINE AND RECIPE Clean the cuttlefish by removing beak, eyes and 'innards'; but reserve at least one of the ink sacs if you wish to serve a dramatically black dish. The mantle (body case) and tentacles and arms, and most of the head, are then cut into serving pieces and may be stewed, with wine if available, or simmered in a Provençal mixture of olive oil and onion and tomato and garlic. A French recipe for grilled cuttlefish is given on page 292.

SQUID

Family *Loliginidae*

Loligo forbesi Steenstrup

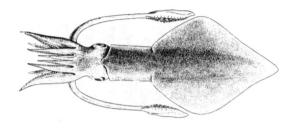

REMARKS   Maximum body length 60 cm. This species belongs to the north-east Atlantic and is the most common edible squid as far south as the British Isles. Further south, and in the Mediterranean, its place is taken by the similar *Loligo vulgaris* (Lamarck), to which the Portuguese, Spanish and French names cited here normally apply.

Squid are able to swim strongly by jet propulsion of water through their funnels, which they can direct backwards or forwards. The fins at the rear of the body are used for steering or for small movements. At the front they have two tentacles and eight 'arms'.

Portuguese: Lula
Spanish: Calamar
French: Encornet
Dutch: Pijlinktvis
German: Kalmar
Polish: Kalmar
Russian: Kal'mar
Swedish: Kalmar, Bläckfisk
Norwegian: Blekkspruter
Danish: Blæksprutter
Icelandic: Smokkfiskur
Other: Inks (a plural name used in the British fish trade)

I show some other edible squid on the next page. *Loligo pealei* (Lesueur) is an American species, common from Cape Cod to Venezuela and known as the LONG-FINNED SQUID or BONE SQUID or WINTER SQUID. Its body may be 45 cm long. Americans of Mediterranean descent provide a limited market for it, which is being expanded by vigorous publicity campaigns. This squid is an important resource, available in heavy concentrations around the outer continental shelf during the winter. But boats from Spain, and even Japan, have been the most active in exploiting it so far.

Alloteuthis subulata (Lamarck), known as the SMALL SQUID (maximum length 17 cm), is landed and sold in some places, including Scotland.

Illex illecebrosus (Lesueur) belongs to a different family, *Ommastrephidae*. Whereas the loliginid squids referred to above are inshore creatures, the ommastrephid squids are oceanic; and indeed constitute one of the large underexploited resources of the oceans. *Illex illecebrosus* occurs in slightly different forms in northern waters on both sides of the Atlantic. Americans call it the SHORT-FINNED SQUID. On the European side may also be found *Todarodes sagittatus* (Lamarck), the FLYING FLUSK, which the French call calmar (but beware, some

Frenchmen use the name for all squid). It is sometimes referred to as 'hard squid', in contrast to ***Todaropsis eblanae*** (Ball), the almost inedible 'soft squid'.

CUISINE   The squid might well have been created expressly for cooks to stuff, so conveniently is its body shaped for this purpose. It has to be cleaned out first, and the head removed, as shown in the drawings on page 244. The tentacles and arms are usually chopped up and incorporated in the stuffing, which may be whatever you fancy. One suggestion is given below; others are in my *Mediterranean Seafood.* However, squid does not have to be stuffed. The cleaned body can be cut into rings and fried. Or you can try the other recipes listed below, the first of which is for the very small squid which the Portuguese call lulinhas and the Spaniards chipirones.

RECIPES

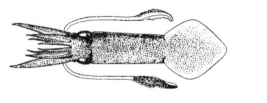

Loligo pealei

Alloteuthis subulata

Illex illecebrosus

Todarodes sagittatus

OCTOPUS

Family *Octopodidae*

Octopus vulgaris (Linnaeus)

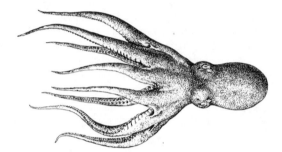

REMARKS The total length of an octopus may be 3 metres, but specimens of this size are rare. The common market length (again, overall) is between 40 and 100 cm.

Portuguese: Polvo
Spanish: Pulpo
French: Poulpe, Pieuvre
Dutch: Octopus
Other: Devil-fish (U.S.A.)

The octopus is common in the eastern Atlantic as far north as the Channel Islands. It is especially common, and highly prized, in the north of Spain. 'Plagues' of the species descend on the southern coasts of England from time to time; plagues in inverted commas because, according to me, a supply of octopus is a blessing, although not yet so perceived by British fishermen, whose lobster-pots and crab-pots it empties. Further north, the octopus seems to be rare or absent. It is also absent from the eastern seaboard of North America, although one species sometimes strays as far north as the Carolinas. Otherwise North Americans must rely on imports or on supplies from the Pacific coast.

CUISINE Cut the muscles which hold the 'innards' in the head; turn the head inside out, clean it and put it back the right way. Beat the octopus (if it is of a fair size) on a stone or with a wooden mallet, to make it more tender. Then proceed according to one of the recipes listed below (or any of the scores in books on Mediterranean cookery). Another possibility, recommended to me in Portugal, is to boil the octopus for a short time only and then to grill pieces of it over charcoal.

RECIPES

Miscellaneous Seafoods

A number of large and edible animals could be mustered for this section of the catalogue. There are the sea turtles, for example, of which several species enter our area. But I have left these out, for various reasons, not least the practical one that one does not find them in fish shops nor catch a specimen while having a holiday at the coast. Moreover, the sea turtles are mostly global in their distribution, and have been described in another book of mine, *Seafood of South-East Asia*, where they sit more suitably (South-East Asia being a region where they are plentiful and more in use as food). It was a tempting idea to include the diamond-back terrapin of the eastern seaboard of the United States; but this is a creature of the salt marshes rather than the sea.

Then there are the whales. But few people nowadays eat whale meat and there is general concern over the risk that certain species of whale will be made extinct. I have therefore left them all out and have allowed them to exclude with themselves the other edible sea mammals, notably the seals. The principles of conservation do not require us to leave seals alone. Indeed, most seal stocks need to be culled regularly to prevent their becoming too large. And I have not forgotten how I once saw a seal being opened up at a fishery station. 'Anyone want salmon paste for tea?' asked the technician jovially, as we passed by. He held up a bowlful of the stomach contents. It was indeed a salmon paste, fresh in aroma, pink in colour and only a little bit chunkier than the product one buys in jars. If seals can gobble as many salmon as they can catch, perhaps man may be allowed to eat seals. But the subject is a sensitive one and the catching and consumption of seals is best left to the Greenlanders and others who have a genuine and traditional dependence on what the seal provides.

These exclusions cause our catalogue to finish with some strikingly uncontroversial items. The sea-urchin is of course a living creature, which belongs to the Order *Diadematoida* and is of pentagonal construction, like the starfish to which it is related. But it has never been invested with even a semblance of the pathetic fallacy and is in no danger of extinction. As for the seaweeds, with which the catalogue ends, they are acceptable even to the most strict vegetarians. My only regret is that I could not go into this interesting field more fully; but it is accompanied by the ,comforting thought that the books by Lily Newton (*Seaweed Utilisation*, 1951) and Euell Gibbons (*Stalking the Blue-Eyed Scallop*, 1964) from which I quote will provide further information for readers who are interested.

SEA-URCHIN, GREEN SEA-URCHIN

Family *Echinidae*

Strongylocentrus droebachiensis (O. F. Müller)

REMARKS   Up to about 8 cm in diameter. There are numerous species of sea-urchin. This one has a circumpolar distribution. Its range in the Atlantic extends down to the English Channel and to New Jersey. Europeans are more familiar with *Paracentrotus lividus* (Lamarck), the main edible species of the Mediterranean, where it is common to see basketfuls on display, with one urchin cut open to reveal the star-shaped orange ovaries

Portuguese: Ouriço do mar
Spanish: Erizo de mar
French: Oursin
Dutch: Zee-egel
German: Seeigel
Swedish: Sjøborrar
Norwegian: Kräkeboller
Danish: Søpindsvin
Icelandic: Igulker

which are the edible part. These can constitute as much as 10 to 20 per cent of the weight of the creature; but even so they make tiny mouthfuls. The main demand for them is in France, which imports some from Ireland, and in Japan, which has been experimenting with shipments from North America. Consumption in North America itself is very small, although sea-urchins from the Bay of Fundy have been marketed in New York. *Strongylocentrus droebachiensis* is abundant on the coast of Maine, but the creatures are there called 'whores' eggs' and regarded with horror. It does not seem to be marketed in northern Europe.

The sea-urchin takes its name from an old English meaning of urchin: hedgehog. (The spines of the sea-urchin are a real menace to bathers. They break off in the flesh and are difficult to remove.) Some of the other names cited above mean simply 'sea-egg'.

The Reverend James Wallace, writing in 1688 about Orkney, observed that: 'The common people reckon the meat of the Sea Urchin or Ivegars, as they call them, a great Rarity, and use it oft instead of butter.' The practice has died out and Orcadians now call the sea-urchin 'scarriman's heid', scarriman meaning a tramp or street child with unruly, spiky hair.

CUISINE   Open the urchin (with a coupe-oursin, if you have one, a most satisfactory possession), take out the ovaries and eat them with nothing more than a drop of lemon juice. Or add them to an omelette.

LAVER (Wales), SLOKE (Ireland)

Family *Bangiaceae*

Porphyra purpurea (Roth) C. Agardh

REMARKS Laver is a reddish seaweed which has for long been eaten in Britain. Camden's *Britannica* refers to it being gathered in Wales, to make 'a sort of food call'd Lhavan or Lhawvan, in English black butter'. Lily Newton gives a pleasant picture of it being gathered in Pembrokeshire in more recent times.

The pickers stride across the sands at low water, bag or bucket on arm, sack tied behind in a waist belt, and proceed to gather the laver with a quick crisp plucking sound, pleasantly reminiscent of the plucking of grass by cattle when eagerly grazing in a lush meadow. Later, very heavily laden, with a full sack balanced on their shoulders, these women return across the shore, with rosy, wind-tanned, broad faces that give a hint of their Flemish ancestry. (*Seaweed Utilisation*, 1951.)

The dried laver was then sent to small factories in Swansea and Gowerton to be boiled (which turns it green), cooled and packed for the market, where it was sold as laverbread (bara lawr). (Why the term bread should ever have been applied to what looks like a purée of spinach is not clear.)

The Welsh remain the great enthusiasts for laverbread, although their formerly abundant supply has dwindled and much of what is sold in Cardiff market now comes from Scotland. The Scots themselves used to make sloke jelly. Marian McNeill (in *The Scots Kitchen*) recalls that Caithness fishermen would take it to sea and eat it with oatcakes. Sloke is also the name in Ireland, where the product used to be treated with ceremony; witness the Georgian silver sloke pot, shown below, from the museum at Dublin. Germans know it as Purpurblatt, the French as porphyrée pourpre. Similar plants are harvested in North America as laver or nori

CUISINE AND RECIPES Buy your little plastic bag of the prepared bottle-green mush. Then follow the Welsh recipes on page 465. Or warm the laverbread in a pan and serve it on toast with lemon juice. It is also good cold, made into a paste with olive oil, lemon juice and black pepper.

CARRAGEEN MOSS, IRISH MOSS

Family *Gigartinaceae*

Chondrus crispus Stackhouse

Portuguese: Carragenina
Spanish: Carragahen
French: Carragheen
Dutch: Iers mos
German: Irisches Moos
Swedish: Karragentang
Danish: Karhagen-tang
Icelandic: Fjørugrøs

REMARKS   This is a small and lovely marine plant. The fronds have a flattened stem, which divides and subdivides in a fan-like manner. In good conditions it grows in dense masses, of a purplish-red or reddish-green colour.

It occurs on the American coast from New York northwards and has been harvested commercially in Massachusetts. But its real home is Ireland, where the village of Carragheen has provided the most common of the names used for it (but often spelled without an 'h'). It is also common on the western coasts of Scotland and its range extends northwards to Scandinavia.

In fact there are two plants which go by the name carrageen. The other is **Gigartina stellata** (Stackhouse), of which a drawing appears opposite, on the next page. Both belong to a group of red seaweeds which are the source of agar (or agar-agar, a Malayan word meaning the gelatinous extract made from various of these plants). This product is important in making liquids viscous or producing jellies and is used in many ways: in the food trade (e.g. for clarifying beer, for giving ice cream the right consistency and to prevent chocolate milk from separating), in medicine, cosmetics, leather dressing and so on.

During the Second World War Britain suffered a shortage of agar and special measures were taken to identify and exploit native stocks of carrageen. Lily Newton, in her book *Seaweed Utilisation*, gives some charming vignettes of this operation, relating how school children gathered the precious moss and processed it in their classrooms and how the biologist-surveyors fared as they looked for it up and down the coasts, working under the aegis of the Ministry of Food.

The housewives of the Hebrides still use carrageen for making a delicious milk jelly which has a pleasant tang of the sea in its flavour. The writer can recall an incident on the Isle of Iona when four botanists sought shelter in a byre from a sudden rain storm. They were taken subsequently to the kitchen of the croft, where, with all the courtly hospitality of the Western Isles, they were given tea, followed by carrageen with sugar and cream. The charm of their hostess and her delightful enquiry – 'What are you for *now*?' – will always be remembered by those who were privileged to eat at her table.

. . . The kindness and hospitality of the coast dwellers everywhere was something that will always remain with those of us who received it. It was epitomised in the words of an old lady of Anglesey, who, having promised beds to two weary surveyors, at the request of the police on a wet night, observed as she led us into her parlour: 'You come along in and I'll give you a little subscription to your Ministry.'

CUISINE It is not always easy to obtain carrageen, but it can often be found in health-food shops. The basic way of preparing it is to steep it, pick it over, boil it in milk or water and then use the strained liquor. The Irish have found many ways of using it in cookery, many of them subsidiary (for example, as an addition to soups or to help set the fruit mixture in a fruit flan). The recipe listed below is one in which carrageen plays the leading role, with cocoa as the surprise second lead, and which I know produces delicious results.

Margaret Roper and Ruth Duffin, in *The Blue Bird Cookery Book for Working Women*, give a similar recipe, but with lemon rind as the flavouring. They also urge sufferers from sleeplessness or indigestion to drink a cupful, hot, before going to bed (which I did, but as I always sleep and digest well in Ireland the experiment yielded no corroboration).

RECIPE
Carragheen dessert, 476

DULSE

Family *Palmariaceae*

Palmaria palmata (Linnaeus) O. Kuntze
Rhodymenia palmata

Portuguese: Alga vermelha
Spanish: Alga roja
French: Algue rouge
Swedish: Rodsallat
Norwegian: Søl
Danish: Rødalge
Icelandic: Sölvum
Other: Dillisk (Irish)

REMARKS   Dulse is a broad-leaved seaweed, crimson in colour, which grows to a length of about 30 cm. It occurs on both sides of the North Atlantic and is harvested commercially in the United States and Canada; especially in the Bay of Fundy, where the island of Grand Manan is a rich source.

The species *Laurencia pinnatifida* (Hudson), known as the pepper-dulse, may be of any colour in the spectrum from yellow-green to red-brown and reaches a length of 18 cm. It is pungent and used as a condiment (in Scotland, for example) rather than as a food. Some Icelanders chew it instead of tobacco, just as the Irish used to chew ordinary dulse. (A Canadian publication during the Second World War stated knowingly that '. . . in Great Britain, chewing dulse is comparable to our habit of chewing gum.' The author must have been thinking of Ireland.)

CUISINE AND RECIPE   Dulse can be eaten fresh; but the sensation is rather like 'chewing on a salted rubber band', as Euell Gibbons put it in *Stalking the Blue-Eyed Scallop*. It is better taken in dried form, or cooked like spinach. Dulse does not become brittle when dry, but remains soft and pliable. Gibbons reports: 'I have found that I could press a number of these soft pieces of Dulse together, like a plug of chewing tobacco, and keep it in my refrigerator . . . This plug could be turned on edge and shaved into fine shreds with a sharp knife. Shredded dulse is very good in salads and slaws.' It can also be added to soups and fish dishes generally. An Icelandic recipe for haddock dressed with dried dulse is given on page 399.

Recipes

Count Rumford has taken much pains to impress on the minds of those who exercise the culinary art, the following simple but practical, important fact, namely; that when water begins only to be agitated by the heat of the fire, it is incapable of being made hotter, and that the violent ebullition is nothing more than an unprofitable dissipation of the water, in the form of steam, and a considerable waste of fuel . . . it is not by the bubbling up, or *violent boiling*, as it is called, of the water that culinary operations are expedited.

(Accum, *Culinary Chemistry*, 1821)

5. General Remarks on Fish Cookery

In my *Mediterranean Seafood* (Penguin, 1972), to which this is a companion book, I included a general essay on cooking fish, which it would be inappropriate to reprint here. I repeat, however, some of the most important points, and add a few new ones.

WHAT DO WE MEAN BY 'COOKING' A FISH?

We all know the answer, in practical terms, to this question. But it is worth knowing the scientific answer. To cook a fish is to raise its temperature, by which I mean the temperature of its innermost parts, to about 145° F (63° C). Doing this brings about the various changes which characterize cooked fish. It is pointless, and in fact detracts from the quality of your dish, to raise the temperature higher or to keep it at that height for a long time.

RULES ABOUT COOKING TIME

It follows from the preceding paragraph that cooking time must depend on the greatest thickness of the fish. Heat travels gradually from the outside to the inside. The further it has to go, the longer it takes.

However, the time taken does not vary in simple proportion to the thickness, but in proportion to the square of the thickness. This principle, of course, applies to other substances, not just to fish; but many people are unaware of it. If it takes 2 minutes to cook a piece of fish 2 cm thick, then a piece 4 cm thick will require 8 minutes, not 4 minutes.

Thus guidance in the form of 'x minutes to the kilo or pound' is likely to be misleading; and the formula 'x minutes per cm of thickness', while less misleading because it takes account of the shape of the fish, can still lead you far astray. (In practice, these misleading formulae cause less havoc than might be expected, because recipes tend to overestimate the time required to cook a thin piece of fish, and are therefore not too far out when it comes to dealing with a thicker piece. But it is better to reach the right result by a correct calculation than to achieve nearly right results by starting from a wrong premise.)

So far as I know, the principle which I have repeated above, having already stated it in *Mediterranean Seafood*, has never been properly explained in any other book about fish cookery in English. It has, however, been set out fully in a Swedish book, *Att koka fisk*, by H. Gyllensköld. This contains a wealth of scientific exposition, graphs and tables, from which I have selected one, reproduced below, to support my contentions. Gyllensköld divides fish into three broad categories, according to how compact their flesh is and how quickly heat penetrates it. He then states the following formulae, which are reflected in the table. If k stands for cooking time and d for the maximum thickness of the fish, then for fish in group I (cod and the like) $k = d^2 \times 0.5$; while for fish in group II (roundfish generally, including salmon) $k = d^2 \times 0.7$; and for fish in group III (eel, herring, mackerel, tuna and flatfish) $k = d^2 \times 1.4$

This table shows what I mean. But it is from a scientific manual and therefore expressed precisely. Please do not start counting the seconds in

COOKING TIMES, IN MINUTES AND SECONDS, OF THREE CATEGORIES OF FISH, IMMERSED IN SIMMERING LIQUID

THICKNESS OF FISH IN CM	GROUP I FISH: COD AND THE LIKE	GROUP II FISH: ROUNDFISH IN GENERAL	GROUP III FISH: EEL, HERRING, MACKEREL, TUNA, FLATFISH
0.2	0.02	0.03	0.06
0.4	0.05	0.07	0.13
0.6	0.11	0.15	0.30
0.8	0.19	0.27	0.54
1.0	0.30	0.42	1.24
1.2	0.43	1.00	2.01
1.4	0.59	1.22	2.45
1.6	1.17	1.47	3.35
1.8	1.37	2.15	4.33
2.0	2.00	2.45	5.30
2.5	3.15	4.30	8.45
3.0	4.50	6.15	12.30
4.0	8.00	11.15	22.45
5.0	12.30	17.30	35.00
6.0	18.00	25.15	50.30
7.0	24.30	34.15	68.30
8.0	32.00	45.00	89.30
9.0	40.30	56.50	113.00
10.0	50.00	70.00	140.00

the kitchen! Remember, also, that the cooking time required for a fish can be greatly reduced if incisions are made in it at short intervals, since this will reduce the distance which the heat has to travel in order to reach its innermost parts.

ADDED FLAVOURS

Fish cooks fairly quickly. Thus, if you are cooking it in water and wish to add flavours in doing so, it is advisable to impart the flavour in advance to the water. The flavour will then have longer in which to impregnate the fish. This is why many recipes call for making a *court-bouillon*, which is simply the flavoured water which you prepare before cooking your fish.

Some of the recipes which follow incorporate their own instructions for making a court-bouillon. Here, however, is a simple and basic recipe for making one. To 2 litres (4 pints) water add 4 tbs wine vinegar (and a little white wine if you have some to spare), 1 tbs salt, a stick of celery, a carrot and a sliced onion, with a bouquet garni and 6 crushed peppercorns. Bring to the boil and simmer for 20 minutes before use.

The court-bouillon may still be of use after your fish has been cooked in it. Reduced by further boiling, and strained, it will provide a suitable liquid for making a sauce, or for use in an aspic. This twofold use of the same flavourings will help to bring about a certain harmony in the composition of the dish.

It is, however, often preferable to have a more concentrated and fishy liquid available for your sauce. This is what is called a fish *fumet*, which is simply water in which fish heads, bones and trimmings, together with such ingredients as go into a court-bouillon, have been cooked; and which has been reduced and strained. It is a good idea to make some of this whenever you have fish trimmings to hand, and to freeze it for later use.

The same principle of advance flavouring applies to fish which are to be grilled or fried. If seasoning and flavours are added beforehand, for example by marinating the fish for 20 minutes in olive oil, lemon juice and garlic (or some such mixture), the fish will already have absorbed the desired flavour before being exposed to the heat of the cooking process. The effect will, of course, be less if the fish is whole and its skin unbroken. A few shallow cuts will promote absorption.

CHOICE OF COOKING METHODS

A principle which I have endeavoured to assert in most aspects of Davidson family life is the 'Fallacy of the Single Right Choice'. The enunciation of the principle has stilled many a vain debate, based on the faulty premise that there must always be one, and only one, 'best' way of performing some activity like dressing for a party, or cooking a fish. A useful feature of fish is that most kinds can be cooked in most ways. In the catalogue entries for the various species, I have made suggestions about how to treat them, but these are not meant to rule out other methods.

Here I should like to say three things.

First, many people forget the advantages of steaming fish. Let Brillat-Savarin (page 299) remind you of these.

Secondly, smoked fish is becoming more and more popular. Remember that, as Scandinavians do, you can simultaneously cook and smoke fish by using a device such as that illustrated on page 262.

Thirdly, it is easy to be misled by loose talk of 'boiling fish'. It is hardly ever appropriate to boil a fish. It should be cooked in a simmering liquid. If the point needs explanation, it will be found in the quotation on page 256. The fact is that, if one excludes certain special operations such as the making of bouillabaisse, the word 'poach' can almost always be substituted for the word 'boil' in directions for cooking fish. It is a pity that we do not have a word which means 'poach in a court-bouillon'. There would be plenty of use for it in a book such as this. The French writer Ali Bab used 'court-bouillonner' as a transitive verb, like sauter or gratiner; but his usage has not become established in France, still less elsewhere.

WEIGHTS AND MEASURES

I have previously used the metric system. I still do in this book. But I also provide equivalent quantities in ounces, pints, etc., for the benefit of all those readers who have not yet metricized their kitchens. The equivalents given in the recipes are in round figures, which in my view are quite close enough. Thus, either 25 or 30 grams will be given as 1 ounce, the true equivalent to which is 28 grams.

I have ignored the difference between teaspoons and tablespoons of various nationalities, and assure readers that they may safely do likewise. The same applies to the cup, a measure which I find very convenient for certain things. The American cup is smaller than the British cup. The difference could be significant in certain contexts, but in those where I have used the cup it is not.

Quantities in cookery have no intrinsic importance. What we are concerned with are *proportions*. My purpose in giving, in most recipes, exact quantities is simply to suggest appropriate proportions. Let no one take these figures more seriously than I intend.

6. Notes on Ingredients and Implements

The great majority of the ingredients mentioned in the recipes are readily obtainable in Europe and North America. A few of the herbs may be elusive in the shops, if they are required fresh; but they can all be grown in the garden. Certain products, such as the smietana of Poland and the smetana of Russia, are only available in an approximately equivalent form – in this instance, sour cream. But the difference is not important, and perfectionists will be able to find the very closest approximation, or even the real stuff, by consulting people of the relevant nationality, who can be counted upon to have gone into the matter.

I must mention here one plant which is difficult to find in Britain, although it used to be as common here as it still is in, say, Poland or Germany. This is Hamburg parsley, referred to in the recipes as parsley root. It is a variant of ordinary parsley, but has a large root, rather like a parsnip. See the drawing on the right. Eleanour Rohde (in her book *Uncommon Vegetables and Fruits*) says. 'This vegetable has so many virtues that it is difficult to understand why it is not grown in every garden.' Grated raw, it has a flavour suggestive of celeriac and parsley combined. It is easy to grow.

Pepper and peppers also require comment. Where I refer to pepper, as in salt and pepper, I mean freshly ground black pepper, unless I specify white pepper. By peppercorns I mean the dark kind, unless I specify white ones. As for the pepper fruits, which are botanically quite different, I refer to the small hot ones as chilli peppers; and it does not matter whether fresh ones are used or dried ones which have been soaked in water. These are not to be confused with the mild peppers which are often known as bell peppers and usually available green, although they will turn yellow and red as they ripen. (Chilli peppers also progress from green to red.)

I turn now to utensils. 'It is not expected that the most expert artist can perform his work in a perfect manner, without a sufficient number of proper instruments; you cannot have neat work without nice tools; nor can your victuals be well dressed, without an apparatus appropriate to the work required.' (Kitchiner, *The Cook's Oracle*.)

If this does not give you good enough reason to go out and buy some new equipment, let me administer a stronger dose of encouragement: 'A surgeon may as well attempt to make an incision with a pair of sheers, or to open a vein with an oyster knife, as a Cook pretend to dress a dinner without proper tools to do it.' (Verral, in 1759.)

Fish kettles, the most important items, have already been illustrated on page 255. Now comes an item of subsidiary, but still considerable importance, the folding metal grid which is used for grilling fish over a charcoal fire.

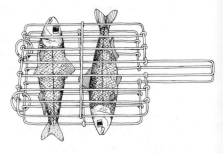

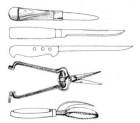

Next, I show a group of knives, and special implements for dealing with shellfish. The filleting knives are flexible ones recommended by a Finnish expert on the art of filleting fish.

Finally, a Swedish fish-smoking box. This useful device comes with easily comprehensible instructions for lighting the sawdust underneath and positioning the fish on the grid, where it will be both cooked and smoked (cf. page 361).

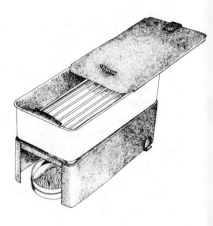

7. Introduction to the Recipes

The North Atlantic region is so rich in seafood recipes that six volumes rather than half of one would be needed to give a full conspectus. But to provide this would be a dis-service to most people, who suffer as readily from a surfeit of recipes as they do from a surfeit of food. Moreover, even when space is severely limited, I believe that it would be a mistake to cram in as many recipes as possible. It is better to have five recipes set in some sort of background, whether personal or cultural or literary or geographical (using the word in a wide sense, to embrace the fauna and flora of a region as well as its coast, rivers or mountains), than to have ten which seem to have sprung naked and unexplained from the author's brow, like Athene from the head of Zeus (or, as we are dealing with seafood, Aphrodite from the ocean foam), and whose real origin and context can only be guessed.

Projecting my own tastes and preferences on to my readers, I have therefore taken the space to say, in many instances, whence a recipe comes, be it a place, a person or a book. But where I have changed a recipe, as a result of trying it out, or amalgamated two or more versions, I have either qualified or omitted the attribution, according to the importance of the changes.

In choosing the recipes, I have looked for those which are typical of the various stretches of coast around the North Atlantic, starting in Portugal, working up to Germany, then anti-clockwise round the Baltic Sea to Sweden, across to Norway, down to Denmark and over to the islands which were or are associated with Denmark, namely the Faroes, Iceland and Greenland; which islands provide for me as they did for the Vikings a natural route to Canada and the eastern seaboard of the United States.

I have also followed some other principles, which have not always been easy to reconcile.

I have tried to strike a balance between the various countries, and between the regions within them; but have thought it right to favour those about which less has been written and less is generally known. The Soviet Union has more pages than France. Wales has as many as

Germany. The other balance which I have deliberately tilted is that between the various species of seafood in the recipes. Again, I have given a little more emphasis to what is less familiar, believing that it will be of general benefit if both fishmongers and their customers become more catholic. 'The harvest of the seas within our reach is so plentiful and diversified that we ought never to be at a loss for variety in our choice and scope to exercise our cooks' ingenuity. Do we take advantage of our opportunities? I hardly think so.' The words of Wyvern (*Common Sense Cookery*, 1894) could be mine, except that I do not have a cook.

I have allowed my natural instincts as a Scot to influence me towards recipes which are economical and practical, while succumbing also to the fascination of certain recipes which are difficult, expensive or exotic, but interesting to read. No one will try to make Surströmming as a result of reading page 368. Indeed, most readers will probably be put off eating it. Yet one could hardly write about seafood in Sweden without mentioning it.

One recipe was chosen by a special criterion. I began to write this book, rather incongruously, in Laos, hundreds of miles from any sea and thousands from the North Atlantic. In such a setting it seemed unlikely that I would have any aid beyond my books. However, I had barely arrived before Peter Ratcliffe was writing from Vientiane to his other home by the Minho River in Portugal to procure for me his recipe for Pescada en geleia. It thus happened that page 269 was the first page of the book to be written.

Peter, who really belonged to another century, probably the eighteenth, abruptly left this one when he and his only close relation were killed in a car crash in Portugal in 1976. Since the news emerged slowly and uncertainly, no public tribute was paid to the qualities and amiable eccentricities which distinguished him. Above all, he had a natural gift for instant and infectious enthusiasm, from which hundreds of people, including myself, drew benefit. One of his greatest enthusiasms was for good food and everything that goes with it. The theme would have figured in the novel which he had planned but barely begun at the time of his death. I am glad that in publishing his favourite Portuguese fish recipe I can say these words about him, and that the recipe comes from someone who had a profound knowledge of food in both the hemispheres between which he divided his life while it lasted.

8. Recipes from Portugal

Fish cookery is a subject of interest to all Portuguese, none of whom lives very far from the sea, and there are recipes for every species to be found in their markets and at the beach auctions which are held in many fishing villages, right beside the colourful fishing boats. But pride of place goes to their beloved bacalhau, salted dried cod, a fish which does not occur in Portuguese waters but which the Portuguese have traditionally fished in distant seas. Equally popular and less expensive are the fresh sardines, the smell of which, as they are grilled over a charcoal brazier, is almost omnipresent in Portuguese coastal towns and villages. The hake (pescada) completes the trilogy of favourites; it is the standard high-class fish.

Other seafood is available in abundance. Squid (lulas, or lulinhas for the little ones) appear on every menu; as do the small clams (see page 234) which are called amêijoas and are so delicious as to make up for the (to me) disappointing quality of the native Portuguese oyster.

Communications within Portugal have been developed slowly; and this may account for the strength of local traditions in cookery. Two magnificent compendia of Portuguese regional cookery are listed in the bibliography under the names Olleboma and Valente; but regional is perhaps the wrong term, for most of the recipes are identified with particular towns or villages, where to this day they are proclaimed as specialities in the restaurants and executed with pride in Portuguese homes.

In touring Portugal, I looked for signs of an influence from Portuguese possessions in the Orient. There are few, although I was surprised to find that fresh coriander (which I knew as Chinese parsley in South-East Asia) is so commonly used. Traces of cooking from Angola and Mozambique are to be found, it is true, but on the whole Portuguese cuisine has remained remarkably pure in its tradition and in its use of native ingredients, one of which must now be mentioned. Portuguese olive oil has a distinctive taste because, unlike the practice in France and Italy, the olives are kept for a week before being pressed. If a Portuguese recipe calls for olive oil and you want the flavour to be authentic, you must use Portuguese olive oil.

Caldeirada

The Portuguese national fish stew   serves eight at least

There must be almost as many versions of this as there are households on the Portuguese coast. This one was demonstrated to me in Lisbon by Judite Jesus de Cabo. I give it exactly as she made it; but with the advice to be flexible in the choice of fish. Conger eel helps to make the liquid pleasantly unctuous; but many cooks prefer a less bony fish. The addition of sardines, cooked separately, is optional. Their crispness provides a note of contrast; but pieces of fried bread, such as adorned a caldeirada which we ate at Peniche, will do the same.

mixed fish, 1¼ kg (2¾ lb)
conger eel, centre cut, ¾ kg (1½ lb)
hake, ¾ kg (1½ lb)
all the above cleaned and cut into sections of 1–2 cm thick
squid, ¼ kg (½ lb), cut up
small clams (amêijoas, page 234), ½ kg (1 lb)
fresh sardines, 8
onions, ¾ kg (1½ lb), sliced
a bunch of parsley
a bunch of coriander

tomatoes, 1 kg (2 lb) ⎫ peeled
potatoes, 1 kg (2 lb) ⎭ and sliced
garlic, 2 cloves, finely chopped
a fresh chilli pepper, finely chopped
fresh red and green peppers, ½ kg (1 lb), cut into strips
black pepper, freshly ground
olive oil, 9 tbs
white wine, 4 dl (⅔ pint)
salt
tinned red pepper, cut into strips for decoration

Take a very large cooking pot and line the bottom with onion slices. Then add further ingredients, in layers, as follows: some of the mixed fish, some conger and squid; some parsley and coriander; tomato slices; potato slices; a spinkling of garlic and chilli; strips of red and green pepper; hake and more mixed fish; a third of the olive oil and almost half of the wine; with occasional grindings of pepper and discreet sprinklings of salt. Repeat, using up all the ingredients (except what you need for the sardines and clams – see below) and finishing up with a layer of onion, a sprinkling of garlic and chilli and second doses of olive oil and wine. Set the pot to cook over a moderate flame for 30 minutes.

About 12 minutes before serving, fry the sardines in 2 or 3 tablespoonfuls of olive oil, with a small quantity of onion, tomato, red and green pepper, parsley and coriander. Six minutes later, set the clams to steam open in a pan with the remaining (2 or 3 tbs) wine and a dash of salt.

When all is ready, ladle the main mixture, juices and all, into a deep serving platter. Put the clams, still in their shells, on top, with the strips of red pepper among them, and the sardines round the side.

Bacalhau Dorado

Salt cod scrambled with eggs and potato   serves six

The Portuguese are great enthusiasts for dried salt cod (page 54). When I was in Lisbon, there was a temporary shortage of it in the shops. The news that a large shipment from Norway had arrived in Oporto was carried under big headlines on the front pages of the newspapers; which was quite right for an item of such immediate interest to all their readers.

The recipe given here happened to be demonstrated to me by a cook from Tras os Montes, but it is popular throughout the country.

bacalhau (dried salt cod), 1 kg (2 lb)	chopped parsley, 2 tbs
potatoes, 1 kg (2 lb), peeled	pepper
vegetable oil for deep-frying	olive oil, 4–5 tbs
salt	margarine, 150 g (5 oz)
eggs, 10	medium onions, 3, chopped
milk, 2 tbs	garlic, 2 cloves, chopped
	black olives, 40 or so

Soak the bacalhau in several changes of water for 24 hours. Then drain it, free it of skin and bone and flake it into smallish pieces.

Cut the potatoes into matchsticks. Heat the vegetable oil in a deep pan and deep-fry them in three batches, each of which will take about 12 minutes. As each batch is done, put it to drain in a bowl lined with absorbent paper and add a light sprinkling of salt.

Meanwhile, break the eggs into a bowl and add the milk, most of the parsley and a little pepper. Whisk the mixture and set it aside.

Next, heat the olive oil and about half the margarine in a large frying pan. (This should be done when the second batch of potatoes is nearly ready.) Add the onion and garlic and fry them over a medium flame for 7 or 8 minutes. Next, add the flaked bacalhau, mixing it in well, and continue to fry for another 7 or 8 minutes, stirring the mixture from time to time. Then spoon it out into a bowl and clean the frying pan in readiness for the final operation.

Melt half the remaining margarine in the pan, then add half the potatoes and half the bacalhau mixture. Stir to mix; and immediately pour in half the egg mixture. Continue to stir and turn and scrape (rather as when cooking scrambled eggs) for 3 minutes over a medium flame, then decant the mixture on to a large, warm serving platter. Melt the remaining margarine and repeat the process. The platter will now be covered with a thick layer of the golden concoction. Dot the olives and sprinkle the rest of the parsley over the surface. Serve at once with a green or mixed salad.

Congro Ensopado à Moda de Bragança

Conger eel stew from Bragança   serves four

conger eel, centre cut, 650–700 g	**a bay leaf**
(1½ lb), sliced	**vinegar, 1 tbs**
olive oil, 1 dl (7 tbs)	**bread, 4 thick slices**
a medium onion, chopped	**egg yolks, 3**
pepper and salt	**a sprig of parsley, chopped**

Heat the oil in a pan and add the onion, pepper and bay leaf. When the onion is golden, add the fish, salt to taste, the vinegar and ¾–1 cup water. Cook for 10 to 15 minutes, until the fish is done. Reserve the broth.

Place the slices of bread, cut to match the slices of fish, on a serving dish, and the fish on top of them. Beat the egg yolks with the parsley and combine this mixture, away from the heat, with a little of the fish broth. Then stir it into the rest of the broth, mix well and let it simmer until the egg yolks are cooked. Pour this sauce over the fish and serve at once.

Lampreia à Moda do Minho

Lamprey in the Minho way   serves four

The village of Monção, on the Minho River, is one of the few places in the world where the lamprey is fished with real enthusiasm. The season is in the early part of the year. This Minho recipe is widely and justly famed.

a lamprey of ¾ kg (1½ lb)	**a marinade of 2½ dl (nearly ½ pint)**
vinegar, 1 tbs	**each of sweet wine (vinho**
olive oil, 1 dl (7 tbs)	**maduro) and dry red wine**
butter, 30 g (1 oz)	**(vinho tinto verde), 2 tbs**
onions, 2, chopped	**brandy, 1 small glass port,**
a clove of garlic	**2 bay leaves, salt, pepper and**
	parsley

Scald the lamprey with boiling water, then scrape it with a knife and rub it clean with a thick linen cloth. Wash it in several changes of water until all viscosity is gone. Next, use a pair of scissors to make a few slits in the head openings. Collect the blood, which will run out, in a bowl with the vinegar. Cut the belly open and pull out the intestines carefully. Then slice the fish and put the slices in a casserole, covered with the blood and all the other ingredients of the marinade. Leave overnight.

Heat the olive oil and butter, add the onions and garlic and cook until transparent. Add the lamprey and some of the marinade and cook gently for 1½ hours, shaking the casserole now and then to prevent sticking.

Pescada en Geleia

Hake (or other fish) in aspic   serves six to eight

This recipe is printed in memoriam Peter Ratcliffe, C.B.E., as I explained on page 264.

Hake is the favoured fish, since it is available daily all over Portugal and is not expensive for its quality. But other white fish with firm flesh will do. You will need a section of cleaned fish weighing 1 kg (2 lb).

for the court-bouillon
a fresh chilli pepper, chopped
a mild green pepper, sliced
a medium onion, finely sliced
lemon (or fresh lime) juice, 3 tbs
a piece of lemon rind
a little each of thyme and basil
several sprigs of parsley
salt, 1 tsp
several peppercorns
celery stalks with leaves, 3

for the aspic
chicken broth, 2 or 3 tbs
gelatine, as required
capers, 2 tbs
lemon juice, 3 tbs
for the sauce
a large cucumber
double cream, $\frac{1}{4}$ litre ($\frac{1}{2}$ pint)
lemon juice, 3 tbs
finely chopped onion, 2 tbs
finely chopped chives, 2 tbs

Cut the pieces of hake into steaks about $2\frac{1}{2}$ cm (1 inch) thick, not more. Take a wide earthenware or other cooking vessel, large enough to accommodate the pieces of fish side by side. Into it put $1\frac{1}{2}$ litres ($2\frac{1}{2}$ pints) water and the ingredients for the court-bouillon. Bring this to the boil and let it simmer for 20 minutes. Then slide in the pieces of fish, bring back to the boil and continue simmering until the fish is cooked (10 minutes or less). Remove the fish, rid it of skin and bone and divide it into bite-size pieces.

Strain the stock. This should yield nearly a litre ($1\frac{3}{4}$ pints). Add the chicken broth. Add the gelatine, following the directions on the packet, as regards quantity and method. Add also the capers and the lemon juice.

Arrange the pieces of fish in an attractive and shallow dish so that they almost fill it. Pour the stock gently over the fish, which it should just cover, filling the dish almost to the brim. A little chopped parsley or some thin slices of cucumber with scalloped edges can be placed on top as decoration. Then put the dish in the refrigerator to set. This will probably take 4 hours, but allow 6 or 8 to be sure.

Bring the fish to table in its dish and serve separately a sauce made as follows. Pare the cucumber and cut it into fine slices or thin strips. Drain these well and pat them dry with a towel. Beat the cream until it is stiff. Add the lemon juice to it gradually, then the onions and chives (with salt if needed), stirring throughout. Combine all this with the cucumber and chill it slightly before serving.

Filetes de Pescada no Forno à Portuguesa

Hake steaks baked with potatoes   serves six

This is the recipe of Maria do Carmo Amaral of Oeiras. It calls for hake, Portugal's favourite fish; but cod or haddock could be used.

Have 1 kg (2 lb) of cleaned hake, cut into steaks; and 18 medium potatoes (3 for each person), parboiled and sliced. Lay half the fish steaks in a buttered oven dish and sprinkle lemon juice, chopped garlic, salt and pepper over them. Cover with half the potato slices. Repeat.

Next, make ¾ litre (1½ pints) white sauce, using butter or margarine and flour, and adding milk, as usual; but then transforming it by adding, while you stir, the juice of half a lemon, a discreet sprinkling of nutmeg and finally an egg yolk. You must stir madly as the egg yolk is added, so that it is mixed in the sauce before it has a chance to cook. Pour the sauce, now faintly yellow and unctuous, over the fish and potato layers and bake in a moderate oven (355° F, gas 4) for 40 minutes.

Carapau de Escabeche

Marinated horse mackerel

The horse mackerel is not the best of fish, but it is abundant off Portugal and is consumed in large quantities by the less well-off. It is grilled, baked or fried; or prepared de escabeche, a technique long practised under similar names (including the old English word caveach) in many parts of the world. It is really a way of keeping fish without refrigeration and tends to go out of the kitchen door as modern appliances come in. But it gives fish a good flavour.

Fry the cleaned fish in olive oil and let them cool. Then fry chopped garlic and onion, add 3 parts of vinegar to 2 of water, lots of salt, a bay leaf and a sprig of parsley. Cook this brew for 15 minutes, then pour it hot over the fish. The dish will keep for several days. It is eaten cold.

Salmonetes Grelhados à Setubalense

Grilled red mullet from Setúbal   serves six

This version of a famous recipe comes from the book of Maria Valente.

Clean 6 red mullet, each of 150–200 g (about 6 oz), and reserve the livers. Season the fish, oil them lightly and grill them on both sides, under a moderate heat, for 10 to 15 minutes.

Meanwhile, mash the livers with 1 tsp flour and a very little water, then cook them briefly in 150 g (5 oz) butter with a chopped sprig of parsley, a little lemon juice, and salt and pepper to taste. Serve the fish with this sauce poured over them, and a garnish of parsley and lemon.

Dourada Assada à Lisboeta

Baked bream Lisbon style   serves four to six

gilt-head bream (dourada, page 100),   chopped onion, 60 g (2 oz)
  1½ kg (3 lb), cleaned   salt and pepper
tomatoes, 6 medium   dry white wine, 2 dl (⅓ pint)
olive oil, 1 dl (7 tbs)   flour, 1 tsp
chopped parsley, 1 tbs   butter, 50 g (2 oz)

Peel, seed and chop the tomatoes. Pour half the olive oil into an oven-proof serving dish and add half the chopped tomatoes, half the parsley and half the onions. Put in the fish, season it with salt and pepper and cover it with the remaining oil, tomatoes, parsley and onions. Pour the wine into the dish, without pouring it over the fish itself. Bake in a moderate oven for 45 minutes, basting frequently. Then remove the dish from the oven, transfer the sauce to a saucepan, bring it to the boil and mix in the flour, which you have worked into a knob of the butter. When the sauce has thickened, remove it from the heat and add the rest of the butter. Rectify the seasoning, pour the sauce over the fish, put the dish in the oven for a few minutes and serve very hot.

Pudim de Peixe com Tres Molhos

Fish pudding with three sauces   serves four

Fish puddings are popular in Portugal. This one, from an old family recipe of Maria Isabel Raposo of Ribatejo, looks dramatic and tastes delicious.

cooked fish, flaked, 350 g (¾ lb)   milk-and-water, mixed, 1¾ cup
vegetable oil, 3 tbs   eggs, 2, separated
a medium onion, chopped   a little butter
salt and pepper   white sauce, ½ cup
white wine, 1½ dl (¼ pint)   tomato sauce, ½ cup
bread, 150 g (5 oz)   mayonnaise, ½ cup

Heat the oil with the onion, and cook until golden. Add the fish, salt, pepper and wine and cook for 10 minutes over a gentle heat, stirring all the time. Meanwhile, soak the bread in the milk and water, add the egg yolks and mix well. Then add the fish mixture and beat all together for 10 minutes (or use a blender) before folding in the egg whites, which have been beaten stiff. Pour the mixture into a buttered oven mould and cook it in a moderate oven for one hour. Turn the pudding out on to a serving dish and pour over it some white sauce, some tomato sauce and some mayonnaise, so that the three sauces partly run into each other. Serve with broccoli or cauliflower.

Roupa Velha de Peixe à Lisboeta

The 'old-clothes' fish dish of Lisbon   serves four

This is an ideal recipe for left-over boiled or baked fish.

left-over fish, ½ kg (1 lb)	a medium onion, chopped
olive oil, 1 dl (7 tbs)	vinegar, 2 tbs
a bay leaf	cooked potatoes, ½ kg (1 lb)
garlic, 2 cloves, halved	salt and pepper

Flake the fish and slice the potatoes. Heat the olive oil, add the bay leaf, garlic and onion and cook until golden. Then add the vinegar and boil for 2 or 3 minutes. Put in the fish flakes and the sliced potatoes and continue to boil, stirring well, so that fish and potatoes absorb the oil and vinegar. Season to taste and serve very hot.

Lagosta Suada de Peniche

'Sweated' lobster from Peniche   serves four

a live spiny lobster of 1½–2 kg (3 to 4 lb)	white wine, 1 dl (7 tbs)
olive oil, 2–3 tbs	dry port, 1 dl (7 tbs)
margarine, 50 g (2 oz)	bay leaves, 2
medium onions, 4, finely chopped	thick tomato sauce, 2 dl (⅓ pint)
garlic, 2 cloves, chopped	piripiri,* 1 tsp
a sprig of parsley, crushed	pepper, ½ tsp
	slices of fried bread

Split the body of the lobster into two, lengthways. Remove the claws entire. Take off the tail and cut it crossways into its segments. Keep all the liquid which emerges from these operations. Discard only the stomach bag from the body.

Heat the olive oil with the margarine in a casserole. Add the onions, garlic and parsley and cook for 5 minutes. Now put in all the pieces of lobster, with the liquid you have saved, and cover the casserole for 10 minutes, so that lobster and onions 'sweat' and release their juices.

Next, uncover the casserole, pour the wine and port over the lobster and add the bay leaves. After the lobster has continued to cook thus for 5 minutes, add the tomato sauce, piripiri and pepper, cover the casserole again and go on cooking gently for a final 10 minutes. Serve the pieces of lobster with their sauce on slices of fried bread.

---

* Piripiri is a hot sauce made by keeping small red chilli peppers in a jar filled with olive oil. One may substitute chopped chilli pepper.

Santola Gratinada

Portuguese crab au gratin   serves four

This dish, cooked for me by Cristina de Freitas, has been a favourite in her family in Lisbon for two generations.

large crabs, 2	pickled onions, 4, chopped
fresh breadcrumbs (see below)	small pickled gherkins, 4, chopped
mayonnaise, 2 tbs	salt and pepper
made mustard, 1 tsp	toasted breadcrumbs, 2 tbs
ketchup, 3 tbs	grated cheese, 2 tbs
hard-boiled eggs, 2, chopped	a little butter

Cook the crabs in boiling water, shell them and reserve the meat. Soak in milk a quantity of fresh breadcrumbs equal in volume to the crab meat.

Mix 6 tablespoonfuls of the water in which the crabs were cooked with the mayonnaise, mustard, ketchup, pickles and eggs. Add the soaked breadcrumbs, after squeezing out excess liquid, and mix well. Season with salt and pepper. Mix in the crab meat. Put the mixture in an ovenproof serving dish, sprinkle with breadcrumbs and grated cheese, dot with butter and cook in a moderate oven (355° F, gas 4) until golden (about 30 minutes).

Vieiras à Moda do Norte

A scallop recipe from the north of Portugal   serves four

This recipe is based on one recorded by Olleboma, who reminds his readers that ewe's cheese would be used in the north of Portugal, where scallops abound and where the dish belongs. However, you may use other suitable cheese.

large scallops, 8, in their shells	a clove of garlic, chopped
butter, 50 g (2 oz)	salt and pepper
thick tomato sauce, 2 dl ($\frac{1}{3}$ pint)	a sprig of parsley, chopped
dry port wine, 1 tbs	grated cheese, 4 tbs

Place the scallops, flat shells upwards, on your cooker's hot-plate. Once they start to open, prise them fully open with a knife, remove the contents and keep such liquid as is released. Separate corals and white muscles as usual, wash them and cut the muscles into thick slices. Fry the corals lightly in half the butter. Place corals, sliced muscles, tomato sauce, reserved scallop juices, port, garlic, salt and pepper in a casserole and cook for 10 minutes, adding the parsley for the last 5 minutes. Clean 4 of the 8 deep shells, dispose the cooked mixture in these, sprinkle the grated cheese on top and dot with the remaining butter. Cook in the oven for 5 minutes, until browned on top.

Amêijoas na Cataplana

Clams in the Portuguese style   serves eight to ten

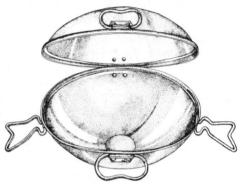

The delicious little clams (page 234) known as amêijoas are a feature of almost every menu in Portugal; and are also used liberally to garnish other seafood dishes. The special utensil used for cooking them, the cataplana, may be of copper or aluminium. What is important is the tight seal effected by the clasps.

Here is a recipe which shows how to use the cataplana.

clams (amêijoas), 2 kg (4½ lb)	butter, 90 g (3 oz)
large onions, 2, sliced	olive oil, 2 tbs
bacon, 200 g (7 oz), in little strips	salt, pepper, paprika
a small Portuguese sausage	a bay leaf
(chouriço), chopped	tomatoes, 2, chopped

Let the clams rest in clear water for a while, allowing them to release any sand. Then place them in the lower half of the cataplana and cover them with all the other ingredients listed above. Seal down the top of the cataplana, set it on a moderate flame and cook for 20 minutes. Then uncover the cataplana and serve at once.

Amêijoas à Bulhão Pato

Clams in broth, to the memory of a Portuguese poet   serves eight to ten

Travelling south through Portugal we kept coming across this item on menus. I looked in my dictionary and concluded that it must be clams cooked in duck stock. Exciting idea! I demanded it and found it good, although I could not pretend to detect the flavour of duck. Then a Portuguese friend told us the truth, that it is not bulhão pato, but Bulhão Pato, a nineteenth-century poet whose name has for long been commemorated in this recipe, for reasons which I hope to learn some day.

Heat a few tablespoonfuls of olive oil in the bottom of a pot and let 3 cloves of garlic, finely chopped, take colour in it. Add ¼ litre (½ pint) water, 2 kg (4½ lb) well-washed clams, a little pepper and chopped coriander. Bring to the boil. When the clams are all open, serve them with the broth.

Lulinhas Estufadas à Narcisa

Tiny squid cooked in Narcisa's way

Narcisa, the lady chef of the Restaurant Casa Mateus at Sezimbra, has perfected this admirable way of cooking very small squid; perfected it perhaps while gazing eponymously at her reflection in the clear waters of the harbour, whose polychrome fishing boats must be the brightest in Portugal. My lyrical appraisal of the dish must make up for lack of details; for Narcisa and I had a communications problem and I had to infer the recipe by studying the made dish as I ate it.

Clean the little creatures, but do not bother to remove their 'pens'. Then heat some olive oil in a casserole and gild therein some sliced onion and chopped garlic and a few small bits of fat bacon. Add the squid, and both red and white wine (of this I am sure, for she showed me the bottles), and snippets of hot chilli pepper and chopped parsley. Let this all simmer, uncovered, for a while, observing how the squidlets take on a pleasing purple hue, and then, when they are tender, serve them with their juices, potatoes at one end of the platter and rice at the other.

Having said thus vaguely what to do with the smallest squid, I should add something about the next size up. Lulas à Minha Moda, which is 'Squid My Way', is a neat, exact and unusual recipe. Take 1 kg (2 lb) of small squid, i.e. about 6, clean them, season them with salt, pepper and lemon juice, and grill them. Lightly fry 150 g (5 oz) smoked ham, thinly sliced, in 60 g (2 oz) margarine, add the grilled squid and serve with boiled potatoes.

Arroz de Polvo

Octopus with rice   serves four

This is a very typical Portuguese dish, especially popular in Lisbon.

octopus, 1 kg (2 lb)	a clove of garlic, chopped
a sprig of parsley, chopped	rice, 200 g (7 oz)
olive oil, 3 tbs	a bay leaf
a medium to large onion, chopped	salt, pepper, lemon juice

Season the cleaned octopus and cut it into fairly small pieces. Cook these, with the parsley, in plenty of boiling salted water for 15 minutes. Meanwhile, heat the olive oil in a large pan, add the onion and garlic and cook them until the onion turns golden; then add at least 6 dl (1 pint) of the octopus cooking-water. When it comes to the boil, add the drained pieces of octopus with the rice, bay leaf and seasonings. Simmer for 15 to 20 minutes, until the rice is fully cooked. The dish will be lilac in hue.

9. Recipes from Spain

The recipes given here are all from the northern maritime provinces – Galicia, Asturias, Santander and the Basque country by the French frontier. A religious pilgrim would make his way through them from east to west, finishing his journey at Santiago de Compostela. I and my wife, as culinary pilgrims, made the journey from west to east, noting first the gentle transition from Portuguese to Galician cookery. This latter is, however, highly distinctive. The charming book *La Cocina Práctica*, published by Sr Puga y Parga at La Coruña early in this century, is still a good guide to it, and is pleasantly studded with poems.

Vigo, with its brown nets, is Spain's greatest fishing port; but I prefer La Coruña, where the nets on the quayside are green and blue and the fishing port has as its backdrop an array of those amazing Galician houses whose upper storeys seem to be all window and white tracery – a combination somehow reminiscent of Venice. And it is at La Coruña that the lover of mariscos (Spanish for fruits de mer) finds his ultimate feasting place. In the narrow pedestrian streets near the port, a whole procession of seafood bars serve crustaceans and molluscs and sardines with the local wines. There is sawdust on the floors, and barrels for tables, round which customers throng, eating with their fingers. One may take one dish in one, a second in another and so on; but the bars are so numerous that no one could complete the course. (The Mesón El Quijote, in Calle Estrella, has an English-speaking patrón, Manuel Toja, who looks like an intellectual version of Laurence Olivier in his youth, and who weaves his way between his barrels with the agility of a ballet-dancer. Try his clams.)

The most common cooking utensil in Spain is the cazuela de barro. The usual translation, 'earthenware casserole', may not give everyone the right idea, so I show a drawing of the real thing. They come in various sizes.

Caldereta

A northern Spanish fish stew

Caldereta is the northern Spanish equivalent of the Provençal bouilla-baisse, the bulavesa of the Spanish Mediterranean coast and the caldeirada of Portugal. It requires very little olive oil, which used to be costly in the north; and does without saffron, which is not grown there.

Fry some garlic in the bottom of a large earthenware pot (caldero – hence the name of the dish) and add tomatoes, parsley, onions, mild red peppers (pimientos) and white wine, followed by a mixture of whatever seafood is available and cheap: fish, molluscs and crustaceans, all prepared as usual. Season with pepper and a very little salt, then add some of the salty broth which you will have produced by steaming open your mussels, clams or other bivalves beforehand.

Cover the pot and cook slowly for about an hour. If you have some walnuts, use the Spanish device of adding half a dozen, peeled, to the caldereta. When they disintegrate, it is ready.

The caldereta should then 'rest', tightly covered, for 15 minutes before receiving a squeeze of lemon juice and being served with the accompaniment of slices of fried bread.

Lubina a la Santanderina

Sea bass, Santander style

This dish is so good that it seemed entirely appropriate to eat it in a palace, the former home of the Barreda-Bracho family in the medieval village of Santillana de Mar, near Santander, and now a parador nacional (state hotel). The chef, Alfonso Hernández, explained the recipe thus, adding that quantities depend on the size of the bass and that the dish can be made with, for example, the rear half of the fish only.

Clean and salt the fish, but do not skin it. Make deep vertical incisions in each side at intervals of 1½ cm. Squeeze lemon juice and pour some olive oil over it, so that it is all well moistened. Then put it in a moderately hot oven (400° F. gas 6).

Meanwhile pound a mixture of toasted almonds, toasted breadcrumbs and a little parsley. After the fish has baked for 10 minutes, take it out and strew this mixture over it. Return it to the oven for another 10 minutes or so, then take it out again and pour a ladleful or more of fumet (concentrated fish bouillon) over it. Five more minutes in the oven and your fish will be ready, sitting all succulent in its orange-coloured and subtly flavoured sauce. Serve it with wedges of lemon.

Bacalao a la Vizcaína

Dried cod in the Basque manner   serves four

This recipe closely follows the version given by Nicolasa Pradera in her book *La cocina de Nicolasa* (1961). Note that the very slow and long cooking of the onions is essential to produce the authentic flavour (although a short-cut is obviously possible here). I mention also that Bacalao a la Vizcaína is often made with tomatoes as well. But the dish should then, strictly speaking, be known as Bacalao a la Riojana.

dried cod, $\frac{3}{4}$ kg (1$\frac{1}{2}$ lb)	large onions, 2, finely chopped
mild red peppers, 8	garlic, 2 cloves, not peeled
olive oil, 3 or 4 tbs	a hard-boiled egg-yolk
ham fat (tocino de jamón), 100 g	chicken or meat bouillon, 1 tbs
(3$\frac{1}{2}$ oz)	salt

Cut the dried cod into uniform pieces and soak these in water for 24 hours, changing the water several times, to get rid of excess salt. The peppers should also be soaked in cold water for a while.

Heat the olive oil and half the ham fat in a large pan. Add the onion and garlic and cook very gently, over the *lowest* of flames, for 4 to 5 hours. They must not brown, but should very, very gradually melt into a purée.

Heat the peppers in a pan of water, but without bringing it to boiling point. Once the peppers are soft, remove their seeds and scrape the pulp from them with a spoon, adding the pulp to the onion. Mash the egg yolk, moistened by the bouillon, into a paste and then add it too. Finally, pass the sauce through a fine sieve.

Carefully scale the pieces of dried cod, taking care not to break or dislodge the skin. Put them in a pan with water to cover and bring almost to boiling point. But, once a scum forms, take the cod out and remove any bones from it.

Heat a little more olive oil and melt the remainder of the ham fat in an earthenware casserole (cazuela de barro – see the drawing on page 276). Add several large spoonfuls of the sauce, followed by the cod and then the rest of the sauce. Set it on a very low flame, after giving it an initial shake, and cook it for 12 to 15 minutes. You may need to add a little more oil, but not much, during the cooking; and should also adjust the seasoning. Serve in the casserole.

This dish will be just as good if reheated on the following day.

Katu-arraya Guisado

Dogfish cooked in the Basque style   serves four

Katu-arraya is the Basque name for the dogfish (*Scyliorhinus canicula*). Ana María Calera, in her 550-page volume on Basque cookery, a splendid work which includes a good bibliography, presents this recipe as one much used by Basque fishermen; 'very tasty and economical'.

a dogfish (page 168) of 1 kg (2 lb)	garlic, 4 cloves
olive oil, 1½ dl (¼ pint)	parsley, chopped
salt	a small hot chilli pepper

Clean and skin the dogfish, if you have caught it yourself; otherwise the fishmonger will have done this for you. Cut it into fairly thin steaks or slices, sprinkle these with salt and leave them for an hour.

Heat the olive oil in an earthenware casserole and cook 2 of the cloves of garlic, chopped, until golden. Put in the fish and strew on top the parsley and the other 2 cloves of garlic, chopped. Add also scraps of the chilli pepper, as much as suits you. Shake the casserole and leave it on a gentle heat, so that the fish cooks gradually and has time to exude its juices. The cooking will take 10 to 15 minutes. Serve in the casserole.

Besugo a la Donostiarra

Bream cooked in the manner of San Sebastián   serves six to eight

Donosti is the Basque name for San Sebastián. This is a Basque dish, which may also be met under the name Besugo a la Vasca (or Basca).

2 sea bream (page 99), each	olive oil, 6 tbs
weighing 1 kg (2 lb) uncleaned	garlic, 2 cloves
salt and pepper	a lemon

Gut the fish, remove their gills, scale them and wash them. Sprinkle them with salt and pepper, then set them aside in a cool place until you are ready to cook them. A Spaniard would hang them up to air (orear), but this is not necessary for those who lack a cool larder and hooks.

About an hour before the meal, anoint the fish with some of the olive oil. Then grill them over glowing charcoal (oak charcoal, if you seek the authentic Basque flavour). Turn them once so that they are well browned on both sides. Meanwhile, fry the cloves of garlic in the rest of the olive oil. Place the cooked fish on a platter, pour the olive oil and garlic over them, followed by squeezes of lemon juice, and serve.

Bonito a la Asturiana

The Asturian way of cooking bonito   serves six

Bonito is often the main dish for Christmas dinner in Asturias. But this popular dish can be made on any day of the year.

bonito (page 132), 1 kg (2 lb), cleaned weight	parsley, 2 sprigs, chopped
	a thread of vinegar
salt and flour	paprika *or* cayenne pepper, ½ tsp
olive oil, 1 dl (7 tbs)	chicken broth, 1 dl (7 tbs)
onions, ½ kg (1 lb), sliced	strips of mild red pepper (fresh,
garlic, 2 cloves, finely chopped	seared and peeled; or tinned)

Cut the bonito into steaks about 1½ cm thick, season these with kitchen salt, coat them with flour and fry them in hot oil on both sides until they are golden in colour. Place the fried steaks in a shallow fireproof dish and keep them warm.

Using the same oil (but having strained it if any of the flour burned), fry the onion and garlic and parsley. These ingredients should not be allowed to become too brown. Then add the thread of vinegar and the paprika or cayenne pepper. Finally, add salt to taste and the chicken broth.

Pour this sauce over the bonito steaks and put them in a moderate oven for 20 minutes. When you serve the dish, decorate it with the strips of red pepper.

Marmite

A Basque fisherman's dish of bonito

This dish may be presented under the name Marmite Kua (or Marmitako). Like bouillabaisse it is by origin a simple dish, but is often presented in restaurants in a sophisticated form. Dionisio Pérez, author of the erudite and charming *Guia del buen comer español* (1929), remarks that a Basque fisherman would be likely to laugh ironically at such 'civilized' versions of his dish, were he to be shown them. He goes on to give the authentic, simple version.

'There is a tradition in the ports that a marmite cannot have full merit unless it is cooked and eaten in the galley of a fishing boat; and there are many people who, knowing this tradition, ask their friends among the fishing fraternity, during the bonito season, to offer them a place and a plate on board such a vessel. Those who have no such friends or are burdened by ridiculous scruples, and cannot therefore enjoy this privilege, lose no opportunity to go at dinner-time to enjoy the appetizing aroma which comes from the numerous marmites which, at dusk, are being cooked in the fishing smacks tied up at the quayside . . .

'Whoever aspires to make a good marmite will put a casserole on the fire and in it oil, onion and garlic. He will cut into slices, not too big, a large piece of bonito. He will put these straight away into the casserole and then add the necessary quantities of water and potatoes, which should all be cooked over a moderate and measured fire. He will put in just the right amount of salt; a pinch of paprika and some canned red pimientos. If these ingredients are complemented by some cubes of bread, when the cooking is well under way, he will have, at the moment of bringing the dish to table, a genuine marmite which will transport him, no matter how far away he should be, to the northern coasts whence the dish had its origin.'

Merluza en Salsa Verde

Hake in a green sauce   serves six

Spaniards like to have fish with a green sauce, in which parsley is usually the sole green ingredient, as in this recipe.

hake, 6 thick steaks	**medium potatoes, 3, thinly sliced**
a lemon	**flour, 1 tbs**
olive oil	**a bay leaf**
garlic, 4 cloves	**chopped parsley, 4 tbs**

Wash the steaks and pat them dry. Then squeeze the juice of the lemon over them.

In an earthenware casserole heat enough olive oil for frying the potato slices. Brown the cloves of garlic in the oil, then remove them and keep them ready in a mortar. Next, fry the potato slices a little; then remove the casserole from the fire while you add the flour with about $\frac{1}{2}$ cup water and the bay leaf. Continue cooking for several minutes until the potato is soft. At this point season the hake steaks with salt and put them in too, followed by the garlic and parsley, pounded together in a mortar with a few drops of water. While the cooking continues, shake the casserole over the fire occasionally, in a zigzag fashion. The dish will be ready in 20 to 30 minutes and is served in the casserole. The sauce will be light green in colour and may be embellished by a sprinkling of fresh parsley at the last minute.

Palometa (Japuta) con Salsa de Tomate

Ray's bream, fried and served in a tomato sauce   serves six

Ray's bream (page 104), 2 or 3	***also needed for the sauce***
weighing 1½ kg (3 lb) uncleaned	**an onion, finely chopped**
salt	**a clove of garlic, finely chopped**
a clove of garlic, crushed	**a sprig of parsley, chopped**
olive oil for frying the fish and for	**tomatoes, 1 kg (2 lb), quartered**
the sauce	**sugar, ½ tsp**

Start by preparing the sauce. Heat ½ dl (3 tbs) olive oil in a pan, add the onion, chopped garlic and parsley and fry these until they are just turning brown; then add the tomatoes and sugar. Cook gently until the sauce starts to thicken, then pass it through a chinois, add salt if necessary and continue cooking until it is quite thick.

Clean and skin the fish. Season them with salt and the crushed clove of garlic, fry them one at a time in hot oil, then put them in an earthenware casserole and pour the sauce over them, followed by a little of the hot oil. Shake the casserole to ensure even distribution. Cook gently for 10 more minutes, covered, and serve.

In Galicia, where wheat is not grown and bread was once a luxury, this dish would be served with 'cachelos', baked potatoes cut in half.

Txangurro Relleno

Stuffed spider crab   serves two

a spider crab (page 205) of ¾ kg	**paprika (pimentón), 1 tsp**
(1½ lb)	**cognac, 3 tbs**
salt	**white wine, 2 dl (⅓ pint)**
a bay leaf	**a scrap of hot chilli pepper (fresh**
olive oil, 4 tbs	**or dried)**
onion, carrot, leek, 50 g (2 oz) of	**tomatoes, ½ kg (1 lb)**
each, finely chopped	**breadcrumbs, chopped parsley,**
flour, 1 tbs	**melted butter, 1 tsp of each**

Bring to the boil, in a pot large enough for the crab, either sea water or fresh water to which you have added salt and a bay leaf. Put in the crab. When the water comes back to the boil, let it boil for 12 minutes, then remove it from the fire and let it stand for 5 minutes. Take out the crab and extract all the meat from legs and body. Put the picked meat into two clean carapaces and reserve all the debris.

Heat the oil in a pan. Add the onion, carrot and leek. When they are tender, move the pan to the side of the fire. Add the flour, paprika and crab debris. Mix well together. Pour the cognac over the mixture and light it. When the flame dies down, add the wine, chilli and tomatoes. Bring all this to the boil, pass it through a mouli-legumes, cook it for a further 20 minutes and pass it through a chinois, using a spoon to rub it all through. Cook it again until it is reduced by half, then pour it over the crab meat in the carapaces and mix well. Finally, sprinkle breadcrumbs, parsley and melted butter on top. Place the carapaces, thus filled, in a hot oven for 5 minutes. The finished dish will be dark brown, with the consistency of a very thick soup.

This recipe is based on that of Sr Don José Castillo, at whose hotel in Beasain I tasted it. Before the meal he led me to the subterranean room in which he writes his Basque cookery books. Passing through the store-rooms I noticed a large stock of spider-crab carapaces. Why? One large spider crab serves two, so you need to have spare carapaces.

Vieiras a la Gallega

Scallops in the Galician style   serves four

The scallop has a special association with Galicia, since it became the emblem of the pilgrims who made their way in large numbers, from the eleventh century onwards, to Santiago to do honour to Saint James of Compostela.

scallops, 18, with their corals	a medium onion, finely chopped
flour, 75 g (2½ oz)	garlic, 4 cloves, finely chopped
olive oil	parsley, chopped
chicken bouillon, 2½ dl (1 cup)	cornflour (if needed)
dry white wine, 2 dl (⅓ pint)	

Reserve the scallop corals. Put the white muscles in a colander and dip them twice in boiling water, then drain them and coat them with flour before frying them in small batches in hot oil. When they are done, remove them to a casserole and cover them with the chicken broth and wine. Bring to the boil and simmer for 5 minutes. Then remove the muscles to a shallow earthenware oven dish, reserving the cooking liquid.

Fry the onion, garlic and parsley in the oil already used. When the onions are well done, add the scallop broth. Reduce this mixture to something like a purée, then add the scallop corals and pass all through a fine sieve, pressing hard. Add a little cornflour if the mixture has to be thickened. Pour the sauce over the muscles, season with salt, heat in a moderate oven for 5 minutes and serve in the oven dish.

Calamares al Estilo del Cantábrico

Squid, stuffed and cooked with their own ink   serves six

This dish is popular throughout the north, but especially in Asturias (less so in Galicia, where the preferred cephalopod is the octopus).

squid, 1½ kg (3 lb)
olive oil
a large onion, finely chopped
raw, dried ham, 100 g (3¼ oz)
garlic, 4 cloves, chopped
a sprig of parsley, chopped
paprika, ½ tsp
white wine, a little (what the
 Spaniards call a chorro, i.e. a
 quick short pour from the
 bottle)
salt

flour, 2 tbs
a small onion, chopped
medium, ripe tomatoes, 4, peeled
 and chopped
a little grated nutmeg
a bay leaf
a little cayenne pepper
soft breadcrumbs, 1 tbs, soaked in
 water with ½ tsp vinegar
slices of French bread fried in
 olive oil

Clean the squid, reserving the ink sacs. Cut the fins and tentacles from the bodies and chop them up finely.

Put a little oil in a frying pan and fry the chopped onion gently in this. Once the onion is soft, add the chopped ham, one of the chopped cloves of garlic and the parsley. Stir all this over a very low heat. Next, put in the chopped fins and tentacles, most of the paprika and the white wine. Add salt to taste, mix all together, remove the pan from the fire and let the mixture cool. This is your stuffing.

Stuff the bodies of the squid with the stuffing, loosely so that they will not burst when cooked; and close them with toothpicks. Flour them lightly with half the flour and fry them briefly in hot oil, without browning them. Then transfer them to an earthenware casserole.

Now fry the second (small) onion in the same oil, with the rest of the garlic, until they are golden. Add the rest of the flour, the tomatoes, nutmeg, salt, bay leaf and remaining paprika, with a little cayenne too, if you wish. Stir together and add a little boiling water. Keep the pan on the fire for 10 minutes, then add as much as you want of the squid's ink, first mixing it with the soaked breadcrumbs. Cook for 10 more minutes, then remove the bay leaf, strain the sauce, pour it over the squid in the casserole, replace the bay leaf and leave the casserole over a low flame for 45 minutes. Check the seasoning, and serve.

The fried bread – for which Spaniards would use 'yesterday's bread', after soaking it in milk – is served with the dish and helps to mop up the Stygian sauce.

Empanada de Pulpo

Galician octopus pie   serves four

This version of a famous Galician dish, the like of which I have not met elsewhere in the world, is that given to me by Señora Pilar Bustamante, whose home in Galicia is at La Coruña. Before I give her instructions, let me make clear that the resulting 'pie' is as wide and flat and thin as a pizza.

Preparing the pastry

eggs, 2   **olive oil, 1 dl (6⅔ tbs)**
salt, ½ tsp   **melted pork fat or lard, 1 tbs**
milk, 1 dl (6⅔ tbs)   **flour, 320 g (12 oz)**

Mix together in a large bowl the eggs, salt, milk, olive oil and melted pork fat or lard. Then add the flour, little by little, so as to form a soft dough (masa blanda). You will know when it is right because the dough will no longer stick to your fingers, although it will still be quite moist. Knead the dough very little. Let it rest, rolled out, while you cook the octopus and prepare the rest of the pie filling.

Preparing the filling

Have a casserole with boiling water and 2 bay leaves in it. Take a cleaned octopus, weighing ½ kg (1 lb), by one end and lower it 3 or 4 times successively into the water, which must continue to boil hard, until the octopus curls. Once it has curled, leave it in the water to continue cooking for about half an hour. Towards the end of the cooking, add a little salt. Remove the octopus, let it cool, then cut it into small pieces.

Meanwhile, chop 2 large onions and fry them very gently, covered, taking care that they do not brown. Next, add 4 large peeled tomatoes (or 2 tomatoes and 1 tbs tomato purée) and let them cook too. Then add ½ to 1 mild red pepper, seeded and chopped, and the pieces of cooked octopus, and continue cooking for 10 to 15 minutes more. Let the mixture cool.

Making and baking the pie

Divide the pastry dough into two. Take a wide and shallow baking tin, e.g. a round one of 30 cm (11½–12 inches) diameter or a rectangular one 24 by 32 cm (9½ by 13 inches). Roll out half the dough so that it will cover the bottom of the chosen tin. Lightly oil the tin. Cover the bottom of it with the pastry dough, so that the dough comes up the sides and overlaps the edges. Spread the filling over this. Roll out the rest of the dough to make the top of the pie, and put this in place, rolling the edges over and crimping them to make a tight seal all the way round.

Cook the pie in a moderate oven (355° F, gas 4) for approximately 30 minutes, until it is a light golden-brown.

10. Recipes from France — Part One, the South-West

The French coast from the Spanish frontier to the Poitou covers about 500 kilometres, which would, I suppose, yield to an earnest gastronomic pilgrim more than 500 different seafood dishes, all good and each the natural and harmonious outcome of local produce.

Starting in Basque territory, where the cuisine is robust and colourful, one comes almost at once to the muted and tranquil scenery of the Landes, whose salt-marshes harbour the fine eels known as anguilles de marais; and thence, suddenly, into the Bordelais country. This is a region from which a really earnest pilgrim might never emerge, so numerous are the experiences which he would wish to undergo. Of all the great wine-growing regions of France, this is the one most closely associated with the sea, indeed doubly associated, for the broad estuary of the Gironde, in which sturgeon still swim, stretches up into its heart. It is exciting to lodge in a town such as Pauillac and eat seafood dishes prepared with wine, knowing that famous vineyards lie less than a kilometre from the salt water and that the happy marriage of ingredients on one's plate reflects this propinquity. Here too, one comes to the first of the famous names in ostreiculture, Arcachon, knowing that the northward journey will lead to others such as Oléron-Marennes.

However, my own favourite region on this northward route is the Charente-Maritime. La Rochelle provides not only superb seafood, but a wholly satisfying ambiance in which to consume it and to learn about it. This is a place where people know about eating the liver of the electric ray, which they call tremblade or tremble. Here is the home of what many consider to be the finest butter in France, the Charentais. In these parts are found the sea salt of the Île de Ré; the pétoncles or small scallops which can only be fished in the vicinity of that island on winter mornings; and the peppery lavagnons (page 238).

The emblem of the Charentais is the cagouille, their word for escargot or snail, which may be taken as referring to their deliberate manner or to the fact that this is a region of slow, prolonged cooking, in which a cooked dish is known as a 'mijhot', that is to say, something which has been mijotté or simmered. Long may this simmering continue.

Anguille Médocaine

Eel in red wine   serves four

A simple recipe, for a large eel, already skinned and cleaned. Cut 4 generous sections off it. Cut into small pieces the white parts of 2 or 3 leeks. Place all this in a casserole just large enough for it, and add red wine (Médoc if possible) to cover. Then put the lid on the casserole, cook gently for 1 to 1½ hours and serve piping hot.

Morue à la Bordelaise

Salt cod in the Bordelaise fashion   serves four

Salt cod is a popular dish in the south-west of France, and each region has its own way of preparing it. The Basques are particularly economical, for they have a soup called Ttoro of which the most primitive version is no more than the water in which salt cod has been cooked, combined with olive oil, bread, garlic, parsley, basil, rosemary and sage. However, Bordeaux is the principal port of entry for the morue which arrives from Newfoundland, and the Bordelaise way of preparing it is perhaps the best.

fillets of salt cod, ½ kg (1 lb)	a bouquet garni (thyme, bay leaf,
olive oil, 4 tbs	parsley)
large onions, 2, chopped	white wine (Graves if possible),
garlic, 4 cloves, crushed	¼ litre (½ pint)
tomatoes, 4, peeled and seeded	tomato purée, 1 tbs
mild green peppers, 2, cut into	sugar, 1 tsp
thin strips	toasted breadcrumbs, 3 or 4 tbs

Desalt the fish for 12 hours in frequent changes of water. Use a trivet to keep it off the bottom of the dish, where the salt will collect.

Bring 1½ litres (2½ pints) of water to the boil in a large casserole. Put the piece or pieces of fish in it, off the fire, and then poach them for 10 to 15 minutes, according to their thickness.

Meanwhile, heat the olive oil and lightly fry it in the onion, garlic, tomatoes and peppers, adding the bouquet garni. All this must simmer for several minutes over a low flame. Then add the wine and an equal amount of the water in which the fish has been cooking. Add the tomato purée and sugar also at this stage. Cook gently for another 10 minutes.

Remove the cooked fish and rid it of any skin or bones. Pour some of the sauce into the bottom of an oven dish, put the fish on this aromatic bed and pour the rest of the sauce over it. Sprinkle the breadcrumbs on top and brown the dish in a hot oven (430° F, gas 7) for 10 minutes.

Alose Grillée, Sauce Béarnaise

Grilled shad with béarnaise sauce   serves four

A shad or other fish weighing 900 g (2 lb) is cleaned, scored on the sides, seasoned, anointed with olive oil and lemon juice, grilled and served with the famous sauce to which the Béarn gives its name.

Put 1½ dl (¼ pint) white wine and the same amount of vinegar in a saucepan with some fresh tarragon, thyme and parsley, a sprinkling of coarsely ground black pepper and 1 or 2 finely chopped shallots. Bring this to the boil and reduce it until there are only a few tablespoonfuls of liquid left. Strain this into the top of a double boiler, let it cool, and then add to it 3 egg yolks previously mixed with a tablespoonful of water. Whisk it while it heats. Once the egg yolks begin to thicken, start adding little by little 150 g (5 oz) melted butter, still whisking. When all the butter has been added, the sauce should be really thick. Pass it through a fine sieve and apply the finishing touches by adding a tablespoonful of chopped tarragon and half a tablespoonful of chopped French parsley, a tiny pinch of cayenne and a thread of lemon juice.

Rougets à la Bordelaise

Red mullet with Bordelaise sauce   serves four

4 red mullet (page 113) of about   **olive oil**
200 g (nearly ½ lb) each   **sprigs of parsley**
salt and pepper   **Bordelaise sauce (see below)**

The fish may be gutted, although many people prefer the gamey taste which they have when cooked whole. Make an incision along the back of each, season them, brush them with olive oil and grill them for not more than 5 minutes on each side. Arrange them on a platter, garnish with parsley and serve the sauce separately.

There are various kinds of Bordelaise sauce and none is entirely simple to make. I suggest for this dish the following. Put 3 dl (just over ½ pint) of white Bordeaux wine in a saucepan with 3 chopped shallots, a tablespoonful of chopped mushroom stalks and a pinch of coarsely ground black pepper. Reduce to one third. Add 3 dl of meat stock (demi-glace) and continue to cook for 40 minutes. Pass the sauce, which should be thick, through a fine sieve. Keeping it off the heat, add 60 g (2 oz) butter and half a tablespoonful of chopped parsley and tarragon. The sauce is then ready.

Meuilles à la Charentaise

Grey mullet in the style of the Charentes   serves four

The grey mullet which are preferred in the Charentes are those of the species *Liza aurata*, which are called 'oreilles jaunes' (page 117), but other grey mullet will do. Local advice is that if you are successful in finding ones which are quite free of any muddy aroma you should, when gutting them, leave the large intestine in place, since it is delicious. I have not had the chance to try this out, but pass on the tip.

4 grey mullet, weighing 200 to 250 g (about ½ lb) each, uncleaned	**garlic, 4 or 5 cloves**
a sprig or two of thyme, a bay leaf, a few cloves, salt and pepper for the court-bouillon	**parsley, 2 sprigs, chopped**
	tomato purée, 140 g (5 oz)
	dry white wine, 1 dl (7 tbs)
butter, 120 g (¼ lb)	**grated cheese, 3 tbs**

Clean the fish. Heat 1–2 litres (2–4 pints) water, with the ingredients of the court-bouillon, in a suitable cooking vessel (the shape of which will determine the amount of water needed). When it comes to the boil, poach the fish in it for 8 minutes, or until done.

Meanwhile, pound the garlic and parsley into the butter, with a little salt and pepper. Melt this in a pan and mix the tomato purée into it.

When the fish are done, drain them and lay them in an oven dish just large enough to take them side by side. Pour the sauce over them, add the wine, sprinkle the cheese on top and leave in a moderate oven (355° F, gas 4) for 15 minutes.

Thon de Saint-Jean

Fresh tuna cooked in the style of Saint-Jean de Luz   serves four

Shrink though one may from its larger neighbours, such as Biarritz, it is impossible not to enjoy the old fishing port of Saint-Jean de Luz.

Take a piece of long-fin tuna (page 131), which the French call thon blanc, weighing about ½ kg (1 lb), flour it and colour it thoroughly on both sides in hot olive oil. Add 3 or 4 green peppers (seeded and cut into slices), some roughly chopped parsley, thyme, 2 teaspoonfuls of paprika moistened with a little water, salt and pepper, and finally 3 or 4 tomatoes which have been peeled and cut up. When all this has started to take colour in the hot oil, add ¼ litre (½ pint) dry white wine, cover the dish and cook very gently for 45 to 50 minutes. Then transfer the tuna steak to a heated platter and pour the sauce over it.

Créat (Esturgeon) Mariné

Marinated Gironde sturgeon   serves six

The Gironde is almost the only river on the European Atlantic coast where sturgeon are still to be taken. Progneaux, in his book on Bordelaise and Girondine specialities, remarks that if you are cleaning such a sturgeon you should take care to preserve the large dark gut, which is 'le meilleur morceau' and should be marinated and cooked with the meat.

sturgeon, 1 kg (2 lb), cleaned weight	butter, 80 g (3 oz)
a marinade of dry white wine (Graves), a little vinegar, a sliced onion, parsley, salt and pepper	shallots, 2 or 3, chopped
	a handful of stale breadcrumbs
	chopped parsley for garnish

Cut the sturgeon into thick slices and leave them in the marinade for 24 hours. Then drain them and colour them on both sides in the butter in a deep cooking pot (cocotte), over a strong flame. Add the onion from the marinade and the shallots. Let it all simmer gently for half an hour.

Next, pour the marinade into the cocotte, add the breadcrumbs, and if necessary a little water and white wine. Cook for a few minutes more, then remove from the heat, garnish with chopped parsley and serve.

Lavagnons Charentais

Small clams prepared in the manner of the Charentes   serves four

The people of Charente-Maritime are proud of this small clam, which they call lavagnon or lavignon. It is a member of the family *Scrobiculariidae* (see page 238) and the treatment here recommended by M. J. Remon of Meschers-les-Bains may be applied to kindred species just as well.

lavagnons, 1½ kg (3 lb)	butter, 80 g (3 oz)
large onions, 2, finely chopped	salt and pepper
olive oil	parsley, finely chopped

Wash the lavagnons well and put them in a covered saucepan, without any water. Place this over a strong flame and shake it about while the lavagnons within open. Then remove and drain them, straining and reserving the juices which they will have yielded.

Meanwhile you will have cooked the onions gently, without letting them brown, in the olive oil. They must be stirred from time to time while they are cooking, and crushed with the back of a fork, to produce a purée called a fondu. When the onions have reached this stage, add to them a soup-ladleful of the reserved juices and continue cooking until this has been reduced by half. Then add the lavagnons (without their shells) and the quantity of butter indicated; the butter would ideally be Charentais. Season to taste when you add the butter, then let the butter melt over a gentle heat, so that it does not cook at all. Once it has melted, sprinkle chopped parsley over the dish and serve it.

Huîtres Farcies à la Charentaise
Stuffed oysters

Strongly though I advocate eating oysters raw, I hesitate when confronted by very large ones. I was therefore pleased to learn that French oystermen have their own characteristic way of dealing with this problem. It seems that sometimes Portuguese oysters are overlooked in the oyster parks, when they are ready to be gathered; and in consequence grow to a larger size than usual. They are then known as 'rapures' and are difficult to open with an oyster knife. This is how the oystermen deal with them.

Place the oysters on a hot plate on the stove and wait until the heat causes them to open. Let them continue heating up while you introduce into each some softened butter which has had finely chopped parsley and either crushed garlic or finely chopped shallot worked into it. Eat them hot.

An alternative method, that of Mme Vialard, is to open the rapures in the heat of the oven; collect their juices and combine these with fresh breadcrumbs soaked in a little milk and seasoned; dry a few cloves of garlic *very* slowly in a small pan, pour a beaten egg over them, and combine this with the breadcrumb mixture; distribute the result over the oysters in their half-shells; brown them in the oven and serve them very hot.

Coquilles St-Jacques au Muscadet
Scallops cooked with Muscadet wine (or cider)

This way of preparing scallops is delicious. Muscadet, with its distinctive flavour, is just right for the purpose; but a medium cider, which might well be used in the cider districts of France, is a good alternative.

Prepare the scallops as usual and place the edible parts in a casserole. Barely cover them with Muscadet, bring to the boil and then simmer gently for 10 minutes. Take out the scallop meats, cut them into slices and keep them hot. Reduce the cooking liquid in the casserole and bind it by adding a little butter into which you have worked some flour; then complete the sauce by adding a generous quantity of cream, seasoning and a little lemon juice. Place the slices of scallop in the sauce, and serve.

La Mouclade

A Charentais dish of mussels   serves six

I first ate mouclade in the Restaurant de la Marée at La Rochelle, a long-established seafood restaurant which is situated not merely near but actually in the wholesale fish market. Despite the lunch-time bustle as some sixty people tackled platters of seafood (which were correctly called Grande Selection de Fruits de la Mer, each containing fifteen different seafoods and measuring up to a metre in length), I was able to ask whether their mouclade contained saffron. The answer was that when real saffron was available at a reasonable price a touch of it would be added at the last moment, but that curcuma (turmeric) made a satisfactory substitute. It certainly did. The mouclade was delicious and subtle; the best mussel dish which I had tasted for years.

mussels, 2 litres (4 pints)	**salt and pepper**
butter, 50 gm (2 oz)	**an egg yolk**
flour, 1 tbs	**juice of 1 medium lemon**
white wine, 1½ dl (¼ pint)	**a touch of saffron or turmeric**
garlic, 2 cloves, crushed	**parsley, chopped**

Place the mussels, well washed and with their 'beards' removed, in a large deep pan over a low flame. Add no water. The mussels will soon open. Remove them and take the surplus half-shells off them. Keep the mussels, each now sitting in its remaining half-shell, warm, for example in the top of a large double-boiler. Strain the mussel juices from the pan.

Melt the butter and stir the flour into it over a low flame. Add the garlic and wine and some of the mussel liquor, enough to produce a fairly thin sauce after 10 minutes' gentle cooking.

Season the sauce, remove it from the fire, add the egg yolk to bind it, the saffron or turmeric, and the lemon juice. Put the mussels into the sauce and sprinkle a little chopped parsley over all.

Blanc de Seiche Grillé

Grilled cuttlefish

This is a Charentais dish, for which you will need fairly large cuttlefish. Clean the body parts and peel them carefully so that you are left with nothing but white meat. The pieces of meat should then be grilled gently over a charcoal fire or under the grill, but not too close to the heat, for half an hour.

Season the pieces of cuttlefish. Melt a large knob of butter in a pan, then add the cuttlefish and stir them around until they are well coated by it.

11. Recipes from France —
Part Two, the North-West

The fishing ports of Brittany include some of the most attractive in Europe. I have a particular liking for Douarnanez and the wild Pointe du Raz to which it leads. But Concarneau, with its 'ville close' and its excellent fishery museum, and Quimper offer rival charms; and Lorient, on a larger scale, is impressive. The seafood throughout Brittany is of a quality which reflects the long traditions of fishing which embellish Breton history; and the Bretons have made one special contribution to seafood cookery in the form of their crêpes or galettes aux fruits de mer (page 302), a sort of northern equivalent to the seafood pizza of Naples.

In Normandy, as in Brittany, we are outside the great areas of viticulture, and in cider country. It is said that it was the Arabs in Spain who began to make cider, with apples from France, as a substitute for the alcoholic drink which they brewed from dates in their own countries. If so, they started a large industry, which takes its place in Normandy beside the dairy industry, which produces the famous beurre d'Isigny and superb cream. Many Norman dishes provide a happy combination of these natural resources with the varied seafood and the wealth of good vegetables which this region, the 'pays gras et savoureux en toutes choses' of Froissart, has always enjoyed.

Hence to the coast of the English Channel, where Dieppe was once the port which supplied most of the fish for Les Halles in Paris. Traces of the route followed by the Dieppois fish coaches can still be seen, such as the suburb of La Poissonière by which they entered the capital. But the importance of Dieppe is now less than that of Boulogne, which has become the greatest fishing port in France. Its fish market, or rather its fish auction-hall, in which the fish are represented only by hieroglyphics on blackboards, may seem old-fashioned – indeed it is part of a World War One aeroplane hangar re-erected by the fish quays, and has what appears to be an almost pre-Marconian telephone system – but that is where the big business is done, by men as deceptively casual as their surroundings and equipment. Perhaps the British excel in understatement, but the French are surely, with the Chinese, the great masters of what might be called underaction.

Saumon en Pain de Caudebec

Salmon 'loaf' from Caudebec   serves six

This is a good summer dish, which can, indeed should, be made in advance.

fresh salmon, a piece weighing 700 g (1½ lb)	**butter, 60 g (2 oz)**
potatoes, ½ kg (1 lb)	**dry white wine or cider, 4 tbs**
fines herbes (chives, tarragon, parsley), washed and chopped	**calvados, 1 tbs (optional)**
medium shallots, 2, chopped	**single cream, ¼ litre (½ pint)**
	salt and pepper
	lemon juice, 2 tsp

Poach the salmon in slightly salted water. Boil the potatoes in their jackets, peel them, mash them and mix into them most of the fines herbes, all the shallots and most of the butter (beurre d'Isigny if possible).

Skin the salmon, flake it and add it to the mashed-potato mixture. Moisten the mixture with the wine or cider and (optional) calvados. Use the remaining butter to grease a 1½ litre (2¾ pint) mould. Put the mixture in the mould, pressing it down lightly. Chill for 6 hours at least, preferably 12. When you are ready to serve the dish, lower the mould into very hot water for a minute, then invert it. Serve with the 'loaf' a jug of cream seasoned with salt and pepper, to which add the lemon juice and the remaining fines herbes (about 2 tbs).

Alose au Four

Shad cooked slowly in the oven   serves four

The long, slow cooking of this dish results in the dissolution of the tiresome small bones which abound in shad. The recipe belongs to the region of the Seine, although nowadays no shad spawn in the Seine itself. It is necessary to choose a shad with plenty of roe or milt, which makes this a dish for the spring or early summer.

a shad, 1 kg (2 lb), uncleaned weight	**parsley and chives, chopped, 3 tbs**
	butter, 90–100 g (3 or 4 oz)
breadcrumbs previously soaked in milk and then squeezed, a quantity equal to half the volume of roe/milt	**dry cider, ¼ litre (½ pint)**
	sprigs of parsley
	slices of lemon for garnish

The shad is to be scaled, gutted and washed. Take out the gills and trim off the fins. Mash up the roe or milt with a fork and mix in the chopped herbs and prepared breadcrumbs. The result should be a fairly thick paste, which you insert as a stuffing in the gut cavity and gill cavities of the fish.

Butter an oven dish, place the fish in it, season it again and sprinkle any surplus stuffing around it. Add 2 tbs of cider and a few knobs of butter on top of it. Cook in a slow oven (290° F, gas 1) for 1½ to 2 hours, basting the fish often with more cider and more knobs of butter.

Aiguille à l'Oseille

Garfish with a sorrel sauce   serves four

This fish is often available in quantity and cheaply, for example in the spring on the coast of Brittany (where it may be called aiguillette).

Buy two fairly large ones, clean them and cut each into two sections. Anoint these with butter or olive oil and grill them over a hot fire until cooked through. Meanwhile, make the sauce. Wash two handfuls of sorrel leaves (or sea spinach, or sea beet – *Beta vulgaris maritima*), dry them and cook them gently in butter until thoroughly soft. Then pass them through a sieve with a little more butter (to help bind the sauce), add salt and pepper and lemon juice to taste, and serve with the fish.

Bar au Beurre Blanc Nantais

Sea bass with the 'beurre blanc' of Nantes   serves six

The famous beurre blanc of Nantes is usually associated with either freshwater fish, such as pike, or fish which ascend rivers, such as shad. The reason for this is that its delicacy would be overpowered by a fish with a strong marine flavour. However, this does not apply to the sea bass, which itself has a delicate flavour and may be taken in waters of low salinity. Buy one weighing over 1½ kg (say, 3½ lb) uncleaned. Prepare it in the usual way and poach it in a lightly flavoured court-bouillon, either whole or after cutting it into sections or steaks.

Meanwhile, make the beurre blanc. This is represented by many authors as a difficult task, but it is fairly straightforward if you allow plenty of time. It must not be hurried. Chop very finely 3 or 4 shallots. Heat them in a pan with 4 tbs wine vinegar and 2 tbs of the court-bouillon. If the shallots are large, increase the quantity of liquid slightly; and in any case strain the court-bouillon which you use for this purpose. The shallots must now be cooked so gently that they 'melt' into the liquid. Add seasoning at this stage and reduce by a quarter. Then start adding ½ kg (1 lb) butter, which should be of the best quality, in very small doses. While doing this, keep the pan over the lowest of heats and beat the mixture continuously. That is all, except that you can stir in a little fresh cream at the end.

Serve the beurre blanc with the fish.

Cabillaud aux Fines Herbes

Centre cut of cod cooked with herbs   serves four

This recipe from Normandy is simple and gives a good taste to the cod. Buy a centre cut weighing ¾ kg (1½ lb). You will also need:

fresh parsley, chives, fennel and   **salt and pepper**
** burnet – or three of the four**   **dry white wine, or dry cider, 3 or**
butter, 30 g (1 oz), softened   ** 4 tbs**

Prepare the piece of cod by making deep diagonal incisions in it, starting from the middle of the side and cutting outwards. Wash the herbs and chop them finely, then work them and the seasoning into the softened butter. The next step is to stuff this prepared butter into the cuts which you have made in the cod. Then place the cod on a piece of buttered cooking parchment or aluminium foil, pour the white wine or cider over it and close it up into a packet. Cook this in a slow oven (290° F, gas 1) for 45 or 50 minutes.

To serve the cod, put it on a warm platter, pour the cooking juices over it, add a little freshly chopped parsley as garnish and surround it with boiled or (better) steamed potatoes.

Poisson aux Tomates, Gratiné

Fish with tomatoes, au gratin   serves four

This is a versatile recipe, which may be applied to a bream or porgy (pages 99 to 101) which has first been poached in a court-bouillon; but is equally suitable for grilled steaks of grouper (page 89), fried fillets of weever (page 123), etc. Whatever the fish, you will need about 700 g (1½ lb), cooked weight; and in addition:

tomatoes, 700 g (1½ lb)   **chopped parsley, 2 tbs**
butter, 120 g (¼ lb)   **salt and pepper**
a clove of garlic, chopped   **stale breadcrumbs, sieved, 2 tbs**

Scald, skin and chop the tomatoes. Melt rather more than half the butter in a pan, cook the garlic in it gently, without letting it brown, then take it out. Add the tomatoes to the hot butter, sprinkle the parsley and seasoning over them and cook gently for 10 minutes to reduce the liquid.

Use most of the remaining butter to grease an oven dish. Pour in half the tomato mixture. Lay the cooked fish on this bed and pour the rest of the tomato mixture over it, or them. Sprinkle breadcrumbs on top, dot the surface with what is left of the butter and cook in a moderate oven (355° F, gas 4) for 10 to 15 minutes, until golden brown on top.

Lançons en Friture

Fried sand-eels   serves six

This is a speciality of Normandy (see page 114) and the northern coast of Brittany. Not everyone can get hold of sand-eels; but the recipe can be applied equally well to many other small fish.

sand-eels, 1 kg (2 lb)	flour
milk, about ¼ litre (½ pint)	oil for deep-frying

Take off the heads of the fish, pulling out the gut as you do so. Rinse them and leave them to soak in milk for 20 minutes or longer. Then dry them lightly on a tea-cloth, flour them and deep-fry them in the oil, which should be good and hot (about 475° F). You should only put a few in at a time, so that the temperature of the oil stays high, and you should take them out once they are golden brown. Salt them lightly before serving them piping hot.

Grondin Gris Farci à la Boulonnaise

Grey gurnard stuffed in the fashion of Boulogne   serves four

This is a 'recette typique régionale', as given to me by M. Hamiot, owner of the bustling Bar Hamiot by the fishing port in Boulogne.

grey gurnard (page 140), a large one, weighing 2 kg (4½ lb) uncleaned	*for the stuffing*
	pork, ¼ kg (9 oz), minced and blanched
butter, 30 g (1 oz)	eggs, 2
shallots, 2, finely chopped	fresh breadcrumbs, 6 tbs
white wine (Macon or Alligote if possible)	fines herbes, to include parsley and chives, chopped, 3 tbs
fish fumet, 1 dl (7 tbs)	a shallot, chopped
fresh cream, 1 dl (7 tbs)	

Gut the gurnard without cutting it open more than necessary. Make the stuffing with the ingredients shown, stuff the fish and sew it up.

Cover the bottom of a buttered baking dish with the finely chopped shallots and place the stuffed fish on this bed. Season it and sprinkle the wine over it, then cook it for about 45 to 50 minutes in a moderate oven (355° F, gas 4). When the fish is cooked, remove it and keep it hot while you strain the cooking juices through a chinois and combine them with the fish fumet. Reduce this by a third, adding more seasoning if necessary. Bind it with the cream. Then arrange the fish on a platter, garnish it with parsley and serve it with the sauce in a sauceboat.

Maquereaux à la Façon de Quimper

Mackerel prepared as at Quimper   serves two to four

I found this recipe in *Le poisson en Bretagne*, published in 1949 by the Syndicat d'Initiative de Cornouaille. It is now a family favourite.

'Have mackerel which are very fresh and of a good size. Gut them and cook them in a strongly-seasoned court-bouillon. Once they are cooked, take them out of the water, let them cool and lift the fillets. Then take a tablespoonful of Dijon mustard and combine this with two egg-yolks which you have broken into a terrine. Mix carefully. Add vinegar, salt, pepper and fines herbes and stir well. Melt a little butter until it is just lukewarm, then pour it into the sauce, which should assume a creamy consistency like mayonnaise. Arrange the fillets of mackerel around a platter, pour the sauce into the middle and decorate the whole with sprigs of parsley.'

Some of the quantities need to be specified, thus. Mackerel, 2 of 30 g (10 oz) each uncleaned; vinegar, 1–2 tsp; fines herbes, 2–3 tbs (use parsley, chives and tarragon – the taste of tarragon should be pleasantly dominant in the sauce); melted butter, 5 tbs.

Thon Froid, Sauce Bretonne

Cold tuna with Breton sauce   serves six

a piece of fresh tuna weighing $\frac{3}{4}$ kg (just over $1\frac{1}{2}$ lb) cleaned *or* the equivalent of canned tuna
materials for a court-bouillon (page 259), only needed for cooking the fresh tuna
medium tomatoes, 6, sliced
canned artichoke hearts, 6, diced
lettuce leaves

for the sauce
olive oil, 3 dl ($\frac{1}{2}$ pint)
wine vinegar, 1 dl (7 tbs)
salt and pepper to taste
spices at your discretion
finely chopped parsley, 3 tbs
finely chopped chives, 2 tbs
small pickled gherkins, 2, finely chopped
capers, 1 tbs
double cream, 1 dl (7 tbs)

The preparation is extremely simple. If you are using fresh tuna, cook it in the court-bouillon for 25 to 45 minutes (depending on its shape and maximum thickness, as explained on page 258). Let it cool. Then set it on a platter decorated with tomato slices and artichoke hearts and lettuce leaves. The lettuce could well form a bed for the fish.

Make the sauce by stirring together vigorously all the ingredients listed, except the cream. If you can include both ordinary and French parsley, so much the better. The sauce should then be lightly chilled. Just before serving it, blend in the cream; then pour half the mixture over the tuna, and serve the remainder separately in a sauceboat.

Turbot à Vapeur

Brillat-Savarin's steamed turbot

Few readers are likely to follow this recipe; but all will benefit from absorbing its lesson and from a taste of Brillat-Savarin's prose.

A very large turbot is not easy to cook whole. The Roman emperor Domitian is said to have consulted the Senate about such a problem. A similar one confronted a French family at Villecrêne, when they were expecting Brillat-Savarin, among others, to dinner. There was no vessel large enough to take the turbot whole and opinions within the family were divided about the propriety of cutting it in half. The dispute still raged and one member of the family actually had a chopper in his grasp, when Brillat-Savarin arrived and quelled the hubbub by announcing with calm authority that the turbot was to remain in one piece.

He then proceeded to the kitchen, followed by the household and their own cook, and inspected the available utensils and the ovens. All were too small for the huge fish; but Brillat-Savarin, espying a large copper wash-boiler fitted on top of its own stove, declared that the turbot would be cooked on that.

And straight away, although it was already dinner-time, I set everyone to work. While some lit the furnace, I made a sort of hurdle, of the exact size of the giant fish, from a fifty-bottle pannier. On this hurdle I spread a layer of roots and savoury herbs, on which the fish was laid, after being well scoured, well dried, and suitably salted. A second layer of the same seasoning was spread on the turbot's back. Then the hurdle with its load was placed over the copper, which had been half-filled with water; and the whole was covered with a small wash-tub, round which some dry sand was heaped, to prevent the steam from escaping too easily. Soon the water was boiling; and before long steam filled the interior of the wash-tub, which was removed at the end of half an hour, when the hurdle was lifted off the copper with the turbot done to a turn, very white and splendid to behold.

Brillat-Savarin remarks that the excellence of the dish should have caused no surprise, since the fish had lost none of its good qualities, as it would have done if immersed in boiling water, but had on the other hand fully absorbed the flavours of the various seasonings.

Filets de Sole aux Morilles, Gratinés

Fillets of sole with morels   serves six

Gastronomie pratique by Ali-Bab is in my view one of the best French cookery books ever published. Ali-Bab is precise, but unfussy; and he never gushes. In referring to this dish he goes so far as to say that it is 'remarquable', especially if one uses freshly gathered morels. Morels, sometimes known as sponge mushrooms, belong to the genus *Morchella*. They can be bought dried, or in tins, for use when fresh ones are unavailable.

soles, 2, each weighing $\frac{3}{4}$ kg ($1\frac{1}{2}$ lb) uncleaned	a bouquet garni
	salt and pepper
white wine, $\frac{1}{2}$ litre (1 pint)	butter, 220 g (7 oz)
water, 3 dl ($\frac{2}{3}$ pint)	morels, $\frac{1}{4}$ kg ($\frac{1}{2}$ lb)
medium carrots, 2	lemon juice, 2 tsp
a medium onion	fine dry breadcrumbs, 2 tbs

Lift the fillets from the soles. Put the heads, bones and trimmings into a casserole with the wine and water; the carrots and onion, cleaned and finely chopped; the bouquet garni and the seasoning. Cook this, uncovered, over a low flame for 30 minutes or more, to obtain a concentrated fish stock (fumet). Strain it through a fine strainer.

Next, cook the fillets of sole in the fumet, after adding to it 25 g (1 oz) butter. Cook the morels in 50 g (2 oz) butter and the lemon juice. Keep both the fillets and the morels warm after they have been cooked. Combine the two lots of cooking liquid and reduce them by a third. Then, without letting the mixture boil again, whisk into it 75 g (3 oz) butter. Correct the seasoning. Your sauce is now ready. Arrange the fillets in an oven dish, surround them with the morels, pour the sauce over all, sprinkle the top with breadcrumbs and dot it with the remaining butter. Brown the dish in the oven and bring it to table in the oven dish.

Sole au Glui

Sole grilled with straw, from the region of Dieppe

Glui means ordinary wheat straw; and this is one of those very old, traditional methods of cooking which has survived to the present day. Even so, I thought to put it in mainly for historical interest. However, when my daughter Caroline tested it, using freshly cut Wiltshire hay as the straw, she reported that it was 'sensationally good' and must be included on its own merits. The flesh of the sole turns a pale Naples yellow and acquires a subtle taste, not slightly acid, as some authors have it, but as it were 'desweetened' and reminiscent of lightly smoked fish.

Gut and trim the sole, but do not skin it. Make a cut right along each side, following the line of the backbone, and smear some good fresh butter into each of these incisions. Season the sole lightly.

Have ready a good charcoal fire and one of those folding metal grids (page 262) which are used for grilling fish. Open the grid and cover one side of it with straw. Put the sole on the straw, then cover it with a second layer of straw before closing the grid over it. Grill the sole, thus prepared, over the charcoal fire. The straw will flare up dramatically almost at once. Allow about 6 minutes for the first side and 4 minutes for the other.

Meanwhile, prepare a cream sauce by placing equal quantities of butter and fresh cream in a saucepan in a warm (but not too hot) bain-marie. Whip these together and, when all is mixed and warm, add salt and pepper and grated nutmeg. Just before the sauce is ready, add 1–2 teaspoonfuls of chopped shallot. Then keep the sauce warm.

When the sole is ready, puff the bits of burned straw off it, put it on a warm serving platter and serve it with the sauce as accompaniment.

Saumonette au Vin Blanc et à la Crème

Dogfish (rock salmon) cooked with white wine and cream   serves four

The treatment recommended here is used in Brittany for a wide variety of fish. It does wonders for the humble dogfish; and also for gurnards.

fillets of dogfish (see pages 168 to 170), $\frac{3}{4}$ kg (1$\frac{1}{2}$ lb)	white wine, $\frac{1}{2}$ litre (1 pint)
shallots, 1 or 2, thinly sliced	butter, 50 g (2 oz)
thyme (or another fresh herb)	flour, 30 g (1 oz)
a bay leaf, shredded	cream, 4 tbs single or 3 tbs double
	tomato purée, 1 tbs

Choose a casserole into which the fillets of fish will fit snugly, and put them into it with the shallot, thyme, bay leaf and wine. Poach them for 10 to 15 minutes, according to their thickness.

Meanwhile make a roux by heating the butter and working the flour into it, without letting it brown. When the fish is done, lift it out and keep it warm. Strain the cooking liquid and add it little by little to the roux in order to produce your sauce. Cook this gently for 5 minutes, then add the cream and tomato purée, stir well and heat through without boiling. Arrange the fillets of fish on a heated platter and pour the sauce over them.

Ormeaux au Beurre Breton

Ormers (abalones) with 'Brittany butter   serves six

A dozen large or 18 medium ormers, having been opened, cleaned and well tenderized (see page 214) are fried in ordinary butter until brown, then drained and laid out in an oven dish.

Meanwhile, you have chopped very finely a small shallot and marinated it in Muscadet for 3 or 4 hours. Combine this with 200 g (7 oz) demi-sel butter, a pounded clove of garlic, 1 tbs very finely chopped parsley and a little pepper. Mix thoroughly, spread over the ormers and put the dish in a moderately hot oven (400° F, gas 6) for 5 minutes. Serve hot.

Galettes (or Crêpes) aux Fruits de Mer

When touring Brittany a few years ago I could never decide which were my favourite products of the crêperies which everywhere confronted and detained us. The galettes with fishy fillings had first claim on my attention; but then the crêpes with fruit seemed equally delicious.

There used to be a clear distinction between galettes and crêpes. The former were made with blé noir (buckwheat), unsweetened, and contained savoury fillings. Crêpes were made with froment (plain wheat) and sugar and held sweet fillings. But the range has widened to include unsweetened crêpes, and the old distinction has become blurred.

Galettes, or crêpes, aux fruits de mer are thin pancakes rolled round a filling of shrimps, mussels, etc., and are quite delicious. Making them is best left to the professionals with their special equipment; or learned from a book such as Simone Morand's *Gastronomie bretonne*. My purpose here is simply to recommend their consumption and to advance the general idea that thin, unsweetened pancakes of any kind, for example the blinis which Russians and others make, are an excellent vehicle for seafoods.

Palourdes Farcies

Stuffed carpet-shells   serves four

This Breton recipe can be applied to other bivalves of comparable size.

palourdes, 24 (page 234)	double cream, 2 dl (⅓ pint)
a shallot, finely chopped	grated cheese, 1 tbs
finely chopped parsley, ½ tbs	toasted breadcrumbs, 2 tsp
butter	salt and pepper

The sauce for 'stuffing' the palourdes is made as follows. Melt sufficient butter in a pan and cook the shallot and parsley in it gently, until the shallot starts to turn yellow. Add the cream, bring to the boil and continue to cook for a minute or so before adding the grated cheese (Gruyère if possible) and breadcrumbs. The sauce, which will now be quite thick, has still to be lightly seasoned and is then ready.

The palourdes may be steamed open or simply opened with a knife. Leave them on the half-shell, coat each with the prepared sauce, sprinkle them lightly with breadcrumbs, brown them under a hot grill and serve at once.

Moules à la Fécampoise

Mussels in the style of Fécamp

This unusual recipe is suitable for large mussels. Begin by heating them in a deep pan with 1 dl (7 tbs) cider. When they have all opened, take them out of their shells and strain the cooking liquid.

Prepare separately a salad of celeriac with a vinaigrette. Arrange this in the bottom of a salad dish and cover it with the mussels. Next, take some mayonnaise and dilute it slightly with some of the strained cooking liquid. Put the mayonnaise over the mussels. Finally, sprinkle on top some very finely chopped herbs, comprising if possible ordinary parsley, French parsley, tarragon and chives.

Pieuvre à la Cocotte

Stewed octopus   serves four

This is a useful recipe from Brittany which gives octopus a delicately different flavour.

an octopus, weighing at least 750 g (1¾ lb) uncleaned	shallots, 3, finely chopped
materials for a court-bouillon (page 259)	garlic, 1 or 2 cloves, chopped
olive oil, 3 or 4 tbs	large tomatoes, 4, quartered
a large onion, chopped	white wine, Muscadet if possible, 2 dl (⅓ pint)
	parsley

Clean the octopus and let it simmer in a court-bouillon for 40 minutes. Remove it and cut it into small pieces.

Meanwhile, heat the olive oil and cook the onion and shallot in it until they are golden brown. Add the octopus and the garlic, followed a few minutes later by the tomatoes, such seasoning as you judge necessary, and the wine. Leave the whole mixture to simmer very gently for at least 20 minutes, then serve it with parsley as the garnish.

12. Recipes from Belgium

Half of Belgium is Francophone; but the whole of the short coastline falls in the Flemish part. So Belgian seafood cookery is essentially Flemish and fits as neatly as part of a jigsaw puzzle between that of Flanders to the south and the Netherlands to the north. It has little which is peculiar to it, but possesses a character of its own. Thus the Visserskaai at Ostend, with its fifty-three restaurants all serving seafood, has an unmistakably Belgian flavour; and even a brief exploration of the fishermen's quarter of Ostend is enough to reveal interesting traditions and the distinctive dialect which survive with Flemish tenacity in this and similar communities. Ostend, after all, was once the east end of the island de Streep which stretched down to Westende; and this stretch of coast still has an insular feel to it.

But when we lived in Belgium it was at Brussels, or Bruxelles/Brussel as the bilingual signs in the capital have it. There, a certain Mme Renard took over our kitchen once a month, preparing therein an economical banquet which usually began with Tomates aux Crevettes. This is a favourite first course in Belgium, and in the Netherlands too, and is so simple that it needs no recipe. (Cut the tops off large tomatoes, scoop out the flesh, stuff them with cooked and peeled shrimps bathed in first-class mayonnaise and sprinkle chopped parsley on top.) And twice a month we would visit one of the unpretentious bourgeois restaurants which abound in Brussels.

One of our haunts was the restaurant Chez Vincent, where, as I wrote in another book which had the distinction of being banned, the original Vincent had set sections of a boat down the room, 'so that one sat in the prow or stern or on the cross-benches amidships, a nautical ambiance which affected the waiters, causing them to sway and glide with the panache of ocean stewards'; and where the pre-1914 tile paintings showed fishing boats and a sandy beach, on which exactly 130 shells and small marine creatures were depicted with *trompe-l'oeil* precision, together with a sou'westered fisherman astride a giant cart-horse in the sea.

This last phenomenon requires explanation. These burly, yellow, oil-skinned fishermen, mounted on their great steeds, used to splosh along in pursuit of their diminutive prey, the shrimps. Only seven of them still do this, at Oostduinkerke, where the charming fishery museum exhibits material about the quaint practice, e.g. the medallion shown on page 305.

Some gastronomic traditions are fading, too. Fortunately, many have been recorded in the superb and encyclopaedic dictionary of the Ostend dialect by M. Roland Desnerck, a lexicographer with a particular bent towards fishermen's lore. I owe the piece on 't zootsje, below, to him.

Like everyone else, Belgians have to make do with fewer herrings at present. They used, however, to consume large quantities. They had one dish called 'Lammeke-zoet', sweet little lambkins. A lambkin was a very lightly salted or smoked herring which had been wrapped in a heavy coat of damp paper and left for a while in a glowing fire or hot oven. The delicacy was served with small potatoes, boiled in their skins, and beer. The other traditional way of eating herring was to buy some, pickled with onion rings, from the tub which stood in every grocery shop. It was fished out of the tub with a wooden fork and eaten at home with bread or in a café with chips.

't Zootsje

This is *un peu d'histoire*, as the Michelin guides say, rather than a recipe which any reader is likely to follow. It is an account, furnished by M. Desnerck, of how fishermen used to cook seafood at sea.

'Zieden' means to cook, 'zoo' comes from the same root and 'zootsje' is the diminutive; a pleasing touch, since the operation is on a massive scale, requiring a great iron cauldron suspended over a source of heat, perhaps the furnace in the engine room. The cauldron is almost full of sea water. A grid is suspended within, just below the bubbling surface of the water, with space at the sides for introducing material below it. This material consists of string bags of potatoes, one for each man, and any available crabs and whelks, which are left to bob about freely. On the grid itself go fish, straight from the net with barely time to stun and gut them.

Each fisherman would have a 'mokke', or enamel mug, with which he would draw out some of the cooking water when he wished to eat. He would at the same time pull up his own bag of potatoes, select a fish and add a crab or whelk. Old fishermen will say that there is nothing which quite matches this dish for marine flavour and for satisfying hungry men.

Oostendse Vissoep

Ostend fish soup   serves ten

In a port which I do not know well I usually ask a fishery official where to find the best fish dishes. At Ostend I was directed to Bij Adelientje, a small restaurant of sober décor which has been functioning since before the First World War and is now run by M. and Mme Lecomte. Their son-in-law, M. Boucquez, is the chef and a native of Ostend. His fish soup is a personal variation on a familiar local theme. I found it excellent. The sombre brown colour with touches of dark green and mysterious hints of purple is in tune with some of the paintings of James Ensor, the Ostend painter, whose house has been preserved as a museum nearby.

fish – heads, trimmings and bones from, e.g., gurnards, angler-fish, turbot – $1\frac{1}{2}$–2 kg (3–4 lb)	unsalted butter, 200 g (7 oz) leeks, 4
celery, 3 bunches	carrots, 6–8
large onions, 4	a pinch of saffron
salt and pepper	tomato purée, 250 g (9 oz)
thyme, $\frac{1}{2}$ tsp	Ricard, 2 dashes per person
bay leaves, 4	powdered garlic, to taste
dry white wine, 1 litre ($1\frac{3}{4}$ pints)	toast, 10 squares 5 by 5 cm
	grated cheese, 5 tbs

Take a very large casserole and put $5\frac{1}{2}$–6 litres (10 British pints) water in it, with the white parts of the celery, 2 of the onions (sliced), salt and pepper to taste, thyme and bay leaves, all the fish heads and trimmings and half the white wine. Boil all this for 20 minutes.

Meanwhile, dice the remaining vegetables. Melt the butter in a second large casserole, add the diced vegetables and the remaining wine and cook gently for 10 minutes. Then add the saffron.

Now pass the fish broth through a fine strainer. Remove all usable chunks of flesh, free of skin and bone, for later incorporation in the soup and discard the debris. Pour the strained broth over the vegetable mixture and boil it all for a further 10 minutes. Then add the tomato purée.

To serve the soup, take a bowl for each person, put some of the saved chunks of fish in each, a couple of dashes of Ricard, a touch of garlic powder (for those who like it) and 2 ladlefuls of the soup. Top each helping with a square of toast covered with grated cheese, which should be Parmesan or Gruyère if possible.

M. Boucquez says that if you have other cooked seafood to hand, as happens in a restaurant, you can add this. He suggests mussels and shrimps. He also says that the soup is even better if prepared on the previous day and reheated.

Paling in't Groen (or Anguille au Vert)

Eel in a green sauce

This famous dish is easily made. It is agreeable to join the Belgians in passionate discussions about just which greens should be used, and I give below what Louis Paul Boon regards as the ideal list; but the important thing is to have several and to be sure to include sorrel, since its flavour should be the most noticeable.

Finely chop and stew gently for half an hour in a little butter, with salt and pepper, the following greens: sorrel, celery tops, parsley, mint, sage, chervil, lemon balm and summer savory. A little minced onion may be added with advantage to this brew.

Meanwhile, select a fat eel, skin it, clean it and cut it into sections. Bring to the boil some water to which a little vinegar has been added. Boil the pieces of eel in this for 5 to 10 minutes, according to their thickness. Then drain them and put them in with the stewed greenery to finish cooking. When the pieces of eel are quite tender, add to the sauce a lump of butter into which you have worked some flour, and bind it thus. Serve hot, with thickly buttered brown bread.

Zeewolf op Zijn Brabants

Wolf-fish in the Brabant way   serves four

This recipe, from the restaurant Au Vigneron at Ostend, suggests a dish of Flemish origin which has been refined by Walloon influences.

wolf-fish (page 121), $\frac{1}{2}$ kg (1 lb), cleaned weight

chicory, $\frac{1}{4}$ kg ($\frac{1}{2}$ lb)

potatoes, $\frac{1}{4}$ kg ($\frac{1}{2}$ lb)

butter, 100 g ($3\frac{1}{2}$ oz)

shallots, 2, finely chopped

salt and pepper

dry white wine, 2 dl ($\frac{1}{3}$ pint)

fish fumet, 2 dl ($\frac{1}{3}$ pint)

Chop up the chicory and potatoes, season them and fry them in half the butter. Use a little more butter to grease an oven dish and strew the shallots over the bottom of it, with a sprinkling of salt and pepper. Lay the fish on this bed, pour wine and fumet over it, cover with foil and cook gently for 10 minutes in the oven at 375° F, gas 5.

Now transfer the potatoes and chicory to a second oven dish, with the fish on top of them, and keep this hot while you make the sauce. This is done by reducing the cooking juices in the first dish, then adding the rest of the butter and seasoning. Pour the sauce over the fish and put the dish back in the oven for a few minutes to give the sauce a glaze.

Kaaksjes en Keeltjes

Cheeks and throats of cods

The title of this dish is in the Ostend dialect. The Ostend fishermen, like their brethren in many other ports, have always regarded the flesh from the head of the cod as the most tasty morsels to be had from that fish. Heads used to fetch a high price. But nowadays, when convenience and quality are often confused, it is the poorer people who bear off the heads, when they are available, and enjoy the titbits for which wealthy epicures would once have been competing.

Buy a couple of cods' heads. Take out the cheeks and detach the throat muscles. Boil them briefly with a sliced onion, salt, pepper and a dash of vinegar. Drain them and serve with boiled potatoes and melted butter.

Do not forget to make a soup from what is left of the heads.

Ingemaakte Rog

Pickled ray

Traditional Flemish eating habits are well described by Louis Paul Boon in his *Eten op zijn Vlaams*. During the week, people liked to have a meal at tea-time, which was 4 o'clock. A favourite dish was the salted whiting which used to hang, on nice windy days, on a pole outside the grocer's shop. It was eaten with bread and strong coffee. However, the Sunday routine called for a sort of high tea at 6 o'clock, at which pickled ray was often served.

Soak pieces of ray for two hours in water to which salt and vinegar have been added. Then bring another litre (2 pints) of water to the boil, with a chopped onion, 2 bay leaves, thyme, $1\frac{1}{2}$ dl ($\frac{1}{4}$ pint) vinegar, whole pepper-corns and salt. Put the pieces of ray in this and bring it back to the boil. Then remove the fish and let it cool before eating it.

The best ray for the above purpose would be a 'ruuder' (*Raja clavata*, page 172). But a 'gladder' (*Raja batis*, page 175) would be used for the fishermen's dish called **Roggelevertjes op Toast**, skate livers on toast. Skate livers, which can weigh as much as $\frac{1}{2}$ kg (1 lb), are not readily available everywhere, but some fishmongers will supply small ones. Allow 75 g ($2\frac{1}{2}$ oz) per person. Wash the livers, and boil them gently for 5 minutes in lightly salted water. Strain them into a colander and let them drain and become lukewarm while you make the toast. Then spread the livers, which will be quite soft, thickly on the pieces of toast. Season with lots of pepper, a little salt and a sprinkling of lemon juice.

Kuit in een Zak

A 'pocketful of roe'

This is how Flemish fishermen have traditionally treated cod's roe. The technique is not exclusive to them; but their name for the result, which comes out in dialect as 'Kiete in e zak', is particularly pleasing.

Take a large cod's roe and wrap it carefully in muslin. Place it in salted water, bring it to the boil, then drain it and let it cool. Unwrap it, cut it into slices, fry these and serve them on toast or bread.

Pladijs met Splets

Plaice with a purée of potato and sorrel

Flemish people often use sorrel (zuring in Dutch, zurkel in the Flemish dialects) in their cookery. This recipe is no more than a suggestion for combining sorrel with potato as an accompaniment for fried plaice or other flatfish. The vegetable combination is known as splets.

Purée of sorrel can be bought in jars in Belgium. To make your own, stew lots of cleaned sorrel in a pot with a little salt, in the water which will exude from the sorrel itself. Then turn it into a purée in the blender.

Mix the sorrel purée thoroughly with mashed potatoes, a little milk, some knobs of butter and a dusting of nutmeg. It is to be served hot with the fried fish; and Flemish practice is to serve browned butter too, which can be poured into little hollows in the purée.

Polderaardappelen Gevuld met Garnalen

Potatoes stuffed with shrimps   serves four

Choose 4 large, evenly shaped potatoes. Boil them in their jackets until they are just about cooked. It will be helpful to have pricked them on top first, so that the skins do not burst. Then lay them in a hot oven for a few minutes, so that they dry out and finish cooking. Cut the tops off them and scoop out enough from each to make room for the stuffing. Reserve the scooped-out potato.

Meanwhile, you have boiled half a medium onion, finely chopped, in 4 or 5 tbs white wine until the wine is reduced to zero. This takes about 15 minutes. Next, add 50 g (2 oz) butter to the onion and let it melt; then 1 dl (7 tbs) single cream, 1 tbs lemon juice, salt and pepper to taste, and $\frac{1}{4}$ kg ($\frac{1}{2}$ lb) freshly peeled, cooked shrimps. I then like to thicken the mixture by mashing some of the scooped-out potato into it, but this is optional. Pour the sauce or stuffing into and over the potatoes and sprinkle 4 tbs chopped parsley on top.

Paardevissersschelp

The horseback fishermen's scallop dish of shrimps   serves four

It is said that the horseback shrimp fishermen (see page 304) would themselves eat shrimps in this way.

Chop a medium onion and 200 g (7 oz) mushrooms and fry the lot together in 50 g (2 oz) butter until the onions are a light brown. Line 4 scallop shells with this mixture.

Next, melt 20 g ($\frac{3}{4}$ oz) butter in a saucepan and work into it 1–1$\frac{1}{2}$ tbs flour, followed by $\frac{1}{4}$ litre (nearly $\frac{1}{2}$ pint) mild brown beer, which you must add little by little, stirring constantly. Once the sauce is smooth, add to it 2 handfuls of cooked and peeled shrimps, heat the mixture through and divide it between the scallop shells. Sprinkle soft breadcrumbs on top, brown under the grill and serve very hot.

Garnaalcroquetten met Tomatensaus

Shrimp croquettes with tomato sauce   serves six to eight

brown shrimp (page 182), 1 kg
   (2 lb), cooked but unpeeled
best salted butter (that of
   Diksmuide if in Belgium), $\frac{1}{4}$ kg
   ($\frac{1}{2}$ lb)
flour, 200 g (7 oz)
white wine, 2 dl ($\frac{1}{3}$ pint)
juice of 3 lemons

eggs, 4, separated
breadcrumbs
beef lard or oil for deep-frying

for the tomato sauce
ordinary butter, 50 g (2 oz)
an onion, finely chopped
tomato purée, 90 g (3 oz)

Peel the shrimps, reserve the meat and set all the debris to boil in water for 5 minutes. Strain and reserve the broth.

Melt the butter in a pan, stir in the flour and add the wine and lemon juice, followed by 3$\frac{1}{2}$–4 dl (about $\frac{2}{3}$ pint) of the strained broth and all the shrimp meat, keeping the pan over a low flame and stirring all the time. The result will be a dough-like mixture. Remove it from the fire, add the egg yolks, mix well and chill for several hours.

Have the whites of egg in a bowl. Take a tablespoonful of the shrimp mixture at a time, form these into the shape of croquettes, dip them in the egg white, roll them in the breadcrumbs and deep-fry them in hot lard or oil (400° F) until brown. You should have 20 to 25 croquettes. They are to be served as a first course and each person will have 3 or 4.

The sauce is easy. Melt the butter, fry the chopped onion in it until it is golden, then add the tomato purée and remove from the fire once the mixture is heated through. It will have the consistency of a thick soup.

Mosselen met Frieten/Moules et Frites

Mussels and chips

This is one of the national dishes, possibly *the* national dish, of Belgium. In Brussels, it may be called simply 'le complet bruxellois'. It is not complicated, but its preparation and the agreeable ritual with which the people of Ostend, in particular, consume it deserve study. I was instructed in the ritual, appropriately, by an Ostend schoolteacher, and in the cooking by Mevrouw Rachel Libin of the same city. She did not join us at table, because there must be someone working continuously in the kitchen to ensure a steady stream of mussels, sauce and chips to the dining-room.

Allow 1½ kg (3 lb) mussels for each person and at least ¼ kg (½ lb) potatoes for each person's chips.

Put the first batch of mussels to open in a large cooking pot with half an onion, chopped, half a glass of white wine or vinegar, a tablespoonful of salt and a sprinkling of pepper. While this is on the flame, fry separately in a pan the other half of the onion, also chopped, and an equivalent amount of chopped celery.

Once the mussels have all opened, remove them to another pot, in which they can be brought to table, pour the fried onion and celery mixture over them and keep them warm while you make the sauce.

Strain the cooking liquid from the mussels. Melt 100 g (3½ oz) butter in a pan over a low flame and stir the same weight of flour into it. Add and stir in enough of the mussel liquid to produce a smooth cream. Add a large quantity (10 tbs or more) of finely chopped parsley, with a smallish onion and 4 little gherkins, also finely chopped. Cook the sauce for one more minute. If the chopping has been done beforehand the preparation of the sauce will take 5 minutes in all.

The chips are deep-fried in the usual way and in ample quantity.

Over to the dining-room, where there will now be a central pot of mussels, a platter of chips, a bowl of sauce and a plate for each diner. The correct procedure is to extract your first mussel from its shell with a fork, dip it in the sauce and eat it; then to use the empty shell as a pair of pincers with which to extract the second mussel, and so on. Discarded shells are arranged in a circle around but not on your plate, each V-shaped double-shell fitting into the previous one. Light beer or lager is the drink. Those who, like myself, drink water, should not take the Ostend tap water, harmless though it is, but Spa bottled water or, better still, water from the natural spring at the Château of Wijnendale near Torhout, the best in Belgium.

The procession of mussels from the kitchen will continue for a long time. It is worth knowing that Ostend fishermen, after eating a large quantity of mussels, will take a little cup of milk to ward off any ill effects.

13. Recipes from the Netherlands

The great fishing ports of the Netherlands are IJmuiden and Scheveningen. We knew Scheveningen well when we lived in The Hague in the 1950s and would enjoy eating simple fish meals in a restaurant on the fishing quay, with glimpses through the window of Scheveningen women going by in their traditional costume. The Dutch capacity for combining progress in technology with a pleasing conservatism was brought home to me on a recent visit to the same restaurant (Restaurant J. van der Toorn), when as I ate my fried sea-wolf I saw the same sight, but this time against the background of the splendid new fish market, where there is a kind of amphitheatre with a huge revolving price clock and the merchants sit at desks and press buttons as the 'Dutch auction' proceeds. Dutch fishermen, by the way, take 80 per cent of the soles caught in the North Sea and the price of these had already soared off the top of the clock by 1976.

The conservatism of the Dutch extends to cookery. Dutch cookery writing is still dominated by the great tomes of the cookery schools – Amsterdam, The Hague, Rotterdam and Dordrecht – which are reprinted again and again in sober format. No one has yet produced a survey of Dutch regional cookery. Most Dutch people say modestly that there is too little of it. In fact, there is some; and several of the recipes which follow are regional specialities. But it is true that the variety, at least in fish cookery, is not great. The Dutch continue to love their herring, as they have done for centuries, and make plain but good dishes of eel, cod and haddock. The influence of Indonesia is apparent in some recipes for curried fish. But the general tendency is to cook fish simply, making use of Dutch dairy products and of the beloved potato.

No recipe is given for my favourite Dutch fish dish, because none is needed. It is simply Dutch smoked eel, in thin fillets or diagonally cut slices, served with lemon wedges and parsley. Nor is there a recipe for fish soup, since the Dutch rarely use fish for this purpose.

The Herring in the Netherlands

The consumption of herring is treated by the Dutch with a properly serious attitude, and the visitor should know what names are applied to this fish in its various guises. Here they are.

GROENE (or NIEUWE) HARINGEN are herring caught at the beginning of the season, in April or May. They are almost completely gutted on board, deboned, lightly salted and allowed to ferment briefly by the action of intestinal enzymes. They used then to be sold thus for immediate consumption. In Amsterdam they would cut up the herring and eat the pieces from toothpicks. In The Hague they would leave the tail on, so that they could lower the fish into the mouth and bite off piece after piece, like mouthfuls of soft butter, taking a little chopped onion between bites.

It was found, however, that nematoids, thread-like worms, sometimes remained in these herring. Freezing kills the nematoids, so the herring must now be frozen before being sold. This new regulation has transformed what had been a seasonal delicacy into one which is available all the year round; and the frozen herring, when thawed, are indistinguishable from fresh ones. So, on the whole, hurrah; especially as the Dutch have retained in this new situation the ancient traditions which involve flag-bedecked festivities at Scheveningen over the arrival of the first groene haringen of the season and which require the captain of the first vessel which lands them to take in person to Queen Juliana a pallet, i.e. 200 or so herring, of his catch.

MAATJES are herring caught while they are feeding vigorously before their spawning season. These fat herring are taken from June until early August and have a special flavour, provided that they have been gutted correctly. Care must be taken to leave in place the caecal appendices of the stomach, since these contain, but only during this period of vigorous feeding, certain enzymes which are capable of 'maturing' the protein in the fish and which produce welcome changes in flavour when they do so.

A PEKELHARING is a brined herring.

A ZURE HARING is a herring pickled in salt, vinegar, spices and onion.

A PANHARING has been fried and then pickled in vinegar.

A BOKKING is a cold-smoked herring. It is mainly for export, although some are eaten by the Dutch. They are smoked whole, so they have a gamey taste and have to be cleaned before they are eaten. Most Dutch cookery books advise simply frying them. However, there seems to have been a tradition at Vlissingen whereby the cleaned bokkingen were chopped up and then fried in butter with eggs and a little stock, the mixture being stirred around until done and garnished with parsley.

Haringsla

Herring salad serves four to six

Of the dishes which the Dutch prepare from herring, this is perhaps the most typical. The recipe comes from *Recepten van de Haagsche Kookschool* (1895).

salted herrings, 6

milk, as required

sour apples, 10, peeled and cored

a beetroot, cooked

cooked veal, 100 g (3½ oz)

hard-boiled eggs, 6

potatoes, 150 g (⅓ lb), boiled and
    mashed

olive oil, 1–2 tbs

vinegar, 1–2 tsp

Soak the herrings overnight in milk or a mixture of milk and water, then bone them and cut the flesh into thin strips. Chop up the apples, the beetroot, the meat and the eggs. Combine all these ingredients with the mashed potato, and moisten the mixture with oil and vinegar. Then put it in a china basin or bowl and press it down so that it will take on the shape of this recipient when turned out on to a platter. It can be covered with mayonnaise.

I like the combination of herring and veal, which echoes the Estonian recipe on page 357; but the veal makes the salad more expensive and it is usual nowadays to make the haringsla without such an addition.

Harlinger Haringschotel

Harlingen baked herring serves four Dutchmen or six others

4 nieuwe haringen (page 313)

butter, 80 g (3 oz)

shallots, 4, chopped

yoghourt, 3 dl (½ pint)

eggs, 4, separated

large potatoes, 4, boiled and
    mashed

sugar, ½ tsp

salt, 2 pinches

Fillet the herring and steep the fillets in cold water for an hour, then drain them and cut them into small chunks. Melt a quarter of the butter in a pan and fry the shallots in this until translucent. Remove them and let them cool, then mix them with a third of the yoghourt and all the fish. (You may, incidentally, use sour cream instead of yoghourt. The Dutch themselves are starting to use it more frequently.)

Meanwhile, melt the rest of the butter in the pan and stir into it the remaining yoghourt, the egg yolks and the mashed potato. Beat the egg whites, then fold them into the mixture, followed by the sugar and salt.

Butter an ovenproof dish and place half the egg and potato mixture in the bottom; on top of this the herring mixture; then the rest of the egg and potato mixture. Bake for ¾ hour in a moderate oven (355° F, gas 4).

Gebakken Spiering met Selderij

Fried smelt with celery   serves four

This is the favourite dish of Dr Dolf Boddeke, a Dutch marine biologist who takes a passionate interest in fish cookery.

smelt, 800 g (1¾ lb)	medium potatoes, 8
celery, ½ kg (1 lb)	vegetable oil for frying

Cut the celery stalks into short sections and simmer them slowly in lightly salted water until they are tender (about 40 minutes). The potatoes are to be done in Dutch fashion. Boil them until they are just cooked but still firm. Then cut them into slices and pan-fry these.

The smelt are small fish, often only 10 or 15 cm long. You will find that you have six or more per person. Take off their heads and gut them. Then either pan-fry them over a high heat or deep-fry them. They should emerge brown and crisp from either treatment. Serve them with the celery and potatoes.

Vis Filets met Kaassaus

Fish fillets with cheese sauce   serves four

This typical Dutch recipe can be used for any good white fish. Thin steaks of halibut respond well to the treatment. So do fillets of John Dory.

'Belegen kaas' is a special matured Gouda cheese, milder than Parmesan but equally hard. A mature Cheddar may be used instead, if necessary.

fillets or steaks of fresh fish, 8 small or 4 large	belegen kaas (see above), 90 g (3 oz), grated
salt and pepper	butter, 30 g (1 oz) for the sauce
butter, 60 g (2 oz) for frying	flour, 2 tbs
butter, a further 15 g (½ oz) for the oven dish	fish stock, 2½ dl (nearly ½ pint)
	cream, 1 dl (5–6 tbs)

Season the fish fillets and fry them gently in the butter until done. Melt the second dose of butter in a large oval oven dish, sprinkle a third of the grated cheese over it and put the fillets in lengthways.

Prepare a sauce with the third dose of butter, the flour, the fish stock and the cream, mix a third of the grated cheese into it and pour it over the fish fillets. Sprinkle the remaining third of the grated cheese on top and put the dish in a moderate oven (355° F, gas 4) until it is lightly browned.

Gebakken Paling

Fried fillets of eel, Dutch style   serves six

This is one of the most popular of Dutch fish dishes. The recipe, which is adapted from the cookery book of the Vlissingen Cookery School, is accompanied by instructions for making the Hollandaise sauce; for which, after all, Dutch instructions seem most appropriate.

This and some other Dutch recipes call for Dutch rusks (beschuiten) as an ingredient. These look like circular pieces of toast, 8 or 9 cm in diameter. What are sold as egg rusks or Tea-Break rusks in Britain will do very well instead. Ordinary toasted breadcrumbs are not quite as good.

eel, 1 kg (2 lb) of a large, thick one, skinned and filleted	crushed rusks (see above)
	butter, 25 g (1 oz)
salt, 25 g (1 oz)	lemon slices, sprigs of parsley,
flour	lettuce leaves

Salt the eel fillets and leave them in a colander for half an hour; then dry them and turn them in flour and crushed rusks. Brown the butter in a pan and fry the fillets quickly on all sides. Garnish them with lemon, parsley and lettuce; and serve them with a dressed salad and a Hollandaise sauce, made thus.

2 egg yolks	100 g (3½ oz) butter
1 tsp salt	1 tbs vinegar
½ tsp pepper	½ tsp lemon juice

Stir the egg yolks with the salt, pepper and butter for 10 minutes or until the mixture has become a thick, whitish mass. Put it in the top of a double boiler, add the vinegar and keep stirring while the mixture heats until it froths. Then stir in the lemon juice and serve at once.

Although the above recipe represents the usual way of cooking eel, there are some interesting alternatives in the provinces. In the north, for example, they make *Gestoofde Paling met Appeltjes*, eel with cooked apples. Sections of eel are baked in the oven with butter, golden bread-crumbs, lemon slices and a little water, then served with boiled potatoes and specially prepared apples. The apples are cored and peeled and cut into large chunks, then cooked in a little water with sugar and cinnamon. After this, they are removed from the pan, the cooking juices are thickened with a little potato flour and the apple chunks glazed with this thickened liquid.

Stokvis

Dried salted cod in three Dutch versions

Stokvis used to be a staple food in the Royal Netherlands Navy and I cherish a copy of the official instructions which governed its preparation, until the Second World War, for naval crews. They stipulate 300 grams of stokvis for each man and inform the purser that 'in order to enhance the meal things like mustard and chutney may be bought with the money allocated for spices'. However, the naval tradition has been lifted on to a higher gastronomic plane by the club of former naval officers who meet in January every year at the De Witte restaurant in The Hague to eat a stokvis dinner. It is their custom to set by each place a Rhine wineglass containing a raw egg. Each diner mixes the egg on his plate and proceeds to help himself to the 'zeven gerechten' (seven courses would be the usual translation, but seven constituents is meant). These are as follows:

1) **100 g (3½ oz) (*much* less than for sailors on active service!) stokvis, which has been soaked as usual to 'reconstitute' it, then tied into little rolls and simmered for 45 minutes before being untied and served**

2) **boiled rice, 'nice and dry'**
3) **boiled potatoes**
4) **a butter sauce**
5) **fried onions**
6) **gherkins**
7) **mustard sauce**

all of which are to be served in the above order, with the optional addition of raw onion. Chutney, piccalilli and Indonesian sambals may be on the table, too. I have tried this mixture and find that it makes a delicious ensemble. If the stokvis is of good quality and has been properly prepared, it should be snow-white and should tremble when put upon the plate.

A book on Zeeland cookery contains traces of a similar tradition there. This time the prescription is of 225 g (½ lb) stokvis for one person, with as much potato and even more rice. These principal elements are accompanied by a mustard sauce, to go with the potatoes and rice; and Zeeland 'epicures stir a raw egg into the rice on their plate'. The mustard sauce, by the way, is best made with ½ litre (1 pint) fish stock, 50 g (2 oz) flour mixed with 2 tbs water, and 1 tbs of made mustard.

Finally, advice from a contemporary housewife, Mevrouw Berserik of Rijswijk. Prepare and cook your stokvis as usual; and boil potatoes and rice separately. Heat butter and allow some tinned anchovy fillets to 'melt' in it, very gently. Mash the potatoes and stokvis together on your plate with a fork, set the rice beside it and pour the anchovy sauce over it. Serve with a dressed salad.

Gestoofde Kabeljauwstaart

Cod's tail cooked Dutch style   serves four

The Dutch like to serve the tail end of a large cod, prepared as follows, and served with boiled potatoes and small carrots. If the cod is of prime quality, the dish is superb.

the tail end of a cod, weighing 750–900 g (1¾–2 lb)	a bouillon cube dissolved in hot water (optional)
salt	butter, 100 g (3½ oz)
a lemon	breadcrumbs

Scale the piece of fish, cut it open on one side and take out the bone. Wash it, salt it lightly and place it in an ovenproof dish with the juice of most of the lemon, and with the dissolved stock cube if used. Put the butter in dabs on top of the fish and cook it, covered, in a moderate oven (355° F, gas 4) for half an hour, basting it from time to time with the cooking liquid. Then sprinkle breadcrumbs over it, put a few slices of lemon on top and continue cooking until the fish is brown.

Schelvis met Mango-saus

Haddock with mango sauce   serves four

This recipe, which I have also met in Germany, invariably calls for haddock as the right fish for the mango sauce. It serves here to represent the South-East Asian influence on Dutch cooking (a different matter from the penetration of the Netherlands by Indonesian restaurants and dishes).

Take a haddock of just over 1 kg (2¼ lb or so), clean it as usual, put it in an oven dish, salt it lightly and sprinkle it with lemon juice. Pour 6 tbs white wine over it, cover it with thin slices of onion, add some knobs of butter and what the Dutch call 'viskruiden' (fish spices, mainly pepper). Cover the dish with buttered aluminium foil and bake it in a moderately hot oven (400° F, gas 6) for 25 to 30 minutes.

Meanwhile the mango sauce is made. A jar of mango chutney (about 2 dl or ⅓ pint) is the foundation. This is warmed, while you peel and thinly slice 450 g (1 lb) sour apples. Add these to the chutney, together with a couple of chunks of preserved ginger, cut up finely, a tablespoonful each of the ginger syrup and of lemon juice, and a sprinkling of powdered ginger. Let all this cook gently until the apple slices are soft. Then serve it in a sauceboat when you bring the haddock to table.

Schelvis met Aardappelen in een Schoteltje

Haddock and potatoes, for Dutch brides of fifty years ago

One of my prized Dutch cookery books is a small undated (*c.* 1920) *Kookboek voor Jonggehuwden*, a maroon volume which was given free to every young lady in The Hague when the banns for her marriage were announced. It was issued by an enterprising shopkeeper and is strewn with advertisements which provide a period seasoning for the rich, filling dishes which it describes; but it is all very Dutch and practical.

'Prepare and poach your haddock in the usual way, then bone it. Meanwhile you have cooked potatoes and sliced them. Cover the bottom of a buttered casserole with a layer of these slices and sprinkle over them salt, pepper and very finely chopped onion, adding a few blobs of butter. Next, put in a layer of fish and sprinkle over this either breadcrumbs or crumbled Dutch rusks, with a little sour cream (which may be omitted). Continue with alternating layers until the casserole is full, taking care that the top layer is of fish sprinkled with breadcrumbs or rusk. Bake the dish in a hot oven for 15 minutes.'

However, a more usual recipe for haddock in the Netherlands is **Gekookte Schelvis met Garnalensaus**, poached haddock served with a sauce made from the local shrimps. Like the Belgians, the Dutch use these small shrimps to make shrimp croquettes (page 310) and to stuff tomatoes (page 304). They also use them often in this sauce, to which they may give a distinctive taste by the use of koffieroom (a sort of condensed milk, unsweetened and yellowish, which comes in bottles) instead of milk or ordinary cream. To make a shrimp sauce without this ingredient, which seems to be peculiar to the Netherlands, prepare a white sauce as usual from butter, flour and fish stock. Then add cooked and peeled shrimps, chopped parsley and a squeeze of lemon juice. Heat through, without bringing back to the boil, and serve.

Gekookte Tarbot met Hollandse Saus

Turbot with Hollandaise sauce

This is the classic Dutch recipe for preparing turbot, and is a traditional speciality of the trawling ports such as IJmuiden and Scheveningen.

The turbot may be poached whole in a turbotière, or cut up first into serving portions. In either event, the poaching should be done in a court-bouillon, which the Dutch prepare in the usual way (page 259) but to which they may add chopped celeriac, the flavour of which they like.

Directions for making the Hollandaise sauce are given on page 316.

Schol op Harlinger Wijze

Plaice in the Harlingen style   serves six

Fishing for plaice in the Netherlands can be a proceeding at once placid and picturesque, as the drawing at the foot of this recipe shows. It comes from Françoise Berserik's book (see Bibliography), and is by her father.

plaice, 1½ kg (3 lb), uncleaned	butter, 150 g (5 oz)
salt	coriander seeds, crushed, ½ tsp
parsley	fresh dill, chopped, 1 tsp
a lemon	fresh tarragon, finely chopped, 1 tsp

Clean the fish and put it in a suitable pan with enough salted water barely to cover it. Bring the water slowly to the boil and poach the fish in it for 15 minutes, until it is ready. Then remove it to a serving platter and garnish it with parsley curls and thin lemon slices, using only half of the lemon.

Meanwhile, you have melted the butter and added the other ingredients to it, together with more chopped parsley, a little salt and the juice of the other half of the lemon. This sauce is served separately.

A cheap fish sauce

The dramatic and Dutch provenance of this recipe accounts for its inclusion here, although it comes from an English book (*Culina Famulatrix Medicinae*, by Ignotus, whose identity is revealed on page 492). Besides, it is essentially an antique (1804) version of what we know as Hollandaise sauce. The book gives two versions, here combined. Spoonful means tablespoonful. Ordinary vinegar may be used. But be sure to make the sauce in the top of a double-boiler, so that it does not curdle.

'To half a pound of melted butter, put the yolks of two eggs well beat, two spoonfuls of elder vinegar, and a little nutmeg and mace. When held over the fire, stir only one way, By constantly moving, the sauce will become sufficiently thick without the addition of flour.

'OBS. this is a good economical sauce, and is much better than those strong sauces that overpower the natural flavour of the fish.

'OBS. This sauce was communicated to Ignotus by a Burgomaster of Amsterdam on his death bed.'

Vissers Recept voor Gebakken Mosselen

How Zeeland fishermen fry mussels

What we learn from the Zeeland fishermen is how to fry *raw* mussels.

'The shells have been washed and scrubbed clean, and the beards removed. The hinge of each mussel is then cut open with a sharp knife, so that the shell can easily be opened by sliding the knife between its two halves. The raw mussels are carefully taken out of their shells with a fork and drained on a clean teacloth and turned one by one in flour, or in crushed rusks. Now brown some butter with a chopped onion in a frying pan. Then put in the raw mussels and sprinkle pepper over them. Fry them quickly; otherwise they become tough. Serve them with some lemon juice.'

The above comes from Heer Aalbregtse's excellent book on Zeeland cookery. He adds that soft-shelled clams (page 239) are prepared and cooked in the same way and eaten with a mustard sauce and buttered bread; all of which must be accompanied by tea (not coffee), served without milk or sugar. A thin mustard sauce (cf. page 317) is in fact the most usual Dutch accompaniment for cooked mussels, which are dunked in it as they are eaten.

Aontjes in Oentjes

Zeeland ways with cockles

The same book on Zeeland cookery has a good passage on cockles. The usual practice is to wash them and leave them in salty water for a while, so that they can 'spit out the sand'. They are then drained and put in a saucepan with salted water to cover and boiled gently for about 5 minutes, until done – no longer, because over-cooking makes them tough. They are served as hot as possible, being brought to the table in the pan, and eaten with bread. In the eyes of a Zeelander, a cockle which has been cooked looks rather like the head of a chicken; which perception accounts for the curious name of this dish, meaning 'cockerels and hens'.

Heer Albregtse continues thus: 'After they have been cooked, they can be washed again, drained in a colander and then fried in butter. One should cover the frying pan with a lid, as they tend to jump out, sometimes as high as the kitchen ceiling. When fried they might be eaten with bread or with potatoes and a sour or sharp sauce [such as that described on page 371].

'Alternatively, one can stew the cockles, after they have been boiled, in a sauce made with melted butter mixed with some water and vinegar, and with a bay leaf. Let the sauce boil for some time, then add some nutmeg and a chopped onion and either breadcrumbs or a crushed rusk. The cockles are stirred into this sauce and stewed over a low flame.'

14. Recipes from Germany

Germany has two coasts, that of the Nordsee (North Sea) and that of the Ostsee (Baltic). The main fishing ports, Bremerhaven and Cuxhaven, are on the North Sea. But German fish cookery is more closely related to that of its Baltic neighbours than to the cuisines of, say, the Low Countries or Britain. True, it shares with the Netherlands, as well as with Denmark, some elements of Oriental cookery, the result of trade with the Indies; but it does so in what seems to me to be an unsystematic and adventurous manner, suddenly inserting pineapple or a dose of curry powder by way of fantasy rather than by a natural absorption of Asian ingredients and techniques. The Germans are at their best when dealing with their own fish in their own traditional ways. The older German cookery books may be hard to read, because of their antique Gothic type, but their contents are sound.

Bremerhaven is the largest fishing port in Europe. A neatly landscaped lock gives access to 5 kilometres of fish quays, through which pass one out of every two fish eaten in the Federal Republic. But the place, perhaps because it was a 'new town' of the early nineteenth century, lacks the vitality of older ports. One misses the bustle and the mess, while admiring the good order and hygiene. And, although one may come across dishes styled auf Bremerhavener Art, these were probably created yesterday. It is to Bremen or Hamburg that one should go in search of culinary traditions. The Schaffermahlzeit, an annual banquet given in the ancient Rathaus at Bremen by shipowners for their captains, has evolved into a social event of wider scope; but the menu still includes Stockfisch as it has done for nearly 400 years, stockfish served with the traditional mustard sauce. The meal ends, oddly, with both cheese and fish again, this time something savoury like Bucklinge.

Hamburg too has its ancient traditions, although Hamburg eel soup, the first of our recipes, is not as old as one might suppose. What is certain is that Hamburg looks ahead as well as to the past. It was there that I first acquired (from *Informationen für die Fischwirtschaft*, No. 4/5 of 1976) some gastronomic recipes for krill, the tiny crustaceans which mass in the Antarctic and may be a food of the future. Krill pasties, already served at one official dinner in Hamburg, sound really good.

Hamburger Aalsuppe

Hamburg eel soup   serves six

North Germans like things sweet and sour. They have excellent pork products; and in the early summer a fine array of fresh vegetables comes into season. So it has been their practice for centuries to make, especially at this time of year, what they call Saure Suppe, which is a sort of sweet and sour soup. It is made from a smoked ham-bone with scraps of ham still on it; fresh vegetables; dried fruit to provide a sweet counterpart to the salty ham; and dumplings to give the soup body.

Hamburg eel soup is achieved quite simply by adding pieces of eel, which have been cooked separately, to this Saure Suppe. It is a relatively recent development. My copy of the manual of the Hamburg Cookery School (*c.* 1910) features Saure Suppe but makes no mention of eel soup. The innovation does, however, date back to the nineteenth century, and it is an excellent one. Apart from the ham-bone you will need:

fresh eel, $\frac{1}{2}$ kg (1 lb), skinned, cleaned and cut across into sections about 3 cm thick

fresh vegetables, $1\frac{1}{2}$ kg (3 lb) in all (peas, carrots, leek, celery, cauliflower, string beans, kohlrabi – the more kinds the better)

dried fruit, 200–300 g (about $\frac{1}{2}$ lb), e.g. prunes, apricots, apple rings, previously soaked in water

small flour dumplings, made from a dough of 225 g ($\frac{1}{2}$ lb) flour, sifted with a little salt, $1\frac{1}{2}$ tbs marrowfat, suet or butter, 1 egg and $1\frac{1}{2}$ dl ($\frac{1}{4}$ pint) water; and poached for 5 minutes

sugar and/or salt to taste

bay leaves, 2

summer savory

a bouquet garni

vinegar

Set the ham-bone to simmer in plenty of water. After 20 minutes remove any scum and add the vegetables, prepared as usual and cut up. Put in last those which require least cooking. Then add the fruit and continue to simmer until the vegetables are cooked.

Meanwhile, poach the pieces of eel separately in water flavoured with a couple of bay leaves, a bouquet garni, summer savory, and a little vinegar.

Remove the ham-bone from the vegetable broth. Take the scraps of meat off it, chop them and add them to the soup. Add the small dumplings and the pieces of cooked eel. Correct the seasoning with a little sugar or salt, if necessary. Simmer for a few minutes, to let the flavours blend, then serve.

German herring cures

Fischwarenkunde, the manual on fish curing by Dr Karl Seumenicht, published by a German fishery institution with a name as long as your fore-arm, describes, along with exotica such as Kippers auf englische Art, the full range of German herring cures. It is indeed a full range, from which I select three well-known items.

BUCKLINGE are hot-smoked herring. Buckling are also prepared in Britain, the Netherlands and Norway. Head and gut may or may not be removed. In Britain, the herring are usually 'nobbed'; this means that after being washed and before being smoked the herring have their heads removed and the gut pulled out by hand, leaving roe or milt in place. In Germany, buckling are usually eaten with Schwarzbrot or Vollkornbrot (black bread or dark rye bread) and butter; often accompanied by tomatoes. They are usually an evening dish, known as the 'poor man's dinner'. In restaurants one finds buckling served with scrambled egg and fried potatoes.

BISMARCK HERRINGS are herring fillets which have been soaked in vinegar with onion rings and seasoning.

ROLLMOPSE (which are called rollmops in English, although this name is the singular of the German name) are herring which have been beheaded, gutted, split open, deboned and left in the form of double fillets, which are rolled up round pickled cucumber and kept in a vinegar or wine and vinegar solution. They can be made at home (see Jane Grigson's *Fish Cookery*), but it is desirable to adjust the salinity, duration and temperature of the marinade according to the fat content of the herring, and most people find it best and simplest to buy ready-prepared rollmops. They are frequently eaten on 'the morning after', as part of a Katerfrühstuck, which is a late breakfast incorporating stimulants and following a night of carousal.

Matjesfilets Lady Hamilton

Herring fillets à la Lady Hamilton   (serves eight as an appetizer)

The English aristocracy seem to have exerted a certain fascination among those Germans who have had the task or taken responsibility for naming dishes. Lady Curzon often appears, usually in connection with a soup to which sherry and curry powder have been added; and a mysterious Sir William, *tout court*, is also prominent. But for me, still puzzling over the Polish 'po Nelsońsku' riddle (page 335), the most intriguing discovery was Lady Hamilton in a recipe title. This, however, was quickly explained; for the first person I asked about it, Peter Frisch, was the very man who had christened the dish. He explained that a certain way of presenting matjes fillets had been named after Lord Nelson (why, he knew not), and that he, having read the account in a book by Hans Leip, *The Lady and the Admiral*, of a journey which Lord Nelson and Lady Hamilton once made down the Elbe from Czechoslovakia – a journey of which the last night was spent just upstream from Hamburg – and having decided as a result of his reading that he found Lady Hamilton more interesting than her lover, resolved to re-create the dish with subtle changes, in her honour rather than his.

matjes (herring) fillets, 8   grated horseradish, 2 tbs
cooking apples, 2   redcurrant jelly, 1–2 tbs
lemon juice, 2 tbs   a bunch of fresh dill
double cream, $\frac{1}{4}$ litre ($\frac{1}{2}$ pint)

Matjes fillets are lightly salted. Soak them for 1 or 2 hours in several changes of water. Core but do not peel the apples. Cut each into 4 thick rings and sprinkle the lemon juice over them. Whip the cream until it is stiff, then combine the horseradish with it.

Dry the matjes fillets, roll them up and place one on each ring of apple. Pipe the cream and horseradish mixture through a forcing bag on to the fillets. Add a little blob of redcurrant jelly on top. Separate the dill into tiny sprigs and plant these in the cream.

Hamburger Pfannfisch

Haddock in the Hamburg style   serves four

steaks of haddock (or similar   potatoes, 600 g ($1\frac{1}{4}$ lb), sliced
   fish), 750 g ($1\frac{1}{2}$ lb)   thinly and parboiled
salt   pepper
butter, 60 g (2 oz)   sour cream, $\frac{1}{4}$ litre ($\frac{1}{2}$ pint)
medium onions, 2, thinly sliced   eggs, 3
     mustard, 50 g (2 oz)

Clean the haddock and cut it into steaks or slices as thick as a finger. Rub these with salt and let them stand for an hour.

Lightly brown the onion in hot butter. Grease a casserole, which should be reasonably deep, with butter. Fill it with alternating layers of fish and potato. In between each layer put some of the onion and a sprinkling of pepper.

Combine the sour cream with the raw eggs and mustard and coat the contents of the casserole with this mixture. Cook over a moderate heat for about 30 minutes and serve with a green salad or a salad of runner beans.

Rotbarsch-Hackbraten

Minced redfish loaf   serves six

Hackbraten means chopped up and cooked, like hamburger meat. It was a daughter of the Weise family of Hamburg who introduced me to this fishy equivalent of the world-conquering meat hamburger. They use redfish, which is very popular in Germany; but other white fish are suitable. They do not themselves add smoked bacon, but agree that it is legitimate.

whole redfish (page 139), 1 kg (2 lb)	salt and pepper
	eggs, 2
smoked bacon, finely diced, 50 g (2 oz)	toasted breadcrumbs, 3 tbs
	lard or margarine, 60 g (2 oz)
medium onions, 2, chopped	flour, 1 tbs
soft white rolls (yesterday's), 3	sour cream, 2 tbs

Clean the fish, leaving the head on, and poach it. Let it cool, then remove the flesh, free of skin and bone, and mince it. Reserve the broth.

While the fish is cooking, fry the cubes of bacon gently in a pan; then remove them and lightly brown the onion in the hot bacon fat. Soak the rolls in water, then squeeze them and crumble them.

Combine in a mixing bowl the fish, bacon, onion and bread. Add pepper and salt to taste, the eggs and the toasted breadcrumbs. Mix all well together and shape the mixture into a loaf.

Meanwhile, you have heated the lard or margarine in a baking dish. Set the loaf in this and baste it with some of the hot fat. Then bake it in a hot oven (430° F, gas 7) for 20 to 30 minutes. After the first 5 minutes add ½ cup of the stock in which the fish was cooked.

Remove the loaf and thicken the sauce with the flour and sour cream, cooking it for another 5 minutes. Serve the loaf with the sauce and with potatoes; and perhaps with red cabbage also.

Fischlabskaus

Seamen's fish hash   serves six

Labskaus is a seamen's dish which belongs to the whole German seaboard and is generally thought to have originated there, although it is also known in Denmark and common in Norway. It is essentially a way of making preserved meat and salted fish, such as ships' crews used to eat on their voyages, tasty. But it lives on in modern times, sustained both by the force of tradition and by its special and hearty flavour. When I was last in

Hamburg, the *Hamburger Abendblatt* held a public banquet of Labskaus to celebrate the anniversary of Hamburg's charter as a port. Thousands paid to attend and to partake.

Labskaus can be made with meat or fish or both. Here is a simple version which readers can treat as a Grundrezept and modify according to the state of their larder.

salted or smoked fish, 200 g (7 oz)	salt and pepper
corned or salted beef or similar	mustard, 1 tbs
preserved meat, 400 g (14 oz)	beetroot juice from a jar of
potatoes, 700 g (1½ lb)	beetroot
medium onions, 3, finely chopped	eggs, 6
fat, e.g. beef dripping, 90 g (3 oz)	pickled gherkins

Prepare, cook and flake the fish. Roughly chop the meat. Peel, quarter, cook and coarsely mash the potatoes. Use a large pan to fry the onions in the hot fat, then stir in the seasoning, mustard and beetroot juice. Add the fish, meat and potato and stir some more, enough to mix up the various elements but not to blend them. Cover and cook until all is hot, then arrange it on a heated platter, decorate it with the gherkins and sliced beetroot, and place a fried egg for each person on top. The dish is to be eaten with a fork alone.

Liverpool readers may like to know that their Lobscouse, from which comes the abbreviated name scouse, meaning Liverpudlian, is this same Labskaus, although I am told that they always make it with meat. And in Newfoundland there is a dish called Lob Scouce; with meat, rice, potato, carrot, turnip and parsnip as the ingredients.

Seezungen auf Bremer Weise

Sole in the Bremen style   serves four

This recipe comes from the *Praktisches Kochbuch* of Henriette Davidis-Holle, originally published around 1880 by Henriette Davidis and officially revised by Frau Holle in 1914. My own revisions of the present recipe, after tests, are minor.

Prepare 4 small soles. Salt them lightly, set them aside for an hour, then pat them dry. Brush them with melted butter, then coat them successively with beaten egg and breadcrumbs; after which pan-fry them.

Mix 120–50 g (4–5 oz) butter with ½–1 tsp anchovy essence, a little nutmeg and 1 tsp each of mustard and chopped parsley. Make a smooth paste of all this and spread it over the cooked soles.

Henriette advises her readers to serve the sole with boiled potatoes *and* a small bowl of potato salad! She does not add that sole cooked in this way is also very good cold; but we have found that it is.

Ewer-Scholle in Speck Gebraten nach Finkenwerder Art

Plaice with smoked bacon   serves four

The recipe given here might just as well be nach Hamburger Art, for it is typical of Hamburg, too; but it is more romantic in the style I have used. An Ewer was a small fishing vessel such as used to bring back fine fresh plaice to the fishing port of Finkenwerder. The once charming scene is now dominated by oil refineries and apartment blocks; but its atmosphere can be recaptured in the novels of Jakob Kinau and Gorch Fock, who wrote movingly of the Finkenwerder fishermen and their families.

4 medium-sized plaice	**smoked streaky bacon, thickly**
a lemon	**cut, 120 g (6 oz)**
salt and flour	**sprigs of parsley**

Clean, wash and pat dry the fish. Sprinkle the juice of half the lemon over them and leave them for 10 minutes, while you dice the bacon and fry it in a pan. Remove it when done, but leave the fat in the pan.

Season the plaice lightly with salt, dredge them in flour and fry them in the bacon fat, for 3 or 4 minutes on each side, until golden brown.

Arrange the plaice on a platter, white sides up, and dispose the bacon on top of them. Garnish with sprigs of parsley and the second half of the lemon, cut in wedges. Serve with boiled potatoes or a potato salad.

Eating the dish at a quayside restaurant in Hamburg, I found that my plaice was heartier fare than usual, thanks to the bacon, and that the combination of flavours was highly successful.

Helgoländer Hummer

Heligoland lobster

The island of Heligoland in the North Sea was famous for its lobsters. Nowadays the majority of visitors are attracted to it by its duty-free status, curiously stipulated when Britain handed it over to Germany in exchange for Zanzibar. The lobster catch has dwindled to what must be a minute proportion of the lobsters served in German restaurants as Heligoland lobsters, most of which come from Norway. But this Heligoland way of serving lobster is still a good one.

Lower your live lobster into 5 litres (11 pints) of boiling North Sea water (or fresh water with 5 tbs of sea salt) and cook it, covered, for 20 minutes. Remove it, let it cool, split it as usual and crack the claws, then lay it on a bed of lettuce leaves and eat it with a mixture of 2 parts mayonnaise to 1 of yoghourt, and with fresh toast.

Grüne Krabbensuppe

Pea soup with shrimps   serves four

chicken or other stock, $\frac{3}{4}$–1 litre   summer savory, 1 tbs
  ($1\frac{3}{4}$–$2\frac{1}{4}$ pints)   tarragon, 1 tsp
a piece of fat smoked bacon rind   fresh or frozen peas, 450 g (1 lb)
carrots, 2, sliced   cooked shrimps, 200 g (7 oz)
onions, 2, sliced   white wine, $1\frac{1}{2}$ dl ($\frac{1}{4}$ pint)

Boil the bacon rind, carrots and onions in the stock for 15 minutes, then remove the bacon rind and put in the savory, tarragon and peas. Bring back to the boil and continue cooking until the peas are really tender. Then strain it all through a sieve, rubbing the peas through, so that you finish up with a fairly thick pea-green soup. Add the shrimps and wine, put the soup back on the flame, just long enough to ensure that everything is hot, and serve.

By following this recipe, adapted from an official pamphlet on shrimp cookery, you will have all the natural flavour of the shrimps, in a soup which offers pleasing contrasts in both taste and colour.

Krabbenbrot

Shrimps on rye bread with a fried egg

This comes from *Spezialitäten aus dem Meer* by Peter Frisch, who sets his recipes skilfully against the background which he knows so well. For each person allow:

a slice of Vollkornbrot (a dark rye   cooked North Sea shrimps, 100 g
  bread)   ($3\frac{1}{2}$ oz)
butter, 25 g (1 oz)   an egg, salt and pepper

'Spread 15 grams of butter on a fresh slice of rye bread and cover it thickly with shrimps. Heat the remaining butter in a frying pan and break the egg into it. Fry it sunny-side up and put it on top of the shrimps. Sprinkle salt and pepper over it.

'With this, at any time of day, is taken a strong cup of Friesian tea, sweetened with Kluntjes [large lumps of candy sugar, such as one used to be able to buy on a string from German grocers] and served with cream.

'This Krabbenbrot is the classical and also the simplest way to eat shrimps. It has as its home the whole stretch of German coast from Husum to Borkum. During the six-week summer season when tourists descend on the coast, one will usually find a bottle of ketchup on the table as well.'

15. Recipes from Poland

Polish fish cookery has in the past been directed primarily at freshwater fish. Poland, after all, has not always had a coastline, or has had only a corridor door into the Baltic. Now, however, an active fishing fleet brings back large quantities of seafood, not only from near-by waters, and there is increasing scope for the Polish cook to practise seafood cookery.

There are mixed traditions in the Polish kitchen. As Edouard de Pomiane has pointed out, Poland is one of those Slav countries which received its Christianity from Rome rather than Byzantium, and therefore has a western outlook in cookery as in other matters. The Italian influence is surprisingly strong. It is largely due to Queen Bona, of the Sforza family in Milan, who was the bride of the Polish King Sigismond I (1506–48), and who brought with her to Poland both Italian recipes and Italian ingredients. To this day, tomatoes are pomidory in Poland, and Poles make a stoufada just as Italians do. It is tempting to think that this good consort, 'gourmande et intelligente', brought ravioli too, and that this developed into the pierógi of Poland, the kolduny of Lithuania and the varenki of Russia; but Lithuanians have an enchanting legend of their own to account for kolduny. Many Lithuanians were, of course, at one time within the Polish frontiers; and the influences from the east are highly visible in Polish cookery. Some were brought by Tartars who settled in Poland in the fourteenth century after being made prisoners of war. More important still were the Jews, who were once so numerous in Poland, and whose culinary influence remains pervasive and beneficial.

Poland is in the heart of that region which uses sour cream and root vegetables – especially beetroot, parsley root (see page 261), parsnip and horseradish. Polish dishes are substantial, to match Polish appetites, which de Pomiane portrays as being 'pantagruéliques' under the influence of the cold Polish winter. Polish fish recipes therefore combine fish with vegetables, or with pasta, or with the buckwheat which they know as kasza, in a manner which stays hunger most effectively. Yet they also have lighter fish dishes, among the hors d'oeuvres which they term zakaski and which match the Russian zakuski. Several of these appear in the selection of recipes, which exemplifies also the frequent use of sour cream, the use of dill in Scandinavian fashion, the Italian influence and the adaptability of Polish cooks when faced with changing patterns of supply.

One other feature has not been illustrated, for lack of space. This is the Polish enthusiasm for serving fish, as well as other things, in jelly or aspic. They have what might be called a *kakoethes aspicandi*, brought fully home to us when we entered a small restaurant in Tczew, not far south of Gdansk, and found its every wall lined with aspic dishes, enough to feed two hundred in a room which seated twenty; everything but everything, fish, meat, poultry and vegetables, had been locked in quivering aspic. One wondered whether the waitresses and even the customers did not risk being themselves so treated by a cook who had gone quite out of control; but then learned the explanation, which was that the restaurant adjoined a cookery school, in which the art of making aspic had been the subject of the morning's work, and the cause of our encountering cod in aspic for the first time; cod which had been garnished with thin slices of lemon and orange and cucumber and parsnip and carrot, together with peas and parsley. This we ate with two forks, in approved Polish fashion.*

There and in other Polish restaurants we noticed that there are two columns of figures opposite the list of dishes. The first gives the weight of the portion in grams, the second the price in zlotys. This is unusual, but logical; although it might strike an inappropriate note in restaurants where one eats for pleasure as well as sustenance.

Sledz w Smietanie

Salted herring with sour cream   serves four

salted herring, 600 g (1¼ lb)   **lemon juice, 1½ tsp**
a large apple, peeled and shredded   **sugar, 1 tsp**
a medium onion, chopped   **a pinch of salt**
sour cream, 1½ dl (¼ pint)   **chopped parsley, 1 tbs**

Soak the herring in several changes of water for 24 hours, then drain and remove the fillets. Cut these into pieces of about 3 cm and arrange them on a dish. Mix all the remaining ingredients, except the parsley, together and pour them over the herring; then sprinkle the parsley on top.

This will serve six or eight people as an hors d'oeuvre.

* I wonder whether it was a Polish influence which brought a similar practice to Boodle's Club in London. a place to which I was once taken by a man who besought me before we sat down to refrain from asking for a fish knife.

Chlodnik z Ryby

Cold fish and vegetable soup   serves six

This is a refreshing summer dish, but also a filling one. It should really be treated as a main course.

I have suggested using redfish (page 139), which is popular in Poland, but almost any white fish with firm flesh will do. A section of cod or hake would be quite suitable. You will need enough to provide at least 750 g ($1\frac{2}{3}$ lb) cleaned flesh.

a redfish weighing rather more than 1 kg (say, $2\frac{1}{2}$ lb) uncleaned	a large cucumber, peeled and cut into strips
medium carrots, 3	chives, dill and parsley, all fresh and finely chopped
a medium turnip	
a medium onion	lemon juice to taste (2 tbs at least)
a large beetroot	
a parsley root, if possible	hard-boiled eggs, 3, quartered
salt, pepper and sugar to taste	sour cream, 1 dl (7 tbs)

Prepare the carrots, turnip, onion, beetroot and parsley root and grate them coarsely. Put them in a large saucepan with water to cover – at least 1 litre (2 pints) – and cook them for 30 minutes. Now, if you wish, you can strain out and discard the vegetables; but many cooks leave them in the soup, which seems to me to be the better course. Whichever choice you make, add salt, sugar and pepper to taste to the contents of the saucepan; and put in the fish, which you have cleaned, scaled and rinsed. Continue cooking for 20 minutes or so, with the pan covered, until the fish is cooked through. Take the pan off the fire, lift out the fish, let it cool, remove all skin and bone and cut the flesh into fairly small pieces.

Next, add the cucumber, chives, dill and parsley to the soup; also the lemon juice (for which Polish cooks would substitute 'pickled' borshch, i.e. borshch left over and stored in a jar, if they had some). Stir well, then chill.

Arrange some pieces of fish and 2 quarters of hard-boiled egg on each soup plate. Bring the soup to table in a tureen and let each person add a dollop of sour cream to his own portion.

Dorsz po Myśliwsku

Cod, hunter's style   serves six

In 1947 the Centrala Rybna (state fish-marketing organization) published a specialized booklet on the cookery of cod. The author, M. Godlewska, has a lot to say about the general principles of preparing cod. In addition to the usual procedures for cleaning the fish, she recommends washing it several times in clean water, soaking it for an hour in a mild solution of vinegar (1 tablespoonful to a litre of water) and then salting it before the actual cooking begins. She explains that the vinegar helps to remove the taste of the sea – that very taste which is prized in most maritime countries but is regarded as a mark of inferiority in countries where freshwater fish have traditionally been preferred. (Poland is one such; Burma another. The Burmese use turmeric in cooking sea fish, to rid it of its salty taste.)

Cooking things in hunter's style, which is not the same as the French *à la chasseur*, is a popular Polish technique. It is applied to meat more often than to fish, but works well for fish with firm flesh.

cod, cleaned weight, 1 kg (2 lb)	flour, 150 g (5 oz)
butter, 100 g (3½ oz)	seasoning to taste (salt and pepper
red wine, ½ litre (1 pint)	or paprika)

The cod, which has been prepared as described and cut into serving pieces, is allowed to brown slightly in the hot butter. You then transfer the cod to a saucepan, add the wine, cover the pan and let the fish simmer for 15 minutes or so. Stir in the flour and seasoning 5 minutes before cooking is completed, to thicken the sauce. Serve with red cabbage; and add prepared cranberry jelly or sauce if you wish.

Dorsz Zapiekany w Smietanie

Cod baked in sour cream   serves four

The numerous Roman Catholic families in Poland eat fish for dinner on Christmas Eve. The tradition is to have thirteen meatless courses, including many fish dishes of which the principal feature will be a carp, bought in advance and kept alive in the family bath-tub until the time comes to cook it. Most of the thirteen dishes will be of this or other freshwater fish, but at least one sea fish is likely to be needed to bring the number of dishes up to full strength. This simple recipe is used by Jean Zwolinska, a Scotswoman long established in Warsaw, for this purpose. She says that the same dish can be made with the addition of mushrooms, fresh or dried.

cod fillets, 500–600 g (1¼ lb)	oil for cooking
seasoned flour, 2 tbs	sour cream, 1 cup

Toss the fillets in the seasoned flour, then fry them until they are lightly browned. Dispose them in a buttered oven dish, cover them with the sour cream and bake them for about 25 to 30 minutes in a moderate oven (355° F, gas 4). I suggest sprinkling a little pepper on top when you take the dish out, partly for appearance and partly to enliven the flavour.

Zapiekanka Rybna

Marianna's fish pie   serves four

Fresh fish is not always available in Poland, but canned fish is. Here is the recipe of a gifted Warsaw cook, Marianna Piasek, for turning any sort of canned fish into a 'pie', delicious, and quickly made.

canned fish, e.g. tuna, 400 g (14 oz)	paprika, 2 pinches
butter, 15 g ($\frac{1}{2}$ oz)	potatoes, 900 g (2 lb), mashed
mayonnaise, 1$\frac{1}{2}$ tbs	grated cheese, enough to cover the
sour cream, 1$\frac{1}{2}$ tbs	dish
small onion, $\frac{1}{2}$, sliced	marjoram *or* dill, as garnish

If there is a lot of oil with the fish in the can, drain off the excess. Then combine the fish with the butter, mayonnaise, sour cream and sliced onion in an ovenproof dish. Sprinkle the paprika over the mixture, then cover it with the mashed potato and add the grated cheese on top. Bake it for about 30 minutes in a moderate to moderately hot oven (375° F, gas 5), so that the top is lightly browned. Serve it with the marjoram or dill as garnish.

Ryba w Szarym Sosie po Krolewsku

Fish with a royal 'grey' [in fact, brown] sauce   serves four

In the present century, and no doubt in earlier ones, too, it has been customary for Poles to serve carp with a grey sauce. However, an early reference to it which I found in *Kucharka Mieyska y Wieyska* (a charming little book on Town and Country Cooking, author not named, Warsaw, 1804) suggests that it was then considered good for sterlet and various marine fish. The version which I have reconstructed from this and other books constitutes an unusual sauce which lends interest to most fish, especially the richer ones. In the instructions which follow I assume that you have prepared separately enough fish for four people, preferably by poaching it.

egg yolks, 2	lemon juice, 1 tbs
gingerbread, 50 g (2 oz)	sugar, 25 g (1 oz)
white pepper, $\frac{1}{2}$ tsp	sultanas, 40 g (1$\frac{1}{2}$ oz)
cinnamon, $\frac{1}{2}$ tsp	blanched almonds, 30 g (1 oz)
red wine, 2 dl ($\frac{1}{3}$ pint)	stoned olives, 30 g (1 oz)

Beat the egg yolks lightly and combine them with the gingerbread, which must first be finely crumbled. Add the white pepper and cinnamon, followed by the wine, lemon juice and sugar. (A little grated lemon rind may also be added at this stage; and 1 tbs honey can be substituted for the sugar.) Mix well and heat slowly until it comes to boiling point. Then remove it from the fire and add the raisins; the almonds, finely slivered; and the olives, finely chopped. Let the sauce rest for at least 2 minutes, then pour it over the fish.

If you do not have gingerbread, use 1 tbs cornflour as a thickening agent, and add 1 tsp ground ginger.

Ryba po Nelsońsku

Fish cooked à la Nelson   serves four
When Poles cook meat or fish à la Nelson, the dish always incorporates mushrooms and usually potatoes and onions, too. But the precise meaning of the expression is difficult to pin down; and its origin, which must have to do with Admiral Lord Nelson, even more elusive.

fish, e.g. redfish (page 139), 750 g (1¾ lb), uncleaned weight	a medium onion, sliced
	potatoes, peeled, 450 g (1 lb)
soup vegetables (an onion, 1 or 2 carrots, a small turnip, a parsley root and parsley leaves)	dried mushrooms, 4–6, previously soaked in water
	salt and pepper
milk, 2½ dl (1 cup)	flour, 1 tbs
butter, 30 g (1 oz)	sour cream, 6 tbs

Clean and trim your fish. Set the head, tail, bones and skin to simmer in about ½ litre (1 pint) water with the soup vegetables, all prepared as usual. You will later need about ¼ litre (½ pint) of this stock.

Cut the flesh of the fish into smallish pieces and put them in a pan with the milk and an equal quantity of water. Place the pan on a warm range, so that the fish warms up, but does not start to cook.

In another saucepan, melt the butter and cook the second onion in it until golden. Add the potatoes and mushrooms, both sliced, and the mushroom water. Continue to cook gently, stirring occasionally. When the potatoes are almost done, add seasoning and transfer the lot to the saucepan which has the fish in it. Work the flour into the sour cream and add this too, together with up to ¼ litre (½ pint) of the fish and vegetable stock. Bring to the boil, then remove at once from the fire and serve. The dish will, by the way, be just as good if reheated and served later.

These instructions are based on Mrs Galecka's book of 'cheap and tasty ways of preparing fish'. For a less cheap but more tasty version, we would follow the great Maria Ochorowicz-Monatowa and add, provided that we were not on a meatless day, one or two chicken bouillon cubes and either a wineglassful of Madeira or a little caramel, to give the sauce a good golden-brown colour.

Ryba Zapiekana z Makaronem

Fish baked with macaroni   serves four

Macaroni is recommended for this dish but any suitable kind of pasta can
be used. The combination of pasta and fish is good. In Italy, whence the
dish must derive, it is more usual to combine other seafoods with pasta,
e.g. small clams with spaghetti; but Pasta con Sarde (with sardines) is a
very common dish in Sicily.

any white fish, $\frac{1}{2}$ kg (1 lb), cleaned weight	butter or margarine, 60 g (2 oz)
a little cooking oil	salt and pepper
macaroni (see above), $\frac{1}{4}$ kg ($\frac{1}{2}$ lb)	sour cream, $1\frac{3}{4}$ dl ($\frac{1}{4}$ pint)
soup vegetables (carrot, onion, turnip, parsley), 225 g ($\frac{1}{2}$ lb)	an egg, lightly beaten
an onion, sliced	Maggi soup seasoning, 1 cube
	parsley leaves, chopped
	strong cheese, grated, 25 g (1 oz)

Cook the macaroni in plenty of salted water, drain it, rinse it with hot
water and mix it with a little oil to prevent it from sticking.

Prepare the soup vegetables, slicing the carrot, onion and turnip. Cook
them all gently in a mixture of oil and water until they are fairly soft.

Make sure that your pieces of fish are clean and free of bone, then cut
them into strips about 2 cm in width. Fry the additional onion in butter
until golden brown. Add the strips of fish to it, with seasoning and $\frac{1}{2}$ cup
water. Cook this mixture for 15 minutes.

Grease an oven dish and arrange a layer of macaroni in it, followed by
the fish mixture and the soup vegetables, and then by the rest of the
macaroni. Pour over this the sour cream, combined with the egg and the
soup seasoning (dissolved in a little hot water). Sprinkle the chopped
parsley and grated cheese on top and cook in a moderate oven (355° F,
gas 4) for about 15 minutes, so that the cheese is slightly browned.

Babka z Ryb Morskich

Sea fish 'babka'   serves four

A babka is a traditional sort of
cake mould, in which Poles confect
their scrumptious and moist
babkas. The drawing shows what it
is like. A jelly mould of the same
general shape will do just as well.

I recommend using whiting or haddock for this dish.

fish, ½ kg (1 lb), cleaned weight	sour cream, 1¾ dl (¼ pint)
a salt herring, filleted	eggs, 3, separated
butter, 60 g (2 oz)	chopped parsley, 1 tbs
medium onions, 2, sliced	salt and pepper
capers, 1 tbs	soft breadcrumbs, ½ cup

Desalt the salt herring fillets as usual. Cut up the fresh fish into fairly small pieces and cook them gently in most of the butter, with the onions, until done. Then remove any bones and pass the fish, onion, herring fillets and capers through a mincer. Mix in with them the sour cream, egg yolks and parsley. Beat the egg whites stiff and fold them into the mixture, followed by the seasoning and breadcrumbs.

Grease your mould with the remaining butter and put the mixture in it, taking care to make the top surface flat and even. Bake it for 35 or 40 minutes in a moderate oven (355° F, gas 4). Then turn the mould out on to a round serving dish and bring it to table with small pickled gherkins and a horseradish sauce.

Kalmar a la Flaczki

Squid cooked like tripe   serves four

Tripe was a favourite dish in Poland, but has become difficult to obtain in recent years. Squid, on the other hand, which was not available previously, is now being marketed in ample quantity. With characteristic adaptability and a shrewd eye for logical substitutions, Poles now cook squid according to their traditional recipe for tripe. This version is based on an official pamphlet on squid cookery. Note the use of the first person plural, typical of modern Polish recipes.

squid, ½ kg (1 lb)	cabbage, 75 g (2½ oz)
carrot, 150 g (5 oz)	margarine, 30 g (1 oz)
parsley root, 50 g (2 oz)	salt and mild paprika
celery, 50 g (2 oz)	marjoram, just a little
leek, 30 g (1 oz)	Maggi sauce (optional)

We grate the carrot and parsley root, and shred the celery, leek and cabbage. Then we place these ingredients in a pot and barely cover them with water, adding the margarine and salt; and we cook them until they are tender. Next, we add the pieces of squid, prepared according to our instructions (i.e. boiled in salted water until tender, then allowed to cool and cut into small strips, like some kinds of pasta) and, in quantities according to taste, salt, paprika and marjoram, and Maggi if we wish. We serve the dish hot with white bread.

16. Recipes from the Soviet Union

(This section has been written by my daughter Pamela Davidson, a fluent Russian speaker who spent the greater part of 1976 in the Soviet Union, conducting research into the fish cookery of north-western Russia and the three Baltic Republics. Her material is based on extensive travel in these areas as well as on conversations and meals with Russian friends and work in the Lenin Library in Moscow.)

THE RUSSIAN ATTITUDE TO FISH

Russians love their fish as much as their women. One of the great terms of endearment for a woman in the nineteenth century was to call her a 'rȳbka' or little fish. Aksakov explains this in his *Notes on Angling*, first published in 1847: 'Almost all young fish, particularly some of the smaller species, are so beautiful or, better, so sweet in appearance, playful and clean, that people in the south of Russia use the term "little fish" as an expression of endearment and tenderness in praise of a woman's beauty and charm.' He then quotes a story by Gogol, in which a young Cossack entices his sweetheart out of her hut with the tender words: 'My heart, my little fish, my necklace . . .'

Fish is mystically associated with bread as a basic food. This is evident in many Russian proverbs and sayings. It is also interesting to note that Russians do not refer to a fish as 'dead', but as 'having gone to sleep' (usnuvshaya).

THE FISH IN THE SHOPS

In fact, not all the fish sold in the Soviet Union have 'gone to sleep'. Trucks labelled 'live fish' (zhivaya rȳba) drive around Moscow, delivering live fish to tanks in the shops. Sometimes one sees a customer emerge from a shop, struggling with a squirming cone of newspaper from which water drips; this is the live fish which he is taking home to fry. If so, he has been lucky. The tanks are usually empty. They constitute, incidentally, a legacy of Stalin, who asked Mikoyan in 1933 whether live fish were still for sale, received an equivocal reply and decreed that the practice should be revived.

These live fish would be freshwater species – carp or sheatfish. In the nineteenth century and earlier it was mainly freshwater species which were fished and eaten by the Russians. In recent times the balance has tilted towards sea fish, as the Soviet fishing fleet has expanded. The old recipes for freshwater fish have been adapted for use with sea fish, and most fish products in the shops now come from the North Atlantic. The fish section of the large Moscow department store G U M displays a huge poster on the wall behind the counter, figuring Neptune rising out of the waves with his trident and crown, proclaiming: 'The gifts of the seas and oceans await you, O beloved customers.' This might lead one to expect a varied and exotic range of fish, but that is not what one finds. A large chain called Okean runs the fish shops in the Soviet Union. However, although frozen, salted, smoked, dried, spiced and tinned fish are always available (the fish which I most commonly observed on sale in one or another of these forms were herring, sprats, sardines, mackerel, sea perch and sea burbot, cod, halibut and tuna), it is difficult to find fresh fish on sale, let alone a wide variety of it. Russians remember nostalgically the abundance of caviar, sturgeon and salmon on sale in the shops until the mid 1950s; since when these have become luxury foods, difficult to obtain and mostly reserved for export or for sale in the special shops which cater for foreigners and the privileged strata of Soviet society.

I saw a satirical reference to this situation in the puppet theatre at Kiev, where Isidor Shtok's play *The Divine Comedy* was being produced. This is based on the creation of the world by God. One of the wittiest scenes describes the creation of fish. God, scratching his head, is wondering how to go about this. A resourceful angel suggests using tins and produces some from his pocket. He passes the tins to God, who reads out the names with doubtful interest and throws the tins down on to earth; herring, sprats, sardines, one by one, are hurled through the firmament and created in this way. Then a tin of caviar is passed along. 'Ha, what's this?' says God, 'they won't be needing this down there'; and he pops it into his pocket. The same happens to a tin of salmon, and one of sturgeon. The audience roared with laughter, thinking no doubt of their shopping problems.

An institution of Soviet life is the avos'ka, a string-net shopping bag which is almost indefinitely expandable (to prove which a Russian friend of mine fitted his nine-year-old son into his avos'ka, which when empty would fit into his pocket). The word avos'ka comes from an old Russian exclamation, avos', meaning 'maybe' with a touch of 'if only', often used of vain or frivolous hopes. No Russian ever goes anywhere without an avos'ka in his pocket or briefcase, in the hope of spotting a queue at a shop where something has turned up with which he can fill it.

COOKERY BOOKS IN THE SOVIET UNION

The disparity between fact and theory in the availability of supplies is one of the factors which pose, for anyone who proposes to write about Russian cooking, the basic dilemma: whether to be idealistic or realistic. One can either produce a mouth-watering selection of recipes based on nineteenth-century cookery books, literary and historical sources; or one can base one's work on what is physically available and possible in the Soviet Union today in terms of money, time, energy and ingredients. The conditions of life of a Soviet woman, combining the problems of house-keeping and queueing in shops with a full-time job, are very different from those of a nineteenth-century housewife with her retinue of servants and plenty of money and leisure.

This basic difference between pre- and post-revolutionary Russia is well reflected in the cookery books of the two periods. The best and most famous Russian cookery book is undoubtedly the work of Elena Ivanovna Molokhovets, entitled *A Gift to Young Housewives*. This work of over 1000 pages, covering all aspects of the art of housekeeping and cooking, corresponds roughly to Mrs Beeton's work in England. The book was first published in 1861 and reached its twenty-ninth edition by 1917; but it has not been republished since the revolution. It is not hard to see why. Molokhovets's book rests on the fundamental assumption that there are plenty of servants around to do the drudge work, and to be fed with inferior food, for which she supplies separate recipes. Corresponding assumptions colour her tracts and books on religion, monarchy, orthodoxy, rationalism and so forth.*

The Soviet period is best represented by the standard cookery book of the Stalinist era, *The Book of Tasty and Healthy Food*, an encyclopaedic compilation of recipes both old and new, illustrated with elaborate engravings of different implements and, significantly, of various food products available to the Soviet consumer. The bouillon and soup section is prefaced by a statement made by Stalin at the eighteenth Party Conference in 1939, to the effect that the Soviet Union was about to enter the second phase of communism and must now overtake the capitalist world in the economic field. The book echoed this political theme by emphasizing the abundance of products already available. Its recipes are sometimes unimaginative, but always practical and detailed; and this

---

* Tarkovsky, the eminent Soviet poet, devoted a whole poem to reproaching Molokhovets for her attitudes to food and servants. He devised for her a fate worthy of Dante's *Inferno*; she sits for eternity under an icy rock while her skull, perched in a colander beside her, endlessly mumbles her reactionary recipes.

is the cookery book most commonly found in Soviet households today.

More recently, over the last fifteen years or so, the trend seems to have been to produce cookery books even more closely related to Soviet products. This applies particularly to fish, the consumption of which is being promoted to make up for the frequent shortages of meat. (There is already one rȳbnȳiden' or 'fish day' a week in Moscow, and in some towns two a week. These are days on which nothing but fish is served in all restaurants and cafés.) I can give an example from Kaliningrad, now one of the main centres for the Soviet fisheries. The cookery book *Gifts of the Ocean* was published there in 1973 and has since been reprinted. It seeks to inform and educate the public, portrayed as faintly conservative and suspicious, about the richness of fish resources and, in particular, to convert them to a fish product which can always be found in every Soviet fish shop: Pasta Okean or Ocean Paste. This is a creamy, pale pink paste, tasting of fish, crabs and shrimp, which is made immediately in the fishing vessels and frozen into bricks of 200 grams or 3 or 10 kilos. The book claims that this paste is 2 to $2\frac{1}{2}$ times more nutritious than eggs, milk or beef and that it is rich in albumen, fat, mineral substances and carbohydrates; and gives no fewer than eighty-six recipes for using it.

Imagination and a sense of pride in national and regional cuisines are not always evident. When I asked a chef in Tallinn what her best and most typically Estonian recipes were, she produced a mammoth book put out in the 1950s by the Ministry of Trade for all catering establishments in the Soviet Union (complete with tables of quantities for 100 people) and started enumerating the standard fish dishes to be found in every Soviet restaurant, such as the inevitable Rȳba Po-Pol'ski (fish, Polish style), a sad combination of fish with hard-boiled egg on top.

In practice, it is virtually impossible to find any cookery book on sale in the Soviet Union. They are in high demand and short supply. Recipes are available, but in a different form; little packs of postcard recipes are sold in most kiosks, often related to the cuisine of particular republics, with a photograph of the dish on one side and the recipe on the other. In addition, most fish shops have an excellent system of pinning up recipes on a board and supplying leaflets which customers can take home, including a short scientific description of the fish.

In compiling the collection of recipes which follows, I have tried to bridge the gap between nineteenth- and twentieth-century fish cookery by consulting all sources, choosing recipes typical of the cuisine of Russia and the Baltic Republics. My friends in Moscow have been invaluable in advising me on this and often in giving me their best family recipes; for the gap which is evident in the changed style of cookery books has been bridged to a large extent by continuity in cookery in Russian homes.

Zakuski

Zakuski are perhaps the most distinctive feature of a Russian meal. The word originally referred to the sweet delicacies and pies served after a main meal. Now it has two meanings: either something light served before a meal, usually with vodka, or by extension a snack, often eaten in a zakusochnaya – a stand-up snack-bar.

In the nineteenth century, zakuski would be laid out very formally on a table, often in a room set aside especially for this purpose and adjoining the dining-room. There is one such room in Pushkin's flat in Leningrad. The company would assemble round this table, propose toasts, clink glasses, down the first glass of vodka in a gulp and quickly follow it with a bite of herring or a caviar canapé. This is an excellent sequence; the vodka cleanses the palate, leaving it fully prepared and stimulated for the taste of whatever follows. The company would then adjourn to the dining-room, where they would embark on the meal proper, starting with a hot soup, continuing with the main hot dish and ending with cakes and chocolates accompanied by tea.

Such an extravagant use of space would be impossible under the more cramped conditions of Soviet life and, as a result, the zakuski ritual has changed somewhat. Nowadays, people sit down at table straight away, in a room which usually acts as bedroom, living-room, dining-room and study. The zakuski are simply served as the first course, but in such quantity that I regularly mistook them for the whole meal until I learned better and reserved some appetite for what was to follow.

Zakuski can be simple – Chekhov once wrote that 'the very best zakuska, if you would like to know, is the herring' – or more elaborate. They fit easily into western eating patterns as light dishes for lunch or supper or, as in the first recipe, breakfast.

Grenki s Seledkoyu k Zavtraku

Herring toasts for breakfast (from Molokhovets)   serves four

fresh herrings, 3, filleted	**olive oil, 2 tbs**
the soft roes of the herrings	**hard-boiled egg yolks, 6**
soft white rolls, 2, sliced	**strong mustard, 1 tsp**
butter, 45 g (1½ oz)	**capers, 1 tsp**

Fry the slices of white roll in butter; this produces your grenki or fried 'toasts'. Mix the olive oil, egg yolks, mustard, capers and soft roes. Spread the grenki with this mixture, chop the fillets of herring over them, pop them in a hot oven for 5 minutes and serve hot.

The drawing, based on one in Molokhovets's book, shows one of her suggestions for an elegant arrangement of zakuski.

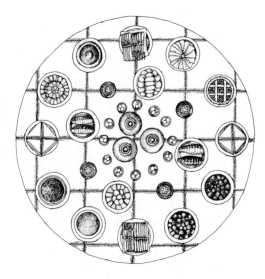

Fal'shivaya Ikra

False caviar

A Russian proverb says that: 'When there is no fish, crayfish counts as a fish.' In making do with what there is in the shops, Russians certainly show considerable imagination. If, as Shtok suggested in his play, God has pocketed the caviar for himself, ordinary mortals must make their caviar out of herring.* The result is not unlike real caviar in appearance, good to eat, and sometimes drily entitled 'Soviet caviar'. The following recipes are from a Muscovite friend.

Red 'Caviar'. Put the following ingredients through a meat grinder, so that they come out about the size of caviar globules: a medium-sized salted herring, cleaned and boned; 2 medium carrots, raw; a 2½ cm cube of processed cheese (the Russians use a brand known as Druzhba, i.e. 'Friendship' cheese); 200 g (7 oz) butter; a medium onion; and a hard-boiled egg. Mix thoroughly and serve in a dish decorated with lemon wedges.

Black 'Caviar'. Follow exactly the same procedure, but substitute finely chopped black olives for the carrots.

* Some caviar is available to ordinary Soviet citizens who apply for it through their institutions on special national occasions; and a couple who are about to be married may ask for authority to buy some caviar for the wedding celebrations.

Russian Fish Soups

A hearty soup is an essential part of a full Russian meal and reflects the love of quantity as well as quality in Russian eating habits. In 1813 Ivan Krȳlov, the Russian La Fontaine, devoted a fable to the Russian passion for huge amounts of soup and the title of this fable has become the common expression for anything excessive: Dem'yanova ukha. In the fable, the host entreats his guest to find room for a fourth helping of the fish soup, described as being 'covered with amber'. Russians do indeed attach importance to the colour of fish soups and take pains, by removing neither too much nor too little of the fat from the surface, to obtain the coveted 'amber sparkles'.

Russians also like their fish bouillon to be properly clear. In the nineteenth century Molokhovets advised her readers, in preparing a sturgeon soup, to clarify the bouillon by stirring in some pressed caviar, which was then discarded! (She also recommended adding Veuve Clicquot champagne.)

The recent and excellent Soviet book on *Fish Dishes*, written by an authors' collective including Academician A. A. Pokrovsky, contains recipes which are more practical, including the following fish versions of three of the most popular and traditional Russian soups: Solyanka, Schchi and Borshch.

Solyanka Rȳbnaya

Fish solyanka   serves four

white fish, ¾ kg (1½ lb) cleaned   **capers, 2 tbs**
salt   **bay leaves, 1 or 2**
butter, 45 g (1½ oz)   **black peppercorns, 3**
onions, 2, finely chopped   **stoned olives, 100 g (3½ oz)**
tomato purée, 2 tbs   **½ lemon, peeled and thinly sliced**
pickled gherkins, 150 g (5 oz)   **parsley, chopped**

Cut the cleaned fish into portion-sized pieces; cover them with cold water and bring to the boil, removing any scum. Then add salt to taste and simmer until done. Remove the fish and keep the bouillon hot. Meanwhile fry the onion in the butter, without letting it take colour, and add the tomato purée to it. Slice the gherkins and add them to the bouillon, followed by the cooked onion mixture, capers, bay leaves and peppercorns. Let it boil gently for 10 minutes, then add the pieces of fish and bring it just back to the boil. To serve, place a portion of fish in each bowl with a couple of slices of lemon and some olives, pour the soup over these and sprinkle with chopped parsley.

The soup is even better if left to mature for 24 hours and reheated.

Schchi Zelenÿe s Rÿboĭ

Fish shchi with sorrel and spinach   serves four

Shchi is usually made with fresh or salted cabbage. This version differs in being made with sorrel (which grows wild in Russian woods and is often used in soups) and spinach.

fillets of white fish, ½ kg (1 lb)	**a bouquet of herbs with a bay leaf**
sorrel, 300 g (10 oz)	**black peppercorns, 4**
spinach, 300 g (10 oz)	**salt and pepper**
butter, 30 g (1 oz)	**a little cooking oil**
an onion, finely chopped	**sour cream, 5 tbs**
a carrot, finely chopped	**chopped hard-boiled eggs, 2**
flour, 2 tbs	**chopped spring onion, 50 g (2 oz)**

Wash the sorrel and spinach, trimming off any thick stalks; cook them gently in a very little water; and make them into a purée.

Fry the onion and carrot in the butter, sprinkling some of the flour on them just before they are ready. Add 1 litre (2 pints) hot water, the sorrel and spinach purée, bouquet of herbs, bay leaf, peppercorns and some salt. Cut the fish fillets into 8 or 12 pieces; salt, pepper and flour them; and fry them in the oil. Then divide them among the 4 soup bowls, pour the bouillon over and add to each bowl its share of the sour cream, the chopped hard-boiled egg and the chopped spring onion.

Borshch s Kal'marami

Borshch with squid   serves four

squid, 450 g (1 lb)	**shredded fresh cabbage, 200 g**
medium beetroots, 3	**(7 oz)**
a carrot	**potatoes, 2, peeled and diced**
a parsley root	**sugar**
salted pork fat, 50 g (2 oz)	**garlic, pounded with salt**
vinegar	**sour cream, 2½ tbs**
tomato purée, 2 tbs	**parsley, finely chopped**

Peel the beetroot, carrot and parsley root and chop them into strips. Dice the pork fat, heat it in a thick frying pan and add these vegetables with a little vinegar and the tomato purée. Cover and stew gently until soft.

Boil the cleaned squid in salted water for 3 to 5 minutes; then remove it and cut it into strips. Add the cabbage to the same boiling water and, 15 minutes later, the potato. When the potato is almost done, add the other vegetables and the squid; bring back to the boil; and add sugar, garlic pounded with salt, and vinegar (all to taste). Serve with a dollop of sour cream in each bowl and sprinkle the chopped parsley on top.

Pirozhki

Russians gó into ecstasies when describing their pirozhki, or little pies. These are usually served with vodka as part of the zakuski course, or with a fish soup. The recipes which follow describe two different sorts of pirozhki. The first is from Molokhovets, who, typically, bids one use a silver tablespoon in measuring out the water.

Sloenÿe Pirozhki v vide Knizhki s Farshem iz Nalima
Puff-pastry 'booklets', stuffed with fish

The dough. Mix $1\frac{1}{4}$ dl (nearly $\frac{1}{4}$ pint) water with 300 g (10 oz) flour, except for a little to flour your working surface. Then roll the mixture out on this to form a round half as thick as a finger. Wash 225 g ($7\frac{1}{2}$ oz) butter in very cold water; beat it quite smooth with a spoon, and squeeze it with a towel to remove excess moisture. Then flatten it into a round half the size of the round of dough. Place it on top of the dough and fold the outer part of the dough over the edge of the butter, then roll the whole thing into a long flat lozenge and chill it for 15 minutes. Next, fold the dough over three times, roll it out once more, cover it with a towel and let it rest in a cool place for 15 minutes. Repeat this procedure five more times. Then keep the dough, rolled out for the final time, in a cool place.

The filling and the baking. Allow about 35 minutes for these operations.

burbot (see page 364) or haddock,	**salt and pepper**
1 kg (2 lb), and its liver	**sour cream, 1 tbs**
butter for frying, 90 g (3 oz)	**egg yolks, 2**
a medium onion, chopped	**parsley for garnishing**

Your fish should be in the form of fillets. Salt them, fry them briefly in some of the butter, bone them and chop the flesh finely. Fry the liver very briefly and chop it too. Use the rest of the butter to fry the onion; then combine onion, fish, liver, seasoning, sour cream and 1 egg yolk. Heat the mixture gently, stirring.

Preheat your oven to hot (430° F. gas 7). Cut the dough into oblongs about 5 by 8 cm. Put a spoonful of filling on the right-hand side of each, then fold the left-hand side over the filling so as to form the shape of a little book – a form which can be emphasized by running the point of a knife along the side of the 'spine'.

Put the pirozhki on a metal sheet brushed with cold water. Mix the second egg yolk with a little cold water and melted butter. Brush the tops of the pirozhki with this, then put them, on their sheet, straight from the cool into the hot oven, so that 'they are suddenly overcome by the heat without the butter having time to melt.' After about 10 minutes, when they begin to turn golden brown and are easy to move from the metal sheet, take them out of the oven. Serve them hot, laid out on a suitable dish over a neatly folded white napkin, decorated with parsley.

Rasstegai s Rȳboĭ

Rasstegai with fish filling

The name rasstegaĭ comes from the Russian verb meaning to unbutton and refers to the fact that the pastry case in which the pie is baked is left, as it were, unbuttoned, i.e. with a small oval aperture at the top, instead of being closed like normal pirozhki. If a large rasstegaĭ is baked, a number of looped openings can be made, and the pie case will then look rather like a tight shirt on which every other button has been left undone.

In his fascinating book *Moscow of the Past*, Ivan Belousov describes the rasstegaĭ pie vendors as he remembers them from his youth in the 1870s, selling their pies in the Zaryad'e market, not far from the Kremlin; a scene still to be witnessed in the 1920s, although nowadays rasstegai are no longer sold on the streets, only baked in the home.

Little rasstegai pies were very common. On meat days they were baked with a filling of meat and onion, and on lenten days with pieces of beluga sturgeon or salmon and with fat, i.e. the soft roe. The filling was not quite covered by the pastry; the pie seemed to be unbuttoned, which is how it got its name. The rasstegai would be put in a little dish, sprinkled with salt and pepper and smeared with a few drops of butter; a fish or meat bouillon, kept in special tin jugs with high and narrow necks, would then be poured over each pie. The jugs were swaddled in rags to keep the bouillon warm. Rasstegai were sold at one or two kopecks each, depending on the size.

To make rasstegai, you can use an ordinary flaky pastry dough. Make a filling with chopped and fried sturgeon or salmon or similar fish, mixed with parboiled rice, salt and pepper and finely chopped hard-boiled egg, parsley and fried onion. Roll out the dough and cut from it rounds about 10 cm in diameter. Place a generous spoonful of filling on each round and do it up from each side, lifting the dough from the sides to the middle, but leaving an oval aperture in the middle. Brush with beaten egg yolk and bake in a hot oven for 10 to 15 minutes, until golden brown.

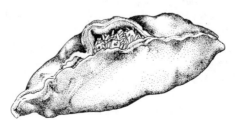

Kulebyaka s Vyazigoĭ

Kulebyaka with dried spinal cord of sturgeon and fish

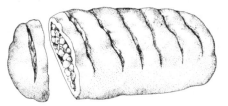

It is impossible to speak of Russian fish cookery without mentioning the kulebyaka; and there is no better introduction to this than the following passage from Gogol's *Dead Souls*. Chichikov has just retired to bed after another gorging session with his host Petukh, but unfortunately his bedroom is next to Petukh's study, and through the wall he can hear Petukh ordering the following day's culinary delights:

'Make a four-cornered fish pie,' he was saying, smacking his lips and sucking in his breath. 'In one corner put a sturgeon's cheeks and dried spinal cord, in another put buckwheat porridge, little mushrooms, onions, soft roes, and brains and something else – well – you know, something nice . . . And see that the crust on one side is well browned and a little less done on the other. And make sure the underpart is baked to a turn, so that it's all soaked in juice, so well done that the whole of it, you see, is – I mean, I don't want it to crumble but melt in the mouth like snow, so that one shouldn't even feel it – feel it melting.' As he said this Petukh smacked and sucked his lips.

A kulebyaka is a pie in which the filling, not necessarily fish, is cooked inside a loaf-shaped envelope of yeast dough. A flaky pastry dough may be used instead, but I do not find this as good. The following recipe was given to me by a friend, and corresponds only to the first corner of Petukh's exceedingly elaborate pie. All of Petukh's general principles should, however, be borne in mind.

There are two parts to the making of a kulebyaka – the dough and the filling. It is wise to start in plenty of time.

The dough

fresh yeast, 20 g (⅔ oz)	eggs, 2, beaten
warm milk, ¼ litre (½ pint)	salt, 1 tsp
sugar, 1 tsp	vegetable oil, 1 tbs
flour, ½ kg (1 lb)	cold milk, ¼ litre (½ pint)

Dissolve the yeast in the warm milk, adding a spoonful of sugar to speed the process. Leave to stand for 10 minutes, then mix with the flour, eggs, salt, vegetable oil and milk. Do not add too much liquid, just enough to bind the dough, which is ready when it is thoroughly kneaded, absolutely smooth, and doesn't stick to the hands or to any surfaces. Cover the dough with a clean tea-towel, and leave to stand in a warm, draught-free place for about 3 hours, or until the dough has doubled in size (the exact length of time will depend on the temperature of the room). Some leave the dough to rise twice or even three times, but in my experience once is enough.

The filling. I must first explain that vyaziga is the Russian term for the dried spinal cord of cartilaginous fish such as sturgeon. It looks unprepossessing – small white curled-up knobbly fragments – but is considered a great delicacy, and the taste and texture which it gives to pie fillings are distinctive and delicious. It is sold ready prepared in boxes in the Soviet Union, and is available in some food speciality shops in the West. But you may make your own in the way described by Molokhovets: 'Remove the spinal cords of a sturgeon, wash them and wipe them dry, and hang them out on a string to dry. When they are half dry, wind them into balls, like a skein of threads, tie them together and dry them out over the stove.'

vyaziga, measured dry, 1 cup
fish, a fillet of 350 g (¾ lb) of a
    good 'meaty' fish such as
    sturgeon, salmon, tuna or
    halibut
butter
an onion, chopped

hard-boiled eggs, 2, chopped
a raw egg
salt and pepper
dill or parsley, chopped
beaten egg *or* strong sweet tea (for
    the glaze)

Soak the vyaziga in plenty of cold water for about 2 hours. It will swell up dramatically, but will shrink again when cooked. Change the water and boil it for 20 minutes, or until soft; then drain it.

Take your fillet of fish, clean it, cut it into small cubes and fry these in butter. Fry the onion until golden, and mix it with the chopped hard-boiled eggs, the fish and the vyaziga, adding a raw egg to bind the mixture and seasoning it with salt and pepper. A little dill or parsley, chopped, may also be put in.

Now take the dough and roll it out into a rounded oblong shape about 1 cm thick. Place the filling in the middle of the dough, and pat it down, but leaving a wide margin all around. Close up the dough, along the middle seam and at the ends, pressing the edges well together. Place the loaf on a metal sheet, seam side down, and brush it with beaten egg, or, as some Russians do, with a solution of strong sweet tea. A design in the style of Russian wooden carving can be made along the top of the loaf with any spare bits of dough, shaped into diamonds or strips. Poke a few discreet holes to allow the steam to escape, and bake in a moderately hot oven (400° F. gas 6) for 30 to 40 minutes, or until golden brown and well cooked.

Treska s Sousom iz Vishen' i Krasnovo Vina

Cod with a cherry and red wine sauce   serves four

In the fish section of her cookbook, Molokhovets devotes a passage of extensive praise to the cod. 'All Northern peoples, nourishing themselves all year with this fish, stand out by virtue of their good health and by the absence of scrofula. One might say that it is the only food, apart from bread which, once one has got used to it, one never gets bored of, without which one could not live and which one would never exchange for any delicacies.' For people who find cod less inspiring than she did, this recipe will do a lot to cheer it up.

cod, $\frac{1}{2}$ kg (1 lb), in 2 fillets	sugar, 1 tbs
milk for poaching the cod	cloves, 2 or 3
unsweetened cherry purée, $\frac{1}{2}$ cup	a pinch of cinnamon
butter, 15 g ($\frac{1}{2}$ oz)	potato flour, 2 tsp
fish stock (or water), 1 cup	red wine, $\frac{1}{4}$ litre ($\frac{1}{2}$ pint)

The fillets of cod are to be poached in milk, while you make the sauce.

Cook the cherry purée (or compote) gently in the butter, then add the fish stock, sugar, cloves, cinnamon and potato flour (dissolved in an equal volume of water). Bring this mixture to the boil and let it simmer for about 15 minutes. Then pour on the red wine and bring it almost but not quite back to the boil. If the two operations, the cooking of the fish and of the sauce, have been properly synchronized, the fish will be ready now. Drain it, pour the sauce over it and serve with hot buttered boiled potatoes.

Rȳba, Zapechennaya v Zemle

Fish baked in earth

The latter section of *Gifts of the Ocean* (see page 341) includes some recipes which, mercifully, do not require Ocean Paste. The following recipe is directed at the Soviet fisherman who has just caught a fish and wishes to eat it on the spot. It can be used for any fish.

Scale, gut and clean the fish. Rub it with salt and fat. Put some fat in the stomach as well, with a little chopped onion if you like. Then soak a clean piece of cloth in vegetable oil and wrap the fish in it, tying the parcel up with string or with 'lȳko', strips of birch bark such as are used to make Russian peasants' shoes. Dig a hole in the ground, the size of the fish, and bury the parcel in it under a covering of earth no thicker than three fingers. Pat the earth down evenly and light a camp fire over the fish. It will be ready to eat in an hour.

Rȳba, Zapechennaya v Smetannom Souse s Grechnevoĭ Kasheĭ

Fish baked with smetana sauce and buckwheat porridge   serves six

This recipe is typically Russian in its use of a porridge (kasha) made in this instance, as for many other purposes, from buckwheat. The recipe comes from *Okeanichyeskaya rȳba v domashnyem pitanii* (Ocean Fish in the Home Kitchen) by Bogomolov and Krasheninnikova. I have amplified it slightly, in describing how to make the buckwheat kasha.

cod or similar fish, 1 kg (2 lb), cleaned weight

salt and pepper and flour

butter or fat for the fish, 70 g (2½ oz)

buckwheat groats, 140 g (5 oz)

a raw egg

butter for the groats, 30 g (1 oz)

a hard-boiled egg, chopped

grated cheese, 20 g (nearly 1 oz)

toasted breadcrumbs

chopped parsley

for the sauce

flour, 1 tbs

butter, 15 g (½ oz)

fish stock or milk, 2 dl (⅓ pint)

sour cream, 1½ dl (¼ pint)

salt to taste

Cut the fish into serving portions. Salt, pepper and flour them lightly, then fry them in butter on both sides.

Buckwheat groats are readily available. Making them into kasha is not difficult, but needs to be done with care. First, break the raw egg into a bowl and fork it lightly. Then add the buckwheat and stir it around until all the grains are coated with egg. This done, transfer the grains to a pan and shake it over a moderate flame until the grains are lightly roasted. Make sure that they do not burn. Next, add the butter and a little salt, and about 3 dl (½ pint) boiling water. Cover the pan, reduce the heat and leave to simmer for 20 minutes. At the end of this time, the water should have been absorbed and the grains should be tender and separate, like cooked rice. You now have your kasha.

Butter a casserole and put the kasha, mixed with the hard-boiled egg, in the bottom of it. Put the fried fish on top of the kasha, followed by the sour cream sauce. This is a white sauce, made in the usual way with the ingredients indicated. The fish stock or milk and the sour cream should be warmed, say the authors of the recipe, before they are added to the flour and butter. The sauce should be cooked for 5 to 7 minutes, until it is thick.

Sprinkle the dish with grated cheese and breadcrumbs and put it in a moderately hot oven (400° F, gas 6) for 10 minutes. Serve hot, with chopped parsley sprinkled over it.

Lithuania

Of the three Baltic capitals, Vilnius is my favourite. It is a mysterious medieval and baroque city, with a rich history and strong Jewish and Catholic traditions. The walls of the Ostra Brama chapel, where to this day a holy image of the Madonna is venerated, are covered with silver hearts laced with inscriptions, reminiscent of the gingerbread cakes on sale in the streets down below. The Jewish influence also remains clearly perceptible; the street known as German Street, once the centre of Jewish life and trade in Vilnius, still stands out among the narrow cobbled streets around it by its air of established prosperity. The most famous Jewish fish dish, gefillte fish, is said to have originated in Lithuania, although it is widespread in all the Baltic Republics as well as at Moscow. Hence my choice of a very simple Lithuanian version of it.

The proximity of Lithuania and Poland, their shared history and shared Catholic traditions have produced many similarities, even in cooking. I tried a fish and potato pie in Vilnius which was close to the Polish dish on page 334, although simpler and enhanced by the accompanying 'kauno duona', the delicious bread from Kaunas.

Finally, two hints. While cooking a Lithuanian recipe you might like to bear in mind the Lithuanian saying that if the dish is over-salted the cook is in love; also that the dish should be tasted with the index finger, since it is this which Lithuanians call the gourmet finger.

Žuvis – Lietuviškai

Fish, Lithuanian style

The Vilnius restaurant is considered by many to be the best in Vilnius. Kristina Vinickiene, who has worked as the chef of the restaurant for the last ten years, gave me this recipe, which she described as a sort of fish equivalent of chicken Kiev.

Take a fillet of fish for each person. Lithuanians would be likely to use perch; but redfish (page 139) would be suitable. Beat each fillet thin and flat, like an escalope.

Finely chop equal quantities of hard-boiled egg, dried mushrooms which have been soaked and then poached, lightly fried onion, and parsley. Mix these with a generous amount of melted butter. Place a good spoonful of this mixture on each fillet, roll it up into a neat sausage shape and secure it with thread. Dip each rolled fillet in beaten egg, coat it with fine breadcrumbs and fry it for 10 minutes or until done. Serve hot, with boiled potatoes and carrots, placing a slice.of lemon, wedged open, over each rolled fillet.

Kimšta Žuvis

Baltic gefillte fish   serves four

This Lithuanian recipe was given to me by a friend who grew up in the Lithuanian/Byelorussian border country. What it produces are delicious fish cakes, served as such and not used as a stuffing. I should explain, however, that many Jews would use the same fish mixture to stuff the whole skin of the fish, or to stuff rounds of skin taken from steaks cut across the fish. This procedure fits the name of the dish, which means 'stuffed fish', but it does make it more complicated to prepare.

The fish used would normally have been freshwater fish such as carp; but the dearth of freshwater fish in Soviet fish shops often makes it necessary to use sea fish nowadays. Whitefish (page 47) or ling (page 66) are among those which would be suitable.

for the fish cakes
a fish weighing 1 kg (2 lb)
a soft white roll
medium onions, 2
beaten eggs, 2
olive or salad oil, 2 tsp
salt, 1–1½ tsp
sugar, ¾ tsp
a pinch of pepper

water, 2 tbs
crumbled matzos (Jewish crackers)
    or toasted breadcrumbs, 1–2 tbs

for the cooking liquid
large onions, 2, chopped
carrots, 3, chopped
parsley, chopped (optional)
salt and pepper

Clean, skin and bone the fish. Mince the flesh in a grinder.

Soak the roll in water or milk, and squeeze it. Mince it and the medium onions, and mix them thoroughly with the minced fish and the remaining ingredients of the fish cakes. If the mixture is not of the right consistency, add some more breadcrumbs. Then form it into 12 round, flattened cakes.

Take a heavy casserole of about 30 cm in diameter. Put in the ingredients for the cooking liquid, and enough water to cover them and two layers of fish cakes. Bring to the boil. Then add the fish cakes, in two layers, reduce the heat, cover and leave to simmer for 1½ to 2 hours.

When the fish cakes are cooked, leave them to cool for a while, but remove them while still warm and arrange them in a fairly deep serving dish. Pieces of the cooked carrot may be used to decorate them. The cooking liquid should then be strained and poured over them. It will form a jelly around the cakes. Chill the whole dish before serving. It will keep for several days, refrigerated.

Jews in Riga would add beetroot to the cooking liquid, while Polish Jews prefer more sugar in the fish cakes.

Latvia

Monday 8 March was International Women's Day. I arrived in Riga off the night train from Tallinn, expecting to find great festivities in progress. However, the streets were deserted; celebrations were presumably taking place in the comfort of the home, perhaps with a bottle of Balzāms, the heady liqueur made in Riga from herbs and bottled in tall thin earthenware containers. It was icy and windy, the town desolate and bare with its combination of little pockets of perfectly preserved seventeenth-century merchants' houses, massive art deco buildings supported by caryatids, and large areas of wasteland, bombed during the last war.

I wandered about gingerly over the ice and was eventually given a lift by the driver of an empty coach to a haven of warmth, the Selga restaurant. Selga is the Latvian for 'open sea', and gives its name to this, the only fish restaurant of Riga. The decor is smart but conventional: small round tables, a bar in the middle, the kitchen at the side and the usual resentful old ladies who take your coat at the door and complain that it lacks a loop by which to hang it.

The chef, a Latvian woman, was introduced to me by name as Sprukule Monika Peteres, and by title as Master Chef of the Republic. The best dishes of the meal which she prepared for me are given below.

Uzkožamais 'Selga'

Selga appetizer

The piquancy of the sauce for this zakuska is just right for whetting the appetite. The fish recommended for this dish would be either Baltic herring, cod, bluefish or 'kapitan' (*Otolithus macrognathus* Bleeker, fished off the NW. African coast and common in Soviet shops). Cook it in water with onion, parsley, salt and pepper. When it is done, remove it from the heat and let it cool. Then drain it and chop it into small pieces. Mix these into a generous amount of sauce made with finely chopped hard-boiled egg, a little horseradish sauce, mayonnaise, a pinch of salt and sugar. Serve on a bed of lettuce.

An alternative salad, *Zivis ar Marinētiem Gurkiem*, uses a sauce made with pickles diced into fine little cubes, mayonnaise, a little sugar and salt. The pickle cubes are pleasantly crunchy.

Zivju Zupa

Latvian fish soup

Choose a fairly firm fish which will not disintegrate in cooking. The Selga recommend cod, which is the easiest for them, and probably for most readers, to obtain.

Prepare a court-bouillon with carrot, onion, parsley, salt and pepper. Bring this to the boil, add your fish (say, ¾ kg or 1½ lb, cleaned weight, but include the head too, if you have it), bring back to the boil and simmer for 15 to 20 minutes until the fish is done.

Meanwhile, boil separately ¼–½ kg (½–1 lb) potatoes, peeled and cut up into small cubes. When the fish is done, remove it, discarding the head, and keep it hot. Strain the broth and add the potato cubes to it. Keep this hot too.

Cut an onion into rings and grate one medium or two small carrots. Fry all this in butter in a frying pan until soft.

Dismember the fish into serving portions and put one in each person's soup plate. Pour a helping of the bouillon and potato over each. Top off with some of the fried onion and carrot, salt and roughly chopped parsley. The addition of the fried onion and carrot transforms what sounds like quite an ordinary fish soup into something distinctive.

Cepts Lasis ar Plūmju Kompotu

Fried Baltic salmon with plum compote

Salmon might be thought rather rich for frying, especially when fried potatoes are to be added, but the acerbity of the compote nicely balances their richness. The chef said that the dish could also be made with sturgeon, but would then be considered somewhat less of a delicacy and would not be so typically Latvian.

Make an ordinary batter out of flour, eggs, salt and pepper, using milk as the liquid. Dip each fillet or steak of fish in the batter, making sure that it is well coated, and then deep-fry them in oil for 5 to 10 minutes, until they are cooked through. The exact frying time will depend on the thickness of the pieces.

Meanwhile, have ready some hot fried potatoes, cut in rounds, and a compote of plums, stewed with just a touch of vinegar or bought ready-prepared, e.g. the excellent Polish bottled plums which are generally available. Serve fish, potatoes and compote together; the gold with the purple, the pleasantly unctuous with the faintly acid.

Estonia

Estonia is the northernmost of the Baltic Republics and the closest in culinary traditions to Scandinavia. It developed largely under Danish and Swedish domination until conquered by Peter the Great in the early eighteenth century. The upper citadel of Tallinn, where a charming librarian, Helle Lont, translated Estonian material for me, still bears witness to the early-thirteenth-century period of Danish domination.

The two staple foods of Estonia were, even in pre-Christian times, salted fish (the Baltic herring and sprat) and bread. The inland peasants bartered their grain for fish caught by the coastal dwellers. Herring was salted in large wooden barrels, with smaller quantities packed in round wooden boxes or containers plaited from strips of bark (shown below – Helle Lont well remembers them from her grandfather's house). Nowadays, of course, fishing and curing have been modernized. In 1959 the fish factory at Parnu pioneered the kippering of Baltic herring. Scottish readers may be intrigued to hear that Estonians consume their kippers chopped up, fried in a batter of egg, milk, flour, a little grated cheese and a touch of sugar, and served with tomato sauce.

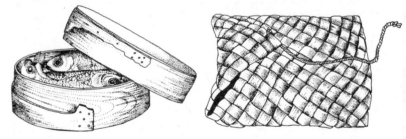

The Baltic herring and sprat remain very important. An entire book devoted to the former, *Zakuski iz sel'di* (Herring Appetizers, Tallinn, 1961), contains 160 recipes ranging from the humdrum to fairy-tale fantasies, such as that which bids you hollow out sections of cucumber, stuff these with a salted herring salad, cap them with tomato slices dotted with mayonnaise and proclaim the result as 'cucumber mushrooms'.

Kiluvõl

Sprat pâté

The most famous and typical Estonian fish is the Baltic sprat (page 31), which is called kilu or Tallinna kilud. The 1914 Baedeker's *Guide to Russia* says that in Tallinn: 'A special branch of industry is the capture and pickling of a small silvery fish resembling the sardine . . . large quantities of which are exported in all directions.' Kilu is still exported in bright blue tins decorated with a picture of old Tallinn. Inside, the little silver fish lie tightly packed, curled in a circle, with a bay leaf on top. They are preserved with thirteen different spices and the flavour is strong, sweet and fishy. Head and gut are not removed, the fish being so small.

But this is the de luxe export version of kilu. It would be too strong for kiluvõl, which is better made with unspiced tinned kilu or plain salted kilu. Finely mince 6 salted kilu and beat them with 100 g (3½ oz) of softened butter until quite smooth, adding a teaspoonful of the salty fish juices. Serve with bread and butter or hot boiled potatoes.

Rosolje

Estonian herring and meat salad serves four as an appetizer

salted herring, 100 g (3½ oz)
cooked pork or beef, 200 g (7 oz)
boiled potato, 200 g (7 oz)
pickled gherkins, ¼ kg (½ lb)
an apple, peeled and cored
hard-boiled eggs, 1 or 2

for the dressing
sour cream, 5 tbs
horseradish sauce, 50 g (2 oz)
vinegar, 2 tbs
mustard, as desired

Dice the salad ingredients. Mix the dressing and combine it with the salad. Mound all this up on a platter. Estonians would decorate the mound with rounds of cucumber, apple, tomato or egg, lettuce leaves and parsley. Serve as a zakuska or light salad.

Silgud Pekikastmes

Baltic herring with pork fat sauce serves four

This recipe again reflects the Estonian liking for dishes which combine meat and fish. It comes from Silvia Kalvir's book on Estonian cookery.

Soak 400–500 g (1 lb) of salted herring (Estonian 'silk') to rid it of excess saltiness, then clean it and cut the flesh into small pieces. Fry 150–200 g (about 6 oz) pork fat, diced, and add to it 1 or 2 chopped onions, 2 tbs flour and seasoning, and cook until brown. Then gradually add 6 dl (1 pint) milk and bring to the boil. Simmer for several minutes, stirring. The sauce will thicken. If it becomes too thick, add a little more milk. When it has reached the right consistency, add the pieces of fish and cook them for 5 to 8 minutes. Just before serving the dish, add 2 tbs sour cream. Serve with hot boiled potatoes.

17. Recipes from Finland

Most countries with a coastline can count a hundred or several hundred species of sea fish in their waters. Not so Finland, which has barely a dozen. The waters in the recesses of the Baltic, where Finland is, are so low in salinity that few sea fish can tolerate them. However, there is some compensation. Freshwater species can come out into and be caught in the sea. This is confusing for writers on seafood. Are they seafood or are they not? It suits me to include some of them here, so I have.

Baltic herring dominate the Finnish catch. Proportions by weight in a recent year were: Baltic herring 73; vendace 9; whitefish 3; sprat 1; salmon 0·7. Cod and flatfish are so few that they barely fin themselves into the statistics. So, as in the other Baltic countries, the preparation of herring is an important part of the cuisine; and on some parts of the coast, as I mentioned on page 29, may be treated as a qualification for marriage. Aspiring brides no doubt swot up *Silakka*, a book containing 145 herring recipes and written, significantly, by a professor of theology.

Buying fish in Helsinki is a joy. The old-fashioned covered market by the port has stalls at which every kind of preserved fish and caviar can be bought. Outside, stretching across the head of the harbour, is an open-air market, blessed to have as backdrop the pistachio, apricot and mushroom colours of Engel's classical buildings and supplying with its own wares the touches of bright red and green which are needed to complete the scene. Statistics may show that relatively few salmon are caught, but last time I was there I saw more than I had ever seen before, laid out on stall after stall to be sliced up and packaged with free bunches of dill for the purchasers, who were numerous. Finns boggle less than most people at the idea of buying fresh salmon. Indeed, it used to be eaten *ad lib* in the north. It may be this familiarity which led to the discovery that the fins of a salmon, when removed, incorporate some rather succulent flesh; and that if the fins are grilled over charcoal they become not merely edible but delicious. This dish, Pariloidut Lohenevät, is a Finnish speciality.

It must be said that most Finnish cookery is hard to disentangle from Swedish cookery, not least because a substantial proportion of Finns are of Swedish origin and Swedish-speaking; or from that of Russia and the Baltic Republics. Thus Kalamureke (page 365) is a fish pudding which probably reached Finland from Norway and Sweden; Kalakukko, the famous freshwater fish pasty from eastern Finland, is clearly related to the Russian Kulebyaka (page 348); and Rosolje, a Finnish herring salad, is very close to the Estonian dish described on page 357.

There is, however, no possibility that the visitor to Finland could be mistaken, whether travelling through the lake-filled countryside or eating in a city restaurant, about where he is. The Finnishness of things Finnish may be difficult to define, but it is remarkably easy to recognize.

Caviar in Finland

The most comprehensive caviar-tasting which I have achieved was in Helsinki, at the Havis Amanda Seafood Restaurant, where I noted the following comparative prices (given in Finnish marks, valid for June 1976):

'Russian' (i.e. sturgeon) caviar	50
Smoked forel (trout) caviar	38/40
Vendace caviar	36
Whitefish caviar	about 32

It is interesting that the disparities should be so limited, but my tasting did not suggest that they should be wider.

Working from the bottom upwards, I tried the whitefish caviar first. The colour is a pleasant orange, the taste good but rather salty.

Vendace caviar is also orange in colour, but smaller in grain, since the vendace is a much smaller fish. It has a good taste and a pleasantly gritty texture. I was told that some people think it the best caviar of all; although still others prefer mateenmäti, burbot caviar eaten with the burbot liver, which is only in season from November to January.

The eggs of the forel (trout) are cold-smoked, separately from the fish, by a process which is still considered secret. They are large and distinct and glistening, bright orange in colour. The flavour is superlatively good. M. Catani, who manages the restaurant, told me that this product freezes well and can thus be available in perfect condition at any time of the year.

The Russian caviar was, of course, extremely good, but did not stand out as unquestionably the best.

All the caviar was served with sour cream and chopped raw onion. There was also a peppermill on the table. I thought that the sea trout caviar was so delicious by itself that it was a pity to add anything. M. Catani agreed, but said that it is excellent if served with thin toast or pancakes (blinis). I agreed with him that the vendace caviar benefited from the sour cream, which tended to diminish its salty taste, and from a discreet sprinkling of black pepper. I did not care for the raw onion with any of the caviar.

Kalakeitto

A simple Finnish fish soup　　　　　　　　　　　　　serves six

fish, 1 kg (2 lb), cleaned and cut
　　into pieces
salt, 1 tbs
onions, 2, sliced
whole allspice, 8
new potatoes, 900 g (2 lb)
flour, 2 tbs

milk (goat's if possible), 4 dl
　　($\frac{2}{3}$ pint)
chives, parsley and dill, finely
　　chopped, 2 tbs
a little thyme
butter, 2 tbs

Bring $1\frac{1}{4}$ litre ($2\frac{1}{4}$ pints) water to the boil with the salt, onions and allspice. Add soon afterwards the potatoes and let them cook for about 10 minutes; after which add the pieces of fish and, a few minutes later, the flour and milk (which must first be mixed together).

Let the soup go on boiling gently until the potatoes are fully cooked. Then add the remaining ingredients and your soup is ready.

Suomalainen Lohikeitto

Finnish salmon soup

This has three invariable ingredients: salmon, potatoes and dill. The question whether milk should be added excites a certain amount of passion among Finns. I think that the soup is very good either way.

The Havis Amanda Seafood Restaurant in Helsinki makes the milkless kind thus. Take the head and tail of a salmon, and some narrow pieces from the flank. Cook these for 15 to 20 minutes with onions, carrots, black and white peppercorns and a bay leaf; then strain it, collect from the debris all the meat which you can find and cut this into bite-size pieces.

The quantity of potatoes should be about equal to the quantity of salmon. Cut them into small pieces and cook them in the strained broth until they are done. Shortly before they are ready, add some chopped leek.

When the potatoes are ready, put the pieces of salmon in with them, add chopped dill and serve.

Now for the version with milk. It so happened that I arrived in Finland to investigate salmon soup just after H.M. the Queen paid her state visit in 1976. I learned that she had gone up country to Jyväskylä, where she was served salmon soup in the forest; and that it was Mr Tarmo Salminen who had organized the 'kitchen in the forest' and made her soup. It is his directions (with quantities 'for one Queen and twenty-four others') which appear below. At this meal, the soup was treated in true Finnish style as the main course. After it came pancakes; and that was that.

fresh salmon, 1¼ kg (2¾ lb) meat, plus head and trimmings	potatoes, peeled, 1 kg (2 lb)
peppercorns, 8 black and 8 white	milk, 1½ litres (2½ pints)
whole allspice, 30	dill, chopped, 100 g (3½ oz)
onion, sliced, 100 g (3½ oz)	salt, as required
	butter, 1½ kg (3¼ lb)

The salmon stock should be prepared by adding the head, bones and trimmings of the fish to 3¼ litres (5½ pints) water, with the whole peppercorns, allspice and onion. Let all this simmer gently for 20 minutes, removing all scum, then strain it. You should have 3 litres (5 pints).

Cut the potatoes into 3 cm cubes and bring them quickly to the boil, to remove excess starch. Drain them and add them to the stock. Cut the salmon into 4 cm pieces, free of skin, and add these too.

Bring the milk just to the boil. When the potatoes are half cooked, add the milk and remaining ingredients. Correct the seasoning and cook for another 10 minutes. You will have 5 litres (8 pints) of soup.

Savustettu Siika ja Muhennetut Korvasieni

Smoked whitefish with morels

This is a simple recipe from the Havis Amanda Restaurant, where they prepare it just as one would at home, using a small Swedish fish-smoking box (see page 262). Remember, in this dish the smoking is the cooking.

Clean your whitefish, but do not scale it. Put lots of rock salt in the gut cavity, with a generous amount of fresh dill.

Have your smoking box ready, using hickory sawdust if possible. Put the fish in and keep it over a high heat for a few minutes, then over a lower heat until it has been smoked for 15 to 20 minutes, according to size.

Finland is rich in edible fungi and the morels (*Morchella esculenta*) are among the best. However, they need to be treated with caution if bought fresh, since it is necessary to boil them for 10 minutes before proceeding to do anything else. (If tinned or dried morels are used, this precaution is unnecessary.) Having boiled the morels, rinse them in cold running water, squeeze out the water and cut them into manageable pieces. Put these in a clean dry pan and heat them gently to banish the last traces of moisture. Then put some butter in the pan with them, adding a little minced onion. When the onion has turned golden, add enough cream to turn the morel mixture into a sauce, let it come to the boil and then simmer for 3 minutes. Finally, add a little salt and white pepper.

The smoked whitefish, which is firm and succulent inside and beautifully 'caramelized' outside, is served with the morel sauce, with the usual delicious Finnish potatoes and the usual fragrant Finnish dill.

Anjovismunahyydyke

Anchovy and egg custard   serves four

Anjovis is the Finnish name for tinned fillets of sprat, but it was with real anchovy fillets that Inger Antell demonstrated this dish to me, while explaining that it could be made with Finnish 'anchovy', or with Baltic smoked herring, or indeed with kipper fillets. This information was imparted under the gaze of her beautiful mother, whose portrait, perhaps the finest by the Finnish art nouveau painter Gebhard, looks down upon her dining table with calm authority. Ever sensitive to my surroundings, I decided that nothing could excel the version with tinned anchovies, which have the advantage of being available everywhere.

tinned anchovy fillets, 12	eggs, 6
milk, ½ litre (1 pint)	salt and pepper

Bring the milk almost to the boil, then remove it from the flame and let it cool a little. Meanwhile, fork the eggs lightly together, with a little seasoning, and combine them with the milk. Stir a little, but do not beat.

Dispose the anchovy fillets in the bottom of a buttered oven dish, pour the mixture over them and set the dish to cook in a bain-marie in a moderately hot oven (400° F, gas 6). It will be ready in 40 minutes.

Hiillostetut Silakat

Charcoal-grilled herring, Finnish style

The typical Finnish method, used also in the north of Sweden, for grilling their Baltic herring is as follows. It can also be applied to muikku (vendace); a real treat on the lakeside in the midsummer midnight sun.

The herring are first cleaned; although some prefer to cook them whole. The heads are left on. The fish are salted, using 3 tablespoonfuls of salt to a kilo (2 lb) of fish, and left for a couple of hours. They are then placed side by side, facing in alternate directions, in one of those double, hinged wire-grids made for the purpose and grilled over glowing charcoal. They are served with potatoes, preferably new, and butter.

In the region of Satakunta, in the south-west of Finland, which some Finns claim has a particularly pure tradition of Finnish cookery, there is an interesting variation. People there would put the grilled herring in layers in an oven dish, with lots of dill and butter between each layer on top. They would add about 1½ dl (¼ pint) water to keep the herring moist, cover the dish and let it stew very gently in a low oven for 1 to 2 hours before removing the fish and eating them.

Silakkapihvit

Herring 'steaks' serves six

The Finnish word for steak has a wide meaning, embracing also what we would call cutlets, rissoles and patties. Here it is used for a pair of herring fillets with seasoning sandwiched in between them.

small fresh herrings, 60	lemon juice, 6 tsp
salt and white pepper	flour (rye if possible)
fresh dill, chopped, 6 tbs	butter for frying

Behead, gut and split open each herring, removing its backbone. Each herring now constitutes a double or 'butterfly' fillet. Lay them out, skin side down, and sprinkle them with salt, pepper and dill. Moisten them with lemon juice and place on every second fillet any of the fillings listed in the next paragraph. Then place the first fillet, skin side up, on top of the second; and so on until you have thirty 'sandwiches'. Add a little salt to the rye flour and dredge the pairs of fillets in this. Then fry them in butter on both sides until they are done (4 or 5 minutes in all).

This is one of the most common herring dishes in Finland. It has a strong resemblance to the Swedish Strömmingsflundror (page 367); but the Finns have a wider range of possible fillings. Professor Teinonen, in his book about the various ways of preparing Baltic herring in Finland, lists the following: (1) horseradish butter, which is butter with raw scraped horseradish blended into it; (2) a mixture of equal quantities of tomato purée and mild prepared mustard; (3) slices of pickled gherkin; (4) fresh chives; (5) tinned anchovy fillets; and (6) a mixture of hard-boiled egg yolks with mustard (to which many Finns would add a little cream).

Another sort of silakkapihvit, closer to Estonian than to Swedish cuisine, is called **Lindströmin Silakkapihvit**. I have not discovered who Lindström was, but his name in the title of a dish indicates the presence of beetroot. This particular dish, again in quantities for six, is made as follows. Buy ½ kilo (1 lb) or a little more fresh herring, clean them and lift the fillets. Put these through a mincer. Then combine the result with 3 pickled beetroots (not the tiny ones, but of medium size) and put it all through the mincer again. Next, combine it with 400 g (14 oz) minced beef, a lightly beaten egg, salt and white pepper. Make the mixture into 6 large or 12 small 'steaks'. Meanwhile, take 2 onions of medium size, slice them thinly and brown them lightly in butter. Add water, barely enough to cover, and let them go on cooking, covered, for about 5 minutes, so that they finish up soft and juicy. While this is going on, fry the 'steaks' in butter on both sides. Transfer them to a hot serving dish, put the onion on top and the juices around them. Serve with mashed potatoes.

Muhennettu Made

Stewed burbot   serves six

The burbot is a freshwater fish and for this reason has not found a place in the catalogue. However, Finnish burbot venture out into the Baltic, and Finnish archipelagites assure me that the burbot from the sea are best, and that this recipe is so important in the cuisine of the archipelago that it must be included here. In Finland it is a dish for the winter, when burbot are in season. Elsewhere it can be applied to other fish.

Burbot, by the way, cannot be scaled, as their scales are too fine.

burbot, 2 kg (4½ lb), uncleaned	**a lemon**
butter, 70 g (2½ oz, or 5 tbs)	**a little sugar**
salt and allspice	**an egg yolk**
flour, 3 tbs	**cream, 1 dl (7 tbs)**

Skin and clean the burbot, reserving liver and roe. Cut the burbot into serving pieces and place these in a buttered pan, sprinkling each layer with salt and allspice and dotting the top layer with butter. Liver and roe are put right on top and water to cover is poured into the pan.

Simmer the fish, covered, for 20 minutes. Then remove it to a serving platter and keep it both warm and moist, which may involve basting it once or twice with a little of the hot broth. Meanwhile, make the sauce. This is prepared by heating 3 tablespoonfuls of butter, working the flour into it and adding a suitable amount of the fish broth. All this must simmer for 15 minutes. Then remove it from the heat and add the juice of half the lemon, with a little sugar. Beat the egg yolk into the cream and add this to the mixture. Then pour the sauce over the burbot and use the other half of the lemon, thinly sliced, to decorate it.

Täytetty Kuha

Stuffed pike-perch

The pike-perch, *Stizostedion lucioperca* (Linnaeus), is another freshwater fish, which does not appear in the catalogue but is admitted here because of its sallies into the Baltic and because Finns prepare it so well.

A pike-perch of 1½ kg (3 lb) is gutted and scaled, rubbed with salt and left to rest for an hour. It is then stuffed with a mixture of 1 cup cooked rice, 2 chopped hard-boiled eggs, 8–10 stoned and chopped prunes, 2 or 3 tbs cream, and seasoning; anointed all over with melted butter and sprinkled with toasted breadcrumbs; and baked in a hot oven (430° F, gas 7) until slightly browned. The oven heat is then reduced to moderate (about 375° F, gas 5) and a little mixed water and cream added, with which the fish is basted while the baking is completed. When the fins pull off easily, it is ready. The whole cooking time will be about 45 minutes. This recipe can be applied to cod, haddock and saithe with good results.

Kalamureke

Fish forcemeat 'pudding'   serves four

This recipe comes from *Keittotaito*, a Finnish cookery book published in 1933, which gives exact figures, such as 1707 or 3002, for the calorie content of every dish in it; an enormous exercise in calculation which was begun by Professor Carl Tigerstedt but had to be finished by others after his death. The fish pudding here described has a count of 2515, or 628¾ per person. In Finland the dish would be made with whitefish, pike-perch or pike; but it is excellent with whiting or saithe.

fish, 1½ kg (3 lb) uncleaned *or*	**potato flour, 1 tbs**
600 g (1⅓ lb) minced fish,	**salt and white pepper**
free of skin and bone	**a little sugar**
butter, 150 g (5 oz), beaten	**cream, 2 dl (⅓ pint) – single in**
eggs, 3, beaten	**Finland, but double is better**

The cleaned, skinned and rinsed fish is minced four times, to make sure that no little bones are left in the flesh. To this, add the remaining ingredients; the cream last and little by little. Beat well for 30 minutes (!) or use a blender to achieve the same result. Then put the mixture into a special kalamureke mould (see drawing), if you have one of these desirable objects; otherwise into a pudding basin. In the former case, put the lid on the mould; in the latter, cover the basin with greaseproof paper tied on securely. Put the covered receptacle in a bain-marie or large saucepan with boiling water surrounding it and keep this boiling for 1 to 1½ hours. Then turn the pudding out on to a dish and serve at once. Sauces recommended in the book are: crayfish, lobster, mushroom or caper. However, a friend whose mother made the dish regularly assures me that Hollandaise is best.

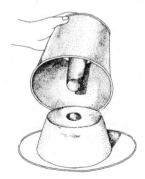

The authors of *Keittotaito* often tell you what to do with left-overs, under the heading Tähteet. In this instance, they advise cutting the left-over part into slices and incorporating it in a smorgasbord. However, the advice is gratuitous. It is always eaten up.

18. Recipes from Sweden

Sweden, for me, is first of all the country to which Linnaeus belonged, where he devised the binomial system of nomenclature for animals and plants, without which this or any similar book would represent the sort of chaos which only William Blake or Lewis Carroll could express. My Swedish shrines are therefore Uppsala, where Linnaeus's house is still preserved and still permeated by his scholarly and amiable personality, and Öland, the island where he did much of his work on the Swedish fauna and flora.

This said, I will name two subsidiary shrines, each worth a pilgrimage.

Stockholm, to my eye the loveliest of European capitals, possesses in the Salu Hall a covered market of exceptional charm. It is not very large, but it includes a number of stalls at which many kinds of fresh, cured and cooked seafood may be bought, the cooked dishes all ready to be carried out in the summer months and eaten *al fresco* beside the flower and fruit market in the adjoining square. That is how I formed my first and favourable impression of Jansson's temptation (page 369) and other Swedish specialities. It is a fine place for sampling small helpings of the numerous kinds of Swedish cured herring, such as glasmästar sill (glassmaker's herring) and Skånsk dillsill (dill herring from Skanes).

Fine though it is, the array of seafood in a Baltic city such as Stockholm would hardly satisfy a Swede from the west coast, accustomed to the greater variety of Atlantic species; and least of all someone from Göteborg (Gothenburg), Sweden's greatest fishing port. This is a sober and delightful city, in which the gentian and calico livery of the trams matches the blue overalls of the porters on the fish quays and the bleached wooden boxes in which they carry the fish; fish so revered that the retail market in which they are purveyed to Göteborgers is built like a church and is indeed called, in the local dialect, the *Feskekörka* or fish church. The atmosphere within, where a gallery overlooks the nave along which shoppers may process, and the merchants stand in stalls like box-pews, is suitably ecclesiastical. Nothing is lacking except organ music and perhaps a few votive candles flickering before whichever is the finest of the day's turbots, turbot being the particular predilection of Göteborgers.

Makrillsoppa

Mackerel soup serves four

A lot of mackerel is eaten on the west coast of Sweden. In his book *Bohusfisk och skaldjur* (Fish and Shellfish of the Province of Bohuslan), Bengt Petersen gives this recipe from the island of Gullholmen, where he lives.

mackerel, 2 or 3, weighing in all	white peppercorns, 10
$\frac{3}{4}$ kg (1$\frac{1}{2}$ lb) uncleaned	a small bunch of fresh dill
water, 1$\frac{1}{2}$ litres (3 pints)	milk, $\frac{1}{2}$ litre (1 pint)
salt, 2 tbs	potatoes, 6–8 (optional)

'The old people in Gullholmen make this soup in the following way.

'Behead the mackerel. Clean and rinse them well, and cut them into sections of about 3 cm. Boil them in the water, to which the salt, peppercorns and dill have been added, for 15 minutes. Then add the milk and boil for a further 10 minutes. Potatoes can also be boiled in the soup, from the start; and if you do this it is called Makrillslura.'

I find this a good recipe, but recommend using half the amount of salt given, and adding the juice of half a lemon with the milk. The rinsed mackerel heads can go in the soup but must be discarded before serving.

Strömmingsflundror

Baltic herring fried to look like flounder serves four

herrings, 8	prepared horseradish (optional)
butter, 30 g (1 oz)	flour, seasoned and mixed with
chopped parsley, 4 or 5 tbs	fine breadcrumbs
chopped dill, 4 or 5 tbs	oil for pan-frying

Remove the heads and tails from your herrings, clean them, open them right out from underneath and remove the backbones, with as many of the smaller bones as you can take out with them. Form each fish into a flat double fillet, or butterfly fillet as it is often called.

Melt the butter and combine it with the parsley and dill; also the optional horseradish, which I think a good idea. Use this mixture as the filling in making 'sandwiches' of the fillets – two fillets together, each with the skin side out and the filling in between. Press each sandwich lightly together. Then dip them in the seasoned flour and breadcrumb mixture and fry them in hot oil on both sides until they are golden brown.

This is the recipe of Fru Sandh of Stockholm, who prepared the dish for me. It is easy to make and good to eat.

Surströmming

This celebrated (or should one say notorious?) kind of fermented herring is produced in the region of Nordingrå, in the north of Sweden, where the clear, dry atmosphere is just right for the process.

Dr Alander of Göteborg used to work in the surströmming region and was told by a local fishery inspector how the practice began. It seems that in the sixteenth century the inhabitants of Gävle on the Bothnian coast were wont to sail forth every spring in search of herring, which they would salt at sea. Their vessel, the *Haxe*, accommodated wives and children as well as goats, empty barrels and a store of salt. Having fished all summer, they would come back and sell their catch at Älvekarleby.

One year they caught more herring than they had salt for; so some of their herring began to ferment and could not be sold to their regular customers. Luckily they found some guileless forest people, of Finnish stock, to whom they were able to sell the faulty produce, confident that they would never see them again. Next year, of course, they took ample salt with them and came back with perfect produce. However, the forest men were waiting for them, and demanded 'the same as last year'.

So the men of Gävle began to ferment herring deliberately for these special customers and thus established a new little industry. Nowadays the fermentation is very exactly controlled. The herring are placed, whole, in closed barrels with about half the normal amount of salt, and the barrels exposed to the summer heat until about 20 August. Then they are opened, to be readied for repacking. Five days later, the surströmming can be sold and there is a stampede all along the coast to get at it.

Another fishery official recalled that as a young man he was in the harbour of the island of Ulvön on the August day when 200 barrels of surströmming were opened. As the smell billowed upwards, birds began to drop dead from the sky. Moreover, the wind carried the fumes over to a distant convoy of tugs hauling barges of limestone along the coast; whereupon every single tugmaster changed course for Ulvön. The small harbour was soon a solid tangle of barges and tugs, from which the crews leaped in a frenzy of desire to secure some of the delicacy.

Cans of surströmming bulge slightly, to accommodate the fermentation. A Swedish naval officer told me that when they ate surströmming on board his ship the cans were always opened on deck, because of the smell. The procedure thereafter is to drain and rinse the fish; to sprinkle some chopped, small red onion over them, to reduce the smell; and to lift off the fillets. These are then served with the small oval potatoes which the Swedes call almond potatoes; thin slices of a special bread, tunnbröd, which the northerners carry about in their wellington boots; and butter.

Sotare

Herrings like chimney-sweeps

This is a well-known way of preparing herrings in Sweden. They are simply grilled until almost sooty in colour and are then served with dill butter and potatoes.

The 'chimney-sweeps' have a good flavour, but an even better one can be achieved by preparing herring for breakfast in the manner of Gastrikland. For this, the fish are cleaned, rinsed, lightly salted and rolled in rye flour. They are then put in a shallow oven dish, with plenty of margarine or butter, and the dish placed in a moderately hot oven (400° F, gas 6). You have meanwhile set fire to some juniper twigs. At intervals of 2 minutes, you thrust these into the oven, where they will 'go out' but emit aromatic smoke which impregnates the fish as it cooks. The fish are turned after the first 6 minutes, then cooked for 4 minutes more.

Janssons Frestelse

Jansson's temptation   serves four

It was the traditional Swedish combination of salted anchovy fillets and potato which tempted Erik Janson (one 's' in life, two in the recipe title). He was a religious enthusiast who emigrated to the United States in the nineteenth century and founded a colony of disciples in Illinois. His principles forbade eating for pleasure, but he succumbed to this dish.

tinned anchovy fillets, 12

butter, 80 g (3 oz)

cooking oil, 1½ tbs

onions, 2, thinly sliced

medium potatoes, 6, peeled

white pepper

fine dry breadcrumbs, 2 tbs

milk, 1¼ dl (nearly ¼ pint)

double cream, 2 dl (⅓ pint)

Heat almost half the butter and all the oil in a pan, add the onions and cook them until soft, but not brown. Drain the anchovy fillets. Cut the potatoes into thin strips, not much thicker than matchsticks.

Use a little butter to grease a baking dish. Arrange a layer of potato strips in the bottom, followed by one of onion and one of anchovy. Repeat twice and finish with a layer of potato. Sprinkle each layer with white pepper and the top layer with the breadcrumbs. Dot the remaining butter over the top.

Heat the milk and cream in a saucepan until not quite boiling, then pour the mixture carefully down the sides of the baking dish. Bake in a moderately hot oven (400° F, gas 6) for 40 minutes or so, until the potatoes are cooked and the liquid almost completely absorbed.

Gravlax

Salmon marinated with dill   serves eight

A dish of great simplicity and great merit. So far as I can discover, it is of
Swedish origin although met, happily, throughout Scandinavia. Salmon
treated in this way will keep for up to a week in the refrigerator.

fresh salmon, middle cut, 1¼ kg	**sea salt, 4 tbs**
(3 lb)	**castor sugar, 1½ tbs**
a large bunch of dill	**crushed white peppercorns, 2 tbs**

Have the piece of salmon cleaned, scaled, bisected lengthways and
deboned.

Choose a glass or enamel casserole of the right size and place one of
your two pieces of salmon, skin side down, in the bottom of it. Add the
dill, chopped if necessary. Combine the remaining ingredients and
sprinkle them over the dill. Then cap the preparation with the other piece
of salmon, this time skin side up, followed by a plate or round wooden
board larger than the area of salmon. Weight this down, and put the
whole in the refrigerator for 36 to 72 hours. The fish is to be turned over,
complete, every 12 hours or so, and basted (inside surfaces too) with the
juices.

To serve, scrape off the dill and the salt mixture, pat the fish dry and
slice it, thinly and at an angle, as you would smoked salmon. It is
accompanied by Gravlaxsäs, a mustard sauce which is made as follows.

Mix together in a bowl 4 tbs mild ready-made mustard, e.g. that of
Dijon, 1 tsp mustard powder, 1 tbs castor sugar and 2 tbs white vinegar.
Then take a wire whisk and beat in, little by little, 6 tbs vegetable oil until
you have a sauce of the consistency of mayonnaise. Into this stir 3 or 4 tbs
chopped dill. This sauce can be prepared in advance and refrigerated, but
should be rewhisked before being served.

Laxpudding med Risgryn

Salted salmon pudding, with rice   serves three or four

Besides making a speciality of Gravlax (above), Swedes also salt salmon,
with a mixture of salt and sugar and nitrate of potassium, to produce what
they call salt lax or rimmad lax. This salted salmon will keep for months.
It is what is used in this recipe for a salmon pudding, but there are of
course others which use fresh salmon. Making a salmon pudding is a good
way of stretching a small quantity of salmon. (It is also economical, in
Sweden, to buy laxpudding ready-made.)

The recipe given here is adapted from that given in *Iduns Kokbok*, a
workmanlike volume in the cookery-school tradition.

salted salmon, 350 g ($\frac{3}{4}$ lb)   salt, 2 tsp
skimmed milk, 1 litre (2 pints)   white pepper, $\frac{1}{2}$ tsp
rice, uncooked, $\frac{3}{4}$ cup   sugar, 2 tsp
unskimmed milk, 1$\frac{1}{2}$ dl ($\frac{1}{4}$ pint)   a little more butter
butter (cold), 50 g (2 oz)   dry breadcrumbs, 3 tbs
eggs, 2 or 3, separated

Rinse the salmon, cut it into slices and soak them in the skimmed milk for 3 hours. Remove, dry well, and cut the slices into cubes.

Bring the unskimmed milk to the boil. Add the rice and cook it, stirring occasionally and adding a little more milk if necessary, until it is almost soft. Then take it off the heat, beat in the cold butter at once and leave it all to cool. When it is quite cold, stir in the beaten egg yolks, the cubes of salmon and the salt, pepper and sugar.

Finally, fold in the stiffly beaten egg whites. Adjust the seasoning, and pour the mixture into the greased and breadcrumbed fireproof dish. Cover it with a tablespoonful of breadcrumbs. Bake it in a moderate oven (355° F, gas 4) for 1 hour. Serve with melted butter.

Inlagd Fisk

Swedish dressed fish   serves four

This is one of the most popular ways of preparing fish in Sweden. Almost any kind of fish can be used. It is first poached or fried. Then, assuming that you have about $\frac{3}{4}$ kg (1$\frac{1}{2}$ lb) cooked fish, proceed as follows.

water, 1 dl (7 tbs)   a bay leaf
vinegar, 1$\frac{1}{2}$ dl ($\frac{1}{4}$ pint)   crushed allspice, $\frac{1}{2}$ tsp
sugar, 140 g (5 oz)   crushed white peppercorns, $\frac{1}{2}$ tsp
cloves, 5

Boil all the above ingredients together for 3 minutes; then allow the mixture to cool. Pour it over your cooked fish, preferably while the fish is still hot, and leave it for 24 hours. Serve it cold with hot boiled potatoes, and with a Skarp Sås (sharp sauce) made as follows.

a hard-boiled egg yolk   French mustard, 1 tsp
a raw egg yolk   a pinch of salt; and sugar, 1 tsp
lemon juice or vinegar, 1$\frac{1}{2}$ tbs   a cup of whipped cream

Mash the cold hard-boiled egg yolk in a bowl and mix in the raw yolk. Add the lemon juice or vinegar, mustard, salt and sugar. Carefully fold in the whipped cream and your sauce is ready. You will find that it is only mildly sharp; and it is very rich, so unsuitable for oily fish.

Torsksoppa från Falkenberg

Cod stew from Falkenberg   serves six

Swedes distinguish between various types of cod. There is the large, light grey cod which is fished in the Kattegat and the Skagerrak; the greenish-grey cod of the fjords, known as grastorsk or grass cod; and the bergtorsk or rock cod, which is taken in inshore waters and around the archipelagos off the coast. This last weighs from 1–6 kg (2–14 lb) and is brown/reddish in colour, blotched and hard to distinguish among the seaweeds. The recipe, which comes from Falkenberg in the province of Halland, calls for 3 *small* cod of this variety; but other small cod (or hake) will do.

Prepare a court-bouillon with 1 litre (2 pints) water, 3 small sliced carrots, a bunch of dill, a sliced onion, salt to taste, 6 white peppercorns, a bay leaf and the juice of half a lemon. Let this simmer for 20 minutes, then add the cleaned fish, cut into pieces, and continue cooking until the fish is done (about 15 minutes). Now add 6 tomatoes cut into thin wedges, 80 g (3 oz) butter and *at least* half a cup of chopped parsley. Continue to simmer the stew for several minutes, correct the seasoning and serve with boiled potatoes.

Stuvad Östersjö-torsk

Baltic cod cooked with dill and parsley   serves four

One of the classic Swedish fish dishes is Stuvad Abborre, abborre being the freshwater perch. How-ever, Hagdahl, author of the greatest cookery book in the Swedish language, which is a sort of culinary national monument, stated therein that the small cod of Baltic waters were suitable for the same treatment. So here is the  recipe, adapted from the perch version given by Tore Wretman in his elegant and learned book *Svensk Husmanskost*. (He can only approve the transferral of the recipe in this way, since it was he who had the honour of writing the introduction to the facsimile reprint of Hagdahl's work.)

small cod, 4   a lemon
butter, 50 g (2 oz)   beurre manié, 30 g (1 oz) butter
fresh dill, lots   with 1 tbs flour worked into it
fresh parsley, lots

Clean the fish, pulling out gills but leaving head and backbone intact. Scale the fish and rinse them in cold water.

Select a pan, large enough to take all the fish side by side, backs up. Butter this pan generously, and strew plenty of chopped dill and parsley in the bottom. Place the fish on this bed and cover them with more chopped dill and parsley. Add salt and pepper.

Put thin dabs of beurre manié on top and pour over everything the juice of half the lemon, mixed with 3 tablespoonfuls of water. Cover the pan with a close-fitting lid, bring the mixture to the boil, then reduce the heat and simmer for about 15 minutes. (When the fin on the back of each fish comes away easily, you will know that the dish is ready.) Adjust seasoning and serve the fish from the pan with boiled potatoes. The other half of the lemon, peeled, sliced very thinly and dipped in chopped parsley will make an attractive decoration and add to the flavour.

If the fish are with roe, boil these in a separate pan, in a little salted water, cut them into slices and place them on top of the fish.

Aladåb på Stenbit, Ägg och Grönsaker

Lumpfish in aspic with eggs and vegetables   serves four

The Swedish cookery book by Jenny Åkerström is called the *Prinsessornas Kokbok* because she taught, at her cookery school in Stockholm, Princess Margaretha of Denmark, Crown Princess Märtha of Norway and Crown Princess Astrid of Belgium. The cover of my copy shows the three young ladies, be-pearled and set in oval gold frames with crowns on top; and they reappear inside, coiffed in white for kitchen work. The recipe which follows is slightly adapted from one in the book. Its interest lies in the fact that lumpfish (presumably the male – see page 142) is deemed worthy of quite an elaborate preparation. Its utility is considerable, since it can be used for many other kinds of fish.

600 g (1⅓ lb) of cleaned lumpfish is poached in a court-bouillon of sliced onion, white peppercorns, ½ bay leaf, salt and sprigs of dill. The fish is then neatly flaked; and the liquid strained, after which a litre of it is reserved, allowed to cool, and skimmed of any fat.

The aspic is made with this reserved liquid, gelatine and 2 egg whites. After it has been strained, twice if necessary to make it quite clear, a tablespoonful of vinegar is added to it. The bottom of a mould is coated with it. When this has set, the pieces of fish, with 10 cooked prawn tails and ½ cup cooked peas are put in and the rest of the aspic poured over. After the aspic has set, the dish is turned out and served with hot boiled potatoes and a sharp sauce (page 371).

Stekt Slätvarsfilé med Kantareller

Fried brill fillets with chanterelles   serves four

This recipe is meant to remind readers that the common mushroom is not the only species with which fish dishes can be enhanced. Scandinavians are well off in this respect. I remember a Finnish friend going off into the woods for 20 minutes and coming back with fifteen different edible fungi. One must of course know which are which, since some are poisonous. Jane Grigson's *The Mushroom Feast* is a good guide for Europeans.

Brill is recommended for this dish by Bengt Petersen in his book on Bohuslan fish cookery; but fillets of other flatfish can be used. And poached morels can be used instead of chanterelles; in which event use a little flour and plenty of cream to make them into murkelsås (morel sauce).

fillets of brill, 800 g (1¾ lb)   **fresh chanterelles, 1 litre (2 pints)**
salt   *or* **about 350 g (¾ lb) preserved**
flour   **ones**
butter, 100 g (3½ oz)   **chopped parsley, 2 tbs**

Salt the fillets lightly, turn them in flour and pan-fry them in butter. Remove them and keep them warm. Put a little more butter in the pan and fry the chanterelles in this for a few minutes. If they are big ones it will be convenient to have cut them up first. Strew the chanterelles and the butter in which they have been cooked over the fish, sprinkle the chopped parsley on top and serve.

Skärhamnsallad

Halibut salad from Skärhamn   serves four

In about 1975 the firm of Svenska Fisk in Göteborg held a competition for fishermen's wives, of whom 150 or so sent in their best fish recipes. The first prize went to Barbro Henning of Skärhamn for this one.

What is known as Västkustsallad (west coast salad) is quite an institution in Sweden and usually comprises a variety of crustaceans and molluscs such as lobster, shrimps, crab and mussels. Getting all these things together and preparing them is not always easy; and the simplicity of this halibut salad is welcome.

poached halibut, ½ kg (1 lb)   *for the dressing*
potatoes, 6, boiled and diced   **lemon juice, 1 tbs**
hard-boiled eggs, 4, chopped   **olive oil, 3 tbs**
pickled gherkins, 2, diced   **salt and pepper**
pimento-stuffed olives, 18 to 24

Cut the cooked fish into small pieces and mix them with the other ingredients. Beat the lemon juice and oil together, and add seasoning to taste. Pour the dressing over the fish salad, mix it in well and serve the salad with a sharp sauce, such as that described on page 371.

Hummer-Pastejer

Lobster pasties serves six

Lobster is such an expensive and rich food that it seems desirable to extend it by a preparation which will allow, say, six people to enjoy one smallish lobster. This recipe provides one such preparation. It comes from the attractive small cookery book by Margaretha Nylander (Stockholm, 1822). She gives only one quantity (5 or 6 eggs of the smaller size then available); so I have added the others by projection from this and by experiment. I have also established that a similar dish can be made with crab or prawns.

a cooked hen lobster of $\frac{3}{4}$ kg **($1\frac{1}{2}$ lb), with its eggs**	**sugar, 2 tsp** **soft breadcrumbs, 3 tbs**
milk, about $\frac{3}{4}$ cup	**double cream, 3 tbs**
butter, 60 g (2 oz)	**eggs, 3, beaten**
	puff pastry

Remove the meat from the lobster and leave it to soak in milk for 2 hours. Clean its carapace well, smash it in a mortar and let the fragments simmer for 15 minutes in $\frac{1}{2}$ cup water. Meanwhile combine the lobster eggs and the butter. Heat the mixture in a frying pan, fry it gently for a few minutes and then add the strained carapace broth. Let it all simmer for 15 minutes, then rub it through a fine sieve. This gives you your red lobster butter. Next, drain the lobster meat and chop it into pieces about as big as peas. Combine this with the lobster butter, sugar, breadcrumbs, cream and eggs.

Divide your puff pastry into 6 or 12 pieces, shaped as in drawing A. Spoon the mixture into the centre of each. Fold over the top and bottom sides to meet each other, so as to produce the shape shown in drawing B. Place the pasties, seams down, on a greased baking tin, bake them in a moderate oven (355° F. gas 4) for about 15 minutes and serve.

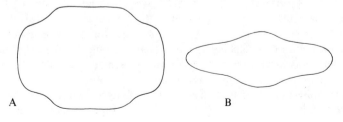

A   B

19. Recipes from Norway

As Norway approaches the 100th anniversary of her separation from Sweden, Bergen will be coming up to its 1000th birthday as a city. The Hanseatic merchants' houses beside the fishing port in Bergen remind us that this city has been for centuries, as it is today, Norway's fish capital.

I am told that Bergen's open-air fish market is but a vestige of its former self, that as the city has grown it has shrunk, that there used to be ten times as many tanks for live fish, and so on. But it still seems to me to be a marvellous place, unique in my own experience. At one end are the surviving fish tanks, with live cod and saithe, a sight which I have not seen elsewhere, although it was usual enough in England a hundred years ago. Then come the stalls on which lie great white halibut, one steak from which serves six; regal salmon barely out of the water; and the glistening mackerel to which Norwegians are so partial. Third, in logical succession, come the stalls of cured fish, where salmon, mackerel and cod reappear in new guises, to be scrutinized by the discriminating Bergensers. (I told one Bergen lady that I planned to buy a piece of local smoked salmon for my family. She was aghast to hear that I proposed to set out solo on this errand. 'Of course,' she admitted, 'all of it is good, but to have the best you must go to the best shop, which is a small one known to me, where the man does his own smoking, and to have the very best you must be accompanied by a Bergenser who will discuss the purchase on your behalf. In short, I must take you.' Which she did.)

Norwegian cookery has more variety than a casual visitor might think. However, I have chosen here to write at length about certain specialities in which the Norwegians excel, rather than to illustrate this variety with numerous short recipes. The best Norwegian dishes are simple, but deserve as much care in explanation as the Norwegians give to making them. As a sign of this care, I cite the fact that Norway belongs to that chain of countries, stretching up from Ireland through Scotland, Orkney and Shetland, in which boiled potatoes are presented in a properly floury state, achieved by partly drying them after the cooking.

The confection of fish puddings and fish balls from fish forcemeat is one area of fish cookery in which Norway stands supreme, her supremacy symbolized by that Norwegian institution, the fiskemat shop or fiskemat-butikk. This is a special kind of shop which sells minced fish; not scraps of inferior fish but first-class fish minced and made into forcemeat for use at home, or already turned into fish puddings and fish balls which can be consumed on the spot or borne away. The old-fashioned ones are especially delightful. Hovland's, at Ladegardsgaten 4 in Bergen, is one of the best to visit, for it lies beside streets of old timber houses painted halibut-white, fish-mustard ochre, rain-sky slate or fjord-blue.

Inquiries which I made in Sweden led me to conclude that the political boundaries of Norway coincide almost exactly with the limits of the fiskematbutikk zone. I hope that this zone will expand. The convenience of buying minced meat is obvious to all. Similar considerations support the provision of minced fish as a matter of course.

I must also mention Rakørret, the fermented trout of which the Norwegians are very proud. This was originally a way of preserving the fat autumn mountain trout for winter use, when lakes and streams were frozen. Now it is applied to salmon trout. The product is so popular, but has such a strong smell, that S.A.S. have special regulations to govern its carriage by passengers leaving Trondheim on their flights.

Rakørret is far less potent than surströmming, its Swedish counter-part; but it is eaten in small quanti-ties only and washed down with aquavit. I first tasted it on the day after I had eaten some superbly fresh salmon trout, overlooking the very fjord which Grieg contem-plated while composing his music. This satisfying experience made me, perhaps, unreceptive to the fermented version; but it certainly has an interesting flavour and I can imagine that it would grow on one.

Cod, however, is *the* fish in Nor-way. and has been for many cen-turies. The illustration shows Norwegians fishing for cod by handline in the early seventeenth century. This method was in use until the latter part of the eighteenth century, when fishing by longline and net came into use.

The librarian of the Maritime Museum at Bergen kindly gave me a reproduction of the picture; the original is in the Historical Museum in the same city.

Bergensk Fiskesuppe

Fish soup as made at Bergen

This is a remarkable soup, which relies on fish rather than on spices or seasoning for its flavour. Professor Knut Fægri, a Bergenser, a botanist and a polymath, invited me to taste it at his hillside home above the harbour, and gave me full details of how to make it. He has done the same for others, only to observe the recipe then published with unauthorized alterations, such as would make his 'forebears rotate in their graves'. Aware of this, I give the recipe here in his own words and with his express approval.

Now, you must imagine yourself to have dined at the Professor's house, to have asked whether some secret ingredient accounted for the excellence of his soup, and to have received thereafter a letter in the following terms.

'A number of friends and acquaintances have asked me what it really is which is so special about that fish soup. I have always answered that there is nothing peculiar about it at all; it's a quite ordinary fish soup such as has always been made in this town, where importance is attached to making good food. The recipe has been quoted in some places, but not quite satisfactorily. So here it is again.

'To make a good fish soup, you need four things: stock, roots, thickening and fish balls.

'*The stock*. If you want a perfect soup, you must put a lot of work into making a good stock; it's no good using any casual fish-water. Allow ¼ kilo fish [½ lb] per person, and add some fish heads if available. Clean the fish thoroughly, cut it into small pieces, put them in cold water and heat them up *very* slowly. When the water reaches boiling point, let them simmer for 20 minutes more. If you leave them longer, a taste of glue may result.

'The fish has to be first-class, what we in this town call first-class; in other words it must be alive until a few hours before you start simmering it. Stock made with old fish corpses doesn't give a first-class soup. The kind of fish is of the greatest importance. The classic choice is, naturally, young saithe. Larger saithe also gives excellent stock, but it's difficult to get them fresh enough. Ling gives good stock, but then it's only away from the towns that you get it really fresh. Otherwise, the remaining fishes of the cod family, including the cod itself, are quite useless for this purpose.

'*The roots*. You need celeriac, carrots, parsnips and parsley root. (Be sure to get the green part with the celeriac and boil it with the fish when making the stock.) Cut these roots up into small pieces measuring about half an inch (just over 1 cm) and boil them separately, which can be done in some second-quality fish stock. Don't boil them too long – they should be quite firm in the soup.

'*The thickening*. Allow 1 tablespoonful of heavy sour cream for each person or, if your sour cream is too "angry", a half-and-half mixture of sour and ordinary cream. Allow also one egg yolk for each person. Put both these ingredients in a heated tureen and beat them well. Very finely chopped parsley is a suitable addition at this stage, if you want it. Then pour in the hot, strained fish stock, while continuing to beat the mixture. The soup itself is now ready; it remains only to add the roots and the fish balls.

'*The fish balls* [see page 381] should be the size of the bowl of a teaspoon and there should be plenty of them [say, 10 per person]. On informal occasions you make bigger ones.

'When you now check the taste of your soup, you should have a little sugar handy. I haven't mentioned salt, since that goes without saying, but you may need a little more.

'And now for the famous veal stock, that so very few people seem to know about. A little [say, 2 tbs per person] strong veal stock does wonders in rounding out the flavour of the soup, without diminishing its fishy taste. It was Holdt, a Bergen restaurateur, who first thought of adding it. But this is such a refinement that it almost deserves to be kept for special occasions.

'I've not added any chives because, as you know, I don't like the onion family. But I'll admit that the addition of a small quantity of chives is something which could at least be discussed.

'As for the fish from which the stock was made, it is of course only suitable for the cat.'

Professor Fægri gave me the following additional comments.

(a) Once the sour cream and egg yolks have been added, the soup must not even approach boiling point; otherwise it will curdle.

(b) The root vegetables can be prepared when in season and frozen in little bags for use at other times of year.

(c) The fish stock can perfectly well be made one day before it is needed.

(d) An optional refinement is to add 1 teaspoonful per person of finely grated cheese before the final heating of the soup.

He also explained that there are, or used to be, three versions of Bergen fish soup: clear, white and brown. The clear one seems to have fallen into desuetude, although Mrs Faegri recalls her grandmother making it. The white version is given above. As for the brown version, the Professor's grandmother pasted into the fly-leaf of her copy of Hanna Winsnes's cookery book a manuscript verse embodying the recipe. This exhibits three different features. Some flour is browned in hot butter and the stock added to this mixture little by little. A generous glassful of sherry and a little cayenne pepper are added when the fish balls go in. And a touch of vinegar is put in with the sugar and salt when the seasoning is adjusted.

Fiskefarse, Fiskepudding, Fiskeboller
Fish forcemeat, fish pudding and fish balls

FISKEFARSE or fish forcemeat. This, rather than plain minced fish, is the raw material for fish puddings and fish balls. To make it, you start by scraping the raw flesh off a suitable fish. Haddock and pollack produce the whitest flesh. Saithe is good if you are going to make fried fish balls, but the flesh is not quite white.

Sarah Dekke, whose Norwegian cookery book of 1938 is the classic work of its time, remarks that the flesh comes off more easily if the cleaned and rinsed fish has been hung up by the tail overnight. For the next stage she recommends taking a 'deep plateful' ($1\frac{1}{2}$–2 cups) of scraped fish flesh, 1 tbs each of salt and potato flour, $\frac{1}{2}$ tsp mace and 30 g (1 oz) cold butter. All this is to be pounded together in a marble mortar (I am told that she would have used one on the floor, wielding a pestle with a handle about a metre long) until the butter has completely 'disappeared'. A blender may of course be used instead. After this, add about $\frac{1}{2}$ litre (1 pint) of single cream to the mixture, spoonful by spoonful. The more you beat (or blend) the mixture between spoonfuls. the better and lighter the forcemeat will be. A little cold fish stock may be added with the cream. The forcemeat should be used very soon after it is ready.

FISKEPUDDING or Fish Pudding. I now turn to Hanna Winsnes, author of Norway's classical cookery book, which was first published in 1845. Hanna was the wife of a clergyman who received his remuneration largely in kind from his parishioners. What they had to offer were fresh salmon, cream, butter, eggs and so forth. Hanna's book seemed to take for granted this wealth of first-class raw material, and she was criticized for extravagance. This upset her and she then pointedly produced a cookery book for less well-off households, in which the recipes were as economical as possible. However, it is her first and main work which I have used.

Her fish forcemeat is prepared on the lines described above, but with some differences. Anticipating her later, more frugal frame of mind, she says that in the absence of sufficient cream you can use milk with the addition of some very finely chopped fat. However, she would have you put a little ground ginger into the mixture, as well as the mace; and she strongly urges the addition of some really good lobster stock to the cream.

Having got your forcemeat ready, according to one prescription or another or following a visit to the fiskemat shop, pour it into a well-greased dish, such as a pyrex one, and gently tap the sides of this so that the forcemeat settles down. Cover it with greaseproof paper and set it in a baking tin half full of boiling water. Place this in a pre-heated moderate oven (say, 355° F, gas 4) and leave it for between 45 and 60 minutes. The water should be simmering throughout and may need to be topped up with a little more boiling water. When a knitting needle goes into the pudding and comes out dry and clean, the pudding is ready. It should be allowed to stand for a few minutes, after being removed from the oven; and any excess liquid should be poured off before you turn it out on to a serving platter.

The pudding is suitably accompanied by Rekesaus, shrimp sauce. To make this melt 50 g (2 oz) butter in a pan, remove from the heat and stir in 4 tbs flour. Add $3\frac{1}{2}$ dl (1 pint + 3 tbs) milk and 2 or 3 tbs cream. Then cook it all over a low heat, stirring continuously, until the mixture is smooth and fairly thick. Season with salt and white pepper, add $1\frac{1}{2}$ tbs lemon juice, the meat from 1 kg (2 lb) cooked shrimp (chopped up, if you wish) and let all this heat through. Finally, add 2 tbs of finely chopped dill and serve the sauce with the pudding.

FISKEBOLLER or Fish Balls are made with the same basic ingredient, fish forcemeat; but for this purpose it can be somewhat firmer. Hanna Winsnes authorizes the addition of a cold, boiled, grated potato, and further remarks that if you are making fried fish cakes of your forcemeat this addition will help them to keep their shape. Fish balls, which are poached, may be small or large, as you please. I give below a self-contained recipe for balls made with young saithe.

PALE-BOLLER IN PALEBU. This onomatopoeic title refers to the best fish balls of all, those made from young saithe. The Norwegian actress Randi Lindtner Næss, contributing to Ingrid Espelid's book, wrote thus.

'In the outermost of the islands of the Bergen archipelago there is a small place called Palebu – and it is so called because they catch so much pale (young saithe) there. The small pale which we get are mostly used for pale-boller.

'Here is the recipe which I inherited from my mother, who used rather small pale. Scrape all the flesh off the fish. Mix it with milk, salt and pepper – in the quantities which seem right to you. Work it well together; if the mixture comes out too runny, you can add a little flour. In our country cabin we mix it with a wooden spoon, but a blender could be used instead.

'However, the *most* important ingredient for these balls is chopped chives – as much as possible! That's what "makes" the balls.

'Prepare your stock by boiling the skin and bones, to which you can easily add a whole (gutted) small pale if you wish.

'Form large fish balls and simmer them in the stock. Eat them with melted butter and good potatoes.'

NORWEGIAN WAYS WITH COD

The Norwegians are the experts of the world in dealing with cod. Here are some, but not all of the things they do.

FRESH COD, NORWEGIAN STYLE. The day which I spent with Professor Fægri in Bergen included a demonstration of how fresh cod is prepared and cooked there.

At 08.15 the Professor was in the fish market, examining the cod and saithe which were swimming about in the fishmonger's tank. Some of the cod had recently spawned and were deemed unsuitable because of their 'spent' condition. But there was one fine seaweed-coloured specimen which swam with vigour and was fat round the neck, as a cod should be. He chose this and the fishmonger netted it. It weighed 3·7 kg (8 lb), just about right for 6 people. It was immediately killed and gutted and the tail fin cut off, to facilitate bleeding. The Professor had correctly foreseen that it would have no roe but a large liver. This was kept separately. The Professor then took the fish to the Botanical Museum, where he had work to do, and allowed it to 'rest' for a full hour, explaining that this repose was a desirable element in its preparation. At 10.00 he laid it on its back and cut it into steaks about 1½ cm across, not quite completing each cut, so that the fish would be easier to carry. The fish was then left under cold running water, to keep its temperature down and to leach out the remaining blood, until the time came (14.30) to take it home.

At home, salted water (3 per cent salt, like sea water) was brought to the boil and half the cod steaks, now completely severed from each other, were put in. Once the water came back to the boil, the pot was removed from the fire. Five or six minutes later, the cod was judged to be ready and was served with floury boiled potatoes and melted butter. The liver, cut in pieces, had meanwhile been poached for a shorter time in a half-and-half mixture of vinegar and water, with a couple of bay leaves and some whole peppercorns. It was served at the same time.

While we ate the first batch of cod steaks, the remaining ones were made ready in the same way, to provide second helpings. The fish was snow-white, tender and delicious. The Professor pointed out that its subtle flavour would be obscured by the addition of almost any second vegetable; he preferred to take a little lettuce afterwards. He also observed that he had not salted the fish at all before cooking it; and that if he had had some whey he would have cooked the cod in that instead of water, thus making the fish even whiter and firmer. In the north they would actually prefer cod a day old but cooked in whey to fresher cod cooked in water.

I have never eaten cod so good.

PERSETORSK (pressed cod). A live cod is bought, killed and gutted. The upper part of its body, above the backbone, is cut off, split open, lightly salted and left under a weighted board, the weight being 2 kg (4 lb), for 24 hours before being skinned and cooked as described above.

ROKERUMPE (smoked tail end of cod). The tail end of a fresh cod is lightly salted and left, but not under pressure, for 24 hours, then cold-smoked for a few hours, preferably over smouldering juniper wood. It should then rest for a day or so on the cellar or larder floor. After this, it is skinned and put in a baking dish, resting on a little butter, basted with plenty of sour cream and accompanied by fresh carrots split lengthways. The fish is cooked in the baking oven at a fairly low temperature (325° F. gas 3) for about one hour. The juices which exude will combine with the butter and sour cream to provide the sauce. This is a more delicate dish than can be made with commercially smoked cod, which has been split.

KLIPPFISK is cleaned cod – or saithe, or ling, or cusk – which has been both salted and dried. Klippe means rock; on the rocks being where the fish were laid out to dry. STOKFISK (or TORRFISK) is the same, except that the fish have only been dried, not salted. These products, which are not exclusive to Norway, have been described in the catalogue (page 54).

LUTEFISK is stockfish prepared in a special way. At first sight or smell, it is a puzzling phenomenon. The stockfish is soaked in water, then in a solution of lye for a couple of days, and finally rinsed in running fresh water before being cooked. The process is only carried out in Norway, Sweden and Finland. In these countries, but nowhere else (except among their emigrant communities), it is part of the Christmas tradition and much is made of it. Why, when stockfish can be reconstituted by simply soaking it in fresh water, do these northerners mess about with lye?

The answer is twofold. First, the lye helps to soften the flesh and assists the full penetration of it by the water. Secondly, in the days before re-frigeration was introduced, the process could only be carried out success-fully in a very cold climate, that is to say during the winter in the Nordic countries and at no time in countries further south. The explanation is neatly rounded off by pointing to the fact that in the Middle Ages lye was the all-purpose cleaning agent: that consignments of stockfish must have occasionally fallen from pack-horses on to dusty roads or into foul ditches; and that when these were cleaned with lye the beneficial effects would have become apparent.

It would seem to follow that if, say, the Portuguese had not been prevented by their warm climate from making lutefisk they would have done so. However, I am not so sure. The product has a slightly gelatinous feel to it and a distinctive taste which many who were not brought up on it find displeasing. When I ate lutefisk in an old Bergen restaurant, I found that it was served with a little jug of melted bacon fat, in which there were scraps of bacon, as well as with floury potatoes and a sort of dry pease pudding. The bacon fat, so it seemed to me, had the role of partly masking a flavour which need not have been there in the first place; for I could recall how delicious plain stockfish can be in the Netherlands (page 317).

ROGN, or roe, of cod is a delicacy. (See also page 308.) A Norwegian geologist who had visited the island of Hitra off the Norwegian coast told me that there, but nowhere else, he had met a dish called Rogn Vaffler. waffles made with mashed raw cod roe incorporated in the batter. He described it as interesting.

Fiskegrateng

Norwegian fish gratin   serves four

Here is one of those simple, family favourites, quite devoid of exotic ingredients and enjoyed by everybody. Marjory Bogstad, who left Scotland for Norway in 1945, has lived in many parts of the country. She acquired this recipe from a Norwegian lady who lived near Tromsø and who was a very good and economical cook.

poached, bone-free fish, such as cod or haddock, $\frac{1}{2}$ kg (1 lb)	grated cheese, mature cheddar or Gouda, 1 cup
butter, 40 g (1$\frac{1}{2}$ oz)	a pinch of pepper
flour, 2 tbs	a pinch of mixed herbs
fish stock or milk, 2$\frac{1}{2}$ dl ($\frac{1}{2}$ pint)	macaroni, cooked, 1 cup
eggs, 3, separated	breadcrumbs
	margarine

Grease a pyrex dish well. Make a fairly thick white sauce with the butter, flour and stock or milk, and let it simmer for 2 minutes. Remove it from the heat and add the yolks of the eggs, most of the grated cheese, the pepper, herbs and macaroni. Then mix in the flaked fish and fold in the whites of the eggs, beaten stiff.

Put this whole mixture in the pyrex dish and sprinkle it with the remaining grated cheese and the breadcrumbs. Dot some margarine on top. Bake the dish in a moderately hot oven (400 ° F, gas 6) for 15 minutes, then reduce the heat to moderate (355 ° F, gas 4) and leave it for another half hour, until well risen and brown on top.

20. Recipes from Denmark

The old fish market in Copenhagen was on the Gammelstrand, where a stocky statue of a lady fishmonger stands on the canal bank, impassively eyeing a pair of famous fish restaurants, Krøg's and the Fiskehuset. These are sempiternal and dignified institutions, where the menus include some of the best-known Danish fish dishes but also reflect a certain deference to the French tradition. This used to be prominent in the cuisine of wealthy Danish households and in Danish cookery books, but it never prevailed in Denmark generally. There is a real wealth of traditional and authentic Danish dishes, a few of which appear in some of the classical Danish cookery books, such as those of Fru Mangor (1837 onwards), but of which no real survey existed before Westergaard's masterly compendium of local Danish recipes (1974).

These traditional recipes include many for seafood. The Danes rank second to the Norwegians, among the peoples of Europe, in consumption of fish per capita. They exploit both the Baltic and the North Sea. They have been inventive and adaptive both in curing fish and in cooking it. Like the Dutch, they had an important trade with the Orient, which accounts for their use of curry (in rather a mild form – a Danish sea captain told me that whenever he put into Grimsby he would buy the stronger curry powder prepared for the English market). However, they have their own condiments. A Danish fishmonger always has handy a bucket of fiskesennep, fish mustard – a mixture of coarsely ground yellow and brown mustard seeds with vinegar and salt – from which most customers elect to have a ladleful. Danish vinegar, by the way, is a mild one, made from molasses. It can be had from establishments like the Danish Food Centre in London.

The oysters (a royal monopoly since the seventeenth century) and mussels of Limfjord are famous, but there are relatively few Danish recipes for molluscs, or indeed for crustaceans. The Danes prefer to eat their lobster *au naturel*; and the same applies to the delicious little shrimp which are often called Tivoli prawns after the Copenhagen pleasure gardens of that name.

Esbjerg is the major fishing port on the west coast; but Skagen, at the northern tip of Denmark. where the Skagerrak and the Kattegat meet (and can usually be seen to meet, for the collision of the two bodies of water is apt to throw up a curtain of spray), is prettier and more interesting and represents an admirable combination of old traditions and new technology. The enchanting Indian-red fish warehouses which were designed by Thorvald Bindesbøll in the last century still stand, but around them is a huge and orderly complex of fishing harbours, spotless auction halls and processing plants, all planned with practicality and harmony. It was there that I discovered how high plaice ranks in Danish estimation (Skagen folk always buy it alive) and there, in a community which has been for centuries and still is devoted to fishing, that I found many of the most interesting Danish recipes, well worth setting down beside the better-known ones of South Jutland and Zealand.

Sødsuppe

A sweet fruit-soup with cod

Danes enjoy soups made with fruit and sago or tapioca, which may be served as the last course. In Vendsyssel, north of Limfjord, there is an exotic version which incorporates cod, and which is thought suitable for celebrating weddings. But it can be used as an everyday dish. Indeed a Danish friend of mine had it literally every day, with either sago or oatmeal.

Bring a litre of fresh fruit juice, including redcurrant juice if possible, to a gentle boil and cook a handful of sago or tapioca or oatmeal in it. Add strips of lemon peel and a little cinnamon; raisins and prunes, previously soaked; and small pieces of boiled cod. When all is hot, serve it.

Stegte Sild i Marinade

Fried, marinated herring   serves four

Most countries where herring is eaten have recipes of this type. The one given here is a classic element in Danish cookery.

herrings, 4, previously fried in margarine	**sugar, 3 tbs**
	freshly ground pepper
Danish (page 385) or other mild vinegar, 2 dl (⅓ pint)	**1 large or 2 smaller onions**
	a few cloves (optional)

Lightly salt your cold, fried herrings. Combine vinegar, sugar and pepper with 3 tablespoonfuls of water, bring quickly to the boil, then allow to cool. Pour this marinade over the fish. If it does not cover them, turn or baste them later. Add also the sliced onions and (optional) cloves.

This dish is at its best if kept chilled overnight and eaten next day. Serve it on buttered rye or wholemeal bread, with beer. Don't forget to eat the onions!

Sol over Gudhjelm

A Bornholm smørrebrød of hot-smoked Baltic herring and raw egg yolk

The egg yolk is the sun (sol); and Gudhjelm (God's home) is a picturesque village on the east coast of Bornholm.

The hot-smoked herring prepared in the island are quite delicious. They are cured in the summer only, over fires of alder wood (*Alnus glutinosa*). It happened that I first met them in a house in Copenhagen which was full of beautiful things from Thailand; and it was perhaps under this influence that I compared the skin of the smoked herring to crinkled gold-leaf.

The herring may be eaten just as they are. But it is enjoyable and rewarding to prepare them according to this traditional recipe. You will need a buttered slice of rye bread for each herring.

Set the herring on its back, remove head and tail, prise the body gently apart and lift out the backbone. Next, disengage the bony edges from each side. Eat them as you do so – the bones are soft enough. Then lift off the two fillets. A little fat will be left adhering to the skin. Scrape this off and eat it too. (Some eat the skin as well.) Now dispose the fillets along the slice of buttered bread. For each pair of fillets have ready one egg yolk, which is to be perched on top of them. The yolk will stay in place if an onion ring is put into position to receive it. But it is just as good to leave the egg yolk in the half eggshell and sit this up between the fillets. On each end of the smørrebrød place garnishing such as finely sliced radish, chopped chives and chopped onion. When you are ready to eat, break the egg yolk so that it runs up and down the length of the fillet – a sort of sun-burst!

Glansfisk i Karry

Curried opah

Skagen is one port where the rare opah (page 82) is landed from time to time. This recipe is based on that given by the Danish author Mogens Brandt, who lived there, in his charming booklet *Skagen og Fisk*.

Buy a large fillet of opah and cut it into slices 1 cm thick. Toss these in seasoned flour. Briefly fry a teaspoonful (or more, if you wish) of strong curry powder in plenty of butter in a pan; and brown the slices of fish in this. Next, take a well-buttered oven dish and lay in it a bed of chopped shallots which have been cooked until they are transparent. Place the pieces of fish on this bed and garnish them with whole peeled tomatoes.

Stir some double cream into the juices in the frying pan, to make a sauce. Pour this over the fish and place the whole dish in the oven, at a low heat, for 10 minutes. Serve with rice, chutney and Indonesian prawn crackers.

Hornfisk Stegt som Kylling

Garfish cooked like chicken   serves four

The Danes eat a lot of garfish (page 77). They make soups of it or fry the fillets or curry them. This recipe provides an interesting alternative.

garfish, 4, of about 225 g (¼ lb) each	**flour, 1 tbs**
a sprig of parsley, chopped	**single cream, 4 tbs**
butter, 70 g (2½ oz)	**chicken stock, 4 tbs**

Clean the fish and lift the pair of long fillets from each, removing the bones as you do so. Sprinkle the parsley and tiny dabs of butter on each fillet, then roll it up and secure it with a toothpick.

Heat the remaining butter in a pan until brown, then add the rolled fillets and turn them until golden brown all over. Let them simmer, covered, for 5 more minutes, then remove them and keep them hot. Meanwhile thicken the pan juices with the flour. Stir in the cream and chicken stock and cook this sauce as usual. Serve it, and boiled potatoes, with the garfish 'chickens'.

Grønsaltet Kuller

'Green-salted' haddock

Clean your haddock, salt it all over and leave it for 12 hours or so. Then give it a quick rinse (no soaking in fresh water or anything like that), poach it and serve it with potatoes, carrots, small onions, chopped or sliced hard-boiled egg and melted butter.

This is much better than ordinary haddock. The carrots are important; their sweet taste complements the somewhat salty fish.

Plukfisk

This is an excellent way of using up bits of boiled white fish. You will also need some new potatoes. cooked and peeled. or left-over larger ones. cut up.

Flake the cooked fish. Make a white sauce according to your usual method, enough to match the quantity of fish and potato, and stir into it as much as you like of the special Danish fish mustard, fiskesennep (page 385), or other coarse mustard. Combine fish, potatoes and sauce, heat through and serve.

Fru Mangor, the classic nineteenth-century Danish cookery writer, gives a version in which white bread is used instead of potato, and a little nutmeg is added to the sauce rather than a lot of mustard.

Maskintorsk

'Machine' cod serves four

The baffling title of this recipe simply indicates the use of a fireproof dish, such as an enamelled iron pot, which device struck Danes of earlier times as constituting a piece of machinery. The instructions given here are an adaptation of those used by Fru Ingeborg Østergaard at her hotel in Skagen.

Butter a fireproof dish 10 cm (4 inches) deep. Cut a bunch of celery into sections, parboil them, drain them and refresh them under cold water. Finely chop a large onion and let it turn transparent in hot butter. Cut ¾ kg (1½ lb) fillets of cod into serving portions. Then fill the dish with these ingredients in layers, starting and ending with celery. Sprinkle toasted and seasoned breadcrumbs on top, sparingly, and knobs of butter, generously. Pour over all 2 dl (⅓ pint) white wine and 1 tbs brandy, then cook in a moderate oven (355° F. gas 4) for 30 minutes and finish off under the grill.

Æbletorsk

Cod with apple

This recipe, from the island of Lyø in South Jutland, is for codling (one per person). But it can be applied successfully to cod steaks.

Clean the codlings and remove their heads and tails. Dredge them in seasoned flour and pan-fry them in butter or oil, adding more as it is needed. When they are almost cooked, add a handful or two of pieces of cooking apple, cored and cut into wedges but not peeled. Cover the pan and leave everything to simmer for 2 or 3 minutes, until the apple is soft.

Kogt Torsk med Smør og Sennep

Poached cod with butter and mustard

This is the standard Danish way of preparing pieces of a large cod. Poach them with a suppevisk (a bouquet of the leaves of parsley, celery and leek) and serve them with boiled potatoes and fiskesennep, the special Danish fish mustard described on page 385, or other coarse mustard.

The traditional accompaniments are chopped hard-boiled eggs, sliced beetroot, shredded horseradish and capers (cf. the accompaniments for Klipfisk, page 390).

This is simple and good. Let a dab of butter melt over each piece of cod, then dip it in the fiskesennep and eat it.

Klipfisk

Danish treatment of salted, dried cod

The shrine, in Copenhagen, to which lovers of klipfisk repair is the Tivoli Hallen, one of those basement restaurants which used to abound in the city and of which several survive in something like their state of fifty years ago. One of the waiters at the Tivoli Hallen has that number of years' service; and the restaurant itself dates from 1791, so I need not fear, in writing about it, that it will have disappeared before my readers arrive there.

The menu says: 'Klipfisk – vor Specialitet – 40 minuten'. But they first need a day and a half, as the lady chef explained, for desalting the klipfisk in three successive changes of water.

The klipfisk is then poached and served with various accompaniments. There is a tray bearing four garnishes: slices of hard-boiled egg; grated strips of horseradish; sliced beetroot; and of course fiskesennep, the Danish fish mustard described on page 385. Diced cooked bacon used to be a fifth element, but it was dropped in mid century.

There is also a bowl of boiled potatoes. There is melted butter, golden yellow. And there is a large, very large, quantity of mustard sauce. This is made by using butter, flour, milk and fish bouillon to create a white sauce into which, after it has come to the boil, fiskesennep is stirred.

Rødspætter Skawbo

Plaice with cranberry sauce

In Skagen they have the pleasant habit of serving fried plaice, or other fried fish, with a sauce or jam made from the red berries called tranebær, which are small cranberries. They prefer these to the larger American cranberry, but accept the latter as a substitute in summer when the real tranebær is scarce.

The plaice are cleaned and cut across into sections about 4 cm wide before being fried. Boiled potatoes with brown melted butter accompany the dish.

Fiskerens Rødspætter

Fishermen's plaice

A friend who has often been to sea with fishermen from Esbjerg told me how they deal with freshly caught plaice; 'a man's way of cooking'.

Gut a plaice of medium size and remove the skin from the back only. Put it in cold sea water to cover and bring this to the boil over a moderate flame. Then turn off the heat and leave it, covered, for 10 minutes. Drain the fish and serve it with potatoes, melted butter and parsley.

Gravad Makrel

Clean some plump, really fresh mackerel, but do not wash them. Bone them and lift the two fillets from each, wiping them dry. Sprinkle each fillet on both sides with a mixture of: ¾ heaped tbs granulated sugar; 1 heaped tbs salt; and some freshly ground white pepper. Next, cover the fillets with chopped dill; place them together in pairs, head to tail; lay them on a bed of dill sprigs and cover them with a further layer of dill. This done, let them rest under light pressure, for example a wooden board with ½ kg (1 lb) weight on it, in the refrigerator for at least 12 hours.

To serve, scrape the dill and seasonings off the fillets and cut them into thin slices, using a very sharp knife and starting at the tail, as you would with smoked salmon. Lay the cut slices on a platter and sprinkle them with freshly chopped dill. The quality of this dish falls short of Gravlax (page 370), but not as far short as you might expect. It is delicious.*

Ræset Makrel

Dried and fried mackerel

This is a recipe with two great advantages. It enables anyone to make practical use of the ancient northern tradition of wind-drying fish. And it makes mackerel both less oily and more tasty.

All you need are some small mackerel, salt and a dry breeze. Behead the mackerel, gut them and split them open, leaving the tails on. Salt them lightly and leave them for 2 hours. Then hang them up by the tails to dry in the wind, but out of the sun, for 2 days (3 for larger fish).

The product can be frozen for later use. Whenever you are ready to eat them, cut the dried mackerel across into 4 or 5 sections each and pan-fry these for a few minutes only. They will cook very quickly. Fru Nielsen of Skagen, who demonstrated the dish to me, recommends using a half-and-half mixture of margarine and lard. Her husband pointed out, as we ate, a third advantage of this cure. All the bones except the backbone itself become edible; indeed eating them and the skin adds to the pleasure.

* I found an echo of this recipe in the Skibereen area of Ireland; a region which has absorbed a number of alien ideas on cookery, and which used to have the only shop in the world for second-hand coffins (a result of the sinking of the *Lusitania*, the American relations of whose victims sent over American-style coffins to replace the hundreds which had been made locally). The herbs used for cured Carrigillihy mackerel are bog myrtle and fennel. Brown sugar and black pepper are employed instead of white. And the fish 'are pressed between two congruent pieces of driftwood'.

DANISH WAYS WITH FRESH EEL

These are manifold. Erik Westergaard's survey of local cookery in Denmark contains dozens of traditional recipes, including various forms of Potteål (jellied eel) and the extraordinary Ålebrød from the Limfjord area (a kind of loaf baked with an eel coiled on top of the dough).

The standard preparation is **Stegt Ål med Stuvede Kartofler**, sections of eel simply fried (but keep pouring away the fat, since the eel supplies its own and the dish tends to be too rich) and served with potatoes in a white sauce. In the country districts one arranges the sections of backbone round the edge of one's plate as one eats. It is almost obligatory to complete one circle; meritorious to make two; and outstanding to finish a third circle. The bill can be computed by the number of circles on each plate.

However, I recommend for small eels the **Ålesuppe** (eel soup) from south Jutland, which is clearly related to Hamburg eel soup (page 323). Cut the prepared eels into pieces 3 cm long and cook these in water with carrots and leeks, celeriac if available, and the bone from a smoked ham (or other meat bone). Allow 20 to 25 minutes for the cooking. For the last 15 minutes add some soaked prunes and pieces of cooking apple. Season to taste with salt, sugar and Danish vinegar (page 385).

A fine large eel may be used for a dish known as **Åleruggepoelse** (eel roll) from east Denmark. The eel should weigh about 2 kg (4¼ lb). Use only the thickest two thirds of it; and cut this long section off the bone into two fillets. Season these with salt, pepper and allspice, then roll each up and wrap it in a piece of gauze to hold the shape. Boil the rolls gently for 10 minutes in fish stock (usually prepared from the discarded parts of the eel), then take them out and let them cool under a weighted wooden board. They may subsequently be sliced, cold, and used for Danish open sandwiches or in a salad.

Ristet Roget Ål med Roræg

Smoked eel with egg

This is a good combination, which is also found in southern Sweden. Roast sections of smoked eel and serve them not with 'scrambled' egg (the usual translation) but with a scrambled egg mixture which has been cooked, undisturbed, in a bain-marie, and which is then cut into slices.

Fiskefrikadeller

Danish fish balls   serves six

The Danes are great ones for meat balls (frikadeller) and for fish balls too. This recipe comes from Karina Sterry of Copenhagen and is suitable for any white fish such as cod, haddock or hake. The fish balls will in any event be deliciously light, but the use of whiting will make them even more so.

white fish meat, $\frac{3}{4}$ kg (1$\frac{1}{2}$ lb)   *optional additions*
butter, 100 g (3$\frac{1}{2}$ oz)   tomato purée, 1 tbs
cornflour, 4 tbs   a little nutmeg
salt, 2 tsp   chopped chives
freshly ground pepper   shredded onion (but only a little)
milk, $\frac{3}{4}$ litre (1$\frac{1}{2}$ pint)
eggs, 4

Mince the fish, which should be free of bone and skin, half a dozen times, combining the butter, cornflour, seasoning and any or all of the optional ingredients with it as you do so. Next, add the milk, little by little, stirring vigorously. Then stir in the eggs. The mixture should now have a firm consistency. Make it into 'balls' by simply scooping up a tablespoonful at a time and fry these in butter or margarine for 5 minutes on each side. Their shape will in fact be more like that of a rissole than a true ball.

In South Jutland housewives traditionally incorporate a little smoked pork in their fish balls and use mashed potato instead of cornflour. The balls may also be made with other kinds of seafood. There is even a recipe for Blækesprutterkroketter. similar confections made with minced octopus! But, if you are not using fresh cooked fish, I recommend using cooked Klipfisk (page 390), which produces excellent frikadeller with a strong flavour.

21. Recipes from Iceland, the Faroes and Greenland

Iceland held surprises for me. The Icelanders, who have recently assumed full title to the world's richest cod fishing grounds, do not themselves eat much cod. They prefer haddock. Reykjavik, the capital, has neither a fish market nor the expected cluster of fish restaurants. 'Where would you go to have a good fish dish?' we asked. 'Home,' they all said.

The fact that so little of the land can be cultivated, most of it being lava fields or glaciers, has been a limiting factor in Icelandic cookery. So has the long dark winter. There are many foods which the Icelanders cannot raise or grow. But they do have their own excellent lamb and dairy products, including the unique and delicious skyr (see page 398). These are not irrelevant to my theme, for mutton fat (see page 399) is an important ingredient in many fish dishes; and whey, which the fortunate Icelanders can buy in cartons at any grocery store, is a traditional preservative for fish as well as for other foods. The art of preserving food for the winter was formerly of great importance. The þorri, or month of sour things, was a period in mid winter when variously preserved foods were eaten in large quantities at special gatherings.

The older Icelandic cookery books reflect all this, but also exhibit marked Scandinavian, especially Danish, influences. One of the most charming was published in 1800 at Leirárgörðum, where Magnus Stephensen, a judge who was bent on 'improving' his countrymen, had set up a printing press. It seems that he himself wrote the book, while stormbound in Norway, but that he thought it unsuitable for a cookery book to come out under a man's name and therefore persuaded his sister-in-law, Marta Maria Stephensen, to lend her name to it. However, the greatest Icelandic cookery writer, Helga Sigurðardóttir, was a real woman writer and one in whom a romantic and classical beauty was united with unremitting industry. Her score of books constitute the best source material on traditional Icelandic cookery and its development from the 1920s to the 1950s. Several of the Icelandic recipes which follow are based on her writings.

Faroese and Greenlandic recipes follow those from Iceland. It would have been interesting to present Shetland in this same group of northern islands, but convention prevails and it will be found under Scotland.

THE GREAT DRIED COD'S HEAD CONTROVERSY

In the old days Icelanders not only ate cods' heads fresh, a common practice in communities where people are really knowledgeable about fish, but also dried them for later consumption. Ponies would carry the cods' heads inland, often taking several days for the round trip. Each carried 120; 60 on each side, 'sticking out into the air like the wings of a small Icelandic Pegasus'. The custom gradually died out; but in 1914 the publication of an old photograph showing ponies thus laden provoked a retrospective attack on it by Tryggvi Gunnarsson, the prominent business-man and banker whose portrait, bland but uncompromising, adorns the Icelandic 100 krónur notes now current.

Gunnarsson applied the criteria of an economist. Taking the ex-warehouse cost of the dried heads, and adding the expenditure on the ponies and the men who guided each convoy, he calculated that the cost of one head, delivered to the inland farmhouse where it would be eaten, had been 7·8 aurar. It would then take an expert $7\frac{1}{2}$ minutes to dissect each head, which would yield on average a mere 67 grams of edible matter. Looked at in this light, the procedure could be seen to be absurdly uneconomical and deserving of condemnation.

Shock waves must have run right through Iceland when this polemic against a cherished tradition was published. However, eleven years passed before Guðmundur Finnbogason, Director of the National Library, was ready to deliver the counter-attack. It was a massive one, in which he deployed mathematical, social, political, moral, linguistic, historical and hygienic arguments in favour of the dried cods' heads. They had been eaten for as long as Iceland had been inhabited. The old belief that if you ate another creature's head your own became more intelligent was probably well founded. He would welcome a trial in which half of a school-class would eat cods' heads while the other half abstained; and was confident that corroboration would emerge.

Finnbogason pointed out that the dictionary of Sigfús Blöndal con-tained 150 different words for parts of the cod's head, illustrated by the great fish expert Bjarni Sæmundsson. (One such drawing is on page 12.) Moreover, one of the greatest American authorities on health had declared that eating hard things improved the teeth. One could say that cods' heads had been Iceland's dentists for centuries, which was a strong economic argument in their favour, quite apart from considerations of human suffering and aesthetics. Besides, the etiquette involved in eating a dried cod's head, which required that the less good parts be eaten first, had inculcated in the population a desirable spirit of perseverance.

In conclusion, Finnbogason invited Icelanders to compare their staple rye bread with cods' heads. What had the eating of rye bread brought about? What virtues had it prompted, with what words had it enriched the language? The answers must be nothing and none. 'Why, anyone was capable, from the very outset, without any instruction and with his eyes closed, of stuffing rye bread into his mouth.' (Game, set and match to Finnbogason.)

SOME ICELANDIC SEAFOOD SPECIALITIES

H Á K A R L is the strangest of the lot. Icelanders have for long pursued the huge Greenland shark, *Somniosus microcephalus*, for the sake of its liver, which is so large that it may yield 3 barrels of oil. The skin of the shark could also be used for making boots and shoes. But the mountain of flesh could not be utilized so readily, since it contained cyanic acid; to consume which is likely to bring on a disagreeable death. It was discovered, however, that if the flesh was buried, whether in the cow-byre or in a gravel bed, and allowed to ferment, the acid was leached out and the flesh became safe to eat. Hákarl is this fermented shark-flesh. It has a very strong and unpleasant smell, but its taste, if it is eaten in thin slivers with aquavit to wash it down, is not so bad. It is bought in smallish pieces, shaped like a side of bacon, with the crinkled black skin looking like a miniature piece of one of the Icelandic lava beds.

Hákarl can be made into H Á K A R L S S T A P P A by picking off the flesh, boiling it, letting it drain overnight and then mashing it up with sour butter or rancid mutton fat. It can be eaten hot; or cold, on bread (canapés of mashed fermented Greenland shark and rancid mutton fat!).

S U N D M A G I are fish sounds, or air bladders, recipes for which abound in old English and Scottish cookery books. Icelanders fry them, whether they are using fresh sounds or dried ones, soaked and drained.

R I K L I N G U R are dried strips of halibut flesh. Like other H A R Ð F I S K U R (dried fish), they are eaten raw, with a little butter.

Lúðusúpa

Halibut soup   serves six

Before publishing her comprehensive cookery book *Matur og Drykkur*, Helga Sigurðardóttir had produced numerous specialized books, such as *160 Fiskréttir* (160 Fish Dishes), which came out in 1939. It is interesting to compare the fish recipes in that work with those in the later one. For this famous Icelandic soup I have followed the earlier version, but incorporated some refinements from the other.

halibut, 1½ kg (3 lb), cleaned
weight
water, 1½ litres (3 pints); vinegar,
2 tbs; salt, 2 tsp; bay leaves, 2
melted butter, 60 g (2 oz)

flour, 60 g (2 oz)
prunes, 20 (or rhubarb, 3 sticks)
juice of ½ lemon
an egg, with 1 tsp sugar stirred
into it

Cut the halibut up into suitable pieces. Bring the water, with the vinegar, salt and bay leaves, to the boil. Add the fish and remove scum when the water comes back to the boil. Continue simmering the fish until the flesh is 'loosened from the bones'. Then strain most of the broth into a second cooking pot, leaving just enough with the fish to keep it hot.

Bring the broth in the second pot back to a gentle boil. Meanwhile, stir the flour into the melted butter and add it, little by little, to the broth, stirring continuously. Let the broth simmer for another 5 to 10 minutes.

The prunes should have been soaked in water for a while and then heated almost to boiling point, with the addition of some slivers of lemon peel (subsequently discarded). If rhubarb, a common food in Iceland, is used instead, it should first be cut into sections of about 3 cm and cooked in a very small quantity of water, with a little sugar, until just tender.

Add the hot prunes or rhubarb, with their juices, to the broth. Pour in the lemon juice. After a minute or two, remove the pot from the fire and stir in the egg. Serve the soup at once, accompanied by the pieces of fish and a dish of potatoes garnished with chopped parsley.

Saltsíld í Kryddlegi með Rúgbrauði

Salted and pickled herring with dark rye bread

In the days when herring was abundant, Siglufjörður on the northern coast of Iceland was a very busy centre for the salting of herring. The cleaned fish would be packed in salt in barrels and kept thus until the flesh came easily off the bone, when they could be eaten.

However, the salted herrings are often marinated before being eaten. Alda Möller, a food technologist from the north, told me that her family would simply put them into a solution of vinegar with some sugar, bay leaves and pickling spices (sildarkrydd, special pickling spices for herring, can be bought in Iceland, but ordinary ones will do). No onion; Icelandic tradition and technical knowledge alike are against including it. It adds nothing to the marinade and itself suffers from being in it. However, fresh onion rings are added when the fish is served.

The accompaniment is dark rye bread with the excellent Icelandic butter. The bread absorbs much of the strong taste of the herring, so that what you eat next will not have an unwanted legacy of herring taste.

Síld með Súrum Rjóma og Graslauk

Salted or spiced herring in sour cream with chives   serves four

fillets of salted or spiced herring   **vinegar, 1 tbs**
  (saltsíld or kryddsíld), 4   **sugar, 1 tbs**
sour cream or skyr (see below),   **chopped chives, 2 tbs**
  2 dl (⅓ pint)

Desalt or drain the herring fillets, depending on which kind you are using. Cut them across into fairly thin slices.

Beat the sour cream and season it with the vinegar and sugar (of which you may use less or more according to taste). Add the chopped chives.

Arrange the herring slices in a dish, so that they are not touching each other. Pour the sour cream mixture over them and wait for 3 or 4 hours before serving the dish. It can be used as part of a cold buffet, or served as a main dish with hot boiled potatoes.

Now a word about skyr. This is something peculiar to Iceland. In the form in which it is now available, in little plastic tubs, it seems like a rather solid and sour yoghourt. It is made from skimmed milk, to which special fermenting agents (rennin and certain bacteria) are added. These curdle the milk. The curds become the skyr and the whey is put to other uses, mainly in preserving foods.

Skyr is served as a dessert. Much is made of the fact that it is full of nutrients but low in calories. However, the benefit of this is lost, much to the consumer's pleasure, by adding sugar and single cream to it. It is an absolutely delicious dessert. However, as soon as I had tasted it, I thought that it must have some use in fish cookery. I asked many Icelanders and they all said no. Then, in the 1800 cookery book referred to on page 394, I found a reference to making an inexpensive fish soup for the servants and found that this incorporated skyr. The skyr of those days was rather different – more of a solid curd which had to be diluted with milk or milk and water before use – but the principle was the same. Triumphant to find myself proved right, I renewed my questioning and found that skyr could also be used instead of sour cream in this herring recipe, with only one difference, that the herring should marinate in the skyr overnight.

Icelanders will tell you of friends from abroad who have gone off with some fresh skyr, hoping to use it as a 'starter' for making their own at home; but that all such efforts have failed. A pity. And skyr cannot be exported, since it only keeps for two days or so. The moral, of course, is that one should pay frequent visits to Iceland.

Soðin Ýsa með Hrognum og Lifur

Poached haddock with its liver and roe   serves four

The way in which Icelanders prepare their favourite fish deserves attention, simple though it is. We start with a whole fish weighing about 2 kg (4 lb).

Cut off the head, tail and other fins. Gut the fish and scale it, making sure that the skin is quite clean. Reserve the liver and the roe, if there is a roe. Cut the fish crossways into sections about 3–4 cm thick. Rinse them, then put them in boiling water and let them simmer for about 10 minutes, or until the flesh is loosened from the bones. Meanwhile, poach the liver and roe separately. The liver will take less time than the fish.

Serve the fish at once when it is done, with the liver and roe, boiled potatoes and melted butter.

In former times, and even now in many Icelandic households, the melted butter would be replaced by rendered mutton fat. There are two kinds of this: hamsatólg, which is unprocessed, and tólg, which has been sieved to clean it. There is also a third possibility, derived from the delicious Icelandic smoked lamb. When this lamb is boiled, fat will congeal afterwards on top of the water. This can be saved and melted down for use later. The special flavour of the smoked lamb makes it a particularly good dressing. It is known as hangikjötsflot.

Ýsa með Sölvum

Haddock with dulse   serves six

haddock, already poached, 1 kg (2 lb)
roe of the haddock, already poached, ¼ kg (½ lb)
mayonnaise, the amount that you can make with 2 egg yolks
pickled beetroot, 60 g (2 oz)
pickled gherkins, 60 g (2 oz)
made mustard, 2–4 tsp
lemon juice, 2–3 tsp
small pastry cups (brauðkollur, bought ready-made in Iceland), 6
a handful of dulse, in the dried strips on sale at health stores

This is a cold supper meal. If you do not have the little pastry cups, you can use scooped-out tomatoes to replace them.

Cut the fish and roe into neat slices and arrange these round the edge of a serving platter. Strew the strips of dried dulse over them. In the middle of the platter arrange the pastry cups. Add to the mayonnaise the beetroot and gherkin, both diced; the mustard; and the lemon juice. Mix well, then pour the mixture into the pastry cups.

ICELANDIC WAYS WITH LUMPFISH

The official Icelandic name for lumpfish (page 142) is hrognkelsi, but the two names in common use are rauðmagi (red belly) for the male and grásleppa for the female. Kristín Guðmundsdóttir, who comes from the northern coast of Iceland, where the lumpfish are most plentiful, described for me how she prepared both male and female.

The female is less good to eat. In the early part of the year, before it is full of roe and its flesh has taken on a jelly-like consistency, it is turned into *Sigin Grásleppa*, a sort of cured or 'hung' lumpfish. Heads and tails are cut off, and the fish are gutted. They are then hung in a cool place until they turn yellowish in colour, presumably as a result of oxidization. Afterwards, they are scored with a knife and poached in salted water for 10 minutes before being eaten.

The male is used to make a dish called *Sodinn Raudmagi*, which simply means boiled male lumpfish. The cleaned fish, or their fillets, are put in boiling water, to which a couple of bay leaves and a little vinegar have been added, and poached for 10 minutes. The vinegar is important; and the fish are sprinkled with a little more vinegar when they are taken out to be served. They are accompanied by boiled potatoes and melted butter.

Rastefisk

The Faroese national fish dish

Small cod must be used for this preparation. Clean them and hang them in the fresh air for about 10 days. This will produce a slight degree of fermentation. (Do not try to do it in the summer, when the warmth would be too great.)

Then simply boil the fish in salt or salted water and serve it with a characteristic Faroese sauce, made as follows.

Take some gatnatolk (fat from around a sheep's kidney, as in the next recipe) and form it into a roll. Leave it to start fermenting, for at least a month. When you observe colonies of green fungus on it, it is ready. It is then melted in a pan with some butter to produce the sauce. (I once met a Faroese fishery expert who was studying in Denmark, where gatnatolk is not available. He experimented in substituting Danish blue cheese and found that the results were surprisingly close to the authentic version.)

Knettir

Faroese fish balls   serves eight

This highly traditional recipe, which is given in the Faroese cookery book by Oluva Skaale and Marius Johannesen (*Matur og matgerd*, 1974), was expounded to me as follows by Jon Olavur Joensen of Holte in the Faroes. He explained that fresh young cod are the best fish to use; but that whiting are also good and that a mixture of cod and haddock is satisfactory. The mutton fat to be used is gatnatolk, to be taken from around the sheep's kidney.

fish (see above), 1½ kg (3 lb)	**salt, 1½–2 tsp**
mutton fat (see above), ½ kg (1 lb)	**pepper, 1 tsp**
a medium onion	**cold water, 1 dl (7 tbs)**

The dish is to be eaten at midday, but the fish balls must be prepared on the previous evening. Clean the fish and separate the flesh from skin and bone. Then put it through the mincing machine with the mutton fat. Next, add the remaining ingredients and put all through the mincing machine again. Knead the result into knettir or balls – quite a large fistful for each, so that you finish up with 8 or 10. Leave the balls to rest overnight.

On the next day they are simply boiled in salted water for 20 minutes, then served with potatoes. Some Faroese offer fish mustard (Danish style – page 385) as an accompaniment; others prefer rhubarb jam.

Kaleragdlit Sulugssugutait Sernartume Kinitat

Marinated halibut fins

This recipe, from Caia Hansen's Greenland cookery manual, is a Greenlandic speciality. Greenlanders would use Greenland halibut (page 155), but ordinary halibut will do; and a fishmonger may well give you the desired pieces for nothing, if trimming fish for other customers.

Cut the edges off 2 large, cleaned halibut, making the cuts clear of the fins themselves. Rub the pieces with 60 g (2 oz) salt and leave them in a cold place (not above 5° C), covered up, for 1 to 2 days. Then rinse off the salt and put them in a marinade composed of 1 dl (7 tbs) vinegar, the same amount of water, 2 tbs sugar, 1 bay leaf and 4 whole peppercorns. Strew an onion, thinly sliced, on top and leave the fins in a cool place to absorb the marinade for 24 hours or so. Then serve them on bread and butter; or as a midday dish with boiled potatoes or potato salad. The fins, of course, have bones; and some people prefer to cut the flesh off the bones before the marinade stage.

22. Recipes from Canada

The origins of Canadian cookery are mostly to be found in Britain and in France. This is certainly true of the Maritime Provinces, although even there one finds, for example, German culinary traditions maintained as well. The local cookery book at Lunenburg is called *Dutch Oven*, Dutch being a corruption of Deutsch; a corruption in which the German families who established this neat town seem to have acquiesced, perhaps despairing of the linguistic ability of their British neighbours.

The pretty name Acadian is applied to that region in the Maritimes which was originally settled by the French, and is used also of their cookery. Despite the expulsion of these original settlers by the British, French cookery has survived in the area and is here exemplified by a recipe for Rappie pie (page 406). It is, however, in the Province of Quebec that French influences in the kitchen are most noticeable; and I give two recipes from that region.

In discussions about the origin of the whole spectrum of clam chowders, a matter also mentioned on page 423, it has been suggested to me that, if any one occurrence can be singled out as the starting point, it could well be the meeting of early French settlers, bringing with them their chaudières or iron cooking pots, and the Canadian Micmac Indians, who were partial to clams but had a primitive batterie de cuisine. Nicolas Denys, writing in 1672, said that they used for their main dishes a huge 'kettle' consisting of a hollowed-out section of tree-trunk, the water in which was heated by the insertion of a series of stones which had been made very hot in a fire. One can see what was likely to happen. And the Micmac did indeed take to the chaudière, while maintaining their own tradition by incising on the outside a pattern resembling the bark of a tree (see the drawing on page 410). And the settlers certainly took to eating the clams. It is all very suggestive; and the hypothesis lends added interest to the Micmac recipe for clam chowder given on page 406. However, the truth may be that clam chowders evolved separately in various places by the triple union of European utensils and know-how, local resources in the shape of the clams, and imported resources such as salt pork and dairy cattle.

Salt pork and, of course, salt cod played a very big role in the cookery of the early settlers; and the role continues to this day in places like

Newfoundland, much of which still wears a newly found and almost virginal aspect, and parts of Nova Scotia. Interesting echoes are found of medieval English dishes such as salt cod mashed with parsnip; and there is also much emphasis, in Newfoundland, on cod cheeks, 'tongues' (throat muscles) and other titbits familiar to all fishing communities.

Perhaps the most famous Newfoundland dish is Fish 'n Brewis. This consists of salt cod; hard bread (brewis, originally ship's biscuits which were soaked to make a porridge or 'brose' – whence comes the name); and 'scrunchions', which are little cubes of fat salt pork, fried until crisp. Another dish of the same genre appears in Nova Scotia under various names (Dutch Mess. House Bankin, Hugger-in-Buff), but always incorporates salt cod, potatoes, onion and scrunchions.

Our Canadian cook's tour starts with one old Newfoundland recipe, not easy to make nowadays, followed in compensation by a very simple one. Then, having sampled French dishes from Quebec, we have an interesting pair of Micmac recipes, an Acadian one from Prince Edward Island, and finally a brace each from Nova Scotia and New Brunswick.

Cod Sound Pie   serves eight

This was contributed by Mrs Stella Boyd of Summerford in Newfoundland to the excellent book *Fat-back and Molasses*, which was edited, printed and published by the family of a clergyman at St John's and is full of local colour as well as local recipes.

'This recipe came from Western Head, Notre Dame Bay, and may originally have come from our great great grandparents who came from England. It was always served for Christmas Eve Supper. The Sounds were brought from Labrador where our fathers fished in the summer months. The Sounds were salted down in wooden butter tubs . . . Today, where Sounds are available, the fifth generation of our family still has "Cod Sound Pie" on Christmas Eve and it really is a delicacy.'

salt cod sounds, 1 kg (2 lb)	molasses, ½ cup
hard bread (see above), 2 cakes	cinnamon, 1 tsp
salt pork, ¼ kg (½ lb)	spice, 1 tsp
raisins, 1 cup	clove, ½ tsp

'Soak sounds in cold water for 24 hours. Drain sounds, and cover with fresh cold water. Cook until tender. Chop in small pieces. Previously soak hard bread for 12 hours in cold water, break in small pieces after draining, and then add to tender Sounds. Cut salt pork in tiny squares, mix in raisins, molasses and spices and pour mixture over Sounds and hard bread. Place all in pan and bake for two hours in moderate oven (350° F).'

Mount Pearl Fish Loaf
serves four

Mount Pearl is in Newfoundland and it is in the cook book of the United Church Women of the First United Church of that good place that this recipe is to be found. It looks and is easy to make, and comes off well with any white fish. We have made it with conger eel.

cooked fish (see above), 2 cups
melted butter, 1 tbs
flour, 1 tbs
hot milk, 1 cup
salt and pepper

eggs, 2, beaten
soft breadcrumbs, 1 cup
hard-boiled egg, 1, chopped
pickled gherkin, chopped, 3 tbs
chopped parsley, 3 tbs

Add the flour to the melted butter and blend well. Then add the hot milk, little by little, stirring. Season and add the remaining ingredients. Mix well together and pour into a greased oblong baking tin, deep enough to give the mixture the form of a loaf. Place this in a bain-marie of simmering water and cook it thus in a moderate oven (355° F, gas 4) for 1 hour. The loaf may be served hot or cold.

Anguille au Vin Blanc
Eel with white wine
serves four

This French Canadian recipe, with its interesting use of lettuce, is attributed, in *L'Art Culinaire au pays des Bleuets et de la Ouananiche*, to an old fisherman.

an eel, weighing $\frac{3}{4}$–1 kg (1$\frac{1}{2}$–1$\frac{3}{4}$
    lb), skinned, cleaned and cut
    into sections
white wine, $\frac{1}{4}$–$\frac{1}{2}$ litre ($\frac{1}{2}$–1 pint)
large lettuce leaves, 12
butter, 100 g (3$\frac{1}{2}$ oz)

petits pois (small peas) with their
    juices, from a tin, about 275 g
    (10 oz)
fresh sage and mint
a bay leaf
flour, 1–1$\frac{1}{2}$ tbs

Put the pieces of eel in a casserole, with white wine to cover, and cook them for 15 minutes. Then transfer them, with what is left of the wine, to a heavy cooking pot. Put the lettuce leaves, torn into long strips, on top of them. Add the butter and the peas and set it all to simmer gently. Add enough sage and mint to flavour the dish, and the bay leaf. When the simmering has continued for 10 minutes, remove a little of the cooking liquid, let it cool slightly and blend it with the flour; then return it to the pot and stir it well in, to thicken the sauce. After another 5 minutes or so, serve.

Ragoût de Lotte

Angler-fish stew   serves six

French Canadians are more catholic than others in their choice of fish.
They eat eels and lampreys, for example, and also the delicious angler-fish
which is otherwise rejected by North Americans.

an angler-fish 'tail' (see page 161), weighing 1 kg (2 lb)	white wine, 1½ dl (¼ pint)
	Madeira, 1½ dl (¼ pint)
olive oil, 4 tbs	small shallots, 3, finely chopped
salt and pepper	tomato purée, 3 tbs
a pinch of cayenne pepper	soft breadcrumbs, if needed

Debone the 'tail' and cut it into 12 pieces. Heat the olive oil in a casserole
and add the pieces of fish and seasoning. Pour the wine and Madeira over
the fish. (If you lack Madeira, use more wine.) Add also the shallots and the
tomato purée.

Bring the contents of the casserole to a gentle boil and keep them
simmering for 20 minutes or a little longer. If the sauce seems too runny,
add breadcrumbs and continue cooking for another 3 minutes.

Namegoss-Mikwamika

Micmac sea-trout jelly

This recipe of the Micmac Indians in Nova Scotia has many uses. It comes
from the excellent collection in *Indian Recipes* by Bernard Assiniwi.

Method. Take 6 sea-trout heads and boil them in 7 cups water with 1½ tsp
salt for 90 minutes. Strain, and add to the strained liquid ½ cup minced,
fresh watercress and 2 tbs cucumber pulp (without seeds) and ¼ tsp freshly
ground pepper. You should have 4 cups.

Uses. Put the mixture in a mould and cool it until it is set into a firm jelly.
This can then be served as a side dish with baked sea-trout or other
seafood.

Use it as a glaze for poached fish, applying it just before it sets; or as an
aspic for any cold fish dish.

Or make *Gigo-Mikwamika*, which means fish poached in trout jelly.
All you have to do is calculate how many minutes your fish or pieces of fish
will need to simmer in order to be cooked through (cf. page 258). Let the
number of minutes be x. Then, after the trout heads have been simmering
for (90 − x) minutes, add the fish and let them simmer until the 90
minutes are up. Fish poached in this special court-bouillon will have a
delicious flavour; and you will still have your sea-trout jelly for use with
the fish or separately.

Micmac Kiniginige

Micmac clam chowder   serves eight

This recipe comes from the Restigouche Reserve in the Province of Quebec. It represents a traditional Micmac recipe which has undergone some modifications. If, as I suggested on page 402, one of the important points of origin for North American chowders was the encounter of the French settlers, armed with their chaudières, and the Micmac Indians, who ate the soft-shelled clams of their coast, this recipe may well represent what might be called one of the first editions of clam chowder. Like the preceding recipe, it comes from Bernard Assiniwi's collection.

soft-shelled clams, 32

lean salt pork, 2 slices cut into very thin strips

wild onions, 6 (or a slightly larger number of shallots)

butter, 40 g (1½ oz)

flour, 3 tbs

white cornflour, 3 tbs

water, 3 cups

cattail roots, (*Typha latifolia*, often called bulrush) 4, diced (or 4 diced potatoes)

salt, 3 tsp (they would have used salt made from the ashes of coltsfoot leaves, but sea salt will do)

freshly ground pepper, 2 pinches

finely chopped watercress, ¼ cup

Steam the clams open and remove the meats, reserving the juices.

Cook the pork in a pan, then add the chopped wild onions or shallots and sauté all together. Add the clam meats to the mixture. Heat the butter separately, mix in the flour and cook for a few minutes, gently. Then add this to the pan, followed by the reserved clam juices, the water, diced cattail roots or potatoes, salt and pepper. Simmer all this for 2 hours, stirring occasionally.

Finally, add the watercress, simmer for 5 minutes more and serve.

Rappie Pie (Rapure) with Clams   serves six

This is an Acadian dish which survives strongly in Prince Edward Island. I learned in Halifax that when students from P.E.I. come back for the start of the university term they will bring some rappie pie with them and offer portions to favoured professors and lecturers.

The secret of the dish is to extract all the liquid from potatoes and replace it by another liquid. Rappie pies can be made with meat or chicken, but there are grounds for thinking that the version with clams may be the earliest. The Acadians, confusingly, used the term 'grandes coques' for the soft-shelled clam (*Mya arenaria*, page 239), but it seems clear that this is the species which they used.

soft-shelled clams, 18–24	salt pork, 250 g ($\frac{1}{2}$ lb)
potatoes, 1$\frac{1}{2}$ kg (3 lb)	pepper to taste

Peel and grate the potatoes. Take a cup at a time and place it in a cheesecloth, which must then be twisted so as to wring out as much liquid as possible. Collect the liquid in a bowl, so that you can measure it; for you will later need the same quantity of clam juices and water. Put the wrung-out potato, which will seem like snow, into another bowl.

Steam the clams open. Reserve the juices and mince the meat.

Dice the salt pork finely and try it out in the bottom of an oven pan, until this is coated with melted fat. Then remove the pieces of salt pork. Meanwhile, add to the clam juices enough water to bring the volume up to that of the liquid extracted from the potatoes. Bring this mixture to the boil, then add the wrung-out potato to it, little by little. The potato will swell up as it absorbs its new liquid. When this operation is completed, place a layer of the potato in the bottom of the oven pan, cover this with minced clams, then another layer of potato and so on – the pie can have three layers or five. Season with pepper to taste, and sprinkle the little bits of salt pork over the top. Bake in a moderately hot oven (400° F, gas 6) for 20 minutes, then reduce the heat to moderate (355° F, gas 4) and continue to bake for another hour or so, when the top of the pie will be brown and crusty.

Nova Scotia Scallop Chowder   serves six

Digby in Nova Scotia is the main base for the Canadian scallop-fishing industry. Scallops are ideal material for a chowder, since the meat is very firm; and this recipe, which comes from Digby, is well calculated to preserve their flavour.

scallops, white meat only, 1 kg (2 lb)	small onions, 2, roughly chopped
	milk, 1$\frac{2}{3}$ litres (3 pints)
butter, 60 g (2 oz)	salt and pepper to taste
medium potatoes, 6, cubed	

Melt the butter in a frying pan and brown the scallop meats on both sides. Then take them out and cut them up into quite small pieces. Return these to the pan and brown them all over.

Meanwhile, cook the potatoes and onions in lightly salted water to cover, until they are done, but not too soft. Add the fried pieces of scallop, with the pan juices, milk and seasoning. Heat the chowder through, but without letting it come back to the boil. Serve it with crackers.

Grenadier Chowder

makes six cups or four bowls

The grenadier (page 72) is a fish which does not figure in traditional recipes. So when I heard from a marine biologist in New Brunswick that he had just returned from a conference in Halifax, Nova Scotia, at which a grenadier chowder had been served for lunch to the assembled experts, I hastened thither and discussed its confection with Cathy Sinott, the home economist who had made it. Her recipe, scaled down for home use, follows.

grenadier fillets, ½ kg (1 lb)
thinly sliced onion, 1 cup
cooking fat, 3 tbs
flour, 1 tbs
potatoes, peeled and cubed, 1 cup
celery, coarsely chopped, ½ cup
carrot, diced, ½ cup

bay leaf, ½
salt (1¼ tsp)
pepper, a pinch
milk, 2 cups
single (light) cream, ½ cup
sour cream, ½ cup

Cut the fillets in serving-size portions. Sauté the onion in the fat until it is transparent. Stir in the flour and gradually add 1 cup of water. Then add the potatoes, celery, carrot, bay leaf, salt and pepper. Cover and simmer for about 15 minutes or until the potatoes are almost tender. At this point, add the fish and simmer 5 minutes longer or until the fillets flake easily when tested with a fork. Add the milk and reheat without boiling. Combine the cream and the sour cream and add this mixture to the chowder. Again reheat without boiling. Finally, remove the ½ bay leaf (if you can find it!) and serve.

Smelts Amandine

serves six

The flavour of almonds goes as well with smelts as with trout.

fresh smelts, 1 kg (2 lb, about 36)
salt
flour, 4 tbs
eggs, 2, beaten

roast ground almonds, 200 g (7 oz)
butter, 120 g (4 oz), melted
lemon wedges

Remove the fin from the back of each smelt, and the five fins on its underside, by pulling them forward and away from the fish. Spread each fish out, opened out butterfly fashion and skin side up. Hit it with a flat heavy object along the back, in four or five places. Then turn it over and you will find that the backbone comes away easily, with the tail. Rinse and dry the fish, sprinkle them inside and out with salt, then fold them back into their original shape. Roll them in flour, shake them, dip them in the beaten egg and let any excess drain off. Then roll them in the ground almonds, and pat this last coating so that it sticks well.

Line a wide, shallow baking pan with foil, grease it and lay the fish in it, side by side. Pour the melted butter evenly over the fish and bake them in a hot oven (450° F, gas 8) for 10 minutes. Serve them at once, garnished with lemon wedges.

This dish has been associated with New Brunswick, but can be made wherever smelts (page 48) are to be had, on either side of the North Atlantic. The St John River shad in New Brunswick are also given an amandine treatment, but of a different nature. Almonds which have been blanched and slivered are cooked in butter until golden brown and then poured over the cooked fish as a dressing.

Salmon Steaks with Fiddleheads   serves four

New Brunswick is blessed with both salmon, thanks to skilful measures of conservation, and a good supply of the fiddlehead fern, *Pteretis nodulosa*. Fiddlehead is really the name for the young fronds, the whole plant being known as the ostrich fern. The tops of the fronds are tightly curled and resemble the end of a violin or fiddle. This unusual vegetable, which also grows in New England, and as far south as Virginia, is available in canned and frozen form; but the season for having it fresh is in May and June. After it has been cooked, it has a flavour reminiscent of asparagus, and goes very well with salmon.

fresh salmon steaks, 4, about 2 cm   **salt, 1 tsp**
(1 inch) thick   **additional flavouring, as desired**
olive or vegetable oil, ¼ cup   **fiddleheads, ½ kg (1 lb)**
vinegar, 1 tbs

The salmon steaks are to be barbecued over a charcoal fire. In preparation for this, grease the grid on which they will rest, and mix the olive oil, vinegar, salt and other flavouring (if and as desired) together. Grill the steaks for 10 to 15 minutes on each side, basting them regularly with the prepared dressing.

Meanwhile, poach or steam the fiddleheads until quite tender. They can be served with the salmon, just as they are; or they can be accompanied by a Hollandaise sauce (page 316) or a mousseline sauce (for which see your favourite French cookery book).

Haddock Chowder, Passamaquoddy Bay

The Centennial Food Guide, one of the best Canadian cookery books, reveals Dr Charles Best, co-discoverer of insulin, as the author of this recipe. The chowder is to be preceded by clams steamed in seaweed and eaten with melted butter and vinegar, 'on a clear September evening beside a towering driftwood fire on the beach at Passamaquoddy Bay, New Brunswick, at half-tide'. The haddock should if possible be freshly caught from the Bay of Fundy. Quantities are for eight at least.

1 haddock weighing 3 kg (6 lb) uncleaned	onions, 2, sliced
raw potato, cubed, 4 cups	milk, scalded, 4 cups
salt pork, diced, ½ cup	butter, 25 grams (1 oz)
	salt to taste

Remove head and tail from the haddock and gut it. Bring to the boil in a fish kettle enough water to cover the fish, then put the fish in (also the head, for additional flavour) and let it simmer for 25 minutes, until cooked through. Remove it, divest it of skin, rid it of bone and flake the flesh. Discard the head and strain the broth, of which you should have 2 cups or a little more. Add 2 cups of boiling water to this, followed by the cubed potatoes. Cook them until they are tender but not soft. Meanwhile, crisp the diced pork in a skillet, and then brown the onions in the hot fat.

Now add to the fish broth and potatoes the contents of the skillet, the flaked fish and the remaining ingredients. Heat almost to boiling point before serving. (Note, however, that the chowder will be even better if chilled and later reheated.) It is left to each person to add pepper.

'Pilot biscuits may be passed around – but the chowder is a meal in itself. Even so we look forward usually to the green-apple pie (made by a family expert) topped with a piece of old Canadian Cheddar which is our next course. The coffee is always made in open kettles over the fire and we are glad to sink back with our pottery mugs full to the brim with a satisfying brew to which salt spray and bits of charred driftwood have added a wonderful but indescribable flavour.' (Dr Best.)

A French seventeenth-century chaudière incised by Micmac Indians to resemble birch bark; from the Nova Scotia Museum.

23. Recipes from the United States — Part One, Northern New England

The eastern seaboard of the United States, from Maine to Georgia, is here divided into four parts. We start in New England, in the north.

Despite doubts about where the southern frontier of New England lies, it would seem natural to treat the whole of it together in the context of seafood cookery. However, the fish themselves recognize a sort of boundary line, corresponding to changes in water temperature, just south of Cape Cod, and it suits me to do the same. There is wealth enough of seafood in Maine and Massachusetts; or there should be.

I say 'should', bearing in mind that Maine, as Richard Saltonstall has put it, '. . . is the place for the sea farmer's wildest dreams to come true'. To expert eyes, its beautiful scenery of bays and islands provides a pattern of 'diverse marine ecosystems, with a stable and geologically ideal set of bottom characteristics, with wonderful water circulation, currents sweeping in continual new amounts of ocean nutrients', and so on. But the conservative attitude of Maine fishermen poses a problem. Remarking that 'the independent manner of these traditional citizens enthralls tourists', the State Planning Office have declared that it is also a major obstacle to the development of aquaculture.

As for Massachusetts, the 'sacred cod' which hangs in the State House, and is shown on the right, reminds us of past glories. But all is not well today.

David Boeri and James Gibson, in their book *Tell it Good-Bye, Kiddo'*, have described and analysed the decline of the offshore fisheries of New England in a vivid manner. 'Everything about the Boston Fish Pier brings back the memory of another era.' True; and in Gloucester, Provincetown, Marblehead, Wellfleet and many other once thriving fishing ports, one has the same impression of a great past from which a worthy present has not ensued.

Foreign competition on the fishing grounds is one reason for the decline. 'Our boys fish for dollars, but those Russians fish for protein,' as one official said to me. Inflexibility in the fishing trade may be another. But a third may be that almost ubiquitous problem, the reluctance of consumers to eat unfamiliar kinds of seafood.

The New England recipes which I offer are mostly traditional ones, of interest to readers elsewhere. New Englanders themselves are invited to look in the recipe sections for the European countries, and to reflect on the popularity of eels in France, the Netherlands and Germany; of angler-fish in Belgium; and of squid in Portugal.

New England Salt Cod Dinner   serves six

My recipe for this is from *Mrs Appleyard's Kitchen* (Boston, 1942).

salt cod, $\frac{3}{4}$ kg (1$\frac{1}{2}$ lb)	**small white turnips, 6**
potatoes, 6	**small beetroots, 6**
onions, 6	**egg sauce, 3 cups (see below)**
carrots, 6	**salt pork, $\frac{1}{4}$ kg ($\frac{1}{2}$ lb)**

'Soak the fish in cold water overnight. Change the water three times. Before you start to cook the vegetables, put the fish in a large frying-pan, cover it with fresh water, bring it to a boil but do not boil it. Set it where it will cook gently below the boiling point until you are ready to use it. Cook each of the vegetables separately. If they are very young and small, allow several of each kind instead of the one apiece called for above. There is of course no harm in cooking some extra anyway, but this is a filling dish and second helpings are not generally needed. While the fish and the vegetables are cooking, make the egg sauce and dice the salt pork fine and try it out until the pork scraps are brown and crisp. When everything is ready put the fish in the middle of a large hot platter and arrange the vegetables around it. Serve the egg sauce in a large bowl and the pork scraps with the pork fat in a sauce boat.

'It is a pretty sight to see Mr Appleyard attack a salt-fish dinner. He takes a potato on his plate and cuts it up rather fine, and then cuts into it the fish and the various vegetables. He keeps on cutting, and works into it some pork scraps and some of the tried-out pork fat, and last of all he takes a generous amount of the egg sauce and cuts that in. The result is a superb mound that fills the plate, in which the different flavors and textures are blended into something that is different from anything that went into it, and yet has the virtues of all its parts.'

The egg sauce is made by adding chopped hard-boiled egg to a white sauce which has been given an onion flavour. Watermelon pickle is an accompaniment which Mr Appleyard also liked.

Scrod Rarebit
serves six

While staying in Dedham, Massachusetts, I studied the local cookery book (*Parish Potpourri*, published by the St Paul's Church Service League of Dedham) and was interested to find the following item, presented as an old family recipe from Mrs William J. Mixter Jr. It is a simple and excellent dish which we have found can be applied equally well to other members of the cod family. This is our adapted version.

cod, cleaned and boned, 1 kg (2 lb)	flour, 2 tbs
	mustard, $\frac{1}{2}$ tbs
salt and pepper to taste	milk, 1 cup ($\frac{1}{4}$ litre or $\frac{1}{2}$ pint)
butter, 30 g (1 oz)	shredded cheese, 1 cup

Place the seasoned fish in an oven dish. Melt the butter over a medium heat, add the flour and mustard and blend together. Then add the milk and cook the mixture until it has thickened, stirring constantly. Finally, add the cheese and continue cooking until this has melted. Spread the mixture over the fish and bake it in a moderate oven (355° F, gas 4) for about 30 minutes.

Gloucester Corned Hake

Cameron's Restaurant in Gloucester, Mass., was formerly a bar-room to which the fishermen came after each voyage to settle up, i.e. to draw their share of the money, part of which they would proceed to drink up on the spot. It is now Gloucester's oldest-established restaurant and plays a fitting part in keeping alive the culinary traditions of this great fishing port. Mr Kelly, the proprietor, serves corned hake every Wednesday and reports a heavy demand for it.

At Cameron's they prepare the dish by simply boiling hake (*Merluccius bilinearis*, page 63) in very heavily salted water. When the water has come to the boil, the fish is ready. It is served with finely cubed salt pork which has been tried out in a pan. The dish is usually accompanied by boiled potatoes and beetroot. The saltiness of the fish combined with the flavour produced by the tiny cubes of salt pork is very distinctive and makes this an outstanding fish dish. It also keeps very well.

There is an alternative way of proceeding, which is to salt the hake, but not too heavily, for a few hours before cooking it. This advance salting firms up the flesh as well as giving it a good flavour.

Fillets of Bluefish Flambé with Gin

serves four

We spent our honeymoon at S'conset in Nantucket, not studying seafood cookery although vaguely aware that the fish dishes of the island were extremely good. More recently, I was intrigued by a recipe in the book by Nancy and Arthur Hawkins and Mary Allen Havemeyer on *Nantucket and Other New England Cooking*. It is for bluefish with gin, and is said to have come by word of mouth from a long line of Nantucketers. Thinking that the effect of flaming the fish with gin might be to reduce its oiliness, which sometimes seems excessive, I tried it and now recommend the following version.

fresh bluefish, 4 fillets, each	pepper, $\frac{1}{4}$ tsp
weighing $\frac{1}{4}$ kg ($\frac{1}{2}$ lb)	salt, $\frac{1}{2}$ tsp
butter, melted, 60 g (2 oz)	gin, 1 dl (7 tbs)
onion flakes, 3 tbs	

Choose a broiler pan just large enough to accommodate the fillets side by side. Grease it and place the fillets in it. Pour half of the melted butter over them and sprinkle the onion flakes, salt and pepper on top. (I assume that in the past people used chopped onion, slightly cooked; but the dried onion flakes are an improvement, since their taste and texture, when charred, are excellent.)

Have your grill (broiler) pre-heated and very hot. Place the broiler pan 3 inches below it and let the fish start to brown. Meanwhile mix the gin with the remaining butter. Remove the pan, pour the mixture on the fish and ignite it. (I had a little trouble doing this. It is probably best to reserve and warm a spoonful of pure gin, to ignite this first and use it to set the rest off.) Now put the pan back under the grill for 3 minutes or so; then turn off the heat. The fish may go on sputtering. It will be ready when the last flame has died.

Broiled Vineyard Swordfish

serves four

Swordfish is a Vineyard speciality, and there are several recipes of European origin for it in *The Martha's Vineyard Cook Book* by Louise Tate King and Jean Stewart Wexler. Like myself, they recommend charcoal-broiling swordfish steaks which have been prepared in a marinade. My own recipe calls for 4 steaks about 2 cm thick. Marinate these in a mixture of 2 tbs lemon juice, 2 tbs olive oil, 2 tsp salt, 1 tsp paprika and 6 bay leaves for at least 4 hours, turning the steaks over several times. Then grill them over a charcoal fire for 5 to 7 minutes on each side. Serve with a dressing of 3 parts lemon juice to 1 of olive oil, into which you have mixed plenty of finely chopped parsley.

Boiled State of Maine Lobster

This is simple. Have 4 inches of well-salted water boiling hard in a kettle large enough to take your lobster. Plunge the live lobster in, head downwards. Cover and let the water come back to the boil. Count 15 minutes from then for a lobster weighing $\frac{1}{2}$ kg (a little over 1 lb); 20 for one weighing $\frac{3}{4}$ kg (a little over $1\frac{1}{2}$ lb). Take the lobster out, lay it on its back, split it clear down the middle with a strong knife or kitchen shears, and remove the gut which runs along the tail and the small sac just below the head. Crack the claws and serve hot with melted butter.

Some people steam their lobsters in a wash-kettle, using little water and putting seaweed in below and above the lobster. But the main thing is to buy a good, lively lobster which feels heavy for its size. Male lobsters are better than females for boiling. (The females can be distinguished by their broader tails.) Very large lobsters make less good eating than small or medium-sized ones.

Fried Clams   serves four

Here is an interesting phenomenon. In Maine 90 per cent of fried clams are dipped in batter before being fried. In Massachusetts, on the other hand, 95 per cent of fried clams are simply breadcrumbed. I do not know what is the historical explanation of the difference; but its practical effect is that you can see the shape of the clam in Massachusetts, but not in Maine. Either way, fried clams are good, so I will briefly give both versions.

To make Maine Fried Clams you will need, besides fat for deep-frying:

clams, 24, shucked and cleaned	melted butter, 1 tbs
an egg, separated	salt, $\frac{1}{4}$ tsp
milk, $\frac{1}{2}$ cup	flour, $\frac{1}{2}$ cup

Beat the egg yolk, combine it with half the milk and add the butter. Sift the flour and salt together and beat them into the mixture. Add the rest of the milk, then fold in the egg white, beaten stiff.

Drain the clams. Dip each in the batter and fry it in deep fat at 375° F until golden brown, turning it several times. Drain the fried clams on absorbent paper and serve them with ketchup or tartare sauce.

To make Massachusetts Fried Clams, which used to be called Fannie Daddies on Cape Cod, take the same number of clams and wash and dry them thoroughly. Beat an egg with a tablespoonful of water. Roll the clams first in dry breadcrumbs, then in the egg mixture, then in the breadcrumbs for a second time. Fry them in deep hot fat, drain them and serve.

Quahog Chowder   serves four

Cap'n Phil Schwind's booklets on seafood are both knowledgeable and amusing. In *Clam Shack Cookery* he describes how Captain Ben Nickerson advertised for a bride, who had to be a good cook and a true Cape Cod girl. He tests the applicants by giving them a bucket of quahogs to cook. Tension mounts as the first applicant, despite having slightly webbed feet and eel-grass in her hair, fails; and so does number two, a red-head who uses some of the Captain's best sherry in her cooking. Now read on.

'The third applicant was a lissome blonde, her hair sun-streaked and neatly tucked in a bun at the back of her swan-like neck. The sun wrinkles at the corners of her faded blue eyes drew attention from the golden freckles sprinkled across the bridge of her snub nose. She wrinkled said snub nose at the bucket of quahogs Captain Ben set before her. "My goodness," said she, "I prefer West Shore quahogs to this stuff you holed in the mud at Nauset Marsh."

'She whittled open everything under three inches and laid the quahogs in their own juice on the half shell in front of Captain Ben. "These you may eat raw, as you should," she said primly.

'She opened about two dozen of the largest quahogs, until she had two cups of dry meats, saving the juice in a saucepan under the strainer. In lieu of a chopping bowl, she minced these fine with Captain Ben's fish knife.

'She cut into small cubes and tried out a chunk of salt pork a quarter as big as her fine-boned, little hand. Some of these she put in front of Captain Ben as a garnish on the last of his remaining littlenecks. The rest she put carefully aside. She sliced an onion into the salt pork fat and fried it a golden brown. She diced two potatoes fine and simmered them in a quart of milk until they were mostly cooked. In the meantime she had simmered the chopped quahogs slowly in their own liquor.

'All these ingredients she put together: the quahogs and their juice, the potatoes cooked in milk, the salt pork scraps and the onions in their salt pork fat. She gently stirred them until they were hot and blended, then she slowly stirred in a dollop of heavy cream.

'Before Captain Ben she placed a hot bowl with a big chunk of butter in, and over this she ladled the chowder. She set the pan on the back of the stove and said quite determinedly, "That will be better tomorrow." Then she retired behind the kitchen range and combed out her long, blonde hair with a comb made of the rib bones of a codfish.'

She won. I need only add that her onion and the two potatoes were all of medium size, that the piece of salt pork was about 2 inches square, and that the chunk of butter was the size of a walnut.

Scallops 'No Name'

The Customs official at Boston Airport showed no interest in my baggage but a lot in my intention to study New England seafood. 'I'll give you a piece of advice. There's a diner on the fish pier where you'll find the freshest fish in Boston. It's called – wait for it, you're not going to believe this – it's called No Name.'

We walked next day, in a freezing and ferocious wind, down the fish pier towards the old Boston Fish Exchange. Half-way down on the right is a plastic green porch, with no name on it, which leads into the 60-year-old establishment. There you do indeed have marvellously fresh seafood, plainly cooked and briskly served by neo-Italian kerchiefed waitresses.

Nick Contos, the proprietor, showed us how he prepared his broiled scallops. He cut them into bite-sized pieces, with which he covered the bottom of a shallow metal tray. Oleo (margarine) was daubed on top, with a discreet sprinkling of garlic powder. The tray was then inserted under the broiler (grill) for 10 minutes, after which the pieces of scallop were beautifully browned on top and swimming, now, in the juices which they had themselves exuded, pale white with golden beads of oleo. They were the best and most tender which we had ever tasted. Why do anything more complicated?

Squid Stew, Cape Cod

This recipe, introduced to me by a New England household in which it is greatly favoured, was contributed to *Foods from Truro Kitchens* by Francis J. Captiva, well known in Provincetown for his skill as a cook.

'Prepare squid by cleaning thoroughly, and cutting into inch sections.

'Brown onions in butter to which has been added salt, pepper and allspice.

'When thoroughly browned add about two bottles of ketchup or slightly diluted tomato paste, and a generous amount of saffron.

'After simmering $\frac{1}{2}$ hour add a dash of Worcestershire sauce and $\frac{1}{2}$ cup of sherry. Add cleaned squid and water to cover amply. When squid is done, drain most of juice into other receptacle. Cook rice enough for all hands in this nectar, and when done serve with the squid stew, garlic bread, and salad.

'Note: Garlic bread is easily made by cutting Portuguese bread the long way, two or three incisions, and spreading with a mixture of butter and crushed garlic, placing in oven for five minutes before serving.'

This recipe is Portuguese-American. The strength of the Portuguese cookery tradition at Provincetown is remarkable. The Portuguese bakery there is a charming and unpretentious expression of this tradition.

24. Recipes from the United States — Part Two, Rhode Island to New Jersey

Further on, when we come to the Chesapeake, the emphasis will be on crab recipes; and for the Carolinas and Georgia we shall be making much of shrimp dishes. In the present section clams hold sway. It was, after all, as 'clamdiggers' that men from Long Island were known to their comrades in the World Wars.

Yet oysters must also figure here, for the eating of oysters reaches a sort of zenith in New York City, where oysters from Long Island vie with those from points north, including the unsurpassable ones from Wellfleet, and points south such as Chesapeake, richest source of all. It is ironic that these creatures, which pass stationary lives, should be assembled in such multitudes to meet their end in a place where all is movement, where the tides of human beings flow more swiftly and sharply than anywhere else except perhaps Tokyo; and that even within this tumultuous metropolis the principal altar on which they are sacrificed should be the oyster bar in the Grand Central Station, whose very *raison d'être* is perpetual motion.

So bivalves are dominant in the recipes which follow; and only the first two offer any indication of the wealth of fish which are to be found around Long Island, for example. The East Hampton Ladies' Village Improvement Society published in 1948 a special edition of their cook book to mark the 300th anniversary of the settlement of East Hampton, and decided – oh, hallelujah! would that others would do the same – to enhance what had been a bare collection of recipes by adding historical and anecdotal material. They even record the consumption of two porpoises stranded nearby in 1947. And the list of the fish which they enjoy reads like blank verse – 'Montauk swordfish, tuna, striped bass, bluefish, snappers, weakfish, seabass, flounders, porgies, fluke, yellowtail, butterfish, blowfish, cod, and eels.' I also like their section on appetizers, which simply says that none are given, because our forefathers had little need of them at any time of day, with so much 'brisk work to do, to work up an interest in the victuals'.

Baked Connecticut Shad
serves four

Sophie Coe, at New Haven, tells me that for her, 'Connecticut river shad is the great spring treat.' She buys two filleted strips, weighing about 500–600 g (1¼ lb) in all, plus the roe. The roe is sautéed in butter first. She then takes a baking pan which will accommodate the fillets side by side (about 9 by 13 inches), lays them in it with the roe, adds up to 1 cup of milk, so that it comes well up the sides of the pan but does not cover the fish. Salt and pepper to taste. Bake in a hot oven (430° F, gas 7) for 10 to 15 minutes, until done.

This is the family favourite. However, left to her own devices, she would substitute white wine, with plenty of chopped parsley, for the milk.

Both these baked dishes are as good as they are simple. But some people prefer the traditional *Planked Shad*, prepared as follows.

For six people, a large shad weighing close to 2 kg (4 lb) is cleaned and split, and then placed skin side down on a greased 'plank'. This should be a piece of hardwood, well-seasoned and large enough for the purpose. Season, brush with melted butter and put in a hot oven (400° F, gas 6) for 20 minutes. Remove, brush a little more butter over the fish, arrange mashed potatoes in a border or mounds around it and return to the oven long enough to brown the potato. Serve on the plank, garnished with parsley.

Stuffed Striped Bass Rothschild
serves six

I have only ever been given one recipe by a Rothschild and this is it. It belongs to the way-out intellectual New Jersey branch of the family. It was delivered to me without quantities but with such an air of casual finality that I realized that it would be up to me to fill in the details, which I have done.

a fresh striped bass, of about 50–60 cm (20–24 inches), cleaned	medium onion, ½, chopped
	fresh cream, 75 ml (¼ cup)
	½ lemon, juice only
fresh spinach, ½ kg (1 lb), washed	fresh soft breadcrumbs

Cook the spinach and chop it roughly. Combine it with the onion, cream and lemon juice. Add enough breadcrumbs to produce a mixture of manageable consistency and then use it to stuff the bass. Bake in a moderate oven for about 40 minutes, taking care not to overcook the fish. Provided that you observe this last precept, the result will be delicious.

Baked Bluefish   serves four

Invited by my hostess in Connecticut to cook the finest bluefish which her son had ever caught. I had recourse to this recipe. Its joint authors are Joan Grice of Wood's Hole and Anne Cohen, a marine biologist at the Smithsonian. Not all ichthyologists take an interest in fish cookery, but those who do – and I have met many such all over the world – usually produce fine and expert recipes, like this one. The stipulation accompanying the recipe is that the fish be very fresh.

bluefish, 4 large fillets	dry white wine, 2 tbs
salt and pepper	grated Parmesan, 2 tbs
butter, 110 g (¼ lb)	paprika, 1 tsp
lemon juice, 1–2 tbs	thyme and chervil, a pinch of each

Season the bluefish fillets. Put the butter in a shallow dish or pan in a hot oven (430° F, gas 7) until lightly browned. (This manoeuvre gives the dish a distinctive flavour.) Then place the fillets, skin side up, in the sizzling hot butter and return the pan to the oven for at least 5 minutes (more if the fillets are very thick).

Next, turn the fillets over with a spatula, baste them with the molten butter, sprinkle over them the lemon juice, white wine, Parmesan, paprika, thyme and chervil. Return the dish to the oven until the fillets are *just* done (about 5 minutes more), when the flesh will be opaquely white and flaky. At this point, run the dish under the broiler for 1 minute. Then give the fillets a final basting with their sauce and serve straight from the pan, with rice as the accompaniment.

Oyster Stew   serves four as a first course

oysters, freshly shucked, ½ litre	milk, scalded, 2 cups
(1 pint, or about 16–20)	chopped shallot, 1–2 tsp
bacon, 4–8 slices	salt, ½ tsp
butter, 2 tbs	pepper, ¼ tsp

Fry the bacon crisp, drain it on absorbent paper and crumble it.

Put the oysters, with their juices, and the butter in a heavy pot and cook them gently until the edges begin to curl (about 3 minutes). Then add the bacon, the milk (or 'half and half' if you prefer), shallot, salt and paprika. Once it is all heated through, serve the stew with oyster crackers.

Oysters Kipling
serves two

May Southworth, in her pretty book of 101 oyster recipes (1907), gives this recipe without explaining how the name Kipling was given to it.

'Mix a half-tablespoonful each of flour and curry-powder with a little cream until smooth. Melt a tablespoonful of butter in a saucepan; add a tablespoonful of finely minced onion and a teaspoon of grated apple and simmer gently for a few minutes. Season with salt and pepper and add the flour and curry and a half-pint of cream and cook gently fifteen minutes; add a pint of drained oysters and cook just till the gills curl. Serve in a border of plain boiled rice.'

Stuffed Clams
serves four

This is a recipe to be used for larger clams; or for ones which look uncouth if presented whole, such as the razor-clam. There is no need to use the shells of the clams which you are cooking. Indeed it is better to have a set of particularly comely shells which have been carefully cleaned and to use these over and over again, oiling them ever so slightly before you use them. Quahog-shells are convenient for the purpose, but scallop-shells, if fairly deep and not too large, also serve well. And there is no reason why you should not use oyster-shells if you have some of a regular shape such as those from Wellfleet on Cape Cod or specially selected grade 000 gravettes d'Arcachon. It is agreeable to revive the memory of an occasion when you ate such oysters by re-using the shells. I often ask a waiter to wash mine and return them to me; but for use in establishments where this would not go down well I carry a plastic bag into which I can pop the shells, to be washed afterwards at my lodging.

The shells can be lightly rubbed with a clove of garlic after they have been oiled; but in this case omit the nutmeg.

15 to 20 large quahogs or other large clams or the equivalent of unhandsome smaller clams	ground nutmeg, 1 tsp
	finely chopped celery, $\frac{1}{4}$ cup
	chopped green pepper, 1 tbs
fresh breadcrumbs, $1\frac{1}{2}$ cups	streaky bacon, 6 rashers

Steam open the clams, shuck them and mince them finely. Strain the broth. Mix the minced clams with all the other ingredients except the bacon, moisten the mixture with a few spoonfuls of the broth, then distribute it between the shells, capping each of them with a piece of bacon. Bake in a hot oven (450° F, gas 8) for 5 to 10 minutes, until the bacon is almost crisp.

Clam Pie

There are many kinds of clam pie, each with its supporters. I like the story of the East Hampton lady who, temporarily in New York, had what she regarded as a 'real' clam pie brought from East Hampton. The cook was told to warm it, but later reported: 'I never had a chance to get it warmed through. Her teeth wuz waterin'.' This is not that recipe, but is a good basic one. You will need about 40 clams, which can be hardshell or soft-shelled, or a mixture of the two; and pastry sufficient for a two-crust pie about 9 inches across and $1\frac{1}{2}$–2 inches deep.

Steam open the well-washed clams. Strain and reserve the liquor. Chop the clams. Next, use a little of the clam broth to cook 3 medium potatoes, diced, with half an onion, finely chopped, and 2 sprigs of parsley, chopped. Drain the vegetables and add to them 25 g (1 oz) butter. Dust them with 1–2 tsp flour; add 1–2 tbs single cream, with a suspicion of garlic. Mix all this with the chopped clams and 1 cup of the reserved broth.

Line your greased pie-dish with pastry. Set a pie-glass (or Welsh pie dragon, page 460) in the centre, pour in the clam mixture and cover the top with the remaining pastry. Bake for 10 minutes in a hot oven (430° F, gas 7), then reduce the heat to 355° F (gas 4) and bake for 40 minutes more.

Steamed Soft-shelled Clams

These may taste best at a clambake, such as that described on page 424, but they are more often prepared at home. Here are simple directions, familiar to Americans but less so to Europeans.

Make sure that all your clams are alive. If the neck or siphon does not retract when touched, discard the clam; and reject likewise any with broken shells. Wash the survivors well under cold running water, place them in a large pot with about 1 cm water, cover and bring to the boil. The steam will open the clams within about 5 minutes.

Line a colander with cheesecloth and place it over a bowl. Put the contents of the pot into the lined colander, liquid and all. Shake slightly and let all the clear, strained clam broth collect in the bowl. The clams themselves, still with their shells, are to be put in large soup bowls, 20 clams for each person. Serve a small bowl of melted butter beside each helping, and a cup of the hot clam broth. Provide napkins too, since the clams are to be eaten with the fingers. The technique is to take the black membrane off the neck or siphon, dunk the clam in melted butter and pop it in. Some people like to add a little lemon juice to the melted butter, but this is optional.

Rhode Island Clam Chowder   serves six

The frontier between Massachusetts and Rhode Island seems to mark the Great Divide between chowders made with milk and those made with tomatoes and water. This is a matter on which strong feelings are easily roused. J. George Frederick, in his *Long Island Seafood Cook Book*, talks of 'Long Island's praetorian gourmet guards, who snorted like whales when an hour-old chowder was offered to them; and might even draw their fish knives menacingly if a milk chowder was even mentioned.' Frederick himself discusses the matter in a calm and illuminating way. He accepts the theory that all these chowders had their origin in the French fisherman's chaudière (which had neither milk nor tomatoes). This dish was brought by the French to Canada (cf. page 402) and soon spread into New England. It was treated as a main dish, and fortified for this purpose by the use of milk. But as it continued its southward progress it entered territory dominated by New York, where a demand grew up for a lighter chowder, which could serve as a first course; where the large Italian community would be predisposed to tomatoes rather than milk; and where tomatoes from places like Long Island were plentiful and eaten on a scale which would not have been practical in, say, Maine. Hence the two main versions of clam chowder: New England and Manhattan, from both of which numerous variants depend.

Frederick calls attention to another difference. Long Islanders and New Yorkers prefer to use soft-shelled clams for steaming and to make clam chowder from small hard-shell clams, such as cherrystones. New Englanders, on the other hand, use the large quahogs or soft-shelled clams. This recipe from Rhode Island offers such a choice.

quahogs or soft-shelled clams, shucked, 24	stewed tomatoes, 2 cups
	crackers, 8
salt pork, diced, 110 g (¼ lb)	creamy milk (top of bottle) or
onions, 4, sliced	'half and half', 1 cup
potatoes, cubed, 3 cups	salt and pepper

Open the clams and remove their dark bellies. Chop the meat coarsely.

Fry the pieces of pork until they are crisp and dry. Drain them on absorbent paper, using the fat to cook the sliced onions until they are tender. Then add the potatoes and the chopped clam meat, followed by the water, and simmer all this gently until the clams are tender. At this point, add the tomatoes and set the mixture aside to 'ripen'.

Soak the crackers in the top of milk. Just before serving the chowder, add the crackers and milk to it, with seasoning to taste. Serve it hot.

A Rhode Island Clambake, *circa* 1890

Mrs Lincoln's Boston Cook Book (1891) is a practical volume, full of wise counsel and clear instructions. Only occasionally, as here, does Mrs Lincoln allow herself to brush in a background to her recipes. The result is so felicitous that one wishes she had done so more often.

'An impromptu clam bake may be had at any time at low tide along the coast where clams are found. If you wish to have genuine fun, and to know what an appetite one can have for the bivalves, make up a pleasant party and dig for the clams yourselves. A short thick dress, a shade hat, rubber boots, – or, better still, no boots at all, if you can bring your mind to the comfort of bare feet, – a small garden trowel, a fork, and a basket, and you are ready. Let those who are not digging gather a large pile of driftwood and seaweed, always to be found along the shore. Select a dozen or more large stones, and of them make a level floor; pile the driftwood upon them, and make a good brisk fire to heat the stones thoroughly. When hot enough to crackle as you sprinkle water upon them, brush off the embers, letting them fall between the stones. Put a thin layer of seaweed on the hot stones, to keep the lower clams from burning. Rinse the clams in salt water by plunging the basket which contains them in the briny pools near by. Pile them over the hot stones, heaping them high in the centre. Cover with a thick layer of seaweed, and a piece of old canvas, blanket, carpet, or dry leaves, to keep in the steam. The time for baking will depend on the size and quantity of the clams. Peep in occasionally at those around the edge. When the shells are open, the clams are done. They are delicious eaten from the shell, with no other sauce than their own briny sweetness. Melted butter, pepper, and vinegar should be ready for those who wish them; then all may "fall to". Fingers must be used. A Rhode Islander would laugh at any one trying to use a knife and fork. Pull off the thin skin, take them by the black end, dip them in the prepared butter, and bite off close to the end. If you swallow them whole, they will not hurt you. At a genuine Rhode Island clam bake, blue-fish, lobsters, crabs, sweet potatoes, and ears of sweet corn in their gauzy husks are baked with the clams. The clam steam gives them a delicious flavour. Brown bread is served with the clams, and watermelon for dessert completes the feast.'

25. Recipes from the United States — Part Three, the Chesapeake Region

'The Chesapeake Bay is the largest estuary in the United States and one of the most useful in the world. It was created in the last 15,000 years by the flooding of the lower valley of the greatest river on the East Coast, the mighty Susquehanna. As a drowned valley, it has hundreds of peripheral rivers, bays, and creeks, a very long shoreline and extensive areas of shallow water.' L. Eugene Cronin thus begins his introduction to *The Chesapeake Bay in Maryland: an atlas of natural resources*, a work which explains in both words and maps the extraordinary importance of this region for aquatic life.

The shoreline of the Bay and its tributaries is estimated to be over 8000 miles (13,000 kilometres). The waters, fed by the Potomac, the Susquehanna and numerous smaller river systems, have a salinity which varies from 0 to 20 parts of salt per 1000 parts of water. The inflow of fresh water from these rivers maintains this pattern of salinity and provides a supply of nutrients (as well as of pollutants). As Cronin says: 'The result is a biological treasure. The nutrients make it possible for plankton and rooted aquatic plants to produce enormous quantities of organic material. These feed the world's largest crops of oysters and clams in water salty enough for them but not salty enough for their worst natural predators.' The waters of low salinity also provide important spawning grounds for striped bass, shad and herring. And it is the principal habitat of the blue crab.

The early settlers found the abundance of seafood almost overwhelming. Captain John Smith wrote in 1608 that: 'We ... found in diverse places that abundance of fish lying so thick with their heads above the water, as for want of nets, our barge driving amongst them, we attempted to catch them with a frying pan, but we found it a bad instrument to catch fish with.' (They did better later in the day, in shallow water, by transfixing fish on their sword-points.)

The Indians, of course, had much to teach the settlers, about the construction of fish weirs, in which sturgeon, for example, could be taken. John Smith makes a tantalizing reference to what sounds like a sort of sturgeon pâté. 'We had more sturgeon than could be devoured by dog or man, of which the industrious by drying and pounding, mingled with caviar, sorrel, and other wholesome herbs, would make bread and good meat.'

The fisheries in the Chesapeake have changed greatly. There was a time when the Bay was embellished by numerous sailing craft of specialized design and great beauty, such as the bugeye (a large oyster-dredger), its successor the skipjack, the all-purpose pungy and the oldest of all, the log canoe. Log canoes were the craft most used for oyster tonging until power boats superseded them. (Two kinds of oyster tong are shown below.)

These changes have occurred in a natural way, and the fisheries have continued to prosper and evolve. Some of the enormous hills of oyster shells which can be seen at Kent Narrows, for example, bear silent witness to the centuries of seafood-gathering; and they are still growing.

Chesapeake was an Indian name meaning 'mother of waters'. The Bay has also mothered many good recipes, of which a few samples follow.

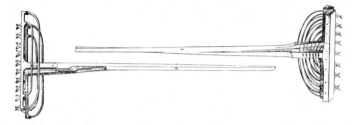

Maryland Stuffed Shad Roe
serves four

Plain shad roe is excellent; but there are occasions when one wants to turn it into something more grand. This recipe based on one in the bicentennial edition of *Maryland's Way*, meets the need.

shad roes, 4 pairs	*for the sauce*
butter, 80 g (3 oz)	**melted butter, 1½ tbs; flour**
lump crab meat, 220 g (½ lb)	**1½ tbs; single cream, 1 cup;**
	salt and pepper

Poach the roes, drain them and let them cool. Then fry them in the butter in a heavy skillet until they are a rich brown on both sides.

Make the cream sauce by stirring the flour into the melted butter over a gentle heat. Gradually add the cream, stirring, until the sauce has thickened. Season it and add the crab meat to it.

Split each half-roe open, taking care not to cut it completely in two. Stuff each with the sauce. Reheat briefly in the oven and serve with, for example, fresh Maryland asparagus and a Hollandaise sauce (page 316).

To Boil Rockfish, by Mrs Mary Randolph

Many of the early American cookery books were, not surprisingly, little more than reprints of or anthologies from the English books which were available at the time. Gradually, however, the impact of a new way of life and the need to deal with new foodstuffs introduced a genuine American flavour into American cookery books. By 1860, when Mrs Mary Randolph had *The Virginia Housewife* published at Philadelphia, there had been plenty of time for this evolution to occur; and her book is a good and interesting one. Here are her instructions for dealing with 'rock' (page 86), a fish found only on the American side of the Atlantic.

'The best part of the rock is the head and shoulders – clean it nicely, put it into the fish kettle with cold water and salt, boil it gently and skim it well; when done, drain off the water, lay it in the dish, and garnish with scraped horse-radish; have two boats of butter nicely melted with chopped parsley, or for a change, you may have anchovy butter; the roe and liver should be fried in separate dishes. If any of the rock be left, it will make a delicious dish next day; – pick it in small pieces, put it in a stew pan with a gill [$\frac{1}{4}$ pint or $1\frac{1}{2}$ dl] of water, a good lump of butter, some salt, a large spoonful of lemon pickle, and one of pepper vinegar – shake it over the fire till perfectly hot, and serve it up. It is almost equal to stewed crab.'

Devilled Crab   serves four

Frederick Philip Stieff described his book *Eat, Drink and Be Merry in Maryland* as an anthology, and ascribed the recipes to their sources. But the art with which he made his selection, the catholic choice of illustrations (even this one from *Punch* – Lady, 'I don't like the look of this haddock.' Fishmonger, 'If it's looks you're after you'd better buy a goldfish.'), the black and red cover redolent of the 1930s, all these things conspire to make this a great cookery book. And with what glee must Stieff have juxtaposed a stilted foreword by the Mayor of Baltimore ('I sincerely trust that this volume . . .') with a letter to himself from Emily Post, recalling in romantic prose his Maryland hospitality, the daily dinner party at three o'clock and the 'black band of wrist between the white cotton glove and pulled-up coat sleeve of Old James, the butler, as he reached over and lifted the huge domed silver cover off of a platter piled high with fried oysters . . .'

However, à nos fruits de mer. Stieff must have deliberated carefully in selecting a recipe for devilled crab, an important dish in the eyes of Marylanders. His choice fell on that of the sober-sounding and manifestly competent Mr H. R. Bowen of the Chesapeake Steamship Company at Baltimore. Here it is.

'1 cup crab meat, ½ cup milk, ⅛ teaspoon dry mustard, ⅛ teaspoon cayenne pepper, ½ green pepper chopped fine, 1 cup bread crumbs, yolks of 2 raw eggs, 1 teaspoon salt, ½ cup melted butter. Mix crab meat with crumbs (which have been moistened with milk) and egg yolks. Add mustard, salt, cayenne pepper, green peppers and butter. Mix well. Fill crab shells with mixture, sift crumbs lightly on top, dot with butter. Brown quickly in very hot oven, being careful they do not burn. Crab shells should be washed and scrubbed in very hot water before being stuffed.'

Crab and Skate Salad

serves six to eight as a first course

This recipe was cunningly devised by Evelene Spencer, co-author of the classic *Fish Cookery* (Boston, 1922) to bring the despised skate on to the American table on the back of the respected crab. The mixture is pleasantly perplexing, since the strands of meat look alike but have different tastes. Her instructions, slightly expanded, are as follows.

crab meat, cooked, 170 g (6 oz), i.e. a small tin, yielding 1 cup or so	**mayonnaise, ¼ litre (½ pint)**
	a lemon, juice only
	salt
skate, poached, ¼ kg (½ lb), i.e. 1 cup of flaked flesh	**paprika**
	lettuce leaves
celery, finely minced, 6–8 stalks, to yield 1½–2 cups	**cream, whipped (optional)**

Mix the crab meat, flaked skate, minced celery and mayonnaise together with a wooden salad spoon. Add the lemon juice, season with salt and dust the top with paprika. Arrange lettuce leaves in little nests. Mould helpings of the salad in an after-dinner coffee cup, pressing down lightly, and turn them out on to the lettuce nests. A top dressing of mayonnaise thinned down with whipped cream may be added if you wish.

Mrs Spencer mentions elsewhere that if one has difficulty in obtaining skate, halibut cheeks may be used instead, since this part of the halibut has meat arranged similarly in long strands. Halibut pretending to be skate pretending to be crab! Was there no end to the deceptions which this good woman was prepared to recommend?

My daughter Caroline tried out the halibut cheeks version and found it highly successful, but recommends adding pepper to the seasoning.

Maryland Crab Meat Cakes

makes two each for four people

Helen Avalynne Tawes, we read on the dust-jacket, 'was born and raised in the seaport town of Crisfield, Maryland, at one time referred to as the seafood capital of the world and situated on the famous Eastern Shore of Maryland. In 1915 she married J. Millard Tawes, a young businessman of Crisfield, who later became Governor of Maryland.' Her book *My Favorite Maryland Recipes* includes menus which she used in the Governor's Mansion, featuring Maryland dishes such as the crab meat cakes for which she gives this recipe. It should be, and is, authentic.

cooked crab meat, 450 g (1 lb)	cayenne pepper, ½ tsp
rich (i.e. creamy) milk, 1 cup	dry mustard, 1 tsp
fresh breadcrumbs, 1 cup	Worcestershire sauce, 2 tsp
an egg	tabasco, 3 drops

'Mix above ingredients well – make 8 individual patties and roll in fine, dry breadcrumbs. Fry in deep fat until golden brown.'

This kind of crab meat cake is not too rich, thanks to the breadcrumbs. Crab or lobster meat prepared Norfolk style, which is to say with nothing else but butter and seasoning, is too rich for some. I have been eating it on and off at Martin's restaurant in Georgetown, D.C., for nearly thirty years, but I plan to give it up on my sixty-fifth birthday.

Maryland Clam Fritters

makes five fritters each for four

This is a favourite dish on the Eastern Shore of Chesapeake Bay and indeed in many other places. Any clams can be used, including the neglected razor clam (page 240).

clams, 24 medium or 12–18 large	baking powder, ½ tsp
eggs, 2	salt and pepper
flour, 50 grams (2 oz)	cooking oil, 2 dl (⅓ pint)
milk, a little (optional)	

Steam the clams open, unless you are using ready-shucked ones. Drain them, but not too thoroughly, then mince or grind them quite finely. Combine eggs, flour, milk if used, baking powder and seasoning into a batter and mix the minced clams into this.

Form the clam mixture into cakes and fry them in batches for 3 or 4 minutes on each side.

This recipe can be applied to mussels and produces quite good results. You would need 36–48 mussels, depending on their size.

Eastern Shore Oyster Soup   serves (?) eight or ten

Josephine Redue ran a private school at Chestertown around the turn of
the century. She also collected recipes, with discrimination, from friends
and neighbours and published these in a little booklet, *The Eastern Shore
Cook Book*, which charmingly expressed her personality and in which she
found space to give general advice, such as to be sure and rest after eating.
'To attempt hard work or close study within an hour after eating, invites
derangement of the digestive organs.'

I copied out this recipe one winter's evening, in an old plantation house
near Chestertown, to the sound of ice floes crashing against the little pier
where peaches were once loaded for Baltimore, and the yacking of
Canada geese as they flew in a skein over the river or settled by the
hundreds on the ice.

'Wash and drain three quarts of oysters; put them on with three quarts
of water, three onions stuck full of cloves and two or three slices of lean ham;
add pepper and salt. Boil until reduced one-half. Thicken with a spoonful of flour, half a cup of cream, and the yolks of six eggs, well beaten.
Boil a few minutes after thickening, taking care that it does not curdle.'

Oyster Crab Omelette

In describing the oyster crab on page 206, I promised a recipe from the
unparalleled collection formed by H. Franklyn Hall. This writer, who
mingles modest disclaimers of scholarship with proud accounts of his
wide experience, and who pledges that 'every receipt in this book is
absolutely correct', had been Chef of the Boothby Hotel Company in
Philadelphia for fifteen years when he published his book in 1901. He
asserts that his restaurants contained 'the generally acknowledged largest
and finest oyster and shell fish department in the world'.

'Oyster Crab Omelets. Take from twenty-five to forty live oyster crabs
for every portion, or person, you wish to serve, and blanch them in boiling
water, drain dry, and add to every twenty-five or forty oyster crabs one
half gill heavy cream sauce, heat hot, and place as much of the crabs and
sauce as you can inside of a three egg, plain omelet, place on a long dish or
platter, pour balance of crabs and cream sauce around edge of omelet,
sprinkle with chopped parsley and serve quickly.'

I wish that there was space to print also Hall's real extravaganza,
Canopy [sic] à la Lorenzo. Each person receives a crouton with a bell-
shaped structure on it, incorporating 50 oyster crabs, $\frac{1}{4}$ truffle, crab meat,
chicken meat and cream, all dusted with green breadcrumbs!

26. Recipes from the United States — Part Four, the Carolinas and Georgia

I have always travelled south by train. This is much the best way, for it gives you an idea of the distance between, say, Washington D.C. and Savannah, Georgia; and it enables you to observe the changes in scenery, vegetation and people at a pace which is just right for perceiving both their gradual nature and their magnitude. It is indeed another world south of Cape Hatteras, for man and for fish.

Down in the Carolinas and Georgia we come to the great shrimping grounds of the eastern seaboard. If the blue crab and the oyster dominate Chesapeake cuisine, the shrimp holds undisputed sway further south. This section of the book is therefore heavily weighted with shrimp recipes. It also reflects one other new factor, the importance of soul food and the culinary influence of the black people to whom it belongs. Only in the south, where climatic conditions and food resources are comparable with those of Africa, could this influence flower.

Life is more leisurely in the south. People do just as much, so it seems to me, bearing in mind the wise observation of the cook Martha on page 436; but are miraculously free of fluster and more able to find time for gestures of courtesy and hospitality. I well remember arriving at a borrowed house on the South Carolina coast and seeing when we were still a quarter of a mile distant the figure of a kind neighbour emerging from her door and setting off, casserole and glass jar in her arms, towards what was to be our door. We arrived simultaneously and she said that she had known we were coming and thought that we would need some lunch. The casserole contained a dish of rice and shrimp; the jar was full of a home-made chutney which suited the shrimp to perfection. Let me find time and space, in southern fashion, to impart the chutney recipe; *much* more useful than another paragraph of superficial generalizations.

Take 2 cups crushed pineapple, 1 cup seedless raisins, $\frac{1}{2}$ cup cider vinegar, 1 cup brown sugar (firmly packed), 1 tbs garlic salt, 2 tbs chopped candied ginger, $\frac{1}{4}$ tsp ground clove, $\frac{1}{4}$ tsp ground cinnamon, $\frac{1}{2}$ cup chopped toasted almonds and a pinch of cayenne pepper. Cook all this over a low heat for 50 minutes, or until thick. Add a few whole almonds. The chutney can be stored in jars or kept in the refrigerator for weeks. (Mrs McTeer.)

Fried Fish Southern Style with Hush Puppies

serves six

Fish and fried fish are almost synonymous in the south. A favourite way of frying them is to coat small fish or fillets of larger fish, e.g. weakfish, in cornmeal and deep-fry or pan-fry them thus. The contrast between the crispness of the coating and the succulence of the fish inside is most agreeable. You need 1 kg (2 lb) of cleaned fish and ½–1 cup of cornmeal for 6 people.

But here I wish to explain about hush puppies. They can be heavy, like lumps of iron ore on the platter – or they can be beautifully light. I owe these directions for the light kind to Horton H. Hobbs Jr, a southerner who works at the Smithsonian.

white cornmeal, ½ cup	flour, 4 tbs (¼ cup)
baking powder, 3 tsp	salt, ½ tsp
vegetable oil, 2 tbs	sugar, 1 tsp
milk, 4 tbs (¼ cup)	black pepper, ¼ tsp
an egg	onion, minced, 2 tbs

Mix the ingredients together and drop the mixture, a teaspoonful at a time, into hot deep fat, using a wire basket if possible. Turn the puppies once with a fork and lift them out when brown, after 2 or 3 minutes.

The scholarly Mr Hobbs insisted on adding that the heavy kind of hush puppy can be made by omitting the baking powder and using less liquid. The only advantage of this is that the puppies can then be shaped as you wish. Another friend explained that a generous addition of red pepper would transform the hush puppies into something which he recalled with pleasure from his childhood as Red-horse bread. These hotted-up hush puppies can be cooked in a skillet in the oven and go well with catfish.

North Carolina Boat Stew

This is a real fishermen's recipe, taught to Alston C. Badger of the Bear's Bluff Field Station when he was fishing with men from Hawker's Island.

Fry some bacon until the grease comes out, then brown some chopped onion in it. Thicken it up with a little flour, previously mixed with water. 'Some can just sprinkle the flour, so they don't have any lumps, but I never could do that.' Leave it to simmer for 20 minutes or so, then add what you have in the way of seafood. Peeled, raw shrimp would be first choice; oysters with their juices second. Cook very briefly, hardly any time at all if you are using oysters, season with pepper and a dash of Worcestershire sauce and, for the shrimp only, a little salt. Mr Badger has taken to adding a pinch of oregano as well. Serve it on rice. 'But those North Carolinians would put it on bread if they didn't have rice made up. Either way, it's real good to eat.'

Frogmore 'Shrimp, Corn and Sausage'

serves four

This recipe comes from Jack Chapman, a shrimp fisherman of Frogmore, S.C. The region, one of salt-flats, quiet creeks and oak-trees hung with Spanish moss, harbours a number of shrimp docks. The shrimp boats berth alongside a row of huts, in which local children, summoned by the bell which announces the return of the boats, assemble to pick the shrimp. When the local people go hunting, they may take the makings of this out-of-doors dish, which is a sort of southern equivalent of the northern clambake.

fresh shrimp, 60-count (i.e. 60 to the lb), beheaded but not peeled, 1 kg (2 lb)

hot (i.e. with chilli) smoked sausage, 400 g (1 lb)

crab boil spices (see page 199), 4 tsp

salt to taste

corn, 4 ears, husked and halved

Cut the sausage into 2 cm pieces and put them with the spices in the bottom of a large pot, with water to cover. Boil for 20 minutes. Add the corn and boil for 5 more minutes. Then add the shrimp, well washed, and bring back to the boil. The dish is then ready. Remove, drain and serve.

Brown Oyster Stew with Benne (Sesame) Seed

serves six

This dish, contributed by Mrs Augustine T. S. Stoney to *Charleston Receipts*, is one of those which show the African influence exerted on southern cookery by the blacks. Benne was originally brought over by slaves, who regarded it as a good-luck plant. The seeds are 'parched' in a heavy pan on the stove, or in the oven, until they are dark brown.

The recipe calls for bacon. In the old days salt-cured 'side-meat' of pork would have been used in this and other southern seafood stews.

shucked oysters, 2 cups

the oyster liquor

bacon, 4 slices

a large onion, sliced

flour, 2 tbs

parched benne (sesame) seeds, pounded in a mortar, 2 tbs

Fry the bacon and onion until brown, then remove them from the pan. Shake the flour into the hot fat and stir until it is brown. Remove the pan from the heat and gradually add the oyster liquor, with a little water if necessary – you need about 1½ cups liquid. Return the pan to the stove and stir the mixture until it has thickened slightly. Add the pounded benne seeds. Lastly, add the oysters and cook them until their edges curl, but no longer. Serve at once on a bed of rice or hominy.

Mulled Down Shrimp with Hominy Grits   serves two

This is real low-country soul food, low-country meaning the coastal areas of the Carolinas and soul food meaning what the black people eat. I like the term mulled down, which expresses well the process of gentle reduction of the gravy, and prefer it to the title Brown shrimp, although that is in common use. 'Half the black people on this island were raised on brown shrimp and grits,' I was told on one of the sea islands, the very ones which gave their name to Sea Island cotton long ago.

Hominy is Indian corn, also called maize, which has been soaked in a weak solution of lye. Ground, it becomes grits. Grits are white or yellow, depending on whether white or yellow corn has been used, and are best when water-ground. The white are the more popular. Most people nowadays use quick or instant grits, of which I recommend the former.

Gracie Reddicks, a real black super-woman, showed me how to make a shrimp and grits breakfast at Coffin House Plantation near Beaufort, S.C.

fresh shrimp, unpeeled, ½ kg (1 lb)	lemon juice, 1 tbs
salt and pepper and garlic salt	*and*
flour, 1½–2 tbs	quick white grits, ½ cup measured
bacon fat, 1½–2 tbs	dry, combined with 1⅔ cup water
a smallish onion, cut up	and seasoned with salt, ½ tsp
green bell pepper, chopped, 1 tbs	

Gracie used shrimp of 100/110 count, which means that you get that number to the pound. She peeled them, deveined them and dried them on a paper towel, then seasoned them with salt and pepper and a very little garlic salt. Then she put most of the flour in a paper bag, added the shrimps and tossed them about until they were well coated.

The quick grits were already cooking. They are supposed to take 5 minutes only, but she prefers to give them 15, on a fairly low flame, and covered.

Meanwhile she had heated most of the bacon fat in a heavy iron pan. She put the shrimps in the hot fat and let them start to brown.

The onion and bell pepper were fried separately in the remaining bacon fat in a heavy iron pan, 'what most people call old-time pots'. After 5 minutes she combined the shrimps with these. She stirred ½ tsp flour into the shrimp pan juices, to thicken them, and then poured in the lemon juice and ⅔ cup hot water and stirred some more. At this point, the shrimp mixture was returned to the pan and left to simmer in the gravy for 5 minutes, covered. After this time the gravy had thickened up and the dish was ready to be served with the attendant grits.

Shrimp in Georgia

I knew many of Ogden Nash's verses by heart when I was a boy, but only recently discovered the one which he contributed as a preface to *The Savannah Cook Book* (1933). It ends thus:

Everybody has the right to think whose food is the most gorgeous,
And I nominate Georgia's.

The quality of the book goes a long way to bear out his claim. I quote first an evocative description of shrimp-sellers in Savannah, followed by a recipe which is superbly untidy but obviously genuine and 'right'.

'Although the fish stalls in the City market are filled with crabs and shrimp brought in fresh daily, the majority of Savannah housekeepers prefer to buy their sea foods from the negro hucksters who come in from the neighbouring watering places, and peddle their wares from door to door – carrying on their heads great baskets of shrimp and crabs and oysters, and filling the morning air with their familiar cry: "Crab by'er! Yeh Swimps! Yeh Oshta!".

'Many efforts have been made by the City fathers to put an end to this street peddling . . . But the plea of the housewife has carried the day, and the presence of the gayly dressed vendors with their buckets of oysters, their baskets of bright shrimp and crabs, and in the spring with swamp lilies, wild honey-suckle and bay flowers, still lends a picturesque touch to streets that are fast losing their charm in the march of progress.

'SHRIMP is the name for this temperamental receipt found in an old cook book. You will have to be a good cook or a good Southerner, or both, to be able to translate it, but it is as good as it is naive.

'A soup plate of shrimp (cut not chop). Dust a mere idea of nutmeg and a little black pepper, a breaking tablespoon of butter and ½ pint of cream, a good handful of bread crumbs. Put in the peppers, sprinkle over with bread crumbs and bake. PS. I forgot to say a wineglass of sherry.'

Shrimp Paste

Some like to flavour shrimp paste with mace, onion juice, etc. But it is hard to beat this simple version, that of Miss Loulie Porcher.

Cream 110 g (¼ lb) of butter until very soft. Take ½ kg (1 lb) of cooked, shelled shrimps and grind them very fine. Mix thoroughly with the butter, add salt to taste and pack the mixture into an oblong pâté dish. Bake in a moderate oven (355° F, gas 4) for about 30 minutes or until the mixture leaves the sides of the dish and is slightly browned on top. Let it cool, then chill it overnight before use.

She-crab Soup

serves six

A crab soup made from female, berried crabs * has a flavour superior to and a texture slightly more glutinous than an ordinary crab soup. It is, however, against the regulations to take berried crabs. I probed into this dilemma while in South Carolina and found that a common interpretation of the regulations was that they applied to commercial crabbing only. It also appeared that some law-abiding people make she-crab soup from plain crabs with the addition of the yolk of a hen's egg. Yet cans of 'real she-crab soup' were available. The situation seemed to defy further analysis. I did, however, have a dish of the real thing and it is very good; and there certainly are places in the North Atlantic area where berried crabs may legally be had. So, with more plausibility than the motor-car manufacturers who offer vehicles capable of 150 m.p.h. 'where traffic laws permit', which to the best of my knowledge is nowhere, I give the recipe as it appears in Blanche H. Rhett's *200 Years of Charleston Cooking.*

This, it seems, was the first book to print it in the form used by William, butler to Mrs Goodwyn Rhett. William's culinary advice is followed in the book, but prefaced here, by an extraordinarily useful observation made by Martha, another black cook who accomplished enormous amounts of work without ever seeming hurried. Asked how she managed, she replied: 'I never does more than one thing at a time. I does a thing and when it's done I goes on to the next thing.'

berried she-crabs, 12	milk, 2 cups
salt	cream, ½ cup
butter, 15 g (½ oz)	Worcestershire sauce, ½ tsp
a small onion, chopped	flour, 1 tsp
a little black pepper	sherry, 1 tbs

Cook the crabs for about 20 minutes in boiling salted water. Remove them and pick off all the meat and eggs. Place these, with the butter, onion and black pepper, in the top of a double boiler and let simmer for 5 minutes. Then add the milk, which you have already heated separately. Stir together and add the cream and Worcestershire sauce. Thicken slightly with the flour, add the sherry and salt to taste. Then continue cooking over a low heat for 30 minutes.

---

* Berried crabs are those which are carrying eggs.

27. Recipes from Scotland

I suppose that the first fish dish which I can really remember was my grandmother's Fish custard (page 441); and that it would be fair to say that one of the contributions which we Scots have made to fish cookery is the concept of a fish dish served at a high tea, a concept not exclusively Scottish but realised for me most satisfactorily in Scotland.

A second Scottish contribution has been the use of oatmeal in cooking fish. This is especially appropriate for fish which have a high content of fat or oil, such as the herring, which was once the principal and glittering prize of the Scottish fishing industry. The great importance of the herring fishery in Scotland led to the development of some eminently successful cures; I think of Loch Fyne kippers (although my own kipperer is Mr Jimmy Fraser of Lerwick, whither one must go to enjoy the product, for he is unwilling to dispatch his kippers by mail). These (and Finnan haddock and Arbroath smokies too) have left their mark on gastronomy; but so did the herring leave its mark on the Scottish people. Memories dim as generations pass, but there are many who can still remember the days of the great herring fleets at sea – and the exploits ashore of the herring girls, of whom a vivid Shetland portrait is printed on page 28.

Shetland and Orkney and the Western Isles are rich in fish cookery traditions, the nature of which was largely determined by the simple cooking equipment in a fisherman's croft and by the pattern of the fish trade in former times. There was in those times no way of sending fresh fish to market from Shetland. So the cod, ling, torsk and saithe all had to be salted and dried. The boats would leave the fish at the curing station minus head, roe, liver, 'soond' (sound or air bladder) and 'muggie' (stomach), all of which were the fishermen's perks. Hence the astonishing dominance in traditional Shetland cookery of dishes made with these ingredients.

In the original edition of Margaret Stout's book on Shetland cookery, published in 1925 under the title *Cookery for Northern Wives*, there were forty-eight entries under Fish; and of these over a third were for fish-liver dishes. Nowhere else in the world have I found a similar phenomenon. Even today, when fish livers are usually discarded at sea, most Shetlanders over forty are ready to discuss with passion the merits of these various dishes. Some were obscure, confined perhaps to one small island, but the two given here (Krappin and Stap, pages 444 and 445) were widely made.

On the mainland, the herring used to be as important in the kitchen as it was in the fisheries. I must mention here one famous old dish, Tatties 'n' Herrin'. Salted herrings, after being desalted, were steamed in a big iron pot, sitting on top of potatoes being boiled in their jackets. The secret of success in this was to drain the potatoes when ready, but leave them in the pot, with a cloth cover, for a few minutes to become dry and mealy. This dish has its counterpart in the Priddhas an' Herrin' of the Isle of Man, which was served with slices of raw onion, and buttermilk.

Another traditional dish, which can be made today and is very good, has the startling title Hairy Tatties. This is nothing supernatural, but salt cod which has been desalted, cooked, flaked finely and beaten into a pot of well-mashed potatoes, with butter and black pepper. The flakes break up into strands not much thicker than hairs; and this explains the name.

All these old dishes are well documented. The standard of writing about Scottish cookery has been consistently high. I quote from some of the best books in the pages which follow, but should like to make honourable mention here of two earlier ones, those of Mrs Dalgairns (*The Practice of Cookery*, 1829) and Meg Dods (*The Cook and Housewife's Manual*, 1826). Mrs Dalgairns analyses, in a sentence worthy of Cicero, the chief requirements of a cookery book, which are: '. . . first, the intrinsic excellence of the precepts it contains; next, their economical adaptation to the habits and tastes of the majority of its readers; and, lastly, such a distinct arrangement of the various parts, that no difficulty can arise in searching for what is wanted, nor any ambiguity in the meaning of the directions when found.'

Meg Dods is not quite so earnest. In her recipes, she anticipated the requirements which Mrs Dalgairns was about to announce; but she rightly saw that there was a further requirement, namely, that a cookery book should be a pleasure to read as well as to use. Hers is certainly both. Thus she tells us how to make a workaday Salmagundi, but adds the following: '*Obs. An ornamental Salmagundi* was one of the frippery Scotch dishes of former times. This edifice was raised on a china bowl reversed, and placed in the middle of a dish, crowned with what, by the courtesy of the kitchen, was called a pine-apple, made of fresh butter. Around were laid, stratum above stratum, chopped eggs, minced herring and veal, rasped meat, and minced parsley; the whole surmounted by a triumphal arch of herring-bones, and adorned with a garnishing of barberries and samphire.' Thank you. I really wanted to hear about that more than the other.

Cullen Skink
serves four

This recipe, with its irresistible title, comes from *The Scottish Cookery Book* by Elizabeth Craig; a book which is based in scholarly fashion on Scots traditions, but is thoroughly practical, as one would expect from someone who wrote about food for Scottish newspapers. (Clippings of her recipes were in my grandmother's kitchen.)

a Finnan haddock (page 61), of medium size
an onion, chopped
milk, ½ litre (1 pint)

mashed potato, as required
butter, 15 g (½ oz)
salt and pepper to taste

Skin the haddock and put it in a shallow pan with just enough water to cover. Bring it slowly to the boil, then add the onion and continue cooking until the haddock turns 'creamy'. At this point, remove it from the pan, rid it of bones and flake the flesh. Return the bones to the pan, which must now be covered. Leave its contents to simmer for 1 hour.

Next, strain the stock and return it to the pan. While it is coming back to the boil, bring the milk to the boil in a separate pan. Add it, and the flaked fish, to the stock. Let it all simmer for another 5 minutes, then add enough mashed potato to make it into a cream soup. Add the butter in small bits, and seasoning.

Elizabeth Craig adds that a tablespoonful or two of cream and a heaped teaspoonful of chopped parsley can be stirred in before serving. I would add that smoked cod could be used in place of Finnan haddock.

Herring Grilled or Fried with Oatmeal

People with whom I stayed in Orkney showed me this simple procedure for Grilled Herring. Buy split fresh herring, wash them and pat them dry with a tea cloth. Lay them skin side down, and sprinkle oatmeal, which must be medium cut, over them. Pat it so that it sticks. Then put the fish under the grill, oatmeal side up, with little knobs of butter or margarine on top. Grill them thus for about 10 minutes, starting with a high heat and then lowering it.

It is more usual to find oatmeal being used for Fried Herring. A coarse cut is then suitable. The oatmeal simply takes the place of the bread-crumbs with which the fish would otherwise be coated. They can be dipped in milk before being coated with the oatmeal, but Marian McNeill says that fishermen's wives would not bother with this, but would simply salt, pepper and oatmeal the cleaned fish.

Jimmy Fraser's Soused Herring   serves six

Invited for 'a cup of tea' in the evening by the proprietor of the Universal
Fish Shop in Lerwick and knowing that in Shetland a cup of tea means a
meal, we wondered what we would be eating. The answer was Mr Fraser's
soused herring, prepared with fish landed that very day.

The recipe is simple. He had taken 13 herring, cleaned them, boned
them, laid them out open and flat on their backs and applied a little salt
and white pepper. He then rolled them up from head to tail and laid them
in a shallow casserole large enough to take them all in one layer. He added
a cup each of water and ordinary white vinegar and cooked the herrings in
a moderately hot oven (400° F, gas 6) for 25 minutes with the lid on and a
final 5 with the lid off, 'to brown the tops'. The result was extremely
good.

Barrie Davidson's Sweet Pickled Herring

This is a distinctive way of pickling herring, the results of which are
enjoyed by guests at the Kilchoan Hotel, Ardnamurchan. My fellow
clansman, whose hotel it is, declares it to be soundly based on a Highland
tradition and so popular that he has to make it frequently in the quantities
here indicated.

fresh herrings, 3¼ kg (7 lb),   a blade of mace, 15 g (½ oz)
   cleaned weight   peppercorns, 15 g (½ oz)
clear malt vinegar, 2¼ litres (2   cloves, 15 g (½ oz)
   British quarts)   large onions, 3, finely sliced
a stick of cinnamon, 15 g (½ oz)   acetic acid, 1 tsp
allspice, 15 g (½ oz)   sugar, 400 g (14 oz)

Combine all the ingredients except the herrings and boil them for 15
minutes. Then add the herrings, filleted, boned and cut into squares of 3
cm (1 inch). Let them simmer for 10 to 15 minutes, when they will be
'setting', i.e. achieving the right degree of firmness. Then leave them to
cool in the liquid.

Barrie Davidson says that the acetic acid, which may be bought at a
chemist's shop, helps the pickled herring to keep well. He also tells me that
herrings often have a good colour of their own, but that sometimes their
flesh is rather grey, even though the quality is excellent. In this event he
adds 2 drops of cochineal when putting in the fish; to restore their natural
colour, one might say.

Whiting in a Parsley Sauce

serves four

This is a good way of dealing with small, fresh whiting. Lady Harriet St Clair (in *Dainty Dishes*, 1856) called it whiting in the Scottish way and said that chopped chives or green onions should be added with the parsley. Later authors just say chives. I suggest neither.

whitings, 4	**chopped parsley, 4 tsp**
flour, salt and pepper	**milk, 1½ dl (¼ pint)**
butter, 50 g (2 oz)	**cream, 1 dl (7 tbs)**

Dip the cleaned fish in seasoned flour, shake off any excess, then fry them gently in the butter on one side, without allowing them to brown. Turn them over after a few minutes and let them cook likewise on the other side. Meanwhile blend the remaining ingredients together. Pour the mixture over the fish and let them finish cooking thus, basting them regularly. The whole cooking time will not be more than 10 minutes.

Fish Custard

serves four

This is a version of the recipe used by my grandmother Marion Davidson, at whose house near Glasgow I spent all my boyhood holidays. The main meal of the day was a high (very high) tea, at which a dish such as this would be preceded by a soup and followed by a profusion of Scots pancakes, raspberry jam, scones, black bun, biscuits and cakes. My grandmother loved cooking and was modestly puzzled by the fact that, through no fault of hers (for she was most generous with recipes and demonstrations), others could never quite match the flavour of her baking; or indeed of her fish custard. Do not, therefore, expect quite the results which she achieved, from these instructions!

Buy 4 fillets of fresh haddock, not too big, and cut them in two lengthwise (a procedure which enables one also to remove the little bits of bone which lie along the centre of the fillets). Roll up the fillets and place them in a well-buttered baking dish with the open end of the rolls uppermost. Into each such aperture introduce a pat of butter, which will melt and spiral downwards within the roll.

Make a custard mixture of 3 beaten eggs and 4 dl (¾ pint) milk, seasoned with salt and pepper. Pour this over the fish fillets, bake the dish for nearly an hour in a slow oven (290° F, gas 1), then serve it as it is, with a little chopped parsley sprinkled over it.

The rolled fillets should be such that a tablespoon will lift one out with some of the custard mixture. Whiting may be used instead of haddock.

Sara Fergusson's Smoked Haddock Mousse

serves four to six

'I take 2 tablespoonfuls of gelatine, soak it in ½ cup cold water and then dissolve it in 1 cup warm water. I always work with a large breakfast cup, by the way, not much different in size from a measuring cup.

'I add to the dissolved gelatine a cup of mayonnaise, 2 tablespoonfuls of lemon juice, a little salt, a pinch of paprika, 2 teaspoonfuls of Worcestershire sauce and ½ tablespoonful of grated onion. Then I fold in a cup of whipped double cream and chill the mixture until it is almost set. At that point I add 2½ cups of shredded smoked haddock and 2 stiffly beaten egg whites, pour the mixture into a greased mould and let it set in the refrigerator.

'I usually need 2 smoked haddocks for this, the pale yellow ones that are still on the bone, *not* the bright yellow smoked fillets.'

The same basic recipe can be used for **Mousse of Smoked Mackerel with Orange**. Use smoked mackerel instead of haddock. Substitute the juice of a whole orange for the lemon juice, and add 2 or 3 tsp of grated orange rind. Leave out the Worcestershire sauce and onion. The result is delicious and its appearance can be enhanced by decorating the top with thin slivers of orange peel.

Arbroath Smokies

'The Arbroath smokie originated in the near-by fishing-hamlet of Auchmithie. Day after day, during the season, the men set out with baited lines after the haddock.

' "With the setting of the sun," writes a native, "the boats come home and in the back-houses the lamps are lit. Up the brae come the creels of fish, and soon every woman and child is gutting, cleaning and salting. Little sticks of wood are stuck into the haddocks gills, and two by two, tied tail to tail, they are hung on little wooden spits high up in the old-fashioned lums (chimneys) . . . curing in the smoke of the fire; then they are taken down, gey black and sooty – but once remove the skins and what a delicious sight you see! Crisp, golden outer flesh paling into pure whiteness near the bone."

'In their picturesque fisher-dress the "luckies" (gudewives) went round the countryside with their creels strapped to their shoulders.

'As the demand grew, "smoke-pits" were sunk in the ground and the fish were hung over halved whisky barrels and smoked over chips of some special wood. (Oak and silver birch are commonly used in smoking fish.)

'Near the beginning of the nineteenth century, a community of Auchmithie fisherfolk settled in Arbroath and continued to practise their ancient craft; but it was not until near the end of the century that the industry as we know it today began to develop, and the name Auchmithie gave place to Arbroath.

'Whereas the finnan-haddie is split and cured to a golden-yellow, the Arbroath smokie is closed and is smoked to a sooty copper.'

The above is what Marian McNeill tells her readers about the origin of Arbroath smokies. Here is the accompanying recipe for serving them.

'Smokies, pepper, butter.

'Heat the fish on both sides (it has already been cooked in the long smoking process), open it out, remove the backbone, mill black pepper over the fish, spread with butter, close up and heat for a few minutes in the oven or under the grill. (In the old days it was brandered.) Serve piping hot.

'The smokie, like the finnan-haddie, makes an excellent savoury.'

Smoked Haddock with Bacon
serves four

My aunt Norah, who lives in Glasgow, finds that this popular dish combines three virtues: it is very easy to prepare, nutritious and tasty. She recommends that the bacon rashers be cut thin and that Wiltshire bacon should be first choice, with Ayrshire as runner-up. The fillets of smoked haddock should be small and it is best to buy the kind which have been skinned. If you have them with the skin on, cook them skin side down.

fillets of smoked haddock, 4 (see above)	bacon, 4 large or 8 small rashers (see above)
	butter

Rub a pie-dish or other shallow oven dish with a buttered paper. Put in the fillets, in a single layer; place the rashers of bacon on top of them, again in a single layer; cover with the buttered paper, buttered side down, and cook in a fairly slow oven (310° F, gas 2) for 30 minutes. Remove the paper for the last 5 minutes, so that the bacon can crisp.

An alternative procedure, only practicable with skinless fillets, is equally easy. Fry the bacon rashers in a pan, then remove them and drain them on absorbent paper. Meanwhile, put the fillets in the pan, just as they are, and fry them for no more than 2 to 3 minutes on each side. Then serve them with the bacon.

Bread and butter accompany the dish.

Krappin and Stap

Fish liver dishes from Shetland

Fish livers are rich in oil, which needs to be mopped up by something if it is to be consumed with pleasure. Krappin is essentially a mixture of fish liver and oatmeal. It is at its best when used to stuff a large fish head (or several smaller ones). It may then be called Krappin (or Krappit) Heid. The quantities given below are for four people and were measured when I made the dish with Mrs Hutchison in her kitchen at Lerwick. But please read the footnote too.

a cod's head weighing 2 kg (4 lb)
haddock livers,* 600 g (1⅓ lb)
oatmeal, 225 g (½ lb)
plain flour, 100 g (3½ oz)

salt, 1½ tsp
white pepper, 1 tsp
more salt to go in the water

Clean the head thoroughly by rinsing it under the tap, letting the water flow through mouth and gills.

Pick over the livers, snipping off any tiny worms on the surface (they look like small gelatinous pimples and are harmless, but should none the less be removed). Knead the livers in your hands in a mixing bowl until the membranes are all broken and you have a thick soupy mixture. Mix the oatmeal (fine-ground or of the breakfast variety) and the flour into this, turning it over and over with a wooden spoon until you have a stiff moist mixture rather like a hamburger-mix in consistency.

Next, lay the head on a board with the mouth up. Prise and hold the mouth open with a wooden spoon (not your fingers, because of the teeth) and stuff the liver mixture down. After two thirds of it has gone in, the head will seem fully stuffed. Lift it up, shake it and give a good pull to the flap of flesh under and between the gills. This will open the jaws further so that the rest of the stuffing fits in.

When the head is fully stuffed, place it in a cooking pot just large enough to take it and add salted water to cover or (if the pot is not quite deep enough) nearly to cover. It is a good idea (although not a Shetland one) to wrap the head in a piece of muslin, so that it can be turned over during the cooking and removed at the end without damage. Bring the water to the boil and let the head simmer for 50 to 60 minutes. (If you are using several smaller heads, the time will be reduced to 25 to 30 minutes.)

* Haddock livers, which are of a pale flesh colour (the paler the better) are thought by many to be the best; but cod livers can be used and ling livers have been very popular in Shetland. The consistency of livers varies. Ling livers are fairly firm, rather like calf's liver. Haddock livers are soft. Even within one species there may be differences which will affect the amount of oatmeal and flour which you add. It is best therefore to add these ingredients gradually until you achieve the right consistency, and to be prepared to use less or more than the quantities given.

Serve the whole head on what the Scots call an ashet (platter – the word comes from the French assiette), with potatoes which have been boiled in their skins, and let everyone compete in excavating choice morsels of flesh (for example, the cheeks) and hunks of stuffing.

This is a substantial dish. Shetlanders observe, with Celtic hyperbole, that after a good helping one needs no other food for twenty-four hours.

Stap is a simpler dish. It is best made with haddock, but other fish will do. Poach the appropriate quantity of fish ($\frac{1}{4}$ kg or $\frac{1}{2}$ lb per person) and half as much of fish livers, picked over and rid of any worms. Flake the cooked fish and mash it up with the cooked livers. Sprinkle with salt and white pepper. That is all. But the result is so good that it has inspired a Shetland poem, by J. J. Haldane Burgess, who recalls how he yowled and wept for stap as a child:

> Oh! weel I mind a schild I sat
> Apo me midder's lap
> An' weel I mind, I yowld and grat,
> An' skirléd oot for stap.

The poet goes on to declare of the dish that 'Hit gies wir young shields soople rigs. Hit gies wir lasses sap', which is to say that it gives young Shetlanders desirable physical attributes. More prosaically, a Shetland acquaintance said: 'It's a very nice feed, something most people can take to.'

NOTE: There are even stranger things to be done with cods' livers. Lillian Beckwith writes: 'One old Bruach fisherman told me that it was usual for the men on his boat to take some of the livers from the cod they caught and put them between two thick slices of bread. Then they would wrap the "sandwiches" in a fold of oilskin and put them on the seat in the wheelhouse where the skipper would be sure to sit on them for a few hours. When they felt peckish they retrieved their sandwiches which of course were now impregnated with the oil squeezed from the livers.'

A Shetland
Yawl

Lobster Bisque (economical)

serves six

Lillian Beckwith's *Hebridean Cookbook* is both practical and readable. This recipe reflects the feeling for economy which we Scots possess and is very useful if you live near a source of lobster debris.

lobster shells, 1 or 2	**butter, 25 g (1 oz)**
water, 1¼ litre (2 pints)	**flour, 1 tbs**
salt and pepper	**cream, 1½ dl (¼ pint)**
a pinch of sweet basil	

'Pound the lobster shell into small pieces and put into the cold water along with the salt and pepper and sweet basil. Bring to the boil and simmer for one and a half to two hours. Sieve the liquid carefully so that no pieces of shell remain.

'Meanwhile melt the butter in a saucepan. Stir in the flour until it begins to froth. Add lobster stock slowly, stirring continuously. Cook for ten minutes. Remove from heat and stir in the fresh cream.

'If you want to be more extravagant you can, of course, add flaked lobster flesh to the bisque.'

Partan, Dressed Hot

serves two to four

A partan is a crab (*Cancer pagurus*, page 194). These can be very big. The number of servings will depend on the size. The quantities given here are right for one measuring 20 cm (8 inches) across the carapace, which will serve four.

a large crab	**lemon juice *or* wine vinegar, 4 tbs**
salt and pepper	**made mustard, 2 tsp**
nutmeg, 2 pinches	**butter, 15 g (½ oz)**
soft breadcrumbs, 2 tbs	

Cook the crab as usual and let it cool, then remove all the edible parts and chop them up in a bowl. Add the remaining ingredients, after chopping up the butter, and beat all well together.

Wash the shell (carapace) very carefully and polish it inside and out with a cloth dipped in a teaspoon of salad oil. Then pack the mixture into it and brown it under the grill (the shell, of course, being on its back, so that the heat plays directly on to the contents). Marian McNeill says that 'the old cottage way was to heat a shovel in the fire and hold it over the pie'; pie being what they would call a partan dressed in this manner.

Limpet Stovies

Commenting on this recipe in her classic work, *The Scots Kitchen*, Marian McNeill says that the contributor was a native of Colonsay who declared: 'I have never seen or heard of the above but in Colonsay, nor have I tasted anything better.'

'Limpets, potatoes, water, pepper, salt, butter.

'Gather two quarts of limpets on the rocks at low tide. Put them in a pot, cover them with water, and bring to the boil. Take out the limpets, remove them from the shells, and remove the eyes and the sandy trail. Take three times their quantity of peeled potatoes, put a layer in the bottom of a large round three-legged pot, add a layer of limpets, season with pepper and a little salt, and repeat the operation until they are all used up. Then add two cupfuls of the liquor in which the limpets were scalded and put pieces of butter over the top, using about half a pound for that quantity. Cover it all with a clean white cloth well rolled in round the edges, bring to the boil, and hang it high up on the crook above a peat-fire. Let it simmer slowly for at least an hour.'

Spoots in Orkney

Spoots are what Orcadians call razor-shells (page 240). The traditional way of eating them is to place them on the girdle iron over the fire. As soon as the shells open, the molluscs within are lifted out and eaten.

Nowadays, however, Orcadians are more likely to use the following method. Place the spoots in boiling water just long enough for the shells to open. Then take the animals from their shells and fry them quickly in butter; barely enough to turn them and coat all sides – the whole process should take no longer than 1 minute, indeed 30 seconds, according to some people.

An Orkney schoolmaster who has made a study of spoot cookery confirms that spoots may be left overnight in a bucket of sea water in order to evacuate their stomachs; but he says that the stomach is so small in relation to the rest of the animal that it is just as easy, and not at all wasteful, simply to cut it off. He is strongly of the view that no recipe for spoots which involves long cooking should ever be recommended by anyone. 'If a spoot is cooked for more than a couple of minutes it comes out like the inner tube of a bicycle tire. This is a mistake often made by "ferryloupers" [i.e. immigrants from the mainland] who as a result are put off spoots for life and cannot imagine why the Orcadians regard them as the best of seafood dishes.'

28. Recipes from England

Scot though I am, England is where I live; which may be why I find it difficult to present a coherent picture of English seafood cookery. The perceptions of a resident are often more blinkered than those of a visitor; and there is the general difficulty that the gap between traditional fish cookery and present practice is, so it seems to me, wider in England than in most other countries.

So I have attempted neither an historical nor a regional survey, but have simply assembled English recipes which please me, laying emphasis on what I think the English do particularly well. I mean things like potted salmon and potted shrimp; fish pies; the cookery of rays, skates and dogfish; and, of course, fish and chips.

Are fish and chips our national dish? Perhaps they deserve the title. But the dish is not of great antiquity. It is true that in the mid nineteenth century many fish fryers were already at work in London, often operating in noisome alleys. ('A gin-drinking neighbourhood suits best,' one coster said, 'for people haven't their smell so correct there.') But the potatoes which they offered with the fish were baked potatoes. Cutting, in *Fish Saving*, states that the practice of selling chipped potatoes began about 1870 and was introduced from France.

The early fish and chip vendors were often ex-stokers, which was fitting, since they did their frying in open cauldrons fired by coal. There were complaints about the smell and the lack of hygiene. But the ruffians kept at it, crying: 'Come on, in your thousands; we are the people who feed the hungry. Come on, pen'orths; stand back, ha'porths.' And the fashion caught on, especially in Lancashire, perhaps (again according to Cutting) 'because with so many women there employed in the cotton mills, a cheap ready-made, hot meal satisfied an urgent social need'. It was also in Lancashire that engineers developed improved frying ranges. But it is in Yorkshire that our most famous fish and chip establishment is located; and it is thence, near my former home in Leeds, that I have drawn the following little essay.

I have not, by the way, forgotten jellied eel. But, having had an eel and pie shop just round the corner for many years, I share the view of most Londoners that this is something you buy rather than make.

Fish and Chips

When you go to Harry Ramsden's at Guiseley in Yorkshire, you can still see the original little green and white shanty where the late Harry Ramsden himself shrewdly started his business, at a road junction which is the gateway to the Yorkshire Dales for both Leeds and Bradford. But the place is now so large that its annual consumption of ingredients is: fish, 400,000 lb; dripping, 150,000 lb; potatoes, 900,000 lb; sauce, 20,000 bottles; tea, 6,000 lb; butter, 13,000 lb; bread, 26,400 loaves; milk, 84,000 pints; sugar, 14,000 lb; salt, 2,000 lb; and vinegar, 9,000 pints.

These figures almost constitute a recipe. The recipe which they follow is in fact very simple. They use prime fresh fish from Grimsby, skinned and filleted. The fillets are dipped in a batter made of 3 lb flour (which comes in bags wittily labelled 'HR Plain Flour', the point being that a secret ingredient is supposedly mixed with the flour at the place of manufacture), 1½ tbs salt, ½ level tsp 'batter powder' and 3 litres of water. (This half-metricized list is what they actually use, and I have left it as it is.) The battered fillets are then immersed in pure beef dripping at a temperature of 370° F for 2 to 3 minutes, after which the temperature is allowed to drop to 360° F for the further 2 to 3 minutes' cooking. And so to table, with chips of sensible thickness (about 1 cm or ⅜ inch).

Although I have lived in both Lancashire and Yorkshire, and thought myself well aware of the differences between them, one had escaped me. In Yorkshire almost all the fish used for fish and chips is haddock. Harry Ramsden's reckon to use about 1200 stone of haddock to 60 of halibut and 40 of plaice. These are the only three species which they prepare; and this is typical of Yorkshire. But in Lancashire cod takes the place of haddock. The division corresponds very closely to the county boundaries, although there are grey areas like Huddersfield, which is in Yorkshire but inclines to cod.

Another thing which I learned at Harry Ramsden's is that the ordinary sort of fish cake is not the only kind. What they make are special *Yorkshire Fish Cakes*. Peter, their potato expert, selects the largest potatoes which come his way and puts them through a machine which cuts them into slices of about 2 mm thickness. Meanwhile, the process of cutting their haddock (into 'specials', which are pieces weighing between 6½ and 7½ oz, and ordinary helpings, from 3½ to 4½ oz) has yielded a supply of small off-cuts. These are minced and used as the filling for 'sandwiches' in which the role usually played by bread is usurped by the potato slices. The entire 'sandwiches' are then deep-fried and emerge as fish cakes. They are very good indeed.

Royal Lamprey Pie from the City of Gloucester

(to serve the Queen, her Consort and twenty-two others)

The Severn used to be famous for its lampreys (page 176), and the City of Gloucester for preparing them. There is still a street there called The Lampreys and a pub called The Lamprey. By long-standing tradition, the city presents to the sovereign on special occasions a lamprey pie.

In 1977, the year of Her Majesty's Jubilee, the authorities at Gloucester adhered to the tradition. Lampreys were caught by Phillip Gaskin of the Severn River Authority, and the pie was planned and baked by Marie Edwards and her colleagues and students in the Home Economics Department of the Gloucestershire College of Education. Here is how they did it.

sea lampreys, 12, average length
20 inches
a marinade consisting of dry white
wine and vinegar in equal
parts, 2 sliced lemons, 6 bay
leaves, 24 peppercorns, 2 tsp
mace, and salt and pepper at
discretion

for the hot water crust pastry:
strong plain flour, 1¾ kg (4 lb);
hard cooking fat, 450 g (1 lb);
water, 11½ dl (2 British pints);
salt, 2 tsp
beaten eggs, for glazing the pastry
gelatine for the aspic
cucumber slices

(1) Behead, skin and clean the lampreys. Cut them into sections of about 2 inches and leave them in the marinade for up to 48 hours.

(2) Cook the pieces of lamprey, still in their marinade, in a covered pot. Allow 45 minutes from when the liquid starts to simmer. Let the lampreys cool in the marinade, then remove them, take out the cartilaginous 'bones' and flake the flesh. Strain and reserve the liquid.

(3) Now prepare the hot water crust pastry (also known as raised pie crust pastry). Sieve the flour and salt into a warm basin. Next, bring the lard and the water to the boil together, then pour it into the middle of the flour and mix rapidly with a wooden spoon. Once it is cool enough to touch, knead it with the hand until quite smooth, adding a little more boiling liquid if necessary. Proceed at once to shape the pie-case, pie-lid and plinth, reserving a little dough for decorations.

(4) Take a cake tin 11 inches in diameter by 4 inches deep. Invert it and cover the outside neatly with greased foil. Using rather more than half the dough, shape the pie-case over the tin, taking care to achieve a uniform thickness and to avoid weaknesses at the edge. Leave it on the tin, ready to bake. Shape the pie-lid over a slightly larger tin, giving it a turned-down rim. Make cuts in this rim at ½ inch intervals, and then turn one piece up

and one down alternately to produce a castellated effect. Shape the plinth in the form of a ring which will just fit outside the pie-case and come about ¼ inch up it. Bake all these prepared pieces in a hot oven (400° F, gas 6) for 1 to 1½ hours. Glaze them with beaten egg towards the end of the cooking time.

(5) Prepare the aspic with the gelatine and the strained cooking liquid. Just before it sets, add the flaked fish. Grease the original cake tin, pack the mixture into it and chill it overnight.

(6) Next day, fill the pie-case. By a series of inversions and re-inversions you must transfer the fish-in-aspic into the case, which it will fit nicely with only a tiny space round the edge. Pour in a little more aspic to fill this space and to cover the top. Set cucumber slices in the aspic on top.

(7) Decorate the pie-lid appropriately. 'On this occasion,' Marie Edwards informs me, 'the City and College crests were chosen, interspersed with Tudor roses – all made from a flour and water paste and previously painted, using culinary colourings.' A jubilee ribbon was then placed round the pie, above the plinth, and the plinth itself decorated with small pastry lampreys and shells.

The finished pie weighed about 5½ kg (12 lb), excluding the handsome wooden base which had been made to support it on its journey in the Mayoral car to Buckingham Palace.

Sceptical members of the press who ate 'off-cuts' left over from the making of the pie confessed that it was delicious. A similar pie may, of course, be made with eel, or salmon, or indeed with white fish.

Red Herrings and Bloaters

The picture below shows the preparation of the famous red herrings of East Anglia; an important British export in previous centuries and a well-loved food. Thomas Nashe, a Lowestoft man, extolled it thus in *Lenten Stuffe, or the Praise of the Red Herring* (1567): 'The puissant red herring, the golden Hesperides red herring, . . . euery pregnant peculiar of whose resplendent laude and honour to delineate and adumbrate to the ample life were a woorke that would drinke drie fourescore and eighteene Castalian fountains of eloquence.' He says that the delicacy was discovered accidentally by a Yarmouth fisherman who, 'having drawne so many herrings hee wist not what to do with all', hung the surplus from the rafters of his hut, above a smoky fire, and noticed a few days later that the fish, 'which were as white as whale-bone when he hung them up, now lookt as red as a lobster'. He proclaimed the news and the process was then refined and developed into a threefold procedure. The herrings, ungutted and unsplit, were first soaked in brine with saltpetre added, then hung up to dry, and finally smoked for 24 to 48 hours over oak, beech and turf.

A. M. Samuel, the East Anglian author of *The Herring: Its Effect on the History of Britain* (1918), wrote this about the red herring:

This fish is not gutted until it reaches the kitchen. The Yarmouth red herring may be eaten, uncooked, during the months of October, November and December. The skin should be peeled off, the head removed, and the fish gutted and cut across into four pieces, dusted with pepper, and eaten with bread and butter. The Yarmouth red herring is locally sometimes called a 'militiaman'; *per contra*, the vulgar Norfolk term for a militiaman in his red tunic . . . was a 'red herring', much as the red herrings sold in the south of Scotland are sometimes known as 'Glasgow magistrates'.

Bloaters are of less antiquity and have a milder cure; no saltpetre in the brine, and smoking for 12 to 18 hours only. Samuel derives their name from the Swedish word blöta, meaning to steep. He also declares that they are 'of the right delicacy and quality only in and near Great Yarmouth'. This is still true, although refrigeration now permits them to be distributed further afield. They can be eaten raw, in the same fashion as the red herring (see above); or grilled and served with butter; or made into bloater paste. Their slightly gamey flavour is most attractive.

Northumberland Potted Salmon

In earlier centuries salmon was much more plentiful than it is now, and old English cookery books contain a wide variety of recipes for it. One of the earliest English fish cookery books (*Fish and How to Cook It*, by Elizabeth Watts, 1866) strays north of the border to mention that on the Beauly in Inverness-shire 'the Frasers, who were lords of the manor, used sometimes to surprise their guests with a voluntarily cooked salmon. A kettle was placed on a flat rock on the south side of the fall, at the water's edge, and kept full and boiling until a salmon fell into it.' I suppose that you could call this 'potting' a salmon. But potting it in the ordinary sense of the word is still useful today, when one may wish to have small tastes at intervals of an expensive piece of the fish, instead of eating it all at once.

Scale your section of salmon, open it out from below and remove the bone. Choose an ovenproof earthenware pot into which the piece of fish will fit snugly. Season it with salt, a little powdered mace and a few cloves; and fit it into the pot. Put half a dozen peppercorns and several bay leaves on top, then cover the whole with a good slab of butter. Tie a buttered paper over the top and bake it in a moderate oven (355° F, gas 4) for an hour or more. Then remove it, drain off the juices, pound the flesh, pack it into clean pots, let it cool and seal with melted butter.

Cod or Other Fish with Samphire Sauce

Any fish with firm, white flesh is suitable for this recipe. It should be poached in the usual way. Do not attempt the dish with fried fish.

Samphire, *Crithmum maritimum*, is the plant illustrated below. It is not a seaweed, but a sea plant, growing on sand dunes and similar ground close to the sea. It used sometimes to be called St Peter's grass.

Friends sometimes bring us a bucketful from Norfolk. For $\frac{1}{2}$ kg (1 lb) fish, we take 350 g ($\frac{3}{4}$ lb) of prepared samphire, well washed and with the hard bits of stalk near the roots cut off, and cook it for 10 minutes in a covered pot with 4 tbs water. Then we drain it and use an electric blender to turn it into a purée, incorporating 80 g (3 oz) butter in it. The purée is then heated and poured over the fish as a sauce. It has a marvellously bright green colour – any other so-called green sauce would go even greener with envy – and a delicious flavour. But it is quite salty, so on no account add salt.

I thought that this was our invention, and indeed it was in the sense that we thought of it ourselves. However, I recently saw that Gerard, in his *Herball* (1597) described samphire as 'the pleasantest sauce, most familiar and best agreeing with man's body'. It is not clear how he made it into a sauce, or for what; but he and his contemporaries were obviously ahead of us. More evidence of this, with fascinating literary and etymological notes, are in Geoffrey Grigson's *The Englishman's Flora*.

One thing is clear, that there is a very old tradition of pickling samphire. The Swedish writer Kalm, in the diary of his travels in England, wrote a long note under the date 3 August 1748 about Englishwomen who were plucking samphire on the banks of the Thames estuary, and preserving it in such a way as to retain the green colour. Erroll Sherson (*The Book of Vegetable Cookery*, 1931) says that it used to be cried in the streets of London as 'cress marine', and gives recipes both for buttered samphire (bacile au beùrre) and pickled samphire. Samphire is still pickled in Norfolk, and in the region of Nantes in France.

In North America there are similar plants, of the genus *Salicornia*, which may be called samphire or glasswort or chicken claws. They can be treated in the same ways.

John Dory with Herbs, Cider and Cream   serves two

Devon is a good county for John Dory and this is a Devonshire recipe, attributed by Elizabeth Lothian (*Devonshire Flavour*) to Mr and Mrs Milne, whose bookshop in Dartmouth I once visited, mistakenly looking for recipes on the shelves instead of in the kitchen.

John Dory (page 80), 4 good fillets of at least 75 g (3 oz) each	**chopped herbs – parsley; fennel leaves; marjoram or basil**
seasoned flour	**lemon juice, 1 tbs**
butter, 30 g (1 oz)	**dry cider, 1 dl (5–6 tbs)**
cooking oil, 1 tbs	**single cream *or* 'top of bottle', 2 or 3 tbs**

Wash and dry the fillets. Dip them in seasoned flour, using freshly ground black pepper. Heat the butter and oil in an enamelled skillet or shallow stoneware dish (not a metal one, because of the cider). Add the herbs and fry the fillets gently, skin side up, for 3 to 4 minutes. Then sprinkle the lemon juice over them, add the cider, turn the heat right down, cover the dish and leave to simmer for 10 minutes.

Remove the skin from the fillets and add the cream to the small quantity of sauce in the dish. Serve the fillets with their sauce straight from the pan, with new potatoes and a green salad.

East Riding Mackerel   serves four

Whitby on the Yorkshire coast was where I caught my first mackerel. Being but twelve years old, I was nonplussed when asked how I would like it cooked. Now I would recommend this recipe, itself a Yorkshire one.

mackerel, 4	**vinegar, about 4 or 5 tbs**
medium shallots, 4, chopped	**a little cornflour**
salt and pepper	**grated cheese, 4 tbs**

Behead and gut the fish, open them out flat from below, remove the backbones and give the fish a rinse. Lay them out, skin side down, in a buttered oven dish. Sprinkle the shallots and seasoning over them. Then cover them with equal quantities of vinegar and water.

Cover the dish with greaseproof paper or foil and bake it in a moderate oven (355° F, gas 4) for 20 minutes. Drain off the liquid and thicken it with cornflour (previously mixed with a little cold water). Pour the liquid back over the fish, sprinkle the grated cheese on top and brown it under the grill for a few minutes.

Fricasseed Skate   serves four

I have met this recipe in twentieth-, nineteenth- and eighteenth-century cookery books. The earliest version which I have found is that of John Farley (*The London Art of Cookery*, 1787). His instructions, whether or not they were the first to be published, have been copied word for word by numerous later authors, usually without either attribution or comment. One wonders whether any of them tried the recipe. We had to do it three times before we evolved a version which was both compatible with what Farley wrote and also successful. In fact this amplified version, given below, is more than successful; it is superb.

wing of skate (ray), 1¼ kg (2½ lb)	**butter, 50 g (2 oz)**
mace, ½ tsp	**flour, 4 tbs**
a good pinch of grated nutmeg	**single cream, 2½ dl (almost ½**
a bouquet garni	**pint)**
salt	**white wine, 2 dl (⅓ pint)**

If what you have is a section of a large wing of skate, dress it so that you have clean pieces, free of cartilage, about an inch across and two inches long. (Don't worry about the exact size or shape. A wing of skate being what it is, you are bound to finish up with some triangles, rhomboids, etc.) If you are dealing with a small wing, it will be simpler just to cut it along the lines of the fibres, from the thick side to the thin side, into strips about an inch wide. The flesh will slip off the cartilage easily enough after it is cooked.

Weigh the pieces of skate, place them in a stew-pan and add 7 dl (1¼ pint) water. Add also a little ground mace and grated nutmeg, a bouquet garni and salt. Bring all this to the boil, cover and leave to simmer for 15 minutes. Then discard the bouquet garni, remove the skate and keep it hot. (Any further removal of cartilage can be done at this stage.) You will find that you have about ¾ cup of cooking liquid left in the pan.

Melt the butter, add the flour, stir, add the cooking liquid and a very little salt. Then add the single cream and the white wine. Bring the mixture back to the boil and let it simmer gently and thicken for 3 to 4 minutes.

Replace the pieces of skate in the sauce and serve hot.

Picnic Skate Pie   serves four

It is always pleasant to read, in cookery books published between the two World Wars, about dishes suitable to be put 'in the car luncheon basket'.

I may be wrong, but I fancy that the British were the people who took their picnics most seriously. The illustrious Mrs Leyel published a little volume of recipes suitable for motorists' picnics; and this recipe might well have been in it, although in fact I do not know whence it comes.

Cook ½ kg (1 lb) of skate by poaching it in a court-bouillon. Take it out when ready and separate the flesh from the cartilage, discarding the latter.

Line a shallow round pie dish (about 10 inches in diameter) with short-crust pastry (of which you will need about 1 kg or 2 lb in all) and dispose the flaked fish on it, adding 2 tbs of your favourite chutney, minced finely and evenly distributed. Carefully break 4 eggs over all, keeping the yolks whole. Then cover the top with the remaining pastry and bake the pie in a moderately hot oven (400° F, gas 6) for 25 to 30 minutes, until the top is lightly browned.

The pie can be eaten hot, but is better cold. I arranged to have it made in Wiltshire, which is good picnic country, and it received top marks from all who ate it. One version of the recipe says that it 'cuts firm', which is correct; and calls it royal skate pie, which makes one wonder whether perhaps at Balmoral or Sandringham, back in the 1920s . . .?

Monkfish and Fried Apples   serves three

This comes from the *Daily Express Prize Recipes for Fish Cookery*, published in the (?) 1930s and full of good things.

monkfish (page 171, *not* page 161), ½ kg (1 lb)	peppercorns, 2
stock or water, 4 tbs	cloves, 2
vinegar, 4 tbs	large cooking apples, 2
salt, 1 tsp	pork dripping or fat, 60 g (2 oz)

'Wash the fish and cut it into convenient-sized pieces. Place in a pie-dish with the stock or water, vinegar, salt, peppercorns and cloves, and cover with greased paper.

'Bake if the oven is being used for other things; if not place it on an asbestos mat over a low gas. Turn the fish over when it is half done. It takes about 15 minutes, and is cooked when the flesh is soft . . .

'Peel the apples, cut them in quarters, and take out the cores. Cut each quarter into 3 or 4 slices. Heat the dripping, put in the apples and fry them slowly till soft; turn them over when half done.

'To serve, place fish on a hot dish with a border of apples and pour in the rest of the dripping.'

Eliza Acton's Baked Soles

I give this recipe in Eliza Acton's own words, since they demonstrate so clearly the thoroughness with which she tested her recipes and the nicety and charm with which she wrote them. This one was evidently a favourite. It is sub-titled 'A simple but excellent Recipe'. I would only add, thinking of the price of soles, that it suits lemon soles too.

'After the fish has been skinned and cleaned in the usual way, wipe it dry, and let it remain for an hour or more, if time will permit, closely folded in a clean cloth; then mix with a slightly beaten egg about an ounce of butter, just liquefied but not *heated* at the mouth of the oven, or before the fire; brush the fish in every part with this mixture, and cover it with very fine dry bread-crumbs, seasoned with a little salt, cayenne, pounded mace, and nutmeg. Pour a teaspoonful or two of liquid butter into a flat dish which will contain the fish well; lay it in, sprinkle it with a little more butter, press the bread-crumbs lightly on it with a broad-bladed knife, and bake it in a moderate oven for about twenty minutes. On our first essay of this receipt, the fish dressed by it (it was baked for twenty-five minutes in a very slack iron oven) proved infinitely nicer than one of the same size which was fried, and served with it. The difference between them was very marked, especially as regarded the exceeding tenderness of the flesh of that which was baked; its appearance, however, would have been somewhat improved by a rather quicker oven. When ready to serve, it should be gently glided on to the dish in which it is to be sent to table. About three ounces of bread-crumbs, and two and a half of butter, will be sufficient for a large pair of soles. They will be more perfectly encrusted with the bread if dipped into, or sprinkled with it a second time, after the first coating has been well moistened with the butter.'

Eliza gives a companion recipe for **Soles Stewed in Cream**. 'Prepare some very fresh middling sized soles with exceeding nicety, put them into boiling water slightly salted, and simmer them for two minutes only; lift them out and let them drain; lay them into a wide stewpan with as much sweet cream as will nearly cover them; add a good seasoning of pounded mace, cayenne, and salt; stew the fish softly from six to ten minutes, or until the flesh parts readily from the bones; dish them, stir the juice of half a lemon to the sauce, pour it over the soles, and send them immediately to table. Some lemon-rind may be boiled in the cream, if approved; and a small teaspoonful of arrow-root, very smoothly mixed with a little milk, may be stirred to the sauce (should it require thickening) before the lemon-juice is added.'

She adds that for 3 or 4 soles you will need $\frac{1}{2}$-1 pint cream.

Cornish Crab Pasty

In *Cornish Recipes, Ancient and Modern* (compiled by Edith Martin, 1929) we read the following: 'The Cornish pasty is, and has been from time immemorial, the staple dish of the County . . . It is said that the Devil has never crossed the Tamar into Cornwall, on account of the well-known habit of Cornishwomen of putting everything into a pasty, and that he was not sufficiently courageous to risk such a fate!'

Oddly, Cornishwomen do not often put crab into their pasties; but it makes an excellent filling.

To make the pastry for Cornish pasties, use 450 g (1 lb) flour, 225 g ($\frac{1}{2}$ lb) lard or suet or a mixture of the two, $\frac{1}{2}$ tsp salt and enough water to mix a fairly firm dough. Roll it out $\frac{1}{2}$ cm ($\frac{1}{4}$ inch) thick and use a plate to cut it into rounds about 15 cm (6 inches) in diameter.

Have your cooked and flaked crabmeat ready, moistened with lemon juice and mixed with some chopped parsley. Take a round of pastry and put it on a floured board. Dispose a helping of the crab mixture on one side, then fold the other side over to make a semi-circular pasty. Crimp the edges down and make a slit in the middle of the top. Then bake the pasties in a hot oven (430° F, gas 7) for about 20 minutes. You will find them very good either hot or cold, and that you only need fingers with which to eat them.

Betsy Tatterstall's Shrimp Paste (or Potted Shrimp)

Dorothy Hartley, in her classic work *Food in England*, gives a beautifully detailed description of the sort of shrimp tea which was served 'up north' and which I can still remember from the 1930s. Betsy Tatterstall not only served shrimp teas but also made the best potted shrimp in her district. This is her recipe.

'Weigh the shrimps, and take an equal quantity of fine flaked white fish. Shell the shrimps, and put heads and shells to boil in enough water to cover. Drain, remove the shells and heads, and now cook the flaked fish in this shrimp water till soft. Let cool, and pound to a smooth paste with a careful seasoning of powdered mace, cayenne and one single spot of anchovy sauce. Now measure, and add an almost equal quantity of butter. When smooth, stir in all the whole shrimps, make all piping hot, press into pots, and flood with the melted butter on the top.

'The effect was a solid potful of shrimps, cemented together with a soft. delicately seasoned pink butter. It was a great delicacy, and always served in fine white china.'

29. Recipes from Wales

Traditional Welsh cookery is elusive. In previous centuries it was over-shadowed by the English cookery which was practised in the better-off households. At the present time, amid the general enthusiasm for re-discovering local and regional cuisines, efforts have been made to recon-stitute a corpus of Welsh recipes; but much of what has appeared in print is pseudonymous and poorly documented and can be traced back to the out-of-print *Croeso Cymreig* (A Welsh Welcome), a book produced by the Welsh Gas Board which had its origin in a general competition for good recipes, whether Welsh or not.

It is fortunate that one person, Mrs Minwel Tibbott of the Welsh Folk Museum at St Fagans, has conducted some systematic, oral research, finding out from older people what they can relate about their traditional methods of preparing food. Two of the recipes below come from *Amser Bwyd*, the book containing the results of her work (also available in English, as *Welsh Fare*).

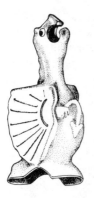

In general, Welsh seafood cookery displays a Celtic character, showing affinities with Irish and Scottish recipes. It also, of course, exhibits some specialization in the kinds of seafood which are or were locally abundant, such as cockles, laver and herring; and, on a higher plane, the magnificent salmon and sewin (salmon trout) which are taken in Welsh rivers. I have illustrated these themes in what follows and have also taken care to include one recipe which uses the Welsh leek and invokes the Welsh talent for baking.

In connection with this last recipe (page 464) I ex-hibit here something which serves both as the emblem of Wales and as a useful aid in the kitchen. It is a Welsh pie dragon, which takes the place of an ordinary pie-glass in the middle of a pie. Like the other, it serves both as a support for the top crust and as a vent for the steam; but has the added attraction that the steam issues from the dragon's mouth.

Berwi Gwyniedyn mewn Llaeth

Sewin (salmon trout) cooked in milk serves four

Wales is famous for its salmon trout (page 45), for which the local name is
sewin. The name Welsh salmon was also applied to it in the past. It used to
be so plentiful that it was not just a luxury food for the English gentry
living in Wales but something which most people would eat from time to
time; and there are, therefore, genuine Welsh traditions for its cookery.
The most popular way of serving it was to cut it into steaks and fry these
in bacon fat or butter. But it might also be steamed or poached, with
fennel. And there is this interesting recipe from Dyfed (formerly
Carmarthenshire), which I have tried and found excellent.

sewin, a piece weighing 600–700 g (1¼–1½ lb) cleaned, to provide 4 good steaks
milk, ¾–1¼ litre (1½–2 pints)
a little salt
sprigs of fennel (optional)
farm (or other) cream, 2–3 dl (about ½ pint)

The amount of milk needed will depend on the shape of your cooking pot.

If the piece of fish fits it snugly, the smaller
quantity will do; but you must have enough
to cover the fish.

Bring the milk to the boil, add a little salt
and lower the fish gently into the pot. If you
wish, you can wrap it in a muslin first, so
that it can be got out easily later. You can
also add fennel sprigs. Let the milk come
back to the boil, then keep it gently simmering for a time (about 30 to 50 minutes) which
will depend on the greatest thickness of the
fish (cf. page 258). When the sewin is done,
lift it out, let it cool a little, cut it into four
thick slices and serve it with hot baked
potatoes and fresh farm cream. I would add
lettuce leaves and a sprinkling of finely
chopped fresh chives.

The dish is also very good if served cold.

The drawing shows a Welsh coracle fisherman, no doubt setting off in search of sewin
or salmon.

Môr-Lysywen o Landdulas

Conger eel as cooked at Llanddulas

It was in the Opera House at Warsaw that someone told me how certain quarrymen in the north of Wales fish for the conger with iron rods. Proceeding therefore to Llanddulas, I found in Dennis Rogers a willing informant. Like his father and grandfather before him, he looks forward every year to the summer months when the conger is to be found close inshore. September is the best month of all; and the combination of a very low tide with a hot and thundery atmosphere offers ideal conditions.

The implement used is an iron rod formed into a handle at one end and a blunt hook at the other. (A sharp hook would tear right through the flesh and is therefore useless.) The one used by Mr Rogers and illustrated at the foot of the page is a little shorter than most, but has been in use for two generations and caught a prize specimen in the 1930s.

The procedure is to go down to the water's edge at low tide and to poke the hooked end gently under large stones or rocks. If a conger is there, it can be felt squirming around. The rod is then manipulated so that with a sudden pull it will engage in the conger's flesh and draw it out. (Spectators who think that the fisherman is looking for crabs are startled almost out of their wits when a six-foot conger shoots out by their feet. Mr Rogers recalls one onlooker who fell full length into the sea, so great was his consternation.)

The conger thus caught is taken home and hung up by a cord around its neck. A careful incision, right round the neck and below the cord, is then made with a razor blade. The cut must go through the skin but not into the flesh. Nippers are then used to roll the skin back from the cut towards the tail. 'It's hard work until you get half-way down – then it comes off like a glove.' The conger, now all pearly white, is gutted and cut across into steaks, ready for cooking.

Mr Rogers then steams the steaks for 20 to 30 minutes, after which he removes them from the steamer and lets them dry out a bit before pan-frying them. He uses pork dripping, a staple in traditional Welsh cooking; just enough to cover the bottom of the pan. And he puts the steamed steaks straight in without any batter or other coating. As the steaks fry, he turns them over and over until they are well done on both sides; and that's all there is to it.

Pennog Picl

Welsh soused or pickled herrings   serves four

This recipe for Soused Herrings was in use in the west of Wales in the not very distant past, and will be worth reviving when herrings are again to be had.

fresh herrings, 4	bay leaves, 2
chopped chives, 1 tbs	whole peppercorns, 4
chopped parsley, 1 tbs	vinegar, as required
salt and pepper	watercress and shredded celery
mixed spices, 2 pinches	salad oil, to taste

Clean the herrings, make each into a double fillet, wash and dry them. Lay them on a board, skin side down, and sprinkle the chopped chives and parsley over them, also salt and pepper to taste. Then roll the fillets up and bind or skewer each one firmly. (Or, if this suits either you or your pie-dish better, you can leave them flat.)

Put the fillets in a pie-dish, sprinkle the mixed spices over them, add the peppercorns and bay leaves and a teaspoonful of salt. Cover the fillets with a mixture of three parts vinegar to one part water. Bake slowly in a moderate oven (355° F, gas 4) for 1 hour.

When the dish is cold, remove the skewers or binding from the fillets, wipe off any spices or bits of bay leaf and arrange the fillets in a serving dish. Garnish them with watercress and shredded celery; and season with salt and pepper and salad oil to taste.

This dish was made for immediate consumption. But the Welsh also have a way of preparing Pickled Herrings, which will keep for some time. This starts on standard lines – the cleaned herrings, with onion rings and pickling spices, are covered with three parts vinegar to one of water – but has a surprise ending. A teaspoonful of black treacle, which used to be the main sweetening agent in Welsh cookery and was sold by the jugful in Welsh grocers' stores, is dissolved in a little warm water and then poured into the mixture. This is followed by a little cornflour which has been blended with cold water. The dish is then baked in a slow oven for a long time, until the small bones have 'melted away'. These pickled herrings would subsequently be served with potatoes baked in their jackets.

Of course, fresh herrings were eaten too. I was told in the north of Wales, not far from Conway, that the vendors of fresh herring used to cry: 'Penwaig ffres – pennau fel plismyn a boliau fel tafarnwyr', meaning 'fresh herring – with heads like policemen and bellies like publicans'. The policemen came into it because the head of a herring, set upright, is shaped like a policeman's helmet.

Casserole of Smoked Haddock (or Smoked Cod)

serves three to four

This unpretentious and convenient little recipe comes from Swansea.

smoked fillets of haddock, ½ kg
  (1 lb)
milk, 2½ dl (½ pint)
water, 2½ dl (½ pint)
margarine, 30 g (1 oz)

finely chopped onion, 1–2 tbs
finely chopped ham, 2 tbs
pepper, to taste
flour, 2 tbs

Place milk, water, margarine, onion, ham and pepper in the casserole. Cover and simmer for 10 minutes.

Cut the smoked fillets into neat, bite-sized pieces and add them to the mixture in the casserole. Simmer for another 10 minutes or so. Five minutes before the dish is ready, mix the flour to a smooth paste with a little milk, add it to the casserole and stir while the mixture comes back to boiling point.

If your fillets had a good colour, the whole dish will come out in a fine van Gogh sunflower yellow. Serve it with mashed potatoes and a garnish of parsley.

Pastai Pysgod a Chennin

Fish and leek pie

serves four

This is an adaptation of a recipe which, I confess, first came to my notice in North America. I think that it must have been taken there by a Welsh emigrant family.

cod or other white fish, cooked and
  flaked, ½ kg (1 lb)
leeks, 4 large or 6 smaller
margarine, 60 g (2 oz)

salt and pepper
white sauce, ½ cup
short-crust pastry, enough to cover
  the dish

Cut the leeks into pieces 4 or 5 cm (2 inches) long. Heat most of the margarine (of which the rest serves to butter your baking dish) and cook the leeks lightly in it, until they are slightly browned. Then lay them in the baking dish, add the flaked fish and seasoning, and pour the sauce over all. (It is not a bad idea to have some grated cheese in the sauce, but this is optional.)

If the baking dish is wide, use a glass funnel or a Welsh pie dragon (page 460) in the middle. Lay your pastry on top in the usual way and bake in a moderate oven (355° F, gas 4) for 20 minutes or until nicely browned.

Gurnard will do quite well for this dish, instead of cod or cod-like fish.

Bara Lawr

Laverbread

Mrs J. Kenney, who lived at Swansea early in this century, used to pick her own laver (page 251). She believed it to be very rich in vitamins, iron and iodine, and always served it for Sunday breakfast.

'It has to be washed well to remove the sand. It is boiled, then chopped finely, made into pats and rolled in fine or medium oatmeal. It is fried with bacon in the bacon fat till golden brown. Eggs or tomatoes can be added to the pan and seasoned with salt and pepper.'

Now this recipe, from an unimpeachable source, will sound familiar to anyone who has read recent books on Welsh cookery. They all say that you should make your pats or cakes or balls of laverbread and then 'coat them with oatmeal'. But when I have tried it with the prepared laverbread which one buys nowadays it simply will not work. The laverbread is too moist to retain any shape. What I do, therefore, is to *mix* the laverbread with oatmeal and form it into balls or pats; then carry on as indicated above. The results are perfectly good, but the puzzle remains – why could you make balls seventy-five years ago, but not now? I think that there must have been a change in the method of preparing the laverbread, but am open to other explanations, including the rather obvious one that I am less deft than Welshwomen.

In Swansea market, Mrs Coghlan, one of the laverbread vendors, told me how she cooked, or rather prepared, it – for, as she pointed out, what she sold had already been cooked by her for 9 hours! She grills her bacon on the grid of her grill-pan, letting the bacon fat drip down into the bottom. When the bacon is done she removes it, and the grid, and puts the laverbread in the hot fat. She makes a hollow in the middle of the laverbread and spoons some of the fat into this; then passes the whole thing under the heat for a minute or two, takes it out, turns the laverbread over and repeats. The laverbread is then ready to be eaten with the bacon.

Mrs Coghlan's laverbread is all Welsh, gathered by herself on the Welsh coasts. She will stir the tub of it for you, to show how the prolonged cooking has 'got the moisture out. That's how people likes their laverbread, it's solid. Now, you goes to some people and what you get is watery . . .' Her eloquence and sincerity convinced me that her laverbread must be the least watery obtainable. But even with this I could not make 'pats' which could be coated with oatmeal.

Welsh Ways with Cockles

The Welsh love their cockles. It is a treat to go into a market such as that in Swansea and to see stall after stall with its little bags of dark green laverbread and its bowl of cooked cockles, which the ladies in charge of this important trade sell by the small glassful, proclaiming them as Gower cockles, which is to say cockles from the nearby Gower peninsula. It is there that the cockle-gatherers of Penclawdd and other villages have for centuries gone down with their little horses and carts to the flats exposed at low tide, to reap their harvest and bring it back to the sheds where the cockles are steamed. 'The Gower', as it is known, is a place of mystery and Gowerians are not always communicative; although on my last visit to Penclawdd, with a rainy mist swirling about the place and her own voice lowered, a woman of the village told me that 'on many a night there's a lorry comes over from King's Lynn', bearing a load of Norfolk cockles to supplement the failing Gower stocks. And why should they not, since Norfolk cockles are excellent? And why not invest the import with an air of stealth, such as becomes a community which used to be involved to a man (or woman, or child) in smuggling?

Cockles may, of course, be gathered elsewhere in Wales. * Justina Evans has given me these recollections, from her childhood, of:

Cockles for Tea

'Cockles, winkles and mussels were a teatime dish. Cockles we picked at the small seaside village of Ferryside, near Carmarthen. They were soaked overnight in a large enamel bowl of water, to which was added a lump of bar salt.

'The following day the tap was left to run on them to remove any trace of sand. They were then boiled in a large iron saucepan on an open fire until the shells opened. They were dished up in the shells in one bowl with another bowl at the side for empty shells. The warm cockles were eaten with homemade bread and yellow, salted Welsh butter.

'Cockles pickled with salt, pepper and vinegar were another teatime meal. They can also be sprinkled with oatmeal and fried with bacon.

'The empty cockle shells were washed and dried and crushed, and used for grit for the chickens which most families kept in their back yards.'

* In *Welsh Fare*, Minwel Tibbott describes the itinerant cockle-sellers: 'Women would go from door to door in many villages in south Wales, selling cockles. Cockles already boiled and taken out of their shells were carried in a wooden pail balanced on the seller's head. These cockles were known as *cocs rhython*. The untreated cockles, still in their shells, were carried in a large basket on the arm and were known as *cocs cregin*.'

Cocos ac Wyau

Cockles and eggs serves four

The cockle recipes in *Welsh Fare* include a tempting Pastai gocos (cockle pie), but I have chosen this easier one, which comes from the seaside village of Cricieth, where I spent several boyhood holidays.

cockles in their shells, 1 litre (1 quart)	**bacon fat, 1–2 tbs**
eggs, 2 large or 3 medium, beaten	**black pepper, to taste**

'Cover the cockles with water and bring to the boil. Boil the cockles for a few minutes only. (Boiling for a long period causes them to become tough.)

'Take the cockles out of their shells, wash them well and lay them out on a large cloth to remove excess moisture. Fry them in a little bacon fat, tossing them well in the fat before pouring the beaten eggs over them. Stir well with a wooden spoon and season with black pepper.'

Mrs Tibbott adds that this mixture was eaten between slices of barley bread or oatcakes in the Porthmadog district. Women would walk from Penrhyndeudraeth to Porthmadog to sell the cockles. 'They would knock on doors, dancing and singing the following rhyme:

Cocos a wya	Cockles and eggs
Bara cerch tena,	Thin oat cakes,
Merched y Penrhyn	The girls of Penrhyn
Yn ysgwyd 'u tina!'	Doing the shakes!'

The Welsh Hermit's Fish Sauce

Lady Llanover's *Good Cookery Illustrated* (1867) is one of the strangest cookery books ever written. It contains relatively few recipes, said to have been communicated to 'The Traveller' by 'The Welsh Hermit of the Cell of St Gover'. This sauce, 'suitable for salmon and every other sort of fish', came from the hermit's family papers.

'One small anchovy well pounded in a mortar, one shallot chopped fine, two tablespoonfuls of sherry, half a tablespoonful of best vinegar, six whole black peppercorns, a little nutmeg and a very little mace. Simmer the above ingredients altogether in a double saucepan, stirring well all the time, until the shallot is soft; then take an ounce of butter in another double saucepan, with as much flour as will make it into a stiff paste; add the other ingredients which have been stewing, and stir it well till scalding hot for about two minutes, then add six tablespoonfuls of cream: stir well and strain.'

30. Recipes from Ireland

One of the many paradoxes which bloom as freely as the shamrock in its native land is this; that the coasts of the emerald isle are rich in seafood, but that the Irish people have on the whole been shy of consuming it. One has only to imagine what would happen on these coasts, if the people of, say, Singapore were suddenly transplanted thither, to realize the extent of this shyness. It is true that the Irish perceived the merits of the Dublin Bay prawn long before the Scots or English did. But they have continually neglected many of the crustaceans and molluscs which are equally accessible to them; they did so even during the time of the Great Famine. And they have a reserved attitude to most species of fish.

The reasons are no doubt manifold. One could be that, for the Catholics, fish has been associated with penance. Another could be the streak of conservatism which runs through the Irish character and which has preserved the country to a large extent from the invasion of foreign dishes and restaurants which has been so noticeable in England.

However, it is well known that no generalization can safely be made about the Irish, and that anyone incautious enough to make one will only encounter further perils if he attempts to substantiate it. I will only make one more, and that is that the Irish are unduly modest about their cookery and their traditional dishes. They have not been forward in producing cookery books. The book by Florence Irwin in the north, the invaluable little volume of *250 Irish Recipes* which the Mount Salus Press (rather to their surprise, as they told me) are constantly obliged to reprint, and the excellent books by Monica Sheridan stand out like lonely beacons on an empty shore. I hope that the wealth of material can be further explored and expounded, and that the following selection of seafood recipes will help to stimulate interest not only in traditional Irish recipes, but also in the new ones which are being developed, of which there are two to be found in these pages. Both come from the Bord Iascaigh Mhara (Irish Sea-Fisheries Service), a fertile and inventive organization, whose work in the field of fish cookery is unsurpassed by that of any sister organizations in larger countries.

Dublin Potted Herrings

As in many other countries, so in Ireland there has been a long tradition of pickling, or 'potting', herrings to preserve them; and this tradition has not entirely died away even now, when fish can be preserved by other means.

fresh herrings	thin slices of lemon
dry mustard	wine vinegar
salt	a bouquet garni
peppercorns	bay leaves
mace	cloves of garlic
coriander	cloves

Remove heads, fins and tails from the fish. Scale them. Wash them well and pat them dry. Slit them open underneath and gut them. Then place each herring on a board with its back upwards, and press down along the back bone until the fish lies flat. Turn it over and you will be able to remove the back bone easily. This done, divide each fish into two fillets.

Each herring fillet is now to be laid out lengthwise, with the skin underneath. Place on it a pinch of mustard and of salt, a few peppercorns, a pinch each of mace and coriander and a few of the thin slices of lemon. Then roll the fillet up and secure it with a toothpick or a fine thread.

Put the prepared rolled fillets in a dish and cover them with a sufficient quantity of hot wine vinegar, which has previously been boiled for five minutes with a bouquet garni. Leave until cold. Then take the rolled herrings out and put them in layers in an earthenware jar, sprinkling over each layer some salt, peppercorns, coriander, cloves, a bay leaf, and garlic. Make sure that there are some cloves at the bottom of the jar and also right at the top. Fill the jar with vinegar and keep it in a cool place for 4 days before use.

A different preparation of the same kind, made at Killybegs, is called **Tipsy Killybegs Herrings**. The first step is to butter an oven dish and put in the bottom of it 3 chopped carrots, 3 chopped onions, as much chopped garlic as you fancy and the same of parsley, with salt and pepper to taste. Cover all this with beer or ale, then add thyme, a bay leaf, 6 peppercorns and 4 cloves. Bring the mixture to the boil and let it simmer until the vegetables are cooked. At this point, put your herrings, which have been trimmed, gutted and washed, on top of the vegetables, cover them with onion rings and add ¼ cup vinegar and more beer or ale to cover. Bake the dish in a moderately hot oven (400° F, gas 6) for 20 minutes, then let the fish cool in the cooking liquid before serving them with soda bread.

This is a good dish, and has the advantage of being ready for immediate consumption. The quantities given are right for 12 small herrings.

Salt Ling with Colcannon
serves six

Salted ling used to be a staple food in Ireland. It can still be found in the west of the country, and is very good when made in the way described below and served with the traditional Irish colcannon.

Cut some salted ling into six portions and soak these overnight. Then put them in a mixture of milk and water (half and half) with some sliced onion, bring to the boil and cook for 25 to 30 minutes. Take the fish out and keep it hot while you thicken the liquid with a little cornflour, thus making a sauce for the ling.

The ingredients required for the colcannon are as follows:

potatoes, 6 fairly large ones	**butter, 30 g (1 oz)**
milk, 1 dl (7 tbs)	**chopped parsley, 1 tbs**
scallions, 6	**pepper and salt**
boiled green cabbage, 1½ cups	

Peel the potatoes and steep them in cold water for an hour. Then put them in a saucepan, cover with cold salted water, bring to the boil and cook until tender. Drain them well and dry them by laying a folded tea-towel on top and putting the pan back over a gentle heat for a couple of minutes. (This business of drying boiled potatoes is very Irish and very commendable. Once you have taken to doing them this way, you will never give up the practice.) Mash the potatoes.

Meanwhile you will have chopped the scallions and scalded them; and brought the milk to the boil. These two ingredients are now beaten into the mashed potatoes until they are all fluffy.

The cabbage, which should be finely chopped, is sautéed in the butter and then added to the potatoes, together with the parsley. Mix it in well and season with salt and plenty of pepper.

Cod Cobbler
serves four

Here is a recipe which allows Irish skill in baking scones to find expression in a seafood dish; and which goes a long way towards providing a 'meal in itself'. It is an invention of the Bord Iascaigh Mhara and all it lacks is a real Irish title. The dish contains cheese, which both is and is not traditional, to state the matter in an Irish way. Dr A. T. Lucas, in his erudite article on 'Irish Food before the Potato' (in *Gwerin*, Vol. III, No. 2, 1960), has shown that it was a standard and substantial part of the Irish diet from the early Christian period until the end of the seventeenth century, but that cheese-making then declined gradually and had almost disappeared in the nineteenth century. 'This extraordinary break in an age-old tradition in food has been difficult to bridge for to the present day cheese still remains an alien thing to the Irish countryman.' Let us hope that cod cobbler will help to remedy the situation.

You will need $\frac{3}{4}$ kg ($1\frac{1}{2}$ lb) skinless fillets of cod (or similar fish), to be cut up and placed in a cheese sauce in the bottom of a round oven dish. (The cheese sauce is made with 60 g (2 oz) each of butter and flour, $\frac{1}{2}$ litre (1 pint) milk and 100 g ($3\frac{1}{2}$ oz) grated cheese.) Meanwhile, you make up an Irish scone dough. Rub 60 g (2 oz) butter into 225 g (8 oz) plain flour with 1 tsp baking powder and a pinch of salt. Add 60 g (2 oz) grated cheese, preferably mature Cheddar or a mixture of that and of Parmesan. Drop an egg yolk into the mixture and add enough milk to make a workable dough. Roll this out into a thickness of 1 cm ($\frac{1}{2}$ inch) and cut it into small rounds with a scone cutter.

Dispose these rounds on top of the sauce, so that they just about cover the surface, glaze them with a little milk, sprinkle some more grated cheese over them and bake the dish in a hot oven (450° F, gas 8) for 25 to 30 minutes, until the scones are golden brown.

Baked Galway Codling with Mussels or Cockles

serves four

The Irish are discriminating in their purchases of cod and are partial to the smaller cod which are often taken by Galway boats. This dish combines codling with mussels (or cockles) in an agreeable way. It may be made with either a whole codling or fillets. Cooking time will be longer if you use a whole fish; and the parboiling of the vegetables should then be briefer.

codling, 1 kg (2 lb), uncleaned	small onions, parboiled
mussels, 3 dozen	butter, 30 g (1 oz), melted
salt and pepper	slices of lemon
chopped thyme	chopped parsley, 1 tbs
small potatoes, 12, parboiled	chopped fennel, 1 tbs

Clean the mussels and steam them open in a pot, with a little water. Remove them from their shells and keep them hot. Strain the liquid.

Lay the cleaned codling in an oven dish. Season it with the salt, pepper and thyme. Lay the potatoes and onions around it. Pour over it the mussel juices and melted butter. Then bake it in a hot oven (430° F, gas 7) for 15 minutes or until done. Baste it several times. Just before it is ready, add the mussels to the dish. Serve with a garnish of lemon slices, parsley and fennel.

Hake, Irish Style

serves four

The Tailteann Cookery Book by K. E. Warren was commended to me as one of the few Irish cookery books. I studied a copy of it in the National Library of Ireland and made some amazing discoveries therein, notably a recipe for Stuffed Haddock à la Syrienne, featuring potato balls, which Syrians would be unlikely to make even if they had haddock in their waters, which they don't. However, I assumed that the recipe for Fish à l'Irlandaise was authentic, tried it out, found it good, stripped it of its French title and now present it to my readers.

hake, ¾ kg (1½ lb), cleaned weight	*for the stuffing*
milk, 2 dl (⅓ pint)	soft breadcrumbs, 3 tbs
a small onion, sliced	margarine, 30 g (1 oz)
potatoes, 6, cooked and sieved	lemon juice, 2 tsp
margarine, 15 g (½ oz)	chopped parsley, 1 tbs
an egg, separated	a pinch of dried herbs
garnish: parsley and lemon	salt and pepper to taste

Make the stuffing with the ingredients shown.

Your hake should be in the form of 2 fillets. Choose a long and narrow oven dish, grease it and place one fillet in it. Put the stuffing on this, then lay the other fillet on top. Pour the milk round the fish and strew the sliced onion over it. Cover it with foil or greaseproof paper and bake it for 30 minutes in a moderate oven (355° F, gas 4).

Combine the margarine and the egg yolk with the sieved potato. Beat the egg white stiff and fold this in. Cover the fish completely with this potato mixture and return it to the oven for 15 minutes to brown lightly.

Garnish the dish as you wish, for example with the usual parsley and lemon slices.

Fillets of Whiting Poached in Cider, with Mushrooms

serves four

The Irish Country Women's Association have published interesting material on Irish cookery, of which my only criticism is that they are allowed to go out of print for long periods. Mrs Segrave Daly of the Goresbridge Guild contributed this recipe, which I have amplified, to the Association's principal cookery book.

Place 8 fillets of whiting, seasoned, in a greased oven dish and cover them with dry cider. Cover the dish, with foil if it lacks its own cover, and poach the fish, which will take 8 to 10 minutes after the cider has begun to simmer.

Meanwhile, fry 100 g (¼ lb) of mushrooms in butter. Remove them from the pan and keep them warm. Add to the butter left in the pan ½ tbs flour and enough cooking liquid from the fish, with a little milk, to make a fairly thick sauce. Sprinkle the mushrooms over the fish, spoon the sauce over all and brown the dish under the grill.

Mackerel with Rhubarb
serves four

Mackerel is an oily fish, best cooked with an edible acid such as certain fruits, vinegar or cider, which will balance the oiliness and make the fish more digestible and tasty. The fruit traditionally used for this purpose is the gooseberry. But the inventive ladies of the Irish Sea Fisheries Board of Dublin propose rhubarb as an alternative. Having tried their recipe, I recommend it in the following version. The pink sauce is striking in aspect, but may be too tart for some palates unless the amount of sugar is slightly increased.

fresh mackerel, each filleted to
 give 2 fillets, 1 kg (2 lb)
margarine, 60 g (2 oz)
a fairly large onion, finely chopped
rhubarb, ¼ kg (½ lb), chopped
pepper and salt
toasted breadcrumbs, 2 tbs

for the sauce
rhubarb, ½ kg (1 lb)
sugar, 2 tbs
water, 2 tbs
a little grated lemon rind

Melt the margarine and cook the onion in it until transparent. Add the chopped rhubarb, season with pepper and salt and continue to cook gently for 5 minutes. Then add the breadcrumbs and stir the mixture.

Now lay the mackerel fillets out flat, skin side down, and spread the stuffing on them. Roll each up, put them in a greased oven dish and cook them in a moderate oven (400° F, gas 6) for 15 to 20 minutes.

While the fish are being cooked, make the rhubarb sauce by placing all the ingredients listed in a saucepan and stewing them until the rhubarb is cooked and quite soft. This will take 10 minutes or a little longer. Then put the cooked rhubarb through a fine sieve or the blender, to make a purée of it. This can be served either hot or cold with the cooked mackerel.

Dublin Bay Prawn Cocktail   serves four

The word cocktail does not sound either Irish or old; but this has been the traditional way of eating Dublin Bay prawns in Dublin, at least from the time my maternal grandmother lived there.

10 to 12 Dublin Bay prawns (page 186), cooked and prepared for use – if buying whole ones ask for ¾ kilo (1½ lb) or just under
lettuce leaves, which may be shredded or left whole, for lining the bowls or glasses
a sprig of parsley, chopped

for the sauce
malt vinegar, 2 tsp
juice of 1 large lemon
horseradish, 2 tsp, grated or from a jar
a little Worcestershire sauce and tomato ketchup, to taste
salt and pepper
whipped cream, 3–4 heaped tbs

Make the sauce by mixing the ingredients together thoroughly.

Shell your cooked prawn tails, remove the thread of gut from each and cut them into cubes or chunks. Combine these with the sauce and chill. Line four small bowls or suitable glasses with the lettuce leaves, then distribute the prawn mixture between them.

If your prawns had corals, these may be sieved and used to garnish the top of the cocktail. Chopped parsley should anyway be added.

Donegal Crab Pie   serves three or four

This recipe is adapted from one in *250 Irish Recipes* (Mount Salus Press).

cooked crab meat, 250 g (½ lb)
puff pastry, 700 g (1½ lb)
white of 1 egg
finely chopped celery, 1 tbs
finely chopped parsley, 2 tbs

dry cider, 1½ dl (¼ pint)
salt and pepper
eggs, 6
milk, 3 dl (½ pint)
grated nutmeg, 2 pinches

Line a pie-tin, 12 inches across and 1 inch deep, with the pastry and chill it in the refrigerator for an hour. A piece of pastry for the top of the pie should also be chilled and then brushed with white of egg.

Flake the crab meat and put it in the pie, followed by the celery, parsley, cider and seasoning. Beat the eggs and milk together and add them and the nutmeg. Put the crust on top and bake the pie in a hot oven (430° F, gas 7) for 25 minutes or so. Serve it at once, so that it has no chance to become soggy.

Clam Soup from Portaferry
serves four

Florence Irwin's book *The Cookin' Woman* is rich in anecdote as well as in recipes which she gathered from people in the north of Ireland. Many of these recipes were published in *The Northern Whig*, often in the words of the people from whom they came (cf. Minwel Tibbott's work in Wales, page 460) and often with the historical and cultural background which makes recipes so much more interesting. Thus, in introducing the chapter on soups in her book, she recalls what Soyer, the famous chef of the Reform Club, did to alleviate the Irish famine of 1848 by initiating the establishment of huge public soup kitchens. This is well known; but I had not heard previously about the resentment which grew up when he published his soup recipes and people realized how economical they were in ingredients. The Dublin *Nation* parodied the witches in *Macbeth*:

'Round about the boiler go,/In twice fifty gallons throw – . . .
Shin of beef from skinny cow/In the boiler then you'll throw; . . .
Scale of codfish, spiders' tongues,/Tomtits' gizzards, head and lungs
Of a famished French-fed frog', etc. etc.

Nor had I realized that when Protestant landowners set up Soyer-type soup kitchens for their peasants, who were mainly Roman Catholics, the acceptance of such fare became a political act which exposed the recipient to being dubbed a 'souper' or religious turncoat. However, let the reader look for more such matter in the book itself. Here is one soup recipe, which persons of any political or religious persuasion may safely make outside Ireland, and which has an interesting affinity with the chowders of North America.

clams, 18–24	butter, 30 g (1 oz)
milk, ½ litre (1 pint)	chopped chives, 6 tbs
potatoes, 4, cut up small	flour, 2 tbs

Wash the clams well. Cover the bottom of a roomy saucepan with water, put the clams in it, cover and boil until the clams open. Remove them from their shells and discard the 'beards' and black parts. Rinse the clams in a cup of water, then strain and reserve this water as well as the liquid left in the saucepan. Chop up the clams.

Put all the reserved liquid in another saucepan, followed by the milk and potatoes. Add also the chopped clams and the butter. Simmer for 30 minutes. Add the chives and simmer for a further 15 minutes. Five minutes before serving blend the flour with a tablespoonful or two of the soup and stir it into the soup to thicken it. Serve very hot.

Carragheen Dessert

Dried carragheen (see page 252 – it seems to be spelled with an h more often than not in Ireland) can be bought in health-food shops and at some chemists. The standard packet contains 3 handfuls of the dried moss.

Take 2 good handfuls of carragheen and leave it to soak in ample cold water for at least 2 hours. Then pick it over, removing any little bits of shell or grit and add it to a mixture of 3 parts milk to 1 of water, about 1 litre (or 2 pints) in all, which you have previously warmed in the top of a double boiler. Heat to boiling point and leave to cook for 1 hour.

Now put the mixture through a mouli-légumes or similar device. If the carragheen was of good quality, just about everything will come through, to form a creamy and slightly glutinous liquid which has a straightforward taste of seaweed. For each cup of this, take 2 heaped tablespoonfuls of cocoa or chocolate powder and $1\frac{1}{4}$ of sugar, mix with a little water and add to the carragheen. Pour the mixture into a bowl, after mixing it well, and leave it to set in the refrigerator. Serve it with Irish farm cream.

I made this dessert with Joan Crichton, whose family recipe it is, in Dublin. We experimented by adding 2 drops of vanilla essence to one batch; and found that this seemed to bring out the seaweed flavour more strongly. To another batch we added 6 drops of almond essence; and this had the effect of banishing the seaweed flavour altogether. I found the dessert delicious in all its versions, but people who do not like the seaweed flavour should clearly use almond essence.

The fact that carragheen tastes of the sea suggests that it could well be used to enhance seafood dishes. It is particularly suitable for producing a seafood aspic, for example *Dublin Bay Prawns in Carragheen Aspic*. Soak 1 good handful of carragheen in water for 15 minutes, then drain it. Set it to simmer in $\frac{1}{2}$ litre (1 pint) fresh water for 1 hour, with a bay leaf, 2 cloves, a sprig of parsley and a little salt. At the end of this period stir into the mixture a teaspoonful of vinegar, then strain it over your prepared prawns in a mould or bowl. Chill it while it sets, then turn it out and serve it with garnishings of your choice.

Carragheen has many other uses. For example, if you wish to thicken any fish or seafood soup, take a little carragheen which has already been steeped in water, put it in a muslin bag and lower this into the soup for a while.

Bibliography

Part One. Works to do with the catalogues of species.

This list of publications from which I have quoted or which I have consulted only includes those directly relevant to the catalogues.

I have only included the name of the publisher where this seems likely to be helpful to the reader.

ABBOTT, R. TUCKER, *Seashells of North America*, New York, 1968.

AFLALO, F. G., *The Sea-fishing Industry of England and Wales*, London, 1904.

ALBUQUERQUE, ROLANDA MARIA, *Peixes de Portugal e ilhas adjacentes*, originally published in *Portugaliae Acta Biologica (B)*, Volume V, 1954–6.

ALLEN, J. A., *Crustacea: Euphausiacea and Decapoda*, in the series on the Fauna of the Clyde Sea area, Scottish Marine Biological Association, Millport, 1967.

American Fisheries Society, *A list of Common and Scientific Names of Fishes from the United States and Canada,* 3rd edition, Ann Arbor, Michigan, 1970.

ANDERSSON, K. A. (chief editor), *Fiskar och Fiske i Norden* (in two volumes, of which Volume I deals with the marine fishes), 3rd printing, Stockholm, 1964.

Anon, 'The History of Trawling', important article in the *Fish Trades Gazette and Poultry, Game and Rabbit Trades Chronicle* of 19 March 1921.

Anon, *Trade Marks of British Herring Curers*, Leslie and Co., Aberdeen, 1909.

ARNOLD, AUGUSTA FOOTE, *The Sea-Beach at Ebb-Tide*, originally published in 1901, Dover reprint, New York, 1968.

BARRETT, JOHN, *Life on the Sea Shore*, Collins, London, 1974.

BEEDHAM, GORDON E., *Identification of the British Mollusca*, Hulton Educational Publications, Amersham, 1972.

BERTRAM, JAMES G., *The Harvest of the Sea*, London, 1873.

BIGELOW, H. B., and SCHROEDER, W. C., *Fishes of the Gulf of Maine* (Fishery Bulletin No. 74 of the Fish and Wildlife Service), U.S. Government Printing Office, 1953.

BONAPARTE, C. L., *Iconografia della Fauna italica per le quattro classi degli Animali Vertebrati*, Tome III: *Pesci*, Rome, 1832.

BREDER, CHARLES M., JR. *Field Book of Marine Fishes of the Atlantic Coast*, Putnam's, New York and London, 1929.

BUCKLAND, FRANK, *The Natural History of British Fishes*, S.P.C.K., London, 1883.

BURGESS, G. H. O., *Developments in Handling and Processing Fish*, Fishing News (Books), 1965.

BURGESS, G. H. O., *The Curious World of Frank Buckland*, Baker, London, 1967.

BURGESS, G. H. O., and others, *Fish handling and processing*, H.M.S.O., 1965.

CADDY, J. F., CHANDLER, R. A., and WILDER, D. G., 'Biology and Commercial Potential of Several Underexploited Molluscs and Crustacea on the Atlantic Coast of Canada', in *Proceedings of the Government–Industry Meeting on the Utilization of Atlantic Marine Resources*, Montreal, 1974.

Canadian Department of Fisheries and Forestry, *Fisheries Fact Sheets*, issued bound together in a single booklet, Ottawa, undated but (?) 1960s.

'CHATCHIP' (MR W. LOFTAS), *The Fish Frier and his Trade*, London, c. 1923.

CHRISTIANSEN, MARIT E., *Crustacea Decapoda Brachyura* (No. 2 in the series Marine Invertebrates of Scandinavia), Universitetsforlaget, Oslo, 1969.

CLARK, ELEANOR, *The Oysters of Locmariaquer*, London, 1965.

COHEN, ANNE C., *The Systematics and Distribution of Loligo . . . in the western North Atlantic*, reprinted from *Malacalogia*, 1976.

CONNELL, J. J., *Control of Fish Quality*, Fishing News (Books), 1975.

Conseil Permanent International pour l'Exploration de la Mer, *Catalogue des poissons du nord de l'Europe, avec les noms vulgaires dont on se sert dans les langues de cette region*, 2nd edition, Copenhagen, 1914.

Conseil Permanent International pour l'Exploration de la Mer, *Faune ichthyologique de l'Atlantique Nord*, Copenhagen, 1929–31.

COUCH, JONATHAN, *A History of the Fishes of the British Islands*, Volumes I–IV, London, 1877–8.

COX, IAN (ed.), *The Scallop – Studies of a shell and its influences on humankind*, Shell Transport and Trading Company, London, 1957.

CUTTING, CHARLES L., *Fish Saving: A History of Fish Processing from Ancient to Modern Times*, Leonard Hill, London, 1955.

DAVIDSON, ALAN, *Mediterranean Seafood*, 2nd edition, Penguin, London, 1976.

DAVIDSON, ALAN, *Seafood of South-East Asia*, Federal Publications, Singapore, 1977, and Macmillan, London, 1978.

DAY, FRANCIS, *The Fishes of Great Britain and Ireland*, Volumes I and II, London, 1880–84.

DE CASTRO, JERONIMO DE MELO OSORIO, *Nomenclatura portuguesa do pescado*, publication no. 39, Gabinete de estudos das pescas, Lisbon, 1967.

DE HAAS, WERNER, and KNORR, FREDY, *Was lebt im Meer an Europas Kusten?*, Stuttgart, 1971.

DE KAY, JAMES E., *The Mollusca*, Vol. 5 of the *Natural History of New York*, Albany, N.Y. 1843.

DEMEL, KAZIMIERZ, *Zycie Morza*, Gdansk, 1974.

DE VOE, THOMAS F., *The Market Assistant*, Orange Judd and Company, New York, 1866.

EDMONSTON, ELIZA, *Sketches and Tales of Shetland*, Edinburgh and London, 1856.

F.A.O. (Food and Agriculture Organization of the United Nations), *Species Identification Sheets for the Mediterranean and the Black Sea*, Rome, 1973.

FARFANTE, ISABEL PÉREZ, *Western Atlantic Shrimps of the genus Penaeus*, Fishery Bulletin, Volume 67, No. 3, U.S. Department of the Interior, 1969.

FARRAN, G. P., *Local Irish Names of Fishes*, reprinted from the *Irish Naturalists' Journal*, Volume VIII, Nos. 9–12, 1946.

FESTING, SALLY, *Fishermen* (of Norfolk in England), David and Charles, Newton Abbot, 1977.

FORBES, E., and HANLEY, S., *A History of British Mollusca and their Shells*, 4 volumes, London, 1849–53.

GANONG, W. F., *The Economic Mollusca of Acadia*, reprinted from Bulletin No. VIII of the Natural History Society of New Brunswick, St John, N.B., 1889.

GASKELL, T. F., *The Gulf Stream*, Cassell, London, 1972.

GIBBONS, EUELL, *Stalking the Blue-Eyed Scallop*, New York, 1964.

GOODE, G. B., and BEAN, T. H., *Oceanic Ichthyology* (a treatise on the deep-sea and pelagic fishes of the world, based chiefly upon the collections made by steamers *Blake*, *Albatross* and *Fish Hawk* in the northwestern Atlantic), published as a Special Bulletin of the U.S. National Museum, 1896.

GOODE, G. BROWN, and a staff of associates, *The Fisheries and Fishery Industries of the United States* (comprising Sections I to III in seven volumes, of which Section I, *The Natural History of Useful Aquatic Animals*, is the most pertinent to the present book), Washington, Government Printing Office, 1884–7.

GOODLAD, C. A., *Shetland Fishing Saga*, the Shetland Times, 1971.

GOUSSET, J., and TIXERANT, G., *Les produits de la pêche*, publication of the official French periodical *Informations Techniques des Services Vétérinaires*, Issy-les-Moulineaux, undated but (?) late 1960s.

GRAHAM, ALASTAIR, *British Prosobranch and other Operculate Gastropod Molluscs*, Academic Press, London and New York, 1971.

HEILER, VAN CAMPEN, *Salt Water Fishing*, Knopf, New York, 1946.

HILDEBRAND, S. F., and SCHROEDER, W. C., *Fishes of Chesapeake Bay*, originally published in 1928 in the Bulletin of the U.S. Bureau of Fisheries, reprinted as a separate book for the Smithsonian Institution, 1972.

HOLDSWORTH, EDMUND W. H., *Deep-sea Fishing and Fishing Boats*, London, 1874.

HOLTHUIS, L. B., *Decapoda Natantia, Macrura Reptantia, Anomura en Stomatopoda*, Volumes IX, X in Fauna van Nederland (ed. Boschma), 1950.

I.C.E.S., *I.C.E.S. List of Names of Fish and Shellfish . . .*, reprinted from the *Bulletin Statistique Cons. Internat. Explor. de la Mer*, Volume 49.

INGLE, RAY, *A Guide to the Seashore*, Hamlyn, London, 1969.

JEFFREYS, J. GWYN, *British Conchology*, 5 volumes, London, 1862–9.

JENKINS, J. GERAINT, *Nets and Coracles* (as used for fishing, especially in Wales), David and Charles, Newton Abbot, 1974.

JENKINS, J. TRAVIS, *The Fishes of the British Isles*, 2nd edition, London, 1936.

JONES, WILLIAM, *The Broad, Broad Ocean and Some of its Inhabitants*, 3rd edition, London, (?) 1884.

JÓNSSON, GUNNAR, *Fiskaliffraeði*, Reykjavik, 1972.

JORDAN, D. S., and EVERMANN, B. W., *American Food and Game Fishes*, New York, 1902.

JORDAN, D. S., and EVERMANN, B. W., *The Fishes of North and Middle America*, in four large volumes, Bulletin of the U.S. National Museum, 1896–1900.

JOUBIN, LOUIS, and LE DANOIS (eds.), *Catalogue illustré des animaux marins comestibles des côtes de France et des mers limitrophes*, Office Scientifique et Technique des Pêches maritimes, Paris, 1925.

KILAJ, ANDRZEJ, and RUTKOWICZ, STANISŁAW, *Atlas Ryb Północnego Atlantyku*, Gdansk, 1970.

KORNHALL, DAVID, *Sydsvenska Fisknamm* (a book on vernacular Swedish names for fish), Lund, 1968.

KREUZER, RUDOLF (ed.), *Fishery Products*, Fishing News (Books), 1974.

KRØYER, HENRIK, *Danmarks Fiske*, Copenhagen, 1843–53.

LANE, FRANK W., *Kingdom of the Octopus*, Jarrolds, London, 1957.

LEIM, A. H., and SCOTT, W. B., *Fishes of the Atlantic Coast of Canada*, Bulletin No. 155 of the Fisheries Research Board of Canada, Ottawa, 1966.

LEWES, G. H., *Sea-Side Studies at Ilfracombe, Tenby, The Scilly Islands, and Jersey*, 2nd edition, Edinburgh and London, 1860.

LIPPSON, ALICE JANE, *The Chesapeake Bay in Maryland, an atlas of natural resources*, Johns Hopkins University Press, 1973.

LOVELL, M. S., *The Edible Mollusca of Great Britain and Ireland, with Recipes for Cooking Them*, 2nd edition, London, 1884.

LOZANO, F., *Nomenclatura ictiolóigica – Nombres científicos y vulgares de los peces españoles*, Instituto Español de Oceanografía, Madrid, 1963.

LOZANO Y REY, L., *Los principales peces marinos y fluviales de España*, 3rd edition, revised by Fernando Lozano Cabo, Madrid, 1964.

MACLEOD, R. D., *Key to the Names of British Fishes, Mammals, Amphibians and Reptiles*, Pitman, London, 1956.

McCORMICK, HAROLD W., ALLEN, TOM, and YOUNG, CAPTAIN WILLIAM, *Shadows in the Sea: The Sharks, Skates and Rays*, Chilton Company, Philadelphia and New York, 1963.

McMILLAN, NORA F., *British Shells*, Warne, London, 1968.

Marine Biological Association of the United Kingdom, *Plymouth Marine Fauna*, 3rd edition, Plymouth, 1957.

MOULE, THOMAS, *Heraldry of Fish*, van Voorst, London, 1842.

MURIE, DR JAMES, *Report on the Sea Fisheries and Fishing Industries of the Thames Estuary*, London, 1903.

MUUS, BENT J., *Skallus, Søtænder, Blæksprutter* (Volume 65 of *Danmarks Fauna*, covering among other subjects the cephalopods), Copenhagen, 1959.

MUUS, BENT J., and DAHLSTRØM, PREBEN, *Sea Fishes of Britain and North-Western Europe*, published in Danish in 1964; English edition, Collins, 1974.

NETBOY, ANTHONY, *The Atlantic Salmon, A Vanishing Species?*, Faber, London, 1968.

NEWTON, LILY, *A Handbook of the British Seaweeds*, British Museum (Natural History), 1931.

NEWTON, LILY, *Seaweed Utilisation*, Sampson Low, London, 1951.

NORREVANG, A., and MEYER, T. J. (eds.). *Danmarks Natur*. Volume 3 (The Sea), and Volume 10 (Greenland and the Faroes). Copenhagen, 1968 and 1971.

O CÉIDIGH, PÅDRAIG, *A List of Irish Marine Decapod Crustacea*, National Museum of Ireland, Dublin, 1963.

O.E.C.D., *Multilingual Dictionary of Fish and Fish Products*, Paris, 1968.

OGBURN, CHARLTON, JR, *The Winter Beach*, Clarion paperback edition, New York, 1971.

OSKARSSON, INGIMAR, *Skeldýrafána Islands*, Volume I, *Samlokur i Sjó*, and Volume II, *Saesniglar með Skel* (Icelandic single shells and bivalves), Volume I, 2nd edition, Reykjavik, 1964; Volume II, Reykjavik, 1962.

PARNELL, RICHARD, *The Natural History of the Fishes of the Firth of Forth and Tributaries*, Edinburgh, 1838.

PARSONS, L. S., MERCER, M. C., WELLER, R., and CAMPBELL, J. S., 'Distribution, Abundance and Biology of Some Underexploited Northwest Atlantic Finfish and Shellfish', in *Proceedings of the Government–Industry Meeting on the Utilization of Atlantic Marine Resources*, Montreal, 1974.

PEARSON, JOHN C. (selected and edited), *The Fish and Fisheries of Colonial North America* (a documentary history of fishing resources of the United States and Canada), in 4 volumes, U.S. Fish and Wildlife Service, Washington, 1972.

PERLMUTTER, ALFRED, *Guide to Marine Fishes*, New York, 1961.

POLL, MAX, *Poissons marins*, in the series Faune de Belgique, Royal Natural History Museum, Brussels, 1947.

RASS, PROFESSOR T. S. (ed.), *Rýbý* (Fish), Volume IV, Part 1, in the series *Zihzn' Zhivotnýkh* (Life of animals), Prosveshchenie Publishing House, Moscow, 1971.

RATHBUN, RICHARD, 'Crustaceans', in the publication of the U.S. Commission of Fish and Fisheries cited under Goode, 1884.

REDEKE, H. C., *De Visschen van Nederland*, Leiden, 1941.

RENDALL, ROBERT, *Orkney Shore*, Kirkwall, 1973.

RICKER, W. E., *Russian–English Dictionary for Students of Fisheries and Aquatic Biology*, Bulletin 183 of the Fisheries Research Board of Canada, 1973.

ROLLEFSEN, GUNNAR (chief editor), *Havet og våre fisker* (a manual of Norwegian sea fish), Volumes I and II, Bergen, 1960–62.

SÆMUNDSSON, BJARNI, *Fiskarnir* (*Pisces Islandiae*), Reykjavik, 1926.

SÆMUNDSSON, BJARNI, *Marine Pisces* [of Iceland]. in the *Zoology of Iceland*, Volume IV, Part 72, Copenhagen and Reykjavik, 1949.

SARS, G. O., *Mollusca Regionis Arcticae Norvegiae*, Christiania, 1878.

SATTERTHWAITE, ANN, 'Fish Mongers in the Concrete Jungle – A Case against Sterilising the Urban Waterfront' (case studies of Washington D.C., Annapolis, Charleston and Boston), unpublished monograph, 1974.

SCHMITT, WALDO L., *Crustaceans*, University of Michigan Press, 1965.

Sears Foundation, *Fishes of the Western North Atlantic* (a continuing series of large volumes of which seven are now available), New Haven, Conn., from 1948.

SIMMONDS, P. L., *The Commercial Products of the Sea*, 2nd edition, London, 1883.

SMITT, PROFESSOR F. A. (edited the revised and completed second edition), *A History of Scandinavian Fishes*, 2nd edition, Stockholm and London, 1893.

STEP, EDWARD, *Shell Life*, Warne, London and New York, 1901.

STEP, EDWARD, *A Naturalist's Holiday – Idle Hours on the Cornish Coast*, Thomas Nelson, London, undated but *c*. 1910.

STEPHENSON, K., *Crustacea Decapoda* [of Iceland], in the *Zoology of Iceland*, Volume III, Part 25, Copenhagen and Reykjavik, 1939.

STREET, PHILIP, *The Crab and its Relatives*, Faber and Faber, London, 1966.

STUXBERG, ANTON, *Sveriges och Norges Fiskar*, Göteborg, 1895.

TEBBLE, NORMAN, *British Bivalve Seashells*, The British Museum (Natural History), London, 1966.

Torry Research Station, numerous pamphlets in the series of *Torry Advisory Notes* on the preservation and marketing of fish etc.

UNESCO, *Check-list of the fishes of the north-eastern Atlantic and of the Mediterranean*, Volumes I and II, Paris, 1973.

USHAKOV, P. V., and others, *Atlas of the Invertebrates of the Far-Eastern Seas of the U.S.S.R.*, Moscow and Leningrad, 1955.

VALLE, K. J., *Suomen Kalat* (Finnish fish), Helsingissä, 1934.

VON KOENEN, A., *Das Norddeutsche Unter-Oligocän und seine Mollusken Fauna*, Berlin, 1893.

WALLACE, F. W., *Canadian Fisheries Manual*, National Business Publications, Canada, (?) 1943.

WALLACE, F. W., *Roving Fisherman: An Autobiography*, Gardenvale, Quebec, 1955.

WARNER, G. F., *The Biology of Crabs*, Elek, London, 1977.

WARNER, WILLIAM W., *Beautiful Swimmers – Watermen, Crabs and the Chesapeake Bay*, Little, Brown, Boston and Toronto, 1976.

WATKIN, GERALD, *British Food Fish*, The Worshipful Company of Fishmongers, London, 1976.

WENT, A. E. J., and KENNEDY, M., *List of Irish Fishes*, 2nd edition, National Museum of Ireland, 1969.

WHEELER, ALWYNE, *The Fishes of the British Isles and North-West Europe*, Macmillan, London, 1969.

WHEELER, ALWYNE (with illustrations by Peter Stebbing), *Key to the Fishes of Northern Europe*, Warne, London, 1978.

WHITEHEAD, P. J. P., and TALWAR, P. K., *Francis Day (1829–1889) and his Collection of Indian Fishes*, British Museum (Natural History), London, 1976.

WHYMPER, F., *The Fisheries of the World* (an illustrated and descriptive record of The International Fisheries Exhibition, 1883), London, 1883.

WILLIAMS, AUSTIN B., *Marine Decapod Crustaceans of the Carolinas*, Fishery Bulletin, Volume 65, No. 1, of the U.S. Department of the Interior, 1965.

WOODING, FREDERICK H., *The Book of Canadian Fishes*, McGraw-Hill Ryerson, Toronto, undated but evidently later than 1972.

YARRELL, WILLIAM, *A History of British Fishes*, Volumes I and II, 3rd edition, London, 1859.

YONGE, C. M., *The Sea Shore*, Collins, London, 1949.

ZINN, DONALD J., *The Handbook for Beach Strollers from Maine to Cape Hatteras*, revised edition, The Pequot Press, Chester, Connecticut, 1975.

Part Two. Works to do with cookery.

The entries here are arranged by country, following the same order as the recipe sections. Titles in languages other than English and French, of which the meaning is not self-evident, are given in English as well as in the original language; or, where this seems more helpful, followed by a brief indication of the scope of the book. I have not included in the list the best-known general cookery books which are currently available in Britain and North America. This seemed unnecessary, although I am of course indebted to such books as well as to the more specialized ones which I bring to the reader's attention here.

Portugal

DE ALMEIDA, ETELVINA LOPES, *ABC da Culinaria* (a general Portuguese cookery book), 4th edition, (?) Lisbon, 1975.

DE SAMPAIO, ALBINO FORJAZ, *Volu'pia a nona arte a gastronomia* (Portuguese cookery and cookery books treated historically), Porto, 1940.

OLLEBOMA, ANTONIO M. DE OLIVEIRA BELLO, *Culinária Portuguesa* (Portuguese cookery), Lisbon, (?) 1936.

ROSA-LIMPO, BERTHA, *O Livro de Pantagruel* (a general Portuguese cookery book). Lisbon, 1945 and many editions thereafter.

VALENTE, MARÍA ODETTE CORTES, *Cozinha regional portuguesa* (Regional cookery in Portugal), Coimbra, 1973.

Spain

Anon, *Manual de cocina (recetario)*, Sección Femenina de F.E.T. y de las J.O.N.S., 15th edition, Madrid, 1965.

CALERA, ANA MARÍA, *La cocina vasca* (Basque cookery); this major work, forming part of *La Gran Enciclopedia Vasca*, was published as a separate book at Bilbao, 1971.

CASTILLO, JOSÉ, *Manual de cocina económica vasca* (Economical Basque dishes, including many fish dishes), 5th edition, Fuenterrabia, 1975.

CASTILLO, JOSÉ, *Recetas económicas de pescado* (Economical fish recipes), Fuenterrabia, undated but (?) 1975.

DOMÉNECH, IGNACIO, *La nueva cocina elegante española*, 6th edition, undated but (?) late 1920s.

GARCIA, GRACIANO (general editor), *El libro de oro de la cocina española*, Volume 4, *Pescados, Mariscos* (the seafood volume in an encyclopaedia of Spanish cookery), Oviedo, (?) 1960s.

PÉREZ, DIONISIO, *Guía del buen comer español* (Guide to good Spanish food), Madrid, 1929.

PRADERA, NICOLASA, *La cocina de Nicolasa*, Editorial Mayfe, Madrid, 1961.

PUGA Y PARGA, MANUEL M., *La Cocina Práctica*, first published (?) in the early 1900s. 8th edition, La Coruña, 1916.

RAMÍREZ, LEONORA, *El pescado en mi cocina* (Fish in my cooking), Barcelona, 1968.

France

ALI-BAB, *Practical Gastronomy*, McGraw-Hill, 1976.
BARBEROUSSE, MICHEL, *Cuisine basque et béarnaise*, Biarritz, undated.
BARBEROUSSE, MICHEL, *La Normandie – ses traditions – sa cuisine – son art de vivre*, Librairie Hachette, 1974.
DAVID, ELIZABETH, *French Provincial Cooking*, Michael Joseph, London, 1960, and in the Penguin series, 1964.
DE CROZE, AUSTIN, *Les plats régionaux de France*, (?) Paris, 1928 (and recently reprinted in a de luxe edition by Daniel Morcrette).
LALLEMAND, ROGER, *La vraie cuisine de la Bretagne*, La Rochelle, 1971.
LALLEMAND, ROGER, *La vraie cuisine de la Normandie*, La Rochelle, 1972.
LALLEMAND, ROGER, *La vraie cuisine de l'Artois, de la Flandre et de la Picardie*, La Rochelle, 1973.
MILLET-ROBINET, Mme, *Maison rustique des Dames*, 12th edition, Paris, 1884.
MORAND, SIMONE, *Gastronomie bretonne d'hier et d'aujourd'hui*, Flammarion, 1965.
MORAND, SIMONE, *Gastronomie normande d'hier et d'aujourd'hui*, Flammarion, Paris, 1970.
OBERTHUR, J., *Poissons et Fruits de Mer de notre Pays* (*Pêche – Histoire naturelle – Cuisine*), La Nouvelle Edition, Paris, 1944.
PALAY, SIMIN, *La cuisine du pays – Armagnac, Pays basque, Béarn, Bigorre, Landes*, Pau, 1975.
PROGNEAUX, J. E., *Les spécialités et recettes gastronomiques bordelaises et girondines*, La Rochelle, 1969.
PROGNEAUX, J. E., *Les spécialités et recettes gastronomiques charentaises*, 6th edition, La Rochelle, 1976.
Syndicat d'Initiative de Cornouaille, *Le poisson en Bretagne*, 1949.

Belgium

BOON, LOUIS PAUL, *Eten op zijn Vlaams* (Eating in the Flemish style), Amsterdam, 1972.
DESNERCK, ROLAND, *Oostends Woordenboek* (a dictionary of the Ostend dialect, dedicated to the Ostend fishermen), 1972.
VAN IMMERSEEL, FRANS, *Garnalenvissers te paard* (Horseback shrimp fishermen), Tielt and Utrecht, 1973.
VERMEERSCH, FONS, *Op zoek naar spijs en drank – Gastronomisch West-Vlaanderen* (a gastronomic tour of West Flanders), Tielt and Utrecht, 1974.
WILLEMS, ANTOINE, *Le poisson – sa cuisine – ses spécialités*, Bruges, 1936.

Netherlands

AALBREGTSE, M. A., *Kezanse Kost* (the cookery of Zeeland), Groede, 1967.
Anon, *Kookboek voor Jonggehuwden* (a cookery book for young brides), Henri Bronsgeest, The Hague, undated (?) about 1920.
BORN, WINA, *Het Groot Visboek* (a book devoted entirely to fish cookery, some Dutch, some international), Haarlem, 1972.

KUIPERS, W. H., and others, *De Welkokende Keukenmeid en Verstandige Huishoudster* (old and new recipes from Friesland), Leeuwarden, 1976.

MANDEN, MEJ. A. C., *Recepten van de Haagsche Kookschool* (recipes from the cookery school of The Hague), The Hague, 1895.

SARELS VAN RIJN, P. J., *Ik kan koken* (the cookery book of the School of Industry and Housekeeping at Vlissingen), 11th printing, Leiden, 1952.

STOLL, F. M., and DE GROOT, W. H., *Recepten, Huishoudschool 'Laan van Meerdervoort', Den Haag* (recipes from the School of Housekeeping in Laan van Meerdervoort in The Hague), The Hague, 1934.

STUIT, MARIANNE, and VAN ES, TON, *Het vokomen visboek* (the fish volume in a series of cookery books produced by Albert Heijn, the supermarket chain), Amsterdam, 1976.

Germany

BAADER, B., BUCHENAU, H., and GEISS, R. D., *Diät aus dem Meer*, Fish Marketing Institute, Bremerhaven, undated but fairly recent.

DAVIDIS-HOLLE, HENRIETTE, *Praktisches Kochbuch* (one of the classic German cookery books), originally published 1854, my copy the 55th printing, Bielefeld and Leipzig, 1925.

FRISCH, PETER, *Spezialitäten aus dem Meer*, Gräfe und Unzer, Munich, undated but recent.

GLEIM, BETTY, *Bremisches Kochbuch* (Bremen cookery book), 11th edition, Bremen, 1869.

GUNTHER, S., *Kochbuch der Haushaltungsschulen der Hansestadt Hamburg* (the cookery book of the School of Domestic Arts at Hamburg), Hamburg, my copy mutilated but date around 1910.

HALLER, OSKAR, *Fischkochbuch mit Atlas der Fische* (a fish cookery book with a coloured chart of the fish), Celerina cookery school, 1929.

HOWE, ROBIN, *German Cooking*, André Deutsch, 1963, and Mayflower paperback edition, 1971.

KATZ, HEINRICH, *Maritime Leckereien; Das Fischkochbuch von der Waterkant* (the cookery book of the chef of the fish cookery school at Bremerhaven), Ditzen and Co., Bremerhaven, 1976.

Seefischkochbuch, publication of the German institute for propaganda in favour of sea fish, (?) Hamburg-Altona, 1921.

SEUMENICHT, KARL, *Fisch-Warenkunde* (fish-curing), an official publication of the German fishing industry, Hamburg, 1959.

Poland

Anon, *Kucharka Mieyska y Wieyska* Town and country cooking), Warsaw, 1804.

DE POMIANE, EDOUARD, *La cuisine polonaise vue des bords de la Seine*, limited edition published by La Société Polonaise des Amis du Livre, Paris, 1952.

GAŁECKA, MARIA, *Jak przyrządzać ryby morskie smacznie i tanio* (Cheap, tasty ways of preparing sea fish), Warsaw, 1916.

GODLEWSKA, M., *Przepisy przyrządzania potraw z dorsza* (Recipes for preparing cod dishes), Centrala Rybna (the state organization for marketing fish), Warsaw, 1947.

MIELCUSZNY, M., *Jedz Ryby Morskie* (Eat sea fish), Morski Instytut Rybacki (Institute of Sea Fisheries), Gdynia, 1936.

OCHOROWICZ-MONATOWA, MARYA, *Universalna Ksiazka Kucharska* (the classic of Polish cookery books), first published at Warsaw, 1912.

SCZYGLOWA, MARIA (general editor), *Dobra Kuchnia* (one of the few recent Polish cookery books to be kept, intermittently, in print), 5th printing, Warsaw, 1976.

SZEPIETOWSKI, DIONIZY, *100 Potraw ze Śledzi* (100 herring dishes), Warsaw, 1966.

ZAWISTOWSKA, ZOFIA, *Ryby na Naszym Stole* (Fish on our table), Warsaw, 1967.

ZERAŃSKA, ALINA, *The Art of Polish Cooking*, Doubleday, New York, 1968.

Soviet Union

AKSAKOV, SERGEĬ, *Zapiski ob uzhen'e rȳbȳ* (Notes on angling), Moscow, 1847.

BELOUSOV, IVAN, *Ushedshaya Moskva* (Moscow of the past), Moscow, 1927.

BOGOMOLOV, T. S., and KRASHENINNIKOVA, A. G. *Okeanichyeskaya rȳba v domashnyem pitanii* (Ocean fish in the home kitchen). Moscow, 1971.

Bureau of Technical Information of the Estonian S.S.R., *Zakuski iz sel'di* (*Herring* appetizers), Tallinn, 1961.

DAUZVARDIS, JOSEPHINE J., *Popular Lithuanian Recipes*, 4th edition, Chicago, 1967.

GOGOL', NIKOLAI, *Dead Souls* (translated by David Magarshack), Penguin, 1961.

ISAEV, V. A., *Darÿ okeana* (Gifts of the ocean), Kaliningrad, 1975.

KALVIR, SILVIA, *Eesti rahvatoite* (Estonian national dishes), Tallinn, 1970.

KRȲLOV, I. A., *Basni* (Fables), St Petersburg, 1819.

LUTS, ARVED, 'Kuidas raim eestlaste toidulauale joudis' (How the Baltic herring found its way on to the Estonian table), in *Eesti Loodus*, No. 5, May, 1969, Tallinn, 1969.

MOLOKHOVETS, ELENA, *Podarok molodȳm khozyaĭkam ili Sredstvo k umen' sheniyu raskhodov v domashnem khozyaistve* (A gift to young housewives, or a guide to the diminution of household expenses), 1st edition, St Petersburg, 1861; 29th and last Russian edition, Petrograd, 1917.

PAPASHVILY, HELEN and GEORGE, *The Cooking of Russia*, Time-Life International, 1971.

POKROVSKY, A. A., LAGUNOV, L. L., and others, *Rȳbnȳe blyuda* (Fish dishes), Moscow, 1973.

SHTOK, I., *Bozhestvennaya Komediya* (The Divine Comedy), Moscow, 1961.

U.S.S.R. Ministry of Trade, *Sbornik retsept blyud i kulinarnȳkh izdeliĭ dlya predpriyatiĭ obshestvennovo pitaniya* (A collection of recipes for dishes and culinary preparations for the use of catering establishments), Moscow, 1955.

Various editors and contributors, *Kniga o vkusnoï i zdorovoï pishche* (The book of tasty and healthy food), Moscow, 1939.
VITSUR, S., *'Atlanticheskie rȳbȳ na nashem stole* (Atlantic fish in home cooking), Tallinn, 1970.

Finland

BENTON, PEGGIE, *Finnish Food*, Bruno Cassirer, Oxford, 1960.
BERGMAN, GÖSTA, *Tuttua ja uuta tuoreesta kalasta* (a manual on the cleaning, boning and filleting fish), Suomen Kalastusyhdistys, No. 68, Turku, 1974.
KÄKÖNEN, ULLA, *Natural Cooking the Finnish Way*, Quadrangle, New York, 1974.
KOSKIMIES, H., and SOMMERSALO, E., *Keittotaito* (a general Finnish cookery book), Werner Söderström, Porvoo, 1933.
REENPAA, LOTTE, and VANHANEN, MAURI, *Fisk och Vilt* (the Swedish language version of a Finnish book on fish and game cookery), Borgå, 1971.
SOIRO, JORMA, *Finnish Cookery*, Hotel Torni, Helsinki, 1963.
TEINONEN, SEPPOA., *Silakka* (Herring), Pieksämäki, 1972.
VIHERJUURI, MATTI, and others, *Finlandia Gastronomica*, 2nd edition, Helsinki, 1974.

Sweden

ÅKERSTRÖM, JENNY, *Prinsessornas Kokbok* (The Princesses' cook book), Stockholm, 1945.
FREDRIKSON, KARIN (chief editor of Swedish original) and ELLISON, AUDREY (translator of English version), *The Great Scandinavian Cook Book* (a work of encyclopaedic scope), London, 1966.
GYLLENSKÖLD, H., *Att koka fisk* (a scientific treatise on the cookery of fish), Stockholm, 1963.
HAGDAHL, DR CH. EM., *Kok-konsten* (Arts of cookery), originally published in 1879, facsimile of 1896 edition by the Gastronomiska Akademiens Bibliotek, 1963.
HOLMQVIST, JOHANNA, *Sill- och Strömmingsrätter* (Herring and Baltic herring dishes), Stockholm, 1913.
JAKOBSSON, OSKAR, *Good Food in Sweden* (translated from the Swedish original), Stockholm, 1968.
NYLANDER, MARGARETHA, *Handbok wid den nu brukliga finare matlagningen* (A handbook of new and practical fine cookery), Stockholm, 1822.
OSTENIUS, ASTA, *Fiskrätter* (Fish dishes), ICA-Forlaget, Västerås, 1955.
OSTMAN, ELISABETH, *Iduns Kokbok* (a general cookery book), Stockholm, 1932.
PETERSEN, BENGT, *Från Västerhav* (From western waters), Göteborg, 1973.
PETERSEN, BENGT, *Bohusfisk och skaldjur* (Fish and seafood from the province of Bohuslan), 3rd printing, Göteborg, 1975 (recipes from this and the preceding book have been published in English under the title *Delicious Fish Dishes*).

WRETMAN, TORE, *Svensk Husmanskost* (an anthology of Swedish recipes, old and new), Bokförlaget Forum, 1968.

Norway

ASKELAND, GUNNAR (ed.), *Norsk Mat fra mange gryter* (a compendium of articles on traditional Norwegian dishes), Oslo, undated but (?) 1960s.

DEGE, HROAR, *Fra Neptuns Gaffel* (a book of seafood recipes – the title means 'from Neptune's fork'), Oslo, 1966.

DEKKE, SARAH, *Hjemmets Kokebok til daglig bruk* (a general Norwegian cookery book, by a Bergenser, which remains in wide use), Oslo, 1938.

ESPELID, INGRID (with the newspaper *Dagbladet*), *Min yndlingsrett* (an anthology of favourite recipes of various Norwegians), Oslo, 1976.

FÆGRI, KNUT, *Krydder pa kjokkenet og i verdenshistorien* (an erudite and beautiful book on spices in history and in the kitchen), Oslo, 1966.

GROTTLAND, KRISTINE LIND, *Daglig brød og daglig dont* (Daily bread and daily work), Oslo, 1962.

LARSEN, DINA, and RABBE, DOROTHEA, *Norske Mat* (Norwegian food), Oslo, 1932 (but a revised and expanded version under the names of Olga Ambjørnud and others was published under the same title at Oslo in 1965).

MEJDELL, ESTER, *Sild er godt* (herring is good – with 193 recipes), Oslo, 1928.

WINSNES, HANNA, *Lærebog i de Forskellige Grene of Huusholdningen* (a textbook of the various branches of housekeeping), 6th edition, Christiania (Oslo), 1857.

Denmark

ANDERSEN, GERDA; BRUUN, ALICE; SKOV, ASTA, and JUL, MOGENS, *Friske Fiskeretter* (Fresh fish dishes), Teknisk Forlag, Copenhagen, 1949.

HERLØV-MÜLLER, E., *Fiskeretter* (Fish dishes), H. Hirschsprungs Forlag, (?) Copenhagen, 1941.

LIND, MOGENS, *I al Beskedenhed: Kogebok for Ungkarle og Lignende* (A cook book for bachelors and suchlike persons), Copenhagen, 1947.

MANGOR, A. M., *Kogebog for Maa Huusholdninger* (A cook book for small households), 6th edition, Copenhagen, 1844.

MANICUS-H., XIANE, and MATHIESEN, ELLEN, *Dansk Mad* (a collection of nearly 350 Danish family recipes), Copenhagen, 1937.

MØRK, KAREN, (Fish dishes), Copenhagen, 1936.

NIMB, LOUISE, *Fru Nimb's Kogebok*, 2nd edition, Copenhagen, 1896.

STEEN-MØLLER, ESTHER, *Sild er Godt!* (Herring is good!), Copenhagen, 1930.

WESTERGAARD, ERIK K., *Dansk Egnsretter* (a survey of Danish regional cookery), Lindhardt og Ringhof, Copenhagen, 1974.

Iceland

FINNBOGASON, GUÐMUNDUR, 'Þorskhausarnir og Þjóðin' (an essay on dried cods' heads), in *Huganir* (a collection of the author's essays), Reykjavik, 1943.

KRISTJÁNSDÓTTIR, ELÍN, *Some Icelandic Recipes* (translated by Hólmfríður Jónsdóttir), Reykjavik, 1975.

SIGURÐARDÓTTIR, HELGA, *160 Fiskréttir* (169 fish recipes), Reykjavik, 1939.

SIGURÐARDÓTTIR, HELGA, *Matur og Drykkur* (the classic general cookery book in Iceland), 4th edition, Reykjavik, 1966.

STEPHENSEN, MARTA MARIA, *Einfaldt Matreiðslu Vasa-Kver þyrir heldri manna Hus-þreyjur* (a simple cookery notebook for gentlewomen), Leirárgörum við Leirá, 1800.

Canada

Anon, *La Cuisine Acadienne* (Acadian Cuisine), Société St Thomas d'Aquin, Charlottetown, Prince Edward Island, 1973.

ASSINIWI, BERNARD, *Indian Recipes*, Copp Clark Publishing Company, Toronto, Montreal and Vancouver, 1972.

BAIRD, ELIZABETH, *Classic Canadian Cooking*, Lorimer, Toronto, 1974.

BOUCHARD, CECILE ROLAND, *L'Art Culinaire au Saguenay-Lac-St-Jean*, Leméac, Ottawa, 1971.

DENYS, NICOLAS, *Concerning the Ways of the Indians – their Customs, Dress, Methods of Hunting and Fishing, and their Amusements*, an account of the Micmac Indians first published in 1672, subsequently issued in translation by the Champlain Society and available from the Nova Scotia Museum.

Department of Fisheries, Ottawa, *Canadian Fish Cook Book*, The Queen's Printer, Ottawa, 1959.

ELLIS, ELEANOR A., *Northern Cookbook*, 'issued under the authority of the Minister of Indian Affairs and Northern Development', Ottawa, 1967.

Fondation Culinaire, *L'Art Culinaire au pays des Bleuets et de la Ouananiche*, Quebec, 1967.

Food Advisory Service, *Food – à la canadienne*, Department of Agriculture, Ottawa, 1970.

GOTLIEB, SONDRA, *The Gourmet's Canada*, Toronto, 1972.

JESPERSON, REV. IVAN F., and family, *Fat-Back and Molasses: A collection of Favourite Old Recipes from Newfoundland and Labrador*, St John's, Newfoundland, 1974.

Ladies Auxiliary of the Lunenburg Hospital Society, *Dutch Oven: A Cook Book of coveted traditional recipes from the kitchens of Lunenburg*, Lunenburg, 1953.

Maple Leaf Mills, *A Treasury of Newfoundland Dishes*, 5th edition, 1964.

MARECAT, CLAIRE, *Le poisson dans la cuisine québécoise*, Montreal, 1972.

Newfoundlanders' Favourite Recipes, Friendship Unit of the United Church Women of the First United Church, Mount Paarl, Newfoundland, undated, fairly recent.

NIGHTINGALE, MARIE, *Out of Old Nova Scotia Kitchens*, 9th printing, place of publication not stated, 1976.

PATTINSON, NELLIE LYLE, *Canadian Cook Book*, first published 1923, new edition revised by Helen Wattie and Elinor Donaldson, Toronto, 1953.

SECORD, LAURA, *The Laura Secord Canadian Cook Book*, McLelland and Stewart, Toronto and Montreal, 1966.

U.S.A.

ADAMS, HARRIET, *Vittles for the Captain: Cape Cod Sea-Food Recipes*, 3rd printing, The Modern Pilgrim Press, Provincetown, Mass., 1951.

A Maine Cookbook (an anthology which includes many recipes from the Department of Sea and Shore Fisheries, Augusta, Maine), 2nd printing, Lewiston, Maine, 1974.

ANDREWS, MRS LEWIS R., and KELLY, MRS J. REANEY, *Maryland's Way*, first published by the Hammond-Harwood House Association, Annapolis, 1963, 8th (Bicentennial) edition, 1976.

Anon, *The Cook Book of the Cosmopolitan Club of Philadelphia*, Philadelphia, 1936.

BEARD, JAMES, *James Beard's Fish Cookery*, Faber, London, 1955.

COLQUITT, HARRIET ROSS, *The Savannah Cook Book*, with an introduction by Ogden Nash, first published 1933, 8th edition, Charleston, S.C., 1974.

DEAN, SIDNEY W., *Cooking American*, Hill and Wang, New York, 1957.

DE VOE, THOMAS F., *The Market Assistant*, Orange Judd and Company, New York, 1866.

DUNAWAY, VIC, *From Hook to Table: How to Clean and Cook Fish*, Macmillan, New York, 1974.

EARLY, ELEANOR, *New England Cookbook*, Random House, New York, 1954.

FISHER, M. F. K., *The Art of Eating: Mrs Fisher's collected gastronomic works*, World Publishing Company, New York, 1954.

FREDERICK, J. GEORGE, *Long Island Seafood Cook Book*, Dover Publications, New York, 1971.

HALL, H. FRANKLYN, *300 Ways to Cook and Serve Shell Fish*, Philadelphia, 1901.

HARLAND, MARION, *Breakfast, Luncheon and Tea*, Scribner's, New York, 1875.

HAWKINS, NANCY and ARTHUR, and HAVEMEYER, MARY ALLEN, *Nantucket and Other New England Cooking*, Hastings House, New York 1976.

HUNT, PETER, *Peter Hunt's Cape Cod Cookbook*, Gramercy, New York, 1962.

JUDSON, HELENA, *The Butterick Cook Book*, New York, 1911.

Junior League of Charleston, S.C., *Charleston Receipts*, first published 1950, 21st printing, 1976.

KENT, LOUISE ANDREWS, *Mrs Appleyard's Kitchen*, Houghton Mifflin, Boston, 1942.

KERR, ROSE G., and BURTIS, JEAN, *How to Cook Oysters*, No. 3 in the Test Kitchen series of the U.S. Fish and Wildlife Service, first issued 1953.

KINDER, BEVIE, and others, *Fripp Island Fare – seafood recipes*, 2nd printing, Fripp Island, S.C., 1976.

KING, LOUISE TATE, and WEXLER, JEAN STEWART, *The Martha's Vineyard Cook Book*, Harper and Row, 1971.

KOEHLER, MARGARET H., *Recipes from the Portuguese of Provincetown*, Chatham Press, Riverside, Connecticut, 1973.

LINCOLN, MRS D. A., *Mrs Lincoln's Boston Cook Book*, Roberts Brothers, Boston, 1891.

Maine Development Commission, *The State of Maine's Best Seafood Recipes*, 1945.

MITCHAM, HOWARD, *The Provincetown Seafood Cookbook*, Addison-Wesley, Reading, Mass., 1975.

NEIL, MARION HARRIS, *The Thrift Cook Book*, British edition published by W. and R. Chambers, undated but (?) 1930s.

PLATT, JUNE, *New England Cook Book*, Atheneum, New York, 1971.

RANDOLPH, MRS MARY, *The Virginia Housewife*, first published 1824, facsimile reprint of a later edition by Crown Publishers, New York, undated, recent.

RATTRAY, MRS ARNOLD E. (ed.). *The Three Hundredth Anniversary Cook Book* [of East Hampton, Long Island], 2nd edition, The Ladies' Village Improvement Society of East Hampton, Long Island, 1949.

REDUE, JOSEPHINE E., *The Eastern Shore Cook Book*, Chestertown, Maryland, undated but (?) about 1905–10.

REED, ANNA WETHERILL, *The Philadelphia Cook Book of Town and Country*, M. Barrows and Company, New York, 1940.

RHETT, BLANCHE S., *200 Years of Charleston Cooking*, Random House, New York, 1934.

RICHARDSON, MRS DON, *Carolina Low Country Cook Book*, 4th revised edition, The Woman's Auxiliary of Prince George, Winyah, Protestant Episcopal Church, Georgetown, S.C., 1975.

RUBIN, CYNTHIA and JEROME, *Cape Cod Cookery*, Emporium Publications, Charlestown, Mass., 1974.

SCHWIND, CAP'N PHIL, *Clam Shack Cookery*, published by the author, 1967.

SCHWIND, CAP'N PHIL, *Clam Shack Clammer*, published by the author (somewhere on Cape Cod, like the preceding book), 1970.

SOUTHWORTH, MAY E., *One Hundred and One Ways of Serving Oysters*, Paul Elder and Company, San Francisco and New York, 1907.

SPARKS, ELIZABETH HEDGECOCKS, *North Carolina and Old Salem Cookery*, 4th edition, Kingsport Press, Tenn., 1974.

SPENCER, EVELENE and COBB, JOHN N., *Fish Cookery*, Little, Brown and Company, Boston, 1922.

STIEFF, FREDERICK PHILIP, *Eat, Drink and Be Merry in Maryland*, Putnam's, New York, 1932.

TAWES, MRS J. MILLARD, *My Favorite Maryland Recipes*, Random House, New York, 1964.

The Taste of Gloucester, 'written . . . by The Fishermen's Wives of Gloucester and the Cape Ann League of Women Voters', Gloucester. Mass., 1976.

U.S. Department of the Interior, *Spiced and Pickled Seafoods*, Fishery Leaflet No. 554, 1963.

WILSON, GUSTY (ed.), *Wood's Hole Cooks Something Up*, Wood's Hole, 1975.
WONGREY, JAN, *Southern Fish and Seafood Cookbook*, The Sandlapper Store Inc., Lexington, S.C., 1975.

Scotland

BECKWITH, LILLIAN, *Hebridean Cookbook*, Hutchinson, London, 1976.
CRAIG, ELIZABETH, *The Scottish Cookery Book*, André Deutsch, London, 1956.
DALGAIRNS, MRS, *The Practice of Cookery*, 2nd edition, Edinburgh, 1829.
DODS, MISTRESS MARGARET, *The Cook and Housewife's Manual*, 15th edition, Edinburgh, undated but (?) about 1880.
FENTON, A., *Traditional Elements in the Diet of the Northern Isles of Scotland*, reprinted by the Scottish Country Life Museums Trust, Edinburgh, 1975; from the *Reports of the Second International Symposium for Ethnological Food Research* held in Helsinki in 1973.
MCNEILL, F. MARIAN, *The Scots Kitchen*, 2nd edition, London and Glasgow, 1963.
MURRAY, JANET, *With a Fine Feeling for Food, Selected and Tested Traditional Scots Recipes*, Aberdeen, 1972.
STOUT, MARGARET B., *The Shetland Cookery Book*, Lerwick, 1968.
WREN, JENNY, *Modern Domestic Cookery*, Paisley, 1880.

England

ACCUM, FREDERICK, *Culinary Chemistry*, London, 1821.
ACTON, ELIZA, *Modern Cookery*, revised and enlarged edition, London, 1860.
AYRTON, ELISABETH, *The Cookery of England*, London, 1975.
BOYD, LIZZIE (ed.), *British Cookery*, Croom Helm Ltd, The British Farm Produce Council and the British Tourist Authority, London, 1976.
COLE, MRS MARY, *The Lady's Complete Guide; or, Cookery in all its branches*, 3rd edition, London, 1791.
COX, J. STEVENS (ed.), *Guernsey Dishes of Bygone Days*, Guernsey Historical Monograph No. 13, St Peter Port, 1971.
Daily Express, *Daily Express Prize Recipes for Fish Cookery*, The Lane Publications, London, undated but (?) about 1930.
DAVID, ELIZABETH, *English Potted Meats and Fish Pastes*, published by the author, London, 1968.
FARLEY, JOHN, *The London Art of Cookery, and Housekeeper's Complete Assistant*, 4th edition, London, 1787.
GRIGSON, GEOFFREY, *The Englishman's Flora*, London, 1955.
GRIGSON, JANE, *Fish Cookery*, London, 1973.
GRIGSON, JANE, *The Mushroom Feast*, London, 1975.
HARTLEY, DOROTHY, *Food in England*, London, 1954.
HEATH, AMBROSE, *Herrings, Bloaters and Kippers*, London, 1954.
IGNOTUS (the nom de plume of Dr John Alex. Hunter of York), *Culina Famulatrix Medicinae, or, Receipts in Cookery*, York, 1804.

KITCHINER, WILLIAM, *Apicius Redivivus, The Cook's Oracle*, 2nd edition, London, 1818.

LEMERY, L., *A Treatise of All Sorts of Foods* (translated from the French by D. Hay), London, 1745.

LOTHIAN, ELIZABETH (compiled), *Devonshire Flavour*, 2nd edition, Newton Abbot, 1971.

LOVELL, M. S., see Bibliography Part One.

MARTIN, EDITH (compiled), *Cornish Recipes, Ancient and Modern*, Cornwall Federation of Women's Institutes, 1929.

PISCATOR, *A Practical Treatise on the Choice and Cookery of Fish*, 2nd edition, London, 1854.

SAMUEL, A. M., *The Herring: Its Effect on the History of Britain*, John Murray, London, 1918.

ST CLAIR, LADY HARRIET, *Dainty Dishes*, 11th edition, London, undated but 6th edition was dated 1866.

WATTS, ELIZABETH, *Fish and How to Cook It*, London, 1866.

WOOLLEY, SUZANNE, *My Grandmother's Cookery Book: 50 Manx Recipes*, Douglas, Isle of Man, 1975.

WYVERN (the nom de plume of Col. Kenney Herbert), *Common Sense Cookery*, first published 1894, 2nd edition, London, undated but (?) late 1890s.

Wales

LLANOVER, THE RIGHT HON. LADY, *Good Cookery Illustrated and Recipes Communicated by the Welsh Hermit of the Cell of St. Gover*, London, 1867.

TIBBOTT, S. MINWEL, *Welsh Fare – A Selection of Traditional Recipes*, Welsh Folk Museum, 1976.

Welsh Gas Board, *Croeso Cymreig – A Welsh Welcome*, Cardiff, 1953.

Ireland

Anon, *250 Irish Recipes*, Mount Salus Press, Dublin, undated but fairly recent and frequently reprinted.

Bord Iascaigh Mhara (Irish Sea Fisheries Board), various booklets and pamphlets containing recipes from their Fish Cookery Advisory Service.

CRAIG, ELIZABETH, *The Art of Irish Cooking*, Ward Lock, London, 1969.

Irish Countrywomen's Association, *The Irish Countrywomen's Association Cookery Book*, Dublin, recent and about to be reprinted.

IRWIN, FLORENCE, *The Cookin' Woman: Irish country recipes and others*, Oliver and Boyd, Edinburgh, 1949.

LUCAS, A. T., *Irish Food Before the Potato*, reprinted from *Gwerin*, Volume III, No. 2, 1960.

ROPER, MARGARET, and DUFFIN, RUTH, *The Blue Bird Cookery Book for Working Women*, The Educational Company Limited, Dublin, (?) 1939.

SHERIDAN, MONICA, *My Irish Cook Book*, Muller, London, 1966.

WARREN, K. E., *The Tailteann Cookery Book*, 2nd edition, Wm Warren and Son, Dublin, 1935.

Index

Part One. Names of Fish, Crustaceans, etc. in the Catalogues

(This index has been designed to combine maximum convenience with minimum size. It does not include obsolete names or names of purely local significance. Nor does it contain names of species which are mentioned only incidentally in the catalogues. Otherwise, it covers all the names which are in the catalogues.

I know that the Icelandic/Faroese letter ð and the Icelandic letter Þ should be treated as separate letters; and that in Scandinavian dictionaries letters with, for example, a diaeresis over them rank after the same letters in plain form. However, I thought that it would be most convenient for the great majority of readers to put all these letters where people unfamiliar with the rules would expect to find them, going by appearance only. *Jennifer Davidson*)

Part Two. Recipes

(This index does not contain systematic groups of recipes under headings such as 'Sweden' or 'haddock'. If you want to find a Swedish recipe, the quickest way is to glance through the Swedish recipe section; and if you want comprehensive advice on cooking methods and recipes for haddock, look up haddock in the catalogue. What are given here are simply the recipe titles in the original language and in English, with one exception and two additions. The exception is that the French recipe titles appear in French only. The additions are as follows:

    All sauces are listed together under the heading 'sauces'.

    All fish soups, chowders, etc. are listed together under the heading 'soups', besides being listed in the ordinary way. Jennifer Davidson)